THE
GRE␣ NORTHERN
␣WAY

THE
GREAT
NORTHERN
RAILWAY

A HISTORY

Ralph W. Hidy, Muriel E. Hidy, Roy V. Scott,

and Don L. Hofsommer

University of Minnesota Press
Minneapolis • London

The Fesler-Lampert Minnesota Heritage Book Series

This series is published with the generous assistance of the John K. and Elsie Lampert Fesler Fund and David R. and Elizabeth P. Fesler. Its mission is to republish significant out-of-print books that contribute to our understanding and appreciation of Minnesota and the Upper Midwest.

First printed in hardcover by Harvard Business School Press, 1988
First University of Minnesota Press edition, 2004

Editorial assistance from Elizabeth A. Burnham

Published by the University of Minnesota Press
111 Third Avenue South, Suite 290
Minneapolis, MN 55401-2520
http://www.upress.umn.edu

Library of Congress Cataloging-in-Publication Data

The Great Northern Railway : a history / Ralph W. Hidy . . . [et al.] ; preface by Alfred D.
Chandler.— 1st University of Minnesota Press ed.
    p.   cm. — (The Fesler-Lampert Minnesota heritage book series)
Includes bibliographical references and index.
ISBN 0-8166-4429-2 (PB : alk. paper)
1. Great Northern Railway Company (U.S.)—History.   2. Railroads—United States—
History.   I. Hidy, Ralph Willard, 1905–1977.   II. Series.
HE2791.G775G73 2004
385'.065'78—dc22
                                                    2003026564

Printed in the United States of America on acid-free paper

The University of Minnesota is an equal-opportunity educator and employer.

14 13 12 11 10 09 08 07   10 9 8 7 6 5 4 3

For John M. Budd

Contents

Preface

The history of this history is a tale of perseverance and patience. The project began more than thirty years ago when John M. Budd, chairman of the Great Northern Railway and Charles W. Moore, the president of the Business History Foundation, signed the agreement to have Professor Ralph Hidy, then of New York University, and his wife Muriel, write the history of Budd's railroad. The company donated the funds to the foundation to support the research and writing. It also agreed to make accessible all of its voluminous archives and to give the authors complete freedom in what they wrote. The project was carefully planned. Research teams were organized. Massive amounts of material were collected and collated. By the late 1960s, the Hidys had completed a long two-volume history, one of the most thoroughly documented stories of a major American business enterprise.

The company then suggested, and the authors agreed, that the completed volumes were too detailed and too specialized to appeal to more than a few academics and railroad specialists. To reach a larger audience the Hidys began condensing the manuscript into a shorter, less detailed single volume. In this work they had the able assistance of Roy V. Scott, professor of history at Mississippi State University, who had been one of the original researchers. As Ralph Hidy became incapacitated by illness, Professor Scott's contribution increased. After Professor Hidy's death in 1977, Muriel Hidy and Roy Scott carried on, with Mrs. Hidy taking the major responsibility for completing the work. During these years she had the invaluable assistance of Elizabeth Burnham. A former member of the faculty of Harvard Business School and knowledgeable in the ways of business and statistical processes and procedures, Elizabeth Burnham made impressive and essential contributions to the final volume. Muriel Hidy continued to persevere, but faltering health following open heart surgery slowed the process of revision. Never fully recovered, she died in 1985.

In the summer of 1984, executives of the Burlington Northern, successsor to the Great Northern, who had shown admirable patience during the years of rewriting, the trustees of the Business History Foundation, and Mrs. Hidy agreed that the manuscript should be completed by another, younger scholar. The foundation was fortunate in obtaining the services of Don L. Hofsommer, a talented and experienced railroad historian who had just completed a history of the Southern Pacific. Dr. Hofsommer began work in 1985 and quickly and efficiently completed the task of revising and condensing what was still an incomplete and unfinished manuscript. Both the foundation and the company are grateful for his most effective performance.

Both also agree that the original two-volume, thoroughly documented history should be made available to scholars and other researchers. So copies have been placed in major historical research libraries. The availability of these copies will permit researchers to follow up leads and to examine in more detail and depth events, issues, and developments described and analyzed in this volume.

Alfred D. Chandler, Jr., *President*
The Business History Foundation

Acknowledgments

During this book's long gestation, the writers have enjoyed astonishing support from a great number of persons without which the enterprise surely would have foundered. Among many others at the Great Northern who granted interviews, provided materials, offered encouragement and suggestions, and assisted in a host of ways were W. B. Irwin, J. C. Kenady, C. A. Pearson, C. E. Finley, Walter N. Norris, William H. Gordenier, E. N. Duncan, Nick Blazovich, H. J. Seyton, George Cottrell, F. L. Paetzold, C. O. Jenks, Margaret Skeene, A. J. Dickinson, I. E. Clary, Jacob H. Marthaler, James Maher, H. W. Kask, Howard H. Hayes, and Frank Gavin. Still others helped similarly and also read various drafts. These included John A. Tauer, John L. Robson, M. M. Scanlan, Anthony Kane, T. C. DeButts, Thomas Balmer, Vernon P. Turnburke, and Herman R. Wiecking. Photographs were assembled by Frank F. Perrin and Patrick W. Stafford, and many of the maps were prepared by Paul Gordenier and Floyd Johnson. Three men— Robert W. Downing, Thomas J. Lamphier, and Charles W. ''Dinty'' Moore—were constant champions of this undertaking and all went beyond the call of duty.

At Harvard, support came from many individuals, including Stanley F. Teele, George F. Baker, Lawrence F. Fouraker, John H. McArthur, Henrietta Larson, William J. Cunningham, Alfred D. Chandler, Jr., Robert M. Lovett, Florence Bartoshesky, Lorna M. Daniels, Rose M. Giacobbe, and especially Elizabeth A. Burnham, a friend of the Hidys and of the business history fraternity at large, who selflessly devoted herself to this venture.

Other assistance came from Charles Purdy, Scott Walton, Robert C. Toole, Helen Kohlmeyer, Richard K. Darr, Lucile Kane, Richard E. Wilkinson, John R. Signor, and Jana McClendon. Professors Albro Martin and Richard C. Overton helped in several ways, as did personnel of the Minnesota State Historical Society, the James Jerome Hill Reference Library, and Ray Palmer Baker and Charles W. Moore of the Business History Foundation.

The writers also acknowledge, with grateful appreciation, financial support from the Burlington Northern and the personal involvement of Richard E. Bressler, Allan R. Boyce, and Thomas E. Harmening.

Most of all, the writers are indebted to John M. Budd, whose dream it was to see a professional business history dealing with the Great Northern and who authorized very significant assistance.

For errors of fact, omissions, and infelicities of style that remain, the writers alone are responsible.

Don L. Hofsommer

Plainview, Texas
March 1986

Introduction

It was a warm summer day when the short train puffed westward out of town. The engine crew waved to happy onlookers, and the melodic report from the locomotive's whistle bounced its call from bluff to bluff across the valley of the Mississippi. On this first trip for revenue in the state of Minnesota, June 28, 1862, the train was headed by the resplendent locomotive *William Crooks*, and was owned by the high-sounding St. Paul & Pacific Railroad Company.

One hundred years later, on June 28, 1962, the Great Northern Railway Company, ultimate successor to the St. Paul & Pacific, put on a fine celebration to commemorate the hundredth-anniversary run of the *William Crooks* between St. Paul and St. Anthony, ten miles west of the capital city and now part of Minneapolis. The morning speeches by Monsignor James P. Shannon, president of the College of St. Thomas, and Governor Elmer L. Anderson built up to presentation of the *William Crooks* to the Minnesota Historical Society. In addition, guests were taken on a commemorative luncheon excursion to Minneapolis and return. That evening over a thousand persons were treated to a dinner program at the Prom Center with a spectacular musical and pictorial presentation on "The First Century of the Iron Horse in Minnesota," led by Skitch Henderson, bandleader and music director for the National Broadcasting Company.

John M. Budd, the Great Northern's president, enjoyed the festivities of that day as much as any. Like Ralph Budd, his father, former president of the GN, the younger Budd held an abiding interest in history. Continuing the legacy of James J. Hill, whose efforts at the helm of the company had earned him the label Empire Builder, he was devoted to building up the railroad and its service area. The festivities, he observed, were a gentle and dignified reminder that the "company had been around a good while, and that it had been a good citizen," looking after the needs of the entire Northwest, and especially Minnesota.

Budd scanned the past and the present, but the future as well; the past pleased him more. The country's railroads, he knew, were a tightly regulated, capital- and labor-intensive industry that had long since lost modal monopoly. It had benefited modestly from the Transportation Act of 1940 and similar legislation in 1958, had firmly embraced internal combustion in lieu of steam power, and was about the business of shedding unremunerative services. Merger, indeed merger on a grand scale, Budd felt, was the next logical step for the evolving industry. Thus, even as he toasted the present by celebrating the past, John Budd was planning for the Great Northern's future—even if it meant extinguishing the proud company's very identity.

To that end, papers had been filed in 1961 with the Interstate Commerce Commission (ICC) for permission to merge the Great Northern and the Northern Pacific, in further combination with the Chicago, Burlington & Quincy and the Spokane, Portland & Seattle, to forge the nation's largest rail company. Budd felt that prospects were good, although his own father and Hill before him had failed in their attempts. Sternly determined forces were out to derail Budd's aspirations, but the ICC eventually agreed that merger to form the proposed Burlington Northern Incorporated was in the public interest. Consummation, with regulatory agency approval, was scheduled for May 10, 1968.

As that day approached, Budd and several senior officers from the Great Northern headed for New York aboard a private jet to meet their counterparts from the other railroads about to be merged. The mood was euphoric. After all, these men had devoted most of a decade to planning the combination. A victory party at the plush Sky Club atop the PanAm building would be followed by signing of corporate and financial documents and then a gala multimedia presentation and reception for journalists and other interested parties. Everything seemed in order. Not quite everything, as it turned out. Opponents filed for a restraining order, and it was granted. The New York proceedings were canceled immediately, and Budd and the others flew home; ecstasy was replaced by emptiness and the episode earned the epithet "false merger."

Delay followed delay. Budd's team labored on, quietly confident and determined to use every hour to better prepare for merger, avoiding the seemingly insuperable problems faced by the recently formed but faltering Penn Central. Finally, the Supreme Court removed the last obstacle and the papers were signed—without flair or ceremony. On March 2, 1970, the Great Northern, the Northern Pacific, the Chicago, Burlington & Quincy, and the tiny Pacific Coast Railroad were merged to form Burlington Northern Incorporated. (Because of short-term tax problems, BNI leased the Spokane, Portland & Seattle.) At 12:01 A.M. on

March 3, the Burlington Northern began combined operations; on M-Day, as it was called, a through freight train left Chicago and twenty-four hours later roared into Montana over the former main line of the Great Northern en route to Seattle. Meanwhile, at the General Office Building in St. Paul, walls separating the former Great Northern and Northern Pacific headquarters were being torn down and doors installed. These events were much more than symbolic; historic dreams were fulfilled.

During the last half of the nineteenth century and two decades into the twentieth, the railroad industry so pervaded American life that writers called ours the "steamcar civilization." In the sprawling northwest quadrant of the country from the upper Mississippi Valley to Puget Sound, no carrier shaped that image more than the Great Northern Railway Company. This is a history of that enterprise, from 1856, when its earliest predecessor received charter authority, to 1970, when the 8,000-mile Great Northern became an integral part of the massive new Burlington Northern.

The first mileage that was to become the Great Northern belonged to pioneer corporations struggling to build and survive in lightly populated Minnesota. Then, in 1879, a strong-minded group of men consolidated the properties of earlier companies to form the St. Paul, Minneapolis & Manitoba Railway Company. The Manitoba quickly enjoyed a success that was generally ascribed to James Jerome Hill, who expanded it into a medium-sized transportation company, including water–rail service from Buffalo, New York to Butte, Montana. The ambitious Hill would not relax. Between 1889 and 1916, when he died, Hill built the Manitoba's successor—the Great Northern

A short train such as this one, headed by the resplendent *William Crooks*, ushered in the steamcar era for the state of Minnesota.

Railway—into a powerful transcontinental stretching from St. Paul and Minneapolis and from the Lakehead at Duluth and Superior on the east to Puget Sound on the west.

Corporations, like individuals, go through phases, usually without sudden breaks between them, because a business organization develops with continuous change: the new is based on the old. Yet, in the Great Northern's experience, a natural dichotomy followed Hill's death in 1916. Thus the first part of this story depicts the company's impressive growth throughout the developing Northwest. In the second the company matures—striving to upgrade property and service as economic, political, social, and technological change surround it.

Those who followed James J. Hill in executive leadership of the Great Northern included Carl R. Gray, 1912–1914; Louis W. Hill, son of the Empire Builder, whose stewardship lasted until 1919; Ralph Budd, 1919–1931; William P. Kenney, 1932–1939; Frank J. Gavin, 1939–1951; and John M. Budd, 1951–1970. Each management period moved without sudden change into the next, but successive presidents left a clear individual stamp on the company as they came to decisions engineered to meet widely differing conditions. Nevertheless, Hill's traditions of efficient operation and thrifty management were hallmarks throughout.

List of Abbreviations

AAR — Association of American Railroads

ARU — American Railway Union

ARE — Association of Railway Executives

AWR — Association of Western Railroads

BLE — Brotherhood of Locomotive Engineers

BLF&E — Brotherhood of Locomotive Firemen & Enginemen

BRT — Brotherhood of Railroad Trainmen

Burlington — Chicago, Burlington & Quincy Railroad

BNI — Burlington Northern Incorporated

CPR — Canadian Pacific Railway

CP — Central Pacific Railroad

CTC — Centralized Traffic Control

C&NW — Chicago & North Western System

CB&N — Chicago, Burlington & Northern Railroad

CB&Q — Chicago, Burlington & Quincy Railroad

CM&StP — Chicago, Milwaukee & St. Paul Railway

D&RGW — Denver & Rio Grande Western Railroad

D&W — Duluth & Western Railroad

Eastern Railway — Eastern Railway of Minnesota

F&S — Fairhaven & Southern Railway

GN — Great Northern Railway

ICC — Interstate Commerce Commission

LS&SW — Lake Superior & South Western Railway

LCL — Less-than-Carload

Manitoba — St. Paul, Minneapolis & Manitoba Railway

Milwaukee — Chicago, Milwaukee & St. Paul Railway or Chicago, Milwaukee, St. Paul & Pacific Railroad

M&StL — Minneapolis & St. Louis Railway or Minneapolis & St. Louis Railroad

M&P — Minnesota & Pacific Railroad

NLRC — National Railway Labor Conference

NP — Northern Pacific Railroad or Northern Pacific Railway

ODT — Office of Defense Transportation

ORC — Order of Railway Conductors

O&T — Oregon & Transcontinental Railroad

OC&E — Oregon, California & Eastern Railroad

OR&N — Oregon Railway & Navigation Company

OT — Oregon Trunk Railway

RLB — Railway Labor Board

RLEA — Railway Labor Executives' Association

RFC — Reconstruction Finance Corporation

StP&P — St. Paul & Pacific Railroad

StPM&M — St. Paul, Minneapolis & Manitoba Railway

S&M — Seattle & Montana Railway

Soo Line — Minneapolis, St. Paul & Sault Ste. Marie Railway

SP — Southern Pacific Company

SP&S — Spokane, Portland & Seattle Railway

SUNA — Switchmen's Union of North America

TPC — Terminal Performance Control

TOFC — Trailer on Flat Car

TSC — Transportation Service Control

UP — Union Pacific Railroad

USRA — United States Railroad Administration

VV&E — Vancouver, Victoria & Eastern Railway & Navigation Company

WPB — War Production Board

WFE — Western Fruit Express

WP — Western Pacific Railroad

Charles E. Perkins, the respected president of the Chicago, Burlington & Quincy, felt that the Manitoba was "probably the snuggest and best of the properties lying beyond St. Paul," with "every mile of it on the best kind of a wheat country." The Manitoba reached Devils Lake, North Dakota, on July 4, 1883 with this elegant excursion train.

(opposite) By December 1905 the name *Oriental Limited* was used to identify the GN's premier passenger train.

PART I

1856
———
1916

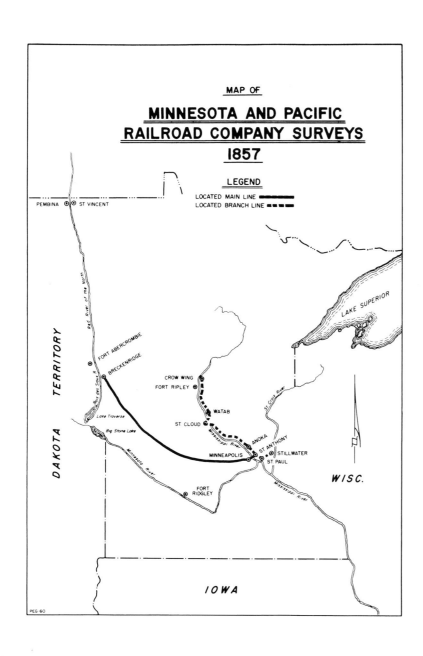

MAP OF

**MINNESOTA AND PACIFIC
RAILROAD COMPANY SURVEYS
1857**

LEGEND

LOCATED MAIN LINE ▬▬▬▬
LOCATED BRANCH LINE ▬ ▬ ▬ ▬

1

The First Ten Miles

Soon after the Minnesota Territory was organized in 1849, local entrepreneurs began to promote varied development projects. Petitions to Congress reflected the need for mail routes, improved river courses and roads, and land grants to encourage railroads to provide simple but essential links between navigable waterways. Several early proposals for rail lines recommended routes from St. Paul—the head of navigation on the Mississippi River—north to Lake Superior, and northwest to the Red River and the "British Possessions." Others urged a line from the St. Croix River at the Wisconsin border west to the Missouri River as part of a northern road to the Pacific.

During the early 1850s, acts of the Minnesota territorial legislature reflected several visionary plans. Laws enabled the building of wagon and plank roads, ferries, and bridges; and between 1853 and 1857 franchises were granted for several railroads. Of these, two had major parts in the history of the Great Northern Railway (GN)—the Minneapolis & St. Cloud Railroad Company, enfranchised by an act of March 1, 1856, and the Minnesota & Pacific Railroad Company (M&P), authorized by law on May 22, 1857.[1]

The Minnesota & Pacific was among several railroads given land grants in 1857. The grant authorized the Minnesota & Pacific to earn still more land by constructing a Main Line from Stillwater, on the St. Croix River, by way of St. Paul, St. Anthony, and Minneapolis northwest to the Bois des Sioux River, and on to the western boundary of Minnesota Territory at the Missouri River. It also authorized a Branch Line from St. Anthony via Anoka and Crow Wing to St. Vincent, on the Red River of the North, near the mouth of the Pembina River and the boundary with Canada.[2]

Fortunately for its welfare, the Minnesota & Pacific Railroad had influential and talented leadership. Company president Edmund Rice was a hardworking lawyer from Vermont who had gained valuable business experience in Michigan before settling in St. Paul. Rice was ably assisted by David Chauncey Shepard, the company's chief engineer.

Shepard gave President Rice an optimistic report early in January 1858. Engineers had located 340 miles of line and filed surveys of the Main Line to the Bois des Sioux River as well as the Branch to Crow Wing with Minnesota's governor. Shepard also enthusiastically asserted that between the Big Woods west of Minneapolis and the Chippewa River lay a "farmer's paradise" of "rolling prairie, woodland, and meadow" that was "watered by a thousand crystal lakes and streams." A settler could "sow with the assurance that he will reap a hundred fold." Moreover, Shepard pictured each of the Minnesota & Pacific's proposed lines as possible links to the West: one could join a projected line across Canada; the other could meet "the railroad to the Pacific," then being discussed in Congress.[3]

Grading began October 1, 1857 between St. Paul and St. Anthony. Even earlier the road's managers had begun the difficult raising of funds. The Minnesota & Pacific was authorized to issue $5 million in stock, but by March 1858, subscriptions amounted to only $604,000. Some shares were bartered for right-of-way, but a 5 percent assessment on subscribers netted only $30,000. Shepard spoke enthusiastically about the potential value of the 2.46-million-acre land grant, estimating that sales would average $8 per acre, aggregating $19,660,800. The engineer was overly optimistic. Company directors quickly learned that the Panic of 1857 had left investors with a dim view of land as collateral for railroad bonds. They also recognized that Minnesota still had a population of only 150,000 (mostly in the southern counties), little capital, undeveloped resources, and a depressed business sector. How soon the projected railroad would be built and how soon land would sell were, one Minnesotan said, matters of "conjecture and experiment."[4]

The state of Minnesota ultimately offered assistance through a complex arrangement intended to safeguard its own credit. The original constitution of Minnesota had forbidden any additional special charters for railroads and loans by the state to individuals or corporations. Yet its citizens were eager for transportation, and after heated public debate and a referendum in April 1858, a month before Minnesota became a state, the constitution was amended, allowing the state to loan its credit to those railroads to which Congress had given land grants. The state then provided a bond issue totaling no more than $5 million. Under this arrangement, any railroad that was given a "loan" of state bonds had to provide security by depositing with the state an equal number of its own first mortgage bonds and to pledge its net income and the first 240 sections of its land grant to pay interest and principal on the bonds. Another element of the amendment, however, delayed marketing of these state bonds: a railroad could receive them *only* after constructing ten-mile units; that is, the company could receive $10,000 in bonds per mile only when the roadbed was ready for ties and rails, and another $10,000 in bonds only when a unit was certified for operation.

These caveats notwithstanding, Selah Chamberlain, who held the construction contract, renewed work early in 1858. His covenant with the Minnesota & Pacific stipulated that he would be paid under a simple formula: $3,000 in state bonds and $20,000 in railroad bonds per mile if he completed the Main Line from St. Paul to St. Anthony and part of the Branch Line by May 25, 1860. Visible progress was evident. Hundreds of men worked on the grade, and the contractor's payroll was a welcome stimulus to St. Paul, which one ebullient newspaper reporter already characterized as "the great railroad entrepôt of the new Northwest."[5]

The local enterprise nevertheless faced grave problems. On July 23, 1858, it executed a mortgage backing its own bonds, and the energetic Edmund Rice hastened to Philadelphia and New York to raise funds. Rice made a few private sales of bonds at low prices, put up some securities as collateral for loans, and paid the contractor in bonds, but neither the state nor the railroad issues found ready markets.

The Minnesota & Pacific, as a result, found itself under fire at home. Early in 1859, the company was accused of not living up to its charter. Detractors pointed out that the road had begun construction not at Stillwater, but at St. Paul, making that city "the focus." In effect, they remarked, the company was building the Branch Line between St. Paul and St. Anthony *before* building its Main Line. The Minnesota & Pacific's management was also accused of "corruption and extravagance" and of being controlled by "the Milwaukee Forty Thieves," Wisconsin investors were minority stockholders of the Minnesota railroad. Company directors lamely countered by pointing out the ill effect of loose and unproved statements about the railroad's campaign to raise required funds.[6]

In 1859, only Selah Chamberlain's faith and commitment made possible any progress. Given an extension of time, he promised to complete the first ten miles by January 1, 1860. Chamberlain also agreed to pay for right-of-way, settle old debts, and meet the company's current bills and obligations, including interest payments on the state bonds. By early spring 1860, graded roadbed amounted to sixty-two miles and ties were on hand for the first ten miles. The absence of further funding, however, delayed delivery of rails.

A change in public policy added to confusion. During summer 1859, Governor Henry H. Sibley announced that Minnesota would issue no more bonds to aid railroads, and in that year's election, George L. Becker, Democratic candidate for governor and Edmund Rice's partner in a law firm, was defeated by Alexander Ramsey. The new governor was himself an incorporator of several railroads, but the Republican legislature "expunged" the constitutional amendment authorizing state aid. The issue of bonds was therefore stopped at $2,275,000.

Chamberlain gave up. No funds were available to pay interest on the state's bonds, and the railroad defaulted the interest on its own bonds. When on March 1, 1860, Chamberlain declared that he could put up no more money,

Edmund Rice faced the unenviable task of raising funds for the fledgling enterprise. *(Courtesy of Minnesota Historical Society)*

the court ordered foreclosure. The legislature then empowered the governor to sell the railroad; on June 23 the state bought its assets.

After lying moribund for nearly a year, the company was reinvigorated in 1861 when legislation restored its franchise. New dates were set for completing roadway, with penalties for noncompliance: Unless the Minnesota & Pacific completed ten miles by January 1, 1862, it would lose $10,000 in earnest money, and its "rights and benefits" would be "forfeited to the State absolutely, and without any further act or ceremony whatever. . . ."[7]

In May 1861, Minnesota & Pacific stock-

holders elected directors, who in turn reappointed many of the previous officers, making one important change. To replace Chief Engineer David Shepard, who had departed with Chamberlain, the directors appointed William Crooks, who had served in that office briefly during 1857. Son of a well-known fur trader and a former student at West Point, Crooks resumed an association that was to be long, if discontinuous, with the railroad.

Soon thereafter, Edmund Rice and Crooks went to Philadelphia, hoping to conclude a major contract with J. Edgar Thomson of the Pennsylvania Railroad. Thomson and several of his associates were interested in western railroads and, in fact, were ready to undertake construction of the entire M&P. Before technical details were worked out, though, the threat of civil war prevented a project that might have become a most significant relationship between eastern and western railroaders.

Rice and Crooks returned to Minnesota disappointed but not empty handed. In fact they found three Ohio bankers—Valentine Winters, Jonathan Harshman, and Elias Franklin Drake—who were willing to finance, build, and equip the ten miles from St. Paul to St. Anthony in return for the railroad's bonds and the land grant to be earned by construction.

Progress was again encouraging. On September 9, 1861, in a drizzling rain, the "ringing of bells" and "screaming of whistles" announced that railroad equipment was landed in St. Paul by the steamer *Alhambra*. The shipment, along with two flat cars, a box car, two hand cars, and about fifty tons of rail, included a splendid locomotive, the *William Crooks*, which was unloaded at the levee in St. Paul and moved over temporary tracks by men pulling it with cables. The *William Crooks* itself supplied the power when a second locomotive, the *Edmund Rice*, arrived a few weeks later.[8]

The euphoria proved temporary. Within a month of the jubilant welcome given the *William Crooks*, the whole enterprise was in jeopardy. Public debate about where the track should terminate in St. Anthony was furious; disputes and an injunction on right-of-way caused delays; low water on the Mississippi blocked steamers carrying rail. Started early in September, tracklaying moved slowly; only 1,400 feet of 45-pound rail were down by October. Legal questions complicated sale under foreclosure of the first mortgage bonds, then trustees of the mortgage claimed a lien on the road. The contracting firm withdrew, the locomotives were stored in sheds made of ties, the January 1 deadline was not met, the road's charter was surrendered to the state, and its chief engineer joined the Third Regiment of Minnesota volunteers.

Early in 1862, the state legislature again raised hopes. An act of March 10 transferred rights and property of the twice-tried Minnesota & Pacific "free and clear of all claims or liens" to a group of associates under a new title—the St. Paul & Pacific Railroad Company (StP&P). With the slate wiped clear of past obligations, the StP&P was given new dates for required completion of specified portions on its line.

Public criticism, however, did not disappear. It remained strongest in St. Anthony, where the city council labored to have the proposed line relocated. Critics elsewhere protested that the company remained in the hands of the same group that had long been "tooting the whistle" without producing any "puff of the engine at the Falls."[9]

Nevertheless, in March 1862, the StP&P's directors made a new contract with Winter, Harshman & Drake, Ohio bankers, who agreed to complete the first ten miles in return for a new issue of $120,000 in railroad bonds with interest at 8 percent and 120 sections of land to be earned by construction.

Accounts of rapid progress enlivened Minnesota's otherwise dreary spring of 1862. As soon as ice was off the Mississippi, rails that had been stored downstream at La Crosse arrived by steamer, and the company's two locomotives were taken out of winter quarters. Tracklaying resumed on April 1. Three months later, on June 28, well ahead of the deadline, the railroad began commercial operations. Despite innumerable delays, the St. Paul & Pacific Railroad Company could claim it was Minnesota's first railroad operation. But that was not the end. In their quarters at the Merchant's Hotel on Fourth Street in St. Paul, officers of the StP&P were preparing to extend the line.[10]

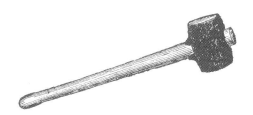

Frustrated by Finance

The St. Paul & Pacific charter gave the company comprehensive construction rights, and in the 1860s amendments expanded its possibilities. To the first authorized routes—the Main Line from Stillwater via the Twin Cities to the present community of Breckenridge, and the Branch Line from St. Anthony to St. Vincent—were added franchises to build from St. Cloud to Lake Superior and from St. Paul south to Winona and the Iowa border. Ironically, however, President Rice actually disposed of some rights, such as the option to build south of St. Paul, which was transferred to railroads that are not a part of the Great Northern's history.[1]

The Branch Line Comes First

Edmund Rice was a remarkable railroad pioneer. As a member of the Minnesota legislature, he had worked hard to obtain a charter for the railroad, and later as senator to have its rights expanded, and to gain extensions of time limits on construction and land grants. As president of the company, Rice traveled broadly in attempts to attract capital. He suffered illness in lonely hotel rooms, rebuffs from bankers, and disappointments when expected contracts did not materialize.

St. Paul was a bustling center of commercial and mercantile importance by the late 1860s. The transportation bounty was shared by the St. Paul & Pacific, the La Crosse & Milwaukee and, of course, navigation companies. *(Courtesy of Minnesota Historical Society)*

The periodic victories that Rice did score were directed toward the Branch Line. Projected to run along the east bank of the meandering Mississippi from St. Anthony to the northwest, the line would serve farms, timber enterprises, and growing towns along that waterway. On the other hand, Rice wrote, the route toward Breckenridge — the Main Line — would require heavy expense for constructing a bridge across the wide Mississippi between St. Anthony and Minneapolis, and, moreover, only a few miles farther west was a wilderness with slight prospect of immediate traffic. Rice and the directors of the St. Paul & Pacific thus determined that the Branch Line would receive earliest attention. After all, the potential for quick reward was much greater there.

In 1862, Rice negotiated an agreement with Electus B. Litchfield & Company of Brooklyn, New York, a financial middleman. In a con-

tract with the StP&P dated May 3, Litchfield agreed to guarantee the construction and equipment for seventy miles of railroad northwest of St. Anthony to near present-day Sauk Rapids. In return, he was to receive all shares issued on that mileage and payments in cash at specified dates, determined by a schedule for construction, to earn the land grant. Work was to be supervised by the railroad's own officers.

To pay Litchfield & Company, directors of the StP&P voted to issue bonds. Each of two series, dated June 2, 1862, was for thirty years and carried interest at 7 percent. The first issue of $700,000 was backed by a second lien on the railroad's first ten miles (there were $120,000 in bonds with a prior claim) and a first mortgage on the next seventy miles. The second issue, for $1.2 million, had a third lien on the first ten miles, a second lien on the seventy miles, and a first mortgage on the 307,200 acres of land grant to be earned by new construction. Rice bartered some of these bonds for rail; others were used as security for short-term loans. In all, he sadly reported, only about a third of this second issue was placed.

In truth, conditions were favorable for neither marketing railroad bonds nor building railroads in Minnesota. The Civil War drained off money and men; rails and labor rose in price; low water on the Mississippi delayed delivery of construction materials; and, in 1862, a Sioux Indian uprising killed settlers, frightened others into towns, and discouraged immigration.

Nevertheless, some progress was made. When 4,500 tons of rail arrived in New York from Wales in 1863, the road's superintendent, Francis R. Delano, was on hand to expedite their shipment to La Crosse by train and then by steamer up the Mississippi to St. Paul,

No. 6. **FIRST DIVISION** No. 6.

ST. PAUL & PACIFIC R. R.
TIME CARD.

Into Effect November 12th, 1866.

DISTANCES.		GOING WEST.		DISTANCES.		GOING EAST.	
		Dep. St. Paul -	10:00 A. M.			Dep. St. Cloud -	10:30 A. M.
10	10	" St. Anthony	10:45 "	11	11	" Clear Lake	11:10 "
7	17	" Manomin	11·15 "	15	26	" Big Lake -	12:05 P. M.
6	23	" Coon Creek		10	36	" Elk River	12:45 "
5	28	" Anoka - -	12:00 M.	5	41	" Itasca -	1:05 "
6	34	" Itasca - -	12:25 P M.	6	47	" Anoka - -	1:30 "
5	39	" Elk River, -	12:45 "	5	52	" Coon Creek	
10	49	" Big Lake -	1:25 "	6	58	" Manomin -	2:15 "
15	64	" Clear Lake -	2·20 "	7	65	" St. Anthony	2:45 "
11	75	Arr. St. Cloud -	3:00 "	10	75	Arr. St. Paul	3:25 "

Trains No. 1 and 2 Meet at Elk River at 12:45 P. M.

Wait 30 Minutes for Delayed Trains.

ST. ANTHONY AND MINNEAPOLIS TRAINS.

LEAVE.	A. M	ARRIVE.	A. M.	LEAVE	P. M	ARRIVE.	P. M.
St. Paul	8:00	St. Anthony	8:45	St. Anthony	12:20	St. Paul	1:00
St Anthony	8:50	St. Paul	9:10	St. Paul	:45	St. Anthony	4:30
St. Paul	11:30	St. Anthony	12·15	St. Anthony	4:35	St. Paul	5:20

Irregular Working and Freight Trains run between St. Paul and Elk River, and Elk River and St. Cloud, and have right to the road, at all hours, except Regular Train time and delayed train time.

LOOK OUT FOR SWITCHES,

Slow Speed to 8 miles an hour over St. Paul Trestle Work, Rice Creek, Coon Creek, Rum River and Elk River Bridges

No Engines allowed on the road except on order of the Superintendent or Master Mechanic.

Irregular Trains slow on curves, and look out for Section men.

In case of doubt, follow the safe course.

[OVER.]

F. R. DELANO, Supt.

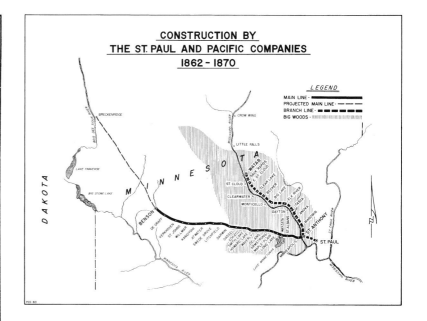

CONSTRUCTION BY THE ST. PAUL AND PACIFIC COMPANIES 1862-1870

the usual route until 1867. By autumn 1863, the Branch Line added nine miles to near Fridley, and by January 1864, it reached Anoka.

Major problems were at hand, however. Litchfield had not been paid as construction proceeded, and presently he demanded additional assurances. Also, a dispute over land ownership in St. Paul was embarrassing to the StP&P, and its bonds were not finding a ready market. To ease financial problems, the directors authorized Rice to issue special stock on designated parts of the franchise and to give control of line segments to parties promising to build. Legislative approval was needed to assure investors, and with President Rice's influence and Minnesotans' generally strong desire for railroads, it was forthcoming in February 1864. Consequently the StP&P gained the right to issue stock in favor of those agreeing to construct specific segments.

Possession of such stock gave its owner control, free of the company's general liabilities; the owner could then form a separate organization and administer his part of the franchise and its land grant. The prospects for trouble were ominous.

On February 6, 1864, Rice signed a new contract with Litchfield, confirming the agreement of 1862, but also authorizing 5,000 shares in Litchfield's name on the Main Line from St. Anthony westward to a point between the foot of Big Stone Lake and the mouth of the Sioux Wood River. This equity carried both the franchise for and the responsibility for constructing that segment of the Main Line on a schedule adequate to earn the land grant. To reach this goal, the First Division of the St. Paul & Pacific Railroad—a captive organization commonly referred to as the First Division—was organized on the same day. This was not an operating division in the accepted sense, but a distinct corporation, building under a part of the StP&P's charter. The First Division of course also took over operation of the ten miles built by the StP&P. (On occasion, where both companies are legally involved, we will refer to the St. Paul & Pacific companies.)

The First Division's president, George Loomis Becker, was one of the most enterprising young lawyers in Minnesota. Born in New York, graduated from the University of Michigan, Becker was a partner of Edmund Rice in the law and private banking business. Becker had been the youngest mayor of St. Paul before suffering defeat as the Democratic candidate for governor, and from 1862 to 1864 he was land commissioner for the StP&P. (Years later he would be engaged in several local railroad projects, and from 1885 to 1901 Becker would serve as state railroad commissioner for Minnesota.)

Meanwhile, work on the Branch Line went ahead. Rails reached Itasca by August 1864, and Elk River, forty-two miles from St. Paul, by 1865. Then another financial crisis threatened. Bonds on the First Division's property were not selling, and Litchfield, who had spent much and hesitated to advance more, neglected to pay interest due on the StP&P's bonds. The company's directors expressed "mortification" at the damage to the StP&P's credit.

Eventually this problem was resolved, peace restored, and steps taken to improve the reputation of both the St. Paul & Pacific and the First Division. A committee of inquiry for the StP&P determined that Litchfield had acted in good faith and expressed confidence in him. Feelings now smoothed, the principals sought a new method to ease financial pressures. Also, Congress voted an increase in land to specified railroads in Minnesota, raising from six to ten sections in depth the grant of alternate sections on either side of the railroad. The StP&P transferred this bonus to the First Division.

Directors of the First Division also authorized a new bond issue to do away with overlapping liens of StP&P issues, to simplify the debt structure, and to raise additional capital for construction. The proposed issue of $2.8 million was designed to provide $780,000 in bonds for construction and the rest to refund earlier issues ($120,000, $700,000, and $1.2 million). Timing seemed propitious. The Civil War had ended, the First Division's value was increased by the enlarged land grant, and a new wave of immigration promised growing traffic. Although some of the earlier bonds had

reached the Dutch market, this time Litchfield approached Amsterdam bankers directly. In 1866, Lippmann, Rosenthal & Company agreed to market them. The new bonds were secured by a mortgage on eighty miles of railroad, 512,000 acres of land, and the railroad's valuable terminal facilities in St. Paul.

Unfortunately, the First Division's $2.8 million bond issue achieved its purposes only in part. The amount taken was a mere $1.1 million, and of this, $354,000 replaced earlier bonds. Opinions held in St. Paul were reflected by reports from Dun & Bradstreet: Bonds of the St. Paul & Pacific companies were not worth more than fifty cents on the dollar. Nevertheless, enough money was raised to encourage Litchfield to finance constructing additional trackage. In September 1866, rails reached St. Cloud, or more accurately and annoyingly for the people of that town, the bank of the Mississippi at East St. Cloud. Two miles added in 1867 brought service to Sauk Rapids, but St. Cloud itself remained devoid of rail service.

The First Division took a new measure to increase its capital on May 2, 1868. No limit had been set by the legislature on the railroad's stock issue, and so directors voted to increase the total to $2.2 million, including some preferred participating stock with a guarantee of an 8 percent dividend. The market, however, was not brisk. In all, stock issued reached $1.5 million, held mostly by Litchfield and his kin.

The uncertain financial picture of the StP&P and the First Division was reflected variously. When bonds were bartered for rails, their quality depended not on choosing the best product but on the manufacturer most pressed to accept securities from a short, unknown pioneer line.

Some American rails, including secondhand stock, were bought in job lots. Indeed, the Branch Line from St. Anthony to St. Cloud ultimately had thirteen types and weights of rails, ranging from forty-five to sixty-four pounds per lineal yard. And ties were not standardized in length or species of timber.[2]

Main Line West

Although the 1864 contract between the First Division and Electus B. Litchfield included his commitment to guarantee construction of the Main Line from St. Anthony to Breckenridge, little was accomplished right away. Litchfield and officers of the First Division were aware that the Main Line would require an expensive bridge across the Mississippi between St. Anthony and Minneapolis, and they knew that population west of Minneapolis was sparse. They also were aware of potential advantages. Right-of-way could be acquired more easily there than in settled areas, construction problems (aside from the Mississippi River bridge) were few, townsites could be located on the company's land grant, and the line would open rich acreage for wheat.

Actual construction west of Minneapolis went slowly, but it advertised the railroad's intent. By 1866, surveyors had located the line through Wayzata, a village on the north arm of Lake Minnetonka, then along its north shore and heading northwest toward "the great prairie." Grading during the year was delayed, however, and when snow fell only fourteen miles had been prepared.[3]

Elsewhere, much attention was given to terminals and yards. St. Paul presented special difficulties. Passengers there had to transfer from a dock some distance from the company's facilities, and transloading freight from water to rail required heavy labor. To alleviate these problems, tracks were extended by a lengthy trestlework — later filled in — and a new station and immigrant workers' houses were built. Between St. Paul and St. Anthony the company began vigorously clearing title to right-of-way and acquiring additional land for yards.[4]

By 1867, extension of the Main Line was evident in Minneapolis and to the west as work of the previous year came into use. At a cost of $90,000, a thousand-foot, seven-span wood trestle crossed the Mississippi at Nicollet Island and carried trains from St. Anthony to the new station in Minneapolis. By August, trains ran to Wayzata and to Lake Minnetonka, where a long-awaited gala celebration, including an elaborate picnic, was held to initiate twice-daily service to that popular summer resort.[5]

As trackworkers returned to the job in spring 1868, the difficult matter of finance again raised its head. Electus B. Litchfield was frankly overextended and looked for relief. At the same time, E. Darwin Litchfield, a brother and London financier who had already advanced more money to this railroad than he had anticipated, wanted greater control and therefore bought the First Division from his brother. Meanwhile the Dutch bankers, already selling bonds of the First Division and eager to sustain its credit, were willing to market additional bonds, but only on their own terms. Lippmann, Rosenthal & Company demanded regular reports on construction, the railroad's freight returns, and proceeds from land sales, and wanted a representative on the railroad's board of directors. The yield of the bond is-

George Loomis Becker, president of the First Division

sue, they declared, must see the line completed to Breckenridge.

During the summer of 1868, E. Darwin Litchfield appointed as his agent President George Loomis Becker and instructed him to employ a competent construction company. Until now on the Main Line, as on the Branch Line, the railroad's chief engineer, D. C. Shepard, had acted as agent of Electus Litchfield and had supervised subcontractors. Now, in June 1868, Becker contracted with Andrew De Graff & Company, which William Crooks had joined after returning from the Civil War, to provide thirty miles of grading from Crow River to a place in Meeker County to be named Darwin. This was the first in a series of such agreements.

9

Frustrated by Finance

Communities such as Atwater, Minnesota, between Litchfield and Willmar, either sprang into being or prospered because of the railroad. *(Courtesy of Minnesota Historical Society)*

Although the new relationship between E. Darwin Litchfield and Becker was put into practice during the summer, it was December 14, 1868, before a formal contract, retroactive in effect, was signed. E. Darwin Litchfield guaranteed completion of the Main Line "fully equipped"; he was to receive, in return, $4.5 million in stock and $9 million in bonds. The railroad was to be completed to Breckenridge by January 1, 1871. Only as segments were ready and equipped for operation would an installment of securities be sent to London. Litchfield in turn would market the bonds through Lippmann, Rosenthal & Company.

Directors of the First Division had arranged for the new bond issue in July 1868. The company issued $6 million of 7 percent thirty-year bonds with a mortgage on 210 miles of line starting from St. Anthony and on 763,000 acres of land grant — subject to prior liens. The unmarketed $1.5 million in bonds of the earlier year were held as collateral for the new issue, explaining why the bonds of 1868 later had a higher market value than the $3 million authorized four years earlier.

Included among terms that Lippmann, Rosenthal & Company demanded before it undertook to market the bonds was joint control of

the railroad. Litchfield agreed and deposited most of his stock with President Becker to be held until the railroad bonds were redeemed. In addition, Leon Willmar, a slender, debonair, sharp-penned native of Liechtenstein but resident of London, became the Dutch bankers' representative on the board of directors of the First Division. Lippmann, Rosenthal & Company was now ready to push the new bonds.

For the First Division, the 1869 season held great optimism and energy. Through the summer and into the autumn, work was pressed with a crew of more than a thousand men. Beyond Darwin the line was in unoccupied territory, except for a handful of settlers who had moved west anticipating the railroad's arrival. In November Crooks congratulated Superintendent Francis R. Delano on establishing "another station on the frontier"—Willmar, midway between St. Paul and Breckenridge. The road thus opened Kandiyohi County, which one source labeled the "greatest wheat field in the world." In a bustling year, the First Division had completed fifty miles of railroad.[6]

All started well next season. Crooks marshaled hundreds of men to make grade west of Willmar, and by July 1870 rails reached thirty miles farther, to Benson. Then construction stopped.

The cause of work stoppage, simply, was financial inadequacy. By the time the road reached Benson all bonds had been turned over to Litchfield and the Amsterdam bankers had sold what they could. On January 1, 1870, Becker bleakly estimated that another $1.8 million would be needed to reach Breckenridge.

A period of almost frenzied finance followed, as all parties sought funds. One proposal indicated how little Europeans understood conditions in frontier Minnesota. In August, Leon Willmar suggested that the railroad's townsite lands from Willmar to Breckenridge be used as security for a new bond issue. He estimated that plotting large towns every five miles with six lots to the acre would make twenty-three towns with almost 112,000 lots. Valued at $50 each, the lots would justify a bond issue of $3 million, enough to complete the road to Breckenridge. President Becker properly responded that such townsites would be too many and too large, and the lots too small. Even farther south where settlers were numerous, town lots sold slowly. Moreover, the townsite lands, yet to be earned by construction, were already pledged under two mortgages.[7]

Circumstances for the Main Line differed little from those besetting the Branch Line: limited funds, unsettled areas providing insufficient revenue, and unrealistic time limits for construction. These conditions resulted in inadequate engineering and superficial construction. At some places the line rose 75 feet to the mile from the horizontal plane; cuts were narrow, ditches were close to tie ends, and for ballast only a little topsoil was applied. Then too, Belgian rails laid in 1867 proved brittle and broke in the rigorous Minnesota winters. De Graff, the contractor, bluntly characterized the road as "built in a cheap way, with heavy

grades and heavy curvature. . . ." This practice, however, was not unusual. Becker correctly maintained that the First Division's lines "were up to the average of western roads. . . . They were in good order and condition for the business they had to do."[8]

As the decade ended, the St. Paul & Pacific companies had compiled a mixed record and faced an uncertain future. They had expanded nicely from the original ten-mile section between St. Paul and St. Anthony, terminals had been improved, the StP&P had rights to build to the Missouri River, and more bonds could be issued if another land grant was obtained. On the other hand, construction had not been completed to meet requirements of the grant the company already had, and, in fact, the St. Paul & Pacific and the First Division remained nothing more than a short local operation carrying a heavy debt on primitive track.

3

Growing Pains

Managing Minnesota's first railroad, isolated for several years without connection to other rail lines, was a trying task. Superintendent Francis R. Delano of the First Division was, he said, "responsible to a greater extent (under our system) than any other general officer for the operation management of the lines of this Company." In fact, ranking next to the president in running the railroad, Delano had charge of both operations and sales. At first only ten miles were under his control, but he soon faced the challenge of managing a growing plant with scarce resources and scant traffic.[1]

Limited service met local needs until traffic grew. Trains made the twenty-mile round trip between St. Paul and St. Anthony in about an hour, and eventually operated three times a day. A controversy arose over Sunday service; it was welcomed by some as beneficial to the working class and denounced by others on moral grounds. Nevertheless, it was eventually established. By late 1862, trains carried ninety passengers a day, the company had gained a mail contract, and it was about to take over the express business.[2]

Freight volume expanded gradually as the Branch Line was extended. When the first

Francis R. Delano served as superintendent of the First Division and was essentially in charge of operations. *(Courtesy of Minnesota Historical Society)*

miles went into operation only 67,000 people lived adjacent to the line, half of them in the Twin Cities, keeping freight traffic light for some time. In the spring of 1863, a newspaper reported the largest train yet run on the local railroad—three box cars and eight flat cars hauling 878 barrels of potatoes, as well as lumber and shingles for transshipment to river steamers at St. Paul.

Although volumes grew slowly at first, anticipated expansion set off energetic activity along projected routes. Anoka was typical. In 1863 farmers there planted more than ever before and employment in the nearby pineries swelled as demand for lumber products soared. In Anoka itself, buildings went "up in all directions," and merchants enjoyed a "lively business." On January 18, 1864, the railroad dramatized its arrival by running a special three-car train carrying 240 passengers to lunch in the thriving little village.[3]

Expansion continued and business gradually increased. Waybills drawn in the mid-1860s reflected the greatly varied freight carried for the military, Indian traders, and settlers. Primary eastbound shipments included lumber, butt headings, barrel staves, grain, flour, furs, and hides. General merchandise, from furniture and agricultural implements to anvils and whisky, led westbound billings.[4]

The new rail service immediately altered traditions of transportation and brought about a curious blend of competition and cooperation among the modes. The railroad's faster, more dependable, and inexpensive service won most of the business from water carriers as well as wagon and stage operators. Some competitors adapted well. J. C. Burbank & Company, proprietors of the Minnesota Stage Company, carrying the North-Western Express and United States mails, evolved continuously. When train service was introduced between St. Paul and St. Anthony, Burbank supplied an "omnibus connection" at each location, and as the railroad built toward St. Cloud, opened new service from the end-of-track to Alexandria and then to Winnipeg.[5]

Passenger volume on the St. Paul & Pacific and elsewhere increased nicely. In April 1866, the First Division showed growth, over that month in the previous year, of 44 percent in passenger traffic between St. Anthony and St. Paul. When the First Division entered Minneapolis in 1867, it immediately advertised "Six Trains a Day each Way" on the "Shortest Quickest & Cheapest route between the three cities." Fares rose to 6 cents a mile, but 1,000-mile "commutation books" sold for $25 —or just 2.5 cents per mile.[6]

Service on the Branch Line by 1870 had grown to two mixed passenger and freight trains daily in each direction, supplemented by work trains that also picked up freight. "Going West" to East St. Cloud, the regular train served seven intermediate towns and made the journey in four hours. Service was reduced in winter because volumes of business were lower.

Offerings on the Main Line were similar. Two mixed trains made the round trip daily between St. Paul and Benson by 1870. During the immigration season, two daily freight trains handled the extra business between St. Paul and Willmar. A special passenger train, the *Delano Accommodation*, left that town each morning for St. Paul, made a trip between St. Paul and Minneapolis at noon, and, serving intermediate stations, returned to Delano at day's end.

As the length of lines and volume of business grew, the company took delivery of more motive power and rolling stock. New locomotives, named for directors, towns, and employees, were more powerful than earlier models. All were built in the East, ranging in weight from twenty-eight to thirty tons. The company similarly received fine new passenger equipment. Late in the decade the First Division paid $7,000 for one car with "patent ventilation roof," and "elegant plush seats" with adjustable "patent flexible backs." Local patrons

between St. Paul and Minneapolis were served by new oak cars "with black walnut molding" and accommodation for fifty-eight on "richly upholstered" seats. A contemporary observer boasted that "the facilities for travel upon this road are equal to any in the United States; as far as car accommodations are concerned."[7]

Although the railroad continued to depend most on eastern suppliers, substantial changes in procurement and delivery were made. After 1867, equipment could arrive by an all-rail route from the East, and local suppliers gradually took form. A St. Paul foundry turned out wheels, and the company's own machine shop not only handled major repairs, but also constructed flat cars and modestly appointed passenger cars.

By 1871, the state's oldest and longest railroad extended from St. Paul to Benson (the Main Line), and from St. Anthony to East St. Cloud (the Branch). The St. Paul & Pacific companies owned 19 locomotives, 171 freight cars, and another 22 cars for passengers, mail, and express. The staff numbered fewer than twenty including officers. Salaries for them were: president ($500 per month), superintendent ($300), assistant superintendent, treasurer, secretary, chief engineer, general freight agent, master mechanic, master of transportation, attorney, purchasing agent, emigrant agent, and five clerks ($50 to $200). Maintenance of way was the responsibility of two roadmasters, one for each line. About three dozen section "bosses" served under them; the road was divided into four- to six-mile

segments, "according to amount of work required on each section." The roadmasters received $75 or $100 monthly, the section foremen $45. Laborers, paid $1.50 per day, ranged from 105 to 225, depending on the season. Operating personnel totaled little more than fifty in 1870; salaries were typical of those paid elsewhere west of Chicago. Engineers, firemen, brakemen, and conductors were compensated "according to distance run per day," brakemen averaged $45 per month, and the few conductors $75. Firemen earned slightly less than brakemen, but when they became engineers their pay was doubled.[8]

Superintendent Delano was also responsible for personnel assigned to the twenty-nine stations and seven flag stops. A few points had three to six employees, but most had only one.

In employing station agents and clerks, Delano considered "the character and ability of the men and their prompt willingness to do any work required of them."[9]

Controlling expenses was especially difficult. Delano faced the constant burden of carrying deadhead construction materials, building new station facilities, and the relatively reduced revenues from per-mile rates on longer hauls. Problems on the First Division were especially pressing. Delano simply could not be satisfied with the volume of traffic that, after expenses in 1870, left the Main Line with a net income of less than $31,000 that had to go toward substantial interest charges. The line's future lay in extension to the Red River, expanded traffic, and increased local settlement.

Settlers for the Land

The railroad's drive for greater traffic demanded serious efforts to attract settlers to its lines and buyers for its land. The credit ranking and the general development of Minnesota also depended on these tasks. Because land served as collateral for the railroad's bonds, proceeds from sales were pledged against securities. As president and land commissioner of the First Division, George L. Becker was answerable directly to the mortgage trustees.

To better carry out his work, Becker studied other railroads' experience and employed a strong associate. In Chicago he received from the Illinois Central ''a full insight'' into the work of its land department, learning that sales lagged until free land was taken up, and that even though the best land sold first, the remainder appreciated when settled. He then engaged Hermann Trott, the well-educated son of a high-ranking German military officer. An affable personality, keen mind, and linguistic ability served Trott well in his essential work.[10]

Becker and Trott soon unveiled a vigorous program. In promotional pamphlets, Trott promised to answer inquiries from other countries in the native language; descriptions of land were meticulous. And the railroad often worked closely with the state in attracting settlers; their interests, after all, were mutual. Minnesota's Board of Immigration distributed thousands of pamphlets in many languages during the 1860s, and Colonel Hans Mattson, who headed the work for Minnesota, traveled extensively in Scandinavia to encourage emigration, doing so in some years on leave of absence from the First Division.

Professional writers were among those em-

Inelegant but perfectly functional coaches were assigned to the *Delano Accommodation*. *(Courtesy of Minnesota Historical Society)*

ployed by the railroad to promote land sales. James Wickes Taylor was assigned solely to the First Division. Another, Edward Pelz, had arrived from Germany in 1848, gaining experience with another railroad before moving west. Still another, Hans Mattson, addressed himself to Scandinavians, but more particularly to Germans. A Dutchman, John H. Kloos, directed his efforts not only to landhunters, but also to possible investors in Holland. Because he had an engineering background, his geological reports on Minnesota later earned him a Ph.D. from the University of Göttingen. Employed by the railroad

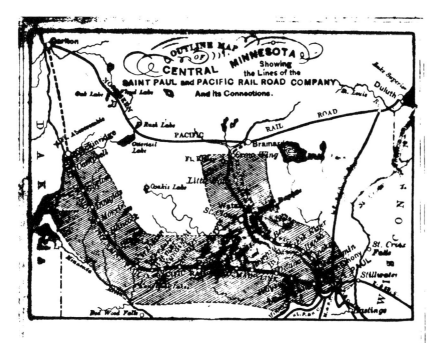

THE FIRST DIVISION
OF THE
ST. PAUL & PACIFIC RAILROAD CO.

For Sale, 1,500,000 Acres
OF
TIMBER, PRAIRIE AND MEADOW LANDS,

Along their lines of Railroad, as shown on the accompanying Map.
Land limits, 20 miles each side of the Railroad.

Prices range from $4 to $12 per Acre for Cash, or on long Credit, with
7 per cent. annual interest.

CASH PRICES ARE ONE DOLLAR PER ACRE LESS THAN CREDIT PRICES.

TOWN LOTS AT PRICES FROM $50 TO $300 PER LOT.

For descriptive Pamphlets and other information, apply to

OFFICE AT ST. PAUL, MINN.

HERMANN TROTT,
Land Commissioner.

The StP&P, unlike its successors who built into the Dakotas and eventually to the Pacific Ocean, received a generous grant of land in Minnesota to aid in construction.

to study soil and to describe land and sell it, he also served as local contact for the Dutch bondholders.

Early advertisements, dealing principally with land along the Branch Line, reflected reality and hope. Information on public roads, schools, and churches was designed to influence wives as well as their husbands. Pamphlets often boasted of flourishing towns, ample water and timber, and the healthiest climate in the United States.

Pleased with selling some 20,000 acres that spring, "mostly to actual settlers," the railroad held a public sale in St. Paul to stimulate further purchases. Terms of sale were attractive, one could pay in cash or in railroad bonds at par, and credit was similarly generous. In the mid-1860s, land on the Branch Line was priced at a minimum of $4 per acre, although some brought more. Other pieces, however, sold for less, for squatters benefited by the state's provision that they need pay only $2.50 an acre.[11]

Boosting sales on the Main Line mattered particularly because there was "scarcely any business in the country which it had to traverse." John Kloos observed that the line was built "on the merits of its land grant, and in the firm conviction that all the country needed for its development was a railroad. Here the road had to *create its own traffic, to induce immigration, and to develop the resources of the country.*"[12]

Even before the Main Line was built, President Becker promoted its route as eventually leading "to the Gold Mines of Idaho," and made long-term credit contracts for land "not yet subject to sale." Until the railroad had earned and received title, sometimes a slow proceeding, the purchaser paid only annual interest. But within a given period he was required to clear, break, and cultivate a specified number of acres. Eager to secure steady and reliable sources of freight, the railroad had no desire to encourage speculators who would hold land solely to benefit from its appreciation. By the late 1860s, prices on the Main Line ranged from $6 to $12 per acre, but a buyer could receive a discount of $1 an acre if he paid in cash. He could also qualify for credit up to ten years at 7 percent, with the privilege of early repayment without penalty. The company's appeal was broad, with special inducements to "persons of small means, who desire to make a home for themselves and their children, as well as to stock raisers and wool growers."[13]

Efforts were also made to attract common laborers. Minnesota had many opportunities for men "lingering around the crowded seaports of the East, with no hope beyond mere subsistence." Indeed, the railroad itself needed workers. In 1869, with ambitious plans for construction, the company's agents circularized Germany and Sweden with glowing pamphlets ballyhooing land in the Big Woods and on the Kandiyohi prairies and promising employment on railroad construction gangs. The $1.75 per day they offered — $4 for a man with a team — when board and shelter cost only $4 a week, made it possible for a man working on the railroad to accumulate funds and "go farming."[14]

Immigrants, the railroad reminded, were under the "protection of the Company" both during the journey and on arrival. Because many immigrants lacked knowledge of the country and the language, and often money, agents helped them along the way, in part to prevent their being diverted to another railroad. A temporary shelter, the "Railroad Immigrant House," was provided at St. Paul,

James J. Hill in 1872

and as the First Division extended into "unoccupied territory," it provided facilities at strategic places where free cooking, washing, and sleeping accommodations were made available to new arrivals.

The railroad also strove to attract those who would build towns. One pamphlet declared that Minnesota offered "more ample and effective water power than New England." This publication further extolled climate, fertility of soil, free schools, and growth of railroads, as well as water transport, highways, and varied scenery that made Minnesota "the state par excellence, to which . . . the man of capital and of enterprise should look."[15]

On the Main Line, the company platted towns upon its own lands. This policy started at Waverly, and assumed greater significance west of Willmar. In Waverly, 90 acres were platted, in Benson 160. The railroad held land for its own purposes, donated or leased lots for churches and schools, and put the rest into a special "townsite account" at $10 an acre. Each acre was divided into five lots, those suitable for commercial and industrial purposes selling for more than the $50 usually asked of settlers for a home site. By the end of 1870, 417 lots had been sold at an average price of $54.75.

In fact, during these early years the railroad had not yet received or sold a great amount of land; it took time to earn it and to secure title. By the end of 1871, the railroad had received deeds for only 858,558 acres; at the end of the previous year it had sold 100,556 acres, all to actual settlers and much of it on credit. Prices rose slightly, but until 1870, sales on the Branch Line averaged $4.93 and on the Main Line $7.25 an acre.

Freight Traffic

By autumn 1865, freight business on the First Division had grown sufficiently to prompt Superintendent Delano to urge that facilities be expanded. Because of the company's small labor force and constant need to economize, Delano urged that, as much as possible, the railroad use "contract work . . . as in such cases the company only pays for what is done and the party doing the work is interested in making all the business he possibly can do." He advised making contracts to erect elevators, warehouses, docks, and levees.[16]

The company followed Delano's advice.

One agreement had both immediate and lasting effects, for it established a close relationship between the railroad and a young, aspiring St. Paul businessman. In March 1866, the *St. Paul Pioneer* published this important announcement:

1866—RAIL AND RIVER FREIGHT NOTICE— The merchants and shippers of freight in Minneapolis, St. Anthony, Anoka, Dayton, Elk River, Monticello, Clearwater, St. Cloud and other points upon or connecting with the First Division of the St. Paul & Pacific Railroad are hereby notified that all freights intended for transportation over said Railroad arriving at this port by steamboat and marked: Care J. J. Hill, Saint Paul, will be transferred from the boats to the Railroad company if landed at the Transfer Depot, or from the Railroad to the boats free of the usual transfer charge at this point. An arrangement has been made by which the merchant or owner of goods will save the sum of five cents per hundred pounds at this point alone, the coming season, if the goods are consigned and delivered as above. Signed: J. J. Hill, General Transportation Agent. St. Paul, Minn. F. R. Delano, Supt. First Div., St. Paul & Pacific R. R. March 15.

James J. Hill had much to recommend him to the railroad. Born in Guelph, Upper Canada, on September 16, 1838, his short but valuable education in Rockwood Academy, a Quaker institution, made him everlastingly grateful to his teacher, William Wetherald. Through his mentor, Hill acquired ease of expression and devotion to applying the discipline of numbers of facts. Persuaded to approach problems analytically, Hill coupled excellent memory with willingness to work long and hard to accumulate facts on which to base judgments.

Hill looked beyond Guelph for opportunity. On the early death of his father, a farmer of modest means, Hill left school at fifteen,

served for more than two years as a store clerk, then started out alone, not discouraged by loss of sight in one eye. After traveling to eastern and southern cities in the United States, he "took a notion to go and see St. Paul." On July 21, 1856, the youth arrived in Minnesota.[17]

In the small, growing settlement of St. Paul, Hill found many possibilities. For three years he was a shipping clerk for J. W. Bass & Company (later Brunson, Lewis & White), a partnership engaged in a general forwarding and commission business, including agency for the Dubuque & St. Paul Packet Company. Following a short stint with another firm, Hill was employed for four years by Borup & Champlin, agents for the Galena Packet Company, and then, for a few months, he gained still wider experience as agent in Chicago for the La Crosse & Milwaukee Railroad (later part of the Milwaukee Road).[18]

With this experience, Hill, at twenty-seven, was ready to start his own commission agency in St. Paul; he knew both river and railroad traffic. He had also established a good reputation, being described as "pleasant, capable and straightforward" and having "commanding abilities and matchless energy." He likewise had valuable business connections, some capital, and excellent credit, being reported by Dun & Bradstreet as "safe for all he would assume."[19]

On this foundation Hill built a respectable commission business. When the Hudson's Bay Company preferred that its agent, Norman W. Kittson, not act for other traders on the Red River, Hill acceded to those lucrative accounts. He routed westbound freight by rail to St. Cloud, then by wagon or cart to Red River flatboats or overland all the way to Fort Garry. He also served as general freight and ticket

agent for the North Western Packet Company (later North Western Union Packet Co.) in the river trade south of St. Paul. Hill advertised his services as a general transportation agent, guaranteeing rapid transit of shipments to eastern cities.

Hill's relationship with the railroad was part of his success. Improvements in transfer facilities at St. Paul reduced costs for the railroad and ended heavy labor; most supplies arriving by steamboat were thereafter unloaded at Hill's large warehouse. His commissions grew steadily. In truth, he performed more than routine tasks. He was an independent businessman acting for others on commission—an expert in obtaining and forwarding freight, using his influence and initiative to increase it. Hill estimated that he was supplying the railroad with almost a third of its volume by the end of the 1860s.

During this decade Hill's partnerships changed and his functions became more diverse. When he first contracted with the railroad, he took into the business (J. J. Hill & Company) a half brother of the Litchfields, and before the 1860s ended, he also entered into agreement with Chauncey W. Griggs, a man with experience in the lumber business and, in Minneapolis, with John A. Armstrong. In 1869, the railroad contracted with Hill, Griggs & Company to supply all its wood for locomotive fuel and for office and station heating.

On another front, as the Main Line began to open the richest wheat lands in the state, it needed more handling facilities. The company did not follow the pattern adopted by some railroads by building, operating, or leasing its own elevators. Rather, it turned the business over to others. On January 1, 1866, William B. Litchfield was granted the right to store grain in the Twin Cities and soon erected elevators of varying sizes. The largest in St. Paul, the "Delano," had a capacity of 150,000 bushels. The railroad had reserved the right to purchase that structure, but when Litchfield left for the East in 1868, transferred the business to those experienced in the trade.[20]

Two contracts with William T. Davidson covered both the Branch and the Main Line and started one of the first grain elevator systems in Minnesota, differing from others in that it stored but did not buy wheat. Davidson, a steamboatman on the Mississippi, had already diversified his investments by building elevators along two other railroads. The First Division committed itself to provide side tracks, to carry fuel at cost, and to transport materials, workers, and agents free of charge. In return, Davidson promised to immediately erect one 10,000-bushel elevator on the Main Line and to add others as needed. The basic rate of 4 cents per bushel, collected for the contractor by the railroad through its tariff, was to be reduced immediately to 2 cents. Provisions also covered long-term storage and handling of grain in bags. The railroad's right to approve inspectors of grain, and stipulations on "adequate facilities," showed its intent to exercise control, as did its option to buy the elevators at a later date. The relationship proved satisfactory. Three dozen elevators were soon operating along the railroad's lines. Of course, 90 percent of the grain handled under contract went to the flourishing mills in Minneapolis.[21]

The railroad had gradually evolved a simple structure of freight rates, regressive with length of haul. Distances were divided into five classes, as were the types of freight. For less than 5 miles, the rate per ton was 32 cents for first class and 16 cents for fifth class (stone). If the distance was from 50 miles to less than 100, the respective rates were 15 7/11 and 3 3/11 cents.[22]

Officers of the railroad were constantly pressed between the bondholders' predictable demands for revenues and customers' equally predictable demands for low rates. New settlers, company representatives argued, needed inexpensive delivery of inbound merchandise and outbound grain. "Upon all these articles it is necessary and expedient to affix low rates of charges." The state legislature initially had little to say about rates, although in granting a franchise directly to the Litchfield elevator operation in 1868, it demanded that freight and passengers on the Branch Line be carried at "reasonable rates." Additional involvement followed. On March 6, 1871, the legislature instituted new and vexing regulations. Company officers bluntly refused to conform: "We cannot carry on our business upon the basis fixed by the act," they said.[23]

The record of the St. Paul & Pacific at the dawn of the 1870s was decidedly mixed. Its prime objective had been to establish itself as the railroad link between the Mississippi River and the Red River of the North—serving the commercial needs of both the United States and Canada. Part of this intent had been accomplished. To be sure, the Branch Line was in service to East St. Cloud and Sauk Rapids, and the Main Line had been thrust west from St. Anthony and Minneapolis to Benson. Nevertheless, the St. Paul & Pacific lacked the wherewithal to accomplish its greater goals. Its credit was low, its condition weak, and the Minnesota legislature appeared cranky. Moreover, other railroads were being formed or already threatened the StP&P. Of problems there was an abundance.

4

Northern Pacific Interlude

Late in the 1860s, railroad promoters and investors in Minnesota faced a rapidly changing environment. Would local railroads retain their independence or come under control of "outsiders"? Would local companies expand or disappear into the fold of growing giants?[1]

At the same time, Canadians wondered whether a railroad connecting their country's eastern centers with the Pacific Coast could be built in time to ensure British Columbia's adherence to the confederation created in 1867. The desirability of such a road was not at issue in Canada, but several difficult questions remained. Should the Canadian government build the line or should it mandate a private firm? Could a railroad be built and operated successfully through the rugged, empty country north of the Great Lakes? Should such a route be built in two segments—Montreal to Sault Ste. Marie, and from the western end of Lake Superior to the Pacific Ocean, using lake vessels or a rail line in the United States for the necessary link?

After years of discussion, meanwhile, the first coast-to-coast rail route in the United States was opened on May 10, 1869, when the Central Pacific (CP) and the Union Pacific

(UP) met at Promontory, Utah. Moreover, years of discussing a second transcontinental —the northern route—from Lake Superior to Puget Sound, had finally led to action. In 1864, a group of New Englanders had obtained a federal charter with a large land grant and had organized the Northern Pacific (NP). Two years later, J. Gregory Smith, a New Englander interested in the Vermont Central Railroad, became president of the NP, and contemplated a cross-continent plan that encompassed Vermont railroads as well as the projected Canadian Pacific. By 1869, a more diverse group took an interest in the project, and Jay Cooke & Company of Philadelphia, which had marketed federal bonds successfully during the Civil War, expressed interest in selling the NP's securities.

Others looked on with interest. One of these was the imaginative journalist James Wickes Taylor, who worked for the First Division and other railroads. Another was Norman W. Kittson, veteran fur trader, former mayor of St. Paul, and agent for the Hudson's Bay Company in Minnesota, whose views would be passed along to Donald Smith, his superior in Winnipeg. The Hudson's Bay Company, after all, yearned for reasonable rates in transporting supplies, furs, and settlers to the twenty-five-million-acre holding it had received in exchange for relinquishing political power. In May 1869, Taylor boldly recommended to Kittson an "international Pacific railway"—a part of which the St. Paul & Pacific had already completed to East St. Cloud and Sauk Centre. Charter rights were available, he pointed out, to extend the line to the Canadian boundary at St. Vincent; from there an extension could take the road to Fort Garry and then west across Canada.[2]

During the autumn of 1869, Taylor had an-

Norman W. Kittson was a veteran fur trader, former mayor of St. Paul, and agent for the Hudson's Bay Company; his views were sure to reach the ears of Donald Smith, his superior in Winnipeg.

other idea. He suggested to Jay Cooke and to the president of the Northern Pacific that the NP could benefit by utilizing two established railroads, the First Division and the Lake Superior & Mississippi River Railroad Company (later the St. Paul & Duluth), which ran from the head of Lake Superior to the Twin Cities. This combination would include in one system "the limits of Lake and River navigation at Duluth, St. Paul and Breckenridge." The NP, Taylor continued, would gain access to the state's capital, quickly earn salable land, hasten construction to the Missouri River, expedite the early development of traffic, and improve its power to attract bondholders.[3]

At that time, however, Jay Cooke opposed purchase of the First Division: the time was not opportune to commit massive funds, for the European market was not ready for American railroad bonds and Congress had not passed legislation that the NP had requested.

President George Becker himself disclaimed any ambitious plans for the First Division, but beginning in 1869 he worked hard to put that part of the St. Paul & Pacific into a strong, independent position from which it could either compete with the NP or enter into a relationship as an equal. At Becker's suggestion a bill was introduced in the United States Senate to provide the First Division with a land grant to build into Dakota Territory from Breckenridge and north to Pembina. He also asked friends in Congress to press for another land grant for the First Division, equal to that awarded the NP—to support construction of a line out to the Missouri River. This extension would facilitate competition with the projected NP line, or at least provide the latter with trackage rights under the First Division's control.

By March 1870, Becker lost hope for his grand plan. He simply had not enough influence in Washington. The bill for a route to Dakota Territory passed the Senate but did not reach a vote in the House, and, worse still, Cooke asked Becker to abandon his plan to build the Pembina line, because it would invade NP's territory.

The NP itself gained vigor. It found valuable support in Congress, selected a terminus at Duluth, determined a route west to the future community of Moorhead, and, in February 1870, began construction. The NP also forged important relationships with other railroads. For a few miles out of Duluth it utilized tracks of the Lake Superior & Mississippi, which it had come to control, and the NP also obtained a franchise to build the St. Vincent Extension, a right originally held by the StP&P.

Becker was acutely aware by fall 1870 that his railroad's bargaining position was wretched. Furthermore, when construction on the Main Line ended at Benson in July, tension with the Dutch bondholders mounted. Leon Willmar criticized Becker for not slackening the pace before contracting a floating debt, for opposing his own townsite plan to raise funds, for negotiating with the NP, for letting the competition win all legislative rounds, and for otherwise disregarding the wishes of First Division stockholders and bondholders. Becker offered to resign if a competent person, after a full investigation, found him to be at fault. He also urged Willmar to visit the Northwest. By October 1870, the First Division was in a truly desperate financial position. Becker and E. Darwin Litchfield frantically searched for funds, but all efforts failed.

At the same time, Jay Cooke favored acquisition of the First Division. Several advantages were readily apparent. The pioneer Minnesota railroad had strong political influence in the state, and purchasing the First Division, with only minimal construction (Brainerd to Sauk Rapids, sixty miles), would ensure NP's entry into the Twin Cities and provide connections there for Milwaukee, Chicago, and St. Louis.

Late in November, E. Darwin Litchfield, Leon Willmar, and NP's William C. Moorhead met in New York. Moorhead, through Willmar, gave the Dutch bankers assurance on four points: their representative on the First Division's board would be retained, the road would be completed to Breckenridge, funds would be provided to pay interest on the earlier bond issue, and a plan would be perfected allowing the First Division—not the NP—to utilize the St. Paul & Pacific's franchise for constructing the St. Vincent Extension. The Dutch banking house of Lippmann, Rosenthal & Company thereupon agreed to market a new issue of bonds.

Under a contract of December 9, 1870, Litchfield sold his stock to the Northern Pacific for $1.5 million in First Division second mortgage bonds and $500,000 in cash. The NP now held in trust the majority of the stock of both St. Paul & Pacific companies, and could essentially control railroad matters north of St. Paul and Minneapolis.[4]

Completing the Main Line

For the Northern Pacific and for the St. Paul & Pacific companies 1871 started with high optimism. J. H. Kloos forecast so bright a future for Minnesota that both immigrants and investors would be attracted. The state, he observed, now had a population of 470,000, almost double that in 1866, and about 1.5 million acres were under cultivation. Industrial growth was everywhere—expanding flour and lumber mills in Minneapolis, granite works in St. Cloud, and many other businesses in newly established communities. In five years the state's railroad mileage had grown from 210 to 1,087, almost a third of it put into operation during 1870.

George Becker remained president of the First Division, but he had less power than when the Litchfield brothers had followed each other as chief stockholders. The NP, of course, had invested in the St. Paul & Pacific companies to make them tributaries. Frederick Billings, then a NP director, explained the relationship: The organization of the two companies (the StP&P and its First Division) "was maintained, but questions relating to their interest were discussed in . . . and the policy and action of these two companies shaped by the Northern Pacific board."[5]

Early in 1871, agreements were reached on two major projects: the Main Line would be extended to Breckenridge and the Branch Line would be lengthened to the Canadian boundary. Thus, while the NP was itself building from Duluth via Brainerd to Moorhead and west in 1871, the First Division finally began to push its line through from Benson to Breckenridge and the Red River. Funds came from a new bond issue. De Graff & Company was the contractor, and by July crews were laying a mile of rail a day. A two-day gala trip to Breckenridge was arranged for "Old Settlers" to mark completion of the railroad 214 miles from St. Paul—"almost to the extreme limit of civilization," according to one account. Daily service for the half-day journey began in December 1871, although operations in that winter were difficult, trains often being delayed by snow.[6]

Francis Delano, as superintendent, was responsible for improvements and new facilities, but his place was taken in 1872 by E. Q. Sewall, a civil engineer trained at Harvard, who had twenty-five years of experience on eastern railroads. The new superintendent quickly ordered fifty-six-pound new steel laid between St. Paul and Minneapolis, instituted regular tie replacement, and completed a fill near the dock in St. Paul. To prepare for winter operations, he ordered plows, built snow fences, and began planting trees along the right of way.[7]

Competition between the First Division and the NP followed the pattern set between the St. Paul & Pacific's two lines. When rails reached Breckenridge, the Hudson's Bay

Company shifted its large business from wagons to the Main Line, but this freight was lost to the NP during the next year because its line crossed the Red River even farther north.

In several practices, though, the railroads worked together. The First Division joined the NP and the Lake Superior & Mississippi to erect a building at the Minnesota State Fair, displaying products from along their lines. They also continued to aid the state in printing and distributing circulars and pamphlets describing the region's attractions and the cost of moving there. Reduced fares were advertised from points within the United States and from twenty-eight European locations. Discounts for emigrants ranged from one-third to one-half of published rates. The cost from Queenstown, Ireland, to Minnesota, for example, was only $50. Regular passenger fares in Minnesota, 4 cents a mile, were likewise reduced for new arrivals.

In land sales, the First Division competed with the NP as well as with other roads and the federal government. Hermann Trott, who succeeded Becker as land commissioner for the First Division in 1869, made new proposals, but the offer of land at low prices, with discounts for cash and interest at 7 percent for long credits, continued. Trott averred that an ambitious man could acquire a productive farm in only a short time. He could save for the down payment, and then supplement a good income from the farm by work away from home, for wheat culture required only a few months of the year. Among the possibilities, Trott counseled, were work on larger farms, hunting game (thousands of deer carcasses were shipped annually from Minnesota), trapping, harvesting ice, cutting and transporting wood for fuel, and working on the railroad.

Eager to increase sales and knowing that for

In 1869, Hermann Trott succeeded George Becker as land commissioner for the First Division. *(Courtesy of Minnesota Historical Society)*

some types of land and crops a large producing unit was most economical, Trott announced a new program in 1872. For those wishing to buy a section or more, the First Division lowered the price to $6 an acre, free of interest and any payment for three and a half years. In a promotional pamphlet Trott specified that he wanted as purchasers neither speculators nor theorists, but practical, experienced men with $5,000 in cash. Settlers needed that amount to meet conditions of purchase — breaking, cultivating, and fencing the land and

planting forty acres in trees, with seeds or seedlings furnished by the railroad.

The requirement that they plant trees was part of the First Division's campaign, initiated in 1872, to make Minnesota's prairie land more attractive. Becker appointed Leonard B. Hodges, an able farmer, superintendent of tree planting. Hodges soon set out arbors to protect track from drifting snow and to beautify new towns and neighboring lakes, and began a campaign encouraging farmers to emulate the railroad's practice. He then wrote a book on the subject, urged the governor and the legislature to support bills encouraging forestation, and supervised the railroad's own campaign.[8]

The railroad sought in many ways to help develop towns, many of which, west of Minneapolis, were on railroad property; the depot was often the first town building erected. At twenty-four such locations, the First Division had platted townsites, laid out streets, and offered lots at prices depending on the size and potential of the hinterland. At some places the First Division donated or leased without charge lots for schools, churches, and parks. To ensure economic growth by "sober residents," early deeds stipulated that purchasers were to improve the properties and refrain from selling intoxicating liquors.

For healthy evolution, towns depended on such factors as quality of surrounding soils, availability of other natural resources, and attractions such as a stream or lake. Local businessmen's enterprise and quality were extremely significant. Storekeepers, hotel men, small manufacturers, stagecoach and freight-hauling operators, bankers, teachers, churchmen, and newspaper editors jointly and severally helped give each community its character and effected its growth. Strong churches often attracted worshipers of like denominations, especially when the railroad's pamphlets stressed their location.

During the prosperous early 1870s, some communities on the Main Line quickly outdistanced others. Designation as the county seat was a distinct advantage; being a crew-change point on the railroad was another. Litchfield, in Meeker County, had a land office, several industrial establishments and churches, and two newspapers. Thriving Delano in 1872 had a flour and grist mill, harness maker, blacksmith shop, furniture factory, newspaper, three hotels, and twelve stores, as well as the customary grain elevator. In Willmar, in Kandiyohi County, was one of the First Division's repair shops; it also had six hotels and boarding houses. Not long after the first train arrived in Breckenridge the town had three hundred inhabitants, four hotels, five stores, and three saloons, not to mention an elevator and railroad facilities at the end-of-track.

The St. Vincent Extension

Construction of a railroad from near St. Cloud to the Canadian boundary, the so-called St. Vincent Extension, had been planned for years. Indeed, President Edmund Rice had written in 1864 of the projected railroad as extending on through British possessions to the Pacific Ocean. Since then the need for rapid, inexpensive transportation to the north and northwest had increased markedly. Development in those regions was dramatized when Manitoba became a province of Canada in 1870 and when Winnipeg was incorporated as a city three years later.

Yet, even as settlement grew, commercial demands increased, and technological advancement progressed, transportation in northwest-

ern Minnesota remained tied to the Red River. Though it was crooked, narrow, and often shallow, steamboating on the Red flourished. The Hudson's Bay Company, which earlier had made long-term contracts with outsiders to move freight, placed its own vessels on the river during the 1860s. These were managed by Norman W. Kittson, Hudson Bay's agent in Minnesota.

James J. Hill also entered the Red River steamboat business. As a freight forwarder handling a growing volume of goods, Hill wanted to be certain of adequate and efficient transport at low rates. To that end, Hill, Griggs & Company authorized construction of a steamboat, and on April 23, 1871, the *Selkirk* made her maiden voyage. As agent for the First Division and as steamboat operator, Hill offered sharp competition for Kittson. In the end, the two men worked out a pooling arrangement, and in 1873 they merged the two properties into the Red River Transportation Company.

Meanwhile, directors of the Northern Pacific were building a line north to Canada and integrating it into their own system. One motive was their desire to participate in the plan to build a Canadian transcontinental, with a portion of it—from the Great Lakes to Winnipeg—in the United States. Rather than use a direct route from East St. Cloud through Crow Wing to the Canadian border, the NP planned a circuitous line utilizing 80 to 120 miles of its own track. The St. Vincent Extension, under this plan, would start near St. Cloud and run to a junction with the NP at Gull River—the length of NP track depending on the point selected for turning north. The NP would then build another segment of road to the boundary under the old StP&P charter.

Those plans did not materialize. Several

considerations caused a change. For one, Leon Willmar, representing the Dutch bankers, wanted a line from St. Cloud to and through the Red River Valley to make best use of the StP&P's land grant, on which the Dutch held many bonds. New surveys, made in 1870 and 1871 by Charles A. F. Morris, chief engineer for the StP&P companies, indicated that for generating traffic a better route could be chosen than that planned by the NP. Another inducement was that politically vocal communities—Melrose, Alexandria, and Fergus Falls among them—had sprung up on the stagecoach route to the northwest. Each promised further growth upon arrival of rail service, each pledged financial inducements, and each lobbied to procure legislative aid. The result was sweet. On March 3, 1871, Congress changed the StP&P route, and the Minnesota legislature concurred. Now the StP&P was enfranchised—if it linked Sauk Rapids and Crow Wing—to build one line from Crow Wing to the NP at Brainerd, and another from Crow Wing to a point intersecting with the lines of the original grant at or near Otter Tail, or Rush Lake, so as to form a more direct route to St. Vincent. All construction had to be completed by March 1, 1873.

During spring and early summer 1871, NP officials took the first steps for this ambitious project. They deemed it impracticable to seek legislation permitting merger of the two StP&P companies, and instead arranged to issue $15 million in bonds with a StP&P mortgage on 438 miles of projected road and anticipated land grant as security. The Amsterdam house of Lippmann, Rosenthal & Company contracted to sell these 7 percent bonds in Europe at or above the railroad's stipulated minimum of 70 percent. In sum, the First Division was to build two extensions—St. Cloud to St.

Officials of the StP&P and guests at Breckenridge, Minnesota, October 1871. The engine *William Crooks*, named after the first chief engineer of the road, was the first in the state. In the group are: (1) Col. A. DeGraff who built most of the railway lines in Minnesota during this early period; (2) William B. Litchfield, president of the StP&P; (3) Col. William Crooks; (4) Leon Willmar who represented the Dutch bondholders of the road; (5) C. A. F. Morris, chief engineer at the time this picture was taken.

Vincent and Sauk Rapids to Brainerd — and lease them to the NP for ninety-nine years.

To carry on both financing and construction, the NP appointed a committee of three. The chairman, William C. Moorhead, exercised control over the whole operation. He was a partner in Jay Cooke & Company, a director of both the NP and the First Division, and a trustee of the StP&P for the $15-million bond issue. He took on this task because the Dutch bankers wished someone to act as middleman between railroad and investors, as Litchfield had done in the past. Moorhead, as agent, purchased track material, accepted rail consigned by Willmar, and, as mortgage trustee, drew bills of exchange on the London representatives of the Dutch bankers to cover expenses reported by Becker. During fall and early winter, Moorhead, not President Becker, signed four contracts with De Graff & Company for major construction, including a bridge over the Mississippi at St. Cloud.

Construction followed a checkered path. The NP carried supplies, including rail, from Duluth to Glyndon, about ten miles short of the Red River, where settlers had established a community of wooden houses and tents. De Graff & Company pushed construction of the extension on two fronts from October 1871, with time out for winter, into the next fall.

The impressive bridge across the Mississippi at St. Cloud was completed during summer 1872, and by September track-layers were approaching Melrose, thirty-five miles west of St. Cloud. The northern portion of the St. Vincent Extension was a little more than a hundred miles in length and ran from a few miles south of Glyndon to north of Crookston. Suddenly, however, construction at both ends stopped. The high hopes of 1871 had given way to the financial realities of 1872.

Lippmann, Rosenthal & Company had prepared the usual prospectus to attract investors to the $15-million bond issue, and on arrival in Holland the securities met a lively market, but it soon turned lethargic. The first $6 million were sold to an "under syndicate" that was slow in collecting and transferring funds,

and the bankers tried to protect the market by repurchases when prices suddenly fell. Sales continued until June 1872, but by that time demand for most American securities had slumped badly.

Although St. Paul & Pacific bonds shared in the general decline, they also suffered from particular circumstances. The sales record of past StP&P bonds had not been good, and the new ones were affected adversely by their close association with NP securities that Jay Cooke & Company was finding so difficult to sell. Also depressing the market for both NP and StP&P bonds was a conflict arising from the ambitions of Cooke and NP leaders to participate in Sir Hugh Allan's scheme for a railroad from eastern Canada running south of Lake Superior and then over NP rails to a connection at the Manitoba border and westward to British Columbia. Groups in Canada so vociferously opposed United States investment in their nation's transcontinental project that in 1873 they precipitated a political battle bringing about repudiation of the entire Canadian-American project.

Tensions and recriminations among all parties contributed to the Dutch investors' reluctance to place their money. Leon Willmar insisted that the StP&P companies' autonomy be retained until the bonds were repaid in full. He further objected to the announcement that St. Vincent Extension securities were being marketed by an agent of the Northern Pacific and to that company's name being displayed on new cars of the First Division. He also disliked the distribution of maps showing First Division mileage as a part of the NP. And the Dutch bondholders, through Willmar, accused both Northern Pacific directors and Becker of favoring the NP.

Indeed, George Becker received the full blast of Willmar's displeasure. Willmar argued that had Becker kept the StP&P financially sound it "should not have been forced to accept with joy the Northern Pacific arrangement, detrimental to all our interests." Willmar later accused Becker of submitting inadequate, late, confusing, and inaccurate accounts that lacked proper form. After William Moorhead had the books of the First Division carefully examined by a professional accountant, however, he urged Becker not to resign and assured the president of freedom to manage the company.[9]

Another cause of ill feelings was confusion about the size of the land grant backing the $15-million bond issue. Where the two railroad lines intersected at Glyndon, overlapping claims and disputes clouded ownership of thousands of acres of land. Not only did doubt about land rights induce Becker to delay sending various bonds to Holland, it also caused potential investors to refrain from buying them. Although Moorhead thought the NP would probably yield to the StP&P, the NP did nothing to justify this belief. To be sure, the controversy over land would encourage litigation for two decades.[10]

By September 1872, conditions had deteriorated further. In Duluth and New York, rails were piling up; storage and interest charges grew. De Graff & Company, which had no payments from the railroad for several months, was heavily in debt and needed immediate help to prevent riots by unpaid workers who threatened to destroy property. Eager to discuss the problem, William Crooks, a partner in De Graff & Company, went to see Moorhead in Philadelphia. The latter had already borrowed money in his own name to advance to the First Division, and refused to provide more funds unless authorized to draw on the Dutch bankers. Frantic cables from Crooks and Moorhead to Lippmann, Rosenthal & Company elicited a reply that no more funds were available from the sale of bonds and that the Amsterdam bankers were already in cash advance and would make no additional commitments.

Moorhead did succeed, however, in providing temporary relief for the hard-pressed De Graff & Company. On Becker's authority and using for security rail stored in New York, the Philadelphia banker borrowed money to meet the payroll. Also, to offer protection for debts owed it, Moorhead gave De Graff & Company a pro forma bill of sale for 2,700 tons of the railroad's rail stored in Duluth.

It was inadequate. On October 5, 1872, Moorhead ordered construction stopped. On the First Division, the line had been extended a mere thirty-five miles from St. Cloud to Melrose. On the second front, in the Red River Valley, the new extension could act as feeder for the NP, but it was only a little more than a hundred miles long and not connected to the St. Paul & Pacific. Elsewhere, work on the Brainerd Extension, little more than a survey and some grading, had been discontinued in spring 1872.

Lack of funding was acute. Accounts of Lippmann, Rosenthal & Company and testimony in later court cases showed the meager results of the $15-million bond issue. Only $10.6 million in bonds (par value) were sold, netting $5.2 million for the railroad after deductions. William Crooks's comment was fatalistic in the extreme: "It had to be done," he remarked, "because it was the only thing, and therefore the best thing."[11]

Northern Pacific executives had attempted too much too soon. Neither their company nor the St. Paul & Pacific companies had enough credit to successfully sell their bonds. Perhaps they could have eventually limped to prosperity, but they were soon overwhelmed by the Panic of 1873, which, ironically, they had helped engender. Disintegration followed. What the pattern for northwestern railroading might have been had the alliance succeeded can only be a matter of conjecture. Union had promised strength, but in the end all participants foundered on the rock of financial collapse. The task of making the St. Paul & Pacific companies into a viable system remained in the category of unfinished business.

5

Legislation and Litigation

People "like to accuse others when a business fails to obtain success," Johan Carp wryly observed in 1873. Carp, a representative of the Dutch bondholders, commented thus on those involved with the St. Paul & Pacific companies. He referred also to the Panic of 1873, a five-year economic depression that seemed especially vicious in the northern heartland. For the StP&P and the First Division, hard times had begun a year earlier, when they lost credit and had to suspend vital construction. Jay Cooke & Company's bankruptcy and the Northern Pacific's financial collapse further complicated matters. And Mother Nature turned nasty as hordes of locusts assaulted crops and reduced production. Each group involved in the affairs of the St. Paul & Pacific roads understandably focused on its own narrow interest, so that stockholders, bondholders, and creditors, especially local contractors, contended for position, often uncertain whether to compromise or to press their full claims.[1]

Conflict in Hard Times

Even before the Panic of 1873, Dutch bondholders had taken steps to protect their interests, with good reason. Cessation of work on the St. Vincent Extension endangered the StP&P's charter and its land grant, and thus the security behind the $15-million issue of bonds. Furthermore, in May 1873, the First Division was forced to stop paying interest on several issues of its bonds. Within a few weeks, businessmen and bankers in Amsterdam formed a committee to represent investors who deposited their securities in exchange for the committee's certificates. The committee then selected the house of J. S. Kennedy & Company as its representative in the United States. That firm's senior partner, astute Scotsman John S. Kennedy, had gained experience in railroad finance with Jesup & Company, New York, before establishing his own firm in 1866.

Kennedy began proceedings for receiverships in 1873 under the various mortgages underlying the St. Paul & Pacific companies' bond issues, and during the following six years of litigation he led negotiations to protect the bondholders' interests. Kennedy and Johan Carp, as a member of the Dutch committee, also painstakingly analyzed the railroads.

A suit brought in the name of Kennedy and his partners against the St. Paul & Pacific Railroad Company, the First Division of the StP&P, the Northern Pacific Railroad Company, and trustees of the various mortgages, elicited widely differing interpretations of the $15-million bond issue. Notwithstanding defendants' objections, it was clear that construction had ceased, that the chief stockholder— the NP—could not give financial assistance, and that the legislative deadline for the StP&P to complete all construction (1873) was at hand. After weighing the evidence, Judge John F. Dillon appointed Jesse P. Farley receiver of the StP&P in August 1873. The court instructed the receiver to take immediate possession of the St. Vincent and the Brainerd extensions, put them in order, and complete them, if possible, by December. To finance the work, Farley was empowered to issue debentures of up to $5 million.[2]

Jesse Farley had two decades of experience in railroading, but he also had liabilities. While acting as receiver of the StP&P, he retained an interest in two Iowa railroads and frequently returned to his home in that state. He had next to no political influence in Minnesota. Although the Amsterdam bankers' assessment of Farley as an elderly and uneducated man was perhaps too harsh, he was nervous, jealous, and often tactless. He especially antagonized the Dutch by bringing his own son and W. H. Fisher from Iowa to assist him rather than having J. H. Kloos, already on salary, monitor the bondholders' interests.[3]

Farley nevertheless worked hard to carry out an almost impossible task. The northern 104 miles of the St. Vincent Extension were a great worry. Earlier, the First Division had laid track from south of Glyndon, where it crossed the NP, to north of Crookston, ending there in "an uninhabited prairie with no human habitation in sight." After minor reconditioning, the northern part of the St. Vincent Extension was put into limited operation. On December 22, 1873, mostly to impress Minnesota politicians, the first "regular" train ran over the Crookston line. No timetable was issued, but the conductor promised service once a week, or "oftener as the business of the road may demand." Local traffic failed to cover expenses, though, and after a month, operation was discontinued until spring 1874.[4]

The solution to the StP&P's problems clearly depended upon public opinion in this country and abroad. For construction the railroad needed extensions of time from both Congress and the Minnesota legislature, and from Holland the company needed financial aid. Throughout the Panic of 1873, however, American credit remained at low ebb; even the solidest American bonds were selling at 50 percent of par. If the railroad did not win the desired legislation and lost its land grant, the Dutch would think Congress dishonest and American credit would sink even lower.

A key question was whether the bondholders and De Graff & Company, both creditors of the StP&P, would work together or oppose each other. Relations between the bondholders' representatives and the contractors started off well. The affable John S. Barnes, Kennedy's partner, visited St. Paul in the summer of 1873, and he, with Kloos and Willmar, had amicable conferences with the Minnesota men. Kloos felt that the bondholders, for their own self-interest, should aid the other hard-pressed creditors. Carp and Kennedy, sensing the political implications, favored making a provisional contract with De Graff & Company.[5]

Personal conflicts within the StP&P, however, soon undermined the potential for reconciliation. Now serving as land commissioner of the StP&P, Kloos made it clear that he had been appointed and paid by Lippmann, Rosenthal & Company to protect the Dutch bondholders' interests. On the other hand, Farley, proud of his authority, felt his position depreciated by the Dutch. He regarded Kloos as "very communicative and unguarded," especially for admitting to the Minnesota legislature that he was an agent of foreign investors. Finally, one representative of the Dutch bondholders, the embittered Willmar, returned to Europe and severed his relations with Lippmann, Rosenthal & Company.[6]

Kennedy soon perceived that Farley's tactlessness had complicated relations with De Graff & Company. Carp reported that Farley had started repairing the railroad without giving a contract to De Graff & Company, and the receiver also had commented on Crooks's work in such a manner as to make "an enraged enemy" of this influential man. Another party, the Northern Pacific, in control of StP&P stock, also harassed the nervous Farley and worried the Dutch investors. Although their company was also bankrupt and financially powerless, NP officials protested that the receiver had done little to improve the StP&P property's condition. They presented their argument to the governor and won significant newspaper support.[7]

After negotiations in 1873 it was clear that the several creditors' interests outweighed mutual needs. Unfortunately, the Dutch bankers wanted a new contract stipulating that all funds to complete the extension would be assured before the first payment to contractors. The De Graffs refused that limitation and the conflict continued.[8]

Laws and Lawsuits

While attempting to raise capital in Europe, the committee of Dutch bondholders received little assurance from either American lawmakers or courts. Criticism of railroads in Minnesota had begun in the 1850s, continued in the 1860s, and grew shrill in 1873 and 1874. Organized farmers demanded relief from allegedly oppressive freight rates and railroad discrimination. In receivership suits, accusations expressed with more venom than objectivity fueled criticism among politicians, state regulatory agents, and the press.

Several commentators criticized railroads in general, but the St. Paul & Pacific companies drew specific attack. One writer claimed that in the 1860s First Division executives had been "too poor to bribe and too weak to domineer," but in the 1870s the company had "grown rich and powerful." It was "cracking always and ever the monopolist's whip . . . with all of the insolence of power derived from wealth," and further practiced "robbing labor of its reward." There was more. On shipments east to Minneapolis and St. Paul the company's charges discriminated in favor of the latter city. Shippers particularly objected to the railroad's contract with Davidson for grain-elevator service and reduced rates on wood given Hill, Griggs & Company.[9]

Before he left the company, Superintendent Francis R. Delano led the railroad's defense campaign. He recognized, he said, the farmer's condition and understood how, pushed to sell his produce at low rates in order to pay his debts, the farmer, feeling abused, blamed others for his plight. Nevertheless, the First Division had no monopoly in purchasing wheat, and the railroad's rates varied less than on any that he knew of. Minneapolis millers enjoyed no rebates or drawbacks but could buy more wheat because they offered a higher price. As to the elevator contract with Davidson, Delano declared that this arrangement saved the railroad from diverting scarce monies into grain-handling facilities. The First Division did exercise control to ensure adequate facilities as well as fair grading and inspection. Delano maintained too that the arrangement with Hill, Griggs & Company reduced fuel costs and, by providing low rates for large shipments of wood, it saved settlers 80 cents a cord in 1873.

Hermann Trott, as First Division land commissioner, also defended the St. Paul & Pacific companies. Because of depressed conditions and competition from free public-domain land, most of the reduced sales volume was on credit. Also, returns from sales of First Division acreage could not be used legally to cover operating deficits because they were pledged to debt redemption.

In the end hard-pressed farmers obviously outvoted bankrupt carriers. A Special Joint Railroad investigating committee was formed in 1871, and legislation followed. Companies had to make annual reports, freight was classified, and rates were set for both goods and passengers. In 1872, several acts amended legislation dealing with rates and obligated the railroads to build fences, supply cattle guards, transfer passengers, and ensure pay for construction workers employed by contractors. A joint resolution in 1873 requested that the attorney general prosecute the First Division because of the alleged exclusive agreement with Hill, Griggs & Company, an "oppressive burden on settlers." The flood would not be stopped. A board of three commissioners with broad powers was directed in 1874 to establish a schedule of "reasonable maximum rates" for each railroad. The burden of proving compliance was on each company.

Minnesota legislators remained in high dudgeon. Legislation in 1874 extended the time for completing the St. Vincent and Brainerd extensions, but to protect contractors added that no land was to be conveyed to the receiver until *all* the railroad's debts to citizens of the state were paid. Although De Graff & Company was the chief creditor, more than a hundred claims by others swelled the litigation. Then, further ensnarling these legal entanglements, the state assembly instructed the attorney general to vacate the company's

THE FIRST DIVISION

—OF THE—

ST. PAUL & PACIFIC

RAILROAD.

WINTER TIME TABLE.

1873 and 1874.

Passengers must get their Baggage checked before it will be carried over the road, and on the arrival of the train at place of destination, must present the check and take possession of their Baggage.

The Company will not be responsible for the safety of any Baggage after its arrival at station for which it is checked, it being no part of the business of this Company to receive and store Baggage, unless a special contract is made to that effect.

E. Q. SEWALL,   J. H. RANDALL,
Superintendent.   *Gen'l Ticket Agent.*

charter and correct alleged abuses in the elevator system.

Farley's reaction was predictable. The Granger interests, fully manifest in Minnesota, were "ready to do anything to blast the prospects of the Railroads," he groused in a letter to Kennedy. And he was suspicious of those closer to the StP&P: Becker, Delano, and De Graff & Company were "determined to ruin if they cannot rule" and he believed Edmund Rice, again a U.S. Senator from Minnesota, was working with them.[10]

Not to be forgotten were the bondholders, persistently attempting to gain control of the First Division by receivership. They would have much to say shortly.

6

The Associates Gain Control

During the mid-1870s, four experienced businessmen, the "associates," as they came to call themselves, resolved to acquire the St. Paul & Pacific Railroad companies in order to establish through rail service from St. Paul to Winnipeg. Three of the four—Donald Alexander Smith, Norman Wolfred Kittson, and James Jerome Hill—first spotted the opportunity in 1873 when the Northern Pacific lost control over the StP&P and its First Division. Their resources were more limited than their ambition, however, and to raise funds they turned to a fourth man, George Stephen, Smith's cousin. Even then, they found much difficulty.[1]

Negotiating a Bond Purchase

Donald Smith (later Lord Strathcona and Mount Royal) understood well how appealing was all-rail service between St. Paul and Winnipeg. An impressive man, thin and above medium height, he had sandy hair, an almost full beard, and shaggy brows over gray-blue eyes. In 1838, at eighteen, Smith had emigrated to Canada from Scotland, spending all his frugal, systematic working life

with the Hudson's Bay Company. A wielder of influence, he had been chief commissioner of his firm since 1870 and at times a member of both the Manitoba and Dominion parliaments. For both company and constituents he sought a rail line between St. Paul and Winnipeg to reduce transportation costs and create a critical link between eastern and western Canada.

The rail link Smith envisioned would also immediately stimulate settlement in the Red River Valley, encourage construction of a Canadian transcontinental, and expedite the sale of nine million acres of land Hudson's Bay Company had received in 1869 for relinquishing political power over Rupert's Land. Furthermore, a St. Paul–Winnipeg railroad promised to be a profitable investment.

Canadian interest in this venture was not new. In 1871, when the Northern Pacific began pushing the St. Vincent Extension northward, Smith, Stephen, and others had acquired charter rights for a connecting railroad to run from the border to Winnipeg, then westward. Implementation was delayed until the NP could demonstrate that it could complete the line, and when that effort failed, the Canadian project too was suspended. The desire for an all-rail line from Winnipeg to St. Paul remained, however.

Smith collected information on the St. Paul & Pacific through Kittson, agent of the Hudson's Bay Company in St. Paul, who asked two specialists in transportation, James J. Hill and Francis R. Delano, to evaluate the road. Kittson and Hill had known each other for several years, of course, and were principals in the Red River Transportation Company. Delano, recently resigned as superintendent of the First Division, was well acquainted with it, as Hill was from his long association as freight agent and supplier of firewood to the company.

Early in 1874, Smith sought out his cousin, George Stephen (later Lord Mount Stephen), who knew Canada's financial standing as well as he did his own. In 1850, not yet twenty-one, Stephen had left his native Scotland for Canada. He soon attained prominence, first as a merchant; then in manufacturing textiles, steel, and railway rolling stock; and finally as a banker. In 1876, he would be elected president of the Bank of Montreal. Tall, thin, with deep-set brooding eyes, he had an air of distinction. Well regarded for prudence and probity, Stephen was, a leading Canadian historian wrote, a man of "infinite resource" and "enormous courage." Although "arrogantly self-confident and impatient of criticism," he was, his biographer judged, "perhaps the greatest creative genius in the whole history of Canadian finance." In 1874, Stephen deemed Smith's dream of acquiring the St. Paul & Pacific unattainable and refused his support. Three years later, however, Stephen changed his mind and joined Smith, Hill, and Kittson.[2]

At first the associates made little headway; their campaign to gain control of the StP&P stood still, their first attempt abortive. Northern Pacific executives offered to transfer that company's StP&P stock to Delano if he would complete a Brainerd–Sauk Rapids line and then give the NP running rights over the Branch Line into St. Paul. In response, several men of St. Paul, including Delano, Hill, and Kittson, organized the Western Railroad Company of Minnesota (Western Railroad) encompassing the necessary route from Brainerd to Sauk Rapids. The incorporators failed to raise adequate funds for this enterprise, but time proved their charter valuable. Kittson and Hill

did succeed in constructing an eleven-mile line from Crookston Junction to Fisher's Landing in 1875. But NP officers, both before and after its reorganization in 1875, plied their influence in the Minnesota legislature to inhibit a north–south line outside their control. One Minnesota law, passed with NP support, even obligated the St. Paul & Pacific companies to pay debts due De Graff & Company and not to construct other trackage before completing both the projected St. Vincent and the Brainerd extensions.

Another Minnesota law of March 1876 gave StP&P and First Division bondholders hope for the future; it enabled mortgagees of a land-grant railroad to purchase the property under foreclosure, to reorganize the company, and to inherit the granted lands.

During 1876, Smith, Kittson, and Hill formulated definite plans to acquire the St. Paul & Pacific companies. On a trip to Ottawa in the spring, Hill discussed with Smith the possibility of interesting Morton, Rose & Company, London investment bankers, in the associates' plan to purchase StP&P bonds. Then, in August, the associates learned that the Dutch bondholders had not ratified the Litchfield Agreement promising compromise between stockholders and bondholders of the railroads. Consequently, bonds controlled by the Dutch committee came back on the market.

In the autumn of 1876, Johan Carp, representing the Dutch bondholders, arrived in St. Paul, and encouraged Hill and Kittson to bid for the First Division's property, excepting the land grant. Although the two Minnesotans wanted no such limited purchase, they offered $3.5 million for those assets in the hope that Carp would make a counterproposal.

While awaiting Carp's response, Hill, acting for the associates but behind the scenes, set

off logrolling to remove any legislative opposition. A pending bill would put aside proceeds from selling 300,000 acres to satisfy the De Graff claim. To promote it, incorporators of the Western Railroad of Minnesota, including Kittson and Hill, accepted an impossible legislative requirement, that the Western Railroad demonstrate intent to build the Brainerd-to-Sauk Rapids line by May 1, 1877. Kittson and Hill thus signaled their willingness to relinquish rights to the Brainerd line; in fact, they ultimately sold that charter to the NP, which eventually finished the line. In March 1877, supporters of the De Graffs and of the NP were finally willing to vote for an omnibus bill repealing restrictions on construction and setting new, workable dates for completing parts of the St. Vincent Extension.

Meanwhile, Hill aided the bondholders' cause, quietly laboring to gain control of the St. Paul & Pacific companies. He avidly collected information on the properties, prices of their securities in the United States and abroad, and the potential of a completed line to Manitoba. Soon Hill was urging the Dutch to finance additional construction and George Stephen to help the three original associates obtain funds to buy bonds of the bankrupt companies.

At Montreal in mid-May 1877, Hill and Smith persuaded Stephen to work with them. Accordingly, on May 26, 1877, Hill and Kittson sent a proposal that the Dutch committee carefully weighed. The phraseology sounded like an offer to buy StP&P bonds, but really requested an option to purchase them. The letter presented a schedule of prices for each of the five issues, leaving the committee free to alter proportions in the categories as long as the aggregate amount to be paid by the associates was not increased. Asked for its coun-

The Alexandria–Melrose stage line would be doomed when those communities were finally linked by rail.

sel, Kennedy & Company advised the Dutch bondholders to consider the proposal. The stage was set for bargaining.

In September 1877, Stephen, accompanied by Richard B. Angus, general manager of the Bank of Montreal, visited Minnesota to better acquaint himself with the properties. Hill had downplayed their value and stressed the locusts' devastation to farming in discussions with Carp, but with Stephen and Angus, he emphasized long-run expectations. Hill argued that, with an estimated investment of $5,540,180 in bonds and new construction, the associates would have a railroad and land holdings worth approximately $19 million. Stephen agreed that the gamble was worth a try.

On January 5, 1878, eager to conclude a purchase, the associates tendered an offer by which the sellers could choose to be paid in cash or in securities of a new company organized after foreclosure sales. They also committed themselves to pay the Dutch committee $125,000 and to advance funds necessary to complete the St. Vincent Extension in time to meet the latest legislative schedule.[3]

Meanwhile, several developments improved the climate for the associates. In January 1878, a preliminary agreement between the Northern Pacific and the St. Paul & Pacific companies provided for mutually satisfactory rates and division of revenues on traffic moving to and from Manitoba. On assurance by Hill that the Chicago, Milwaukee & St. Paul Railway (Milwaukee) was not backing the associates' project, the president of the Chicago & North Western Railway (C&NW) ordered his company's partisans in Holland to cease opposition to the proposed bond purchases.

In 1878, Hill also won favorable decisions from the Minnesota legislature, and by agreeing to pay the De Graffs later, he eliminated both protective legislation for that firm and its support for the NP's obstructive tactics. The legislature also changed the dates for completing the Melrose–Sauk Centre line from July 1 to August 1, 1878; the Melrose–Alexandria line to December 1, 1878; Fergus Falls and St. Vincent to January 1, 1880; and Glyndon-to-Fergus Falls a year later.

After procuring these important changes, the four associates signed an agreement on March 13, 1878 to buy the bonds and coupons controlled by the Dutch committee. Paying $3,753,150 for the bonds, the associates also assumed several other obligations. Starting December 22, 1877, they were required to pay 7 percent interest semiannually on the contract price of the bonds and on the cost of the Red River & Manitoba Railroad (the Breckenridge Cutoff, twenty-nine miles, Breckenridge to Barnesville in far western Minnesota, to tie the Main Line to the Branch). From that date they were also liable for legal costs for executing the agreement and pending suits, including foreclosure actions. To compensate the Dutch committee for its expenses, the associates agreed to pay $280,000 earnest money as soon as the bonds were put in the custody of Kennedy & Company. Finally, they were obligated to complete the St. Vincent Extension in 1878.[4]

Shortly after signing the purchase agreement, the associates formalized previous understandings on their respective shares in this ambitious venture. All four assumed joint and several responsibility for repaying money borrowed or advanced in executing the enterprise and, they understood, they were to share equally in ownership of the corporation to be formed after they had control of the St. Paul & Pacific properties. Each associate, however, was to receive only a one-fifth portion—the final fifth to be put in Stephen's hands, at first on the assumption that he would need it to obtain funds in London to carry out the agreement with the Dutch committee. Later, this sum was turned over to John S. Kennedy as compensation for his aid in consummating the project.

By June 8, 1878, the contract was in effect. The partners' expectations were high. They were acquiring properties that were bankrupt but potentially of great value. On the other hand, they were risking their reputations and their fortunes.

Completing Rail Links

Several problems plagued the management of, and construction for, the St. Paul & Pacific companies before the foreclosure sales. Working through the mortgage trustees and Receiver-General Manager Farley, the associates labored to keep their promise by completing the two remaining segments of the St. Vincent Extension (from near Melrose to Alexandria, and from Snake Hill, north of Crookston, to the international boundary) in 1878. At the same time, the partners looked for a Canadian road to connect with the St. Vincent Extension, assured themselves that the Dominion government employed Canadian

contractors to lay rail from Pembina, at the boundary, to Winnipeg (actually to St. Boniface, across the river from Winnipeg), and lobbied for an exclusive contract to run trains over this route.

Working out adequate and productive relationships with other railroads in Minnesota was still another task that demanded the associates' attention. Conflict and competition remained active between the NP and the StP&P companies, and the associates were vigilant to prevent any intervention in the StP&P companies' affairs by either the Milwaukee or the C&NW. While moving toward ownership, then, the associates needed to work through the current StP&P companies' management to safeguard their future.

Stephen and Hill led in moving the associates' plans to fruition. Kittson, in poor health, was away from St. Paul for several months; and, not having backed the successful candidate in the Dominion election of 1878, Smith was out of favor politically and had to stay in the background. The new prime minister, John A. MacDonald, whose goodwill was priceless to the associates, took office in September, determined to help complete some kind of Canadian transcontinental. Stephen, consequently, took the lead in arranging financing, obtaining political support in Canada, and negotiating with the NP and the Litchfields. Hill primarily acted the strong local manager who simultaneously sought political influence in Minnesota's legislature.

Hill was joined by Kittson, though, in assuming positions of influence in corporations informally related to the St. Paul & Pacific companies. In June 1878, the two were elected directors of both the Red River Valley Railroad (Crookston to Fisher's Landing) and the Red River & Manitoba Railway (Breckenridge

Cutoff), and the board of the latter elected Hill president. Hill and Kittson also purchased almost all outstanding shares of the Red River Transportation Company from minority stockholders.[5]

The associates found it necessary to provide collateral for their loans in several ways. Each man, in fact, put up every transferable security he owned. Hill sent his shares in the Red River Transportation Company and the deed for his Iowa coal lands. Stephen sold businesses netting him between $30,000 and $40,000 a year, and Hill disposed of his share of a fuel business in Minnesota, which, with other investments, had been producing a yearly income of $15,000.

Meanwhile, Hill had helped receiver Farley win authority from the United States District Court, on May 31, 1878, for the StP&P to issue debentures covering construction costs, no higher than $10,000 per mile, and secured by a first lien on all new road built. Not until the track was completed could the securities be issued, and then only for the amount expended. Within a week, John S. Kennedy, as trustee in possession of the railroad, instructed Farley to begin construction.

To expedite construction, Kennedy, at Hill's request, urged Jesse Farley to relinquish his authority. Kennedy suggested that the receiver lease both old and new parts of the St. Vincent Extension to the Red River & Manitoba Railway and also urged him to grant Hill and Kittson the contract for laying rails on the unfinished portions of that line. The lease would give the associates control of all operations on the Extension, free them to run it in such a way as to facilitate construction, and enable them to channel earnings into the corporation they managed.

Farley, however, initially insisted on keeping control of the StP&P companies, and his slowness in prosecuting construction worried the associates. Alert to the possibility of losing the land grant, Hill traveled often to the end-of-the-track with Farley, whom he regarded as dilatory and inefficient. Under stern pressure from the associates, Farley finally agreed to let Hill and Kittson take over responsibility for construction of the St. Vincent Extension in September 1878.

Yet, rather than being controlled, the work seemed to do the controlling. Suppliers lagged in delivering materials; October floods covered land and track; construction trains were delayed when locomotives were deprived of water because balky windmills failed; workmen drifted off the job; and snow, with extreme cold, came early.

Despite frustrating delays, the First Division met Minnesota's legislative deadlines in 1878. The nearly 105 miles added in one year was more new track than had been laid by the St. Paul & Pacific companies for some seasons. In fact, since 1872, the only construction by companies related to the StP&P had been from Crookston to Fisher's Landing in 1875, and the Breckenridge to Barnesville cutoff in 1876. Service reached Alexandria by November 5, and the *St. Paul Pioneer Press* exuberantly declared that the railroad was entitled to the ''gratitude of the state.'' Soon track-laying was completed from Warren to St. Vincent, adding another sixty-two miles, and on November 10, 1878, the first train from St. Vincent pulled in to St. Paul. Among other cars in its consist were elegant new sleepers, the *St. Paul* and the *Minneapolis*, which carried Farley, Hill, and their friends. A gap remained in the St. Vincent Extension from Alexandria to Barnesville, but the Breckenridge Cutoff provided a temporary alternative.[6]

Meanwhile, rail service north of the border was proving difficult to introduce. The Canadian government had awarded a contract to build north from the boundary to Winnipeg, but growing delays in construction became obvious. To expedite the work, Hill persuaded the First Division to sell the Canadian contractor a locomotive and ties and a supplier to deliver fifteen flat cars. All obstacles were finally overcome, and the last spike was driven on December 2, 1878. Four days later the first revenue train left St. Paul for Winnipeg via Breckenridge.

Eliminating Potential Competition

Throughout this frenetic, frustrating period the associates labored to acquire securities of the St. Paul & Pacific companies that were not in the hands of the Dutch committee. The partners' heavy commitment in money and effort made it imperative that they strengthen their position in relation to the two companies so that no other contender could gain control, either before or at the foreclosure sales. Most of these securities were held by two parties. Charles B. Wright, president of the Northern Pacific, held much of the StP&P's stock, and Edwin C. Litchfield, the family spokesman, held bonds and was the major First Division stockholder. Although the nearly valueless bond issue of 1871 could be ignored, investors, apart from those working through the Dutch committee, owned $2,880,000 par value of the others. Even if minority bondholders did not fight foreclosure suits, their delaying tactics could subvert the entire undertaking.

Stephen adopted a strategy of selective emphasis. In Holland, purchasers of some of the $3-million issue drove the price above the $30 stipulated in the associates' agreement with the

Dutch committee, but Hill countered by persuading the mortgage trustees first to refuse to accept unpaid coupons of StP&P bonds in payment for land, and then to suspend all sales of land. The strategy worked: by January 1879, Stephen had control of about seven-eighths of the several issues.

Somewhat earlier, the associates had sought to resolve conflicts between the Northern Pacific and the St. Paul & Pacific. With the StP&P's Breckenridge Cutoff open for business, NP's control of rail transport in the Duluth–St. Paul–Winnipeg triangle was weakened, although its managers were determined to salvage all possible influence. Knowing that Stephen's group needed the StP&P shares, NP executives decided to seek a large concession in exchange for stock held by their President Wright. To this end they supported Litchfield and the De Graffs; argued over claims, trackage rights, rates, divisions, and interchange of cars; and took the StP&P to court over contested land grants.

Amid this nasty business, the NP's Wright asserted that charges to his road for running rights were too high and threateningly added that Alexander Mitchell, chief executive of the Milwaukee and a director of the NP, had offered to have the Milwaukee join the NP in building a competitive parallel line from Sauk Rapids to St. Paul on the west bank of the Mississippi. Indeed, Wright did more than threaten—he ordered surveys for lines along both the Red and the Mississippi rivers.

Mortgage trustees of the First Division, vigorously encouraged by Hill, eventually agreed with NP's Wright to arbitrate their differences on interchanges of traffic and division of rates. In short order the arbitrators stipulated that on joint rates between points on the NP and the Twin Cities, divisions were to be prorated ex-

The *Minneapolis Tribune* sobbed that St. Paul seemingly had become "the chief railroad . . . metropolis of the Northwest," but business on the StP&P at Minneapolis was clearly very good as this view from 1874 demonstrates. The passenger station, at Washington Avenue and Third Avenue North, is at left with the freight station in the center. *(Courtesy of Minnesota Historical Society)*

cept for shipments originating or terminating at five locations—Bismarck, Fargo, and Jamestown, North Dakota and Moorhead and Glyndon, Minnesota—where specific schedules of rate divisions were set. Revenues on grain shipments from Glyndon to the Twin Cities and to Duluth were to be pooled and all grain from Glyndon to St. Paul and to Minneapolis was to be routed over the First Division's Main Line.

These important agreements notwithstanding, the associates and the NP's Wright continued to spar over other points at issue. During summer 1878 the NP encouraged outsiders to form a new company—the Minneapolis, St. Cloud & Sauk Rapids Railway—to construct a competitive route along the west bank of the Mississippi between Minneapolis and St. Cloud. Wright also let it be known that the NP would lease the line if completed. Greatly upset, mortgage trustees of the St. Paul & Pacific urged the associates to make concessions. Wright pressed his advantage, demanding joint ownership of several properties held by the StP&P: the line north of Glyndon, that from Sauk Rapids to St. Paul, and terminals at St. Cloud, Minneapolis, and St. Paul. Hill and Stephen refused to discuss any joint arrangement in the Red River Valley and threatened to survey a line west from Grand Forks to the Missouri River, parallel to the NP.

Progress came, but slowly. Hill suggested that agreement might be reached through joint utilization of the Branch Line from St. Paul to St. Cloud and Sauk Rapids, each company bearing costs proportional to use, and Wright accepted the idea as a basis for discussion. Stephen knew that the NP desired some land owned by the First Division in St. Paul, another point for bargaining. Factional differences, though, appeared among the NP directors. One group, led by Wright, considered it imperative that the NP have an independent entry into Minneapolis; another faction, headed by Frederick Billings, chairman of the committee negotiating with Stephen, opposed any such expenditure because

the NP needed every penny for building its main line to the West Coast. Backed by St. Paul businessmen, who pledged to withdraw all shipments from the Milwaukee until assured that no new line would be constructed from Sauk Rapids to Minneapolis, Hill persuaded Alexander Mitchell, chief executive of the Milwaukee and a director of the NP, to support Billings's position.

Exploiting this split within the NP directorate, Stephen made his "final" proposition to the NP on November 8, 1878; he won a "treaty of peace" ten days later. The deal encompassed three agreements, one allowing the question of disputed land-grant properties to be settled in the courts. The second, a preliminary protocol, was a detailed, formal contract for settling major differences between the NP and the Stephen group. The NP agreed to build neither a line on the west bank of the Mississippi, nor lines within twenty miles from the west bank of the Red. In return, the NP gained ninety-nine-year running rights over the Branch Line from Sauk Rapids to St. Paul, and use of the passenger depot and a gift of ten acres for a freight warehouse and tracks in St. Paul. Most important to Stephen at the moment was the third element of the "treaty": the NP promised to relinquish to the associates its StP&P shares, to drop all opposition to foreclosure suits, and to support Stephen in his negotiations with the Litchfields.

Local newspaper reactions reflected specific if parochial interests. The *St. Paul Globe* exultantly called on the citizenry to provide the NP "with all the facilities which the terminus of such a gigantic highway requires." Fuming in defeat, the *St. Cloud Journal* declared that to the people of Minneapolis and St. Cloud, St. Paul had done "all the injury in her power by killing" the west-bank line. And the *Minneapolis Tribune* complained that St. Paul seemingly had consolidated its position as "the chief railroad, commercial, manufacturing and political metropolis of the Northwest."[7]

With agreement between the StP&P and the NP ensured, interest was now concentrated on the "Litchfield matter." Until late 1878, the associates' strategy in dealing with the Litchfields was, Hill wrote, to act as if "we expected nothing except what the courts gave us." In October 1877, fearful that the majority stockholder of the First Division, E. Darwin Litchfield, would apply earnings of the Branch Line to pay interest in arrears on bonds issued on those miles and then assert control, Kittson

and Hill persuaded Kennedy, as mortgage trustee, to have the principal on the First Division's mortgage declared due at once. Alleging fraud in the StP&P's obligations under the $15-million bond issue, Hill's lawyers in mid-1878 also instituted legal attachment of all E. Darwin Litchfield's stock and personal property in Minnesota, mostly virgin land along the Main Line. Later in the year the associates began similar proceedings in New York. Stephen wrote Edwin C. Litchfield, in October 1878, that he had heard "nothing will satisfy you but to litigate to the end, and our plans are laid accordingly."[8]

Finally, on February 6, 1879, a deal was struck with the Litchfields. The associates agreed to pay $200,000 in cash and $300,000 in bonds of a new company they planned to form. In return, the Litchfields relinquished all bond holdings in the St. Paul & Pacific companies, all but a few shares, agreed to assume claims by George Becker, and promised to abide by judgments in foreclosure suits. On the evening when the agreement was signed, all former directors of the First Division resigned and new ones, including John S. Barnes of Kennedy & Company, Stephen, and Hill were elected. The new directors elected Stephen president the next day.

The timing was excellent. Earlier, Hill had estimated that the First Division's operating revenues for 1878 would exceed operating expenses by $500,000. The actual figure was substantially higher; the First Division was becoming a profitable operation.

Tag Ends of a Long-Tailed Kite

After delay that seemed interminable, decisions on the foreclosures came in March and April 1879. Four were handed down in a

Minnesota District Court between March 15 and 31, and the fifth, April 11 in the United States Court by Judge Dillon. Each decree included orders for holding a sale, minimum price to be paid, and stipulations on methods of payment. Specific protection for minority bondholders was included.

On May 23, 1879, amid these foreclosure sales, the associates formed the St. Paul, Minneapolis & Manitoba Railway Company (StPM&M or Manitoba) under the general laws of Minnesota. This organization, led by President Stephen, now controlled the former St. Paul & Pacific properties.

For the associates to meet contractual obligations, they needed control of the new corporations' securities. The StPM&M arranged for $15 million in common stock and two bond issues of $8 million each. The major part of these securities was allotted to the associates for money they had paid out and for new risks they were taking, but much of the first issue went to make payments to others. The total capitalization was set at $31,486,000.

Part of the StPM&M's common stock was used to pay for property previously acquired. Of the 150,000 shares issued in 1879, 2,500 were used to purchase stock of the Red River & Manitoba Railroad, which the Dutch had financed. Another 2,000 shares went to pay stockholders of the Red River Valley Railroad Company. That corporation owned not only the eleven miles of rail from Crookston to Fisher's Landing but also almost all the stock of the Winnipeg & Western Transportation Company, Ltd., successor to the Red River Transportation Company.

At the time these arrangements were perfected, the associates were still responsible for completing lines from Alexandria to Barnesville and from Fisher's Landing to Grand

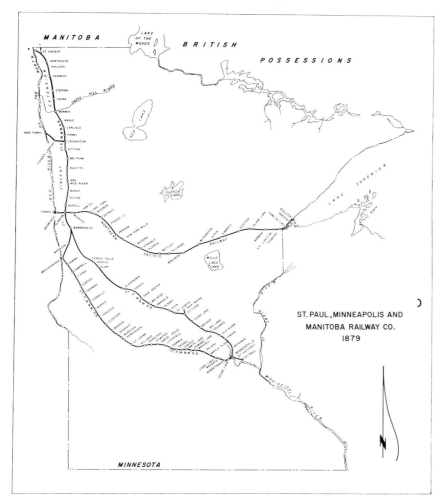

ST. PAUL, MINNEAPOLIS AND
MANITOBA RAILWAY CO.
1879

Anthony Falls Water Power Company, shares and bonds of the Minneapolis & St. Paul Elevator Company, stock of the Winnipeg & Western Transportation Company, Ltd., and a few bonds issued by the town of Fergus Falls.[9]

In a sense, however, the accounting was not final for many years. Until the 1890s, the associates would have many anxious moments from a welter of claims arising from acquisition of properties that went into the Manitoba. The De Graff claim, finally closed out with others for $150,000 in 1881, was minor. John S. Barnes could philosophically observe to Hill that the partners "should expect all sorts of tag ends to such a long-tailed kite," but the four associates who had struggled so long and so hard to get possession of the StP&P companies found slight balm in these words.[10]

Disturbing as these problems were, the associates were much more concerned and for a much longer time, over the actions of Jesse P. Farley. Shortly after the associates' purchase agreement was concluded with the Dutch bondholders in 1878, Farley wrote Kennedy, claiming that Hill and Kittson had offered him an interest. In rebuttal, Kennedy argued that acceptance would be inconsistent with Farley's obligations, as receiver and general manager of the railroad, to the trustees and the bondholders. A year later Farley again asserted that Kittson and Hill had promised him participation in the purchase contract with the Dutch committee, and asked $100,000 compensation for services rendered. Hill refused, saying that salaries paid to Farley as the general manager and receiver were adequate reward. Barnes expressed his opinion freely. He regarded Farley's behavior as a "rascally thing," particularly because Farley already had been "paid ten times more than his services" were

Forks. They were also personally responsible for making extensive repairs, improvements, and additions. To finance these projects, the associates "loaned" the company $2,700,000 in Manitoba bonds as collateral. By December 1879, the construction tasks had been completed and improvement programs were under way.

Six months later, on May 12, 1880, the final accounting between the StPM&M and the associates as individuals was made. In settlement, the associates transferred the $2,700,000 in bonds mentioned above. Of this amount, $2,200,000 was "in full discharge of their [the associates'] said liability for the construction and equipment" of the two lines. For the remaining $500,000, which the partners had lent in excess of their obligations, they received from the StPM&M some of the securities that it held in local organizations: stock of the St.

worth. Even though Hill, being "a loose talker" and "inclined to make messes of negotiation," might well have given Farley "ground to indulge in hopes" of the "vaguest sort," Barnes believed that Stephen should dismiss the claimant without a penny.[11]

Kennedy and Stephen preferred to establish the facts and to appease Farley, if possible. Kittson and Hill admitted privately to Kennedy that they had offered an "interest" to Farley, and Stephen gave his commitment to carry out anything that Hill and Kittson had promised. Stephen even suggested that Farley be given stock of the StPM&M to qualify as a director of the company, but Kennedy reminded them that, as receiver and general manager of the St. Paul & Pacific companies, Farley could not sit as a director of the new corporation. Farley then commenced suit. He asked to be given a 20 percent share in the associates' enterprise, basing his claim on reputed promises by Hill and Kittson. In detailed expositions of their actions, the defendants omitted mention of their early offer to Farley, and denied making him any binding promises of participation. They won round after round, but Farley carried the case to the U.S. Supreme Court, which on December 11, 1893, upheld the validity of the District Court's decree in dismissing his bill of complaint.[12]

Gaining control of the St. Paul & Pacific companies had been a major accomplishment for the associates. And at long last rails ran from St. Paul to Winnipeg. The great challenge ahead was making the new company an integrated and profitable railroad system. The real value of the property would depend not on its circumstances in 1879 but on its ultimate earning power, which at last rested in the competent hands of new owners.

7

The Manitoba

When it was organized in 1879, the St. Paul, Minneapolis & Manitoba Railway Company faced an uncertain future. For almost a quarter of a century the railroads that were consolidated under its banner had experienced a checkered history, and their properties remained in generally shaky condition. St. Paul newspapers editorialized, however, that with "ownership" management, "a new age of success henceforth dawns on this important sectional and international commercial thoroughfare." It was far from clear, nevertheless, that purchase of the properties by the associates—George Stephen, Donald Smith, Norman Kittson, and James J. Hill—would prove a sound investment. To their credit, these men understood that success required organized, systematic management to complete the construction promised the Dutch bondholders, to expand the StPM&M system in an orderly and efficient fashion, and to develop a profitable volume of traffic by promoting settlement in the Red River Valley and by building up commerce with western Canada.[1]

Men and Organization

As could be expected, the associates dominated among company directors and officers. The board included Hill, Kittson, Smith,

and Stephen; two attorneys, Horace R. Bigelow and Reuben B. Galusha; and John S. Barnes, partner in J. S. Kennedy & Company, formerly the representative of the Dutch bondholders and now the Manitoba's fiscal agent in New York. Stephen was elected president and Kittson vice president. The only man in the group experienced in transportation, James J. Hill, was named general manager.

Although residing in the East, as did presidents of many western railroads in that era, Stephen remained chief executive officer until 1882. Kittson, ranking officer in St. Paul, was old, in poor health, and relatively inactive in company affairs. Stephen visited the property occasionally and was consulted regularly by Hill, but left most operating decisions to the general manager or quickly accepted his recommendations. Stephen's major responsibilities included negotiating with British investors, bargaining with the Northern Pacific, and dealing with the Canadian government for a contract to build the Canadian Pacific Railway (CPR).

From the beginning, Hill realized that he had to improve the road's management. In 1878, he told Stephen that an "entire change of method and discipline" was needed. Stephen agreed and urged Hill to get rid of "any barnacles" and to discharge Farley, who was not only an expense but a "nuisance." Hill complied.[2]

Only forty-one years old, healthy, and full of vigor, Hill drove himself unremittingly. He felt responsibility for all local affairs: legislative actions, legal problems, community and labor relations, solicitation, operations, and construction. His first step was to institute an intensive economy drive, believing that great savings could be gained with care in purchasing. Hill was busy with decisions large and small, day and night. On one occasion he told Stephen that he had not left his office before midnight for weeks. Appointing a purchasing agent and a tie and fuel agent slightly eased his burdens, and Hill optimistically hoped "to get matters into a better system" so that his tasks would "not be such hard work."[3]

Stephen expressed sympathetic understanding, and encouraged Hill to proceed with confidence: "I know how much you have to do and to think of and how difficult it is for you to overtake all the work cast upon you. . . ." When performance was not up to expectations, Stephen wrote: "I know full well that you are doing almost a superhuman amount of work. . . . It would be almost a miracle if some mistakes were not made and some important things overlooked."[4]

When Stephen became convinced that Hill was working too hard, he resolved to strengthen the resident team. Kittson resigned as vice president, and the post was filled by Richard B. Angus, general manager of the Bank of Montreal. Angus and Hill made a good team. The vice president soon reported that he was "more in the railway work day by day and the utmost harmony prevails." Each man brought different experiences and abilities. Hill instructed Angus in the intricacies of railroading, and Angus educated Hill in matters of financial management.[5]

Stephen meanwhile won a major contract with the Canadian government to construct the Canadian Pacific Railway west of the Great Lakes. In this project, Angus and Hill would carry heavy responsibility on behalf of the CPR, serving on its board of directors and, as western representatives of its executive committee, handling local affairs. Hill was pleased when the route he recommended as "shortest and best" through southern Manitoba was cho-

sen, and he reminded CPR's chief engineer that in British Columbia the directors wished the line to go "no nearer the Boundary Line than in the neighborhood of 100 miles." During spring 1881, Alpheus B. Stickney, who had been the Manitoba's superintendent of construction, was sent north to fill the same position on the CPR. Stephen also accepted Hill's recommendation to appoint as CPR general manager William C. Van Horne, who had been general superintendent on the Milwaukee. Late in 1881, Hill personally escorted the new officer to Winnipeg.[6]

Other personnel changes followed. Angus left the Manitoba to devote full time to CPR affairs in Montreal. With Angus in Montreal, Hill's task in western Canada was lightened, but his burdens in Minnesota were increased. Stephen now had less time to devote to the StPM&M, and so Hill was elected vice president; Allen Manvel, with twenty-five years' experience on the Chicago, Rock Island & Pacific, became general manager. Yet Hill found it difficult to delegate authority—even to the talented Manvel—saying to Stephen: "I am much happier in feeling it move forward than if I should leave it to others." Stephen was properly apprehensive. Hill, he said, was "only a little softer than steel," and was endangering his own health, without which "everything else becomes valueless."[7]

Reflecting Stephen's assessment, Hill was elected president of the Manitoba in August 1882. At that time, the directors, along with Hill, were Angus, Smith, Stephen, the lawyer Galusha, and two new members—John S. Kennedy and D. Willis James, both of New York and both experts in finance. Because monthly meetings of the directors were difficult to arrange, that provision of the bylaws was repealed, and an executive committee of

four, which included Hill, made necessary decisions between sessions of the board.

After Hill's election as president, the management team was further enlarged. By late 1883, John S. Kennedy turned his New York firm over to his nephew, J. Kennedy Tod, and devoted more time to his new position as vice president of the StPM&M, specializing in finance. At St. Paul, two departments arose under the general manager. The operating department was headed by a general superintendent, who with an assistant general superintendent, supervised three divisions: Breckenridge, Fergus Falls, and Northern. Jurisdiction of the traffic (sales) department fell to W. C. Alexander, general freight agent, supported by a new assistant general passenger agent. By 1883, this small group of officers supervised 5,800 employees operating 1,350 miles of railroad.

The task of recruiting, training, disciplining, and retaining workers was difficult because of time and place. About a third of the company's employees worked in or out of St. Paul. At the shops, more skilled workers were hired to care for the growing fleet of locomotives and cars, and at stations along the line, telegraphers doubled as station agents. After gaining experience in this way, though, young men often left the company to grasp opportunities elsewhere. Their reasons for leaving varied widely; the record often cryptically carried the word "quit," but one explicit note stated: "Resigned to make more money producing No. 1 hard wheat & did."[8]

Semiskilled workers on the StPM&M—section hands, maintenance men, and construction laborers—were a cross section of nationalities who were settling Minnesota. New immigrants, most of them farmers looking for cash to develop their land, found employment on

Track crews constituted a cross section of nationalities that were settling Minnesota. *(Courtesy of Minnesota Historical Society)*

the railroad, and many who had teams spent part of their time as subcontractors. They needed only a few months of the year for wheat production, and the railroad tried to plan work not to interfere with planting and harvesting.

Train service personnel—engineers, firemen, conductors, brakemen, and baggage men—often had experience on other railroads; usually they were young men who had migrated west. Of the 660 on the payroll in 1882, 80 percent were native born, more than half of them from the upper Midwest, and the others from the Northeast. Most of the foreign born came from Canada, Ireland, or England.

Conductors and brakemen had an uneven record for reliability. During the years 1879 to 1882, the StPM&M's 126 conductors were on

the average younger than its engineers. Many were discharged, usually in clusters following efficiency tests, indicating that new strict controls "caught" men not accustomed to discipline. Some were dismissed for "knocking down" fares, but more often they were discharged for disobeying orders or neglecting duty. Among young brakemen, who performed difficult and dangerous tasks, the accident rate was higher than for conductors, and dismissal was more frequently for drunkenness. Of the 227 hired, 20 percent were fired for reasons including "general worthlessness," "indecent language," and "putting arm around female in coach." Other brakemen were promoted or quit to work for another railroad.

Engine crews had a better record for dependability. A typical engineer had eleven

years of railroading elsewhere and was young and vigorous. In 1882, only two were over fifty and the average age was thirty-one. Almost a third of the 148 engineers listed in that year had served the antecedent St. Paul & Pacific companies and had an excellent record for compliance with orders and freedom from accidents. Firemen averaged twenty-four years of age, some with experience on boats or in mills, but usually they came to the Manitoba with experience on other railroads. Few of the 141 firemen were older than thirty, and very few suffered personal injury or were discharged.

Those who worked on locomotives had their position more clearly defined than that of any other group. Although the Brotherhood of Locomotive Engineers dated from 1863, it had no contract with the StPM&M, although in 1888, an agreement was signed between an affiliate and a committee of its engineers. In 1883, the company's master mechanic had announced an ''agreement with employees'' handling motive power. For a month of 360 hours or less on a switch engine, a fireman started at $52.50 and an engineer at $85, with a program for increases. For a day of 100 miles or less on the road, a fireman received $2.25 and a ''first-class engineer,'' $3.90. Seniority was defined, and those suspended or discharged were to have fair and impartial hearings.

Generally positive relationships between the company and its operating crafts contrasted with the difficulty the Manitoba had with its shop workers. Strikes were called for varied reasons, but efforts to effect discipline caused as much discontent as the workers' desire for improved wages. During autumn 1879, one strike followed a new master mechanic's reducing the daily wage for boilermakers from $2.50 to $2.40, and in summer 1880, roundhouse employees in St. Paul walked out, followed by about three hundred in the shops. They accused the master mechanic and two foremen of being unnecessarily exacting and of favoring new men from Canada. Hill, then general manager, addressed the disgruntled men, declared his willingness to hear individual grievances and to right wrongs, but he did not agree to negotiate with a committee. All dissidents returned to work, but shop workers remained disaffected. In August 1881, the boilermakers, blacksmiths, and their helpers walked off the job. Helpers returned when offered a 7 percent pay increase and a company commitment to supply fuel for their homes at cost, but the others stayed out. Hill angrily complained that the boilermakers were paid as much as those in other shops, and sent to

Montreal for replacements. In December he again refused an increase, stating that the railroad would ''be subject to another rise whenever they took a notion to demand it.''[9]

Both Hill and Manvel rigidly enforced rules and were unwilling to deal with organized labor, but both showed solicitude for those who gave faithful service. They regretted ''catching'' a good worker in a minor infraction or an isolated instance of carelessness, and they exercised clemency or quietly tried to place such a man with another railroad. They repeatedly advised superintendents to give every man a fair hearing. Hill rewarded diligence and zeal on the company's behalf with praise, pay raises, and occasionally a bonus. Employees frequently wrote to him of personal problems and trouble with supervisors; rarely were their requests ignored. Discipline was required, but Hill and Manvel, both prodigious workers themselves, expressed respect and understanding for a fellow employee who was dedicated to the company.

Construction and Relations with Other Railroads

Immediately after organizing the Manitoba, the associates prepared to complete construction that had been promised the Dutch bondholders. Hill had pushed work from Melrose to Alexandria in 1878, but a seventy-seven-mile gap remained between Alexandria and Barnesville. To prepare that route, Hill contracted in May 1879 with Langdon, Harrison & Company. That firm enjoyed the services of David C. Shepard, who, after serving briefly as chief engineer of the Minnesota & Pacific, had gained wide experience in railroad construction. Under various partnerships, he would build most of the Manitoba's mileage.

In spite of difficulties, the Alexandria–Barnesville line was finished before the end of 1879. The StPM&M could finally offer direct service on two trunk routes—the former Main Line and the former Branch Line—west and north from the Twin Cities.

Elsewhere, motivation was strong to build a short branch from Crookston, Minnesota, to Grand Forks, Dakota Territory. In the summer of 1879, Hill estimated that, after favorable harvests and two seasons of low water on the Red River, a quarter million bushels of wheat awaited the first train to Grand Forks. Contractors pushed a temporary bridge across the river to start service, planning to erect a more lasting structure later. Before the end of the year, the associates had met their promise to the Dutch bondholders, and the StPM&M established a foothold in Dakota Territory.

Furthermore, as long as the company conformed to territorial laws, it could expand westward. Indeed, directors were already planning other lines. Two factors charged this decision: the ominous prospect of competition and the desire to occupy new territory. News reached the directors that Delano, the ''Old Man'' of the St. Paul & Pacific, was grading north of Casselton, Dakota Territory, and soon rumor had it that this line was actually planned to join another south from Winnipeg. The Northern Pacific, they knew, was behind both projects. It was true that NP President Frederick Billings had not been willing to concede in the 1879 pact between the NP and the Manitoba that the StPM&M was to be a north–south system and the NP an east–west road. Yet Hill stubbornly persisted in that understanding. During the early 1880s, in any event, the two companies expanded in both Dakota Territory and Minnesota; a railroad commissioner in Minnesota commented that the two systems were "interlocking and lapping" on each other.[10]

In 1880, the Manitoba concentrated on four new routes. That from Morris to Brown's Valley (47 miles) opened a rich farming area that the railroad was to be awarded "in lieu of" land grants earned but not available along its trunk lines because of early settlement and claims by other railroads. The StPM&M's building there also was motivated by the desire to head off the Milwaukee, which coveted the area too.

The greatest undertaking by the StPM&M, in 1880, however, was on three lines in the northeast corner of Dakota Territory, where it clashed grandly with the Northern Pacific. Angus accused the NP of planning "to rob its weaker neighbor," and Frederick Billings protested that the Manitoba's expansion west of the Red River was contrary to agreement. One new StPM&M line ran from Breckenridge to Durbin (48 miles), and another was a short extension from Grand Forks west to Ojata (12 miles). The longest new line pushed from Barnesville through Moorhead and Fargo to Reynolds (82 miles) to occupy the land just west of the Red River. Moorhead would be a point competitive with the NP; that company adopted a familiar delaying tactic: it sought an injunction to restrain the StPM&M from crossing NP tracks. After Angus found that the NP had failed to obtain a legal right-of-way at the point of crossing, the StPM&M resumed construction. "If the Nor. Pac. continues hostile," Hill assured Kennedy, "we will make ourselves felt in a way they cannot misunderstand."[11]

Rivalry between the two railroads intensified during the next years. The NP's management had great plans for expansion and pushed them vigorously after Henry Villard, through the Oregon & Transcontinental Railroad Company (O&T), acquired control of the NP in 1881 and replaced Billings as president. Using the O&T's leverage, Villard purchased the majority of stock in the Manitoba & South-Western Colonization Railway Company, a road strategically located to link NP's Casselton line with Winnipeg. In Minnesota, the NP itself planned two lines to cut across the Manitoba's trunk routes, one from Little Falls southwest to Morris, the other from Wadena via Fergus Falls to the Black Hills in Dakota Territory. The NP also started a branch from Fergus Falls up the Pelican Valley.

Meanwhile, the StPM&M's expansion campaign soon confirmed predictions in the *Minneapolis Tribune*, stating on December 13, 1880, that the railroad desired to "branch about generally" in Minnesota, Dakota, and Manitoba. The company's directors indeed authorized several specific extensions in Dakota Territory. The StPM&M occupied the area immediately west of the Red River in 1881–1882 by completing the road from Reynolds, northwest of Fargo, to Neche on the Canadian border, from Grand Forks 68 miles west to Bartlett, and from Breckenridge to Durbin, which was lengthened northwest another 82.6 miles to Hope. In 1882, still another new line was started from Sauk Centre, Minnesota, reaching northeast to Browerville (25.5 miles). To counter NP moves in Minnesota, the StPM&M also threw up a roadbed east of Morris, and announced plans to build west to the Missouri River; in 1881–1882, Shepard graded some 40 miles west of Wahpeton. When Hill's forces began grading northward from Carlisle up the Pelican Valley toward Red Lake Woods, however, they met NP workers—NP trackmen in an area regarded by the StPM&M as "absolutely within the territory of the Manitoba according to all railway usage." And, as the StPM&M built from Carlisle Junction to Elizabeth, the NP constructed a link from Fergus Falls to Pelican Rapids (21.7 miles).[12]

Other significant strategic decisions followed. For instance, the Manitoba announced plans for a line along the west bank of the Mississippi from Minneapolis to St. Cloud. Several considerations inspired this. Settlers in the area had long suggested it, the NP coveted the route for an independent line into the Twin Cities, and the Milwaukee was known to be negotiating with persons in Minneapolis about a new line west from that city and it, too, might select this corridor. By year's end Manitoba rails reached Clearwater and were extended to St. Cloud by the next.

The StPM&M similarly found good reason to strengthen its connection with Duluth. Farmers west and southwest of the Twin Cities were known to be interested in a more direct route to Lake Superior, and the StPM&M was itself desirous of finding a way to avoid expensive rates on coal from Duluth. Although the company had already invested $210,000 in Iowa's Climax Coal Company, it still depended on fuel shipments from West Virginia and Pennsylvania via the Great Lakes. These moved, Hill groused, from the Head of the Lakes via the NP, either to Glyndon or to Sauk Rapids. Other factors had to be considered. Angus pointed out that competition among routes around Lake Michigan (that is, Chicago) and those via Lake Superior (in other words, Duluth) was fully joined. Who then were to be allies?

Senior officers of the Manitoba pondered options; concrete plans followed. First, with two others—the Chicago, Milwaukee & St. Paul and the Chicago, St. Paul, Minneapolis

& Omaha—it jointly purchased control of the St. Paul & Duluth (formerly the Lake Superior & Mississippi and owned by the NP for a short time prior to 1873) and immediately made vital traffic agreements with it. This purchase was, in a sense, defensive. Hill, disturbed by the Milwaukee's announcement that it was planning to extend from Minneapolis west to Ortonville, near the boundary of Minnesota and Dakota Territory, was clearly pleased to share control of the St. Paul & Duluth with that company, for the Milwaukee might otherwise come to control it or join with others whose pooling arrangements would favor Chicago over Duluth. The second move was made unilaterally. In 1881, the Manitoba purchased the charter of the Minneapolis & St. Cloud Railroad Company from Joseph P. Wilson, founder of St. Cloud, who had been trying since 1856 to finance construction for that local road. Wilson's threat to sell his rights to the Northern Pacific induced the StPM&M to spend $30,000 to satisfy the discouraged owner. Surveys from St. Cloud northeast to a connection with the jointly controlled St. Paul & Duluth at Hinckley were followed by construction of the 66.5 miles in 1882.[13]

Elsewhere, carrying construction materials and the growing revenue traffic strained both men and equipment. Especially on the new Northern Division between Fergus Falls and the international boundary, a succession of superintendents struggled against both natural and man-made obstacles to improve operations. The northwest winds of the Red River

The northwest winds of the Red River Valley piled up snow in a series of bitterly cold winters; that of 1879–1880 was reportedly the worst in twenty years. Men suffered and locomotives failed.

The Manitoba opened the famous Hotel Lafayette on beautiful Lake Minnetonka in 1882. *(Stereoptican card and poster)*

Valley piled up snow in bitterly cold winters; that of 1879–1880 was reportedly the worst in twenty years. Men suffered and locomotives failed. Spring thaws and rains, coupled with inadequate drainage, caused flooding of low-lying track. Finally, incoming settlers, forced to wait for the land to dry out before unloading their "movables," created a scarcity of yard facilities, side tracks, and cars.

The inadequate supply of labor was another problem. In 1880, Superintendent John L. Sullivan reported difficulty in keeping "a regular set of engineers," and in one month he had to discharge six freight conductors for irregularities. In April 1881, Sullivan's frustration was acute. He had just nine road engines to handle freight and switching assignments on the 202 miles of line under his supervision. Emigrant trains were "dropping in," and "odds and ends of cars" were scattered at stations where they had been left because of inadequate power. Some men were sick, others absent, and a bad derailment at Rothsay added trouble. Full freight trains were being pulled north, full empties moving south, and it was time, Sullivan moaned, to start seasonal work on the track.[14]

By July 1882, yet another officer was wrestling with operating problems. Incompetence was rife in many of the crafts, company rules were disobeyed, and whisky was "freely used." Morale had been hurt by too many new superintendents, who had fired men impulsively and brought in "followers." Although "a few good men" worked on the Northern Division, too many "loafers" and "scalawags" had been "passed up" to "the north." Train dispatchers issued orders to conductors at variance with company rules and timetables; housing for overnight stopovers was scarce; and trainmen had to pay 50 cents for poor accommodations or sleep in box cars. Furthermore, they were paid less than their peers on the neighboring CPR or NP. Still another superintendent recommended that the company provide better housing, send more married men, promote from within the company, and delegate more decisions to his of-

The Great Northern Railway: A History/Part I 1856 to 1916

The St. Paul Union Depot opened for business in August 1881 and gave the community a note of elegance. *(Courtesy of Minnesota Historical Society)*

fice. He also believed the idea "that cheap men can be kept up here" should be abandoned.[15]

Other ramifications grew from Northern Division operating difficulties during the early 1880s. To be sure, friction erupted with the Canadian Pacific, which had taken over track built by the Canadian government from the international boundary to Winnipeg. The CPR had also acceded to the Manitoba's contract of June 8, 1880, providing for exclusive transfer of all traffic at the international boundary, division of rates, and mileage charges for cars. Among other things, the CP objected to delays in moving immigrant and freight cars through Minnesota, rightly claiming that they incon-

venienced settlers and businessmen alike. The Manitoba also found reason to complain, especially when the CPR returned rolling stock slowly and in poor condition.

Complaints about the storage of cars, congestion, and division of rates peaked in the busy spring of 1882. A heavy traffic in immigrants and their movables, as well as rails and construction equipment consigned to the CPR, moved slowly on both sides of the border, and a particularly rainy spring even necessitated transferring some passengers and freight to Red River steamboats. By mid-June, several miles of loaded cars were stranded between St. Vincent and Winnipeg, where storage facilities were already filled. The Manitoba and the Ca-

nadian Pacific nevertheless were forced to depend on each other. The StPM&M, after all, was the CPR's link on the east, and the Canadian road provided the Manitoba with no less than a third of its freight volume and 40 percent of its gross revenue.

Meanwhile, the Manitoba needed to iron out at least some of its problems with the Northern Pacific which remained the chief rival. The tension had several sources. Their crossing at Glyndon caused continuing litigation over ownership of land-grant acreage there; at several other locations they tilted for traffic; in places they were building competitively; and, under the 1879 agreement, the NP depended for access to the Twin Cities on rights over the

Manitoba from Sauk Rapids to St. Paul.

Northern Pacific's new president, Henry Villard, took a hard line on all issues. At times, Stephen feared that "Villard's vanity" might make him "reject any treaty of peace" that did not "gratify his vain desire to obtain triumph." Indeed, Villard was adamant about the NP's "territorial rights" in the Pelican Valley, along the Casselton Branch, and from Wadena to the western Minnesota boundary. Moreover, to strengthen its primary system, the NP wanted to buy a charter from the Manitoba enabling it to build an independent line from Sauk Rapids into the Twin Cities. Negotiations were tedious. Villard was willing to concede the Red River Valley to the StPM&M, but only if the latter withdrew from west of Moorhead and Fargo.[16]

Manitoba officers presented varying points of view. Hill sarcastically asked NP's Thomas F. Oakes if the NP planned to concentrate on its transcontinental enterprise or on the "construction of lines resulting in the greatest investment of capital for the lowest revenue." On the other hand, Stephen's usual conciliatory tone was manifest in his efforts for "joint and harmonious action." Both railroads, sometimes pressed by outsiders, he commented, admittedly had undertaken construction calculated to annoy each other, yet of "little commercial value." The StPM&M outwardly expressed no ambition to go "beyond its present boundaries," yet it clearly considered the Red River Valley its own territory; the NP's Casselton branch and its projected line to Canada were nothing less than an invasion. Stephen thought likewise about the Pelican Valley line.[17]

As time passed the Manitoba found its bargaining position stronger. The Northern Pacific was at a disadvantage because its traffic to and from Duluth and points in the Red River Valley and western Canada had to be transferred at Glyndon and the Manitoba's growing strength, especially its recent arrival at the lakehead, threatened NP's traffic base. Most important, though, the NP was financially strapped by its expensive campaign to reach the Pacific Coast.

These many pressures left the Northern Pacific little choice but to resolve issues. As to Minnesota traffic, the Manitoba and the NP agreed on pooling and division of rates. Charges from Glyndon, Fargo, and Moorhead to Lake Superior were to be no less than those between these towns and the Twin Cities. The two further promised to maintain rates at competitive points and not to offer special inducements or employ special soliciting agents, except at St. Paul. For three years, or until the NP completed its own line from Sauk Rapids to Minneapolis, its trackage rights on the StPM&M line, granted in 1879, were to remain in force. The NP also gained terminal rights in the Twin Cities.

The Manitoba and the NP likewise exchanged properties that complemented the former's vertical axis and the latter's east–west orientation. The NP sold to the StPM&M, for cost plus interest, two lines, one from Fergus Falls to Pelican Rapids, and the other from Casselton to Mayville. It transferred the majority of stock in its Canadian corporation, the Manitoba & South-Western Colonization Railway Company. Reciprocating in kind, the StPM&M sold the graded portions of two lines to the NP. The first ran forty miles west from Wahpeton and could be used for a line the NP planned from Wadena via Fergus Falls toward the Black Hills, and the second from Morris east toward Sauk Centre. The StPM&M additionally granted to the NP trackage rights over its route from Morris to Brown's Valley. Hill was pleased with these territorial adjustments and what he hoped was the end of "disastrous competition": As he put it, "the desirability of this exchange has been fully justified by the harmony that has since existed in conducting business between the two roads and has prevented the construction of unnecessary lines by either party into the territory of the other."[18]

The Manitoba's construction program from 1883 through 1885 was more limited than in the years immediately preceding, but it did tie into the system the lines bought from the NP and it completed other work. In 1883, a line from Shirley (near Crookston) running 22 miles east to St. Hilaire opened free government land and forest areas, and another short branch of 34 miles from Moorhead Junction to Halstad collected wheat and preempted territory between the Red River and the StPM&M's trunk line to St. Vincent. Completing the route from Sauk Centre to Eagle Bend enabled the StPM&M to ship ties and lumber from its recently purchased 26,670 acres of Todd County timberland. In 1884 the only new lines of any length were those from Portland to Larimore (30 miles) and from Park River Junction (later Hanna Junction) near Larimore to Park River (35 miles). Both reflected the company's policy of extending service into new farming territory west of the Red River. Apart from short mileage to integrate the Casselton Branch into the system, other construction was for local improvement. In 1885, only 15 miles were added.

The Manitoba engaged in another form of expansion during 1882, however, opening the famous Hotel Lafayette on beautiful Lake Minnetonka west of Minneapolis. This impressive spa was operated by a former manager of the well-known Hotel Brevoort on Fifth Avenue, New York; some considered it the finest and largest resort hotel in America. To serve this attractive area and to compete with the Minneapolis & St. Louis Railway, which already had a line on the south side of the lake, the Manitoba built the North Shore line. Boating was an added attraction; the StPM&M soon owned a share in a small fleet, including the *Belle of Minnetonka*, largest vessel on those waters.[19]

Terminals in the Twin Cities

Meanwhile, the StPM&M was devoting great energy to providing adequate terminal facilities in St. Paul and Minneapolis — an effort that required working out long-term relationships with city governments, numerous business firms, and several railroads. Here was proof that the Manitoba was growing physically and expanding its volume of business, that management was recognizing competitive forces, and that Hill intended to plan for the future. For instance, the fledgling Minneapolis & St. Louis Railway offered Minneapolis interests a means of competing directly with those of St. Paul; and in November 1880, the Milwaukee, boasting the only double track in the state, announced a twenty-seven-minute run over its new short line between the state's principal cities. Politicians, businessmen, and both communities' newspapers uniformly called for even better railroad facilities. Hill was awake to all of it.

In St. Paul, the immediate focus was on passenger service. After ten years of talk about a union passenger station, the seven railroads entering that city finally agreed in January 1879 to establish the St. Paul Union Depot Company. Its first president was S. S. Merrill of the Milwaukee, and its initial vice president

was James J. Hill. By purchasing stock, participating railroads were to share in the proposed plant's ownership, management, and revenues. Membership was open to "all railroads now constructed or which may hereafter be constructed." To erect a "very large and commodious passenger station and train shed" on Sibley Street, the St. Paul Union Depot Company agreed to spend about $200,000, but tracks and other facilities would require additional outlays. When the main building was opened in August 1881, its colored-glass skylight, oak trim, Vermont marble, iron railing, large fireplace, and steam heat gave St. Paul a note of elegance. A fire on June 10, 1884, destroyed the station house, but it was quickly rebuilt. In the late 1880s, St. Paul's Union Depot was said to have more business than any other station in the country; some other cities had more traffic but none of comparable size had a union station.[20]

The Manitoba likewise cooperated in another venture serving the Twin Cities' needs, the Minnesota Transfer Company. Hill and the president of the Milwaukee had earlier obtained a long, narrow strip of land between St. Paul and Minneapolis, which they turned over at cost, plus 6 percent, when the transfer company was organized in 1881. Two years later, when five railroads jointly owned it, facilities included several miles of track, a stockyard, stable, warehouse, and loading platforms. By 1884, some 218,000 cattle were handled there annually, and in the early 1890s one officer characterized Minnesota Transfer's 200 acres and facilities as "the most commodious and convenient and economical plant and system for transfer that there is in any large city . . . in the world . . . ."[21]

To these joint ventures, the St. Paul Union Depot and Minnesota Transfer companies, Hill

added numerous independent betterment programs on behalf of the Manitoba. Land along the Mississippi River in St. Paul was filled to erect freight-handling structures, and at the corner of Wacouta and Fourth streets, the company built a four-story office building and in April 1880 moved its headquarters there. It also established an auxiliary yard on the flats near Como Avenue, and to effect economies in handling its growing fleet of motive power and rolling stock, opened the Jackson Street shops in December 1882.[22]

At the same time, numerous issues had to be resolved before the desires of the railroad and of nearby Minneapolis could be reconciled. In that aspiring community, owners of wholesale and manufacturing firms, especially lumber and flour mills, wanted "better rail access" for their properties and additional rail outlets north and west to bring the hinterland more effectively into the Mill City's sphere of influence. The StPM&M station there was shared on a rental basis with other railroads, but was now inadequate. When Stephen, in his March 1879 visit, failed to convince the board of trade and others that the associates would soon be able to provide all desired facilities, local government voted $250,000 to reactivate the Minneapolis & Northwestern Railway Company, which projected three narrow-gauge lines radiating from the city. It was no idle threat; grading began shortly.

With the specter of a municipally aided competitor in the background, and sure that other roads would move if the Manitoba did not, Hill took part in several planning sessions during 1879 and 1880. W. D. Washburn, president of the Minneapolis & St. Louis Railway, proposed joint operations, and others talked of a "grand central" passenger station jointly owned by users, as in St. Paul. Some urged that all rail improvements in the city be undertaken by a cooperatively owned Eastern Minneapolis Transfer Company. Hill and Angus opposed any collective venture, citing the difficulties and delays they had experienced over the St. Paul Union Depot project, admitting privately that they wanted the StPM&M to continue to own its Minneapolis facilities and the revenue therefrom. They also wished to protect local investments. The Manitoba had already acquired control of the St. Anthony Water Power Company, to have that firm's land for their use and to increase supplies of water power essential for the industrial development in Minneapolis.

Settlement came during the summer of 1880. Other railroads withdrew their objections when the StPM&M pledged to share new passenger-station and auxiliary facilities. To that end, the Manitoba agreed that, after right-of-way and street-crossing questions were settled, it would erect a magnificent station building, direct its main line through the city, and build two double-tracked bridges, one at St. Anthony Falls and another just north of the existing bridge.

While waiting for final agreement with Minneapolis interests, the Manitoba commenced work on allied projects certain to please the Mill City. To carry the increasing traffic of the StPM&M and its tenant companies between St. Paul and Minneapolis, the Manitoba began major improvements there—two main tracks with right-of-way for two more. In Minneapolis, the site of the new depot was selected, and a separate but wholly owned affiliate, the Min-

neapolis Union Railway Company, was formed to carry out the Manitoba's commitments. As president of the new company, Hill kept watch for the interests of the StPM&M, and C. A. Pillsbury on the board of directors handled those of the millers.[23]

After the right-of-way and other real estate was acquired, a double-track line was built from the stockyards, and the Union line was extended over a new stone bridge to Minneapolis, where it connected with track adjacent to the mills and other Manitoba properties. Designed and located by Charles C. Smith, the StPM&M's chief engineer, the stone-arch structure erected for the Minneapolis Union Railway near St. Anthony Falls was, according to the *Railroad Gazette*, "one of the greatest specimens of engineering skill in the country." The 2,300-foot bridge stretched diagonally across the river in an arc composed of splendid arches. Ohio granite gave strength to its piers and limestone from local quarries gave beauty to its surface. On April 16, 1884, the first revenue train passed over this magnificent structure.[24]

In April 1885, after six months of partial use, the new passenger depot on Hennepin Avenue in Minneapolis was officially opened. Hill assured company stockholders that it was "substantial and first class," sufficient with its waiting and immigration rooms "for the wants of this Company and others using the same for years to come."[25]

Financial Management

While Hill and Manvel made contracts for construction and improved operations, Angus brought money-management control to St. Paul. At the same time, Stephen built confidence among investors, especially in the Brit-

ish Isles. In New York, Kennedy used his extensive knowledge of railroad securities and his skill in the money market to raise funds and to enhance credit—essential to maximizing the short-term profit of the associates and to the Manitoba's lasting health.

The initial capital structure of the StPM&M was simple compared to that of its predecessors. Earlier, the 422 miles of the two St. Paul & Pacific companies alone had carried the weight of $39.5 million in securities ($6.5 million in stock and $33 million in varied bond issues). By the end of 1879, the StPM&M owned almost 60 percent more miles of line (656), represented by 20 percent lower capitalization—a total of $31,486,000, of which $15 million was stock. Under the funded debt of 1879, the company was responsible for StP&P bonds amounting to $486,000, which was reduced to $366,000 within twenty-four months. Each of the two new series of first and second mortgage thirty-year bonds issued in 1879 was for $8 million.

For more than a year the associates held all StPM&M stock because they wanted full control while they met commitments. Also, because the second-mortgage bonds did not quickly find a market, Stephen advised the directors to retain the common stock in case they needed to substitute consolidated bonds for those already issued. By the autumn of 1880, however, the time seemed favorable to market Manitoba stock. Although these transactions were for the associates' account, not that of the company, good sales improved the corporation's credit. To J. S. Kennedy & Company, the associates transferred 30,000 shares, including 11,644 of Stephen's 57,815 shares. In May 1881, Kittson sold his 28,823 shares to Stephen, Angus, Hill, Kennedy, and Smith to form the "second syndicate," out of which stock was gradually offered publicly. The original stockholders also individually disposed of some of their holdings.

Although willing to partly share ownership of the StPM&M, the associates had no intention of selling the railroad or even a majority of their respective holdings. Stephen, referring to an offer from the Milwaukee to purchase the StPM&M, stated in 1881 that he was

The new passenger station at Minneapolis, conveniently located on Hennepin Avenue, was opened early in 1885. *(Courtesy of Minnesota Historical Society)*

"fully resolved on holding on *together* and doing my best to aid in making the property what I believe the future (near) has destined it to be. (It is always a good thing to have destiny on our side.)"[26]

Meanwhile, Kennedy & Company was slowly breeding a market for bonds. Those offered came from three sources—the Dutch holders with $3,444,900, the company itself with $2,700,000, and the associates with $9,855,100. Of the last mentioned only $1,855,100 were under the first mortgage. The capital market was selective in 1879, making

difficult Kennedy's job of selling bonds of a new company that replaced those of dubious record. From mid-1880, though, the StPM&M's profitable operations, its impressive record in expanded construction, and its potentially remunerative relationship with the CPR aided sales. Under a November 1 indenture, the company was authorized to issue up to $6 million first-mortgage Dakota Extension bonds at 6 percent, and by the end of June 1883, $5,676,000 of bonds had been issued.

Although it was reassuring to investors that a piece of line had been completed before the

Dakota Extension bonds on it were issued, the practice created difficulties. Kennedy, having contracted in advance for the marketing, impatiently awaited their arrival. Also, because payment for construction fell due before the sale, short-term financing was necessary and floating debt might hurt the railroad's credit. By late 1881, Stephen commented that, although the line's success was "astonishing everyone," he was eager to put the "house" in a more "snug" and "weatherproof condition financially."[27]

One problem was that the StPM&M was undercapitalized. Its outstanding stock and bonds did not represent fully the increase in value of the property accruing from new construction and improvements. The Manitoba had utilized several charters for building new lines in Minnesota, and it had advanced the required funds and held the stock of the affiliates, but the full investment was not represented by StPM&M securities. Transporting the company's own materials for construction and repairs was not charged for, and so this expense was included neither in income to the railroad nor in cost of construction. Angus explained that repairs that might have been charged to capital account were included in operating expenditures. Much net income was plowed back into roadbed and track, renewal of bridges, buildings, new machinery, and replacement of iron rail with steel over most of the system. None of this expense was represented by stocks or bonds.

In 1882, a change was made in the practice of building new lines under charters of proprietary companies with money advanced by the StPM&M. To carry out the expensive improvements planned in Minneapolis, for instance, the Minneapolis Union Railway Company, wholly owned by StPM&M, issued its own bonds. Under an indenture of March 1, 1882, provision was made for $3 million, half to be marketed immediately. This method of financing through bonds of an affiliated company, with interest and principal guaranteed by the parent, set a precedent later utilized several times by the StPM&M and its eventual successor.

In June 1882, directors of the StPM&M voted to increase the company's stock issue by $5 million in order to raise funds for new extensions and to acquire existing lines con-

Railroad Gazette called the Manitoba's stone arch bridge "one of the greatest specimens of engineering skill in the country."

structed under proprietary companies with advances. Issued at par, this paper was apportioned to stockholders in the ratio of one share for three. Although the sale brought in $5 million, it raised StPM&M's stock issue to its legal maximum of $20 million, which left bonds as the only resource for additional financing of capital investment.[28]

In August 1883, stockholders approved plans for consolidating the company's affiliated lines and an increase in funded debt. For these and other purposes, the StPM&M would issue $50 million in consolidated bonds to mature in fifty years, rather than the usual thirty, carrying interest of not more than 6 percent. One category, amounting to $10 million, would be issued immediately to represent the stockholders' equity in revenue-producing investment. Net income that could have been distributed to stockholders in dividends had been reinvested in "large and valuable properties and lines of railway" and in "extensive improvements and additions to its other properties," without corresponding issues of bonds. To be reimbursed for this "plowing back of profits," stockholders had the privilege of acquiring consolidated bonds amounting to 50 percent of their stock at the price of 10 percent of par; that is, an owner of $2,000 in stock could buy a $1,000 bond for $100. The bonus offer brought a welcome $1 million into the treasury; it also increased debt by about 50 percent.[29]

This last element stirred immediate controversy. Press comment was vicious, critics calling the action a "bond grab" or "cutting a melon." Hill contended, however, that the decision was "wise and for the best interest of the company." To reassure investors that these securities were not just watered bonds, he pointed out that stockholders received $9 mil-

lion in bonds to represent an investment in property worth $13 million.[30]

During its formative years the Manitoba proved a remarkably successful enterprise. Officers and directors had brought to their tasks diverse experience and skills and worked in close harmony. Under their close watch, leaders of the StPM&M—aided by a booming economy and by the extraordinary carriage of construction materials for the CPR—had converted a small, lackluster property into a middle-sized railroad paying regular dividends from 1881 on, and enjoying excellent credit. In addition, James J. Hill foreshadowed his later dynamic leadership. His abilities, though, were to be put to severe test in the mid-1880s.

8

Consolidations and Adjustments

The years 1883 through 1885 encumbered the new St. Paul, Minneapolis & Manitoba with critical issues that could not be ignored. A general slowdown in economic activity turned into a recession; heavy flows of traffic north to Manitoba and the Canadian West dropped off; Canadian Pacific interests came into direct conflict with those of the Manitoba; and the associates' harmony lessened, though without a total rift. James J. Hill was forced to simultaneously initiate policies that would carry the StPM&M through a recession and find new supporters who could make possible renewed expansion.[1]

The Canadian Pacific

By the summer of 1883, friction between the Manitoba and the Canadian Pacific was palpable. Constant quarrels over division of rates and interchange of cars were painful, but a greater injury was the CPR's construction policy. In the fall of 1882, without telling Hill (one of its own directors), the CPR announced that it would build a line from Port Arthur, on Lake Superior, to Winnipeg. Thus the monopoly that the Manitoba had enjoyed in carrying CPR's construction supplies for the

Pacific extension would end, and the two companies would be competitors. The CPR's Port Arthur–Winnipeg line would also be a crucial link in its all-Canada transcontinental aspirations.

Those plans, so warming for Canadian hearts, were confirmed in 1883 when the CPR board—against Hill's strenuous objections—pledged to press westward through the desolate country above Lake Superior to link up with the Port Arthur–Winnipeg line and thus truly tie the western provinces to eastern Canada. Hill argued that a route in such rough country would not be profitable for many years, but other directors favored building the line at once, partly because the Canadian company was legally committed to construction and also because it offered rich subsidies and land grants.

During 1882, Hill had sold some of his CPR stock to ease financial burdens; now he resigned from the board of directors and sold his remaining shares. Stephen, who facilitated the sale, thought Hill's action would ''go a long way toward placing the relations between the two companies [CPR and StPM&M] on easier footing.'' Indeed, Stephen continually sought to resolve conflicts. ''It will simply be a scandal and reflection on the sense and wisdom of all concerned if foolish and hostile views gain the ascendancy,'' he wrote to Hill. The two railroads were ''so linked'' in the public mind that the ''very appearance of a disagreement'' between them would do ''infinite harm to both.'' Stephen enthusiastically emphasized the roads' mutual dependence, and when a rumor circulated that the Milwaukee was going to move into the StPM&M's northern territory, Stephen planted a counterstatement sure to be repeated: The connection between the StPM&M and the CPR, ''no mat-

ter what might be said by some to the contrary, was a *family* one and would be strengthened as is always the case in domestic matters by any outside attempt to interfere.''[2]

One point of friction disappeared in 1884. As part of the settlement to forestall its projected north–south route in Minnesota, George Stephen had agreed that the Manitoba would purchase the NP's Casselton line in Dakota Territory and pay the NP's Oregon & Transcontinental Company for control of the Manitoba & South-Western Colonization Railway Company, the NP's proposed connection north of the border. Resolution followed in January 1884, when the CPR acquired the Manitoba & South-Western stock from the StPM&M.

Meanwhile, delayed interchanging of cars at the boundary south of Winnipeg worsened after CPR's line opened from Port Arthur. The Winnipeg Board of Trade complained of the Canadian road's slowness in picking up cars from the Manitoba, and some shippers suspected the CPR of purposely impeding traffic routed via the StPM&M. In turn, the CPR accused the Manitoba of attempting to divert traffic to its own line.

The CPR's Port Arthur route also set the stage for sharp conflict over rates. In the spring of 1883, the Northwestern Traffic Association, responding to new CPR schedules, announced lower tariffs from midwestern points through St. Paul to the boundary. In 1884, while the Canadian company was vigorously denying that its rates from the border at St. Vincent to Winnipeg were excessive, Hill complained that the CPR had promulgated, without notice, lower Port Arthur–Winnipeg charges; Hill viewed this change as a violation of an understanding between the two companies. When the Canadian line accused the StPM&M of rate cutting, Kennedy assured

John S. Kennedy provided wise counsel and a steady hand.

Stephen that the Manitoba was only following CPR's lead.[3]

Negotiations between the two protagonists dragged on. In late 1883, StPM&M directors instructed General Manager Manvel to start discussions with the CPR to better facilitate the interchange of business. Delays continued and Manvel concluded that Van Horne was an uncompromising man, but Kennedy supported Stephen in advocating an amicable agreement, stating that the companies would do better in harmony than acting in ''a jealous and hostile manner.'' Finally, in July 1885, Angus and Van Horne met Hill and Manvel in St. Paul. The concordance that they signed was more limited than Hill and Manvel desired, dealing primarily with pooling freight and dividing revenues on westbound shipments to Winnipeg. It excluded much—lumber, coal, livestock, immigrant effects, and materials for railroad construction—and would be in force for only one year. Rates from Port Arthur, Duluth, and St. Paul to Winnipeg were to be uniform; the StPM&M was to receive 12 percent of the gross earnings on Canadian pooled freight carried by the CPR from Port Arthur, and, if routed via St. Paul or Duluth, the StPM&M's share was to be 52 percent; on American pooled freight by these two routes the StPM&M would receive 20 and 60 percent, respectively. Another stipulation pledged the CPR to discourage building of rival connecting lines south of the border and to quote rates for exchange of traffic exclusively with the StPM&M.[4]

Despite limitations, the Manitoba's management hoped the agreement would remove most sources of irritation. Some issues had been laid to rest, at least temporarily, and Manvel thought face-to-face conferences and airing of views with Van Horne would reduce frustrating delays at St. Vincent and generally improve relations between the two railroads. It was peace, albeit temporary.

Strengthening Credit

At the same time as the Manitoba was trying to improve relations with the Canadian Pacific, Hill carried on a multipronged campaign to strengthen the company's board of directors and fortify the road's reputation and credit. Urging board members to attend a meeting in September 1883, he wrote: "I am determined to have the Board know more of the property and its condition." Some of these directors were new. John Kennedy had joined the board, and in 1882 two others were

elected: D. Willis James, an expert in iron, steel, and railroads, and Marshall Field, the Chicago merchant. After Angus resigned from the board in 1884, Samuel Thorne, a New York financier, was elected. When Hill severed his relations with the CPR, Stephen and Smith discussed resigning from the StPM&M board, but decided not to do so because of strained relations between the two companies. Kennedy favored Stephen's continuing as a Manitoba director because he wanted to deter the former president from suddenly throwing his stock on the market, to prevent a rupture in relations between the two companies, and to kill injurious rumors about lack of harmony among the old associates. As it developed, Smith and Stephen continued on the board but seldom attended meetings.[5]

Hill usually worked well with board members, but at times he felt that they tried to usurp his prerogatives and put a brake on his plans. When an executive committee vote on a minor matter in New York went against his judgment, he wrote: "So long as I am president of the Company's Board of Directors no further change of policy must be made after an understanding by the Board without an expression of the Board, except in cases of extreme emergency, when a telegram might be sent. . . ." Thorne, a wholehearted Hill supporter, tactfully smoothed ruffled feelings. An exchange of views led to expressions of confidence in Hill, but the incident emphasized that the active directors were concentrated in New York.[6]

Despite their differences, all hands cooperated to stabilize the Manitoba's stock price. Early in July 1883, the company's shares took a sudden tumble. Bears were supported by rumors on Wall Street and in the press that crops were poor, dividends would be passed, Hill

Samuel Thorne, a New York financier, joined the Manitoba's board in 1884.

and Kennedy were selling their holdings, and Vanderbilt had bought in only to sell later. Stephen was "convinced it is a great mistake allowing the market to run itself—we ought in my judgment to take steps to keep the market steady." With no more than 70,000 of the StPM&M's 200,000 outstanding shares "floating," the market could in fact be controlled. Consequently, the five men established a pool of 40,000 shares, each contributing in proportion to his holdings. As manager of the pool, Kennedy bought and sold shares as circumstances warranted, "the object being, not to accumulate more stock than necessary, but to keep it in good repute and steady in the market." When raiders made another attack in the autumn of 1884 on a rumor that the Chicago,

James J. Hill labored to make the Manitoba's credit as solid as the road's stone arch bridge at Minneapolis.

traffic fluctuations and its dependence on hauling wheat—20 percent of its freight in 1884. Rates were lowered several times; those by the Northwest Traffic Association in 1883 were general, and the StPM&M added cuts of its own, 10 percent for wheat in 1884. In that same year, Hill announced that the company's policy was "to reduce as rapidly as possible the rates on those commodities which would most assist the settlers." The StPM&M's average freight rate per ton mile dropped 25 percent between 1882 and 1885, but the volume of traffic and revenue did not rise commensurately.[8]

Reacting to declines in revenue, the Manitoba was forced to reduce its quarterly dividend rate, which had been set at 2 percent in the autumn of 1882. Kennedy recommended a cut in 1884 because funds were scarce and he believed a lower dividend would attract conservative investors rather than speculators. In the autumn, the rate went to 1.5 percent.

The Manitoba also established a reserve fund, an unusual practice among railroad companies at that time. On December 16, 1884, the board of directors voted "that all surplus income after providing for the payment of fixed charges and a dividend of six percent per annum on capital stock be placed to the credit of 'Reserve Guarantee Fund' until not less than $2,500,000 should be accumulated." The company soon would have cash in hand to pay dividends for two years even if conditions further reduced earnings. Hill thought this action would not only attract investors but also discourage competing railroads from invading the Manitoba's territory.[9]

Rock Island & Pacific was moving into StPM&M territory north and west of the Twin Cities, Kennedy gladly bought enough shares "to give the bears a twist."[7]

While holding raiders at bay, Hill and the others reduced expenditures, made extra efforts to increase traffic and revenues, and restricted new growth. Attention to efficient operation was not new, but the nation's economic doldrums led to still more cost cutting. Salaries were reduced, wages were lowered, and a few positions on the small staff were eliminated. On another front, the Manitoba emphasized reducing rates to gain and hold freight traffic. The decline in Canadian shipments accentuated the railroad's seasonal

Throughout these uncertain times, Kennedy continued to manage finances in New York. With construction curtailed, only a few new bonds were marketed. An issue by the affiliated Minneapolis Union Railway to complete improvements to the station in Minneapolis was sold in parcels at satisfactory prices. Kennedy disposed of small amounts of Consolidateds but held most of these for a more favorable market. Although the StPM&M had to resort to short-term loans during the recession, Kennedy sought to completely avoid carrying floating debt. In 1884, he eliminated all borrowing from outsiders, preferring if necessary to put up personal funds for short periods.

The Manitoba's stock proved more worrisome, for it had not yet attained a wide investment market and was still vulnerable to attack. As Kennedy explained, "the talk of the Street" was that Manitoba shares were held in large blocks on borrowed money, and an increase in price would result in heavy sales. These would "put the price down and probably shake confidence" in the company. "So long as this opinion prevails," Kennedy added, "and so long as it is really the case we can hardly look for any great advance though I have confidence that it will all work right in time." At the moment, however, he was aware that the Montreal associates had sold some of their StPM&M's shares and might market others. Who would the buyers be?[10]

Boston Investors

By 1885, Hill and Kennedy were eager to attract to the Manitoba a new group of strong and conservative investors. Thus would they squelch rumors about the Manitoba's changed relationship with the CPR, make the company's stock less speculative, discourage raids, provide a friendly market for shares the Canadian associates wanted to sell, and help attract a larger following.[11]

Fortunately, the opportunity for a desirable alliance was at hand. Since 1882, Boston investors in the Chicago, Burlington & Quincy Railroad (CB&Q or Burlington) had been interested in adding a line between Chicago and St. Paul. The Bostonians were not just interested in local business; they also sought a friendly connection for long-haul traffic. The Manitoba and the Northern Pacific were the likely candidates for such an association, and they ordered studies of each. After a trip over the two roads in 1883, Charles E. Perkins, respected president of the CB&Q, reported that the Manitoba was "probably the snuggest and best of the properties lying beyond St. Paul," with "every mile of it in the best kind of a wheat country." During the next year young Henry D. Minot, of a Boston banking family, carefully investigated both the NP and the StPM&M for the Boston investors. The Minnesota legislature meanwhile had granted to the Chicago, Burlington & Northern Railroad Company (CB&N), a subsidiary of the Burlington, a charter for construction to St. Paul.[12]

At the same time, Hill and Kennedy clearly understood how the potential advantages of a strong relationship with the Boston group could help. With investment in a company committed to a strong line between Chicago and St. Paul, the Bostonians would share interests with the Manitoba as harmonious as until recently the StPM&M had enjoyed with the Canadian Pacific. An intimate association with stockholders of the CB&Q would also strengthen the Manitoba in its rivalry with other Chicago-based carriers — the Milwaukee, in particular, which already extended west of St. Paul. As a result, negotiations began in earnest between Hill and Kennedy, on one side, and Lee, Higginson & Company, an investment banking firm representing the New England capitalists, on the other.

Negotiations dragged through the summer, until Hill and Kennedy grew impatient. Competition was rising or was threatened: the Milwaukee had moved into Fargo, Minneapolis millers were supporting a new road to be built north and west of the Twin Cities between the StPM&M's two main routes, and the Chicago & North Western appeared to be on an expansionist course. Thus the need for alliance with the Burlington and its CB&N was imperative — so that, according to Kennedy, the "jealous neighbors" of the Manitoba would "be careful what they do for they must know the inevitable consequences should they provoke a conflict."[13]

Finally, after frank discussion covering many points, a sale was consummated. Acting as agent for Smith and Stephen, on August 3, 1885, Kennedy agreed to sell 12,500 shares of StPM&M stock to Lee, Higginson & Company, with an option for an additional 7,500 shares to be provided by Kennedy (4,750) and Hill (2,750). To strengthen this new community of interest, Hill and Kennedy soon acquired small quantities of CB&N stock made available by its president, A. E. Touzalin.

Changes soon clarified the understanding. In August, Henry D. Minot replaced Marshall Field as a director of the Manitoba. With Minot on the executive committee with Hill, Kennedy, James, and Thorne, the Boston investors could be sure of participating in all the company's major decisions. To outsiders, Hill was coy. The Manitoba directors, he told an Amsterdam banker, "made no particular alliance" with the Chicago, Burlington &

"The Burlington"

The Pullman Vestibule Line from Minneapolis and St. Paul to Chicago and St. Louis.

TRAVELERS Take "The Burlington" because it makes connections in Union Depots at Chicago, Peoria, St. Louis, Kansas City, Council Bluffs, Denver, St. Paul, and Minneapolis.

ONLY DINING CAR AND VESTIBULED LINE TO ST. LOUIS.

GEO. B. HARRIS, Vice President.　　　W. J. C. KENYON, Gen'l Pass. Agt.

Northern, "and do not propose to sacrifice to any other corporation the independence of our property."[14]

After some delay, in May 1886, the CB&N won agreement on use of facilities in the Twin Cities. Purchase of stock in the St. Paul Union Depot Company gave the road participating ownership and joint utilization of that property; the Manitoba granted to the CB&N trackage rights from St. Paul to Minneapolis and joint use of the Minneapolis Union Station; and land for a freight house in St. Paul was proffered by the StPM&M. Touzalin suggested that a fair spirit in making and carrying out agreements was "productive of the best results."[15]

In spite of forecasts to the contrary, for several years the CB&N failed to meet expectations held by either the CB&Q or Hill and Kennedy. Financial and other problems held off construction until 1885; not till August 1886 did the CB&N accept through freight, and full passenger service was offered only in October. Neither did cutting rates allow the CB&N enough business to be profitable, for it shared Chicago–Twin Cities traffic with five earlier established lines. Nevertheless, the CB&Q took full control of the unprofitable Chicago Burlington & Northern, quickly integrating it into the system.

The years 1883 through 1885, though not a time of great expansion for the Manitoba, nevertheless represented an important watershed. The CPR and StPM&M, going their separate ways, now had an acceptable working relationship; the Manitoba had stabilized its dividend policy and strengthened its financial reputation; and the Bostonians had chosen to invest in the Manitoba. By 1886, the road was prepared to build a broader traffic base.

9

From Butte to Buffalo

As the economy shifted in the mid-1880s from recession to recovery, James J. Hill urged directors of the St. Paul, Minneapolis & Manitoba to support a bold expansion plan. The Manitoba, he argued, needed new lines to reduce its dependence on fluctuating wheat shipments from the Red River Valley and to avoid being fenced in by competing railroads' accelerated construction programs. At the same time, Hill urged organizational improvements in the company.[1]

Systematizing Administration

For the first time since R. B. Angus returned to Montreal four years earlier, Hill had an able policymaking assistant with him in St. Paul—Henry D. Minot, the twenty-seven-year-old banker. A young man in a hurry, Minot's passion was analysis and system. At seventeen he had written an authoritative book on ornithology, demonstrating his grasp of detail, his powers of perception, and his ability to organize. He attended Harvard, studied law, and in his family's banking firm intensively studied several railroads, including the Mexican Central, the Northern Pacific, and in 1884, the Manitoba.

Circumstances favored Minot's growing influence on company policy. Overworked and impaired in health, General Manager Manvel took a leave for recovery; Minot had a free hand. Contracts that had "long lain neglected" were gathered and filed, and the by-laws were rewritten. Minot's compilation, *Records of St. Paul, Minneapolis & Manitoba Railway Company of Minnesota*, gathered "into convenient compass" various documents, company charters, pertinent legislation, mortgage indentures, and maps.[2]

Minot was also responsible for the significant booklet, "Code of Organization for the St. Paul, Minneapolis & Manitoba Railway Company," effective January 1, 1887. Its twenty-seven pages established governance for the railroad, responding to Hill's request for a "working code of rules governing the relations of the different departments of the road to each other and the duties of the respective officers." The new code carefully defined functions, and began the difficult stating of relationships among departments. It especially strengthened disciplines and controls, such as the requirement for reporting, record keeping, and channels of Authority for Expenditure (AFE).[3]

Although establishing and maintaining an efficient organization required continuous adjustment, President Hill hailed Minot's work as "introducing a more exact system." One day all the company's affairs would be so "thoroughly systematized and put in such order" that it would be "comparatively easy to know every week and month in exact form just what we are doing." This work "has now to be done," he wrote to Kennedy, "by my keeping close watch of what is done and what is to be done."[4]

Generally pleased with the railroad's organization, Hill was less satisfied with the quality

of his board of directors. Hill's ideal was a group of men vitally interested in, fully informed about, and active in the affairs of the company. The 1885 board, he thought, failed to meet that standard. Hill, Kennedy, James, and Thorne generally worked well together, though without the harmony of earlier years. Jealousy among rival investment groups on the board was obvious, as were tensions arising from rapid expansion and financial burdens.

Strained relations between Hill and Kennedy on the one side and the Canadian directors, Stephen and Smith, on the other, had not let up since 1883. Neither Hill nor Stephen regularly attended board meetings held in New York, and by 1886 they had not seen each other in two years. Stephen complained that no one had alerted him to a plan to market a large bond issue, and Kennedy left one board meeting "burning with indignation" because he had been accused by Stephen of selling company bonds at too low a price. Other directors regretted that Stephen and Smith were less and less active, but when either was at a meeting it was awkward, for Stephen was also president of the Canadian Pacific (to 1888). When he was in attendance, it was obviously improper and impolitic to discuss the Manitoba's strategic plans. More awkwardness followed when Stephen and Smith invested in a rival road — the Minneapolis & Pacific, sponsored by Minneapolis millers — which had built northwesterly between the Manitoba's two lines, and was presently extending toward Dakota Territory. In 1888, this company became part of the Minneapolis, St. Paul & Sault Ste. Marie Railway, or Soo Line.[5]

In the autumn of 1887, the StPM&M board began a period of rapid change. Minot, Smith, and Stephen were not reelected. Their vacancies were filled by F. P. Olcott, president of

Henry D. Minot, described as a man in a hurry, had a passion for analysis and system.

the Central Trust Company; David C. Shepard, railroad contractor and close friend of Hill; and Greenleaf Clark, prominent St. Paul attorney. Strangely, however, all three newcomers departed within a year. The faithful Manvel was placed on the board, and Minot was returned. T. Jefferson Coolidge, a large investor from Boston, was added.

The Manitoba list of officers differed little from those of other railroads comparable in size (president, first vice president, second vice president, secretary, treasurer, land commissioner, general solicitor, and general manager). The six "local departments" (operating, traffic, engineering, supply, general store, and accounting) were supervised by the general manager. The land commissioner was salesman for the railroad's land holdings, and was

The long march to Montana *(Courtesy of Minnesota Historical Society)*

also responsible for returns to the trustees under mortgage indentures.

The vice presidents too underwent change. After Kennedy resigned to leave for Europe and rest, Manvel was briefly first vice president until he resigned to head the Atchison, Topeka & Santa Fe. His successor as general manager was A. L. Mohler, promoted from within the company. In March 1887, Hill persuaded William P. Clough, a lawyer of calm and sound judgment, to leave the Northern Pacific and devote his skill in public and legislative relations to benefit the Manitoba. John N. Abbott, with a quarter century of experience on the Erie Railroad, filled the unusually significant position of assistant to the president.

The Long March to Montana

The Manitoba had not yet built beyond the Red River when Hill received suggestions that the railroad be extended westward across the high plains of Dakota and Montana territories—"a virgin field and a big one," one enthusiastic writer described it. Indeed, the country west of the Red offered diversity: grazing land, millions of acres ready for the plow, forests rich in timber, and vast, nearly untouched mineral resources. Among the many who urged Hill to action during the early 1880s, none was more influential than Paris Gibson. Wool buyer, rancher, importer of purebred sheep, and later a founding father of

Great Falls and senator from Montana, Gibson constantly deluged Hill with information about the territory. His imagination was particularly stirred by the confluence of the Sun and Missouri rivers; with waterpower from the Missouri falls and the promise of nearby coal resources, it was certain to become a thriving commercial and smelting center. Gibson urged that Hill visit the area: a "view of the country might change your future policy."[6]

Hill remained circumspect. Noncommittal in 1879, he wrote that Montana "is at present quite remote from our line," but added that it "may not always be so. . . ." By 1881, however, he admitted that he had "some notion of 'going west.' " Years later he interpreted this decision as retaliation for the Northern Pacific's move into the Red River Valley. Perhaps. After all, the truce of 1882 between the Manitoba and the Northern Pacific was less than a year old when the NP pressed feeders westward into fertile regions of Dakota Territory, and at approximately the same time Hill privately joined Paris Gibson in ownership of a large land holding at the great falls of the Missouri.[7]

Hill visited Montana for the first time in 1884. Ostensibly on a hunting trip, he explored the countryside and talked with Gibson, William G. and Charles E. Conrad of Fort Benton, and Charles A. Broadwater of Helena. Montana, Hill discovered, was still very much a frontier, but it appeared on the verge of sustained development. Its population, down after the placer-mining rush of the 1860s, had increased since the late 1870s to about 40,000. Cattle and sheep ranching were firmly established, and the agricultural potential was enormous. Many were certain that the wheat culture would transform Montana as it had the Red River Valley. At the moment, though, mines and ore-processing plants were the main business.

The central Montana mining enterprises and opportunities impressed Hill. Gold, silver, lead, and copper deposits were being exploited, promising dramatic expansion in the future. Butte was already a lively silver and copper center, and the Drum Lummon mine, first to attract British capital, was producing silver and gold at Marysville. Near Helena, silver deposits were being opened, and Hill knew of other mining possibilities at nearby Rimini.

Railroads were new in Montana, but their expansion was imminent. The Utah & Northern Railroad Company's narrow-gauge line had reduced reliance on Missouri River steamers and wagon freighters, having been built northward from the Union Pacific (UP) to Butte in 1881 and on to Garrison in 1882. In 1883, the Northern Pacific, as it drove west toward the Pacific, passed through Helena, the substantial trading center. It was inadequate. The country's citizenry hungered for more rails; a town might have one railroad but wanted another. At Fort Benton, businessmen promoted a local road, hoping the CP would build south to it. Elsewhere, Sir Alexander Gault, producer of coal across the border at Lethbridge, Alberta, was eager to negotiate with any railroad that would haul fuel to Montana smelters. If Hill wanted to extend the StPM&M into Montana, he needed to act promptly.

Hill made his first move into Montana railroading as a private investor. In 1885, he joined with friends in the East to acquire stock in three related enterprises: the Red Mountain Consolidated Mining Company at Rimini, the Great Falls Water Power & Townsite Company, and the Montana Central Railway Company, designed to connect Great Falls with Helena and Butte.

Organized on January 25, 1886, the Montana Central had a territorial charter and local incorporators. Charles A. Broadwater, a versatile frontier businessman, was elected president. He consulted with Hill, but was no rubber stamp. Widely known as provisioner of army posts, owner and manager of an extensive wagon freighting business (the Diamond R Freight Company), investor in mines, president of the Montana National Bank of Helena, and owner of a large hotel bearing his name, Broadwater acted in Manitoba territory as Samuel Hauser did for the NP. Both were knowledgeable men, with wide local experience and political influence.

Montana Central engineers surveyed the proposed route northeast from Helena even before the company was formally organized; graders were not far behind. To thwart other aspirants, they had to preempt narrow canyons. Working through the winter of 1885–1886, Chief Engineer E. J. Dodge located a satisfactory line through Prickly Pear Canyon and along the Missouri River. Along Ten Mile Creek, on the short branch from Helena to Rimini, an encounter between Montana Central and NP engineers created legal conflict and dramatic newspaper copy; but, before 1886 ended, the Central's grading between Helena and Great Falls was almost complete, and the line from Helena to Butte was being located, along with work on the branches to Rimini and to Marysville. With right-of-way secured, Kennedy advised Hill to negotiate with NP representatives to obtain their goodwill "and not have them in a state of chronic hostility towards us." The NP, Kennedy said, had already quoted a rate for rail to Helena that discouraged the Montana Central's immediate completion.[8]

Despite constant rumors connecting the Montana Central with the Manitoba, Hill and others on the Manitoba's board studiously explored options. Early in 1886, Hill prepared the "War Map," including "actual, probable, and possible" routes the StPM&M could follow. Each line had to be considered on its own merits; some would be "necessary under some conditions" but not others. The directors at first favored a cautious policy, but were soon caught up in Hill's enthusiasm for diversifying the railroad's traffic base and acting promptly to forestall competitors, especially the NP. Kennedy eventually expressed a consensus reached among New York directors: "Without being aggressive or giving any just cause of offense to our neighbors, we must go forward boldly."[9]

57

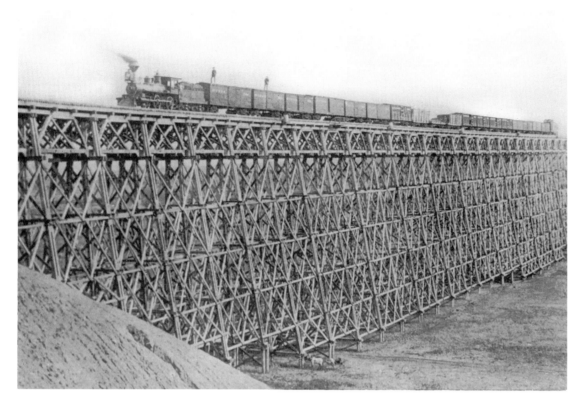

The 1,609-foot trestle across Gassman Coulee —just west of Minot—required thousands of board feet of timber that had to be delivered from pineries well to the east of the "front."

One of the opportunities that company directors considered was purchasing the Montana Central and extending the Manitoba westward to a junction with it at Great Falls. To embrace that option, however, would require great courage. Hill noted the presence of the Northern Pacific and the Union Pacific, both of which were hostile to the Montana Central. Moreover, rumor suggested that the Union Pacific—which had brought the Utah & Northern under its wing—had paid the Northern Pacific not to go into Butte; if true, this won only postponement, for the NP shortly arrived in that bustling community of miners and smelters. Offering a bit of self-serving advice,

the president of the Union Pacific suggested that the StPM&M stay out of Montana and devote itself to building branch lines in Dakota Territory as it had in Minnesota. Directors of the Manitoba, nevertheless, urged acquisition of the Montana Central, and Manitoba stockholders approved.

Early in 1886, the Manitoba started west from Devil's Lake, Dakota Territory. While engineers selected location, D. C. Shepard & Company started grading, scattering 2,000 men in groups of twenty-five to thirty along the survey under subcontractors. Most of the graders were Scandinavian farmers who, anticipating the railroad's extension, had settled as

much as twenty-five miles west of Devil's Lake and now found an opportunity to earn cash. Skilled Irish track-layers were right behind, completing 121 miles by reaching the second crossing of the Mouse River on October 4. Surfacing was done with dirt; ballasting could wait. At the end-of-track, the town of Minot, named to honor StPM&M's second vice president, began its history as a stockpiling center for the next year's construction.[10]

Hill stressed to Manitoba directors that the line must be pushed on from Minot to Great Falls during the next year; his mind was "fully bent on the long march forward." The Manitoba, he declared, must build more than 700 miles in eight months during the next year "to insure our position of advantage." This mileage, being built from only one end, the east, was double the StPM&M's construction for 1886 (366 miles) and was "more track than has ever been laid in ten months elsewhere." Hill was convinced that results would justify the effort. "I feel sure that the future of the Company depends on our work during the coming year," he commented to the cautious D. Willis James, "and that with a vigorous policy actively carried out we will have the future strength and prosperity of the company well assured."[11]

The affable Thorne supported Hill, realizing, though, that the "herculean" project of pushing the railroad from North Dakota into Montana required "extraordinary good management and executive ability." Vast quantities of material had to be ordered quickly before prices rose prohibitively, and support for the plan must be obtained in Washington, for the StPM&M still lacked right-of-way through military and Indian reservations (Berthold and Blackfeet). The Blackfoot Reservation covered so much of the northern Dakota and Montana territories that, unless the Indians accepted smaller reservations, much of the land along the projected railroad would be closed to settlement.[12]

Ordering rails and arranging for their shipment was a huge task. The StPM&M purchased rail in Germany as well as England; ordering abroad also helped keep from others the extent of the railroad's plan. United States purchases were divided among several mills to obtain favorable terms and to avoid depending on one manufacturer should production problems arise.[13]

Advance contracting helped, but scarcities marred 1887, especially for wood products, which the railroad required in vast quantity. Hundreds of thousands of feet of lumber and piling had to be found for bridges and trestles, not to mention three million ties. Low water in streams meant that logs could not be rafted in the required masses, and some contractors failed to deliver their quotas. The necessity of providing some 600,000 bushels of oats for horses in construction service suggests the scope of supply problems.

By March 15, 1887, the Manitoba's decision to build to Great Falls had been spread on the minute books, and difficult relations with Indian groups were being settled. By April, the village of Minot had become a remarkably bustling staging area for the great march West. The late movement of crops and a hard winter had put extreme pressure on motive power, delaying the arrival of materials, but still stocks of rail, ties, spikes, and other construc-

tion supplies covered acres and acres of neighboring countryside. Carloads continued to pour in, eventually totaling 16,000. From Minot, dispatchers sent to the front an unending stream of trains, each laden with materials to build one mile of track. The town, with a population of 400 early in the year, soon housed twice that many transients alone. Saloons flourished above all, but Minot also had stores, a school, a Park House (hotel), and two churches.

The 545 miles of line from Minot to Great Falls was located in 1887. From the second crossing of the Mouse River, the new route climbed through the Berthold Indian Reservation, to Williston and the Missouri River Valley, and beyond through terrain that engineers described as the "four-tenths maximum grade division." Leaving Fort Buford, it crossed the Poplar River, dipped into the Milk River Valley, and crossed that stream thrice before reaching Fort Assiniboine, southwest of Havre. There the line turned southwest, crossed the Marias River, passed near Fort Benton, and proceeded over coulees to Great Falls.[14]

Earthmoving subcontractors hit their stride in May 1887. When the job peaked, 8,000 men and 6,600 horses ground away just at grading. Charles Dudley Warner, Mark Twain's friend, wrote: "Those who saw this army of men and teams stretching over the prairie and casting up this continental highway think they behold one of the most striking achievements of civilization." These great forces graded 100 miles a month until the last 200 miles, when crews raced at seven miles a day.[15]

Track-laying was a raucous symphony of men and horses, ringing iron, and hammering blows. Hordes of men moved mountains of

Construction forces, deployed as far ahead as the camera eye carried, were pushing the St. Paul, Minneapolis & Manitoba Railway westward in 1887 when this picture was taken in Montana Territory.

ties from the construction train to massed wagons, whence they were hauled to the graded roadbed, onto which ties were unloaded and precisely spaced; rails were hauled on low iron cars from Minot to the end-of-track. Burly workers hoisted rails onto ties; others distributed angle bars, bolts, and spikes; finally came the spikers. Hill described the effort: "The work is immense and requires every possible provision against delay."[16]

Before the construction year ended, rails joined Minot and Helena. Track-layers arrived in Great Falls on October 16, 1887; the next day they started for Helena, covering ninety-seven miles of the Montana Central by November 19, when work stopped for the winter. Butte would be reached later. Service to Great Falls began October 31 and went on to Helena in the next month.

The Manitoba had made an enviable record of track-laying. It did not equal, nor did it sur-pass the Central Pacific's incredible one-day feat, laying more than ten miles. Nevertheless, as D. C. Shepard observed, ''No railroad had yet been constructed as rapidly as this, where the work could be reached and carried on only from one end, and it is doubtful whether 643 continuous miles of track will ever be laid again in seven and one-half months at the rate of 3¼ miles per day for each working day and by one gang of workmen throughout.'' Nor could anyone claim that the construction was of dubious quality. For its ninety-seven miles, the Montana Central insisted it had achieved advantages over any other Rocky Mountain line heretofore constructed in grades and curvature. Into its construction had gone 3,000

Irishmen made up the bulk of track-laying crews who moved from location to location as the Manitoba inched westward. *(Courtesy of Minnesota Historical Society)*

The arrival of the first train at Jasper, Minnesota—on the Willmar & Sioux Falls—was a reflection of Hill's desire to tie a broad area southwest of the Lakehead to a Duluth gateway.

oak ties per mile and seventy-five-pound steel rail.[17]

The long stretch from Minot to Helena was just a part of the 940 miles that made 1887 a record construction year for the Manitoba. Work in northern Minnesota and northern Dakota Territory included a line from Moorhead to Wahpeton (42 miles) to take the place of the old Glyndon Cutoff and to compete with the Milwaukee's new Fargo line. North of Grand Forks, the Manitoba was pressured by farmers, who, having settled and planted crops fully anticipating that rails would come, wanted transport to a market without delay. Two short branches were therefore built north of the main line in Dakota—Park River to Langdon (39 miles) and Rugby Junction to Bottineau (38 miles). Farmers between Church's Ferry and St. John (55 miles) would have to wait until the next year.

Eastward to Buffalo

As the Manitoba made its long march to central Montana, it also undertook significant expansion on its eastern flank. During the 1880s, the cities at the Head of the Lakes —Duluth and Superior—and traffic on the Great Lakes grew significantly. Coal moved west to serve a growing market, the Standard Oil Company built a large bulk distribution station at Superior, lumbermen in the Cloquet –Duluth area were expanding output of their product, and prospects for iron ore production were promising. More immediately telling was the increased volume in wheat and flour that flowed when the prime growing areas in western Minnesota and Dakota Territory were opened. Taking advantage of lower waterborne tariffs, Duluth buyers offered higher prices for wheat than their competitors in Chicago could, and farmers in the southern part of Dakota Territory, seeing this differential in price but dependent on railroads oriented to the Twin Cities and Chicago, clamored for direct rail connections to the Head of the Lakes.

Hill, aware of this demand as early as 1884, discussed the possibility of building toward the southwest from the Breckenridge line, but he had to balance a number of considerations precluding such a step at that time. Had the Manitoba any obligations to other railroads, expressed or implied, to avoid construction in that direction? What did two new board appointments on rival roads—William Rockefeller to the Milwaukee and Marshall Field to the Rock Island—mean? At the time, Kennedy wanted to avoid stirring up ''any hostile feeling on the part of these companies or any others that are our neighbors, lest they should immediately adopt retaliatory measures for which at the moment we are hardly prepared.'' Moreover, the mid-1880s economic doldrums precluded a positive climate for construction projects.[18]

Convinced, however, that in time roads would be built from the southwest to Duluth and Superior, Hill was determined that the Manitoba would be in the thick of it. He wrote to Kennedy early in 1886 that ''local demands of southwestern Minnesota and southern Dakota will force lines across to Lake Superior.''

Henry D. Minot was president of the Eastern Railway Company of Minnesota, organized in August 1887. Capital investments included Mogul locomotives and an impressive roundhouse at Superior.

Hill was firm: "We should by all means see that they are located for our benefit and not against us." Henry Minot, dispatched to survey possible projects, soon recommended aggressive action. Building in the area was certain and economic conditions were improving: the StPM&M needed to move quickly to preempt the best routes and keep costs down: "Construction of new lines is always better done to advantage at the beginning of such periods rather than in the middle of them," counseled Minot. Did this aggressiveness antagonize other railroads? "As a matter of policy," he asserted, "it is probably better to strike out all around at once, thus making retaliation more difficult and preventing forestallment."[19]

The Manitoba did not "strike out all around at once," but competitors did make overt moves, leading Hill to react quickly. When the president of the C&NW inquired about Hill's intentions, he was told that rate competition by the Milwaukee Road was forcing the Manitoba's hand. Even before Minot submitted his report on construction possibilities for southern Dakota Territory, the Manitoba was shortening mileage between its two northbound trunk routes in Minnesota, the Breckenridge line and that via St. Cloud. The southwest-to-northeast Willmar–St. Cloud shortcut (58 miles) was completed under franchise of the affiliated St. Cloud, Mankato & Austin Railroad Company, which sold its property to the StPM&M in 1886. Other communities were brought closer to Duluth in 1887 when the Manitoba constructed a thirty-two-mile line from Tintah to Evansville.

Local organizations shared in shaping the StPM&M's actions in Dakota Territory. Such groups were often helpful in obtaining franchises, rights-of-way, and station grounds. Hill's attitude was revealing—he would rather work with able, local residents than have them as competitors. He explained to Kennedy: "We keep our place [in negotiations] so that if anything occurs to give them [local plans] the breath of life we will be around at the Christening."[20]

From 1886 through 1888, the Manitoba arranged for construction of three lines to the west and southwest that offered access to Duluth. Contractors finished a road from Yarmouth, on the Breckenridge line, west through Rutland to Aberdeen, Dakota Territory (119 miles) in 1886, and in the next year built another branch from Benson to Watertown (92 miles) and extended it in 1888, under the terri-

Freight and passenger cars were combined on this Eastern Railway train that paused for water and a portrait between Hinckley and Superior soon after the line was opened.

torial charter of the Duluth, Watertown & Pacific Railway Company, to Huron (70 miles).

Minot strongly endorsed the third line, from Willmar to Sioux Falls, Dakota Territory, submitting a detailed assessment dealing with grades and curvature, location of highways, local settlement, agricultural production, competition, and ownership of land. Sioux Falls was already a community of 7,500 with rising real estate values. To obtain terminal facilities with "a first-rate location for doing business," Hill acted promptly. Constructed as the Willmar & Sioux Falls Railway Company, the 147-mile line linking the two cities of its namesake connected with the Willmar – St. Cloud Cutoff, built two years earlier. An agreement with the locally encouraged Sioux City & Northern Railway Company covered interchange at Garretson for all traffic not otherwise consigned, giving the Manitoba indirect access to Sioux City, a leading commercial center in western Iowa.[21]

Relationships with another Iowa railroad did not result in the same corporate affiliation. In 1885, the StPM&M ended operations at its Climax Coal Company mines along the Minneapolis & St. Louis Railway near Angus, in central Iowa, but Hill still closely followed his personal investment in coal mining in nearby Webster County. Consequently, in 1886, with Kennedy and others, he bought the 92-mile Mason City & Fort Dodge Railroad Company, built as an outlet for Webster County coal. Meanwhile, the StPM&M acquired a narrow-gauge railroad between the Twin Cities and Hutchinson, Minnesota (52 miles), and converted it to standard gauge, starting a line that seemed meant to connect with the Mason City & Fort Dodge. Hill instead became disillusioned with the Iowa railroad and sold it, so that the Manitoba's line ended forever at Hutchinson.

The company again focused on the Head of the Lakes. The Manitoba already had a line between St. Cloud and Hinckley, and rumor suggested it would soon be extended to Duluth. Practical reasons dictated otherwise — for a while. During the depressed mid-1880s, traffic was light, the area above Hinckley promised little immediate business, and funds for construction were scarce. Moreover, the Manitoba remained part owner of, and had favorable traffic arrangements with the St. Paul & Duluth Railroad, with a direct route between the state capital and the Head of the Lakes, and the StPM&M connected with it at Hinckley.

Conditions had changed by 1886, however. The StPM&M objected to poor service on the St. Paul & Duluth, to its tariffs on coal, and

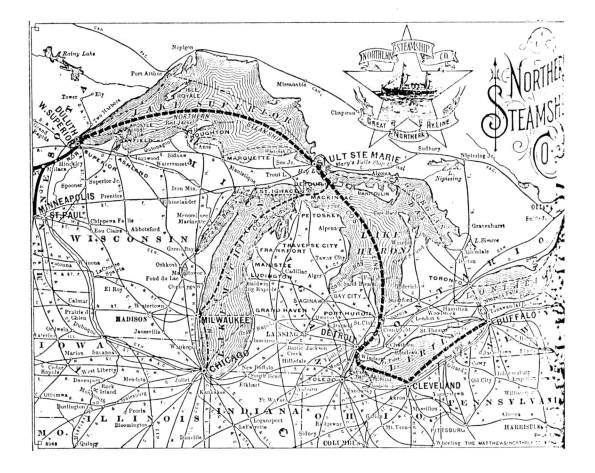

during the mid-1880s, the Manitoba provided for its own terminal location at nearby West Superior with the Lake Superior & South Western Railway Company. Organized in August 1886, under President John H. Hammond, the firm was to hold property already purchased, acquire more land, and build a short line, a dock, a warehouse, and an elevator.[22]

The Manitoba's massive elevator "A" was particularly noteworthy. This impressive structure was leased for operation to the Great Northern Elevator Company, the first related firm to carry the name soon to be used by the entire railroad system. With a storage capacity of 1,750,000 bushels, this huge grain-handling facility could handle "as many cars daily as all the elevators combined on the Duluth side," according to the Manitoba, and one Chicago grain dealer enthusiastically characterized the structure as "the best elevator in the World." Hill was pleased, and soon planned another.[23]

As freely predicted, Hill eventually recommended, and the board approved, construction of an extension from Hinckley to give the Manitoba an independent entry to Superior and Duluth. Less expected was the company's announcement that it would also acquire a fleet of steamers to ply between Duluth, Minnesota and Buffalo, New York.

Organized in August 1887, the Eastern Railway Company of Minnesota (Eastern Railway) bore a name reminiscent of the well-known Eastern of Massachusetts—presumably to attract Boston investors. Henry Minot, president of the new company, arranged financing early in 1888 by floating $5 million in twenty-year bonds marketed by Lee, Higginson & Company of Boston. The Manitoba received Eastern's $5 million in stock and turned over

to the division of rates on joint traffic. Farmers and country elevator operators also complained of that railroad's inadequate car supply, insufficient storage at Duluth, and delays in delivery. The tripartite agreement of 1881, under which the StPM&M had joint ownership of the local company, was abrogated in 1885, and the StPM&M's board in the following year authorized disposal of the Duluth road's stock. The Manitoba also built a line from Elk River through Princeton to Milaca (32 miles) to shorten its route between the Twin Cities and

Hinckley, but the St. Paul & Duluth clearly retained a more direct route from the Twin Cities.

Hill continued to develop the Manitoba's interests in northeastern Minnesota. Always wanting adequate terminals and handling facilities, he not only petitioned the federal government to improve the harbor at Superior, but urged the Northern Pacific to build a drawbridge from Rice's Point, Minnesota, across St. Louis Bay to the Wisconsin side to make additional sites accessible to shipping. And, ownership of the West Superior terminal facilities, held by the Lake Superior & Southwestern, which itself was merged with the Eastern. The Eastern Railway was also given running rights over the Manitoba from Hinckley to St. Paul, use of terminal facilities there, and a traffic agreement further defining the relationship.

As sale of the Eastern's bonds proceeded, construction did, too. By the end of February 1888, surveys were complete and orders placed for construction materials and equipment. In March, grading commenced under general supervision by Foley Brothers. Kerrick & Watson did the heavy bridge work, including the Nemadji River bridge, which alone used 1,200,000 feet of timber and 70,000 pounds of steel. At one time, 3,000 men were busy along the Eastern Railway while other workmen were improving dock facilities, adding a new slip, and building a second elevator at West Superior.

Work proceeded haltingly. Much of the sixty-eight-mile line between Hinckley and the Head of the Lakes ran through unoccupied, rough, and heavily timbered land. Spring 1888 was particularly wet, making the red clay of northeastern Minnesota hard to handle; in places it ran like melted butter. A bad sinkhole near the north end of the line would continue to consume carloads of fill for years. Construction was expedited, however, because the Eastern was "virtually a part of the Manitoba system." Considerable finishing remained for the next season, but by September 23, 1888, the line was hauling revenue freight, and nine months later, on July 17, 1889, it began regular passenger service despite Hill's doubts aroused by a rough trip over the line.[24]

The Manitoba then turned to its maritime requirements. Fortunately, Hill was no stranger to water transport. He had been part owner of the Red River Transportation Company, and the railroad continued to operate a fleet of pleasure boats on Lake Minnetonka near Minneapolis. Hill entered the Great Lakes steamship business because of rates and their control. The number of lake vessels was inadequate to demand, he correctly observed, and as a consequence, rates charged by owners were so high as to negate the attractiveness to shippers for the Manitoba's new routes from the southwest. Furthermore, Chicago-based railroads and the eastern trunk lines remained powerful in rate making and routing. Thus, in a very real sense, Hill and the Manitoba were forced into waterborne commerce. Despite tariff reductions by the Manitoba, "the through rate from interior points to Buffalo, or the seacoast, will not be materially reduced . . ." Hill explained, "unless the StPM&M has its own boats." If competitors lowered their tariffs, then "we would be able to maintain rates on the Manitoba road" and by cutting charges on "the Lake line would be able to equalize the reduction." Some trunk lines in the East were reported to own or control much steamer tonnage and the newly established Interstate Commerce Commission lacked authority over water transportation, perhaps also influencing his thinking. Hill therefore felt that the lakes vessels were not only a promising financial investment but "a powerful ally in controlling traffic and rates for the country served by our railroad line."[25]

Accordingly, the Northern Steamship Company was formed on June 12, 1888. Hill had contracted a year earlier with Mark Hanna of Cleveland's Globe Iron Works for six steel vessels capable of holding 2,700 tons each. These 310-foot steamers were designed especially for handling coal, iron ore, and other heavy bulk freight. The first, the *Northern Light*, began her maiden voyage June 18, 1888, six days after the corporation was organized. By next April, it was joined by sister ships *North Wind, Northern King, Northern Wave, North Star*, and *Northern Queen*. John Gordon, in charge of their operation, reported that for the 1889 season, the steamers carried 42 percent of the flour going east from Duluth to Superior and in westbound freight "our competitors are completely demoralized."[26]

These developments pointed to the future, as did another of the Manitoba's new lines in northern Minnesota. In 1888, The StPM&M ran only forty-five miles from Crookston Junction eastward to Fosston, but railroad journals reported this as part of "the proposed line from Crookston" to the Head of the Lakes, and time proved them correct.[27]

The Manitoba thus extended its influence west, east, and southwest, but in the north it was mostly unsuccessful. The Canadian matter was complex. Opposed to a monopoly by the Canadian Pacific, provincial legislators in Manitoba had chartered the Red River Valley Railway Company to build south from Winnipeg toward the border. Its route was located, but funds for construction were not. Though StPM&M and NP managers had discussed acting jointly to take over the project, each company eventually made a separate proposal to the Province of Manitoba. The debate in Winnipeg was long and fiery. In the end, the StPM&M's elaborate plan, including branch lines, was turned down, perhaps because of the road's earlier relation with the CP, and the NP offer was accepted; to Hill's great consternation, it built through the Red River Valley to Manitoba.

By 1889, the Manitoba system included six proprietary companies, owning and operating a growing inventory of equipment with which it served 3,326 route miles in five states and on the Great Lakes. At the same time, James J. Hill matured as a railroad leader. He learned to delegate responsibility, to systematize the division of labor, and to share the formulating and implementing of policy with men as diverse in personality and talent as Kennedy, Minot, and Manvel. With their aid, he expanded the primarily intrastate Manitoba of 1885 into an interstate regional rail and water carrier serving an expansive territory from Butte, Montana, to Buffalo, New York. The system's strength, however, was founded on its network connecting the Twin Cities with points in the Red River Valley, Winnipeg, Duluth, and Sioux Falls. In this part of the Upper Mississippi Valley, the Manitoba concentrated its efforts to expand traffic and to serve the predominantly agricultural population, competing with increasingly strong rail rivals.

10

Tensions in Finance

The St. Paul, Minneapolis & Manitoba's rapid expansion in the late 1880s eventually created a crisis in financial management. The officers and directors shared responsibility for raising funds, but the New York experts in money-market intricacies necessarily did the leading. Gradually, tension grew between the ever-optimistic frontier expansionist James J. Hill and the conservative eastern financiers led by John S. Kennedy.[1]

A New Problem

Both operators and financiers were justified by the Manitoba's early financial record in sustaining a mood favorable to expansion of the system. Operating revenue rose from nearly $2.9 million in fiscal 1880 to more than $9 million three years later. Despite the decline in construction supplies to be hauled for the Canadian Pacific, the StPM&M's revenues stayed above those of 1882 even during the depressed years 1884 and 1885. At the same time, despite many capital outlays in maintenance account, operating expenses were held at levels that were low relative to operating revenue. Consequently, net operating income rose from less than $1.5 million in 1879–1880 to more than $4.4 million in 1882–1883

and exceeded $4.25 million in each of the next two years. Prior to June 1885, the company paid cash dividends of $5.6 million as well as a bonus of $9 million in bonds, and credited $5.6 million to surplus.

In deciding how to raise money, officers and directors understandably agreed that they must come up with adequate and timely financing at reasonable cost to meet obligations and maintain the company's positive reputation. The increase in bonds relative to stock was not ideal, but the company had reached the legal limit of its stock issue; marketing bonds, all agreed, was preferred over seeking to revise its charter. Managers and directors further considered that a railroad with relatively low fixed charges and low capitalization was in an advantageous position compared with those having large capitalization per mile and long-term, noncallable bonds bearing high rates of interest.

Opinions varied on other matters. In 1886, John Kennedy and D. Willis James held that the company should discontinue its policy of first making large commitments for sizable expenditures and then trusting to "luck to get the money to meet them." Strikes, short crops, political troubles, or saturation of the railroad bond market, they pointed out, might delay raising funds. Several railroads had recently marketed bonds before they expanded, but, under the consolidated bond mortgage of 1883, the Manitoba had to show certified evidence of construction before floating new issues. Kennedy thought the road should arrange to issue bonds bearing a lower interest rate because holding down service charges on the company's debt would leave a profit even when business was reduced. Moreover, Kennedy's experience indicated that investors preferred buying bonds below par with a lower rate of interest rather than paying a premium on securities that carried a higher rate.[2]

During summer and fall 1886, Kennedy put some of his ideas into action by persuading a group of bankers to make advance commitments. The first contract was for $300,000 in consolidated 6 percent bonds taken by Kuhn, Loeb & Company, 50 percent; Brown Brothers & Company, 25 percent; and J. Kennedy Tod & Company, 25 percent. Kennedy anticipated that this contract would pave the way for other consolidated bonds, enhance the Manitoba's financial position, and improve the standing of all company bonds. In autumn 1886, he reported that the syndicate had agreed to take $5,400,000 of new 4½ percent consolidated bonds and had signed an option for an additional $2,700,000 of the same issue. The transaction appeared to substantiate his position that a lower interest rate would prove attractive.

Hill, who had urged the Manitoba's directors to approve building into Montana, was annoyed at the large option Kennedy granted. "Our work for next year is already so large and subject to great perils . . .," Hill complained, that "we cannot afford to give options which, doing us no good, tie up our resources and place our whole enterprise in unnecessary danger." Because the consolidated bonds could not be issued until mileage was completed, he felt that meeting the bonds' delivery date might push him into constructing lines in Minnesota and Dakota rather than those in Montana. "I am anxious to do all we can next year but you seem to assume there is no limit to what we can do," Hill exploded to Kennedy.[3]

Kennedy staunchly defended his position. In a rapidly changing market, buyers were unwilling to commit themselves to firm promises for a larger total at a distant date, hence bonds could be delivered only as construction was completed. The StPM&M had made large commitments to build new lines and bond prices were declining — Kennedy had to act promptly. He was pleased with the low interest, the good price, and a firm relationship with a syndicate of bankers able to create a market for the bonds in Europe.

Kennedy's position was justified. On November 12, 1886, the syndicate advertised StPM&M 4½ percent consolidateds in New York, Hamburg, and Berlin, and all were taken on the first day; by June 30, 1887, the entire lot of $8,100,000 consolidateds was sold. These transactions also helped build the StPM&M's credit with the important London banking house of Baring Brothers & Company.

Meanwhile, Manitoba directors, upon committing the road to expansion as far as Great Falls, decided to raise funds by still another bond issue. The Montana Extension mortgage was intended to finance both immediately projected and future construction in that territory. It provided for issuing no more than $25 million in fifty-year bonds with a maximum interest of 6 percent. The first of the $7 million 4 percent issue was offered to stockholders at 80 percent of par. The bonds sold well, a total of $7,468,000 within two years.

Dissension, 1887–1889

Soon after negotiations with the syndicate in September 1887, tension grew between Hill and his eastern financiers, partly because of the cumulative fatigue that both Kennedy and Hill were showing. Kennedy was nervous and harassed. "I think what fools we are," he lamented to Hill. "You and I have got all we

Hill complained of a "weary feeling" and the company's financial headaches must have been a great burden, but in characteristic fashion, he plunged ahead.

need and a great deal more besides, then what is the use of toiling and laboring night and day to increase it?" In the summer of 1887, Hill complained of neuralgic headaches and a "weary feeling," and expressed his unwillingness to "continue to give unremitting attention to the Company."[4]

On the other hand, the New York directors also went through an "anxious depressing time," E. T. Nichols wrote. This junior officer did not hesitate to state his views privately to Hill. Nichols was worried not about Hill's large personal investments, which he was helping to manage, but about the state of the stock market and the Manitoba's circumstances

James J. Hill relied on E. T. Nichols for candid advice.

relative to it disturbed him. The market, having absorbed millions in railroad bonds like a sponge, warned Nichols, was saturated. Wall Street thought the West generally had "best grow up to its rails," and the StPM&M seemed a special target for attack. Its stock, which had held up well, suddenly fell; bears, busily circulating marked copies of unfavorable newspaper articles, were selling short. "In plain words," Nichols confided to Hill, "it seems to me that we must cease for a time to expand, husband our resources as much as possible and sail as close to the wind as we can."[5]

By late 1887, members of the finance committee felt that Hill's expansion program was out of hand. Samuel Thorne had looked forward to "the great relief of mind that comes when one knows that the money is on hand to meet every obligation," only to see Hill's expenditures increase. New estimates escalated, and when the figure in November was $1.9 million higher than that of August, Kennedy was alarmed. He knew the market was taking few railroad bonds and he feared a panic.[6]

On November 16, 1887, the finance committee demanded that Hill call a meeting of the entire board to discuss the financial situation. As Kennedy viewed it, the company's reputation required safeguarding, current obligations had to be met, and Hill's plans for construction in 1888 suggested careful scrutiny. For more than a year, Kennedy had felt that the railroad's credit was being strained "pretty severely" by large issues of bonds. Even friends thought that the StPM&M was "going too fast," and that it had a "great many bitter enemies" who seemed "never to lose a chance of saying false and bitter things." As to plans for 1888, Kennedy stated flatly: "It will not do to undertake work unless we have the ways and means provided to meet it."[7]

The directors earlier had discussed other means of raising funds; several had suggested increasing the stock issue. Although Kennedy knew that the Manitoba was not one of the railroads critics castigated for laying rails to carry bonds, not freight, he believed that the ratio of its bonds to shares should be changed: 3 to 2 in 1884, it was rapidly moving toward 3 to 1. Furthermore, although bonds added to the growing burden of interest, dividends on shares could be reduced in hard times. With a larger issue and more stockholders, T. Jeffer-

son Coolidge thought the company would be in "a safer and stronger condition" to resist others' attempts to gain control. Others stressed the need for a stock issue that more accurately represented the increased value of the railroad's property, including that of affiliated companies.[8]

In principle Hill did not oppose issuing additional stock; he did feel it inopportune. If the company asked to revise its Minnesota charter so as to increase its stock issue, hearings would follow and the company's strategic plans would have to be divulged. The grangers, who had already criticized the StPM&M for building into the western territories, would be opposed. Permission to increase the stock might be withheld, or, if granted, be restricted. Hill thought either result would harm the railroad's credit.

Problems mounted. In December 1887, Shepard, Winston & Company, pressed by subcontractors, was "extremely importunate for payments"; Haskel, Barker & Company wanted its money for cars; bills from the Globe Iron Works for the lake freighters and vouchers for the StPM&M's new office building added pressure; and monthly payrolls and fuel costs had to be met. Heavy snows in January, the worst since 1873, prevented passengers and freight from reaching the railroad's lines. Revenues almost dried up; on one day the general office in St. Paul received only $1,000 from agents and conductors. Hill and Kennedy took steps to meet the immediate troubles. Much as Kennedy disliked a floating debt, during the winter he quietly negotiated loans, and Hill even put up some of his own securities as collateral for part of the railroad's short-term obligations.[9]

Reminiscing later with Lord Mount Stephen about the four or five times in the railroad's

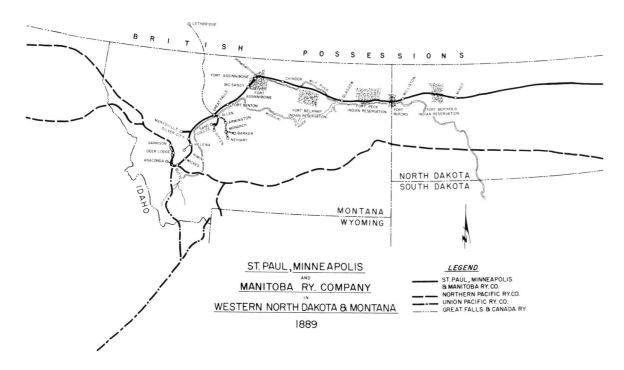

ST. PAUL, MINNEAPOLIS
AND
MANITOBA RY. COMPANY
IN
WESTERN NORTH DAKOTA & MONTANA
1889

LEGEND
— ST. PAUL, MINNEAPOLIS
& MANITOBA RY. CO.
– – – NORTHERN PACIFIC RY. CO.
–·–·– UNION PACIFIC RY. CO.
········· GREAT FALLS & CANADA RY.

BERTHS IN FREE SLEEPING CAR.

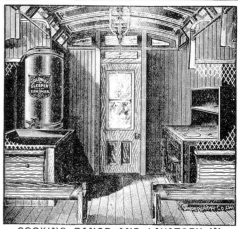

COOKING RANGE AND LAVATORY IN
FREE SLEEPER.

history when the directors "might have gone astray," Hill recalled one board meeting, probably in January 1888, when Kennedy proposed that a corporation be organized in Dakota to buy the StPM&M and related companies "at an advance, in other words, to make a melon and sell out." This "was the time I locked the door on the Board of Directors and served notice on them that they might vote for the plan, but that would be as near as they would ever come to carrying it into effect."[10]

Significant changes followed in New York. In January 1888, Kennedy resigned as vice president, his health having deteriorated under the strain, and he soon departed for Europe. Kennedy remained one of the largest stockholders, of course, and for a number of months a director of the railroad, but his place

on the finance committee was taken by F. P. Olcott of the Central Trust Company. Later in that year, E. T. Nichols, strongly endorsed by Kennedy, was appointed treasurer of the StPM&M. His quick, analytical mind and access to Wall Street facts, rumors, and gossip made him an efficient treasurer and he kept Hill well informed on financial affairs.

Throughout 1888, however, the Manitoba's financial position was subject to divergent interpretations. An optimist like Hill could point to new construction completed or in progress. Although it would take some time to develop the country contiguous to these lines, the railroad could anticipate significant new sources of income. For the StPM&M alone, revenue in fiscal 1888, highest in the company's history, already exceeded that of 1886 by 30 percent, and net railway operating income was

also rising. Critics, though, commented that the company was "marching at too rapid a pace in the extension of its system" and that the collateral trust loan appeared "hardly of a nature to strengthen confidence." European investors too raised questions about the new bonds, backed as they were by securities of roads connecting little-known centers.[11]

Even the railroad's friends evinced concern at the increase in funded debt and carrying

Table 1. Bonded Debt of the St. Paul, Minneapolis & Manitoba Railway Company, 1885 and 1889

Bonds	June 30, 1885	June 30, 1889
First Mortgage	$5,350,000	$4,480,000
Second Mortgage	8,000,000	8,000,000
St. Paul & Pacific	366,000	366,000
Dakota Extension	5,676,000	5,676,000
Consolidated Mortgage (6%)	13,044,000	13,344,000
Consolidated Mortgage (4½%)	——	13,651,000
Montana Extension	——	7,468,000
Collateral Trust	——	8,000,000
	$32,436,000	$60,985,000

Note: This list does not include bonds issued by proprietary companies: Minneapolis Union, $2,700,000; Montana Central, $6,500,000; Eastern Minnesota, $4,500,000; Willmar & Sioux Falls, $2,625,000; Duluth, Watertown & Pacific, $1,375,000. On June 30, 1889, the StPM&M held $500,000 of the MC bonds and all those issued by the W&SF and DW&P. The figures are the remainder of the $8-million issue after redemption with net proceeds of the sale of granted lands.

Sources: StPM&MAR, 1884–1885, p. 21, and 1888–1889, p. 23.

charges. Without counting guaranteed interest on bonds of affiliated companies, the Manitoba's annual interest charges rose more than $1.25 million between June 1885 and June 1889. The bonded indebtedness, which had been $32,436,000 at the end of fiscal 1885, climbed to $60,985,000 by June 30, 1889. The ratio of bonds to equity increased to 3 to 1, exclusive of the $17,700,000 of bonds issued by proprietary companies. (See Table 1.)

Although ownership remained concentrated, the number of stockholders grew astonishingly. Just over 150 in 1885, they increased to more than 750 just four years later. Geographically, the stock was more widely dispersed than it had been earlier, but 82 percent was held domestically—46 percent was held in New York City, reflecting brokers' accounts, although Boston boasted more individual holdings than any other center. Of the 18 percent foreign ownership, almost half was in Montreal, held by George Stephen and Donald Smith. By far the largest owner in Europe was the Dutch Administration Office, but large accounts were held in England and Scotland.[12]

Feelings of uncertainty were accentuated by the Manitoba's financial performance during the last years of the 1880s. Operating revenue bottomed at $7.3 million in fiscal 1886 before moving to a new peak of $9.6 million in 1888. A drop of 10 percent in 1889, occasioned primarily by a decline in wheat shipments, was a special blow. New mileage placed in service during 1886–1888, accompanied as it was by tariffs reduced by greater competition, had as yet failed to generate a much-desired sustained increase in operating revenues. Moreover, with increased mileage, operating expenses grew more rapidly than revenue, from $3.3 million in 1884–1885 to $4.7 million four years later. Such outlays averaged more than $4 million for the three years 1887 to 1889. Reflecting the deteriorating relationship between expenses and revenue, total income (the sum of net railway operating income and nonoperating income) of prosperous 1888 was almost $300,000 less than that for 1883; the average for the four years 1886 to 1889 ($4.5 million) fell short of the average for the comparable preceding period ($4.7 million). (See Table 2.)

Other disquieting news included rumors circulated early in 1889 that the Union Pacific and the Northern Pacific were attempting to work together by putting control of their associated branches into the hands of trustees. If true, the venture threatened to bottle up the Manitoba at Butte and Helena. Nichols wondered too if Henry Villard was behind an anonymous Boston banker who reportedly wanted to control the StPM&M. Clearly this was, as Kennedy said, a time to "be wise as serpents and ever on the watch."[13]

The situation would have disconcerted Hill all the more if he had not been moving to strengthen his control in order to prosecute yet another ambitious expansion plan. Hill, Smith,

Table 2. Financial Statement of the St. Paul, Minneapolis and Manitoba Railway Company, 1879–1889

(000 omitted)

	1880	1881	1882	1883	1884	1885	1886	1887	1888	1889
Railway Operating Revenues	$2,885	$3,653	$6,578	$9,003	$8,184	$7,776	$7,322	$8,028	$9,562	$8,586
Railway Operating Expenses	1,300	1,746	3,321	4,343	3,735	3,316	3,659	4,099	4,406	4,751
Railway Operating Income	1,585	1,907	3,257	4,660	4,449	4,460	3,663	3,929	5,156	3,835
All Taxes	—	110	195	252	195	194	180	215	264	249
Net Railway Operating Income	1,498	1,797	3,062	4,438	4,254	4,266	3,483	3,714	4,892	3,586
Nonoperating Income	650	276	947	1,021	706	198	521	930	272	914
Total Income	2,148	2,073	4,009	5,459	4,960	4,464	4,004	4,644	5,164	4,500
Nonoperating Expenses	1,592	1,341	2,049	2,078	2,749	2,112	2,350	3,186	3,816	3,431
Net Income	556	732	1,960	3,381	2,211	2,352	1,654	1,458	1,348	1,069
Dividends Paid and Accrued	—	—	975	1,725	1,600	1,300	1,200	1,200	1,200	1,200
Carried to Profit and Loss	556	732	985	1,656	611	1,052	454	258	148	(131)

Note: Some adjustments necessary to make entries consistent throughout the period. Subheadings changed to present terminology; e.g., Railway Operating Revenue for Gross Earnings.

Sources: St. Paul, Minneapolis and Manitoba Railway Company, 1880–1889, Income Accounts. The fiscal year ended June 30.

and Stephen had gradually purchased additional stock, including some from Kennedy. Stephen, who had been off the StPM&M board for two years and had recently retired from the CP presidency, was intrigued by Hill's suggestion to press westward with the Manitoba either by gaining control of the NP or by building a new transcontinental to the Pacific Coast.

Tension on the board became painful early in 1889; financial practice and Hill's continuing calls for expansion were points at issue. Operating revenues, running below those of fiscal 1888, and net income, held down by a record outlay of $3,256,000 for interest, threatened to be insufficient to pay the regular 6 percent dividend. (To make the previous quarterly payment, funds had been drawn from profit and loss.) Lack of harmony prevailed not only between eastern and western directors but between Boston and New York. A resolution of March 8 approving the sale of additional bonds of the affiliated Eastern Railway Company elicited a resounding "no" from D. Willis James; on March 9 no quorum was present; and, on March 12, two resignations were accepted. Kennedy's was not unexpected; in Europe, he had been inactive for some

months. Coolidge explained his departure by citing preoccupation with other affairs. James refused to vote on some resolutions on that day and left the meeting early. The election of William H. Forbes, Henry Minot, and his brother, William, Jr., gave New England investors the three places on the board they had long desired. At the board meeting on April 24, 1889, Hill, as expected, won unqualified support.

During these months of financial strain, Hill saw to the erection of physical structures as expressions of achievement and of his optimism for the future. In August 1888, a stronger and larger Manitoba occupied a new office building on Third Street near the St. Paul Union Station. Constructed of red brick, with entrance through a massive rough-stone arch, it was a statement of substance. At the same time, Hill was supervising every detail in a family mansion being constructed, with rough-stone trim, on a site near the east end of Summit Avenue giving him a clear view of downtown St. Paul and the Mississippi River Valley. These outward symbols of accomplishment implied much more: the Empire Builder was ready to launch another campaign of expansion.[14]

11

On to Puget Sound

In 1889, James J. Hill and his associates determined to extend their railroad to the Pacific Coast, a decision requiring substantial courage to say the very least. Builders of western railroads could no longer expect government aid, and transcontinental roads hardly inspired investors by their performance. Nor was 1889 a particularly encouraging year for the Manitoba Road. Its expansion had been rapid, several new arteries were still in the early stages of developing traffic, and operating revenues were 10 percent less than in the previous season. Nevertheless, Hill had long dreamed of building on to the Pacific and to him the time seemed propitious. The Northern Pacific was becoming more aggressive, and sooner or later other roads would undertake construction that might well restrict the Manitoba's options. Either expand now, Hill concluded, or be forever contained.[1]

New Dress

The Great Northern Railway Company (GN), which was to become Hill's transcontinental, was neither a new company nor a reorganization; it was merely a new name for a corporation. Hill had earlier acquired the charter of the Minneapolis & St. Cloud Rail-

Critics thought Hill was moving too quickly into the northwest, but this train on the Montana Central between Great Falls and Butte suggests that business was ample.

road Company, incorporated by the Minnesota territorial legislature in 1856, and had used its powers to build some of the Manitoba's lines. Now the old charter was to be used for a broader purpose, and on September 16, 1889, the Minneapolis & St. Cloud became the Great Northern. Hill had already used the words "Great Northern" for a grain elevator at Superior, and he and his associates were well aware of the excellent reputation that England's Great Northern Railway had. Moreover, its projected service area made the new designation clearly appropriate.

Plans called for the Great Northern to lease current and future Manitoba properties for 999 years. The GN was authorized to issue $40 million in stock, half of it preferred, and owners of the StPM&M were invited to subscribe. Only preferred stock was issued. For each $100 share held in the Manitoba, a holder was entitled to purchase $100 of preferred stock in GN, issued at par. The price in cash was $50 a share, the other half being provided by transfer to the GN of $22 million in securities held by the StPM&M. The GN then undertook to pay off $8 million in collateral trust mortgage bonds of the StPM&M and to provide for taxes, assessments, interest on bonds, and other obligations, including 6 percent annual dividends on stock. This arrangement gave the Manitoba's shareholders strong incentive to buy GN stock, and most took advantage.

Hill and his associates quickly worked out final details. The lease of the Manitoba by the Great Northern began at midnight, January 31, 1890. Writing to stockholders of the Manitoba five months later, Hill summarized the changes: Control and operation of the StPM&M had been transferred to the GN, said Hill, and "Your Company has, therefore, ceased to be an operating company." The

Manitoba would build west, but its new lines would come under lease to the Great Northern.[2]

At the annual GN stockholder meeting in October 1890, a new board, enlarged to nine members divided into three categories, was elected. Three-year terms went to James J. Hill, William P. Clough, and Samuel Hill, a son-in-law of the president, who had substantial legal and financial experience. Named to two-year terms were Stephen and Smith, long Hill's associates, and George Bliss of New York. Elected for one-year terms were J. Kennedy Tod, nephew of J. S. Kennedy and still an important stockholder, and two officers of the company, M. D. Grover, general solicitor, and Edward Sawyer, treasurer and assistant secretary.

During the early 1890s, changes among this group were few. In 1892, with the organization well launched, George Stephen (Lord Mount Stephen) and George Bliss gave way to more active members. Their successors were Jacob H. Schiff of Kuhn, Loeb & Company and Edward T. Nichols, GN's secretary and assistant treasurer. Meanwhile, seven GN directors served also on the board of the Manitoba, an arrangement that facilitated coordination.

Many of the men who had managed the StPM&M now held similar positions on the GN. Hill was president and William P. Clough vice president; M. D. Grover was general solicitor; A. L. Mohler, general manager; the traffic department was headed by P. P. Shelby; and C. W. Case headed the operating department. Elbridge H. Beckler of the Montana Central was assigned chief engineer for the Pacific Extension. It was to the construction of that enterprise that these officers gave their primary attention.

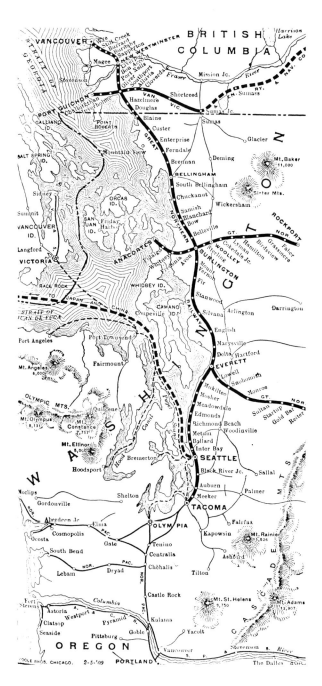

Engineering Challenges

Four months after the Great Northern leased the Manitoba, the former authorized the latter to undertake construction of some 800 miles to Puget Sound. As Hill explained, he preferred that the extension be built in the name of the Manitoba, which owned most of the GN's system, because he did "not like the idea of having the main line cut into two half way across the continent."[3]

Although GN directors wanted the road pushed westward "as rapidly as possible," they defined the proposition in only general terms. Its route, said the board, should generate local traffic and be located in a way that distance, grade, curvature, and construction costs would be balanced so that the finished product could be operated efficiently. It was to start at some "point on the Montana Extension line" near the crossing of the Marias River and proceed westward by a "suitable route, to be hereafter determined" through Montana, Idaho, and Washington "to some suitable point upon the water of Puget Sound."[4]

It fell to Elbridge H. Beckler to locate an acceptable course. In his mid-thirties, short, modest, and scholarly, born in Boston and raised in Maine, Beckler was a graduate of that state's land-grant college. His engineering career included service with the Northern Pacific and the Canadian Pacific as well as with the Hill properties. In 1887, he had been named chief engineer of the Montana Central; in October 1889, he assumed his new duties.

Beckler's tasks as chief engineer of the Pacific Extension were many. Reconnaissance work had to be completed before preliminary lines could be run to gain the detailed, accurate data. Next, exact locations of line had to be made in order to classify work into sections for contractors. Finally, Beckler and his subordinates had to time, push, and inspect the work. The job, Beckler later recalled, required the "attention of more than fifty educated men for three years with an army of followers."[5]

Beckler's primary goal was to plot the most feasible route across the Rockies and the Cascades; no decision was more critical to the company's lasting health. Beckler studied four prospective paths. Reconnaissance showed that one of these, extending along the North Fork of the Sun River and into the Flathead Valley, was longer than the others and lacked compensating advantages. The second, running west from Butte across the Bitter Roots and other mountains, was rejected because the terrain was rough and because much of the line would be "too near the region of perpetual snow." More promising was a route following the South Fork of the Sun River, crossing the Rockies at Rogers Pass, then paralleling the Big Blackfoot to Missoula. From there it proceeded to Mullan, Idaho, where the GN might make connections with the Oregon Railway & Navigation Company (OR&N) or build its own line northwest to Spokane.[6]

A fourth alternative was a more northerly line, starting near Fort Assiniboine, where the Manitoba's line turned southwest to Great Falls. Beckler himself undertook reconnaissance of the region from Spokane Falls east to the Kootenai River, and he was convinced that construction would be less difficult than he had feared. The area also was clothed with heavy timber and appeared to have potential for mining and water power.

Meanwhile, two of Beckler's subordinates were studying the territory beyond Fort Assiniboine. One of them worked eastward from Flathead Lake and the other, John F. Stevens, surveyed the area west of Fort Assiniboine.

Like Beckler, Stevens had been raised in Maine; he, too, was a widely respected railroad engineer with outstanding accomplishments from Canada to Texas. He would soon add to his reputation. Proceeding from Fort Assiniboine in a buckboard, he reached the Blackfoot Agency and reported to Beckler: "distance 130 miles; nothing steeper than 1% grades." But now he came to the critical portion of his task: locating a pass through the Rockies. Leaving the Blackfoot Agency, he scoured the mountains, found the headwaters of one stream, and another that drained toward the west. Returning to the summit, he tramped throughout the night of December 11, 1889, to keep from freezing in the minus 40-degree temperature. Stevens had found Marias Pass, its summit at only 5,214 feet. This altitude was lower, said Beckler, "than any pass that I have heard of in the range crossed by a Railroad." Others had known of Marias Pass, no doubt, but Stevens was the first to explore it as a location engineer, to judge its feasibility for a railroad, and to make his findings public.[7]

By the spring of 1890, Beckler was focusing on the northern option. Compared to the Dearborn–Missoula–Mullan route, the northern survey would require less heavy construction and fewer tunnels, would have less rise and fall, had better alignment, would give the GN its own line to Spokane Falls, promised fewer helper engine districts, and was a shorter route between competing points. The distance would be greater than by the southern route, but Beckler estimated that construction costs would be less. The climate was similar; both had heavy snow but the northern route probably had more rain. With its lower elevation the northern route might have more agricultural development. The Dearborn route

John F. Stevens was assigned by Elbridge H. Beckler the task of studying the territory west from Fort Assinniboine.

crossed the Coeur d'Alene district, but there also appeared to be substantial mining potential farther north. Finally, the northern line would open virgin territory the full distance to eastern Washington; traffic generated along it would not have to be divided.

Beckler's attention was similarly drawn to the west edge of the Rockies and a shield-shaped, arid valley bounded on three sides by streams leading from the Rockies and a spur of the Cascades. The Columbia River — on the northwest and northern rims — dominated and gave the valley its name: the Columbia Basin.

The Spokane bounded the area on the eastern edge of the north rim, and the Snake formed part of the southern border until it joined the Columbia at Pasco. With abundant water from these streams, Beckler correctly calculated that irrigation would make the broad region flower for agriculture.

The chief engineer also remarked on the beautiful scenery in the Marias Pass – Spokane region, but Hill did not so regard it: "We do not care enough for Rocky Mountain scenery to spend a large sum of money in developing it," he wrote Beckler. "What we want is the best possible line, shortest distance, lowest grades, and least curvature that we can build. . . ." It was vintage Hill. Beckler understood exactly what his boss meant and assured him that the northern route met all requirements. The decision was made: the Great Northern would go west from Pacific Junction, just west of today's Havre.[8]

With that major decision behind them, Hill and Beckler turned to the next major task — locating a pass through the Cascades. Here again John F. Stevens would prove his abilities. Beckler placed Stevens in charge and dispatched him to Waterville, Washington. Hill was his typically impatient self, but dense forest and a dearth of trails on the east slope of the Cascades made difficult and dangerous work. Stevens tramped for miles through the rough country, following streams and examining passes. Finally, he found a creek (later named Nason) that came from the west and emptied into the south end of Lake Wenatchee. Noticing its relationship to a low crest in the mountains, he sent a subordinate, Charles F. B. Haskell, to make the survey. After accomplishing this assignment, Haskell carved the words "Stevens Pass" on a massive cedar tree in the heavy forest, memorial-izing the engineer's name on the famed pass that became a vital segment in the Great Northern's transcontinental route.

"Head of the Rake"

Locating low-grade mountain passes through the Rockies and the Cascades was indispensable, and so too was establishing prime terminals on the Pacific Coast. Other railroads were strongly entrenched at several locations. The Canadian Pacific was in Vancouver, with marine connections to Seattle and trans-Pacific points. The Northern Pacific had direct access to Tacoma, its western terminus, with branches to Seattle and to Portland. It also reached Portland from Spokane, partly on its own tracks and partly over rails of the Oregon Railroad & Navigation Company, and had favorable contacts with oceanic shipping companies operating to Alaska and the Far East. Another powerful competitor, the Union Pacific, reached Spokane and Portland by the way of the OR&N. Finally, the Southern Pacific had a major route into Portland from the south and dominated transportation in western Oregon.

To reach major entrepôts in the Northwest, argued Hill, the Great Northern would require a vertical axis line, from Portland north to Vancouver. Such a line would gather traffic and feed it to the GN's east – west route for the long haul to St. Paul and beyond. Hill picturesquely described it: the north – south line would be the "head of the rake," the transcontinental its "handle."

With that cryptic but useful metaphor in mind, Hill could say when pressed for an early decision on locating his company's western terminus that "we shall strike at every point." Still, there would have to be a focal location.

Construction of this gigantic trestle at Two
Medicine Creek—along the eastern edge of
what became Glacier National Park—posed
significant engineering problems.

Hill said the community selected would have to have at least two qualities, a "safe, deep harbor" and "a live energetic people." Several places met those qualifications, at least so their respective inhabitants thought, but Hill took a dry-eyed approach. Information was gathered from many sources, and company representatives undertook on-site inspections. On perhaps the most important of these tours, early in 1890, Vice President Clough and Chief Engineer Beckler went to Puget Sound. The latter studied engineering matters, and Clough evaluated business and legal climates. Among other businessmen whom he met was Thomas A. Burke, an energetic Irish-American attorney who typified the enterprising spirit that the railroaders found in Seattle, and who proved influential in Hill's decision to make Seattle the Great Northern's western terminal.[9]

In retrospect, Seattle was the logical choice. Its fine harbor was already an important port for the coastal fleet; it was the economic and legal center of Washington, which had achieved statehood in the previous year; and its people demonstrated their energy by their rapid recovery after a disastrous June 1889 fire. Hill apparently picked Seattle during the spring of 1890, but his frequent threats to go elsewhere kept the issue in doubt and local residents nervous. Not until 1900 did the decision appear secure, and terminal facilities were not completed for another six years.

Meanwhile, Hill pondered alternatives as he planned for the GN's head of the rake. Every hamlet presented its claim for service, and every local businessman had something to sell. Moves produced countermoves, rumors flew, and the major carriers watched each other and the GN interloper with dark suspicion.

In this confused environment, Hill eventually determined that the best way to gain a line southward from Seattle into Portland was by cooperating with the Union Pacific. After extensive discussions, the GN and the Oregon Short Line (OSL) and Utah & Northern Railroad—UP subsidiaries—entered into a contract during late 1890 by which a jointly owned Puget Sound & Portland Railroad Company would construct a new line between Seattle and Portland in competition with the Northern Pacific. That project proved abortive. Both the UP and the GN sent engineers to make surveys, and for a time men and teams bustled on the surveyed line; expenditures exceeded $1 million. But Hill approved of neither the location nor the costs, which he considered excessive. He also worried about the health of the UP; it soon passed into receivership. On the other hand, UP officers complained that the GN was slow in making its payments. In the end, construction stopped, and the GN would have to wait several years to make its entry into Portland.

Hill did better in securing that part of the rake lying north of Seattle, making his first move in 1889. Fairhaven (South Bellingham) enjoyed a favorable location on Bellingham Bay and had attracted a dynamic population, including Nelson Bennett, builder of the NP's Cascade Division and Stampede Tunnel. In 1888, Bennett and others had obtained a charter for the Fairhaven & Southern Railroad, and by November in the next year that company had built twenty-five miles of line running from Fairhaven southeast toward bituminous coal fields on the Skagit River. Early in 1889 Hill's GN bought the property, and in 1890–1891 the Fairhaven & Southern was completed from Fairhaven north to the Canadian border and south to near the town of Burlington. A seven-mile branch led to the coal fields. It might have appeared insignifi-cant, but the tiny road actually was a major element in Hill's aspirations.

Arrangements with Nelson Bennett also permitted the GN to enter Canada. In 1889 Bennett had obtained a British Columbia franchise for the New Westminster & Southern. Ultimately he agreed to allow the GN use of this charter, and twenty-five miles of line were promptly built, from the south bank of the Fraser River through rich farmlands to the international boundary.

The Great Northern's entrance into Canadian Pacific territory generated little enthusiasm among Canadians, although Hill had invited the CPR to participate in the new line. Perhaps CPR President Van Horne was disturbed by the GN's decision to become a transcontinental. In any event, GN officers were soon complaining about CPR's traffic policies, and in March 1890 the CPR ordered the GN to withdraw all its rates from the Twin Cities to points on the CPR west of Winnipeg and to retain in the East only the tariffs that were competitive with those of the Northern Pacific. Moreover, the CPR was in no hurry to arrange for easy transfer of passengers at New Westminster and rumors said that, through a traffic agreement with the independent Spokane Falls & Northern Railroad, the CPR was planning to solicit competitively in Washington.

Meanwhile, Great Northern's managers were taking steps to obtain land for terminal and other facilities in Seattle. At the northern edge of this city, between Smith's Cove and Salmon Bay, sixty acres were purchased for $1,000 an acre; here eventually would be the GN's yards, machine and car shops, and docks. South of the business district, in the tidelands, the railroad received a gift of land from those eager to benefit from the appreciating value of neighboring property.

The next move was to obtain right-of-way tying the two properties together. At an executive meeting of the Seattle city council in March 1890, the Great Northern was granted 60 of the 120 feet of Railroad Avenue. Thomas Burke viewed the ordinance as "the strongest in the public interest of any ever passed" by Seattle's council, but critics' opinions were less friendly. The secrecy in these proceedings was denounced, and some observers commented that within months Acting Mayor D. E. Durie, who signed the franchise, became editor of Burke's *Seattle Telegraph*, described by rivals as "the Great Northern Democratic Daily." Northern Pacific officers appeared in great numbers at subsequent council meetings, and efforts to revoke the GN grant went on for years. The city fathers' urgency, however, probably was inspired by their intense desire to convince Hill that Seattle should be the GN's premier western terminal.[10]

At the same time, Hill and his associates arranged for construction north from Seattle to meet the Fairhaven & Southern as it built south from the international border. To facilitate this work, they obtained a charter for the Seattle & Montana Railway Company. Local citizens were the incorporators and a Washingtonian, Daniel H. Gilman, was the first president, but it was no secret that the GN held 99.5 percent of the company's stock. The Seattle & Montana built seventy-eight miles of track north along Puget Sound, about half of it nearly at water level.

Celebrations followed completion of the coastal line above Seattle. On Valentine's Day 1891, the last spike was driven on the northern segment at Blaine. On November 27, a train with 275 passengers in decorated cars ran all the way from Seattle to the Fraser River at South Westminster. There a Seattle Chamber of Commerce official heralded the accomplishment with contemporary flamboyance: "Every rail is the pathway to prosperity," he proclaimed. "Blest be the tie that binds our hearts and towns with business love." Enhancing the future of the Great Northern, Hill had fashioned a goodly portion of his head of the rake.[11]

Sterling Bonds of 1890

While engineers were hunting easy grades and the Great Northern was getting a toehold in Washington, directors were arranging for funds to build the Pacific Extension, a major task. Hill, after all, proposed to construct almost a thousand miles of line, much of it through undeveloped country, with no land grant to offer as security.

In February 1890, engineers estimated that building the Pacific Extension would cost $25 million. Hill suggested that the Manitoba issue bonds in approximately that amount, timing them to bring in $2 million or $3 million a month. The GN and its friends might take about 20 percent; the balance could be sold. Partly because the New York money market was unsettled during 1890, Hill and his associates decided to try capital markets abroad. Reports from London were hopeful, and interest there was expected to grow as investors learned that the GN had found favorable passes over the Rockies and the Cascades and that progress was being made on the Pacific Coast. In May, Hill wrote to Baring Brothers & Company that everything "looks well from New York to the Pacific Coast, and I feel certain that our enterprise will do fully as well for its owners as the Manitoba did."[12]

Under deed of July 1, 1890, the Manitoba's Pacific Extension mortgage provided for an issue of fifty-year, £6,000,000 gold bonds, at 4 percent. A third of the total was to be issued at once, with additional amounts to be authorized as mileage was completed and equipped. By spreading sales over a longer period, the company hoped to take advantage of a changing money market and to dispose of the bonds when the price was most acceptable.

In the spring of 1891, Hill and his associates moved to dispose of another portion of the issue. Hill calculated that the railroad needed a million pounds sterling to carry construction to spring 1892, another million by the following August, and the final two million by May 1893. Conditions, unfortunately, were not as favorable as in 1890. Hill wrote in August that "there will be no confidence in the large money centers of the world, in the financial plans of this Company, until the fear of losing our gold ceases; and this may, through a want of understanding of the situation on the part of Congress, take a turn that will temporarily bring disaster upon the whole country." Nevertheless, sales eventually brought in $3,699,146.[13]

Disappointed by this yield, Hill altered the GN's financial plans by adopting as expedient a shorter-term collateral trust bond; the contract between the Manitoba and the GN was changed in 1892. Under the new arrangement, the StPM&M paid the GN the remaining £3,000,000 bonds in return for construction. For some years these sterling bonds served as security for the GN's own first issue. Great Northern Collateral Trust gold bonds, bearing 4 percent, were for ten years but redeemable at any time after 1893. Offered to GN stockholders at 72½, they produced a net of $10,834,575 and were all paid by September 1, 1898.

After the Collateral Trust bonds had been redeemed, the GN was free to market the sterling bonds. By waiting carefully for an opportune time to sell, the company succeeded in meeting a much better market. Taken together, the £6,000,000 sterling issue netted the GN $25,943,676.

Unlike Demersville, which perished when the railroad passed it by, Libby's life was assured by the Great Northern.

Building the Transcontinental

In July 1890, Hill summoned Chief Engineer Beckler to St. Paul. He was ready to go over estimates, take bids from contractors, and work out details for constructing 800 miles of line that would be the Pacific Extension. Hill decided that the work would be accomplished by independent contractors to GN standards and be checked by company engineers. Beckler would supervise the entire job.

On August 1, 1890, the first of many agreements was signed. D. C. Shepard, who had built many lines for Hill, had taken his son-in-law into the firm, which was now known as Shepard, Siems & Company. The GN's contract with this firm covered both grading and track-laying for 185 miles to the summit of the Rockies, which was to be completed by April 1, 1891. The rate for track-laying was $200 a mile; for surfacing, $175 a mile. The railroad, of course, supplied rails and other track materials.

The "business district" at Martin Creek attracted the lumberjack, track-layer, and others working on the railroad in the Cascades. The building in the foreground advertises "Beds" and the other, the Cascade Saloon, is also a restaurant boasting "Meals, Cheapest And Best In Town."

Ahead of the contractors, right-of-way agents performed their tasks. Acts of 1875 and 1887 covered corridors through government and Indian lands, but details remained to be resolved. In areas such as the Flathead country, agents frequently found hardy pioneers who also proved to be skilled land speculators. Occasionally, they ran into casual squatters. In Idaho and Washington, the GN purchased lands from the NP, which proved easier to deal with than some of the ranchers.

Still other factors had to be considered. Four miles east of Pacific Junction, where the new line would begin, a supply of water was found; the future town of Havre was established there. Beyond that place, as the line continued westward, several wells were drilled, but for immediate needs the railroad ran water cars. Meanwhile, engineers calculated that passing tracks should be located about twelve miles apart and as near water as possible. During the first year of construction, these were not built at regular intervals, but Hill did establish their length—1,600 feet between the frogs—indicating that he anticipated that long trains would be operating on the line.

Locating station sites mattered as well. Numerous factors had to be weighed in making these decisions, including the distance between stations and physical characteristics of the countryside. To give station agents and telegraph operators an adequate view of trains, Hill urged that depots not be built on curves or

at the bottom of grades. The GN also attempted to avoid locations in which land speculators were plying their trade, and company rules strictly prohibited employees from taking "advantage of any information gotten through their service with the Company. . . ."[14]

Some towns were built by the railroad; it destroyed others. North of Flathead Lake was Demersville, an established community that Beckler hoped to serve but grades argued against it. Moreover, the Kalispell location had much in its favor, including a good water supply; when rails reached that point, the merchants of Demersville moved there, and the old town disappeared.

By the late summer of 1890, supply trains were moving west. Track-laying began at Pa-

cific Junction on October 20, 1890, and continued with few interruptions until January 7, 1893. In some parts of Washington, Idaho, and western Montana, work went from west to east, but most was done by crews working from east to west. Rail was generally sixty-pound, though heavier sections were employed in the Rockies and over the Cascades.

Contractors constantly needed an adequate labor supply, meaning that men were recruited all along the line, in cities to the east, and elsewhere. Swedish workers were common, but as construction moved westward, Italians became more numerous. Living conditions on the job were primitive. Graders generally lived in tent camps, which contractors tried to place close to the work. Boarding cars were home

for track-laying crews. Weather was a constantly threatening challenge, but men soon learned to cope with cold rains and deep snow. In all cases, contractors found endless difficulty in retaining those hired. Harvest season tempted many away.[15]

Building the Pacific Extension produced its share of railhead towns, with attendant evils. Typical perhaps, near the summit of the Rockies, was McCartyville, a collection of forty log shacks that one visitor labeled "a seething Sodom of Wickedness." But the front moved on; McCartyville was deserted and disappeared from the map, replaced by other quickly forgotten centers where briefly smoke arose from chimneys, outlining the trees, and men sought release from hard work and loneliness.[16]

During the winter of 1890, plans were made for the next year's work. Construction from the summit to the Columbia River was to be accomplished by Shepard, Siems & Company for cost plus profit. A contract was made for lumber, and the St. Paul firm of Porter Brothers agreed to put up necessary buildings. Much subcontracting for grading went to small firms or to individuals, for short distances. Beckler set schedules that he thought "would be as high as it would be necessary to pay . . . and permit subcontractors a reasonable profit." Timing counted too, for these contractors would probably take a lower price after spring came. The standard rate for men was $2.25 a day, and for teams $5.[17]

Grading in the Rockies started as soon in

While construction gangs approached the crest of the Cascades from the east, work also progressed from the west.

1891 as snow melted and frost left the ground. Soon men were at work on the summit, and from there to the Flathead River the route was covered with grading outfits. The work was especially difficult because most of the country was inaccessible: heavy machinery could be used very little and, because it was expensive to bring and feed horses, some small subcontractors worked without them. To carry dirt short distances, men often moved big trays along greased poles; they removed earth from cuts in "Swedish carts," hand-drawn vehicles directed from behind by manipulating long poles.

The laying of rail resumed on April 24, 1891, and continued through the year. Among the innumerable problems slowing the work was scarcity of workers, and progress was delayed for a month during the summer while crews completed bridges, including a spectacular structure spanning the Two Medicine River. By mid-September, the rail crew had laid sixty miles and had started down the west slope of the Rockies. Autumn rains then impeded work, causing unpredictable slides; in the mountains temperatures fell rapidly, and the men had to labor in horrible conditions. By the end of November, Beckler informed Hill that crews had registered only seven miles of new construction during the most recent week. Before the year was out, though, track-layers were at Kalispell. In all, they had built 157 miles of road in 1891. Hill, rightfully pleased with the work and with prospects for the future, said to a stockholder, "We are getting a first-rate line—better than I supposed was possible—through the broken country in the Rocky Mountain sections."[18]

Hill's insistence that the line through the Cascades be completed quickly required construction of tortuous switchbacks.

Driving of the last spike in construction of the Great Northern Railway's transcontinental line took place January 6, 1893, near the present station of Scenic, Washington, in the Cascade Mountains.

Seattle eagerly greeted the Great Northern. This view is of Railroad Avenue, now Alaska Way, between Marion and Columbia streets.

The first months of 1892 were marked by uneven progress. Several times, crews worked day and night shifts to push grading ahead of track-layers; slides, snow, bridge construction, and missing manpower delayed the job. East of Bonners Ferry a wreck killed four men and destroyed several boarding cars. The push to Spokane was helped, however, by west-to-east construction of eighty-six miles from Albeni Falls, Idaho, to near Troy, Montana. Rails and other construction materials reached this stretch via the Northern Pacific.

By June 1, 1892, the Pacific Extension reached the small, busy city of Spokane, already a mining, flour milling, and railroad center. The NP and the OR&N already served the city, along with local roads, and at the close of the 1880s, D. C. Corbin had begun to extend his Spokane Falls & Northern Railway toward the Canadian border. Still, Spokane, eager for another railroad, set local leaders working to attract the GN to their city.

These men, in fact, had feared that the GN would bypass Spokane some distance to the north. From an engineering point of view, the city's physical features presented problems, and land prices there were subject to inflation. To offset these liabilities, Hill, wanting the city to contribute a right-of-way, had visited Spokane in February 1892. A stirring speech before a mass meeting helped, and in the end he received the aid he wanted. As a temporary expedient, Hill arranged for trackage rights from the east side of town to the west over rails of the Seattle, Lake Shore & Eastern and the OR&N.

Hill continued vigorously pushing the entire Pacific project, fearing that in the Cascades weather would force delays. Instructions to Beckler grew ever more pointed, but the chief engineer faced many difficulties. Steel workers went on strike, bridge iron was difficult to get, and grading on the east slope of the Cascades was handicapped when about 2,000 laborers departed for other opportunities. Nevertheless, when track-laying started west of Spokane on July 18, 1892, it went well enough. On August 13, near Harrington, the daily record for the Pacific Extension was set—4.07 miles. Meanwhile, an arrangement had been worked out for temporary track and a ferry that would serve until a bridge could be thrown over the Columbia River at Wenatchee in May 1893. Sectioning and grading were under way in the tough Tumwater Canyon west of the Columbia. Ahead loomed the peaks of the Cascades.

When Charles Haskell located Stevens Pass, he recognized that approaches to it would take heavy grades, sharp curves, and a lengthy tunnel. All this was necessary, Beckler agreed, to achieve the company's plan for low-cost transcontinental operation—the hallmark of Hill's long-term business strategy. Hill was impatient, however, and for the first time he demanded that speedy construction take precedence over quality of line. Beckler had therefore to plan a cumbersome and expensive-to-operate, if temporary, twelve-mile complex of switchbacks to carry the GN over the Cascades summit.

While construction gangs approached the

crest of the Cascades from the east, work progressed from the west. In November 1891, a contract had been signed with the Shepard firm for grading from Everett to the summit; work began in spring 1892 and progressed nicely through summer and fall. Building a railroad through the Cascades as winter approached, though, proved to be enormously difficult. The predictably harsh weather alternated between rain and snow, flash floods frequently washing away bridges; interruptions were many. "The only track made today was our tracks in the snow," a disgruntled worker wrote after a particularly trying day. Still, the work went on. In mid-December track-layers from the west were approaching the summit, and on January 6, 1893, after building over the crest, the crew from the east met the other at Madison, Washington (later renamed Scenic) — 1,727 miles from St. Paul. The Pacific Extension was at last complete.[19]

Constructing more than 800 miles from near Havre, Montana, to Everett, Washington — over challenging and difficult terrain — in only two and a half years was an amazing accomplishment, properly earning Beckler high praise from engineering colleagues, who knew that the project had been "pushed in a manner heretofore unequalled in railway building and tracklaying."[20]

Ironically, completion of this great task inspired no immediate celebration. The dead-of-winter top of the Cascades was no fit place for festivities. Illness confined Hill to his St. Paul home, and Beckler, having done so much to complete the Pacific Extension, was leaving the railroad. In the end, only two GN officials watched the conventional spike-driving ceremony. Six months later, however, on June 7, 1893, the Twin Cities held a colorful pageant celebrating completion of the new transconti-

nental. Seattle had its own celebration on July 4, two weeks after the first GN passenger train arrived from St. Paul.

If residents of St. Paul and Seattle were enthusiastic, so were many financial writers. Prospects for the Great Northern were good. It was sure to face vigorous competition from the Northern Pacific but, as one observer put it, "on account of the excessive capitalization and higher operating expenditures of the Villard Line," the contest would take "place under conditions decidedly favorable to the Great Northern." In addition, except for the temporary switchback over the Cascades, the Great Northern clearly owned a route that was superior to that of its rival in terms of engineering and cost of operation. The new transcontinental's greatest asset, however, was its president. James J. Hill was described by one analyst as a "master of detail" with "extraordinary capabilities as a practical railroad man, as an administrator, and as a financier." Subsequent developments would prove the validity of those assessments as to the man and the company that he led.[21]

Creating an Empire

With the Pacific Extension completed in 1893, James J. Hill stated that the Great Northern's construction work was practically at an end, an assessment that proved premature. In the next two decades the GN would grow significantly and Hill's overall railroad interests would expand dramatically. Reacting in part to challenges by aggressive and powerful competitors and inspired always by a profound desire to protect investments, Hill went on to create a railroad empire of which the GN was just a part.[1]

Expansion in Minnesota

Hill, preoccupied by the Pacific Extension, postponed but did not diminish his determination to design a more expansive rail system for the Great Northern in Minnesota. During the early 1890s, the company added a few short branches, all in the western portion of the state. The most meaningful was an extension of the Sauk Centre – Eagle Bend line northwest to the pine country near Park Rapids. Later, the GN built thirty-two miles of road north of Moorhead, completing the route between that place and Crookston via Halstad.

Hill was ever alert to further possibilities. The state's abundant iron ore had been first exploited when the Minnesota Iron Company, organized in 1882 on the Vermilion Range, introduced the first practical development of Minnesota's mineral wealth. Subsequently, those entrepreneurs had organized the Duluth & Iron Range Railroad to haul ore to docks at Two Harbors, north of Duluth on Agate Bay. As early as 1892, shipments there exceeded a million tons. Farther to the west, meanwhile, the Merritt brothers, with Leonidas Merritt as president of the Mountain Iron Company, were opening the Mesabi Range. In 1892, the struggling Duluth & Winnipeg Railroad (D&W) hauled its first Mesabi ore to Lake Superior.[2]

That local road got Hill's interest up. Organized in 1878, at first its movement toward uniting the cities of its namesake was slight, but by 1892, the recently created North Star Construction Company had built a hundred miles of line between the St. Louis River and Deer River, and the affiliated Duluth & Superior Terminal Company had constructed a dock at Allouez Bay on Lake Superior to handle ore into lake steamers. In others' hands, the D&W could be dangerous, Hill said: it was the "only line that could be built in unoccupied territory that could materially injure our business." The property could, though, be a good investment in itself, for it ran close to newly opened mines on the Mesabi Range, sure to provide substantial business. The Duluth road was in financial difficulties and Hill acted.[3]

Unfortunately for Hill's plans, though, the D&W was attractive to others as well. The Canadian Pacific had already acquired control of the Soo Line as well as the Duluth, South Shore & Atlantic Railway; the former was es-

pecially strong in northern Minnesota; the latter operated 410 miles of line between Sault Ste. Marie and Duluth. If the D&W reached completion as planned, it would, CPR strategists understood, complement both of these properties. By January 1893, friends of the Canadian company had taken control of the D&W.

The new owners of the Duluth & Winnipeg failed to carry out plans to extend it, however, and the road's financial condition further deteriorated. The Panic of 1893 added insult to injury and completion of the rival Duluth, Missabe & Northern to Lake Superior deprived

the D&W of some of its recently acquired ore traffic. By 1894, the road was in receivership and two years later it was sold under foreclosure. During the next month the property was transferred to a new corporation, the Duluth, Superior & Western Railway Company (DS&W). Control, nevertheless, remained in the hands of those associated with the CPR.

In 1895, Hill decided to try again; bargaining with President Van Horne of the CPR went on for two years. Hill remained, after all, convinced that the entire Lake Superior mining area was inestimably valuable; he enthusiastically recommended it to investors be-

In 1892, the Duluth & Winnipeg, predecessor of the Great Northern, hauled its first Mesabi ore to Lake Superior.

cause the "ores could be laid down at the furnaces for less than any other ores in the country." In his negotiations with Van Horne, Hill fortunately had the support of his old friends, George Stephen, now Baron Mount Stephen, and Sir Donald Smith, but Van Horne was coy, and not until April 26, 1897, did Hill and the president of the CPR come to terms.[4]

By this agreement, the Great Northern acquired the Duluth, Superior & Western as well as affiliated interests, including the Duluth & Winnipeg Terminal Company with its dock at Allouez Bay and the North Star Construction Company. In exchange, the CPR gained significant traffic agreements. The GN, for instance, promised to exchange business with the Soo and the South Shore "on as favorable terms as are accorded its most favored connections."[5]

Soon after the Duluth company was acquired, another opportunity presented itself. In 1892, Amni W. Wright and Charles H. Davis, lumbermen from Saginaw, Michigan, had constructed the first logging railroad in Itasca County. Beginning at Mississippi Landing, it ran north to Swan River Junction on the Duluth, Superior & Western (née Duluth & Winnipeg). Three years later Wright and Davis's company, the Duluth, Mississippi River & Northern Railroad, reached Hibbing. Near that community, the rich Mahoning mine was discovered on land owned by the loggers. Wright and Davis shortly determined to sell not only their forty-five miles of railroad but also 25,000 acres of land opened for mining.

Hill moved quickly. On May 1, 1899, he bought in his own name all the Wright and Davis properties, including lands and the logging road, paying $4,050,000. Hill explained that his primary object was "to get control of the transportation of that ore. . . ." For others, too, the purchase was meaningful. Edmund J. Longyear, a Mesabi pioneer, claimed that Hill's action was "one of the most dramatic happenings ever to occur on the Mesabi."[6]

Purchase of the Duluth, Superior & Western and the Duluth, Mississippi River & Northern put the Great Northern in the business of hauling iron ore in a big way. Both properties were assigned to the Eastern Railway of Minnesota, which, with its parent, planned vigorous expansion campaigns in northern Minnesota. Most vital was completing the Fosston line to connect the Head of the Lakes with the Red River Valley. Available for use were forty-five miles of line from Crookston east to Fosston and a hundred miles of the newly acquired DS&W reaching as far as Deer River. About a hundred miles of new line remained to be built, and Hill pushed the work energetically. The Crookston–Fosston line was upgraded, and much of the former DS&W between Cloquet and Deer River was rebuilt. To avoid heavy grades on the old route east of

In 1897, the Great Northern acquired important properties at the Lakehead. These included a dock on Allouez Bay where whalebacks took on heavy tonnage of Mesabi ore.

Cloquet, a new line of twenty-eight miles was built from Cloquet to a junction with the Eastern Railway at the Nemadji River, thirteen miles south of West Superior. This extension lengthened the distance to the ore dock at Allouez, but provided a better approach with a lower grade. The completed line between the Red River Valley and the Head of the Lakes was opened September 25, 1898.[7]

Hill soon added other lines in Minnesota. In 1899, the Eastern Railway completed a new one from Coon Creek, north of Minneapolis, to Brook Park, southwest of Hinckley. (From there it paralleled a GN line another eighteen miles to Sandstone.) The new Coon Creek–Brook Park route cut the distance from St. Paul to Superior by about twenty-five miles. Another line, which earlier had inched northward from Sauk Centre, by May 1899 was pushed through to Cass Lake on the new Fosston line.

The Eastern Railway undertook still more construction on the Mesabi Range. By 1905, to handle increased ore tonnage, the main line west of Superior (the railroad changed its internal designation from West Superior to Superior in 1903) to Brookston was double-tracked. After it had taken over the Duluth, Superior & Western, the Eastern Railway improved that line from Swan River northeast to Hibbing and in 1899 extended it through Ellis to serve newly opened mines at Virginia. And as ore movements increased, the company found in 1901 it had to connect Ellis, on the Virginia line, with Brookston. Short stretches of new track also ran from Kelly Lake to Nashwauk on the western side of the Mesabi Range and from Kelly Lake to Flanders.

The character of terrain and the nature of handling ore often resulted in high construction costs. Some lines ran over peat bogs, re-

quiring endless attention to ditching and surfacing. At the mines, most of which were open pit, ore was dumped into cars by steamshovel; spurs serving the mines had constantly to be moved. As Hill described it, "Where the track was today a week hence the ore would be shoveled out maybe 25 feet below it."[8]

Acquisitions and new construction transformed the Eastern Railway into a major carrier. In 1890, it had 72 miles of line; by July 1907, its mileage grew to 503, and capitalization had to be increased accordingly. The Eastern's stock issue grew from $5 million in 1897 to $16 million in 1900, most of it held by the GN. Outstanding First Mortgage bonds amounted to $4.7 million in 1898, but in April of that year $15 million in Northern Division First-Mortgage, fifty-year bonds were authorized. A third of this amount was issued to the public to raise funds for construction, but much of the balance was used to refund the twenty-year bonds of 1888.

After the turn of the century the Eastern Railway's position also changed vis-à-vis the GN. To centralize management and to simplify operating and accounting procedures, the GN leased the Eastern in 1902. For rental the parent paid interest on the Eastern's bonds, its taxes, and a 6 percent dividend on its stock. The latter payment, of course, was merely a bookkeeping transfer, because the stock was held primarily by the GN and the Manitoba. Finally, in July 1907, the GN bought the Eastern Railway of Minnesota, terminating its existence as an operating carrier.

Control of the Northern Pacific and the Burlington

When the Northern Pacific fell into receivership in 1893, Hill recognized a golden opportunity. The NP, of course, had been the GN's leading competitor, challenging incessantly from the Twin Cities and the Head of the Lakes to Puget Sound. In the short run, receivership would make the NP an even more dangerous rival, but with control of the property, Hill could nullify its temporary advantage in rate making, temper its aggressive tendencies, and manage the two roads with benefit to both. That this would make him the dominant figure in transportation between the Twin Cities and the Pacific Northwest was not lost on Hill, but neither was it lost on his competitors, or the public.

Ironically, Hill was actually asked by persons interested in the NP to take part in its rehabilitation. Soon after receivership was publicly announced on August 15, 1893, NP bondholders established a reorganization committee, supported by J. P. Morgan & Company and headed by E. D. Adams of New York. A group of German investors formed the nucleus of the committee, holding $6.5 million of NP bonds, and represented by the Deutsche Bank of Berlin. One of the bank's officers proposed a plan by which the "Northern Pacific would practically disappear and be absorbed by Great Northern."[9]

The NP's problems, however, were such as to give pause to anyone considering control. Baron Mount Stephen wrote that the NP's steep grades, tight curves, light rail, and inadequate bridges, as well as business's general depression resulting from the Panic of 1893, made it a "matter for grave consideration whether we ought to touch it on any terms." Hill shared these somber views, but also understood that most of the NP's difficulties derived from high operating costs. In 1894, another GN official sarcastically remarked that the NP ran enough extra train miles to make several trips to the moon, apparently "for advertising purposes," because "no correspondent increase in revenue" resulted. Many of

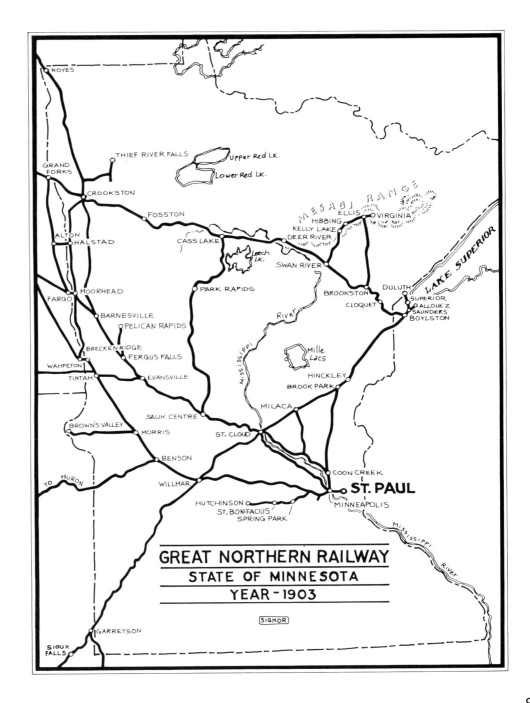

GREAT NORTHERN RAILWAY
STATE OF MINNESOTA
YEAR - 1903

Creating an Empire

these problems, Hill thought, could be solved in time.[10]

The German investors correspondingly concluded that the NP's territory would yield good revenue if the carrier had better management. The Germans felt that the NP bankruptcy was caused mainly by unwise decisions; its management, they believed, had made errors of judgment in moving corporate headquarters to New York, building unprofitable extensions and branches, and arranging a high-cost lease of the Wisconsin Central to gain access to Chicago. Signs of financial anemia were evident as early as 1890; the Great Northern's arrival at Puget Sound simply administered the coup de grâce.

Regardless of problems that control might present, Hill decided to move ahead. Lengthy discussions followed among Hill and his friends, New York bankers, and representatives of the German bondholders. Finally, the GN group agreed to take the lead in reorganizing the Northern Pacific; on May 10, 1895, the so-called London Agreement was signed. The GN pledged to guarantee principal and interest of $175 million in gold bonds of a new company. Bonds for any new mileage were to be issued at no more than $20,000 per mile, and new issues were not to exceed $200 million. In return, the GN was to receive and hold half of the NP's capital stock and was to name a majority of members to the board until a dividend rate of 5 percent upon the entire capital stock of the new company had been paid for two consecutive years.

This arrangement won less than universal approval. Henry Villard disliked it, and Brayton Ives, NP president, opposed almost every element. E. V. Smalley, former editor of *Northwest Magazine* and currently president of the St. Paul Chamber of Commerce, contended that the Northern Pacific's and its stockholders' interests should not be submerged by those of the GN. Groups from Wisconsin to Washington also feared losing "rights" associated with the NP, and instituted litigation in state and federal courts.

The chief obstacle, however, proved to be a question over power of the Great Northern, under Minnesota law to make guarantees required by the London Agreement. One of New York's most prestigious law firms affirmed that full control by the GN over the embarrassed NP was legal, but counsel for the reorganization committee and Morgan & Company took a contrary view. Under the circumstances, Great Northern executives probably welcomed a suit brought by Thomas W. Pearson, a GN stockholder, asking for an injunction against the London Agreement.

With no settlement in sight, the principals considered alternatives. E. D. Adams proposed that a company be created to hold the stock of both the GN and the NP. By September 1895, Mount Stephen was convinced that GN managers should concentrate on their own company, for the "stronger . . . we can make it, the greater will be the anxiety of the N.P. bondholders to get into alliance with us." Jacob Schiff suggested that Hill and his friends wait until NP bonds declined in price and then get control by purchase. For his part, Hill believed that the GN should not oppose an independent reorganization of the NP by Morgan & Company and suggested that the GN's large shareholders buy at least half the outstanding NP consolidated bonds. By doing so, they might yet establish a "community of interests."[11]

It was not to be. Indeed, Hill had decided to abandon the London Agreement even before the Supreme Court ruled that he must do so.

Legal bungling, he thought, had produced a "pitiful jungle in the courts." The decision in the Pearson case, handed down March 30, 1896, denying under Minnesota law the legality of the proposed joint arrangement on parallel and competing lines, merely sealed Hill's private conclusion.[12]

Meanwhile, J. P. Morgan & Company joined with the Deutsche Bank to draft another reorganization plan for the NP. This one would create the Northern Pacific Railway Company, a Wisconsin corporation, control of which was to be vested in a five-year voting trust in the hands of Morgan & Company. On April 2, Hill and representatives of Morgan and the Deutsche Bank abrogated the London Agreement and accepted NP reorganization independent of the GN or any other road. Hill and his associates also agreed to discourage any opposing schemes and to enter "a permanent alliance" with the NP "with a view of avoiding competition and aggressive policy and of generally protecting the common interests of both Companies." Business competitive between the two roads was to be divided on "equitable terms" and tariff wars and rate cutting were to be "absolutely avoided." Neither railroad was to "ingress into the other's territory by new construction or purchase of acquiring control of existing lines."[13]

Hill and his closest associate, Baron Mount Stephen, agreed to purchase securities of both the old and new NP companies. In all, they took consolidated bonds and stock in the old company amounting to $3 million, and they ultimately acquired 19,549 preferred and 258,341 common shares of the new NP for a total outlay of $7.8 million.

Regardless of this investment by the Hill group, control of the reorganized NP rested squarely with Morgan & Company and the

Deutsche Bank. The latest agreement provided that during the five years after the trust was terminated, each of the two groups would propose candidates for the board of new NP company in proportion to their holdings of stock, each to vote for the other's nominees.

Almost immediately, the always impatient and frequently impetuous Hill disagreed with Morgan & Company decisions. Hill's objective was to put the Northern Pacific on its feet as soon as possible and then take control of it, but at the moment he and his friends did not even have a representative among NP's directors. Worse, Morgan upset Hill by choosing as president Edwin P. Winter, who in Hill's opinion lacked "any marked ability as an operating man." Soon Hill was complaining that the new management was extravagant and inefficient. Much to his dismay, differences in NP and GN procedures continued, and Hill became suspicious that the NP might undertake new construction in North Dakota, violating the 1896 understanding. Meanwhile, Hill made available to the NP's general manager the GN's system of management and personnel to explain it. Hill wanted the NP to reduce operating costs so as to increase net income; specifically, he urged more vigorous generation and movement of traffic, improved accounting, and better statistics, all carried forward with close, demanding supervision. But when acceptance of his ideas came slowly, he called belligerently for a management cordial and sympathetic to him—a new, aggressive president, a strong general manager, and three directors of his nomination.[14]

By the spring of 1897, members of the Morgan firm began to listen to Hill, at least on some points. In June, Hill recommended Daniel S. Lamont for the presidency, but Morgan had him elected vice president and chose Charles Mellen for the top position. Hill was at first satisfied with this compromise. In the fall, he felt that Mellen was doing very well; he had "unlimited business sense and a level head and judicious tongue." By the end of the first quarter of 1898 NP losses were being replaced by gains. "The inauguration of our method of accounting and securing early information as to the details of operation has greatly facilitated the economic operation of the Northern Pacific," Hill reported, "and in time, when it is thoroughly understood and applied, the results will be still more gratifying."[15]

Hill's early and rather positive assessment of the NP's future was soon replaced by a plainly censorious view. Wanting to control the NP not only for power and profit but also to protect the GN, Hill undertook to convince Morgan & Company that the voting trust should be terminated. Focusing his antagonism on Mellen, Hill denounced him by mid-1898, for "unwarranted" expansion of the NP and for invasion of the GN's "rightful" domain. Despite an agreement to purchase jointly securities of the Spokane Falls & Northern, for instance, the NP bought them alone, thrusting itself into GN territory, a step reversed only by Morgan's direct order.[16]

When Morgan refused to surrender the voting trust or to indicate when it would end, Hill decided to be firmer. In a formal letter of protest, dated September 27, 1898, Hill complained bitterly of NP transgressions, called for reduction in its capitalization, and outlined alternatives open to him and his friends if nothing changed: they could dispose of their securities at a profit, letting the NP "drift into a position where another re-organization would be called for." At the very least, if the voting trust were continued, Hill asked that George F. Baker, John S. Kennedy, and John Sterling be elected to the board. If he could not have control, he wanted to be "more fairly represented."[17]

In reply, Morgan & Company quarreled with Hill on almost every point. Still, it was obvious that Morgan wanted peace, and shared with Hill a willingness to engage in "frank discussion of matters of interest between the two corporations" that would be "conducive to a continuation of harmonious relations." Negotiations proceeded accordingly. Hill complained again of unnecessary friction generated by the NP, and the GN's traffic department reported that NP agents were quoting reduced rates on "our lines and very distant from the lines of the Northern Pacific." Mellen had also acquired property desired by the GN in Seattle and had sought control of the Union Depot at Spokane. But the primary contention between Hill and Morgan was how to define "reasonable time" for termination of the voting trust. Hill calculated the time was now; Morgan disagreed.[18]

For the moment, Morgan prevailed. Early in 1899, much to Hill's dismay, the NP began paying dividends on common as well as preferred stock. On the other hand, at Hill's suggestion, J. S. Kennedy went on the NP's board of directors in mid-1899, and individuals to whom Hill objected departed from the directorate and from higher managerial positions. Various changes in operation also pleased Hill. Most important, in 1900, the NP concluded a $6-million sale of timberland in Washington and Oregon to the Weyerhaeuser Timber Company. Funds thus available were used to retire NP bonds.[19]

The turning point in Hill's drive to control the Northern Pacific came early in 1900. Relations between Hill and Morgan & Company improved sharply after the death of C. H. Coster, who had represented the banking firm on the NP's board. He was replaced by E. Robert Bacon, another Morgan partner, but one who seemed "reasonable and disposed to consider matters fairly and conservatively." More to the point, he appeared to be willing to listen to Hill's ideas. Hill commenced to woo Bacon, hoping to influence Morgan through his partner.[20]

In fact, Morgan's attitude toward Hill did soften. Ironically, it changed partly because of Hill's work in rehabilitating two eastern railroads. In September 1898, at Jacob Schiff's request, Hill joined a syndicate of financiers who purchased enough Baltimore & Ohio shares to gain control of that company. Hill served on the board of directors and the executive committee until 1901. Also, impressed more and more with Hill as a railroad manager and eager to forestall threatening moves by Edward H. Harriman, Morgan asked Hill for advice in running the Erie Railroad. Hill was pleased to comply.

Before the end of 1900, Hill had won his long campaign for control of the Northern Pacific. At a meeting on Morgan's yacht that fall, the banker agreed to relinquish control. Further indicating his faith in Hill's abilities, Morgan agreed to purchase personally 10,000 shares of GN from Hill's own holdings. The voting trust was terminated January 1, 1901, and Hill was finally free to manage the two northern transcontinentals in ways that he thought beneficial.

Even as Hill labored to strengthen his hand in the West, he looked eagerly to his eastern flank. He was particularly interested in the Chicago, Burlington & Quincy Railroad, a granger carrier that served Chicago, St. Louis, Kansas City, St. Paul, and Minneapolis, and

had lines covering sizable portions of western Illinois, northern Missouri, southern Iowa, and Nebraska, and stretching into Wyoming, Colorado, and Montana. Since 1890, Hill had considered purchasing all or part of the CB&Q. Other projects caused delay, but by 1901, with the NP now in his hands, the time was opportune. Acquiring the Burlington would give Hill's northern lines controlled access into Chicago, facilitate the flow of Pacific Coast lumber to vastly expanded markets in the Middle West, and encourage movement of midwestern grain and southern cotton to the Pacific Northwest for consumption there or for export to the Orient. Ownership of the CB&Q would also open the southern Illinois coal fields to Hill's roads. Finally, the Burlington was itself a profitable enterprise and therefore an attractive investment.[21]

Unfortunately for Hill, another erstwhile contestant also coveted the CB&Q. With help from allied investors, Edward H. Harriman had taken control of the Union Pacific in 1898, and in 1901 substantially expanded his domain by gaining control over the sprawling Southern Pacific. Harriman recognized that Hill's acquisition of the Burlington would strengthen the northern lines in their struggle with his properties; on the other hand, the Burlington would be a valuable adjunct to the UP, giving it a line into Chicago. Finally, the UP and the Burlington had many parallel lines, and so combination would permit large economies. Motivated by these and other factors, Harriman tried several times in 1900 to buy the CB&Q or at least obtain control by stock ownership. His efforts failed, but they were enough to energize Hill.[22]

Early in 1901, in alliance with Morgan & Company, Hill began to purchase Burlington stock and to seek an arrangement that would

be acceptable to Burlington's management. Negotiations continued until April 20, 1901, when the Great Northern and the Northern Pacific formally offered to purchase not less than two-thirds of outstanding Burlington stock at $200 a share, paying either in joint GN–NP 4 percent twenty-year bonds or cash. Burlington directors urged acceptance of the offer. By May, 91 percent of CB&Q's stock was deposited; by November the percentage rose to 97.

Hill now had the Burlington. The problem was keeping it, for Harriman and his friends refused to accept the fact. Direct control of the CB&Q by Harriman was now precluded, but a tantalizing opening remained. Harriman understood that he might yet achieve his goal, albeit indirectly, by gaining control of the Northern Pacific. To this end he and his friends quietly launched a campaign of acquisition; in a short time they had acquired more than half of NP's common and preferred stock. Unfortunately for the Harriman interests, however, control of common stock was the critical factor, because the 1896 NP reorganization provided that common stockholders could vote to retire the preferred stock on January 1 of any given year.

This pattern of activity touched off a titanic and well-known contest between Hill's and Harriman's interests. Soon NP common reached $1,000 a share. Many short operators were caught, and complaints arose that the giants were behaving irresponsibly. By May 9, when the battle ended, the Hill–Morgan forces held a majority of common stock, but the Harriman–Kuhn Loeb group held more common and preferred combined. Thus the Hill group had won a victory of sorts, but a board of directors still had to be elected that would protect the victory. If Harriman won that contest, he might be able to postpone retirement of the preferred stock. The result was a compromise: Harriman and selected associates were chosen for both the NP and the Burlington directorates, in effect establishing a temporary community of interests among the Hill and Harriman railroad systems.[23]

Nevertheless, Hill and his friends determined to devise a means for protecting their position in the GN–NP–CB&Q companies. For that purpose, on November 12, 1901 the Northern Securities Company was launched. Capitalized at $400,000,000, and with Hill as president, the new firm was a holding company, established to control the northern lines and through them the Burlington. It accepted NP shares at $115, those of GN at $180. Harriman and his friends sold their 781,080 common and preferred shares in NP to the new company, and on January 1, 1902, the NP retired its preferred stock in such a way as to maintain for the Hill–Morgan group its previous proportion of NP common stock. By March 1902, Northern Securities held about 96 percent of the NP's authorized capital stock and roughly 76 percent of the GN's.

In the public authorities' opinion, though, the Northern Securities Company did violence to the law. As a consequence, the attorney general of Minnesota brought suit in federal court charging breach of state antitrust laws. Meanwhile, inspired by Theodore Roosevelt, Attorney General Philander C. Knox also initiated action against the Northern Securities Company. Both cases ultimately reached the Supreme Court, which remanded the Minnesota case to the state courts, but agreed to consider the federal suit. Eventually the court accepted Knox's argument that it was not necessary to prove that competition between GN and NP had been suppressed, but that the "offense which the law forbids is the obtaining of the power." The justices, by a 5 to 4 vote, found that Northern Securities violated the Sherman Act.[24]

The decision against Northern Securities generated another clash between Hill and Harriman. Because dissolving the holding company would undermine his influence in Burlington matters, Harriman argued that he should receive the same amount of NP stock as he had handed over to Northern Securities. Hill insisted, instead, on allocating NP common shares in proportion to Northern Securities' holdings *after* retirement of the preferred, leaving the Harriman group in a minority position. That controversy soon progressed to the Supreme Court, which in a decision on March 6, 1905, rebuffed Harriman. In the end, Hill's group retained control of the Great Northern with 24 percent of outstanding stock and of Northern Pacific with 25 percent. The Harriman proportions were 19 and 20 percent.

Perhaps Hill's victory over Harriman enabled Hill to be more philosophical about losing Northern Securities. In a 1910 newspaper interview he said: "If a combination has been effected in violation of the law, it will have to dissolve. What then? The property is all there just the same. What is the difference whether the owners have one green certificate to represent their interests or two red ones?" Hill's reasoning was good, of course, but more important, the Burlington remained firmly welded to the Hill system, with 97 percent of its stock held by the Great Northern and the Northern Pacific.[25]

Jockeying for Position in the Northwest

When the Great Northern completed its transcontinental line to the Pacific and tied it to the north–south line from the Fraser River south to Seattle, the company was in a reasonably satisfactory position to generate traffic to and from the Pacific Northwest. Still, the arrangement was not completely to Hill's liking. Much territory remained to be tapped, strong competition stood at major points, and relationships among carriers were often unstable.

Throughout the 1890s, the Oregon Railway & Navigation Company's circumstances were a major worry. Its main line ran along the south bank of the Columbia River from Portland to Wallula, Washington, connecting there with the Northern Pacific. Another line extended south from Umatilla, Oregon, to Huntington, where it met the Union Pacific's Oregon Short Line; together, these roads—the OR&N and the OSL—made the UP's route from Ogden, Utah, to Portland. The OR&N also had branch lines penetrating several major districts, including the Coeur d'Alene, and it operated steamships along the Coast from southern British Columbia to San Francisco and on the Columbia, Willamette, and Snake rivers. Not only did the OR&N provide both the UP and NP with their routes to and from Portland, but at several places it competed with each of them and with the Great Northern and the Canadian Pacific as well.

Hill watched the OR&N fall into receivership during 1893 with apprehension and perhaps anticipation. Two years later, in September 1895, Morgan & Company's reorganization plan for the OR&N, including a five-year voting trust, was approved. Under that arrangement, the OR&N acted as an entity tied to no major carrier. Others, including the GN, predictably evinced strong interest in it.

By 1897, Hill decided that this arrangement was unsatisfactory; he was displeased with the OR&N's overcapitalization, its banker-ap-

E. H. Harriman fought tenaciously to control a territory he perceived as a legitimate preserve of the Harriman Lines. *(Courtesy of the Southern Pacific Company)*

A. L. Mohler, OR&N president, was a former GN general manager who retained healthy respect for Hill's views. Moreover, on August 5, OR&N and NP officials signed the so-called Portland Protocol, agreeing to avoid competitive building and to take no action impairing each other's revenues.

Unfortunately for Hill, problems sprouted quickly. All parties, in fact, soon promoted their own special interests and several experienced internal conflict. Particularly vigorous bickering broke out between the NP and the OR&N over their respective "rights" in the Snake River Valley and adjacent areas. Meanwhile, Hill tried to retain the GN's share of traffic to and from the Clearwater, Palouse, and Walla Walla areas. The GN, Hill threatened, would build into disputed territories and would construct its own line between Spokane and Portland if it could protect itself in no other way.

The Union Pacific and the Oregon Short Line soon became stronger players in this drama. Harriman appeared at first willing to work out arrangements guaranteeing to protect GN interests relative to the OR&N, but in 1899 he induced Morgan & Company to dissolve the OR&N voting trust, a decision quickly ratified by the stockholders. In effect, Harriman's UP had regained control of the OR&N and quickly integrated it into its system, forming "an unbroken line" from the "Missouri River to Portland and the Pacific Coast."[26]

Hill had been outmaneuvered. The NP sold its OR&N shares to the UP; the GN followed suit—its pain somewhat dulled by a profit of almost $700,000 on the sale. Early in 1900, Hill proposed to Harriman that the GN, NP, and UP jointly guarantee OR&N fixed charges and 4 percent on its stock, a suggestion that

Harriman politely rejected. Hill lost this round in the Pacific Northwest, but would have ample opportunity to tilt with Harriman again.

In fact, the contest between Hill and Harriman was nearly constant, especially in the relatively untapped area west of the Rockies from southern British Columbia through Washington and Oregon to California. Growth in the Pacific Northwest as a whole indicated that more railroads would soon be needed there. The GN and the NP could either double-track some lines in Washington or build new ones. The latter alternative seemed more logical, because so much territory lacked railroads and both companies had long wanted direct access to Portland from the east. Many observers recognized that a Hill railroad along the north shore of the Columbia River might well be only the first step toward central Oregon and perhaps even to California. Constructing such a line would breach the so-called Harriman fence, and was certain to arouse strong SP and UP reactions, both of them Harriman roads.[27]

Managements of the GN and the NP each had long contemplated building to Portland along the Columbia River as part of their transcontinental aspirations. Other considerations had dictated other routes, so that by 1904 the Hill roads' only controlled access to Portland was the single-track NP line from Seattle. That one, however, was taxed to the limit. Furthermore, a direct, low-grade water-level route to Portland from the east was all the more desirable when compared to costs for operating trans-Cascade routes. Hill was ready to take the plunge. To undertake construction, the GN and the NP agreed to own in equal shares the Portland & Seattle Railway Company, incorporated in August 1905 and in 1908 renamed the Spokane, Portland and Seattle Railway (SP&S). The new subsidiary was authorized to

pointed management, and its friction with the Northern Pacific. Those in charge of the NP apparently shared his views. The GN then joined with the NP in authorizing Morgan and Kuhn, Loeb & Company to purchase stock of the OR&N. Hill hoped that owning these shares would permit settlement of actual and potential conflicts among the GN, NP, and OR&N, and for a few months, it seemed his ambitions for achieving a modus vivendi might be realized. Among the company's new directors were two spokesmen for GN interests, and build from Seattle to Portland, but, much more important, from Portland to Spokane. Actually, the NP had proposed that the SP&S use its main line from Spokane to Pasco, to save building 147 miles of duplicate line, yet Hill would have none of it, arguing that the NP had undesirable grades and curvature.

The announcement generated great enthusiasm in Portland and a boom in real estate values, but it also inspired Harriman to respond. If he could not stop the project, he would slow it as much as he could and increase its costs. Paper railroad companies appeared in remarkable number, followed by injunctions, condemnations, and court battles. During December 1905, a dramatic confrontation in North Portland had SP&S forces fighting to obtain a crossing of OR&N tracks. In a related move, the UP threatened to build north from Portland to Seattle.

These harassing tactics only delayed construction of the SP&S without preventing it. On March 11, 1908, a Golden Spike Special carried 400 excursionists to Lyle, Washington, to celebrate completion of construction. Eight months later the entire line from Portland to Spokane was formally opened to traffic, and eventually a large general-purpose terminal was dedicated near Astoria, at the Columbia's mouth, 107 miles west of Portland.

Strategically important in itself, construction of the SP&S also opened possibilities for the Hill lines in central Oregon. If Hill wanted to extend rails in that direction, however, he would have to do so quickly. Both the UP and SP were active there; Harriman seemed ready

James J. Hill, shown at left, with Howard Elliott of the Northern Pacific and his own son, Louis W. Hill, was greatly relieved when the Spokane, Portland & Seattle finally entered revenue service.

to enter and occupy central Oregon from all points of the compass. Early in 1909, Louis W. Hill, son of the Empire Builder, recommended immediate action.

James J. Hill turned again to John F. Stevens, who recently had retired as vice president of the New York, New Haven & Hartford Railroad. On a sub rosa evaluation trip, Stevens explored the Deschutes River and checked other possible locations into central Oregon. These explorations convinced him that the valley of the Deschutes was the most feasible route for an extension south of the Columbia. Moreover, he discovered that the Oregon Trunk Line, Inc., a Nevada corporation formed in 1906, had already surveyed and

located a line along that stream, and early in 1909 had initiated grading. Hill moved quickly. In August, the SP&S purchased the Oregon Trunk, renamed it the Oregon Trunk Railway Company (Trunk), and promptly started construction at various points.[28]

These actions precipitated the so-called Deschutes Canyon war. The Deschutes Railroad Company, a Harriman corporation, had also planned to build in the canyon; it now stirred to action. A grading and track-laying race, much friction, and a near shoot-out followed, but in May 1910, the contending forces worked out a compromise. The OT would be allowed to build southward to Bend, in central Oregon, but the Deschutes Railroad Company

would be permitted to use portions of the new line, and they would have joint terminal facilities at Bend and at Metolius. Under this arrangement, the Trunk began service to Bend on November 1, 1911, and scheduled the first train over the new bridge spanning the Columbia at Fallbridge (later Wishram) on January 4, 1912.

While the SP&S was supplying funds for constructing the Oregon Trunk, in 1910 it was also acquiring in western Oregon the United Railways (Portland to Wilkesboro) and the Oregon Electric Railway. The latter had been completed from Portland to Salem in 1907,

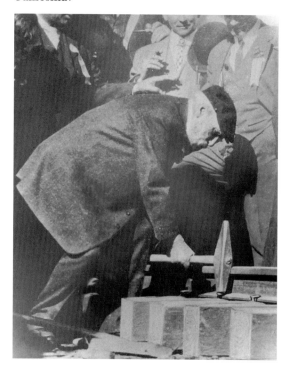

James J. Hill drove the golden spike at Bend, Oregon, on October 5, 1911. Was this the first step in a calculated campaign to reach California?

and in 1912 the new ownership extended it to Eugene, precipitating a flurry of SP activity in electric lines throughout the area.[29]

By the time Harriman died in 1909, Hill could reasonably assert that he had won leadership for the northern lines in the Pacific Northwest. He had succeeded in building a low-grade route from the east to Portland, had breached the Harriman fence in central Oregon and pointed the way to California, had penetrated SP territory in northwest Oregon, and had prevented the UP's Oregon & Washington from building north from Portland to Seattle. (Hill was forced, however, to grant the UP entrance to Seattle from Portland, mainly by trackage rights over the Northern Pacific.) Allied or company-owned steamships connected these points and ran to California and abroad, generating traffic for the long haul to St. Paul and on to Chicago over the CB&Q. Hill had indeed forged the head of the rake that he had outlined almost two decades earlier.

These accomplishments were not without their costs and disappointments, of course, and their influence on transportation in the Pacific Northwest was somewhat lessened by a new rail competitor in that region, the Chicago, Milwaukee & St. Paul Railway. Inspired perhaps by fear of Hill's power after 1901, officials of that granger railroad made one of the least sound decisions in railway history when in 1905 they decided to build to the Pacific Coast. Construction costs proved high, the country through which much of the line ran had little potential, and competition from other roads and later the Panama Canal was fierce. Through service was instituted in July 1909, to Spokane, Tacoma, and Seattle, in part by working with Harriman companies, but the Milwaukee Road failed to reach Portland.

Extension of the Milwaukee into the North-

west understandably forced the Hill roads to take protective measures. In eastern Washington, Milwaukee officers eyed the Spokane & Inland Empire Railroad, an electric road running south from Spokane to Moscow, Idaho, as a possible route to Spokane. The northern lines preempted that property in 1909, but the Milwaukee entered Spokane otherwise, and succeeded in making the acquisition an expensive one. Farther east, in Montana and North Dakota, Milwaukee activity caused GN's directors to authorize construction of a new line from Moccasin, Montana, toward Williston, N.D. — the western portion of a projected second main line from New Rockford, N.D. to central Montana. Elsewhere, near the middle of the so-called New Rockford Cutoff, a line extended southward from Snowden on GN's main line to Fairview, and from there lines ran west to Richey, Montana, and east to Watford City, N.D.

Continuing Skirmishes with the Canadian Pacific

Along the international boundary, as in all other locations, Hill worked for territorial division and stable rates. He regarded purchase of the Duluth, Superior & Western in 1897 as a victory for his principles. That acquisition and completion of the Fosston line in the next year had the added benefit of creating an effective block against incursions by the CPR and preserved both northern Minnesota and the western Iron Range for the GN. Special traffic arrangements given the Soo and the South Shore, he thought, were a small price to pay for those gains.

Elsewhere, critics of the CPR found adequate cause for complaint. By showing an interest in the Seattle & International, the CPR

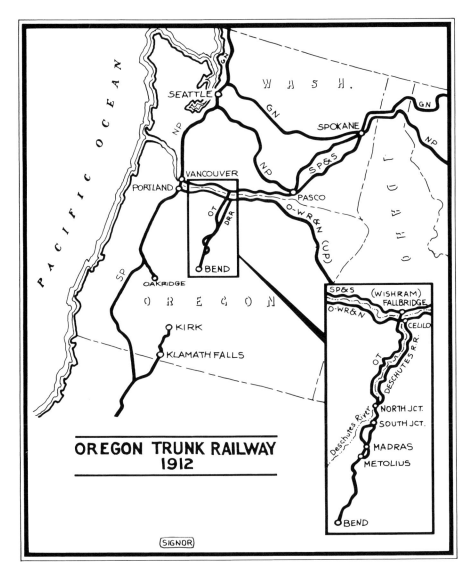

OREGON TRUNK RAILWAY 1912

(SIGNOR)

the South Shore. The latter in particular complained that it was not getting a fair share of wool shipments from Montana to New England. Van Horne was also disturbed about reported GN plans to build into southern British Columbia from Bonners Ferry, Idaho. Earlier, Hill had complained of Soo's construction in North Dakota. Such conduct, he thought, constituted "aggressive warfare" and did "not belong to the present era of Railroading." Peace on GN's northern frontier was obviously elusive.[30]

Indeed, until his death in 1916, Hill fought a running battle with the Canadian Pacific, his one-time ally. Skirmishes occurred on both sides of the border from the upper Midwest to Puget Sound. The root of the conflict was Hill's obsession with offsetting the CPR's advantage—through its Soo Line—in rate making from midwestern points to the Pacific Coast, his determination to set up GN affiliates in Canada comparable to CPR's Soo in the United States, and his eagerness to protect and extend the northern frontiers of his empire.

At the beginning, the CPR was in a strong position. The Soo Line proved a powerful weapon, drawing substantially more traffic from south of the border than the Hill roads were able to pull from Canada. Meanwhile, the CPR was energetically protecting its own service area. From Winnipeg west its construction policies were designed to prevent the GN or other interlopers from direct competition within the Dominion. Hill's properties were able to challenge the CPR effectively only in Manitoba where, through an affiliate, the NP owned lines from the border to Winnipeg, from there west to Portage La Prairie, and from Morris, on the Winnipeg line, northwest to Brandon. On the Pacific Coast, GN rails had reached South Westminster, British Co-

had induced the NP to pay too much for it. A similar flirtation with the Spokane Falls & Northern inspired the NP to buy that company's securities as well. Finally, many observers accused the CPR of starting a rate war. Whether the CPR was guilty was a matter for debate, but competitors accused it of such villainy, especially on passenger rates, and retaliated with sharp reductions of their own.

Other issues were equally troublesome. William Van Horne accused the GN of violating the 1897 traffic agreement with the Soo and lumbia, but GN passengers still had to cross the Fraser River by ferry and then take an interurban tram to reach Vancouver and connections there with the CPR. To the east, extensions north of Spokane and Bonners Ferry allowed the GN to meagerly assert its presence in the area adjacent to Kootenay Lake.

For some time, Hill had regarded penetration of the Kootenay region as a major bargaining chip to offset Soo's advantage in rate making. As early as 1897, he had indicated willingness to turn over his interests there to the CPR if it would withdraw from the United States. When the CPR steadfastly refused, Hill decided to fight the Canadians on their own turf.

To that end, Great Northern interests acquired the charter of the Vancouver, Victoria & Eastern Railway & Navigation Company (VV&E) in 1900. With it and other local properties that he acquired, Hill undertook to build a line from Vancouver to the Fraser River, then eastward up that stream and over the Hope Mountains through the southern part of British Columbia to a GN connection north of Spokane. A bridge across the Fraser River and new trackage allowed the VV&E to enter Vancouver in 1904, permitting through train service from Seattle, but other portions of Hill's dream progressed haltingly. Crews started eastward along the south bank of the Fraser, finally reaching Sumas Landing in 1916. At the eastern end of the line, GN interests commenced laying rail from Curlew, Washington, a junction point on the Marcus–Republic line. The new route crossed the international boundary five times—because of rugged terrain—between Marcus and the Similkameen Valley north of Oroville, Washington, and so another GN affiliate, the Washington & Great North-

ern Railway Company, built the portion south of the 49th parallel.

Competition was occasionally mixed with cooperation. Strange to say, the CPR reacted very slowly to Hill's penetration of British Columbia; not until 1913–1914 did the CPR's Kettle Valley Railway Company punch through a line competitive to the VV&E west from the Kootenay region to Princeton. By that time, though, a decline in mining traffic and World War I pressures thrust the combatants into cooperation. The Kettle Valley Railway granted the VV&E joint use of its tracks from Brookmere over the Coquihalla Pass to Hope, and the VV&E gave the Kettle Valley the same privilege over its rails from Princeton to Brookmere. Later, the Canadian Northern Pacific Railway accorded the VV&E joint use of its tracks from Hope to Sumas Landing, permitting completion of GN's through route from Vancouver to the Kootenay country and Spokane.

At other points, too, the GN jousted with the CPR. In 1901, to compete with the CPR in handling coal and coke from southeastern British Columbia, and to gain an adequate supply of locomotive fuel for the GN's western operations, Hill personally purchased a minority interest in the Crow's Nest Pass Coal Company and then organized the Crow's Nest Southern Railway to haul its production. Building north from Jennings, on the old main line via Kalispell, that company's tracks reached mines at Swinton, Fernie, and Michel by 1908. Farther east, in 1901, the GN purchased the Canadian-owned Great Falls & Canada Railroad, a narrow-gauge company extending from the border to the GN's main line near Shelby and on to Great Falls. Rebuilt in 1902 to standard gauge, the line opened for traffic in January 1903. Hill's interests were similar in Manitoba.

The GN took control of the NP's line from the border to Winnipeg in 1901, and two years later the Midland Railway Company of Manitoba, jointly owned by the GN and the NP, was organized to build within the province. It constructed two lines, one from the border near Neche, N.D., to Portage la Prairie, and the other from GN's Walhalla Extension north of Morden. The GN also bought the charter of the Brandon, Saskatchewan & Hudson's Bay Railway, which had been organized by Canadians, and used it to construct a line north from St. John, N.D., to Brandon. These lines opened for service in 1907. Somewhat later, the Manitoba Great Northern Railway Company would take over the Portage la Prairie and Morden lines; the Midland Railway Company of Manitoba was left with responsibility for developing terminal and other facilities in Winnipeg. By adding all this property the GN was in an enviable position to tap the rapidly growing wheat traffic of the prairie provinces. It was also better able to compete with the CPR on rates between that region and midwestern points.

Meanwhile, the CPR was not idle. In addition to its Kettle Valley line in southern British Columbia, the CPR took several other steps to protect itself. In 1905–1906, it secured entrance to Spokane by acquiring D. C. Corbin's Spokane International Railway; trackage agreements with the Union Pacific's OR&N opened the way for through service to Portland. The CPR thus blocked GN extension north of Sweet Grass, Montana. More important, in 1909, the Soo Line leased the Wisconsin Central (lost earlier by the NP), which gave the CPR its long-desired access to Chicago.

Hill's activities in Canada and his own broad statements led to wide speculation that he intended to build another through line from Winnipeg west to the Pacific Coast. Indeed, in April 1906, Hill wrote to the Winnipeg Board of Trade that "We are now undertaking to build a . . . new transcontinental line through the Canadian Northwest. . . ." Furthermore, Louis W. Hill stated that "if our Canadian plans do not miscarry I expect, within the next ten years, to have a railroad system that will be almost an equivalent of the Great Northern system as it is today in the United States." In fact, throughout the previous winter five hundred men had been "busy in the Northern Minnesota woods" cutting "ties to be used by the Great Northern in building its extension in the Canadian West." The new line reportedly would touch Winnipeg, Brandon, Regina, Calgary, Edmonton, Prince Albert, and perhaps would run on through the Peace River country.[31]

The CPR's officials called these plans "pure wind," but the semiretired Sir William Van Horne, who had much experience with Hill, was more philosophical. "I don't know what Mr. Hill's plans are," he said. "I know that he is a very able man, and when he talks about doing what is clearly a foolish thing, it is safe to assume that it is a cover to something that is not foolish."[32]

By 1911, Hill apparently had abandoned this dream and had decided to settle for alliances with CPR's Canadian competitors. In 1912, the Midland Railway of Manitoba acquired running rights between Lynne and Winnipeg as well as over the Canadian Northern and Grand Trunk Pacific to a new union passenger station in Winnipeg, giving the Great Northern entree for its own trains to and from that important city. During the next year, the GN opened for operation twenty-two miles from Niobe to Northgate, N.D., connecting at

the border with the Grand Trunk Pacific, which had excellent access to adjacent wheat lands.

These ventures were not always profitable. When Hill died, the GN had an investment of more than $36.5 million in Canadian and associated companies. None of the several properties in British Columbia—except for the Crow's Nest Southern—paid dividends, and in reality, many of Hill's ventures in Canada were costly failures—the investments written down or written off.

If Hill failed to achieve all his objectives in Canada, he was dramatically successful elsewhere. Indeed, Hill had come to head a railroad empire that consisted of several companies and 26,000 miles of line, roughly a tenth of the American rail network at that time. From the Pacific Northwest, where the head of Hill's rake now extended from Bend and Eugene in Oregon north to Vancouver, the Hill empire stretched eastward, forming a giant triangle. Resting upon the parallel lines of the GN and the NP, and east from central Montana on the tracks of the Burlington, it touched such distant points as Winnipeg, Duluth–Superior, Chicago, St. Louis, and Kansas City. A Burlington line also reached the Ohio River, and Burlington subsidiaries, the Colorado & Southern and the Fort Worth & Denver City, acquired in 1908, ran from Wyoming into Texas. Nevertheless, at the center of the Hill empire stood the 8,050-mile Great Northern.

13

Developing the Northwest

After the Great Northern reached Pacific tidewater in 1893, its great challenge was developing the region through which the new line extended. With only slight exaggeration, *Northwest Magazine* reported that the new transcontinental ran 1,500 miles through a wild country with only three "important" freight-producing centers—Kalispell, Bonners Ferry, and Spokane. A few branch lines in North Dakota were generating traffic, but the task of attracting settlers to much of that state and to Montana remained; Idaho was lightly populated, and except for the coastal areas, Washington was pretty much an open opportunity. If the GN were to prosper, millions of acres of land would have to be occupied and businesses of all kinds would have to be established.[1]

Organization and Development

During the 1880s, passenger and land-department agents were responsible for promoting colonization. This arrangement, Hill decided, was unsatisfactory, and in 1891, Max Bass, who was to give his name to a North Dakota town, became immigration agent. Born in Bohemia and educated in Vienna, Bass had

Great Northern Railway Lands.

1,500,000 ACRES,

→ IN ←

Park Region and Red River Valley.

BARNYARD, RED RIVER VALLEY, MINNESOTA. (*From a Photograph.*)

No state presents a greater combination of advantages for the home-seeker than Minnesota.

The soil is deep, fertile and productive. It produces No. 1 hard wheat, the best in the world.

It is the native heath of the most nutritious grasses.

Vegetables grow freely and of superior quality.

It is particularly adapted to mixed farming, dairying and poultry raising.

It is a natural stock raising country. All animals enjoy singular immunity from diseases.

It is one of the best beef and mutton raising and wool producing sections of America.

Water for all purposes is of the best, abundant and easily obtained.

It has an unequaled surface water supply,

there being thousands of lakes and numerous rivers and streams.

It has the largest forests of hard wood and pine in the Northwest. Timber for fuel, building purposes and fences is found on every side.

No state has such timber, mineral and water privileges in close association with farming and grazing lands.

Market towns are scattered all along the various lines of the Great Northern throughout the state.

The Park Region and Red River Valley districts are within easy distance of the great markets of the Twin Cities.

It has one of the finest school sytems and the largest school fund in America.

The Great Northern Railway has 1,500,000 acres of farming and grazing lands for sale on low prices and easy terms.

FOR MAPS, PUBLICATIONS AND OTHER INFORMATION, APPLY OR WRITE TO

W. W. BRADEN,

Land Commissioner, St. Paul, Minnesota.

emigrated to the United States in the 1870s, and became deputy commissioner of immigration for Dakota Territory in 1883. After joining the GN, he was stationed in Chicago to recruit homeseekers from the older Middle West. In 1896, Bass was given an assistant and the new title of general immigration agent; which he held until his death in 1909. His successor was E. C. Leedy.

Soon after 1900, Hill ordered new activities calculated to strengthen and improve farming in the GN's service area. This program was handled for a time by subordinates under direct supervision by Hill himself. Thomas Shaw was an agricultural educator who became the GN's authority on dry farming. Fred R. Crane, a soils expert from the University of Wisconsin, was similarly retained to oversee several demonstration plots. Then, in 1917, the colonization and agricultural development functions were combined as the Agricultural Development Department and placed under Leedy's direction, with headquarters in St. Paul.

The campaign was highly competitive: every carrier west of the Mississippi had an active colonization program, and their work was supplemented by that of state and territorial immigration agencies as well as a multitude of local groups and real estate promoters. Moreover, some roads had the advantage of huge land holdings. In January 1894, the Northern Pacific still had for sale more than 36 million acres; the Canadian Pacific also had a princely domain. By contrast, the GN had little more than a million acres, the remnant of grants made to predecessor lines; consequently it was forced to advertise the millions of acres of federal and state land that lay along its lines. Some privately owned lands, held in large blocks by cattlemen, one-time bonanza farmers, and speculators were also available for purchase.

The entire campaign was too important to be "left to chance or good intentions," Hill maintained, and should be prosecuted in a "careful, thorough, and intelligent manner. . . ." North Dakota, he argued, required people "who have from three to ten thousand dollars, good farmers, to take the place of the more shiftless material that occupies so much land on the frontier." Either native Americans or the foreign born were acceptable, but Hill believed all prospective settlers should have farming experience in the United States, and they should be interested in diversified agriculture. He also believed peoples of the same religious or other background were desirable in a location, for like-minded persons supported each other during difficult periods of adjustment on the raw frontier and made it easier to develop community spirit.[2]

The GN's Max Bass labored effectively among several religious groups seeking settlers. As early as 1891, he placed a few Mennonites in Minnesota and North Dakota. Bass's efforts with German Baptists, commonly known as Dunkers or Dunkards, mattered more, however. In 1893, he attended a meeting of Dunkers at Muncie, Indiana, and persuaded a group of them to visit GN territory. A favorable report in the church's *Gospel Messenger* and open support from a prominent minister made it possible to move 350 Dunkers from Indiana and Ohio to Cando, N.D., in 1894. Other groups came later. In 1895, Bass reported locating 460 Dunkers in North Dakota. By 1900, the number had grown to 10,956.

Encouraged by this success and by an expected improvement in the Northwest's economy, the GN stepped up its efforts. The number of clerks in the Chicago office and of traveling immigration agents gradually rose, and the volume of promotional literature also grew. Advertisements appeared in company timetables as well as in religious periodicals, farm magazines, and newspapers. At land shows, state and county fairs, and special exhibitions, agents talked to farmers, distributed literature, and whipped up enthusiasm for the West.

Results of this work in North Dakota and elsewhere can be assessed only by impression. Immigrants who moved by special train could be counted, but Bass reported that they were only a part, perhaps a tenth, of those who settled along GN lines. From 1896 through 1898, when 8,138 colonists traveled by special trains, the company estimated a total settlement of 95,000. As another measure, Bass calculated that during the years 1893 to 1901, homeseekers in North Dakota had taken more than 5,000,000 acres through federal land offices.

Accomplishments in the 1890s set the stage for the westward surge coming between the turn of the century and World War I—the last great land rush in American history. The GN understandably wanted its share. Vast stretches of country served by the road still awaited the plow in 1900. Less attractive cut-over lands in northwestern Minnesota were available, and in North Dakota settlement was moving out beyond the 100th meridian. Eastern and northern Montana remained mostly untouched, and construction of the Spokane, Portland & Seattle and the Oregon Trunk in central Oregon opened promising territories, to which Bass and his subordinates turned. These efforts differed little from those of the 1890s. Immigration agents carried essentially the same message—land was available for the asking. Near Minot improved ground could be had for $10 to $15 an acre; it was, boosters said, as productive as land in Iowa that went for as much as $100 an acre. To the small midwestern farmer or those with little capital, the appeal was compelling.

That the GN generated interest was shown by the reception given an exhibition car sent to the Midwest and the East during winter 1910–1911. Carrying a corps of immigration agents and a sampling of crops, the car was designed to convince skeptics that agriculture in the West could be profitable. Hundreds of people streamed through the car at some stops, where they viewed the exhibits, asked questions, and heard lectures by railroad agents.

The atmosphere was similar at great shows that flourished in the years before 1917. Typical, perhaps, was the 1911 Land and Irrigation Exposition held in New York's Madison Square Garden. There the GN had a huge display of products from the Northwest, and James J. Hill personally awarded a silver cup for the best exhibit of wheat grown in the United States that year. The show, according to one observer, indicated that "the railroads had abandoned the worn-out style of flamboyant exaggeration and now bend their energies all to the demonstration of actualities." The similar Northwestern Land Products Show attracted 93,000 to St. Paul, also in 1911. The event, said Louis W. Hill, was "a tremendous object lesson for all of us." It showed "what a great empire the Northwest . . . is, and . . . imparted . . . some idea of the methods and industry that produce the success of each state."[3]

During these years of the early twentieth century the GN made a concerted effort to settle the state of Washington. The company's first item of promotional literature for that state, a large map, appeared in 1894, and such material flowered after 1900. A Washington book was issued in 1909, and folders described specific sections of the state. As in North Dakota, contacts with Dunkers proved useful, and a leading churchman visited Wenatchee as early as 1901. By 1905, a colony of Dunkers had been established nearby. Later, the same colonizing techniques were focused on the Okanogan Valley. In 1916, one agent devoted his full time to contacting prospective homeseekers, conducting tours, helping to arrange land purchases, and promoting fruit growing in the valley.

None of this activity was without potential liability. In settling western North Dakota and northern Montana the GN, along with many others, fell into a trap prepared by nature. West of Minot to the slopes of the Montana Rockies stretched millions of acres of arid or semiarid land long considered unsuited for agriculture, except, of course, in relatively small areas that might be irrigated. Railroaders willingly accepted this view and had put their early hopes for development on irrigation. Soon after the turn of the century, however, authorities began to question accepted wisdom. By that time Hardy W. Campbell and others had developed dry-farming methods, and agricultural experiment stations were busy testing them. Pushed perhaps by the Milwaukee Road's enterprising colonization campaigns, officials of the Hill lines soon convinced themselves that western North Dakota and northern Montana were little different from the country farther east. They saw no reason that would keep a system of diversified, small farm agriculture comparable to that in Iowa and growing essentially the same crops from developing in those areas.[4]

James J. Hill never doubted that idea's validity. "The yields of most of the cereals are the highest per acre in the country," he wrote to a friend in 1914. "What she [Montana] needs now is a larger population, to which end immigration should be encouraged. . . ." Hill was equally certain that "it is upon the development of her agriculture that her [Montana's] future depends."[5]

Nature itself temporarily conspired to give credence to Hill's assessment. For ten years before 1917, annual precipitation in Montana substantially exceeded the long-term average. This abnormality combined with high crop yields from virgin soil convinced many authorities that traditional midwestern farming techniques and crops could be employed on the northern plains. That pioneers had failed in comparable areas elsewhere faded from the memories of these optimistic men, and the rush was on.

Beginning in 1908, the GN aimed a spectacular colonization program at Montana. Immigration agents visited scores of state and county fairs and other exhibitions and expositions around the country, and with literature and lectures carefully explained federal land laws and announced state land sales and the opening of Indian lands. The status and prospects of major irrigation projects in that state —Lower Yellowstone, Sun River, and Milk River—received extensive coverage, but most effort was aimed at settling the rolling bench lands in eastern and northern Montana.

Especially enthusiastic about the productivity of Montana soils, the GN quoted U.S. De-

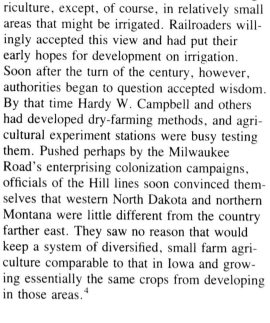

Hill was frequently on the stump, promoting favored agricultural topics. Here he addresses a group of farmers at Litchfield, Minnesota, in 1914.

102

partment of Agriculture data showing that in 1915 Montana's average yield per acre of several major crops exceeded the national average and most often was higher than the average in eleven Midwestern states. The same source indicated that from 1900 to 1915, average yields of wheat had never fallen below 20 bushels per acre, of potatoes 120 bushels, and of oats 35 bushels.

The GN, of course, was not alone in booming Montana. Literature flooded from the Montana Bureau of Agriculture, Labor and Industry. Scores of local promotional groups and real estate men were active, too. Every town had its booster club, and land companies sprang up to peddle former grazing land. Indigenous newspapers, such as *Marvelous Montana*, constantly ballyhooed the state's virtues. Even the federal government contributed to the rush when, in 1909, Congress doubled the permissible homestead acreage to 320—a measure that later observers believed "merely tempted farmers into lands where they could not exist. . . ."[6]

All this urging produced a mighty movement of settlers. Montana homestead entries totaled 5,173,929 acres through 1909, and added 34,744,678 acres by 1919. The number of farms increased from 26,214 in 1910 to 57,677 a decade later. But by that time signs were ominous. In 1917, drought began, and in 1919 the average wheat yield in the state was less than three bushels an acre. Settlers began to decamp, a plague of bankruptcies wiped out local businessmen, and the Montana boom came to an end, leaving the state's agriculture to face difficult adjustments in the 1920s.

The Great Northern operated a constant flow of demonstration trains. This one is at Ephrata, in Grant County, Washington.

Improving and Strengthening Agriculture

Simply placing settlers on land, James J. Hill had known all along, was not enough; farmers had to succeed if the Great Northern was to prosper. Recognizing that symbiotic relationship, Hill had broadened his views of what farming required in the Northwest, and he earned the well-deserved reputation of a powerful voice calling for sweeping changes in agricultural practice. Hill advocated producing more livestock and dairy products, better tillage, use of pure seed and adequate fertilizer, rotating crops, and producing legumes. Land conservation and reclamation became major goals, partly because Hill was now convinced that population would inevitably outrun agricultural output unless use of land was improved.

Hill took special interest in livestock. Late in his life, he decided that so-called dual-purpose cattle would best meet the needs of farmers in GN territory. Some authorities doubted that such an animal existed, believing instead that cattle must be bred for either meat or milk, but Hill persisted. In 1913 and 1914, he imported from Europe fifty Milking Shorthorn bulls and distributed them to farmers scattered through the service area. Hill also launched almost singlehandedly the American Milking Shorthorn Breeder's Association.[7]

Other problems of livestock producers also caught Hill's fancy. Corn did not grow well in northern Minnesota and North Dakota, handicapping their livestock production. Hill therefore conducted a search for an early maturing variety, found one in Connecticut, and promoted its use in the Northwest. He encouraged scientific study of hog cholera, one of the

swine producer's scourges, and contributed $50,000 to the work. In addition, he studied and tried to ease the problem of credit for livestock producers. Partly for that reason, Hill purchased two banks in St. Paul in 1912, and then added the Northwestern Trust Company, creating the largest financial institution in Minnesota. Through it, Hill experimented with agricultural credit and urged other bankers to lend money on livestock.

Hill and the Great Northern were similarly active on related fronts such as the farmers' institute movement in the Northwest, providing free transportation for lecturers, and Hill himself became something of a feature on state and county fair circuits. Short courses held by agricultural colleges were encouraged. Hill, in fact, enthusiastically boosted land-grant colleges and agricultural experiment stations; he recognized how these institutions could lead in dealing with farm problems. For years the company gave reduced rates to farmers and their wives who attended meetings at the University of Minnesota and other agricultural colleges. And Hill gave 480 acres near Crookston, Minnesota, for a branch experiment station. Later, he was a warm friend to

the rural youth movement that led to modern 4-H clubs, providing prizes for club winners in Minnesota and sponsoring the first boys' and girls' corn-growing contest in Montana. For a time, Hill also gave an award to one farmer in each congressional district served by the GN who excelled in the types of agriculture that he favored. Meanwhile, company spokesmen advocated growing sugar beets in the Red River Valley, helped to introduce durum wheat in the Northwest, and urged northern Montana farmers to plant Sudan grass. As early as 1893, the railroad helped North Dakota farmers recruit seasonal workers and transported them to the wheat fields at reduced rates.

The Great Northern also operated demonstration trains, the technique most commonly used by railroads in the first decades of this century to stimulate agricultural improvement. In 1906, a seed-improvement train toured company lines in North Dakota, and others appeared in that state and elsewhere. But by 1911, Hill expressed doubt that these trains could do enough to bring about as much change as he thought necessary.

The GN then turned to a method that Hill thought more effective. Railroads had used

It was ironic, given what happened later, that the Great Northern gave constant and enthusiastic support to the Good Roads Movement. Louis W. Hill is shown above with a group of GN officers at Twisp, in north central Washington.

model or demonstration farms for years, and the Hill roads had provided funds to establish several dry-land plots as early as 1906. By 1911, however, Hill concluded that farmers could best be instructed in small plots on their own land. Accordingly, the GN launched an agricultural teaching program that observers claimed was the largest private agricultural extension system in the nation.

Late in 1911, the GN put a soils expert in charge of its undertaking, which was modeled after Seaman A. Knapp's demonstration work in the South. Farmers who agreed to cooperate grew crops on five-acre tracts of their own land, following instructions given them by the railroad. Soils of all plots were first tested in Hill's private greenhouse; the railroad provided fertilizer and the proper variety of seed. By 1914, the lesson had been driven home to a sizable number of farmers that improved methods would produce sharply better returns.

Because the GN program was similar in methods and objectives to the new county extension agent system it was understandable that Hill would use his influence to attract government agents for counties on the line. As an example, Hill contributed $15,000 in the name of the GN to the North Dakota Better Farming Association, which employed the state's first county agent in 1912. Hill also served on the advisory committee of the National Soil Fertility League.

The GN participated in the corollary good roads movement—not foreseeing the devastation that railroads would eventually suffer from hard-surfaced roads and rubber tires. This movement originated in the 1880s and 1890s with groups such as the League of American Wheelmen, and the federal government joined in 1893 by creating a public roads office in the Department of Agriculture. Better roads, of course, were perceived by rail leaders not as potential competitors but as feeders to rail lines. Industry officials contended that good roads would encourage immigration, help farmers diversify their operations, and lead to a stabler flow of traffic. It became almost an article of faith among managers that a direct and measurable relationship connected the condition of roads and the volume of rail traffic.

The industry's most notable contribution to this movement was the good-roads train—essentially a demonstration train. Manufacturers provided road-building implements; the National Good Roads Association, the federal government, and other agencies provided experts; and railroads made available rolling stock for transporting both machinery and personnel. Thus, when government officials asked Louis W. Hill in 1902 to provide a special train to carry men and machinery on a tour from Chicago to Seattle, he was all too eager

to comply. The first major program was in St. Paul, where experts built a stretch of macadam road in conjunction with the Minnesota state fair.

Finally, Hill and the Great Northern were eager proponents of irrigation. Western railroads generally shared that interest, at least until officials decided to convert the high plains to general farming. "The importance of irrigation as a means of developing the arid districts, with the resulting increase in railroad traffic in all kinds, can hardly be overestimated," a trade journal editorialized in 1905. "That the railroad interests and irrigation go hand in hand is duly appreciated by railroad management throughout the West." Certainly those sentiments reflected James J. Hill's ideas. Indeed, one admirer contended that he had "done more for the United States in the promotion of irrigation . . . than Congress."[8]

One of the most energetic advocates of irrigation, Hill spoke widely on the topic, urged that both federal and state legislation be enacted, and invested considerable money in privately owned irrigation works. The nation must put its land to the best possible use, Hill declared, and reclamation was one means to that end. "Land without population is a wilderness," he said, "and population without land is a mob." Irrigation was a proper and feasible approach to "certainty, abundance, and variety" in agriculture.[9]

By the late 1890s, many authorities had concluded that an effective irrigation system required new federal legislation. The Desert Land Act of 1877 and the Carey Act of 1894 had proved less than satisfactory, and high construction costs and the interstate character of many irrigable valleys suggested that federal help was needed. To promote that end, the GN, the NP, and three other railroad com-

panies each gave $5,000 a year to the National Irrigation Association, an educational organization formed in 1899 by George H. Maxwell. Partly because of that organization's work, both major political parties adopted planks in 1900 calling for federal construction of irrigation works, and in 1902 Congress enacted the Newlands Act.

Although Hill and the GN enthusiastically supported a greater federal part in irrigation, they were prepared to give substantial aid for private projects. Hill viewed such outlays as seed money, believing that successful ventures would encourage local residents to undertake others and demonstrate that irrigation was generally feasible and practical on a larger scale.

That was the problem in the Columbia Basin, where the Great Northern ran for miles through country that would hardly support grazing cattle. Quite plainly, if most of the Basin had any agricultural future at all, it would rest on irrigation. When in August 1895, J. D. McIntyre organized the Cooperative Irrigation Company to serve about half a township between Stratford and Ephrata, Hill was ready to help. The GN agreed to purchase from the company 2,500 acres of land and water rights and to provide transportation for construction equipment and supplies.

The project proved a fiasco. The GN gave more aid, but in 1899 the railroad found it necessary to take over the company's assets. By 1903, when the ill-starred firm was dissolved, the railroad had lost about $73,000, and GN management concluded that the Columbia Basin could be irrigated only by a great federal project—although for the next twenty years it gave support to several other private irrigation projects that were launched there.

The Great Northern's assistance produced

better results elsewhere. In 1893, Hill rejected a proposal to finance construction of an irrigation system near Wenatchee, but he was willing to extend aid if others took the first step. Such a promoter was Arthur Gunn. In 1891, Gunn had organized the Wenatchee Development Company and later the Wenatchee Water Power Company to irrigate his lands and those belonging to neighbors. When Gunn found it difficult to sell bonds of the waterpower company, he turned to the GN, which in 1897 took $15,000 of them. The railroad subsequently lent another $10,000 and encouraged the company in other ways. By 1900, the GN owned one-fourth interest in the Gunn enterprises, which irrigated some 12,000 acres that became prime orchard land.

Soon after the turn of the century, the GN became involved in yet another irrigation project in the Wenatchee area. In 1901, two local men organized the Washington Canal Company, designed to take water from the Wenatchee River to canals on bench lands around the town, irrigating in all about 6,500 acres. Construction started in 1902, and the system was operational a year later. It provided more water than could be used near at hand, and so the company's promoters announced a proposal to carry the surplus across the Columbia River to 15,000 acres east of that stream. Two companies were established in 1906 to implement the plan: The Washington Bridge Company, with capitalization of $125,000, for building a bridge across the Columbia to carry vehicular traffic as well as the company's water pipes; and the East Wenatchee Land

Hill used his own monies and those of the Great Northern to promote irrigation. After all, increased agricultural production would bode well for the long-term interests of the railroad.

Company, capitalized at $200,000, and essentially a real estate firm. Both were backed by a syndicate that included Hill and some of his New York financial friends. Neither firm was notably successful financially. In 1911, the Washington Bridge Company sold its assets to the state for bonds that went for almost $50,000 less than the bridge cost to build. Nor was the East Wenatchee Land Company more fortunate. The GN managed to retrieve its investment but no more; its goal, of course, had been not earnings but traffic. In that sense, irrigating 30,000 acres was a real victory.

Elsewhere, a GN line constructed along the Columbia and Okanogan rivers between Wenatchee and southern British Columbia aroused the railroad's interest in proposed irrigation projects along those streams. Several were studied by company engineers, but for various reasons no aid was extended to them. On the other hand, the GN became deeply involved in construction in the West Okanogan Irrigation District south of the Canadian border. The GN had the project surveyed, managed relations with landowners, arranged for a contractor to build the works, and took $10,000 in the district's bonds. This project was completed in 1916, and in the next year GN officials reported that 7,000 acres were under cultivation.

In other ways, too, Hill and the GN promoted irrigation from North Dakota to Puget Sound. Hill was a regular speaker at meetings to hammer a favorite message: land was in short supply, the rising population would inevitably place great pressure on food supplies, and irrigating land that was tillable only by artifically applying water was an absolute necessity. At gatherings such as the National Irrigation Congress, Hill and other GN officers were much in evidence; the railroad helped to arrange some of these conclaves and often provided free transportation. Similar aid went to state and regional irrigation meetings. In 1903, Hill spoke to the North Dakota Irrigation Congress, where he argued that irrigation could add 100,000 acres to that state's farmland.

After the Newlands Act became law, the GN used its influence to have the federal projects located in its territory, encouraged their prompt completion, and offered varied assistance. The company was a special advocate for the Milk River project in northern Montana, active in every stage of its early development.

By these and other means, Hill and the Great Northern attempted to strengthen the economy of the vast country lying between the Twin Cities and Puget Sound. Results of these efforts could be ascertained with statistical precision in only a few instances. Most developmental programs were designed for the long term; the multiplicity of agencies and groups working toward similar ends also made determining the GN's effectiveness difficult. Nevertheless, in a general way it is clear that the GN contributed significantly to settlement in the northern tier of states, and in developing a stabler and more productive agriculture. By 1916, tillable virgin land, for all practical purposes was gone, and during that last surge, the Hill roads were "credited with carrying more colonists than any other Western system. . . ."[10]

The results of the GN's efforts are more clearly evident when viewed from the perspective of traffic carried. Hill's campaign to create on the bench lands of northern Montana a copy of the small-farm, diversified agriculture common farther east had proven to be only a dream, but grain shipments on the GN from Montana increased 1,600 percent between 1909 and 1917. Efforts to promote irrigation and fruit production in central Washington could be assessed similarly. The first apples had moved from Chelan, Douglas, and Okanogan counties in 1901. Seventeen years later, the company hauled 8,338 cars from that district, and during the next decade shipments would average almost 16,000 cars annually. By such measures, Great Northern's programs had been both successful and significant.

14

Men and Mallets

To reach corporate maturity, James J. Hill knew, the Great Northern must properly equip and efficiently manage both the transcontinental line and also the company's growing system of branches and feeders. At the same time, Hill insisted that the GN guard its frontiers and devote itself to an energetic policy of attracting freight traffic.[1]

Men and Organization

Struggling to create an effective, systematic organization, Hill made numerous changes between 1890 and 1916. That quarter century brought great fluidity in managerial personnel. The talented young Henry Minot, in whom Hill had so much faith, died tragically in 1890. Rival carriers enticed away other able officers, and still others quit, unable to bear Hill's domineering style. These steady losses gradually swung Hill to his sons, James N. and Louis W. Hill. Both had graduated from Yale and taken jobs with their father's railroads. At twenty-seven, James was managing the Eastern Railway of Minnesota, and in 1899 became a GN vice president. When poor health made him withdraw from active participation in company affairs early in the new century, his father turned to Louis. In 1907,

Louis became GN president, and five years later was chairman of the board.

Other important changes were made in the officer corps during the mid-1890s. General Manager A. L. Mohler resigned in 1893, to be replaced by C. W. Case, a veteran of many years with the Chicago, Milwaukee & St. Paul. But Case, severely disagreeing with Hill over labor matters, resigned in 1894. His successor was C. W. Warren, comptroller of the GN since 1889; this appointment probably reflected Hill's growing interest in statistics. R. I. Farrington was then promoted to comptroller and soon had a major voice in the company. In 1892, P. P. Shelby was promoted to vice president and assigned responsibilities in the West.

First Years as a Transcontinental

Among the plethora of present and future issues and problems that James J. Hill faced, few were more pressing than the need to develop traffic in freight and passenger to support and then yield profit for the Great Northern. Competition from other carriers was stiff, and for the moment, business deriving from long stretches of the Pacific Extension was not significant. To generate freight traffic in this vast, thinly populated area, Hill cut rates as soon as the line was open for through traffic. The Northern Pacific, though, had already reduced its tariffs from Seattle to St. Paul on lading such as lumber and shingles, from 93 cents per hundredweight (phw) in 1883 to 55 cents six years later. Now the GN quoted 40 cents phw for these commodities and set a special low rate on fir lumber. Offering such low rates, Hill hoped, would stimulate greater production and thus heavier shipments.

Louis W. Hill followed in his father's footsteps, becoming president of the GN in 1907 and chairman five years later.

Company officials gradually grew optimistic. Every day several cars were sent to Bonners Ferry to pick up ore destined for San Francisco, and in Seattle shippers were now willing to route traffic over the GN. Officials believed that the railroad could move enough consigned freight and company coal west to carry east no fewer than twenty-two loads of lumber and shingles each day. They also estimated the system's potential gross earnings on freight, destined to or originating on the Pacific Coast, at $162,000 a month.

The institution of through passenger service

was held off until June 1893. Hill had been eager to begin operations earlier—this was the year of the Chicago Fair—but the Northern Pacific, ever alert for a chance to thwart the interloper, had recently reduced its Coast to St. Paul run to seventy hours, a schedule that the GN could not yet match. An officer stated that it would have been "suicidal for us to undertake to do the business in view of the service other people are giving, unless we can somewhere nearly approach what they are doing and maintain it." Nevertheless, he said, the outlook was encouraging, "unless the present business depression should grow much worse."[2]

The depression did worsen. Hill reported to President Grover Cleveland in May 1893 that planting was extensive and conditions promised a large crop; on the other hand, country merchants were buying little, farmers lacked money, and local lenders could give no aid. New York banks were sustaining rural financial institutions, which in turn helped mercantile customers, but incessant pressures were bringing down many country banks, including some in which GN had funds. These collective problems were reflected by the country's railroads. The neighboring Northern Pacific announced its bankruptcy in August, and by the time the depression reached its depths, a third of the Class I railroad mileage in the country was operated by receivers.

Not surprisingly, the GN suffered, too. Hill did what he could to rebuild confidence, to alleviate distress, and he used his influence to secure loans for healthy country banks and to obtain funds from other banks to move the wheat crop. Later in the year billings of wheat on the GN proved large. Hill reported that this was because "we were able to get money for our large elevator companies, which has been

more difficult for the companies on other lines and has resulted in helping our business." Having good credit, when its competitors did not, was one key to weathering the storm.[3]

In truth, the 1893 crisis hit the GN somewhat differently than it did other roads. Compared to many other western carriers, the GN had a marvelously efficient profile (except for the Cascade switchbacks), a talented and enthusiastic management team, and, not to be ignored, the appeal peculiar to a new enterprise.

This did not imply the absence of difficulties. The company was confronted by the heavy expense deriving from its dramatic expansion, the simultaneous cost of gathering necessary traffic, and the responsibility of servicing debt piled up over several years. As the depression deepened and unemployment increased, units of Coxey's Army roamed the West. Railroads were one of their targets, but no GN trains were commandeered. Uncertainties, confusion, and fear of property damage, however, delayed opening GN's Spokane shops, and the American Railway Union, led by Eugene V. Debs, struck the GN on April 13. A settlement was reached on May 2, but the Pullman strike followed in June. The GN was not affected directly, although stoppage of trains in Chicago and elsewhere did cut into traffic. In autumn a devastating forest fire in eastern Minnesota, fanned by wind, swept through the village of Hinckley, destroying lumber, mills, homes, and people. In all, about 500 lost their lives. Heroes in the disaster were an Eastern Railway engineer and a conductor, whose passenger train arrived at Hinckley on the afternoon of September 3. Acting quickly, the two men gathered terrified people and took their train north over burning ties and bridges, through flaming forests, to safety.

The depression lingered, but by 1896 good fortune, good management, and an efficient plant brought the GN prosperity. The 1895 harvest was exceptional. South Dakota, though nearly caught in a crop failure a year earlier, had good production; Minnesota and North Dakota increased their yields of wheat by almost 40 percent. By the end of October business was heavy, putting every locomotive and car into service. Unprecedented traffic and effective economies combined to elevate Hill to euphoria. "The Great Northern is certainly a most remarkable property to earn money," he rejoiced. Net income jumped 33 percent from fiscal 1894 to fiscal 1895, and a spectacular 66 percent in the next year. "Our company is the only Pacific line paying a dividend on its shares," Hill wrote, "while three out of the five lines other than our own are in process of reorganization, which must wipe out a great many millions of capital invested in those enterprises." While other railroads were consuming capital, the Great Northern was accumulating it. Consequently, Hill's railroad was in a position to expand.[4]

Fleshing Out

When the Pacific Extension opened in 1893, Hill told stockholders that the "completion of this line practically finishes the work of construction for the Company, except so far as greater development of local territory served by your lines may demand the building of some local branches." Hill greatly understated reality, for within five years he embarked upon a huge construction program that, with brief pauses, would continue through his life. Branches were built to open new farmland, for access to standing timber, to serve new mines, and for outflanking opponents.

Another motive for expansion was to provide a cutoff or air line to shorten mileage and reduce costs of operation.[5]

Before building into an area, managers made comprehensive studies. Location had to be considered relative to existing or possible rail lines and towns. Estimating the potential of a region, especially if it was not settled, was a complex task, necessitating the study of natural resources, the extent of nearby arable land, the quality of soil, and the quantity of rainfall and water supply. In some areas timber resources and mineral potential were important factors. Political and economic considerations were many. Was free or cheap government land available? At what price was improved land held, and in whose hands? The existence of an Indian reservation would have a marked influence on the rate of growth, and immediate development would be adversely affected if land prices were high and ownership was in the hands of speculators or pioneer cattlemen. The caliber of people already settled in an area—their energy, ambition, intelligence, and willingness to work—would affect its attraction and thus influence growth. In more established areas, existing traffic patterns were important: Would the line attract shipments to markets that the GN reached on a single-line basis or through friendly connections?

During the early 1890s, Hill had no general plan to extend into Iowa and Nebraska, or to add lines in South Dakota. On the other hand, he was willing to encourage local promoters if their projected roads would generate traffic for the Great Northern or its affiliates. One such local road was the Sioux Falls, Yankton & South Western Railway Company, incorporated in 1889 to build from Yankton, S.D., to Sioux Falls, southern terminus of the GN's Willmar-to-Sioux Falls line. This road would give farmers in that area a direct route to Duluth and provide traffic for the Eastern Railway of Minnesota. When this short line had financial difficulties, Hill loaned it funds, and before the railroad was completed in 1893, it became part of the GN system, adding fifty-eight miles of line to the Willmar & Sioux Falls Railway.

Several years passed before the GN collected more mileage in South Dakota, despite any number of rumors that the company would build toward the Missouri River and perhaps even to the Black Hills region. Finally, in 1916, it expanded there by acquiring the South Dakota Central Railway Company. Between 1904 and 1907, this tiny 103-mile pike had linked Sioux Falls with Watertown.

The Great Northern also extended itself into Iowa. A. S. Garretson and others who wanted access to the Duluth market from Sioux City, Iowa, had tried to interest Hill in their plans for a railroad during the early 1890s. Hill, at that time preoccupied with the Pacific Extension, but was willing to arrange for interchange of traffic, and, when Garretson got into financial trouble, to give him aid. He also introduced Garretson to J. Kennedy Tod & Company, which helped market the Iowa railroad's bonds, and the GN became owner of

Branches were built to open new farm lands, serve mines, outflank pretenders, or—as here at Bonners Ferry, Idaho—to tap timber reserves.

some of its securities. Garretson properties actually consisted of three companies: the Sioux City & Northern Railroad Company, extending 96 miles from Sioux City to Garretson, S.D., where it connected with the Willmar & Sioux Falls Railroad; the Sioux City Terminal Railroad & Warehouse Company; and the Sioux City, O'Neill & Western Railroad Company, which ran west from Sioux City 129 miles to O'Neill, Nebraska. When depression threw the Garretson lines into receivership, it worried Hill, and by 1900 he announced that these properties had been acquired by the Willmar & Sioux Falls Railway. Seven years later, however, the GN disposed of the Sioux City – O'Neill line to the Chicago, Burlington & Quincy Railroad.

Hill's policy regarding the construction of branch lines was clear. He explained it to a partner of Morgan & Company in 1900: "I do not mean to spend money on lines of railway in advance of any possible requirements of the country. . . ." At the same time, though, he wanted to protect territory that he perceived as the GN's domain from encroachment by other railroads. The Sheyenne River was the "natural boundary" between GN and NP country, in his view, and when the NP talked of building a branch southwest of Devils Lake, Hill pointed out that "We have no objection to your building West and South of the Sheyenne River, but the line you propose is directly competitive and the building of it would necessitate our making such reprisals as might be necessary. . . ."[6]

It was the Minneapolis, St. Paul & Sault Ste. Marie, or Soo Line, however, that in the

The Great Northern determined to blanket northern North Dakota with a system of branches. One of these served the heavy grain-producing area around Bottineau.

early years of the twentieth century proved to be the competitive nemesis that caused the GN to undertake what might be called protective construction. One of Soo's predecessors, the Minneapolis & Pacific, had built west from Minneapolis to Lidgerwood, Dakota Territory, in 1886, and after the Canadian Pacific assumed its control and formed the Minneapolis, St. Paul & Sault Ste. Marie in 1888, the Minneapolis & Pacific became the starting point for an extension to Portal, N.D. and a connection there with the CPR. This line, when completed in 1893, crossed the GN main line at Minot, and served an excellent wheat-producing country. More important, it was integral to a joint CPR–Soo route under Canadian Pacific

control—designed to compete with the GN for long-haul as well as local traffic.

Soo's aggressiveness increased in 1903 when it undertook a bold program of expansion in northern Minnesota and North Dakota. An extension from Glenwood, Minnesota, to Winnipeg passed through Thief River Falls and reached Noyes, Minnesota, on the international boundary, in 1904. In so doing, the Soo connected with an existing line of the CPR and thus completed a second through route to the competitive disadvantage of the GN.

The GN found more that was disturbing in 1905, in a grain-gathering line built 300 miles from Thief River Falls to Kenmare, N.D.,

Heavy snow and snow slides required frequent and expensive use of rotary plows on the Cascade switchbacks.

Moving trains in either direction over the Cascade switchbacks was tedious and expensive: a 7-car passenger train required 3 locomotives.

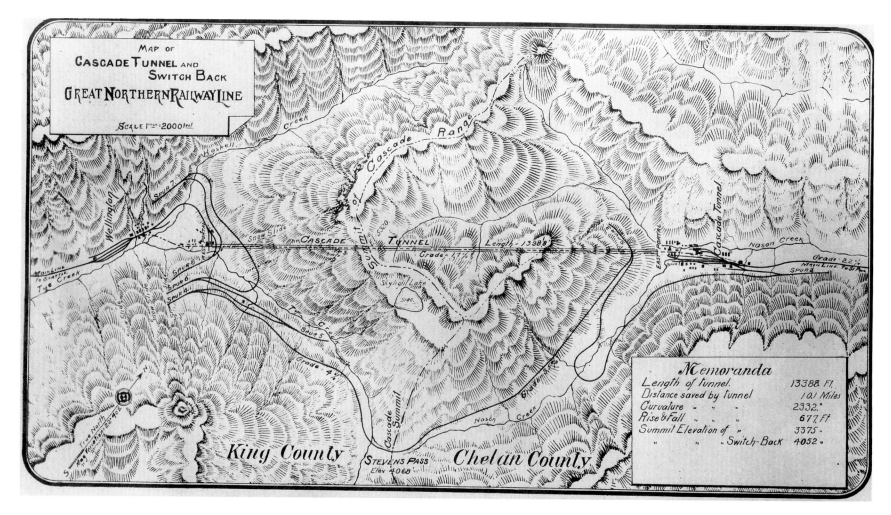

MAP OF
CASCADE TUNNEL AND
SWITCH BACK
GREAT NORTHERN RAILWAY LINE

SCALE 1 inch = 2000 feet

Memoranda

Length of tunnel		13388 Ft.
Distance saved by tunnel		10.1 Miles
Curvature	"	2332.°
Rise & Fall	"	677 Ft.
Summit Elevation of	"	3375 "
"	" Switch-Back	4052 "

King County

STEVENS PASS
Elev 4068'

Chelan County

near Portal. About halfway between the GN and the Canadian boundary, it cut across numerous GN branches. Still another Soo artery was driven from near Portal to Whitetail, Montana.

The Soo Line's actions were not simply harassment but a shrewd strategy calculated to challenge the GN in the grain-carrying trade and the GN and the NP for transcontinental business via Sault Ste. Marie, the Twin Cities, Winnipeg, and Portal. It was also the latest round in the historic campaign between Hill and the CP. When attempts at negotiation failed, the GN began active retaliation. L. W. Hill wrote, "If we take care of some of the extensions . . . the [unoccupied] territory will not be so extensive." Company officers especially wanted to protect the country between the main line and the Canadian border, and so they resolved to blanket the territory with a generally north–south system of branches, resembling bent teeth of a comb. From the time frost left the ground in 1905, North Dakota was the scene of railroad construction projects.[7]

From 1910 through 1913, another surge of construction added even more North Dakota trackage. In 1910, Hill approved construction of the Fargo–Surrey Cutoff, designed as an air-line route from the Red River Valley to near Minot. Completed two years later, this route opened nine counties to GN service and shortened the transcontinental line by sixty miles, clearly strengthening the GN's competitive position. A number of branches were extended as well, and a line constructed from Fairview to Arnegard and Watford City in the western part of the state implied that management was considering a second main route from New Rockford, on the Surrey Cutoff, to Lewistown, Montana.

Branch construction in Montana followed many of the same patterns as in North Dakota, but later. Except for the Pacific Extension little was added during the 1890s — less than a hundred miles. Between 1900 and 1916, however, more than 800 miles were built. North of the main line, GN's strategy called for a system of branches sweeping to the international boundary, but only a few were completed. The first of these started from Bainville and ran fifty-three miles northwest to Plentywood, reaching it in 1910; it was extended westward forty-five miles to Scobey three years later. In the far northwest corner of the state, a new route left the Pacific Extension at Columbia Falls, swung west to Whitefish, and reached Rexford in 1911. There it met a line built north from Jennings in 1901 – 1902 and shortly became the new main line, replacing the original route through Kalispell and Marion.

In central Montana, the GN system was now a giant wheel, with its hub at Great Falls and spokes in all directions. Already there was the line running southwest from Pacific Junction through Great Falls and Helena to Butte. Later a secondary main line drove southeast from near Great Falls to Billings, connecting there with the CB&Q from Kansas City and Denver. Together with the recently standard-gauged line northward from Great Falls to the

Pacific Extension at Shelby, this was a route with favorable grades offering effective competition with the Northern Pacific for traffic to and from the Pacific Northwest. From each of these, branches reached into fertile valleys and promising mining country. In 1912, the GN built a thirty-mile extension from the Great Falls – Billings line at Moccasin to Lewistown, and in the next season built a forty-three mile feeder from Power, on the Great Falls – Shelby line, to Bynum.

Elsewhere, if the tedious switchback operation over the Cascades was an anomaly, the decision to replace it with a line change and tunnel was in perfect keeping with Hill's well-known philosophy of investing in plant for greater operating efficiency. Work began in 1897 on the Cascade Tunnel; the 2.6-mile bore and attendant approaches were placed in service in December 1900. This massive project eliminated more than eight miles of line, reduced summit elevation from 4,059 to 3,383 feet, and eradicated all grades greater than 2.2 percent. All was not well, however, as smoke and gas from laboring steam locomotives in the tunnel presented a lethal threat. Consequently, on July 10, 1909, the GN completed a short three-phase electrification program through the tunnel that required time-consuming exchanges of motive power at either end, but solved the problem of safety.

Traffic Generation and the Ore Lands

The 1897 purchase of the Duluth, Superior & Winnipeg Railroad brought to Great Northern stockholders not only an interest in hauling ore but also direct participation in developing Mesabi mining. Hill had also obtained with the DS&W a vital subsidiary that held more than 10,000 acres of land on the

Mesabi Range. To these lands others would soon be added. When Hill bought the Duluth, Mississippi River & Northern Railroad in 1899, 25,000 acres of land partly opened to mining was included in the purchase. Eventually Hill and his sons were able to build vast holdings of ore properties, some in freehold, some jointly with others, and, by lease, still others. In 1912, Hill gave the total of these lands as 65,000 acres, or about a third of the Mesabi Range as then defined.

Hill had several reasons for keeping the ore properties separate from the railroad. For one thing, the charter under which the GN operated did not authorize mining, but perhaps a more compelling impulse was to prevent mixing the mining and railroad revenues and "to avoid the charge of earning too much money." Although Hill himself bought many of these iron-ore properties, he considered them as belonging to GN stockholders. "The Great Northern never owned them," he explained, "but it was a transaction that came to me in dealing for the company, and I did not want any personal interest in anything that was mixed up in the company's affairs, and I turned those lands over to be held for the benefit of the stockholders of the Great Northern Railway."[8]

In 1899, Hill saw to the organization of the Lake Superior Company, Ltd., and transferred to it the iron-ore properties and securities of companies that were "not strictly a part of the Railway system." His thinking changed in 1906. The mineral properties, Hill believed, were becoming too large and valuable. They were separated from other holdings and turned over to a new trust, the Great Northern Iron Ore Properties. Soon thereafter Hill negotiated to lease substantial holdings to the United States Steel Corporation. For that company the arrangement guaranteed a supply of ore for its vast mills, for the owners it provided handsome royalties, and for the GN it ensured a heavy volume of ore traffic to the docks at Allouez.

Others, however, were displeased. The Minnesota House of Representatives criticized the arrangement, and one minority stockholder, a gadfly, instituted suit in Minnesota, asking that the ore properties be restored to the railroad and then sold for the stockholders' benefit. A bigger objection appeared in a federal government investigation of the entire steel industry. With the Great Northern Iron Ore lease, U.S. Steel controlled 75 percent of Mesabi holdings when that range was producing about two-thirds of the iron ore used in the United States. Shortly after the government began its examination, U.S. Steel canceled the contract, effective January 1, 1915. Pressed to explain this event, Hill observed, probably with justice: "I think they were frightened to death . . . they had buck fever." During the life of the lease, however, U.S. Steel paid the trustees $45 million in royalties.[9]

These dealings were reflected by operations of the Eastern Railway of Minnesota, and after 1907—when it was fully absorbed—by its parent, the Great Northern. Successful handling of ore, company managers learned early, required careful planning. Hill called it "close and accurate" work. Operating officers constantly needed motive power and equipment to handle the rapidly growing yet fluctuating output of ore. Cars were gathered from the mines and assembled into trains at Virginia and later at Kelly Lake. These flowed regularly to the classification yard near Allouez, where they were sorted according to ownership and grade. Finally, the cars were shoved onto the docks, where their contents were dumped into pock-

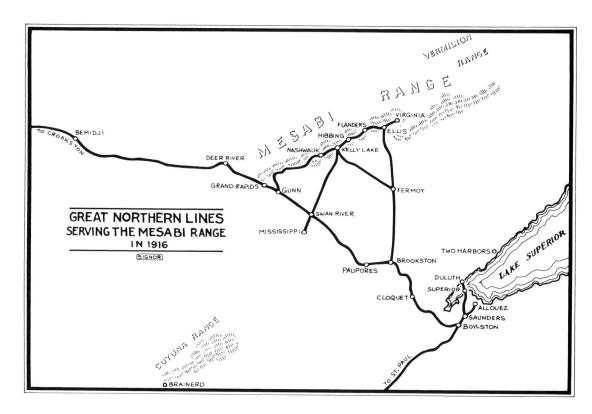

GREAT NORTHERN LINES
SERVING THE MESABI RANGE
IN 1916
(SIGNOR)

ets, which in turn were emptied into the holds of lake vessels, in accordance with the requirement to blend and mix each order.[10]

Weather and other forces beyond railroaders' control complicated the task. Late opening of navigation or storms occasionally delayed arrival of the lakers, backing up loaded cars at the yards and ore docks. An early winter could catch the railroad with cars of frozen ore, which had to be moved to the hothouse or to pipes for steaming. Always, unloading balky ore into pockets at the dock called for workers with great strength and manual skill with poles and hammers.

Hill took special pride in the railroad's Mesabi operations. "I will undertake to say that

never in the whole world has the same amount of track moved the same tonnage, or approached it," he declared. "No man living can demonstrate that there is any other way to handle this business than to have the largest capacity for the cars and engines." Old wooden twenty-ton cars soon were replaced by the steel car, the average 1906 load for which was 39 long (2,240 pounds) tons.[11]

Between 1907 and 1916, the Great Northern gradually expanded its investment on the Mesabi. The increased number of mines, the growth in size of open pits, and heavier output called for additional capacity. In 1907, a twenty-three-mile line was built from Kelly Lake to Fermoy on the Ellis–Brookston line, shortening the route from Kelly Lake to the main line, and with easier grades making possible trains with higher tonnage. Earlier, no more than sixty cars could be handled via Ellis to Brookston, where ten additional cars, hauled by a "turn-around" train, were added. Now routed via Fermoy to Brookston, one locomotive could haul seventy cars all the way from Kelly Lake. Elsewhere, a twenty-two-mile line from Nashawauk to Gunn, completed in 1909, served the western part of the Range and added a third route leading to the main line, its double track extending to about thirty miles west of Brookston by 1913. Additional passing tracks, block signals, heavier rail, and deeper ballast collectively improved movement of heavier and heavier ore trains.

This burgeoning business inevitably built pressure on terminal facilities, which were again expanded to meet demand. At Kelly Lake, the engine house was enlarged, and improvements were made in powerhouse, storehouse, and facilities for servicing locomotives. Similar improvements were made at Superior. And at Allouez a new ore dock, No. 4, was built of concrete and steel in 1911; it was 1,812 feet long with 151 pockets on each side, having a capacity of 106,304 tons. Reportedly the largest structure of its type on Lake Superior, it combined with the Allouez Bay Company's three newly rebuilt wooden docks to provide an aggregate capacity of 378,630 tons for storage and loading.

Hill, dedicated to efficient production of ton miles, made sure that bigger and bigger motive power was assigned to this territory as quickly as possible. In 1898, the Eastern Railway had ordered various locomotives and used several types in iron ore operation. Consolidation (2-8-0) and Prairie (2-6-2) types were among the first employed, but in 1910 the GN placed an order for unusual 2-6-8-0 articulated locomotives to haul the heavier trains.

Great Northern ore shipments showed general growth from 1897 to 1917, but rates for hauling and handling fluctuated. Shipments climbed through 1902, were irregular until 1908, and then showed rapid gains. From 1898 through the end of the 1916 shipping season, the GN handled 120 million long tons. On December 11, 1911, following the lead of the other railroads on the Mesabi, the GN voluntarily reduced charges for transportation and dockage from 80 to 60 cents per ton. The next reduction was inspired by an ICC order, following an investigation of general conditions on the Range. Questions arose on valuation of property, depreciation, division of joint costs, and apportionment of outlays to operating expenditures or capital investment. Railroaders emphasized that mining properties have finite lives, that heavy investments carrying great risk, and that mining traffic is highly seasonal, requiring expensive equipment for only about five months each year. The Mesabi country's rapid development implied that the rate was reasonable, they said, and, indeed Hill declared that the earlier 80-cent rate was the cheapest ore rate in the world. The ICC decided in 1915, however, that it should be reduced from 60 to 55.

Motive Power, Rolling Stock, and Rates

The handling of ore, operations in mountainous country, and general growth in business that occurred throughout the system's service area after 1890 required a vast increase in the company's locomotive fleet and rolling stock. In 1889, the Manitoba had owned only 256 locomotives, most of them American types (4-4-0), and Moguls (2-6-0), but by 1896, the total number of GN locomotives had jumped to 397, and new types were on the roster. Between 1891 and 1893 alone, the company bought more than a hundred locomotives. Included were Ten Wheelers (4-6-0), Consolidations (2-8-0), and Twelve Wheelers (4-8-0).

The move toward faster and more powerful engines continued. When the increasing weight of passenger trains required more power, the GN shifted to Pacific (4-6-2) types, purchasing six from the American Locomotive Company in 1905. During the next year, along with more Pacifics, the company ordered from the Baldwin Locomotive Works fifty Prairie (2-6-2) types, ten Atlantic (4-4-2), and five Mallet articulated (2-6-6-2) engines for pusher service over the Cascades. With a tractive effort of 69,000 pounds, the 2-6-6-2s performed so well on the slopes of the Cascades that in 1907 and 1908 the GN ordered another forty-five locomotives of the same design. These were followed in 1909 and 1910 by the thirty-five 2-6-8-0s for use on the Mesabi Range, and in 1912, another order was placed, for twenty-five Mallets with a 2-8-8-0 wheel arrangement and a tractive effort of 93,250 pounds. In 1911 came the first Mikado locomotives, later to form a large fleet. Built by Baldwin, these 2-8-2s developed 60,900 pounds of tractive effort and were faster than the Mallets. Between 1911 and 1916, the GN acquired ninety-five of these sturdy machines.

Changes in passenger and freight car fleets were comparable. By 1895, the GN, Montana Central, and Eastern Railway passenger fleet had 318 cars. In 1906, those three roads counted 600 passenger cars and 1,184 by 1916. Freight cars for the system increased from 13,818 in 1895 to 34,954 in 1906 and to

55,963 in 1916. More specialized cars were added, and capacities grew. A few older box cars carried no more than 28,000 pounds, but by 1916, the average capacity of the company's freight-car fleet had risen to 37.7 tons.

Greater operating efficiencies that came with the use of larger cars and more powerful loco-motives clearly reflected the operating philosophy of James J. Hill. Reductions in train miles and increases in car and ton miles resulting from employment of heavier rolling stock, Hill knew, was certain to generate larger earnings. At least that was true if rates could be maintained at favorable levels. Unfortunately, the rate issue was one over which Hill and other rail managers had very little control. To be

In 1889, most of the company's locomotives were of the American Standard type. This one, all decked out for a special occasion at Crookston or Barnesville, was representative.

The Great Northern Railway: A History/Part I 1856 to 1916

sure, government intervention in the matter of rates charged for transportation had increased markedly and had greatly altered the environment within which railroads had to operate.

The Interstate Commerce Act of 1887 actually changed tariffs little during the following decade. Market forces controlled, leaving a strong downward trend. The causes were disorganization in the railroad industry, vigorous competition, and an economic depression that pushed many railroads into receivership. The average revenue per ton mile fell from .941 cent in 1890 to .742 cent in 1899. To stabilize charges, carriers placed new emphasis on traffic-association agreements, only to see these outlawed by the Supreme Court in the Trans-Missouri case of 1897. Railroads also tried consolidations and communities of interest to prevent further decreases in rates.

The Progressive movement in the first years of the century brought additional regulation, vigorously if intemperately enforced, and an attack on mergers. Indeed, the unfavorable Northern Securities decision discouraged consolidation so thoroughly that the matter was not quickly revived. Communities of interest too were questioned, leading the Pennsylvania, for one, to begin disposing of its holdings in other railroads.

Strengthening competition, the Progressives and President Theodore Roosevelt believed, was not enough; they insisted that regulation needed further expansion. The Elkins Act of 1903 made departing from published tariffs a misdemeanor, and the Hepburn Act of 1906 gave rate-making powers to the Interstate Commerce Commission by authorizing it to set maximums. Similar legislation followed in a steady stream. In 1910, the Mann-Elkins Act revitalized the long- and short-haul clause of the Interstate Commerce Act and empowered

The GN's 4-8-0s were reliable and powerful, if not elegant.

the ICC to suspend proposed changes in rates pending an investigation on reasonableness. The Valuation Act of 1913 authorized the ICC to place a value on railroad property, and a Bureau of Valuation spent twenty years and much public money to determine that, in the main, railroads were not overcapitalized, that dividends were not being paid on watered stock, and that railroads were not making excessive returns on investments in them. Meanwhile, the Locomotive Boiler Inspection Act of 1911 extended the ICC's power over safety, and the Panama Canal Act of 1912 gave the ICC jurisdiction over joint rail and water transportation and prohibited railroads from owning coastwise ships using the Canal.

For many years it was not clear how rate legislation affected the country's railroads. Conventionally, Progressive legislation was supposed to be a victory for the people over private interests and the railroad industry's subsequent problems were thought to be caused by mismanagement, excessive capitali-

zation, and financial manipulation. Recently, however, scholars have argued that the Hepburn and the Mann-Elkins acts in truth reduced the industry's attractiveness to investors, starved the carriers of capital, and initiated the railroad's decline in the United States.[12]

These estimations are correct. After the Hepburn Act was enacted, the ICC in effect froze rates at the 1906 level, just slightly above that of 1889, and the inflationary trends of the times, plus organized labor's growing strength, and the attitudes of both the ICC and state regulatory agencies clamped the country's railroads in an economic vise from which they could not escape. Costs were rising rapidly by 1907. Railroads appeared prosperous, but the investment curve began a downward trend. By 1910, railroad stocks were off substantially, and before 1912 new investments fell rapidly. Earnings in 1910 did not equal those of 1907, though railroads were carrying 10 percent more traffic. Operating ratios rose, standing collectively at 72 in 1914.

Hill and other railroad leaders were fully aware that rate structures needed adjustment to rising costs of operation. In April 1910, twenty-four carriers, members of the Western Traffic Association, asked for a general increase—a new departure, for previously the carriers had acted individually. They were soon joined by eastern roads, but the request was rejected. In 1913 and 1914 the country's railroads tried again. After extensive hearings the Commission granted a 5 percent boost—but only for roads in eastern trunk-line territory. The western roads agreed to try again. Hearings revealed that operating ratios in the West had risen from 69 in 1901 to 79 in 1914, but the ICC decided that only a tiny increase was justified. Indeed, the ICC held the status quo in rate matters after 1906, permitting no significant increases during the decade before America entered World War I—even though operating costs had risen dramatically. Revenue per ton mile fell to .719 by 1916, an all-time low. Spokesmen for the industry argued that operating expenses per train mile were 42 percent higher in 1914 than in 1910, but revenues per train mile had risen only 33 percent. Productivity increased by more powerful engines and larger freight cars had not compensated for the disparity between rising costs and stable or declining rates. All in all, it was a grim picture.

Few railroad men knew more than James J. Hill about prevailing trends in rates and their effect on the rail carriers. In the 1895–1896 annual report, he pointed out that in the previous twenty-four years "the price of no commodity . . . has fallen so fast or so far as that of rail transportation." His assessment was correct. The average revenue per ton mile in 1880–1881 was 2.88 cents; in 1895–1896 it was only .976 cent, and it would go lower.

Meanwhile, wages increased an average of 45 percent. Constructive regulation would be beneficial to all, Hill believed, but he feared that, bearing their prejudices and lack of knowledge about railroad operation, legislators might well produce counterproductive policy. Too many politicians, he thought, considered railroads' net profits as a tax levied on the mass of the people for the benefit of the stockholders.[13]

Hill's reputation as an industry leader make understandable his frequent appearances before legislative committees, and his views were well stated. Because a railroad could prosper only as the territory it served prospered, Hill insisted that rates could not rise beyond the level that would permit commodities to reach markets at prices profitable to producers. At the other extreme, no railroad could long afford rates inadequate to pay expenses, interest, taxes, and a justifiable return to stockholders. In fact, he said, rates had fallen so rapidly in the 1880s and 1890s that few people continued to object to high rates; discrimination was the real issue.

Regardless of Hill's views on these matters, federal legislation passed during the so-called Progressive Era inspired many state legislatures to place on the books their own new regulatory laws. Perhaps the most objectionable tendency was mandating maximum rates. Minnesota, as an example, established passenger rates at a mere two cents a mile; five other states in GN territory enacted similar legislation. Minnesota also set maximum rates on shipments of grain, coal, lumber, livestock, and other commodities. Company executives believed these state-imposed maximum rates unreasonably low, but because the law carried severe penalties for violators, the Great Northern placed them in effect. A group of disgruntled stockholders, however, instituted a suit in

federal court, seeking an injunction to block implementation of the Minnesota law. The Supreme Court ultimately received the Minnesota Rate Case, as it was known, but in June 1913 upheld the constitutionality of the Minnesota law and the tariffs provided under it.

Hill's devotion to low grades and easy curves, high-capacity cars and heavy-duty locomotives allowed the GN to compete effectively even in an environment beclouded by governmental intervention. If there was little he could do to modify the political mood, he could do much to improve the Great Northern's traffic base, passenger as well as freight.

15

Locals, Limiteds, and Liners

The quarter of a century beginning in 1890 was the golden age of railway passenger operations. Volume of traffic expanded rapidly; equipment was steadily improved; modal competition was slight; and, until late in the period, public regulation was limited and generally ineffective. During those twenty-five years, the Great Northern expanded its service, and intensified its efforts to attract customers, as shown by the passenger department's growth. As early as 1906 it had three dozen passenger agents, holding various titles and scattered from London to Los Angeles. In New York City the company's ticket office was moved to Broadway: the GN's reputation had risen.[1]

Expansion and Improvements

When the St. Paul, Minneapolis & Manitoba became the Great Northern, it already had a well-established passenger service. Between St. Paul and Minneapolis and to nearby Lake Minnetonka, trains were provided so frequently that it was really a commuter service. Most branch lines were served by passenger trains, daily or daily except Sunday, although a few lines had tri-weekly service.

Other trains made longer runs. To some cities such as Winnipeg, Duluth, and Red River points, more than one train a day offered convenience. Still others ran from the Twin Cities to Willmar and from there on to Breckenridge, Aberdeen, Huron, Sioux Falls, and Sioux City. On the far eastern end of GN's territory, two trains ran daily from St. Paul via Elk River and the new Princeton cutoff to Hinckley and on to Superior and Duluth.

Transcontinental offerings especially underwent change. Before the GN finished its own line to the Coast, the railroad offered through service in conjunction with the Canadian Pacific. Then, in 1893, the GN inaugurated its direct transcontinental passenger service, the first westbound train leaving St. Paul on June 18 for the seventy-two-hour run to Seattle. Shortly thereafter the GN also arranged to run through cars to and from Chicago over the Chicago, Milwaukee & St. Paul, a railroad which had not yet entered transcontinental competition and with which Hill then had friendly relations. Growth followed predictably. In 1903, the GN added a second transcontinental train, and by December 1905, the name *Oriental Limited* was in use. Meanwhile, the GN's new relationship with the Burlington made possible a third transcontinental train. When the GN completed its Billings line, cars from the Burlington's *Northwest Limited*, which originated in Kansas City, began to run through Great Falls and Shelby to Seattle.

The GN did not shirk expense in establishing cross-country service. Cars on the transcontinental train that began operating in 1893 were new and among the best available; diners were finished in polished oak, as were sleepers. The buffet-library observation car was adorned with rich carpets, wicker chairs, wrought-iron design work, and colorful curtains and ornate lamps — all in contemporary Victorian fashion. Its Booklover's Library earned praise from many travelers, including Vice President Adlai Stevenson, who wrote that the car "is one of the greatest conveniences to tourists in making long journeys. It is a comfortable thing to find a library of books . . . daily newspapers, writing materials, easy chairs, a bathroom, a barber shop, and smoking-room. . . . It is club-life carried through the journey."[2]

In the early years of the new century the GN purchased many new cars and modernized its older equipment. The roster of observation-compartment cars climbed to thirty-five, and when new parlor cars arrived, older ones were converted to business cars. By 1908, the shops were busy installing electric lights and storage batteries to replace acetylene gas lamps. Steam heat was added to older cars and others were equipped with full-platform vestibules.

Motive power for passenger service underwent similar change. Some of the company's Ten Wheelers were converted into Pacifics, with greater tractive force, and in 1914, forty locomotives specifically for passenger service — twenty-five Pacifics and fifteen Mountain type (4-8-2) — were delivered. The two gasoline-electric motor cars that arrived in 1913 were a harbinger. Costing $25,000 each but much cheaper to operate than steam power, they were expected to replace locomotives on branch lines and suburban runs where traffic was light.

Of Things Nautical

To improve the company's competitive position and to generate more volume, the Great Northern also entered passenger business

The *North West*, which entered service in 1894, was handsome in every respect.

on the Great Lakes. Hill had been interested in maritime matters since launching his *Selkirk* on the Red River in 1870, and the company's Great Lakes freighters had long carried passengers. He was thus receptive to Mark Hanna's suggestion in 1891 that the GN acquire passenger steamers. Consequently, late in 1892 the Northern Steamship Company contracted with the Globe Iron Works for two vessels. These twin-screw, 5,500-ton steamers were powered by two quadruple-expansion engines; they were 386 feet long, and could accommodate 758 passengers, 544 in first and 214 in second class.

The *North West* went into service in 1894; the *Northland*, a year later. They proved to be fast and luxurious, with accommodations equaling those of fine hotels. Some staterooms even had private baths, and electric dynamos supplied lighting. According to William McKinley, then governor of Ohio, the *North West* was "a veritable floating palace," and years later both ships were remembered as the "last word in fresh water transportation."[3]

Operating results, however, were mixed. At first the steamers provided semiweekly service from Buffalo to Duluth, where passengers could make connections with GN trains for the West Coast and intermediate points. Later, the *Northland* plied between Buffalo and Chicago, where it connected with the Burlington. The vessels rarely showed a profit, but they did generate rail traffic for the northern lines and they did create a favorable image. An official

of the steamship company wrote in 1911: "While I am aware that the investment is not a profitable one, I consider the value of the business and contribution rendered to the entire Great Northern System . . . and the advertisement that goes with it a good thing."[4]

Hill also turned to water transportation at the western end of his empire. Since 1896, the GN had exchanged passengers and freight with a Japanese steamship line, Nippon Yusen Kaisha. Encouraged by this association and hoping to build a greater market for American exports, especially wheat and cotton, Hill placed an order for two large ships, the *Minnesota* and the *Dakota*, which entered service in 1903 and 1904. Sailing to Philippine, Japanese, and Chinese ports, the Great Northern Steamship Company catered to both passengers and freight. Its 28,000-ton vessels were equipped with elegant staterooms, electric lights, and telephones. Baron Jutaro Kamura of Japan called the *Minnesota* a "floating hotel," an apt description.[5]

Finally, in 1915, the GN began maritime operations along the Pacific seaboard. The Great Northern Pacific Steamship Company, jointly held by the GN and the NP, commissioned two large steamers. The *Great Northern* began service between Flavel (Astoria), Oregon, and San Francisco in June; the *Northern Pacific* followed shortly after. Both carried freight as well as passengers, and they were sufficiently speedy to make a strong bid for coastal business. Despite supplemental winter cruises to Hawaii, the ships were not financially successful. During World War I, the federal government purchased them for use as troop transports.

122

Passengers on the *Oriental Limited* coming into Seattle on this day were treated to a view of both the *Minnesota* and *Dakota* tied up at the Great Northern's Pier 89.

Advertising, Glacier Park, and Rocky

New stations, better rolling stock, and a steadily improved track structure were supplemented by promotional policies calculated to attract even more travelers to GN trains. To encourage discretionary travel, the GN produced a flood of pamphlets and other materials extolling its territory. In 1894, the company issued *Valley, Peaks, and Plains*, followed in the next year by *Great Northern Country; Being the Chronicles of the Happy Travellers Club*, which described the scenery and productivity of the country between Minnesota and Puget Sound. After Hill had concluded a contract with Nippon Yusen Kaisha in 1896, another company publication urged travelers to visit the Orient. During the gold-rush excitement, *Alaska, Land of Gold Glacier* pointed out advantageous rail and steamship connections as well as the Klondike's beauty.

Other advertising was focused on the company's name trains. When the *Oriental Limited* went into service, GN salesmen eschewed modesty in describing its glitter: the train was "one of the greatest," and covered "the shortest, the easiest, the most interesting route across the Continent." Indeed, they went on, "the track of the Great Northern is noted for its solidarity, long tangents, and easy curves; the rails are of the heaviest steel, the ballasting of rock; the train swings as smoothly over the Montana mountains as it does over the prairies of North Dakota; the jumps, jerks and bumps have all been worked out of the roadway—a spoonful of coffee always reaches the passenger's mouth intact from his cup despite the fact that a 160-ton engine is whirling the train along at 40 miles an hour."[6]

Elevating Louis W. Hill to the presidency in 1907 made an unmistakable impact upon pas-senger advertising. Always more of a marketer than an operating man, artistic and lover of the West, especially the Rocky Mountains, Hill combined his personality and interest with promoting passenger travel. "See America First" became his slogan. With Louis Hill in full support, GN passenger agents promoted richly varied vacation opportunities—the Lake Park Region of Minnesota, Lake McDonald in Montana, and Hayden Lake in Idaho among them. Soap Lake, in Washington, was another; a stage ran to it from the Ephrata station. Sixty-mile-long Lake Chelan had fine hotel accommodations and could be reached by steamer from Wenatchee. Other attractions were the Pacific Coast cities and Alaska.

Louis Hill's interest in the West and in the GN's passenger offerings led to his enthusiastically participating in the campaign to establish Glacier National Park. After all, he chafed, other roads boasted service to such parks—the Northern Pacific to Yellowstone, for one—and the Great Northern should have a similar drawing card. Hill counseled only one logical location—in northwest Montana where the GN's main line skirted magnificent mountains, placid lakes, and breathtaking glaciers. In 1907, Senator Thomas H. Carter introduced a bill to establish a park there, a proposal supported enthusiastically by Louis Hill, who lobbied in Washington on its behalf. The rewards were sweet: on May 11, 1910, William Howard Taft signed legislation setting aside 1,400 square miles to create the famed Glacier Park.

Government appropriations for the park were small, and so the GN was soon doing far more than providing just rail transportation to its two stations, Midvale (East Glacier) and Belton. A company-employed timber cruiser laid out trails, and in the first season six tent camps were set up. Visitors could follow a

A new Great Northern station on Hennepin Avenue in Minneapolis was opened on January 27, 1914. Two years later, the facility handled 125 trains and 5,700 passengers daily. The station was also used by the Northern Pacific, the CB&Q, the Chicago Great Western, the Chicago, St. Paul, Minneapolis & Omaha, and eventually the Minneapolis & St. Louis.

route that, starting at the east entrance, went over Gunsight Pass to an independent hotel at Lake McDonald near Belton. Expenses for the walking tourist were three dollars a day, including meals. Each year facilities were improved. By 1912, tent camps remained, but Swiss log chalets had been built on the shores of four lakes, and others followed. On June 15, 1913, a large hotel, later named Glacier Park Lodge, was opened near East Glacier, and the GN built a road to St. Mary's Camp and to the Many Glacier Hotel, opened in 1915. The company also provided boat transportation on three of the park's lakes.

Expanding the GN's work at Glacier Park required changes in corporate organization and management. In 1914, the Glacier Park Hotel Company was incorporated; its charter was broad enough to cover ownership and control of GN properties at the park, including hotels and chalets, camps, restaurants, garages and

livery stables, boats, and automobile lines. The company, held indirectly by the GN, soon had investments of more than $2 million.

Once Glacier National Park was created, the GN's passenger advertising had a major new theme. Beginning in 1911, GN timetable covers played up Glacier and its many attractions. "See America First, Great Northern Railway, National Park Route," was the crisp, concise message. By 1914, the company was spending almost a third of a million dollars a year to promote the park. The campaign used many media, including newspapers, magazines, and booklets, billboards and window displays, as well as stereopticon lectures in more than a hundred cities and towns.

For another major advertising campaign, Louis H. Hill retained well-known painters — Winold Reiss, W. L. Kinn, and John Fery among them — to portray the "glories of the West." Their work graced GN advertising from playing cards to wall calendars, distributed throughout the service area and beyond. Into many such promotional materials were woven images of local Indians colorfully attired.

A visual element that evolved in these campaigns was the Rocky Mountain goat that became the company's famous symbol. "Rocky" appeared on freight cars all over the nation, attractively rendered with the slogan,

"See America First, Glacier National Park." Rocky lived more than a half century, his countenance periodically "modernized."

Express, Mail, and Silk

A signficant part of passenger revenues was derived from express business. The industry had no consensus on whether a carrier should delegate that activity to independent companies or handle it within the organization. Both ways had advantages, but by the 1880s, most express was solicited and handled by outside firms. The Manitoba had used such companies, but they never completely satisfied management. "The Revenue we derive from Express business . . . is less in proportion to the cost to us and the service rendered by us than any business we do," Hill complained in 1880. Nevertheless, in July 1889, the company contracted with American Express for service on all its lines. That arrangement proved temporary. Being unable to control business when it was in others' hands and believing that the railroad itself could do better, the GN established the Great Northern Express Company. A wholly owned subsidiary, it assumed responsibility for the system's express business July 1, 1892. In time, it built much traffic over other lines as well as those of the GN; both gross and net income trended upward, and contributions to passenger-train revenues were substantial.[7]

Carrying federal mails generated even more passenger-train revenues. As new lines were opened, the Post Office Department authorized mail service, and because of its shorter and more efficient route between St. Paul and Seattle, the GN won coveted transcontinental postal contracts. The business brought controversy, however. Every four years the mail was weighed to determine the amount on which rates should be charged, and Hill—along with most industry spokesmen—thought the government often parsimonious. Despite bickering, gross returns from mail service rose. As Hill commented in 1899: "There is probably no better illustration of the growth of the Western country than the increase in mail earnings."[8]

One very special commodity, silk, required both passenger equipment and passenger-train speeds. Products manufactured from raw silk increased rapidly early in this century, and the GN's many contacts with the Orient elevated it to major carrier of this commodity eastbound from Seattle. Because of its high value and its tendency to deteriorate rapidly, however, silk

had to be moved promptly—exactly the kind of challenge Hill thrived on. Special trains were often called for. In 1911, one precious eight-car movement made the Seattle–St. Paul trip in only 45 hours and 16 minutes, a record unequaled for more than a decade. The silk business produced excellent revenues and even better grist for company publicists.

Pricing the Service

Rate making in the passenger trade was highly complex because it involved sleeping- and parlor-car charges, first- and second-class fares, and lower rates for settlers and their belongings. Fares were quoted for many more features—duration of return privilege,

stopover rights, and possible alternate routing on the return trip—among others.

Transcontinental rates that were low in 1890 and would go lower disturbed Hill; he complained that the business was thoroughly demoralized. Both the Transcontinental Association and the Western Traffic Association, to which the GN belonged, had failed to maintain rates, and Hill declared in 1892 that passenger business west of Chicago did not pay "relatively, the cost of hauling the passen-

"See America First, Great Northern Railway, National Park Route," was the crisp and concise advertising message that L. W. Hill approved in 1911. Trains, like this one shown at Belton, brought thousands of people to Glacier Park.

gers and maintaining the equipment." Conditions were worst, Hill believed, in the first-class business. For railroads in the Transcontinental Association, first-class fares made up only 8 percent of revenues, and another 12 percent came from reduced round-trip or excursion rates. The remaining 80 percent was second-class travel, which differed little, Hill said, from first-class service. Thus he urged competitors to agree to charge first-class fares on first-class trains and to reduce the spread that he considered unreasonable between first- and second-class fares. Getting no action, he decided to move unilaterally. In 1892, he announced that the GN would withdraw from the Western Traffic Association, informing other roads that he was prepared to cut rates: "our new line will get the benefit of the reduction . . . through advertisement on the part of our competitors."[9]

Hill's policies quickly touched off a rate war. The Northern Pacific had normally charged $60 for first-class and $35 for second-class St. Paul–Seattle tickets, but Hill slashed prices to $35 and $25, respectively. On June 19, the NP met those rates, and two days later cut them to $25 and $18. Rates charged by other roads were similarly reduced; the Canadian Pacific posted San Francisco–New York tariffs of just $50, and included berths and meals on those parts of the journey made by ocean and lake steamer. Peace was gradually restored. By the end of 1894, the GN, NP, and UP had come to agreement, but competition with the CPR and its Soo connection remained vigorous, especially in the summer season.

Another area almost constantly in conflict was that of handling of immigrant traffic. Whether a new arrival to the Northwest came from an eastern state or from Europe, he ex-

pected low-cost transportation and cooking facilities aboard a tourist sleeper. He also wanted inexpensive rates for his farm equipment and personal possessions. Like other roads, the GN labored most earnestly in pursuing this business. For Europeans aspiring to emigrate, its agents said, the GN formed a chain all the way from their homelands to the New World. The business, however, was controlled by rate-cutting steamship lines and contending commission agents. Accusations and

counteraccusations over sending settlers on roundabout routes and diverting them to rival lines were constant. These were not the only problems. Should passes or reduced rates be given to independent agents and others who influenced settlers to use a road? If special rates were given to colonists, how could railroaders recognize those who were bona fide travelers?

For the immigrant business, Hill consistently favored reducing rates, vigorously re-

The Great Northern missed no opportunity to advertise its reliable and expeditious handling of silk by special train from Seattle to St. Paul.

Table 3. Passenger Traffic of Great Northern, 1895–1915

	1895[a]	1900	1905	1910	1915
Miles of railroad	4,496	5,283	6,023	7,020	8,061
Passenger-train miles[b]	2,176,297	4,010,799	6,617,297	11,454,315	12,655,880
Passengers carried	1,058,798	2,407,312[a]	4,711,234	6,343,557	8,468,317
Passengers carried one mile	72,700,446	195,505,382	335,524,414	649,317,544	575,020,556
Passenger revenue	$ 2,371,718	$ 4,974,364	$ 8,319,649	$14,911,000	$13,164,867
Passenger-service train revenues[c]	$ 3,005,240	$ 6,021,439	$ 9,979,758	$17,635,662	$18,166,875
Averages					
Passenger-service train revenues per train mile	$ 1.1676	$ 1.2192	$ 1.5081	$ 1.486	$ 1.435
Revenue per passenger per mile	2.551¢	2.378¢	2.384¢	2.204¢	2.289¢

a. The statistics for 1895 compiled from reports of separate companies are not fully comparable and probably include some double counting. For passenger revenue the figure here is lower than the $2,541,126 from the annual report. See GNAR, 1894–1895, p. 12, and GNAR, 1900–1901, p. 33.

b. Mixed train miles for the earlier years were included in freight-train miles: 927,024 for 1900 and 581,311 for 1905. For the later years they are included in passenger-train miles: 783,000 for 1910 and 1,064,778 for 1915.

c. Passenger-service train revenues include passenger revenues, those from Mail and Express, and some miscellaneous revenues, such as baggage.

Sources: GNAR, 1895 to 1915, especially 1900–1901, p. 33, and Almanacs.

jecting arguments by those who favored eliminating all special fares for homeseekers, believing that it mattered much more to people the company's service area than to gain short-run profits from ticket sales, and that railway earnings would eventually grow following the arrival of productive settlers. Accordingly, in the spring of 1899, the GN cut St. Paul–Seattle fares to $25 and the round-trip ticket to $40. Eastbound Seattle–St. Paul fares were reduced to $18 before the year was out; Klon-

dikers and others returning east occupied the seats used by westbound settlers.

In the new century, the GN continued to advertise these opportunites. At times, the GN was a price leader; at other times it offered rates in cooperation with connecting roads; and ICC rules occasionally shaped policies. The pattern was infinitely varied. In 1900, *Railway Gazette* credited the GN with "radical reductions" in settlers' tickets. For six days in spring 1902, the GN sold St. Paul–Williston

tickets at less than a penny a mile. In the fall of the same year, the GN, NP, the Soo, and those several roads operating through the Omaha gateway agreed to quote uniform daily reduced fares for settlers: $22.50 to Spokane and $25 to the Kootenay Country and points west of the Cascades. In 1902, also, the GN gave a special St. Paul–Minot harvester's rate of $5.

By such actions, the GN and other roads attracted substantial traffic to their lines. After a lull during the Panic of 1893, immigration to and movement within the United States reached new highs. During the spring of 1902, 102,000 settlers arrived in the Northwest; emigrant movables traffic on the GN doubled in that season. One company official estimated that during the ten years before World War I, the GN hauled 600,000 settlers and 25,000 cars of emigrant movables. Such was the immigrant business for which the GN and its rivals competed (see Table 3).

Rates for all types of passenger service were constantly subject to market forces, which often forced them down. In 1898, the NP cut the maximum in Washington and Idaho from five to four cents; the GN followed. Two years later, both roads lowered the maximum in other states to only three cents. *Railway Age* observed that ''the farmer on the lonely prairies of Dakota and the lumberman in the wilds of Washington'' could now travel as cheaply as men in Ohio and Illinois. In 1901, the GN and others extended the three-cent rate to South Dakota, and in 1903 both the GN and the NP reduced their maximum rate in Montana to three cents—two years before the state legislature set that limit.[10]

As this century progressed, state legislatures became more active in setting rates, a trend that Hill disliked intensely, because already the margin of profit on passenger service was distressingly low. He had followed the practice of reducing rates, he declared, not only specifically to attract settlers but also to increase the density of traffic. Admittedly, though, some voluntary reductions were inspired by public opinion. When Montana was considering restrictive legislation in 1899, Hill suggested to E. H. Harriman that the UP's Oregon Short Line reduce its fare: the GN and the NP had already done so, and Hill hoped to prevent Montana from imposing ruinous price reductions. By 1907, however, legislatures were in a more belligerent mood. In Minnesota, a new law cut the maximum rate to two cents a mile, and in that year alone five other states in GN territory passed similar legislation. North Dakota and South Dakota reduced the maximum from three to two and one-half cents, Nebraska, Iowa, and Wisconsin from three to two cents.

Hill understood that these changes would precipitate drastic decreases in passenger revenue, aggregating perhaps as much as 10 percent, or more than $1 million. If the maximum rates were lowered, the remunerative part of the business would yield less and cut the average below cost. Furthermore, changes in state maximums would necessitate upward adjustments in interstate fares.

On one issue, though—free passes—railroaders welcomed legislation. Politicians and

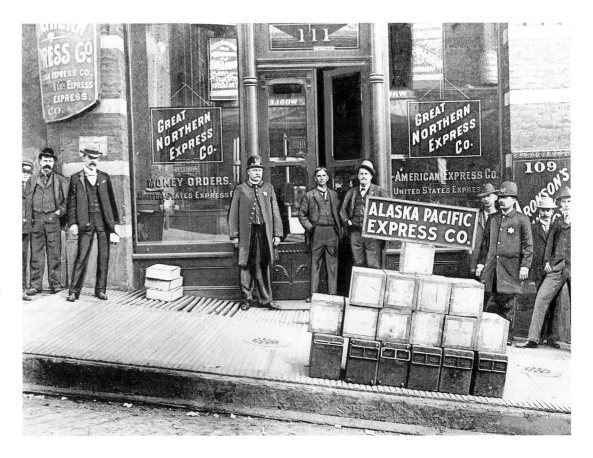

The Seattle office of the Great Northern Express Company was an extremely busy place at the turn of the century.

publishers were especially prone to demand and get free transportation. Ignatius Donnelly, the firebrand from Minnesota, had a pass, and politicians generally had a distressing tendency to denounce railroads while traveling at their expense. According to one GN spokesman in 1894, "almost every official of the country, from United States Senator down, travels upon passes, on official business, and at the same time draws full mileage from the Government." Ethics aside, for years GN's management had complained about the "promiscuous use of free transportation," and had tried to curb it. In 1899, when presented with a request from Washington state politicians, Louis W. Hill complained that passes were "a burdensome tax on the company," and that recipients did not "appreciate the favor" but took it "as a privilege." Nevertheless, he forwarded the passes. Understandably, GN executives did not object to new regulations on the matter.[11]

If passenger business before 1916 was highly competitive, at least it was not yet subject to intense modal competition. Nevertheless, hints of events to come were noticeable. In 1891, when streetcar companies serving St. Paul and Minneapolis merged and changed from horse to electric power, the GN found that its business between those cities dropped rapidly. In the same decade, the bicycle adversely affected revenues from the run to Lake Minnetonka. But not until 1917 did the passenger department feel it necessary to refer to the automobile's influence. The cloud of rubber tires and hardtop roads was on the horizon, but when World War I broke out, the shadow was still very small.

James J. Hill commented in 1900 that "our passenger business is excellent everywhere," an assertion with foundation. The high quality of the GN's service was well recognized not only by the traveling public but by the Post Office Department as well. Indeed, the GN had become the premier carrier of mail to the Pacific Northwest, reflecting the company's tradition of high operating standards. This status also mirrored the Great Northern's admirable financial condition—a circumstance that, after all, allowed the road to turn in sterling performances.[12]

16

Corporate Structure and Finance

The Great Northern's success depended on several factors, not the least of them its efficient formulation and administration of financial policies. This relation was not lost on James J. Hill. His devotion to operational efficiency was now a matter of clear and perfect record. Less well known and appreciated were his relentless efforts to increase the entire property's value by effective financial management.[1]

Early Experience

With the corporate organization established under contract of February 1890, Hill and his associates worked on enhancing the Manitoba's credit and establishing that of the GN with minimal interference from regulatory bodies. Simultaneously, the GN's 100 percent ownership of proprietary companies gave it flexibility in making rates and thus advantageous flow of dividends to the parent.

Although GN managers succeeded in holding down the interest rate on the system's publicly held bonds between 1890 and 1893, debt increased substantially. Under authority to match not only currently redeemed First Mortgage 7s but also those paid off since 1883, the

Manitoba issued and sold $4,695,000 Consolidated 4½ percents. The Manitoba also issued Montana Extension bonds at 4 percent; of these it sold $148,000 to the public, and another $11,502,000 served as backing for the Pacific Extension 4s and were never marketed. During the same period, the Montana Central issued $2 million in 5s, of which $1.5 million were sold and $500,000 exchanged for the same amount of 6s held by the GN, and the Willmar & Sioux Falls also issued 5s to replace the $2,625,000 of 6s in the GN's portfolio. The Minneapolis Union sold an additional $100,000 in 5s, and $200,000 of Eastern Railway 5s went into public hands. Thus, all new issues of the GN system were brought out at 4 to 5 percent, but the funded debt held by the public was increased by $34,325,755.

Great Northern accounts in fiscal 1894 also showed acquisition of $490,000 par value of shares and $900,000 in bonds of the Butte, Anaconda & Pacific Railroad. This acquisition entailed no current cash outlay but was Marcus Daly's reimbursement for aid in earlier construction of a railway to compete with the Northern Pacific. Daly's railroad, after all, carried ore for Anaconda Copper to Butte and a connection there with Hill's Montana Central to the smelter at Great Falls.

Despite the extreme austerity that President Hill ordered during the Panic of 1893, the GN had to adopt extraordinary measures to pay a 5 percent dividend in fiscal 1894. Net operating income dropped 23.5 percent (from $5,812,000 in 1893 to $4,445,000 in the following year), and failed to cover fixed charges, but using its power over wholly owned affiliates, the GN expanded dividends received from them from $70,136 in 1893 to $1,084,607 in 1894 — thereby increasing non-operating income from an average of $1 million to almost $2 million. Finally, when net income fell shy of the required amount for the GN dividend, the directors voted to take $104,000 from surplus. Nevertheless, the year's results confirmed, Hill said, the "great vitality" of the GN.[2]

The GN's financial circumstances were no great problem after 1894 (see Table 4). Net railway operating income began rising in 1895 and continued upward with only a slight decline in 1897. Sizable dividends from proprietary companies provided marginal funds to meet fixed charges and to pay GN's 5 percent dividend in 1895, but nothing unusual was needed thereafter. In fiscal 1897, the GN even felt free to invest $1,108,491 in shares of the Oregon Railway & Navigation Company for leverage in negotiating with the Union Pacific and the Northern Pacific.

Meanwhile, between 1893 and 1897, the equity-to-debt ratio for the GN system was changed. The Duluth, Watertown & Pacific's $1,375,000 6s were relegated to the GN's treasury, and the Manitoba retired $2,721,900 First Mortgage 7s, but marketed $2,916,000 Consolidated 4½ percents and $291,000 Montana Extension 4s. Other affiliates also added to the system's debt. The net growth in publicly held bonds of the system for 1893–1897, when added to increases taken on between 1890 and 1893, totaled $35,656,855, and the equity-to-debt ratio that had stood at 43 to 57 in 1890 was 30 to 70 in 1897.

Table 4. Selected Comparative Income Statistics, 1890–1916, Great Northern Railway Company

(000 omitted)

	Net revenue from railway operations	Railway tax accruals	Net railway operating income[a]	Other income	Income available for fixed charges	Fixed[b] charges	Net income
1890	$ 4,857	$ 274	$ 4,583	$ 881	$ 5,464	$3,656	$ 1,808
1891	5,118	300	4,818	924	5,742	4,103	1,639
1892	5,471	368	5,103	940	6,043	4,099	1,943
1893	6,187	376	5,812	1,019	6,830	4,648	2,182
1894	4,857	412	4,445	1,991	6,436	5,353	1,083
1895	5,963	459	5,504	1,308	6,812	5,373	1,439
1896	7,398	528	6,870	805	7,675	5,383	2,292
1897	6,821	502	6,375	1,463	7,808	5,381	2,457
1898	9,324	586	8,795	2,424	11,219	5,397	5,822
1899	9,661	759	8,989	2,587	11,576	4,138	7,438
1900	10,305	774	9,623	4,513	14,136	3,710	10,426
1901	8,772	745	8,128	4,146	12,274	3,688	8,586
1902	14,253	984	13,349	2,636	16,085	3,742	12,343
1903	19,307	1,345	18,152	1,650	19,802	3,993	15,809
1904	17,963	1,283	16,896	1,407	18,303	4,186	14,117
1905	20,202	1,385	19,108	2,089	21,197	4,366	16,831
1906	23,126	1,606	21,803	1,920	23,723	4,259	19,464
1907	20,446	1,883	19,008	2,970	21,978	4,418	17,560
1908	18,605	2,288	17,209	2,956	20,164	5,174	14,990
1909	21,383	2,570	19,402	2,934	22,336	4,848	17,488
1910	25,427	3,570	22,170	563	22,733	4,941	17,792
1911	23,863	3,300	20,715	1,960	22,675	5,158	17,517
1912	28,651	3,488	25,568	2,548	28,116	6,462	21,654

The Great Northern Railway: A History/Part I 1856 to 1916

Table 4 (continued)

	Net revenue from railway operations	Railway tax accruals	Net railway operating income[a]	Other income	Income available for fixed charges	Fixed[b] charges	Net income
1913	32,955	4,279	28,483	2,544	31,027	6,459	24,568
1914	29,085	4,792	24,365	2,550	26,905[c]	6,451	20,454
1915	30,335	4,630	25,766	1,328	27,066[c]	6,448	20,618
1916	37,348	5,132	32,337	1,736	34,044[c]	6,443	27,601

a. Data entered in this column for the years 1890–1896 are for Railway operating income, not Net revenue from railway operations, and to get the Net railway operating income for the years 1897–1916, entries for equipment rents and joint facility rents, in addition to Tax accruals, have been subtracted from NRRO.

b. Fixed charges are almost entirely for rent of leased roads and equipment, 1890–1907, and for interest on funded debt, 1908–1916.

c. From the sum of Net railway operating income and Other income, small Miscellaneous deductions were made to get the income available for fixed charges, 1914–1916.

Sources: GNAR, 1890–1916

Consolidating Properties

As early as 1894, President James J. Hill and his associates discussed ways of improving their enterprise's corporate structure. The 1893 stringency had prompted E. T. Nichols to suggest that the GN buy all properties of the Manitoba. The parent corporation's relatively small amount of property provided an inadequate base for credit, he thought. Also, if the GN met some bad years and failed to earn enough to pay dividends, the leased property would revert to its stockholders and carry with it all the proprietary companies. Additional incentives for change were present. The steady rise in earnings after 1894 minimized fears about simplifying the corporate structure, and several rate cases pending in state and federal courts promised to specify more clearly the legally acceptable basis for rate making. Hill observed, in 1898: "All of our property today is capitalized for very much less than it would cost to reproduce it, and limiting our earnings to a reasonable return on our present capitalization would destroy about all the railroads west of Chicago."[3]

By 1896, Hill agreed to a plan designed to achieve consolidation of properties associated with the GN and thus structure a better balance between share capital and funded debt. To activate his program, Hill waited until 1898, after the Smyth v. Ames rate-making decision, in which Justice Harlan held that a company is entitled to "a fair return upon the value of that which it employs for the public convenience." J. S. Kennedy thought the decision was "as strong and satisfactory as could have been expected"; Hill considered it "just in all respects."[4]

Consequently, in 1898, stockholders agreed to take $25 million of the company's shares at par. With the current market price at $125 for the stock, still called preferred, the proposition was quite attractive. Of that issue, $15 million served to retire the same amount of GN collateral trust 4s, thus freeing £3 million of the Manitoba's Pacific Extension 4s for sale when a favorable market offered. The remaining $10 million of new shares were exchanged for the entire capital stock ($12,500,000) of the Seattle & Montana Railroad Company, which had recently been vested with the properties and securities of the Pacific Coast lines acquired and built since 1889, and already part of the GN system. The Seattle & Montana's mileage was free of debt, the original advances for purchases and construction having been made by the GN on behalf of the stockholders for whom the shares of these affiliated lines were held in trust. By Hill's estimate, the $10 million was "well within the present cost of the property," and gave the GN direct operating control of lines from Seattle to the Fraser River in British Columbia, plus a branch to coal fields at Cokedale in the Skagit River Valley, and an interest with the Union Pacific in the Portland & Puget Sound Railroad Company, which hoped to construct a line from Seattle to Portland.[5]

The $10 million GN shares paid to stockholders for their rights in Seattle & Montana stock constituted a merited stock dividend, the capitalization of earnings that could have been paid out as cash dividends. Some newspapers, however, called the stock issue a "melon," although the editor of New York's *Commercial Advertiser* pointed out that it was not water but the outcome of actions by a master of "scientific transportation." Hill predictably thought the program "the best and strongest thing we have ever done'' for GN sharehold-ers.[6]

In October 1898, GN directors and stock-holders approved three other elements of Hill's plan. Having already voted a 6 percent divi-dend in the last quarter of 1897, they now ap-proved an annual rate of 7 percent. Second, they relinquished authority to issue common stock, making all shares ''of union character and having uniform rights.'' Third, the stock-holders approved a second $25-million issue of GN stock to be exchanged for the $20 million in outstanding shares of the Manitoba. In that way, the GN came to own almost all the Man-itoba shares. Nichols now could relax; the GN not only leased the StPM&M but exercised control by ownership of stock.[7]

With proceeds of an additional $15 million at par in new GN shares distributed to stock-holders, management further prosecuted its plans. In the West, part of the funds was used to pay the Northern Pacific for securities of the Spokane Falls & Northern Railway Company, allowing the GN to control and operate all lines north from Spokane and in southern Brit-ish Columbia as an integral part of its system. To the east, the GN invested remaining funds in 75,000 shares of the Eastern Railway of Minnesota.[8]

During the ten years up to 1907, the com-pany had issued $125 million in new stock, making a total of $150 million outstanding. The GN had acquired either 100 percent own-ership, or nearly that amount, of the system's major components, including the Manitoba. At

the same time, however, the GN's funded debt had risen drastically, although not as much as its capital stock. In 1901, Hill more than dou-bled the railroad's funded debt obligation by purchasing, in collaboration with the NP, the stock of the Chicago, Burlington & Quincy. The two companies paid $200 per share in joint GN–NP 4 percent, twenty-year bonds, GN's responsibility being $107,577,200 in 1902, and raised to $107,613,000 five years later. New issues going into public hands from 1897 to 1907 totaled $121,039,383. Bonds re-tired aggregated $19,663,400. Publicly held funded debt thus rose by $101,376,084, the amount outstanding on June 30, 1907 being $207,517,929. The ratio of shares to funded

debt was now 42 to 58 if the GN–NP joint 4s were included; if they were not, as Hill liked, the figures were 64 and 36.[9]

Meanwhile, statistics for the entire system's performance recorded noteworthy growth. The GN's own net assets grew from $3,572,000 in 1890 to $99,367,000 in 1907, those of the system from $114,376,000 to $480,629,000. Net revenues from operations increased from $4,857,000 in 1890 to $20,446,000 seventeen years later, operating income from $4,583,000 to $19,008,000.

Stockholders could not be other than happy with the system's earnings and the portion al-located to them. Net income grew from $1,808,000 in 1890 to $17,560,000 seventeen

Carl R. Gray (center) was president of the Spokane, Portland & Seattle before assuming the same post on the GN in 1912. Gray is flanked on the left by James J. Hill and on the right by L. W. Hill and a reporter from the *Boston American*.

years later. Stockholders were paid dividends ranging from 4.75 percent in 1891 to 7 percent in 1907, and until late in 1898, GN stockholders who held Manitoba shares also received 6 percent annual dividend on those. In addition, shareholders divided in 1898 a stock dividend held in trust for them, and in 1902 another $5 million in GN shares for an equal amount of Manitoba improvement bonds. Two .5 percent cash dividends (1901 and 1907) on shares in the Lake Superior Company and $1,500,000 in shares of the Great Northern Iron Ore Properties in 1906 also went to GN stockholders.[10]

By 1907, the time had come for the "ultimate consolidation" of GN properties that Hill had visualized. The parent company held nearly all shares of major operating units; minority holdings were too small to offer effective opposition to contemplated changes. To promote consolidation then, the directors in December 1906 authorized issuance of another 600,000 of GN shares. As of July 1, 1907, the GN purchased the properties (securities, rail lines, equipment, and all other physical assets) of fourteen affiliates in the United States; those of the Manitoba were added four months later. Payment took several forms. The GN assumed the affiliates' outstanding bonds, wrote off advances, assumed and discharged all other liabilities and obligations, and paid cash in specified amounts. For the Manitoba, the GN assumed funded debt of almost $95,000,000, including $11,900,000 in unmarketed improvement bonds, and paid minority stockholders $175 per share.

Although now direct owner of all major properties of the system, the Great Northern continued to act as a holding company. It held the stock of its railways in Manitoba (one jointly with the NP) and of eight British Columbia concerns, and it also owned outstanding stock of three companies in the United States whose properties were operated in conjunction with but not as part of the GN system. It had minority interests in four other small depots, terminals, and shipping firms, and owned 48.5 percent of the CB&Q's shares. Among other investments, the GN held stock of two steamship companies, one lumber company, one coal company, a bridge company, and a land company.

Shareholders had good reason to salute James J. Hill. They "made over and above their dividends a profit of about one hundred and fifty million of dollars," he observed in reviewing the record from 1879 to 1904. Although some of this profit was made on Manitoba shares, much was the product of GN stock, which, if acquired directly from the company, cost par or less. The market price for GN shares was above 100 after 1891; the low in 1905 was 236. Not surprisingly, the number of GN stockholders rose from 212 in 1892 to 15,000 in 1906.[11]

Finances of a Maturing Railroad

Between 1907 and 1917, the Great Northern moved toward effective institutionalization of its financial affairs. Financial managers tidied up accounts and arranged for closing out or transferring numerous corporate activities. During 1907 and 1908, transactions were completed for the GN's purchase of the Billings & Northern Railway Company (Laurel to Armington, Montana) from the CB&Q and the GN's sale of the Sioux City & Western (Sioux City to O'Neill, Nebraska) to the CB&Q.

Debt management was almost routine. Four issues were redeemed in full at maturity between 1908 and 1911, and in the same years, increases were recorded in bond sales of three affiliates. In all, sales of GN bonds and those of its affiliates totaled $59,677,819, producing a net increase in debt of $43,370,819. The GN financed some growth by issuing stock. A total of 400,000 shares were sold to holders at par, giving them a very good deal, though no longer a bonanza; market prices of GN stock ranged from 126 in 1912 to 135 in 1914.

The GN's total publicly held funded debt rose to $250,889,258 in 1916, but this figure was conservative for a railroad that had grown by 1,484 miles in nine years. Bonded debt per mile increased from $15,356 to $17,786, comparing favorably with that of any other major railroad in the United States, and, for that matter, total capitalization per mile was only $48,824 in 1916.

Great Northern accounts in 1914 for the first time reflected a new technique for financing purchase of equipment — advances to and shares of the Great Northern Equipment Company. This corporation used funds to purchase, hold, and lease rolling stock until the parent company was ready to take possession.

Also in its fiscal affairs, the Great Northern used available funds to favor local bankers and thus generate business. In the depressed fall of 1907, to aid farmers and to promote wheat traffic — and incidentally to stimulate exports of grain and bring gold into the country — the GN and the NP each extended to shippers $1,000,000, amounts matched by banks in the Twin Cities, Duluth, and New York City. And, responding to local bankers' requests and to the .5 percent higher interest rate in the upper Midwest during 1911 and 1912, Comptroller G. R. Martin left larger than normal amounts of current receipts on deposit with Twin City and Duluth banks instead of forwarding them immediately to New York.

Financial management from 1890 to 1916 proceeded mainly as Hill had planned. Dividends were paid every year, at 7 percent from 1899 on. Simplified corporate structure provided more straightforward accounting and corrected undercapitalization; issuing large amounts of capital stock and restrained use of new bonds resulted in a 1 to 1 ratio between the two. As handled, the new stock issues from 1898 to 1907 were a bonanza to stockholders, and profitable even at post–1907 prices. Net income supplied a high percentage of funds for expanding the system, almost 50 percent after 1907, and it was not yet clearly recognized that the large investment in Canadian lines, especially in British Columbia, was a losing proposition. Small wonder that Wall Streeters hailed James J. Hill as an extraordinary railroader.

17

"Leading the Band"

At a banquet honoring his seventy-fifth birthday in September 1913, James J. Hill commented that to manage effectively "a great big machine" such as the Great Northern required that "somebody must lead the band." He referred, of course, to his own leadership. "Now, it has not been the easiest thing in the world," he observed on another occasion, "to play first violin in the Great Northern band." Indeed, Hill's role in "leading the band" of GN employees required a most difficult balancing act. On the one hand, he had to contend with constant fluctuations in the business cycle, and on the other he had to deal with organized labor's growing demands. The record set by Hill and the GN in this regard might be considered a case study for the entire industry.[1]

Basic Principles

James J. Hill's philosophy on employee relations was well formed by 1890. Economic conditions and the demand for railroad service, Hill thought, should govern wages and salaries, as well as the size of the work force, and management alone should make those determinations. Moreover, if investment

in plant could displace labor, Hill chose that path, as illustrated by one incident. When coal chutes with increased storage capacity were recommended in 1897, General Superintendent Ward explained: "It is cheaper to spend more on pockets than to hire a night man." Hill agreed.[2]

Hill ultimately established company policy, but in practice he delegated most personnel matters to subordinates. Despite this authority, employees frequently appealed decisions to Hill. He would investigate with care, though he most often upheld the subordinates' judgments. Writing in 1893 to a man complaining of unfairness, Hill typically declared: "You are discharged because, in the opinion of your foreman, you are incompetent. . . ." For a few decisions, though, he found himself torn between strict principles and his reluctance to punish a veteran employee. A worker might be temporarily removed from his post but soon reinstated or employed elsewhere on the system. For a locomotive engineer discharged because of a collision, Hill asked Henry Minot of the Eastern Railway to take him because the man was "entirely steady and competent, and has had to pay the penalty of bad luck."[3]

Outsiders and subordinates alike described Hill as an "exacting" and "hard master," an "austere manager," and a "difficult overlord." In moments ruled by impatience, he would occasionally give vent to monumental wrath, a trait for which he never apologized. A driver of men as well as a leader, Hill inspired employees by his own example. Most men would retain lifelong respect for Hill. "I find as thousands have found before me that a college course under that Master Mind of J. J. Hill is a great help in many lines of work," one man wrote long after leaving the GN.

Others thought of Hill as "the worst slave driver they'd ever worked for, but they all had a liking for him anyway."[4]

Certainly Hill's methods made him a remarkable teacher. He became almost as famous for the railroad leaders he "trained and lost" as for his other achievements. Several of the ablest railroad executives in the country—Presidents Allen Manvel of the Santa Fe and A. L. Mohler of the Union Pacific to cite only two—were "graduates of the Hill school," as one newspaper reported, and "most of them left after severe personal disagreements with their chieftain." Many others survived Hill's training and stayed with the GN, among them an outstanding vice president of operations, Charles O. Jenks, and two future presidents, Ralph Budd and William P. Kenney.[5]

To provide systematic day-by-day management of the railroad, definitions of functions and rules emanated from executive offices regularly. Codes of organization in 1896 and 1912 defined responsibilities expected of executives and other supervisors. Some rules governed employees' behavior. Hill stated in 1891 that "no person drawing the Company's pay can be mixed up in any way whatever with right-of-way or real estate operations for any private or personal account. . . ." The company also demanded that employees manage their personal finances responsibly. The GN had to follow the law on garnisheeing wages, but no excuse would be "accepted for more than one attachment or garnishment in any one year, unless the circumstances of the case are exceptional." Rules against use of liquor were difficult to enforce but were strict. In 1894, a special circular stated flatly that no "person addicted to the use of intoxicating liquors . . . shall hereafter be employed or continued in the service of the Company." Repeated in 1909, this rule made newspaper headlines: "Hill Roads Bar Drinkers."[6]

Employees understood that management expected the rules to be followed, and they also knew that opportunity awaited those who followed them and otherwise performed well. Whenever possible, supervisory and officer personnel were recruited from the ranks. "I have always tried to give everybody . . . opportunity to rise and take a step forward and upward in his own behalf," Hill asserted in 1913. Several men in prominent positions, he declared, "were born in section houses on Great Northern. . . ."[7]

A few exceptions appeared, however. In 1892, after service with the Western Traffic Association, W. W. Finley became general traffic manager of the GN. Four years later W. H. Newman came from the Chicago & North Western to be GN's second vice president. Another, J. M. Gruber, had served on the Rock Island and the Burlington before he was appointed to succeed F. E. Ward as GN's general manager. Perhaps most unusual was Carl R. Gray's election as president in 1912; he came from vice presidency of the St. Louis & San Francisco and a brief stint as president of the Spokane, Portland & Seattle.

For several significant appointments, James J. Hill ignored the otherwise rigidly enforced rule "against the employment of relatives by officers of the Company." His eldest son, James, rose to a vice presidency before going to similar posts on the CB&Q and the NP. Two of Hill's sons-in-law, Samuel Hill and George T. Slade, served in responsible positions on the GN or proprietary companies, and another son-in-law, E. C. Lindley, in 1910 became general solicitor for the GN. Louis W.

Hill, of course, moved up the administrative ladder quickly, becoming assistant to the president in 1898, president in 1907, and in 1912 chairman of the board.[8]

As far as the record shows, these family members were satisfactory managers. Louis W. Hill upheld his father's standards, but with a less forceful personality he had difficulty in applying the Empire Builder's imperious techniques. Subordinates would accept, often with pride, a tongue-lashing from James J. Hill, but not from the less majestic son. And, because Louis W. Hill failed to train a successor for the presidency, the company's directors had to turn to an outsider in 1912.

No doubt James J. Hill demanded of relatives as much as he did from others. All workers should give their wholehearted effort to the company's welfare. He asked no more than he gave, devoting himself so completely to the railroad that he could not be expected to sympathize with subordinates' failures and human frailties. Nor could he be expected to understand fully the divided loyalties required of employees who were union members.

Union – Management Relations, 1883 – 1893

Although Hill found it difficult to reconcile his understanding of employee responsibility with unionism, he made early collective agreements to buy peace and stability. During the early 1890s, agreements applied only between the carrier and train-service employees. Contracts were negotiated with engineers and firemen in 1890 and with conductors, brakemen, and yardmen in the same year. These understandings were usually made with repre-

The *William Crooks* was brought out of retirement on James J. Hill's 70th birthday, September 13, 1908. Hill, sixth from the left, is flanked by officers and employees of the company.

sentatives of the GN's train-service employees, functioning as union negotiating committees, not with national brotherhoods.[9]

Soon after the GN was organized, a committee representing several groups of enginemen asked for changes in rules regulating pay, computation of time, seniority, and other "rights." Negotiations produced an agreement with the engineers effective November 1, 1890. Their classification into four groups remained the same as an agreement of 1885 — first-class, newly appointed, switch, and transfer — but changes in computing time and pay improved their lot. For the first two classes, the basic day was cut from twelve to ten hours or a hundred miles or less. For engineers on switch and transfer jobs, the basic day remained twelve hours, although overtime was calculated after ten hours. First-class and transfer engineers continued to receive $3.90 per day, but the overtime rate was raised from 35 to 39 cents an hour. Other provisions in the 1890 contract gave those with more seniority greater rights and privileges in choice of runs, promotions, demotions, and transfers. The company agreed to employ no more engineers than were necessary "to move the freight with promptness and dispatch," and the number constituting a "surplus" was to be determined by the master mechanic and a committee of engineers. If an engineer was discharged or suspended for causes that he considered unjust and improper, he could get a hearing before the master mechanic and a committee on adjustment.[10]

No GN labor contracts prior to 1894 had separate schedules for firemen. They were treated as apprentice engineers, from whose ranks promotion was made to engineer. The Eastern Railway contract of 1889 was unusual in that it included a schedule for firemen.

In 1892, the GN signed contracts with trainmen and yardmen. Under this agreement, passenger trainmen had fixed runs, so that they received monthly salaries: conductors $125, baggagemen $70, and experienced brakemen $60. Only on extra runs with layover days did they earn overtime. Freight trainmen were paid according to mileage: conductors three cents per mile and brakemen two. Except for those on work trains, who continued a twelve-hour day, the day was defined as ten hours, and overtime pay was one-tenth the rate per day for each extra hour.

Conductors and other trainmen made further gains. When a general reduction in salaries was instituted in 1893, salaried trainmen sustained no cut, and in a new contract of August 1, 1893, some won slightly higher pay. Conductors and brakemen assigned to switchback service in the Cascades were raised respectively from 3 to 3.6 cents per mile and from 2 to 2.4 cents. Crews also received actual mileage for "doubling hills" — taking half a train up in each trip. This contract was especially significant in that it was signed not only by GN employees but also by national union officers of the Order of Railway Conductors (ORC) and the Brotherhood of Railroad Trainmen (BRT).

Yardmen had less clout. Yardmasters asked for monthly salaries and other concessions, but the GN, regarding them as officials of the company, refused to sign union contracts until 1925. Yard foremen and helpers were given a basic ten-hour day, hourly pay, and pro rata for overtime, which, if of 35 minutes or more, was to be counted as an hour. Management agreed to a request for a two-cent differential for night crews but rejected the request for a long-desired geographic differential, a cause for later problems.

The ARU Strike and Its Aftermath

During the summer of 1893, Hill set off a chain of events that led to a major labor crisis. Convinced that business would get worse before it got better, he resolved to slash expenditures. Hill telegraphed A. L. Mohler: "take whatever steps are necessary to reduce track, machinery, station, and other services to lowest point possible. Take off all extra gangs everywhere, except those relaying steel. Reduce wages section foremen to forty dollars East and forty-five West, and of section men to one dollar East and one dollar and quarter West." In October, Hill could report: "We have reduced our force to the lowest possible point. . . ." The GN had also cut compensation for all salaried personnel from 15 to 30 percent, the higher rate applying to the seven men earning $5,000 and more per year.[11]

Negotiations to reduce compensation of engine and train-service employees were much more difficult and prolonged. When engineers resisted altered rules on hours as well as wages, discussions almost broke down. Early in March 1894, however, negotiators signed a contract that cut the daily rate for engineers on road engines by 25 cents and of switch engines 20 cents. These and other changes left many enginemen discontented, although the contract promised a return to the wage schedule of April 1, 1893 as soon as the company's annual gross earnings amounted to $4,500 per mile.

The contract with conductors and other trainmen was nearly ready for a vote when, on April 1, 1894, the trainmen's committee chairman raised an issue that led directly to crisis. He pointed out that although switchmen in the Butte yard of the Montana Central had not been covered by an earlier agreement, Mohler had promised them wages equal to those paid locally for the same service by other carriers. When the new general manager did not respond immediately, though, some men walked off the job. Hill wired from Europe that he knew of no such promise, and that the men who had struck should be discharged. On April 4, General Manager Case signed an agreement with the BRT fixing wages for switchmen at Butte significantly higher than elsewhere on the GN, but his refusal to rehire the strikers angered some of the Montana Central yardmen, who turned from the BRT to join another organization.

Feeding on the frustration and unrest among workers discharged or suffering wage cuts during the onrushing depression, the American Railway Union (ARU) rode the crest of a rising wave. Eugene V. Debs, formerly a sincere and dedicated supporter of the brotherhoods, had become convinced that salvation for railroad workers lay in one all-embracing union, the ARU. By January 1, 1894, the new organization that Debs headed reportedly had organized several roads—the Union Pacific and the Santa Fe among others—and spokesmen claimed more than forty locals on the Southern Pacific and twenty-two on the Northern Pacific.

Three days after Hill returned from Europe he was faced with a strike. On April 13, 1894, a spokesman presented the ARU's demands: restoration of wage schedules and rules prevailing prior to August 1893; union scale for switchmen at Butte, Helena, and Great Falls; and agreement by management to meet with ARU representatives at Minot. Management was given less than three hours to reply; none was forthcoming, and the strike began at noon on April 13 across the Montana and Kalispell divisions of the GN and on the Montana Central. Although the ARU promised not to interfere with trains and offered to handle those moving mail, if no passengers or freight were carried, Hill ordered that all trains be stopped at the nearest station. Business on the system came to a standstill.

Hill, with mixed sentiments, was indignant that men he had trusted and with whom the GN had signed contracts had seemingly turned against him and the company. Moreover, their demands threatened the GN's good health at a time when many other railroads were plummeting into bankruptcy. On the other hand, he was acutely aware of the need to retain the workers' loyalty and respect. But he was convinced that the ARU spoke for relatively few employees, and that loyal members of the brotherhoods, unhappy as they might be with reduced wages, were adamantly opposed to interference by a rival union. It seemed a jurisdictional dispute: "While the Company desires to deal with all or any of the men on its payrolls," he observed, "it has been asked to violate agreements now in existence with the different classes of its men, against the will of those who made such agreements, and to enter into new agreement with the American Railway Union."[12]

Accordingly, Hill first adopted a "strictly legal" approach. Following his general refusal to use strikebreakers, he asked national officers of the Brotherhood of Locomotive Engineers (BLE), the ORC, and the BRT to "take such action as will carry out your representation that an agreement with the Brotherhood binds its members." The grand chiefs denounced the strike, declared that those who struck had placed themselves outside the organizations, and initially tried to persuade members to return to their jobs.[13]

Hill then combined reason with veiled threats. To the mayor of Helena, he asserted that the GN had "at all times been willing to discuss with its employees, or their duly authorized representatives, all questions affecting their wages or other terms of employment." The men who quit had mistaken the company's intentions, Hill wrote to the secretary of the ARU, and "upon a little reflection" they would no doubt return to their jobs "and thereby relieve the Company from the necessity of hiring others to take their places."[14]

Some trains began to roll. Four days after the strike began, shopmen at St. Cloud returned to work and many enginemen and conductors, especially those on the eastern end, were willing to work if protected. At the company's request, court injunctions were granted in Minnesota and North Dakota to restrain interference, United States marshals enforced the orders, and local sheriffs generally preserved the peace and protected property. By April 20, passenger trains were running in Minnesota and in North Dakota as far as Minot.

Simultaneously, Hill was trying to settle the wage issue in Montana. On April 19, he authorized Marcus Daly, chief executive of the Anaconda Company and mayor of Butte, to announce that the GN was willing to pay trackmen and carmen the same wages as paid by other companies. He also suggested it was possible to arbitrate the dispute, providing that the men returned to work at once. If they preferred the ARU to the brotherhoods, the GN would accept their wishes.

Events soon caused Hill to alter his tactics. Federal and other authorities pushed for termination of the strike, and on April 21, the Solicitor General of the United States issued an opinion that "it was an offense for anyone to obstruct or retard the passage of a train carrying the mail." This departure in federal policy encouraged the GN to start one through mail train in each direction, but fears of disturbance by Coxey's army of the unemployed, which was attempting to march on the nation's capital, frightened many. Conditions were tense; violence was in the air. In St. Paul, Governor Knute Nelson and other public officials urged Hill to settle the strike. Debs appeared before the governor and the St. Paul Chamber of Commerce, favorably impressing them. If Hill had arranged these meetings expecting that Debs would weaken his cause, that hope was dashed.[15]

Deciding to deal directly with Debs, Hill invited the ARU committee to his office for a conference on April 25, angering heads of the brotherhoods, who denied that either the ARU committee or Debs himself represented the men in GN's employ. Nevertheless, Hill proposed that all employees return to work and that rates of pay be taken up with the company by representatives chosen by the workers; all matters not promptly settled would be referred to a three-man board of arbitration made up of disinterested railway men, its findings to bind all parties.

When Debs rejected that proposal, Hill acted quickly. He dispatched a freight train to the West and notified sheriffs that he expected them to prevent interference. The ARU then ordered a strike in St. Paul and Minneapolis, and, on April 28, Hill asked President Grover Cleveland for troops because United States marshals were "prevented by turbulent mobs from serving the civil and criminal processes of the United States courts, and from taking any steps to prevent interference with United States mails on trains of the Great Northern Railway." Despite Hill's request, an order for troops was given only for North Dakota, and that too late to be significant.[16]

F. E. Ward was forced to settle with local committees when the boilermakers struck for increased pay early in the century.

The strike, though, was moving rapidly toward settlement. Debs knew that the GN's eastern division was returning to normal. Also, on April 28, men on the Cascade Division announced they were ready to work. At the same time, a group of Minneapolis business leaders proposed a settlement based on the points Hill had made four days earlier, but with a five-member board of arbitration. Debs and Hill accepted this proposal, and the board, headed by Charles A. Pillsbury, sat down to hear both sides' arguments. On May 1, the board made its award. Debs and his associates accepted the findings and drew up a memorandum of agreement listing the conditions under which GN employees would return to work. Hill added only brief qualifications, which Debs accepted. All parties signed the final document, Debs for the ARU, Hill for the GN, and Samuel Hill for the proprietary companies. Thus the strike ended, with Debs rejecting a proposed celebration banquet and Hill congratulating the ARU leaders on their "shrewd management" of the affair.[17]

Both sides professed to be pleased. According to Hill, the strike was settled with the company's proposals accepted on most issues, the balance being arbitrated. Wages of train-service personnel remained unchanged and shop workers had 75 percent of their reductions restored. At some deferred date, switchmen in Butte, Helena, and Great Falls were to have identical wage schedules. Hill figured that the settlement resulted in a net reduction of 4¼ percent from the wages paid prior to August 1893. At the same time, an ARU spokesman claimed that group had won 97½ percent of its demands and an aggregate wage increase of $146,000 per month, apparently calculated from the reduced schedule after August 1893.

Several developments complicated or threatened to complicate return to normal operations. First came spring rains and floods along the line. Then, in late June, the Pullman Company was struck by the ARU, affecting all railroads using Pullman service, though not the GN directly. Some workers threatened to walk off their jobs on Hill's roads, but the ARU lived up to its contract and did nothing to obstruct the running of trains. The Pullman Company, and not the ARU, eventually prevailed.

One new practice, partly the result of the ARU strike, was centralized control of GN workers. Within six weeks after signing the ARU contract, the company established an Employment Bureau to compile and maintain records on all skilled employees; common laborers would not be included until more than

By 1913, the Great Northern had explicitly recognized national brotherhoods in the operating crafts, but many other crafts were forced to bargain at the local level.

forty years later. In 1898, the company took another step to systematize relations with workers. Henceforth, most of those seeking jobs were required to complete an application form for the Employment Bureau, and any employee's engagement, transfer, or promotion was confirmed by the assistant to the president.

Other actions inhibited the growth of unionism, although they were not so intended. Because common labor was scarce, the company signed a contract in February 1899 with the Oriental Trading Company to supply Japanese workers for maintenance on the western divisions. They were paid less than Caucasian laborers, performed well, and showed no interest in unions. Elsewhere, hiring immigrant groups further delayed unionizing. By 1912, an estimated 75 percent of summer gangs were Italians and Slavonians.[18]

Another new approach to employee relations was the Great Northern Employee Investment Company, a limited partnership, formed in 1900 for workers interested in the railroad's welfare. Under this program, an employee could purchase certificates in any multiple of $10 up to $5,000. When the amount received from an employee reached $100, the investment company purchased at par one share of GN stock to be held in trust for the subscriber. By 1909, 595 employees had taken advantage of the investment opportunity.

Toward Parity with Competitors, 1900–1916

In 1901, General Superintendent F. E. Ward asserted that one worker request "leads to another," and "on some roads that have yielded to demands for recognition of various unions it has come to a point where even sec-

tion laborers have formed a union and secured a contract with the railroad company. When such a state of affairs is reached the time of officers is mostly taken up listening to grievance committees."[19]

Despite such convictions, Ward and his successors accepted change. Officers responsible for employee relations recognized the general rise in consumer prices, the railroad unions' growing strength and demands, and the concessions made to them by rival carriers. Ward himself made decisions breaking with past practices. By a misunderstanding, a subordinate in Montana made one-year agreements in 1901 with national unions representing boilermakers and machinists. Ward considered repudiating the unauthorized contracts, and tried to avoid making any schedules in the next year. When the boilermakers struck, however, he settled with local committees for increased pay. In 1902, GN yardmen asked that the Switchmen's Union of North America (SUNA) be allowed to represent them, and Ward acquiesced, insisting, though, that a contract between the Twin City Railroad Association and the union be signed by representatives of GN employees, not by union officers. Thus, Ward upheld the company's tradition of refusing to recognize national unions as representatives of GN shop employees, but he abandoned Hill's earlier denial of bargaining rights for organizations of other than train-service workers.

Ward also made an agreement with locomotive engineers that was a substantial change in policy. A 1902 contract implicitly recognized the BLE and the Brotherhood of Locomotive Firemen (BLF, soon to be the Brotherhood of Locomotive Firemen & Enginemen, BLF&E) as agents in collective bargaining. It was signed by local officials of those organizations,

and Ward specifically agreed that these men could serve as union officers while employed by the company.

Ward soon found himself dealing with the unions' national officers. In 1902, the ORC and the BRT demanded of all railroads a 20 percent increase and double pay for trainmen on trains of more than thirty cars pulled by more than one locomotive. The unions' demand was frankly triggered by the GN's emphasis on heavy trains to achieve low cost per ton mile. Ward negotiated reluctantly. In the contract effective September 1, 1903, he succeeded in retaining the right to determine lengths of trains and allocation of power, but he granted pay raises and acceded to concessions on rules and procedures.

George T. Slade, following Ward in 1903, was more responsive than his predecessor in recognizing workers' positions. Slade negotiated full agreements with boilermakers and machinists and new schedules with enginemen —including those on both the Montana Central and the Willmar & Sioux Falls, breaching the practice of separate agreements for proprietary companies. In the contract with enginemen and in one with trainmen, representatives of the BLE, BLF, ORC, and BRT signed in their local fraternal capacities, according greater recognition to the national organizations.

After years of piecemeal alterations in bargaining practice, the GN made major changes in 1907. A year earlier, the BLE, BLF&E, ORC, and BRT presented demands to the western railroads; they particularly wanted eight hours as the basic day in freight service. Although the GN was not a member of the General Managers' Association of Chicago, Ward was invited and took part in the bargaining. In the resulting agreement, dated January

16, 1907, the basic day remained at ten hours, but freight engineers received higher rates than those in passenger service, and switch engineers got substantial increases. Comparable arrangements were worked out with the others.

By 1913, the GN had explicitly recognized the national brotherhoods as representatives of its employees in collective bargaining and also in disciplinary actions and in allocating men to new runs. The first such recognition came in 1908, when the GN signed an agreement accepting the recently enacted federal hours-of-service law. Four years later the company specifically agreed to allow the ORC and the BRT to act as agents for the GN's conductors and trainmen, and in 1913, the company accorded the BLE and BLF&E representation of its engineers and firemen, respectively.

For unorganized workers, though, GN managers continued to make unilateral decisions on pay, rules, and conditions of work. These groups were often aided, however, by pressure from those who were organized. Shopmen received the nine-hour day in 1907 because the GN wanted to retard unionization, and some raises in pay and reductions in hours for non-union personnel were made to maintain preexisting relationships in rates among groups and to eliminate disparities.

In some categories, GN wages were substantially below those of competing carriers. Its pay levels for section foremen were beneath those of the NP and the Milwaukee, and even some of the Soo wages were better than those of the GN. For accounting clerks, the GN's highest rate in 1916 was only 64 percent as high as that of the UP, partly because the GN lagged in adopting Hollerith and other machines that called for specialized skills. (See Table 5 for average GN wages from 1893 to 1913.)

Although the lower-paid groups were required to work long hours and were granted few vacations, their conditions did improve somewhat over the years. During the early 1890s, clerks had seven paid holidays a year; their work day began at 8:00 A.M. and ended at 6:00 P.M., six days a week. Changes were made in the mid-1890s when the day of the office picnic was added to the holidays; the clerk's day ended at 5:30 P.M., and in summer on Saturday at 1 P.M. In 1916, heads of departments continued to authorize vacations and sick leaves as they thought proper, no uniform rules having been set for this practice.

The company's practices on accidental injuries and death of employees continued with little change. The GN offered no insurance plan of its own, but encouraged workers to take out accident policies, permitted first one and later two companies to solicit business, and deducted premium payments from wages. For accidental death, the GN often paid expenses, although it bore no legal responsibility for doing so. Many inexperienced new employees, growing traffic, and faster trains led the GN to pay $787,865 for "injuries to persons" in 1916.

Some programs were meant to encourage cohesion and loyalty to the company. Company athletic teams and picnics helped, but the Veteran's Association, strongly encouraged by the Hills, was more effective. Organized in 1913, it was open to employees with twenty-five or more years of service. And the generous policy on passes for employees, especially to union members, showed an unsurpassed "degree of liberality," according to Carl Gray. On the other hand, the GN was slow to set up a formal retirement program, granting only a few small pensions to selected needy, long-term, and loyal employees. On September 16, 1916, the company finally implemented a plan, endowed at $1,000,000.[20]

The Great Northern's employee-relations policy in 1916 blended old and new. Company executives held many of GN's pay schedules and general labor costs below those of competitors, but at least for most operating crafts they had come to recognize the national brotherhoods as bargaining agents. Granting the nine-hour day and occasional raises in pay to nonunion workers helped maintain an effective force and minimize employees' departure to higher-paid jobs elsewhere. These arrangements would be put to severe test, though, when rising costs of living and World War I pressed greater demands on the Great Northern and the rest of the country's railroads.

Table 5. Average Daily Compensation, Selected Groups of Workers, 1893–1913

	1893	1898	1903	1908	1913	% change 1893–1913	% change 1908–1913
General Office Clerks	$2.59	$1.83	$2.00	$2.29	$2.26	−13	−01
Station Agents	1.92	1.76	1.84	2.36	2.40	25	02
Other Stationmen	1.93	1.50	1.49	1.84	1.98	03	08
Engineers	3.94	3.94	4.13	4.49	5.02	27	12
Firemen	2.33	2.29	2.35	2.91	3.34	43	15
Conductors	3.11	3.24	3.22	4.06	4.62	49	14
Other Trainmen	2.13	2.00	1.78	2.55	2.84	33	11
Machinists	2.85	2.69	3.27	3.71	4.25	49	15
Carpenters	2.53	2.36	2.52	2.75	2.81	11	02
Other Shopmen	1.93	1.76	1.85	2.18	2.29	19	05
Section Foremen	1.62	1.46	1.61	1.98	2.13	31	08
Other Trackmen	1.33	1.29	1.53	1.79	1.78	34	0
Switchmen, Flagmen, and Watchmen	2.02	2.13	1.58	1.89	1.80	−11	−05
Telegraph Operators and Dispatchers	2.07	2.08	2.08	2.64	2.71	32	03

Sources: ARGN-ICC, 1893, 1898, 1908, 1918.

PART II

1916
1970

Introduction

James Jerome Hill had delegated formal titles if not total managerial control to his son Louis W. Hill, but he did not ignore the Great Northern Railway and the many other enterprises and subjects that interested him. He remained outspoken on the need for a continuous capital program for the GN's main line—such as a much longer Cascade Tunnel—and con-

James Jerome Hill
1838–1916

tinued to speak out on topics as diverse as animal husbandry and international affairs. Indeed, Hill grew exceedingly anxious over the ultimate effects World War I would have—a conflict of calculated attrition, he concluded early. Strangely, however, Hill was much less anxious about his own good health, although for several years physicians had warned that he faced potentially severe problems. They were not surprised when he fell ill on May 17, 1916, was restricted to bed a few days later, and died of infection on May 29 at seventy-seven.

The "Empire Builder" was gone, as were his "associates." Their lasting legacy was the Great Northern Railway. Moreover, Hill's philosophy, values, and beliefs—a tightly operated system, turning out ton miles at a cost lower than that of your competitors, the need for a well-rounded mixture of traffic and a balance between equity and debt—were already institutionalized as the foundation of the Great Northern's corporate culture.

Also absent from the national landscape following Hill's death were the era of heroic entrepreneurship and, just as importantly, the railroad industry's near modal monopoly. Their replacements were professional managers, severe and subsidized competition from other forms of transport, and frequently ill-conceived and often heavy-handed government regulation. The history of the Great Northern to 1916 had essentially been that of forging a major transcontinental railroad; its record thereafter would be judged by how well the company's managers adapted to the new environment. The challenges were, in a word, monumental.

18

World War I and the USRA

World War I, raging in Europe since 1914, drew the United States inexorably into its web three years later. The impact on the country and on its transportation net was both dramatic and long term. For the Great Northern, the "war to end all wars" meant strong increases in the shipment of foodstuffs, iron ore, and war materiel. The conflict also brought governmental control, as it did to most of the country's railroads.[1]

The Heritage

Louis W. Hill's first major public statement after his father's death in 1916 reflected the company's traditional management philosophy. The organization was "splendid," nearly everyone in it had grown up with the road, and all had "as earnest an interest" in it as they would "in their own personal affairs." Louis Hill believed that the company served a truly "wonderful country." Opportunities for growth were "still very great," and the railroad was "pushing out new lines to serve undeveloped sections." Those extensions were "by no means doubtful as to results," boasted Hill, for settlers were still "coming in rapidly," and "large new areas" were being put under cultivation.[2]

Financial analysts agreed. One writer considered the Great Northern "one of the best managed and one of the rich railroads" in the United States. Its management was "able, both in the technical sense and also in its financial acumen"; few railways had "a more moderate bonded debt ahead of the stock, or a simpler financial structure." Furthermore, running through "a rich and growing country," the road had "opportunities for development beyond the dreams of avarice."[3]

Great Northern officers nevertheless had reason for unease. The company was suffering from the usual growth pains and some investments were slow to show profit. Key properties also needed upgrading, the GN had inadequate fleets of cars and locomotives, and a better Cascade Mountain crossing remained an unfulfilled dream. From a comparative standpoint, passenger service to the Pacific Coast was less attractive than that offered by the Northern Pacific.

Labor costs were another difficulty. To retain employees, the GN had been forced into piecemeal upward revisions in salary and wage schedules since 1914, but even more disturbing were new demands from the operating unions. For more than a year they had been demanding eight hours as the basic work day, as well as modified work rules and conditions of work, and, hoping to achieve their goals by legislation, they had declined to have the issues submitted to an impartial body of arbitrators.

Railroads in general were in the difficult position of being unable to adjust rates commensurately with changing times. Walker D. Hines wrote, "private management was management only in a partial sense." The Interstate Commerce Commission, after all, controlled interstate rates, and in some of the states, rates

were fixed "absolutely"; in others, they were set by carriers only with state approval. By mid-1916, all roads experienced unpleasant pressure on freight rates, imposed by regulatory as well as competitive forces. During the previous year the GN had made "no less than thirty" changes, mostly downward, affecting "nearly every kind of business and nearly all localities." For the company the most significant had been the ICC order in June 1915 reducing iron-ore rates from 60 cents to 55 cents per long ton.[4]

All of this reflected changed and changing circumstances for the nation's carriers. About one-sixth of rail mileage was in receivership, and the Newlands Committee, established in 1916 by President Wilson's request, sought "explanations" and was expected to propose legislative remedies. Before the Newlands group had begun its work, however, the brotherhoods, after a bitter confrontation with management, won passage of the Adamson Act for an eight-hour day. This legislation provided that a worker had to be paid at the same rate for eight hours as formerly for ten; it also meant increasing payment for work beyond the normal work day as well as for work on Sundays and holidays. For employees covered by this law, compensation would rise by 25 percent or more, and no operating employee could be asked to work more than sixteen hours in any twenty-four. Louis Hill estimated that these new requirements would add $100 million to the operating expenses of the nation's railroads.[5]

Meanwhile the GN, like other carriers, faced massive problems in operations. By September 1916, President Louis Hill realized that the nationwide shortage of freight cars was critical. In mid-October, more than 19 percent of cars owned by the GN were off-line, and

available foreign equipment often was not in good condition. For lack of rolling stock, half a million bushels of grain were piled up at GN stations in Montana, and by late November the company was unable to fill 50 percent of requests for transporting coal.

The Great Northern's experience was simply one element in the growing transportation crisis. On December 1, 1916, the ICC asserted that congestion, delays, and shortages of cars had marred the entire year. The commission subsequently observed that in the West, "mills had shut down, prices advanced," and perishables had rotted because cars were "being held" away from home roads. Meanwhile, in the East "there had been so many cars on the lines and in the terminals . . . that service had been thrown into unprecedented confusion." The commission not only condemned lax observance of car service rules, but called for a major expansion in railroad facilities to ensure adequate response to shippers' demands.[6]

Immediately after America entered the war, executives of leading railroads, as members of the American Railway Association (ARA), agreed to create a "national railway system" by coordinating their operations and reducing competitive activities. Responsibility for such cooperation was given to the Association's Special Committee on National Defense. It, in turn, delegated power to the Railroads' War Board, whose members strove to induce railway companies to observe rules for servicing cars, to pool box cars, to load cars more fully, and to discontinue unnecessary passenger trains. This board also adopted measures to expedite export shipments, and at the Great Lakes ports to ensure timely movement of ore eastward and coal westward.

On its own behalf, GN management expanded orders for new equipment. Late in

1916, the company ordered 50 locomotives, 15 steel mail cars, and 2,000 freight cars. To this list, during the next twelve months, it added 44 locomotives and 20 steel baggage cars. From July 1, 1916, to December 31, 1917, expenditures for motive power and rolling stock reached almost $5.3 million, compared with $1.1 million for fiscal 1916.

Upgrading of roadway and structures, although done selectively, ranged over the entire system. The roadbed was improved on more than 1,000 miles of line, 154 miles of main track were relaid with ninety-pound rail, and in Montana the GN installed a second main track at several places. Terminal facilities in the heart of Vancouver, British Columbia, were brought into full service, and at St. Paul, the GN built an 800-foot freight depot. These and other improvements were designed, of course, to relieve congestion and smooth the flow of traffic.

At the same time, the GN brought a few miles of new line into service. The Great Falls & Teton County Railway added 8.7 miles from Bynum to Pendroy, and the Montana Eastern, 23.8 miles from Lambert to Richey, Montana. Construction from Wildrose to Grenora in North Dakota extended the Stanley Branch by 36.32 miles. All opened new land for producing wheat.[7]

Throughout 1916 and 1917, GN officers concentrated on meeting increased demands rather than generating new traffic. The GN's expenditures for agricultural development were curtailed, but the program was continued. E. C. Leedy, who had headed this work since 1909, reported that his department was "encouraging this movement [of farmers to virgin lands] in every possible way and [we] are advising settlers to put in every possible acre."

In one three-week period early in 1916, the GN carried 3,000 people with 600 cars of immigrant movables to Montana; in 1917, the federal land office at Havre listed 7,500 entries, more than twice the number for 1912.[8]

Meanwhile, the rising cost of materials and increased taxes were general difficulties, but GN managers became thoroughly alarmed by huge leaps in labor costs. Total compensation rose from less than $31 million in 1916 to almost $37 million in 1917, partly because the average number of employees had grown modestly, but most was attributable to pay raises made mandatory by the Adamson Act and by stiff competition for labor from war industries.

The carriers sought compensating rate increases, but in June 1917, the ICC rejected requests for any general advance. It did, however, agree to periodic selective escalations. The one that mattered most for the GN was the increase from 55 cents per long ton of iron ore to 63.5 cents, effective July 27, 1917. This rise of more than 15 percent on a commodity furnishing more than 40 percent of the company's tonnage and about 13 percent of freight revenue made a decided difference. In general, though, concessions by the ICC were unrealistically low compared with increased operating costs.

By many measures, the GN, along with other American railroads, made a creditable record in 1916 and 1917. Tonnage handled jumped from 23,453,000 in fiscal 1915 to 30,651,000 in 1917; most of this growth was in manufactured products and iron ore. The number of passengers declined slightly, but they traveled farther, and passenger miles went up 16 percent.

Nevertheless, revenues fell behind in the race with expenses. Railway operating reve-

William P. Kenney became federal manager of the Great Northern during the period of USRA control.

nues showed a gain of 22.6 percent from 1915 to 1917, but railway operating expenses rose more than 57 percent. From 1915 through 1917, the GN's operating ratios (operating expenses to operating revenues) were 52.3, 58.3, and 66.9 percent, respectively. During the same period, net revenues from operations dropped almost 15 percent, and net corporate income more than 8 percent ($25,156,000 to $23,040,000). Although the company continued to pay its stockholders dividends of 7 percent, the downward trend in net corporate income was not encouraging.

Despite strenuous efforts, the GN shared in the rail carriers' ultimate failure to meet wartime demands. By voluntary cooperation, they had reduced passenger service, pooled freight equipment, eliminated much congestion at eastern terminals, and minimized car shortages. During fall 1917, however, heavy harvest traffic, early cold weather, and a crisis in coal shipping made the need for equipment desperate. By November 1, 1917, the number of cars awaiting unloading at eastern ports was unprecedented. The GN had wrenching shortages of equipment for shipment of lumber, apples, potatoes, hay, feed, and coal — especially west of Williston, N.D.

Both lasting and immediate factors contributed to the carriers' inability to perform adequately. Unfavorable money-market conditions had reduced funds for purchasing new equipment after 1913, the federal government requisitioned rolling stock for overseas use, and scarce labor hindered repairs. Furthermore, conflicting priorities applied by the Army, Navy, Shipping Board, and other government agencies showered confusion on all railroads. Frequently the lack of ships, worsened by losses to German submarines, compounded congestion at eastern ports. The Railroads' War Board tried to arrange unification and pooling, but was inhibited by congressional refusal to suspend antitrust laws and by antipooling provisions in the Interstate Commerce Act. Furthermore, it was clearly unrealistic to expect railroad executives, without some guarantee that their stockholders would not suffer, to release equipment in substantial quantities to other lines.

The ICC recognized how bad the shortages were, and declared early in December 1917 that unifying railroad operations was indispensable to "their fullest utilization for the National Defense and welfare."[9]

Great Northern under Federal Control

Although the Railroad's War Board presented a last-minute appeal for voluntary unification of service, President Wilson proclaimed that as of January 1, 1918, the government would take possession and control of privately owned railroad properties. He named as Director General of Railroads the Secretary of the Treasury, William G. McAdoo, who immediately set up the United States Railroad Administration (USRA). McAdoo immediately divided the country into seven operating regions, each administered by a director. Within a region were districts served by specific railroads, each company being headed by a federal manager, usually the former president. On March 21, 1918, Congress passed the Federal Control Act outlining financial and other terms under which the Director General was to make agreements with the railroads.

Government operation significantly changed the GN's leadership. When Louis W. Hill refused to take a government job, the directors designated William P. Kenney as their nominee for federal manager. They also elected him president of the GN, a post he held from February to July, 1918. Kenney, born in Wisconsin of Irish descent, had started his career as a telegrapher and joined the GN in 1902. Promotions followed, and ten years later he was vice president of traffic, a position he held until named president. At midyear 1918, the USRA decided that separation between government and private corporate loyalties was desirable. Thus, Chairman of the Board Louis W. Hill resumed the presidency, but Ralph Budd, executive vice president since February 12, 1918, acted as chief executive officer.

Kenney, like other federal managers, was governed by the Federal Control Act. Compensation for each company was to be a "standard return" equivalent to the average net railway operating income for a three-year "test period" ending June 30, 1917. Because each company's circumstances differed from all others', the Control Act provided for adjustments according to several factors, including enlargement of system, exceptional additions to equipment, and the like. The USRA agreed to continue operating local and through service, to maintain way, structures, and equipment, and to make accounting adjustments later. It also took over the operating revenues, operating expenses, taxes other than war levies, and rents on equipment and joint facilities. For its part, the GN received nonoperating income and the standard return; from the sum of the two, it paid its corporate expenses, rents, miscellaneous and war taxes, interest, other charges, and dividends. The key item in the contract, as in those with other carriers, provided for the railroad to be returned to the corporation "in substantially as good repair and in substantially as complete equipment" as on January 1, 1918.[10]

Following USRA policy, Kenney practically stopped immigration and agricultural development work, discontinued solicitation of traffic, closed off-line ticket offices, and did no promotional advertising. The GN accepted such curtailment of passenger operations that those responsible for that function felt that "the passenger business of the Great Northern Railroad was sacrificed beyond that of any other Western line in the supreme effort to win the war." The American Railway Express Company, organized to conduct the express service of railroads taken over by the government, also leased the property of the GN's wholly owned

Great Northern Express Company. The latter was never revived. The GN joined the Milwaukee, the Soo Line, and the Northern Pacific in consolidated use of various terminals. For economy, freight was rerouted among the several railroads, but traffic lost by the GN was more or less compensated for by that gained.[11]

While the GN's federal manager was forcing economies under USRA orders, he was losing the fight against rising cost of supplies and labor. Fuel consumed by locomotives in both 1918 and 1919 declined in comparison with 1917, but the cost of that fuel rose by 34 percent in 1918 and dropped but slightly over the next twelve months. At the same time, while the average number of employees in GN service rose 5.4 percent, total compensation increased 48 percent. For average hourly earnings of railroad workers in the nation, exclusive of officers, the index number (1915 = 100) stood at 129 in December 1917, at 198 a year later, and at 225 for the first quarter of 1920.

Director General William G. McAdoo and his successor, Walker D. Hines, argued that the USRA raised wages no more than conditions demanded. After all, they said, during the twenty-six months of government operation, the cost of living rose more rapidly than increases in compensation for railroad employees. Moreover, all pay raises were approved not only by labor spokesmen but also by management representatives working for the USRA

A national climate for labor relations was a more lasting change. McAdoo also established a special Board of Railroad Wages and Working Conditions, representing both labor and management, and responsible for specific categories of railroad work. Boards of Adjustment decisions in interpreting contracts and settling

disputes brought to the attention of *all* railroad unions and spread into practice rules and conditions of work that had been accepted by *some* railroad companies.

Broad changes were made in just a few months. The USRA recognized railroad employees right to unionize and to have collective bargaining and accepted seniority as the guide for pay and promotion. That agency also abolished piecework in the shops. For all railroads and their workers, the USRA extended the eight-hour day, time-and-a-half pay for overtime, and standardized and detailed job classifications that would in the end be unproductive. Nonoperating employees made clear gains when five of their unions concluded national agreements with the Railroad Administration.

For the GN and other railroads the most disturbing immediate result of the new compensation policy was an abrupt increase in operating expenses. The GN's operating expenditures rose 46 percent from 1917 to 1919, but its operating revenues increased by only 20 percent. Consequently, the company's operating ratio went from 66.9 in 1917 to 83.8 a year later, falling back only to 81.4 in 1919. The peaks were higher and spreads greater than those of many other railroads.

The primary reason for inadequate growth in operating revenue was that the USRA authorized increased passenger and freight rates only once during the twenty-six months of federal control. Because expenses rose more sharply than revenue, the GN fell far short of making its standard return. Instead of $28,777,361, the yearly average in the ''test period'' (fiscal 1915–1917), the company reported net railway operating income of only $11,978,791 in 1918 and $12,459,618 a year later.

In service performed, the record was mixed. Tonnage hauled by the GN in 1918 was slightly above that for 1917, but for 1919 it declined 11 percent from that of 1918. In contrast to changes in freight tonnage, the number of passengers carried in 1918 fell 13 percent below that in 1917, then rose 17 percent in 1919.

Return to Private Operation

Throughout this period of government control, the GN's senior officers—Louis W. Hill and Ralph Budd—had been caring for company affairs outside Federal Manager Kenney's jurisdiction. They supervised and acted as banker for nonoperating subsidiaries; eleven subsidiaries received advances amounting to $1,050,000 in 1918. Various other actions reduced costs and investments. By an agreement with the Milwaukee early in 1918, the GN acquired trackage rights in perpetuity over eighteen miles of road between Monroe and Tolt, Washington, enabling the GN to remove its line between those stations, and the same two companies agreed to jointly construct a line in Montana from Lewistown and Grass Range to Winnett. During 1919, the GN also began slowly reducing its unprofitable investment in rail lines serving British Columbia. The company removed track between Hazelmere and Port Kells, abandoned forty miles of the Vancouver, Victoria & Eastern Railway when the mine at Phoenix closed, and sold VV&E properties on Vancouver Island to the Canadian National Railway.

The GN additionally completed disposing of its maritime operations. The *Dakota* had been lost to accident several years earlier, leaving the *Minnesota* the GN's only steamship in the trans-Pacific trade. In 1917, the railroad sold her to the Atlantic Transport Company, and thereafter depended on contracts with the Nippon Yusen Kaisha of Japan for connecting service to the Orient. The Great Northern Pacific Steamship Company, jointly owned by the GN and the NP, terminated coastwide service when the *Great Northern* and the *Northern Pacific* were commandeered for military service and purchased by the federal government in September 1917. Even before, the GN's Northern Steamship Company, which had operated on the Great Lakes, sold its *Northwest*, and when this subsidiary disposed of the *Northland* late in 1918, the last steamship affiliate ceased to exist. Some of the vessels to which James J. Hill had devoted so much personal attention continued separate lives, however: serving as a troopship in two world wars, the *Great Northern* would be at Omaha Beach on June 6, 1944.

Financial management during federal operation proved relatively easy. The largest outlays went for distribution of dividends ($17,463,000 annually, the rate remaining at 7 percent), payment of interest (more than $11,736,000 annually), and purchase of Liberty bonds ($5,025,000). The sum of $3,089,000 was appropriated for and invested in physical property. Revenues came from several sources: advances against rentals due from the USRA, dividends on Burlington stock earmarked for paying interest on the joint NP–GN bonds issued in 1901, smaller amounts from rentals, dividends and interest from funded and unfunded debt of several affiliated firms, and more than $1 million in cash from sale of Liberty bonds.

Through the last twelve months of federal control the USRA and the carrier corporations (including the GN) argued over apportioning expenditures for betterments. The difficulty lay

in agreeing on which outlays were for current operation, and so to be borne by the USRA, and which were properly to be charged against capital account, the railroads' responsibility. To fortify contentions about inadequate federal maintenance, Ralph Budd drew up in August 1919 a detailed report based on extensive inspection. Budd said the Minot Division was in "much poorer condition" than earlier, and rail on the Kalispell Division was too light for cur-

The *Great Northern* eventually became the *H. F. Alexander*, operated by the Pacific Steamship Company.

rent locomotives and the volume of traffic. In places, as on the Cascade Division, the track was in acceptable shape. Everywhere, however, curtailed maintenance of roadway threatened future GN efficiency.[12]

As he pondered claims for postwar settlement, Louis Hill supported campaigns for two kinds of federal legislation: to define conditions under which the railroad properties were to be returned to private operation, and to establish policies and powers for the ICC and other regulatory agencies. To these ends, the GN gave its support for a program advocated by the Association of Railway Executives (ARE). Organized around a nucleus of the wartime Railway Executives Advisory Committee, the ARE created a standing Committee of Twenty-five to campaign for desired legislation.

The ARE was one of many interest groups suggesting plans for the future of the country's railroads. One month after the armistice on November 11, 1918, William G. McAdoo proposed continuing government operation for five years before returning the properties to individual railroad companies. More threatening by far were Glenn E. Plumb's ideas. Speaking for the four train-service brotherhoods, he vigorously recommended that the federal government purchase the carriers' properties, create a national operating corporation, and lease these properties to it. Among other interested groups were the Interstate Commerce Commission, the National Association of Owners of Railroad Securities, the National Industrial Traffic League (a shippers' organization), and many who supported scientific management for railroads. All the last-mentioned groups opposed nationalization, but all wanted stronger regulation.

Congress obviously had to reconcile widely conflicting ideas. Members listened to and weighed proposals by investors, shippers, and railroad employees, as well as the Association of Railway Executives. Congressmen generally concluded that the time was not opportune for

experiment and relied heavily on "tutelage" by the ICC. Thus the Esch-Cummins Act, known also as the Transportation Act of 1920, was a compromise measure leaving the door open for pragmatic solutions. After some days of indecision, President Wilson signed the document on February 28, 1920.[13]

The ARE and the companies it represented won acceptance for at least part of their program. Above all, on March 1, 1920, the railroads were to be returned to private operation. Esch-Cummins recognized two grand principles: regulation should assure the carriers of adequate earnings to restore the railroads' credit, and federal regulatory authority would be supreme when in conflict with state decisions. Specifically, the ICC was empowered to make rates that would allow "carriers as a whole," or in groups, to earn "an aggregate annual net railway operating income equal, as nearly as may be, to a fair return upon the aggregate value" of the railroad's property. For the first two years after March 1, 1920, the "fair return" was set at 5½ percent, which the ICC might raise later to 6 percent.[14]

The new law further extended federal control to certain competitive practices. The ICC was empowered to set minimum rates, to permit pooling under prescribed circumstances, and to regulate new construction. It also gained authority over abandonment of lines, use of joint terminals, and even issuance of securities. The commission also received comprehensive powers over rules for car service at all times and over movement of traffic in emergencies. Most welcome for the carriers was the provision giving the regulatory agency ultimate authority over intrastate rates, if and when they conflicted with the new interstate policy.

In yet another departure the Transportation Act of 1920 vested the ICC with power over acquisitions by and consolidations of railroad companies. Of more lasting importance, the regulatory agency was instructed to prepare and adopt plans for consolidating the country's railroads into a few systems of relatively equal earning power. In making such plans, the ICC was to preserve competition as fully as possible and maintain present routes as far as practicable.

In another area, the law required creation of the Railroad Labor Board, on which employers, employees, and the public were each to have three members. Disputes over grievances, rules, or working conditions, if not resolved in conference, were to go to local, regional, or national boards of adjustment formed by voluntary agreement between carriers and labor. If no understanding was reached, the controversy was to go directly to the Railroad Labor Board, as were wage disutes if not settled in conference. Decisions of the board, which was primarily an arbitration agency, were to be enforced by nothing more than public opinion.

As GN officers and directors prepared to resume control of the company's property, they could review the years since 1916 with mixed pride and unease. Despite great handicaps, the company had carried, in peace and in war, more freight and passengers than during any comparable period in its history, and it had met, with relative success, its customers' demands for service. While under government control, however, the maintenance of property, except motive power, had deteriorated to the point that, for effective performance in the future, massive investment was necessary. The USRA had also established a labor policy enhancing the unions' power and so increased railway operating expenses that profitability was undermined. As GN managers looked to the future, they realized that upgrading property and performance was essential, but they could only wonder if profitable operation was possible under conditions imposed by the Transportation Act of 1920.

19

Of Good News and Bad

Railroad officers across the country looked forward eagerly to resuming private management on March 1, 1920. They had accepted federal operation as a matter of patriotic obligation, but few wanted to remain government employees. The Great Northern's managers shared this attitude and, several months before the United States Railroad Administration was scheduled to relinquish control, they began to plan for changes essential to the company's future welfare. When control was transferred, it proceeded smoothly, but during the first years of private management adverse economic conditions forced postponement or modification of many plans.[1]

Preparing for Control

Because Louis W. Hill did not choose to be the company's chief executive officer, directors had to elect a new president, and chose Ralph Budd. The October 9, 1919 decision surprised Budd, who had expected William P. Kenney to be named, but it surprised few others. Born August 20, 1879, Ralph Budd spent his childhood on a farm in central Iowa, attended high school in Des Moines, and studied civil engineering at Highland Park College, graduating in 1899. Following varied service

with the Chicago Great Western, the Chicago, Rock Island & Pacific, and the Panama Railroad, Budd joined the GN in 1909. Starting as an engineer for the Oregon Trunk, he became chief engineer of the Spokane, Portland & Seattle in 1910, and on January 1, 1913, moved to the GN at St. Paul as assistant to the president. Already knowledgeable about the company's property in the Pacific Northwest, Budd was soon acquainted with all phases of the GN's operations, and in 1918 was named vice president. James J. Hill himself had groomed Budd for a top managerial post, instilling in

Ralph Budd was chosen president of the Great Northern on October 9, 1919.

him the idea that the "prime objective of a railroad is to produce the maximum transportation service with the minimum amount of effort."[2]

Budd was omnivorous in absorbing facts, cool and detached in analysis, quick and decisive in judgment. He had the rare ability to delegate authority but at the same time to keep himself fully informed. Subordinates regarded the new president as firm but fair; they also commented that he was not as arbitrary as J. J. Hill, or as unpredictable as L. W. Hill, or as explosive as W. P. Kenney. He was at ease in the work of making decisions, and had a well-developed sense of history; years after an event he could give full credit to those who had suggested new policies or carried through significant programs. Jackson E. Reynolds, who for some years headed the First National Bank of the City of New York, and was an authority on railroads and the men managing them, believed that Budd was the best railroad officer of his generation and that he would have been a top executive in any field.[3]

As his chief assistants Budd chose two of the ablest men in the GN organization. W. P. Kenney agreed to assume again the office of vice president-traffic, a position for which he was well suited. For vice president-operations, Budd's choice was Charles O. Jenks, son of Cyrus H. Jenks, a division superintendent and long a trusted favorite of James J. Hill. The younger Jenks had held GN positions ranging from clerk to assistant general manager.

Jenks came to be one of the most feared, yet one of the most respected of GN officers. Fiery by temperament, he had little patience with incompetence. He drove himself and his men unceasingly, praising them for accomplishment but discharging them summarily if they failed to live up to his expectations. Jenks

particularly prided himself on recruiting executive trainees from among college graduates, especially those from Yale University, one of the few institutions offering courses in railroad transportation. The subsequent success of these young men, many of whom earned high positions with the GN and other railroads, enhanced Jenk's reputation as one of the nation's most competent operating officers.

Charles O. Jenks, though he had wit, was often sardonic. On an inspection trip, one time, he got word that a switch engine at Crookston, Minnesota, had wandered without apparent reason into the turntable pit. What should be done? asked the local official. Jenks immediately ordered that another switch engine at the location assist the "big hook" (wrecker) in extricating the first locomotive. Later, as his inspection train rolled onward, a wayside station telegraph operator hooped up another message. Now, reported the local official at Crookston, the hook too was in the pit. Should another wrecker be summoned? "Hell no," scribbled Jenks on a company telegraph form, "there's no more room in the pit at Crookston!"[4]

Most of the GN's top officers served throughout Ralph Budd's tenure as president. Along with Jenks and Kenney, they were E. T. Nichols, financial guide extraordinary in New York; angular and soft-spoken F. L. Paetzold, secretary and treasurer; and meticulous comptroller George H. Hess. Luthene C. Gilman was made vice president-executive department in Seattle during the first year of Budd's administration and held that position until 1937.

Continuity held together the board, at least its nucleus, in these years. At its center were L. W. Hill as chairman, with his continuing interest in finance and the passenger business,

and Budd, Nichols, Kenney, Edward E. Loomis, and F. E. Weyerhaeuser. With these members, group meetings could be in either New York or St. Paul. Representation continued among leading businessmen in the Twin Cities and over the years others from the railroad's territory, chiefly bankers, served on the board, as did financial experts from New York. Arthur Curtiss James, a large investor in the GN and other railroads, provided sage advice as had his father on the board of the St. Paul, Minneapolis & Manitoba in the 1880s.

To Budd and his associates, as they prepared to take control, the immediate objective was clear: they had to provide service at a level that would enable the company, after paying its traditional 7 percent dividend, to generate funds needed for major improvements. They understood that labor would remain costly by prewar standards, so the company would have to achieve greater efficiency—mainly by running longer and heavier trains. This would require improvement of road and structures to facilitate larger locomotives and cars, and a much better crossing of the Cascades.

Some indicators gave reason for optimism, others were mixed. Heavy traffic—both passenger and freight—in the last six months of 1919 implied prosperity for the following year, and agricultural production, though unsatisfactory in Montana and western North Dakota, was high elsewhere in GN territory. In fact, rolling stock and personnel were so strained to meet demands for service that railroaders, including those of the GN, could watch relatively unperturbed as modal competition grew. Truck rates, though, were already competitive with rail tariffs in some areas for distances up to one hundred miles, and intercity travelers were taking to their automobiles or to motor

A heavy volume of traffic during the last six months of 1919 implied prosperity for the following year.

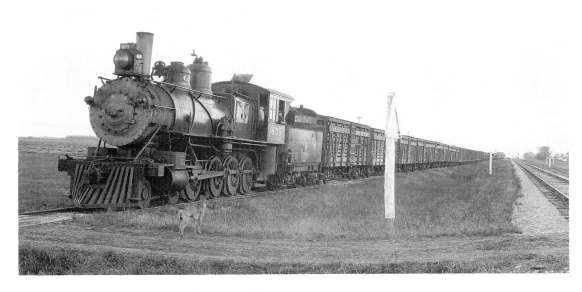

buses. Nevertheless, railroaders still saw highways primarily as feeders for rails.

In this environment, the GN moved to meet the first of its many needs after resuming private management. The board authorized purchase of 30,000 tons of rail and fifty locomotives "to keep up with the demands of our territory and to increase earnings." Additional plans were made to acquire freight equipment, and they gave some thought to upgrading passenger cars. The budget for 1920 stipulated capital expenditures for improvements of more than $11 million, greatly exceeding the average spent in each of the preceding two years.[5]

The Great Northern could tap several sources for funding. It could sell its Liberty Bonds or use its plentiful supply of unpledged securities as collateral for short-term loans. Equipment trusts might well replace the Great Northern Equipment Company as a means for financing purchase of rolling stock, but the most attractive of founts was the federal government, which still owed the company about $4,950,000 for the period of government operation. The government could make advances to the GN on a guaranteed standard return for six months ending August 31, 1920, and it could lend the company some of the $300 million from a fund created under the Transportation Act of 1920.

Frustrations and Realities

During the first months of private operations, officials discovered again that expectations do not always square with realities. The transition from federal control went smoothly enough, but a sharp divergence from the anticipated economic climate resulted in a record of performance quite different from that envisioned in 1919.

William P. Kenney, as head of the traffic department, once again emphasized vigorous and personal solicitation for business, and by May 1920, he believed that progress was being made, although he expected that it would "take some time to get back all that we have lost during two years of federal control." Kenney also reactivated programs for stimulating immigration and agricultural development.[6]

Meanwhile, property was upgraded according to plan. Capital expenditures for equipment in 1920 were $17.4 million, including $7.1 million to purchase from the Great Northern Equipment Company rolling stock acquired in earlier years. Additions and betterments for roadway and structures in 1920 showed a net capital outlay of $5.2 million, used to renovate several yards, to lay 221 miles of ninety-pound rail, to improve water-supply facilities, and to build a new wharf at Seattle.

Despite these efforts, results were less favorable than Budd had hoped. Fuel costs rose by more than $3 million, and tax accruals went up 26 percent. Car supply was a constant headache. Not even Budd's threat to take GN out of the American Railway Association did much to increase the return flow of company-owned equipment that circulated off-line.

The cost of labor gave far greater trouble. In 1920, the company employed an average of 41,400 workers, 7.3 percent more than in 1919, and paid them $71.3 million, a devastating jump of 30 percent in aggregate compensation. Managers attributed 46 percent of this growth to 1920 Railway Labor Board decisions that raised railroad pay rates 22 percent. Railway wages, like wholesale prices, now were 240 percent higher than in 1900, but freight rates were up only 30 percent. Occasional adjustments in passenger and freight rates compensated only in part. Passenger fares were raised 20 percent in August 1920, and at the same time, the ICC granted general increases in regional freight rates, ranging from 25 to 40 percent.

The GN's record for 1920 was mixed. More passengers were carried than in 1919, but freight tonnage went up a more satisfying 20 percent because mine products grew in volume by 40 percent and manufactured items 14 percent. Still operating revenue failed to keep up with operating expenditures. The former rose 15 percent in one year, but the latter rose 31 percent, pushing the operating ratio from 81.4 in 1919 to 91.2 a year later, highest in the company's history. Budd understood the ramifications. Because the GN had not been able to control costs, net operating income was so low

For the Great Northern there was too little of this activity in 1921. A sharp recession forced many mills to shut down entirely.

as to bode ill for the future. Moreover, the economy was turning sour.

Fighting Recession

By the last quarter of 1920, Budd recognized that the nation was in a sharp recession. Long-range plans for improving the railroad and setting it on a proper course for the future had to be interrupted. Also, low earnings impaired the GN's credit just when the company needed its best reputation to obtain low interest rates for refunding Chicago, Burlington & Quincy Joint GN–NP 4 percent bonds maturing in June 1921.

The recession's severity was attested by numerous indicators. In 1913 dollars, wholesale prices for all commodities slid from an index of 227.9 in 1920 to 150.6 in 1921. Retail prices declined somewhat less. Raw-material and farm-product prices fell almost to prewar levels. The country's gross national product dropped only 6.6 percent, but the number of unemployed at the nadir was estimated at 4,754,000. Bankruptcies reached about 100,000.

The GN's freight customers were primarily producers and processors of farm products and basic raw materials, exposing the company to the full weight of recession. At the beginning of 1921, West Coast lumbermen were shutting down mills, and iron and steel producers had curtailed output by a third, foreshadowing substantially reduced iron-ore shipments. Meanwhile, the dramatic collapse in prices for grain, combined with four dry years on the northern high plains, crushed many farmers. Of the estimated 453,000 forced to give up their land, a disproportionate number were in GN territory.

The bad news rolled on. Shippers demanded reduced rates, traffic was lost to the Panama Canal (in full peacetime operation for the first time), and the price of coal for locomotive fuel continued to rise. At the same time, union leaders strongly opposed any cut in wages or change in wartime work rules, and the new national system for resolving railway labor disputes was so ponderous that the carriers could effect modifications only with great difficulty, if at all.

President Budd struggled to generate business while reducing expenditures at every turn. W. P. Kenney doubled the advertising budget and hired more traffic solicitors, for Budd thought it would be "very shortsighted to curtail forces of the Traffic Department" or do anything that would hinder "that department in going after business." And, to increase trans-Pacific shipments, the GN signed a new agreement with the Japanese steamship company, Nippon Yusen Kaisha, renewing a relationship formed in 1896.[7]

Kenney's chief method for attracting business was adjusting freight tariffs. To that end the GN reduced rates on many commodities, including smelter products in Washington; sand, gravel, and low-grade ore in Montana; coke in Minnesota; and all freight to western Canada. Between March and December 1921, either on its own or at ICC behest, the GN cut rates on lumber to every section of the United States, removed about half the increases over 1920 levels, cut another 10 percent on grains, and even more on livestock. Tariffs on farm commodities thus remained relatively low compared to those on manufactured goods, a disparity which, Ralph Budd thought, created an "unfortunate rate situation in the Northwest compared with the East."[8]

While Kenney battled for every scrap of traffic, Charles O. Jenks fought to hold down the cost of handling it. The company made only one major purchase of equipment in 1921 — 500 refrigerator cars — and held equipment expenditures on capital account to a mere $1,285,000. Outlays for maintenance of equipment were 21 percent below those of the previous year, and Jenks canceled much scheduled work, permitted little new rail to be laid, and directed his engineers to equip no more than fifty-five miles of line with block signals. Tie and rail renewals almost equaled those of 1920, but most came from inventory purchased earlier. In 1921, outlays for maintenance of roadway and structures dropped 46 percent.[9]

Caught between constantly escalating wage scales and less and less adequate rates, officers of the nation's railroads scrambled for relief. Rail workers, however, were in no mood to give up their large war-period gains, and their leaders pledged to resist management requests. In the end, the Railway Labor Board reduced wages about 12 percent, leaving them some 100 percent above those of March 1, 1920. Union leaders with the operating brotherhood in the van, immediately asked for and won approval for a strike. When the RLB pointed out, however, that employees who struck would voluntarily remove themselves "from the classes entitled to appeal" for "relief and protection," the unions reluctantly accepted the verdict.[10]

On the Great Northern, the average number of employees and their aggregate compensation declined about a third in 1921, but the average annual pay per employee remained more than twice as high as in 1916, and salaries and wages still absorbed 58 percent of expenses.

Accounts for 1921 showed net income of $28.5 million, but that included large chunks of "other income." The most significant was the Burlington's dividend of $21.8 million — more than $17.5 million greater than the GN had received from the CB&Q in 1920. Only in that way was the GN able to pay its usual 7 percent dividend. The GN's credit fell embarrassingly. Writers in financial periodicals and other observers remarked that the road was really paying dividends out of surplus, and even the hometown St. Paul *Pioneer Press* advised a widow to sell her GN stock "without delay in spite of the small loss which you will have to accept in the transaction." Not since 1890 had shares sold as low as 60, the bottom quotation for the postwar depression.[11]

Resuming Course — with a Difference

Budd was disappointed by GN's operations in 1921, and yet he remained optimistic because he assumed that the economy would soon recover, as it did. Agricultural output increased and manufacturers resumed producing to meet rebounding demand. In GN territory, production on farm and ranch as well as in forest, mill, and mine either held steady or increased; Oregon and Washington put out almost 50 percent more lumber from 1921 to 1922.[12]

Budd's optimism, combined with his belief that the GN would help significantly in stimulating recovery, caused him to move forward with capital plans. In all, the GN pledged to spend $15 million in 1922 for rolling stock and roadway improvements. Budd was true to his word. Four locomotives of the Mikado type were built in GN shops, using parts of dismantled Mallets; older engines were rebuilt as modern Pacifics; more were converted from coal to oil; and still others were improved to increase tractive effort and fuel efficiency. Shop forces also overhauled nearly a hundred of the company's older coaches. Other improvements included 175 miles of automatic block signals, as well as new culverts and steel and concrete bridges to carry the new, heavier rolling stock.

One very dark cloud appeared, however. Budd's hope for continued improvement in the GN's labor relations was dashed at least temporarily by a long and expensive nationwide strike by shop craft unions. After erupting on July 1, 1922, it dragged on through the summer. The controversy arose from managements' pressure to reduce wages and the unions' disaffection with that idea. While negotiating unsuccessfully with several unions for new contracts, the country's railroads requested that the RLB authorize cuts in wages, to become effective simultaneously with reduced freight rates. After long deliberation, the board announced that the railroads might put into effect, on July 1, reductions ranging from 2 to 9 cents an hour for several categories of workers: clerical and station forces, employees on stationary engines, workers in boiler rooms, and those in the signal department. Signalmen and maintenance-of-way employees accepted the decision, but the Railway Employees Department of the American Federation of Labor refused to accede and called the shop employees' strike.

Violence broke out almost immediately. When strikers seized control of some GN properties in Montana, the company hired strikebreakers and guards, encouraged friendly workers to report to management on strikers' activities, obtained injunctions against strike

activity, and issued an embargo on freight in Montana. The company also contracted with an outside firm to rebuild 3,500 box cars. After guards killed a striking brakeman, the GN asked futilely for aid from the Montana militia, but did receive help from federal marshals. Meanwhile, rail service deteriorated, although trains continued to run.

Bitter as the long shopmen's strike was, occasional incidents demonstrated GN employees' traditional underlying loyalty toward their employer. The men who ordinarily handled the wrecking outfit stationed at Whitefish were on strike, of course, but after a serious derailment nearby they contacted the division superintendent and offered to help in restoring service. They did just that, but as a matter of principle, they refused to make a claim for their work.

Disagreement over policy divided all parties; managers were not unanimous in their views and neither were union leaders nor government officials. President Warren G. Harding intervened, but ineffectively. For weeks Attorney General Harry M. Daugherty refused to ask for a federal injunction, but finally, on September 1, he requested and received court orders to restrain the shop crafts and other union workers associated with the strike. Great Northern General Counsel M. L. Countryman labeled a supplementary order "the most sweeping and drastic injunction ever granted against organized labor."[13]

Faced with federal government power, labor surrendered. By October, the GN's car shops were functioning, with about 90 percent of the jobs filled. Acting on a suggestion by the RLB, a majority of the company's shop workers voted to create the Associated Organization of Shop Craft Employees – Great Northern Railway, a company union that agreed to wage

schedules set forth by the RLB. Strikers reemployed before October 1 were assured pension rights and pass privileges; those not rehired on that date were promised restoration to the GN's payroll as openings occurred.

The Great Northern and other railroads had won the battle, but costs were high for all. Workers lost substantial income and gained little or nothing in enhanced wage schedules; GN shopmen now had a company union, the value of which was questionable. On the other side of the conflict, accountants estimated the GN's loss at $5 million in revenue, and another $2 million in extraordinary costs associated with the strike.

Freight rates were quickly reduced to stimulate general economic recovery and to fulfill agreements. In December 1921, all tariffs in Canada were cut to levels only 20 percent above those prevailing before September 1920. After the ICC ordered reduction in rates ranging from 10 to 13 percent on grain, grain products, and hay, and 20 percent on coarse grains as of January 1, 1922, the GN itself lowered tariffs on other farm products by 10 percent and on long-distance shipments of cattle by 20 percent. Finally, on May 16, the ICC stipulated that any rate not already brought down at least 10 percent below those of August 1920 must be so reduced, effective July 1, 1922. As carriers had urged in hearings, and promised in union negotiations, lower wage scales were introduced coincident with the decline in tariffs.

Although the GN's 1922 returns from railway operations surpassed those of 1921, they were still disappointing. Tonnage went up 40.5 percent and net ton miles by almost 20 percent; significant gains were registered in almost all categories except wheat. Freight revenues rose $3.4 million, but passenger train revenues dropped more than $1 million, leaving railway operating revenues in 1922 only 2 percent above those in depressed 1921.

No improvement appeared in the all-important category, net income. During 1922, the GN's net earnings fell to less than $11 million, 62 percent below those of the preceding year. A decline in dividends from the Burlington and increased interest on funded debt contributed to this disappointing result. The latter reflected $30 million in 5½ percent General Mortgage Gold bonds issued in January 1922. Faced with disappointing net income, GN directors decided to depart from the traditional 7 percent dividend, voting 5¼ for 1922 and 5 percent for the next year. Just to make payment on the lower rate in 1922, the GN took $2,252,000 out of accumulated surplus.

By lowering the dividend rate, those who directed GN affairs tacitly admitted that the company faced a climate radically unlike that before 1916. Indeed, all railroads would have to function within an increasingly rigid federal regulatory framework, created in part by the carriers themselves. Despite management's isolated victories over labor, wage schedules would remain much higher than before World War 1. Moreover, with few exceptions, labor problems would henceforth be worked out nationally with strong unions, supported by the government. Having lost its ability to respond to cyclical changes by adjusting outlays for wages — its major expenditure — in the future the GN would be required more than ever to invest in technology to hold down costs. Moreover, return to the prewar operating ratio was extremely unlikely, as the 79.5 for 1921

and 77.0 for 1922 indicated. The 7 percent interest rate on the General Mortgage bonds of 1921 also meant that company managers would have to live with higher fixed costs.

Ralph Budd and his subordinates, hardly pleased with the new environment, felt essentially justified in pressing on with long-range plans outlined earlier. The recession was nearing its end, major labor issues seemed at least partly resolved, and the ICC surely would reduce freight rates no further. Thus, if economic conditions improved, as they anticipated, GN officers felt they could finally turn to projects calculated to enhance the railroad's strength and profitability.

The astonishing growth in the size and complexity of steam power is demonstrated by the juxtaposition of the *William Crooks* against one of the GN's 2-8-8-2s.

20

Polishing the Operation

In a 1928 speech, Ralph Budd observed that two main paths led to successful railroad operation. One, he said, "lies through reduction of costs," which could be achieved only by a company "able to reduce its grades, improve its roadbed, and best equip and maintain its line." The other lay in substantially expanding a company's volume of business. The two, of course, were intertwined to form a general policy designed to attract and hold business. Budd's views, not unique, were valid. Fortunately for the Great Northern, he practiced what he preached.[1]

Upgrading Plant and Equipment

In allocating funds, GN's management gave first priority to motive power and rolling stock. Between 1919 and 1931, the company purchased or built in its own shops 158 locomotives. Most of these, including fifty Mikados (2-8-2) purchased in 1919–1920, and thirty Santa Fes (2-10-2), acquired in 1923, were for freight service. During the next year, the GN ordered four simple articulated (2-8-8-2) giants, each weighing almost 600,000 pounds, and, including tender, 107 feet long. With the same 2-8-8-2 wheel arrangement, but even more powerful, were twenty-six machines built between 1927 and 1930 in the GN's Spokane (Hillyard) shops, at a 20 percent savings over the $100,000 asked per unit by commercial locomotive works. These monsters went into service in mountain districts because even over the difficult Continental Divide between Whitefish and Cut Bank they could handle 4,000-ton trains.

New power was also acquired for passenger service. To replace older Pacifics, the GN in 1923 ordered twenty-eight Mountain-type (4-8-2) locomotives. Ralph Budd thought these new "long-limbed, racy" engines "about the finest things on wheels." Late in the 1920s, to meet the projected schedule of a new transcontinental passenger train, the GN needed still more power. Consequently, the company ordered twenty Northerns (4-8-4) from Baldwin in 1928 and 1929 for use across the Montana Division and between Spokane and Wenatchee where, for long stretches, conditions were favorable for high speed.[2]

New motive power was the conspicuous manifestation of the GN's improvement program, but rebuilding older steam locomotives and converting others to more serviceable types was equally important, if more mundane. All 128 of the cumbersome 2-6-6-2 compound Mallets acquired early in the century were either scrapped or rebuilt as Mikados or as simple articulateds with increased power and flexibility and lower operating

The GN's P-2 Mountain-type locomotives proved to be marvelously reliable.

costs. Meanwhile, installing locomotive boosters, superheaters, and brick arches increased power or fuel efficiency or both. At the same time, many new devices—including exhaust steam injectors, feed water heaters, automatic fire doors, power-grate shakers, mechanical stokers, and power-reverse gears—improved performance, saved fuel, and raised engine crews' morale.

And so the company's locomotive fleet was transformed. As late as 1923, the commonest engine on the roster was still the 2-8-0, with average tractive effort of 37,500 pounds. But by 1931, only 150 of these old reliables remained. In that year the company had 411 modern locomotives, with average tractive effort ranging from 63,000 pounds for the 2-8-2s to almost 144,000 for the 2-8-8-2s. Although the number of steam locomotives declined from 1,391 in 1919 to 1,087 in 1931, the average tractive effort per engine was increased by 30 percent.

To experiment with another type of power, the GN acquired in 1926 the first diesel-electric locomotive in the Northwest. This 600-horsepower machine, used for yard service, performed well. Diesel equipment, however, was not to be used generally for more than a decade.

Similar betterments were made in the freight-car fleet. While the company increased its gross inventory only slightly, from 54,125 in 1920 to 54,889 in 1931, the average capacity per car jumped 11 percent to more than forty-three tons. Changing needs meant more refrigerator, gondola, and stock cars, and fewer flat, box, and ore cars. The company purchased some equipment from manufacturers, but built a great number of cars in its own shops; in fact, of the more than 18,000 box cars placed in service during the decade, fewer than 3,000 were acquired from outside sources. Company workmen modernized many other cars by rebuilding them with improved draft gear, better couplers, and steel underframes and center sills. Several obsolete types, all the twenty-ton, and most of the thirty-ton cars, were scrapped or modified. New gondolas of seventy-ton capacity handled bulk commodities.

Refrigerator cars presented special problems. In 1919, the GN owned 4,694 of these and added more later, but because of seasonal demand and the difficulty of getting them returned, the company often encountered shortages. In an attempt to ameliorate the problem, the GN in 1923 organized a wholly owned subsidiary, the Western Fruit Express Company (WFE), leasing to it both the reefers and necessary service facilities. WFE introduced improved methods of harvesting and handling ice, utilized new mechanical devices, and established an association with the Fruit Growers' Express Company, a similar firm owned by eastern roads. Three years later the CB&Q's Refrigerator Express Company joined the cooperative effort under common management. Among other advantages, all participants benefited from joint use of shops as well as joint inspection of shipments on all member roads. This cooperation enabled the GN to draw upon a large pool of cars to meet sea-

Boy Scouts lined up atop a 2-8-8-2 at Hillyard to suggest the relative size of this monster.

sonal needs, and also to earn income on its own cars in service elsewhere during periods when the perishables business in the Northwest was slack.

Improvements to track structure and roadway were corollary and represented the philosophical legacy of James J. Hill and the wisdom of Ralph Budd. On a year-by-year basis, it was essentially a policy of a little here and a little there. In the aggregate, however, these efforts resulted in impressive savings in costs of maintenance and operation. Fills were widened and tiled, cuts drained, and old ballast was replaced by washed gravel, the new standard. From 1924, ties usually were treated with creosote, and were increased in size and their number per mile. Additional rail anchors

and larger, heavier tie plates were installed, and over the years rail weight was increased. In 1920, ninety-pound rail was the heaviest, but eleven years later the standard for main lines was 110-pound, although some 130-pound section was also utilized. Bridges and trestles were similarly upgraded to increase capacity. Wood was replaced by steel, and fills replaced trestles where feasible.

Improved safety was implied in several programs. Crossings at grade were fewer and automatic interlockers at railroad crossings were more numerous. Yard switches were changed to remote control, and by 1926, the GN completed a system of block signals protecting its main line from St. Paul to Seattle (via the Surrey Cutoff), the world's longest unbroken in-

stallation at that time. Meanwhile, the GN adopted colored light signals as standard, replacing semaphores, the ancient symbol of railroading. These new devices were subject to fewer mechanical failures, required less maintenance, and were more easily visible under most conditions.

The Great Northern's managers also attended to miscellaneous structures essential to railroad operation. At Bellingham, Washington, a new brick depot was typical of many that the GN put up in small but growing towns. Several engine houses were enlarged or

Fierce looking, high-stepping 4-8-4s were assigned to passenger service across the Montana Division and between Spokane and Wenatchee.

A paragon of ugliness was this first diesel unit on the GN, but it heralded an incredible change soon to come in motive power and train operations.

new ones built and other maintenance and repair facilities were erected. Old-style coal chutes were replaced by more effective balanced-bucket loaders. For an adequate supply of water treatment plants were built, and, in Montana, large reservoirs. A new wharf at Seattle facilitated business there, and an additional elevator at Superior greatly expanded capacity for storing wheat there.

Especially important among several other structural improvements, was that of ore-handling facilities at Allouez. Of the four docks there in 1920, only No. 4, the newest, was constructed of steel. The others, all timber, required reconditioning or replacement. Between 1921 and 1923, the GN rebuilt No. 2 with steel and concrete; when completed, it was reported to be the most modern dock on the Great Lakes. Two years later the GN undertook similar renovation of Dock No. 1, so that by the end of the decade only No. 3 was still a timber structure. New machinery and changes in organization also reduced costs. Air hammers helped laborers dump stubborn ore, and electrical devices loaded vessels more efficiently.

Reducing Costs

Upgrading motive power, car fleet, roadway, and structures opened the way to more efficient operation. Ralph Budd understood that these improvements, coupled with high standards for maintenance, would assure shippers of swift and reliable service and thus strengthen the GN's competitive position and increase its traffic. He also knew, however,

that to generate satisfactory earnings — while burdened with significant outlays for labor, taxes, and fixed charges — required an effective and unceasing attack on costs at every level. This awareness, too, was a James J. Hill legacy.

Because locomotive fuel accounted for 15 percent of operating costs, it received special attention. Through the decade steam locomotives provided most of the GN power, 97 percent of it as late as 1931. Thus, starting in 1921, when oil prices fell rapidly, the company gradually converted many of its locomotives to that fuel. By 1931, on almost a third of GN engines, firemen no longer shoveled coal.

Still, coal remained a major cost. In purchasing supplies, buyers for the railroad had much to consider: characteristics of the fuel, especially its BTU value; cost of transport from various sources; expense of handling ashes and cinders; and influence that orders might have on coal suppliers who were also important commercial shippers. During the decade, coal came from British Columbia,

Montana, Illinois, Kentucky, and even West Virginia.

Other fields were fertile for tightening efficiency. Locomotives were reassigned to take maximum advantage of their capabilities, capacities of tenders were increased, underutilized water and coaling stations were closed, the number of operating divisions was reduced from sixteen in 1920 to eight in 1935, and extraneous supervisory positions were abolished.

Further savings were achieved by abandoning little-used lines. Of about 300 miles removed during Budd's presidency, two-thirds were in Canada, including the Portage La Prairie Branch in Manitoba north of Neche, North Dakota, and several short stretches of track in southern British Columbia. Obliquely, the GN thus signaled that it had given up on James J. Hill's energetic plan for a direct route from Spokane, Washington, to Vancouver, British Columbia, through the border area. Also, the old rumor that the GN would run a line through Canada from Vancouver to Winnipeg was finally put to rest.

Perhaps the most graphic example of Ralph

Box car capacity rose quickly from 20 to 44 tons.

Budd's business philosophy was cutting the number of GN employees, consequently reducing wages and salaries. Innovations in roadway maintenance during the 1920s allowed a 55 percent slash in section men, and although a comparable cut in the rest of the work force was not achieved, in 1929 the average number of employees was 28,258, down from 41,388 in 1920. Expenditures for labor also fell, but less sharply. Although average annual compensation per employee rose about 5 percent, from $1,721 in 1920 to $1,796 in 1929, the outlay for labor fell impressively from $71.3

million in the former year to $50.7 million in the latter.[3]

Striving to increase productivity, Budd simultaneously tended to the workers' morale. Like James J. Hill, he took clear interest in his fellow officers as well as in contract employees, and backed suggestions that might create team spirit. The *Semaphore*, a periodical published by the company in the early 1920s, was filled with informative articles and newsy personnel items to interest workers in the GN's history and in current developments. Employee organizations flourished at the General Office Building in St. Paul and along the line, all implying joint concern for the company's success. In 1923, the GN modified its stock-purchasing plan by arranging payment by payroll deductions, and introduced a group plan with Metropolitan Life Insurance Company, sharing premiums between the railroad and its employees. Four years later, 7,750 GN personnel had some protection.

Homely illustrations from Minnesota's iron range suggest the important and close relationship of improved plant, increased power, worker morale, and productivity. In 1920, crews normally required nearly seventeen hours to operate an average train of 110 empty cars from Allouez to Kelly Lake, pick up as many loaded cars, and return to the classification yard near Superior with an average of 4,789 long tons of ore. In 1922, elapsed time for the round trip of 198 miles rose to twenty-one hours. C. O. Jenks was enraged, challenging crews to improve performance. One engineer, J. Arten, a full-blood Chippewa Indian, soon thereafter made the run in fourteen hours and ten minutes after Jenks asked him to "show those white men" that an engineer could eat both breakfast and supper at home. By 1931, dedication by skilled workers, as well as improved track and increased power,

cut the round trip to eleven and a half hours and increased the average load hauled from the mines to 171 cars, carrying 9,727 long tons.[4]

Conquering the Cascades

A major challenge facing Ralph Budd was to improve the Great Northern's difficult crossing of the Cascades in western Washington. In 1892 and 1893, James J. Hill had ordered the line built through those challenging peaks with 4 percent grades and formidable switchbacks. To eliminate the latter, the company in 1900 had completed and placed in service its first Cascade Tunnel, a 2.63-mile bore. Nine years later the GN solved the troublesome smoke problem by substituting electric locomotives to power trains for a mere three miles. Exchanging locomotives at each end consumed time and money, however; the grades and curvature remained excessive, and fires and lumbermen denuding slopes above the line made snow slides on the approach ever more dangerous. To alleviate some of these problems, the GN built almost twelve miles of short tunnels and snow sheds, but these held smoke from steam engines, reduced visibility, and exposing crews and passengers alike to unpleasantness, were expensive to maintain.

A longer main tunnel at a lower elevation seemed the obvious solution. A 1912 engineering study showed that a 14.5- or 17.5-mile bore, costing about $27 million, would be both adequate and feasible. World War I postponed a final decision, but rising costs thereafter rendered the lengthy passageways prohibitive. By the mid-1920s, however, the possibility of acquiring more powerful electric

Construction of a new and much longer Cascade Tunnel promised to make redundant many snowsheds and trestles.

locomotives and extending the catenary made a major reduction of summit elevation less important. Company officers decided that a shorter tunnel would suffice.

As plans matured, Budd's Cascades improvement project took on a three-sided character. Most important was construction of a straight single-track tunnel to extend 7.79 miles from Berne, on the east slope of the Cascades, to Scenic, on the west. This would avoid the most dangerous snow-slide area west of the summit, reduce elevation moderately, and cut both curvature and distance.

A second part of the project was line relocation along the slopes where winding track had been rushed to completion during the early 1890s. Changes were designed to effect a more uniform and relatively easy grade with less curvature. This, in addition to the tunnel, would collectively eliminate snow sheds and cut costs of maintenance and operation. More important, these improvements would contribute to safety.

The third element involved improvements in electric operation including: its extension from Wenatchee west for seventy-two miles to Skykomish; replacement of the old three-phase power, double-trolley system with a modern single-phase, single-trolley system; and the acquisition of new and more flexible electric locomotives. This would eliminate all smoke problems and make possible heavier trains, greater speed, and better economy. Budd informed Louis W. Hill that these changes would "leave us for all times in the future with an up-to-date, modern line that can be operated cheaply . . . ."[5]

The executive committee enthusiastically approved all of this on November 19, 1925, and within a week the GN made a contract with A. Guthrie & Company, a St. Paul-based con-

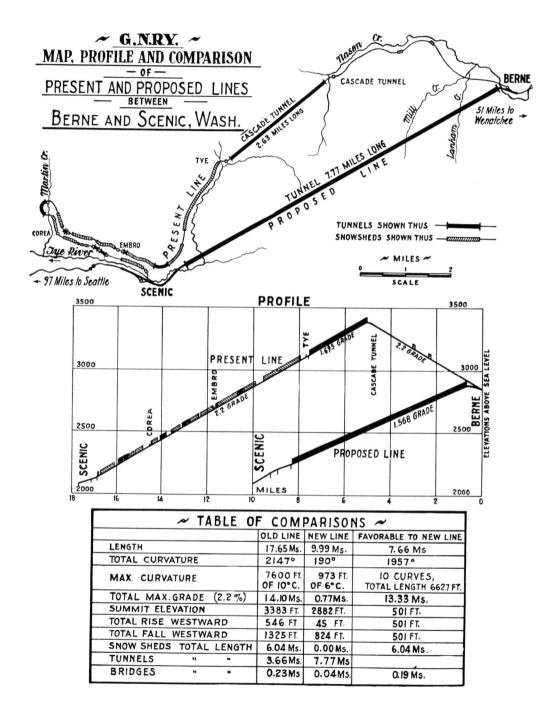

~ G.N.RY. ~
MAP, PROFILE AND COMPARISON
— OF —
PRESENT AND PROPOSED LINES
BETWEEN
BERNE AND SCENIC, WASH.

TUNNELS SHOWN THUS
SNOWSHEDS SHOWN THUS

~ MILES ~
SCALE

PROFILE

~ TABLE OF COMPARISONS ~			
	OLD LINE	NEW LINE	FAVORABLE TO NEW LINE
LENGTH	17.65 Ms.	9.99 Ms.	7.66 Ms
TOTAL CURVATURE	2147°	190°	1957°
MAX. CURVATURE	7600 FT. OF 10°C.	973 FT. OF 6°C.	10 CURVES, TOTAL LENGTH 6627 FT.
TOTAL MAX. GRADE (2.2%)	14.10 Ms.	0.77 Ms.	13.33 Ms.
SUMMIT ELEVATION	3383 FT.	2882 FT.	501 FT.
TOTAL RISE WESTWARD	546 FT	45 FT.	501 FT.
TOTAL FALL WESTWARD	1325 FT.	824 FT.	501 FT.
SNOW SHEDS TOTAL LENGTH	6.04 Ms.	0.00 Ms.	6.04 Ms.
TUNNELS " "	3.66 Ms.	7.77 Ms.	
BRIDGES " "	0.23 Ms.	0.04 Ms.	0.19 Ms.

struction firm, to build the tunnel at cost plus a flat fee. In the middle of December workers moved the first dirt at the tunnel site.

To construct this longest railroad tunnel in the western hemisphere, the contractor had to balance several necessities. First, the railroad was impatient: the task must be completed in three years. Second, engineering was difficult. The bore was to descend on a 1.6 percent grade from east to west, presenting Guthrie & Co. with possibily heavy flows of underground water. The Denver & Salt Lake Railroad's Moffat Tunnel in Colorado had been slowed by such flows, requiring major changes in plans. Third, the isolated location might make it difficult to attract and hold a work force.

These problems in large measure dictated calculations for construction. The first step was to divide work into segments and sink a 622-foot shaft to intersect the tunnel 2.41 miles west of the east portal at Berne. This shaft, from the floor of Mill Creek, gave the contractor two additional working faces. Meanwhile, from the west portal to the Mill Creek shaft, engineers would push a pioneer work tunnel, parallel to and sixty-six feet south of the projected main bore. To the main tunnel from the work bore, engineers made twenty-one cross-cuts; crews then attacked several faces simultaneously and for most of the way drove the work up grade. On the longer (5.28 miles) western portion of the tunnel, the pioneer bore also eased movement of equipment and materials, and it carried air pipes and power lines. Finally, this work bore drained up to 9,000 gallons of water a minute from the various construction faces.

Work progressed nicely, though laborers found conditions most adverse, "thousands of feet under ground . . . at times in water knee deep." According to one report, the men

Electrification reached 72 miles from Wenatchee to Skykomish.

"changed shifts at the handles of the drills. . . . A constant battering was kept up . . . every day and every night for thirty-five months. . . . Drilling, blasting, mucking out the broken rock, then over again; eight feet gained at each round, five rounds in 24 hours. . . . There was no letting up. . . ." In all, 923,000 cubic yards of rock and earth were removed in slightly less than three years.[6]

By such herculean efforts the contractor completed the impressive new Cascade Tunnel on schedule; workers poured the last cement lining December 24, 1928. It was a monumental achievement, accomplished in a remarkably short time. The St. Gotthard Tunnel in the Swiss Alps was only 1.49 miles longer but took nine years to complete. In Colorado, the Moffat Tunnel required five and a half years to construct, though 9,000 feet shorter than the GN's Cascade bore.

At ceremonies on January 12, 1929, President-elect Herbert Hoover, with an engineer's

The last cement was poured on December 24, 1928.

The Great Northern Railway: A History/Part II 1916 to 1970

appreciation for the huge project, hailed it as a victory for all Americans. Without such braggadocio, Ralph Budd fitted the accomplishment into the GN's own heritage: "The completed tunnel symbolizes the main idea behind the railroad career of James J. Hill; namely, the importance of economy and efficiency in railway operation."[7]

As promised, the tunnel and other improvements in the Cascades increased efficiency of operation and effected large economies. Maximum elevation was reduced by 502 feet to 2,881, practically the same as Northern Pacific's 2,852—but with far better approaches—and only 312 feet higher than the Milwaukee's superior crossing of that range. Curvature and grade were sharply reduced; miles of troublesome, expensive snow sheds were eliminated; constant anxiety over slides was greatly reduced; and operation through the Cascades was now nearly as reliable as on the remainder of the GN's route. Passenger and freight schedules from St. Paul to Seattle were immediately cut; the GN was now in an even stronger competitive position.

Conquering the Cascades was expensive, though: $25.6 million were spent to build the tunnel, relocate the line, and expand electrification. To justify all this improvement, the railroad needed an ever-growing volume of business.

Building Freight Traffic

Freight business formed, as always, the cornerstone of the Great Northern's income account. During the 1920s, about 81 percent of its railway operating revenue derived therefrom. Thus, management's success rested upon its ability to maintain or improve that service.

Vice President William P. Kenney held responsibility for this area. Hard-driving and convivial, he was a strict taskmaster. Stimulating freight salesmen was his specialty. Sales offices in twenty-four on-line and sixteen off-line cities were staffed by up to half a dozen representatives each, and at all stations GN agents were expected to do all possible to attract business. The company reestablished its foreign office in the Orient in 1922, primarily to solicit shipments of raw silk from Seattle to Chicago over the GN and the Burlington.

In the day-by-day business of generating traffic, Kenney saw that personal relationships between railroad men and shippers were the secret. "Good service must be given," he wrote, but a tremendous amount of business was "controlled by personality." Still, a salesman could not simply call on a prospective customer, hand him a cigar, and ask him to ship via GN. Instead, Kenney demanded that traffic representatives understand the customer's business and combine personal friendship with genuine assistance.[8]

Kenney too actively solicited traffic, by close and friendly contact with Montana wheat growers, Wenatchee apple producers, and officials of large firms throughout the country. He understood how extending courtesies to important shippers registered. For example, while visiting New York in 1923, he entertained GN customers at a fulsome banquet and at the renowned Dempsey–Firpo prizefight, explaining that these customers "have given us a nice business . . . and it gives us a good chance to . . . repay them the only way we can. . . ."[9]

Kenney applied energetic solicitation, but found careful rate making at least as vital. Setting rates in the 1920s, as it had always been, was indescribably complex, enmeshing the railroad, its customers, and also conflicting interest groups, including the Interstate Commerce Commission, state regulatory agencies, middlemen, and consumers. All carriers needed rates high enough to cover operating costs plus a reasonable profit, yet low enough to attract traffic and still market goods profitably. After the 1920 general increase in freight charges, rates declined during the decade. To stimulate traffic in the postwar depression, the nation's railroads voluntarily reduced rates, and the ICC imposed mandatory reductions for selected items, among them 10 to 13 percent cuts on charges for grain products and hay, and about 20 percent for coarse grains.

Several analysts contended that such reductions could only be described as extreme. Moreover, these rates discriminated against roads such as the GN because they deducted from the Mountain–Pacific companies "a larger proportion of the advances accorded in 1920 than was taken away from any other part of the country except the South." Certainly the rate structure left northwestern roads with net incomes far short of the fair returns stipulated under the Transportation Act of 1920, troubling the ICC not at all. When in 1925 the carriers asked the ICC for a horizontal increase of 5 percent, the reply was a flat refusal. Not until 1932 did the railroads score even a small gain.[10]

Since the ICC decision of 1922 was the last general reduction in the decade, the prevailing downward trend for rates in that period resulted from a multitude of decreases made on single commodities or groups. These came from decisions by the federal regulatory agency, state commissions, and the carriers themselves. In the rates and divisions office of the GN, for instance, there was a general understanding that the company's customers, after all, frequently had to compete with producers who were advantaged by being closer to markets. Consequently the GN had no choice but to keep its own operating costs low so that it could quote rates allowing on-line shippers to contend for those distant markets. To cite only one example, in 1923 the GN voluntarily reduced rates on Wenatchee apples destined for points on the Southern Pacific via Portland in order to expand the growers' potential sales territory and in that way to enhance the railroad's revenues.

Meanwhile, Kenney and his staff increasingly had to concern themselves with modal competition. One of the most serious challenges came from increased use of the Panama Canal. The loss of eastbound lumber shipments from the Pacific Coast was substantial. Also under the prevailing rate structure eastern shipping lines could reach inland competitively as far west as Chicago for cargoes of manufactured goods destined for the Pacific Coast, thereby taking business from the GN and reducing the company's westbound shipments needed to balance eastbound movements of lumber, wheat, and perishables.

Water competition could have been met, for one thing, by offering on westbound freight to coastal cities rates lower than those to intermediate points. Such long- and short-haul pricing, though, was prohibited by Section 4 of the Interstate Commerce Act, except under such specific exemptions as the commission might authorize. Twice in the early 1920s, northwestern carriers asked for relief, only to be rebuffed by the commission, vociferously encouraged in its stand by inland points such as Spokane. Subsequently, the transcontinentals resorted to reducing rates on specific westbound commodities, including canned foods, iron, steel, tires, brass, bronze, and copper goods.[11]

Competition from trucks was at first less extensive than that from water carriers. Kenney simply dismissed the subject in 1921: there "is not much concern . . . because the short-haul merchandise business has not given the railroad any profit." Even Ralph Budd grossly underestimated rubber-tired competition. Eventually, he predicted, "the motor truck will take its proper place in the transportation service of the country, and it should not seriously affect a transcontinental line to have some of its short-haul freight handled by truck." As the decade wore on, however, managers were disturbed more and were less philosophical about competition on the highways. With other railroads, the GN urged state legislatures to apply regulation and taxation to the new industry, and to reduce rates, in particular areas and on specific commodities. Combined with intensive solicitation, these steps were effective at times, occasionally driving trucking firms out of business. Later, hoping to minimize truckers' inroads, the GN tried innovative changes, among them handling LCL freight on passenger trains, better scheduling of way-freights to provide early morning delivery, and experimentally, pick-up-and-delivery service. As depression descended on the Northwest after 1929, though, management recognized that no completely satisfactory answer to highway competition was ready.[12]

By the end of the 1920s, Ralph Budd's emphasis on the "two main paths" to successful railroad operation had borne fruit. Compared to their condition ten years before, the company's rolling stock, motive power, and fixed properties were vastly improved; the new Cascade Tunnel was the most dramatic manifestation. Moreover, Budd's insistence on modernizing and improving service, combined with the GN's sharpened marketing, lowered costs, increased business, and achieved a pleasant improvement in the operating ratio.

21

Passenger Business and Change

The Great Northern—and the nation's railroads generally—faced sharply changing conditions in the passenger-carrying trade during the 1920s. Prosperity at mid-decade stimulated long-distance vacation travel, but depressed economic conditions later forcefully reduced this business. Competition among railroads, always strong, grew more intense, and the rapid growth of travel by private automobile and commercial buses, especially for trips of short distance, caused a dramatic drop in coach riders. Another long-term trend was foreshadowed by the introduction of air transport.[1]

In 1920, more passengers used GN service despite a 20 percent advance in fares. The road's passenger revenue alone totaled $20.5 million, and passenger-service revenue (including fares, baggage, express, and mail) reached $30.4 million, about 25 percent of aggregate revenue from rail operations. To handle a demand that appeared to be rising, GN managers felt compelled to improve rolling stock. In 1920, the GN owned 1,206 passenger cars, but many of them were antiquated. A third of its 150 sleepers were of the tourist type, all of its diners antedated 1912, and only 25 of its 403 coaches were built of steel. Almost alone among Class I railroads, the GN until 1916 had owned and serviced all its sleeping and parlor cars. In that year the Pullman Company began to supply for a year at a time some cars and services for the GN's transcontinental trains; a long-term contract was yet to be arranged.

The St. Paul Union Depot

For a decade and more prior to 1920, both the railroads and the public saw that St. Paul needed a new passenger terminal. The city, a metropolitan area with more than a quarter of a million people, was a major transfer point for passengers, express, and mail. The large prewar westward flow of immigrants and heavy commuter traffic kept business strong despite competition from interurbans and street cars. On a peak day in 1916, more than 500 trains used the city's facility. Express and mail tonnage had much more than doubled in ten years, and, except for Boston's South Station, no railroad terminal in the nation handled more mail.

Improvement had started early in this century. In 1903, James J. Hill purchased real estate needed for expansion, and three years later directors of the St. Paul Union Depot Company appointed a committee to study the matter. In the same year city officials established a Union Depot and River Harbor Commission that reviewed the community's transportation needs.

During the years of study and preparation, demand for a new station reached a state of public clamor, and then, ironically, on October 3, 1913, the old structure caught fire. St. Paul's fire marshal condemned the partly restored building and local newspapers described temporary facilities in a nearby wholesale

house as unsanitary, inadequate, and unsuitable. In January 1914, when the GN opened its imposing new station in nearby Minneapolis, the mayor of St. Paul called a public meeting, and a Citizens' Terminal Depot Committee subsequently gathered thousands of signatures in protest over St. Paul's unseemly facilities. One newspaper asserted, "Never has public sentiment been so thoroughly united."[2]

Progress followed. From 1914 through 1916, railroad planners and their companies agreed to build on the site of the original sta-

Railway Age described the St. Paul Union Depot as one of "monumental proportions and classic design," but onlookers here seem more captivated by the monumental proportions of the GN's 2030.

tion, plus land purchased earlier by Hill, rather than on another location in the Midway district between St. Paul and Minneapolis. Charles S. Frost of Chicago was appointed architect, and he, together with the superintendent of the St. Paul Union Depot Company, thoroughly analyzed terminals in North America and abroad.

The depot company finally reached satisfactory arrangements with member railroads in 1916, advertised for construction bids, and explored sources of funds.

Work on the new depot had to avoid, as much as possible, interrupting railroad operations. Construction was divided into six parts, each completed section being promptly put to use. The headhouse (passenger-station building) was opened April 5, 1920, with a gala dance, but major construction continued on other portions of the massive facility. Strangely, not until 1923 were arrangements made for long-term financing through a bond issue of $15 million to replace earlier short-term notes. The size of the loan reflected both high standards for work and rising costs.

When completed, the St. Paul Union Depot was described in *Railway Age* as of "monumental proportions and classic design." It did not look out on a fine mall as James J. Hill had visualized, but the gray Bedford stone exterior, large Doric columns, and Tennessee marble interior were patently striking. Changes in the grade of Sibley Street made it possible to reach lower levels of the concourse and other parts of the plant from the street. A special feature of the building was a large space equipped to accommodate the many needs of immigrants.[3]

Highway Competition

Even as St. Paul's grand new station was being completed, the business of passenger trains began to change. Revenue from ex-

Ironically, railroads made good net revenue on the delivery of automobiles like this one being unloaded just outside Seattle's King Street Station, but automobiles increasingly swept patrons from branch trains and locals.

press and mail rose, but from travelers—especially for short hauls—it declined after 1920. The average distance traveled on the GN was 80 miles in 1920, but by 1924 it was 107 miles, and it lengthened to 202 miles by 1931.

Conditions after World War I favored a shift to highways. Until 1919, United States intercity travel by auto was almost negligible. By 1923, though, motor-vehicle passenger miles were about three-fourths as great as train passenger miles, and by 1926 surpassed the latter. Road improvement was stimulated by the Federal Aid Act of 1916 and by inexpensive concrete after the war. The individualistic American's relatively high standard of living and easy credit put him in his own automobile, enjoying its convenience, flexibility, and freedom.

In the early 1920s 90 percent of auto travel was by personal vehicle, but a few entrepreneurs were attracted to the bus business. "Jitney" and "automobile-stage" operations multiplied rapidly. Owners needed comparatively little capital, drivers worked for low wages, and many of the owners, lacking knowledge of cost accounting, offered attractively low fares.

The GN studied this new competition, especially in Minnesota, where train travel had peaked in 1914, six years earlier than in the country as a whole. The decline in local passenger business there had a marked affect on the GN, since the company owned a quarter of the state's total rail mileage, with half of its 2,100 miles in short branches. Relative to population, the number of private passenger autos in Minnesota exceeded the national average, and by 1923, thirty-three intercity bus lines operated on routes paralleling GN lines. A study of selected stations on the GN showed

Business was good on trains like the *International* between Seattle and Vancouver, British Columbia, but in the hinterlands, the GN was forced to offer an increased volume of mixed or "hog and human" trains such as this one below in North Dakota.

Fierce competition raged between crews of GN silk trains that raced between Seattle and St. Paul in the 1920s. One of these trains is shown taking on fuel and water at New Rockford, North Dakota, in 1925. Townspeople, who knew of the impending arrival via telegraph, gathered to watch crew members hastily servicing the *Marathon.*

an average drop in ticket sales of 64 percent during the early 1920s.

To stem the tide, the GN tried various approaches, tightening schedules and making concessions in fares, although Budd generally opposed this approach. "One of the worst diseases passenger men get is the urge to cut fares," he commented. "It has cost railways millions of dollars." Nevertheless, the company had success with special weekend round-trip tickets in Minnesota and elsewhere. Special coach fares for homeseekers were continued, usually on Tuesday, but a low rate for migratory harvesters failed to draw them out of their automobiles. Significant questions remained. Did a special rate create traffic or merely shift it? Would temporarily reducing fares to meet bus competition lead to permanent cuts? Would reduced rates spread to long-distance travel? Would low rates create enough business to increase net income, or would they add more to cost than to gross revenue?[4]

Involved in the question of rates and costs was the prickly matter of dividing expenses between passenger and freight operations. Passenger service traditionally was charged with expenses directly incurred in its performance, but also with a portion of so-called common expense, including taxes and cost of capital. In

Pooling passenger service with the Soo Line and Northern Pacific between the Twin Cities and Duluth–Superior began in 1927. Here a GN train headed by a 4-4-2 has left Duluth en route to Superior and beyond.

1914, the Interstate Commerce Commission devised a general formula for apportioning costs, but the 27 percent it allocated to passenger service and 73 percent to freight was already dated in the 1920s, when freight produced an ever-greater percentage of traffic revenue. Some argued that passenger business should be regarded as a by-product of freight operations and that in assigning railroad expenses, little more than the out-of-pocket cost for providing passenger service should be charged against resulting revenue.

The GN could not change the ICC formula, but it could strive to reduce the cost of carrying passengers. Increasing mixed train service lowered passenger train miles, and where volume of patronage on a short run did not require a steam locomotive, the GN introduced lighter, less expensive power. In 1922, it acquired four gasoline motor cars with trailers, and two years later added a couple of gas-electric units, each capable of pulling a car at one-third the cost for steam; by 1931, the GN had thirty-five of them. On runs where passenger business fell off sharply, the railroad asked state authorities for permission to drop service.

Pooling passenger business with other railroads also reduced costs. A prime area was on the 182 miles between Seattle and Portland. Here, the Great Northern, the Northern Pacific, and the Union Pacific in 1910 had operated eleven trains each way daily, but in 1925 the Pacific Highway was opened, draining traffic. Simultaneously, the public demanded faster train service. Ultimately the ICC allowed the three companies to form a pool, and the railroads then put on fast trains, but reduced runs to six and then to five in each direction. This happy experience led officers of the GN, the NP, and the Soo Line in 1927 to similarly pool passenger operations and earn-

ings on the 160-mile run between the Twin Cities and Duluth–Superior. By dropping one round trip a day on that route, the GN saved 117,000 train miles per annum.

In a related matter, President Budd strongly advocated the use of buses by railroads. An internal study in 1921 urged that because buses and trucks were "here to stay," the railroads should engage "in short-haul business [on the highway] as part of their transportation activities." The GN, however, stayed out of the bus business in Minnesota as long as such transport was not regulated in that state. Meanwhile, its officers watched the Spokane, Portland & Seattle experiment with buses in the Portland area. As the GN made preliminary preparations in Minnesota, Budd stayed informed about public opinion. In April 1925, the state legislature gave the Railroad and Warehouse Commission responsibility for issuing certificates of convenience and necessity and for carrying out other regulations affecting highway transport. Budd then consulted Louis Hill, and on May 15, 1925, the GN's board approved the railroad's entry into the motor-transport business.[5]

The nucleus of the GN's newly established Northland Transportation Company was the Mesabi Motor Company, organized and operated by C. Eric Wickman. In 1916, Wickman had begun a jitney business to serve Virginia and Hibbing, mining communities on the Mesabi Range. The GN bought this and other bus lines, obtained franchises, merged them into Northland Transportation, and retained Wickman as manager. The railroad held 90 percent of the stock, but Wickman retained a minority interest. Budd informed GN stockholders that the purchase was neither "advanced" nor "radical" but "purely defensive and essential." The regulatory legislation made "it

practicable for the first time in this state [Minnesota] to provide a complete transportation system correlating the use of the railways with that of the highways."[6]

In coordinating bus and train service, said Budd, the prime objective was to give the "maximum of service with the minimum of cost." Buses and trains both operated on some runs, but where patronage was inadequate, the GN sought to discontinue rail service in favor of Northland buses. In a few places where the bus company did not already run, and the GN wished to remove a passenger train, the railroad paid Northland its costs, plus 2 cents per mile, to provide service. In 1928, the GN had 700,000 passenger train miles fewer than in 1924. Because running a bus cost about a fifth as much as a steam train, significant savings were achieved.[7]

Through Northland, the GN by 1928 had become the largest railroad-owned operator in the country, as well as one of the most successful. With a capitalization of $3 million, Northland continued to buy and consolidate companies and to add service. Its principal business was in Minnesota, but lines stretched from the Twin Cities to Eau Claire, Wisconsin; Port Arthur, Ontario; Fargo, N.D.; and Sioux Falls, S.D. In 1928, Northland had 3,300 miles of routes, carried more than three million passengers, and contemplated acquiring a line from Chicago to St. Paul.

In 1929, however, despite Northland Transportation Company's promising record, the GN sold most of its stock to the founder of Greyhound, the railroad retained only a 30 percent interest in the renamed Northland Greyhound Lines. The bus industry had grown greatly since 1925, and its leaders wanted to create a "close alliance between various bus companies operating coast to coast." Budd,

Cut flowers from the GN's own greenhouse adorned tables in the dining car of the *Oriental Limited*.

ardently favoring consolidation, did not oppose "so important a transportation development."[8]

The GN's management frankly took little interest in the bus business beyond Minnesota. For example, Budd thought Montana's population too sparse to justify operating two modes of passenger transportation in that state. On another front, he could not induce the NP and the UP to join the GN in providing highway transportation between Seattle and Portland.

Despite gas-electric trains, pooling, and buses, managers could not agree on the future of passenger business. Kenney hoped that better service and reduced fares would get travelers back on the trains. Budd was more realistic. He anticipated that "each form of transportation" would find its "economic sphere" and function only "therein." Later, he said the best "way to make money in local passenger business is to get out of it as soon as local passenger trains fail to pay their way." His outlook on long-distance train travel was much more optimistic, and he was determined that the GN should get its share.[9]

Upgrading Transcontinental Travel

Ralph Budd resolved to create a new image for the company's transcontinental passenger service. He wanted to improve it, not only to increase revenue but also to attract to the railroad and its territory shippers and others who might be impressed by opportunities in the Northwest. Budd remarked that "the Passenger Department is the show window of the railroad, and contributes more to its successful operation than actual passenger revenue."[10]

The task was not without difficulty. The idea persisted, *Railway Age* editorialized in 1924, that "James J. Hill did not look with favor on passenger business." But the statement was not wholly accurate. Hill could hardly have been indifferent to the source contributing at least a fifth of the GN's revenue from railroad operation. Furthermore, he had stressed attracting and carrying settlers, and had emphasized economical passenger transportation. Especially in the first decade of the new century, Hill and son Louis had given close attention to improving passenger trains, and they had provided luxury travel on the Great Lakes, the Pacific Ocean, and, jointly with the NP, along the West Coast from Oregon to California.[11]

Now, in the early 1920s, the steamships were gone and the GN needed to polish its reputation—at least that of long-distance passenger service. Years of economies, interrupted business during the war, and then pressure for other expenditures had cut the company's outlays for passenger equipment. Budd recognized that it would be "an up-hill job to make a popular passenger line out of the Great Northern,'' but he urged Kenney to use ''every effort'' and ''every possible ingenuity'' to accomplish that task. Louis Hill enthusiastically concurred.[12]

By 1924, ''new oil-burning passenger locomotives'' provided a clean, smoother, and faster trip for premier passenger trains, for the transcontinental mail train (''the fastest long-distance train in the world''), and for trains carrying raw silk from Seattle to St. Paul. Insurance, as well as interest on the investment in silk, a high-value, perishable product from the Orient, demanded rapid delivery from western docks to eastern manufacturers. The GN had long since built a reputation for care in preparing and handling these special trains, and the company's image was further enhanced in July 1924, when its 1911 speed record was shattered. Starting from Seattle with a coach and ten baggage cars loaded with raw silk, the train ran the 1,748 miles to St. Paul in just 38 hours and 50 minutes. Between 1925 and 1929, the GN averaged forty-three silk trains a year, including one that hauled a cargo valued at $5 million. These exotic movements were significant in GN business until 1933, when the depression and synthetic textiles reduced demand for silk to shipments that could be handled in cars attached to regular passenger trains.[13]

In a matter unrelated to the carriage of silk, but of great importance to its long-haul passenger business was a change made by the GN with the Pullman Company. On May 1, after years of short-term arrangements, a five-year contract became effective. Under the new agreement, by April 1925, Pullman agreed to supply and service almost all observation cars and sleepers on the GN. This enabled the company to reduce its ownership of sleepers

from 207 in 1920 to 27, which in 1931 were used on a few short runs.[14]

The GN greatly improved its transcontinental passenger service by inaugurating on June 1, 1924, the new *Oriental Limited*: ''as wonderful as the country it served,'' this ''Pullman equipped flyer'' offered a daily trip each way between Chicago and Seattle on a seventy-hour schedule. Pulled by oil-burning steamers and by electric locomotives in western Washington, the *Oriental Limited* boasted ''the longest cinderless mileage of any railroad in the Northwest.'' And the GN was also able to make good on its admonition to ''See More of

Despite fine trains such as the *Oriental Limited* and the *Empire Builder* and the scenery in northwestern Montana, Budd was dismayed by lower and lower boardings.

America'' by coupling open-top cars to the rear of the train for its spectacular trip through the Montana Rockies.[15]

The *Oriental Limited*'s dining cars and the cuisine served aboard them got special attention. Prices were kept low but food and service were kept high in quality: a broiled chicken dinner cost 75 cents, and later, as costs rose, a table d'hôte dinner was only $1.50. Cut flowers from GN's own greenhouse

In order to "See More of America," the GN attached open-top cars to the rear of the *Oriental Limited* through the Montana Rockies.

in Monroe, Washington, adorned tables, and patrons received a complimentary recipe book, *Great Northern Secrets*.[16]

There was more. On June 10, 1929, the GN introduced an entirely new train, The *Empire Builder*, honoring James J. Hill and dramatizing the advantages of the newly opened Cascade Tunnel. Budd and Jenks supervised details down to appointments on the new diners—even the electric refrigerators and dishwashers. The sun parlor and observation car, with its "card room," was "the longest of its type in existence," but oldtimers regretted loss of the open platform. The new train's diners were named for states, and observation cars memorialized historically important persons.[17]

As the *Empire Builder* became the company's premier train, the *Oriental Limited* was downgraded in status though not quality. Now the GN had two first-class, modern transcontinentals to compete for long-haul business. The traveling public applauded the GN's devotion to "the last detail" in creature comfort. As if in proof, the *Builder* in summer months slowed each day so that the Stryker, Montana telegraph operator could hand up a package of freshly caught mountain trout to dining-car personnel, who quickly prepared them for appreciative dinner patrons.[18]

Throughout the 1920s, the Great Northern increased transcontinental passenger-train speeds. Part of this reflected the need to meet or exceed the performance of other rail car-

On June 10, 1929, the GN introduced an entirely new train—the *Empire Builder*, here posed at St. Paul Union Depot.

riers and part mirrored a recognition of competition from a new mode. In 1928, the passenger department blandly noted: "Expansion of airplane service, with dependable year-round schedules, is beginning to have its effect." The company responded by seeking cooperation, instituting a plan "effecting the savings of a business day" by arranging for two of its trains to connect at St. Paul with Northwest Airlines service between St. Paul and Chicago. The GN, in fact, fostered air travel by selling the airline's tickets and carrying its advertisements in timetables. Years later Budd recorded his disappointment at being unable to interest other western railroads in joint ownership of an air-transport company.[19]

Advertising and Promotion

Having spent heavily for new equipment, the GN opened an extensive campaign to sell travel to the Northwest, employing national and local newspapers and magazines, informative timetables, folders, booklets, window displays, color slides, lectures, radio, and motion pictures. The purpose was to create new business "and to direct such traffic as was bound to move somewhere, such as vacation or pleasure travel, to our line and to the territory it serves."[20]

In line with Budd's own interest and knowledge, the GN's advertising stressed the history in the GN's service area. The *William Crooks*, first locomotive in Minnesota, made several trips under its own power to fairs and similar events, and Grace Flandrau wrote interesting

The GN unveiled a statue of John F. Stevens at Summit, Montana, on July 21, 1925. The man who had located Marias Pass was there in grateful appreciation.

pamphlets on the history of the Northwest, to which President Budd, from his own extensive reading and exploration of the Upper Missouri, contributed many suggestions.

Louis W. Hill suggested an unusual twist: that the names of smaller main-line stations in Montana be changed to romantic-sounding western designations better suited to promotion. Thus, for instance, Kilroy became Spotted Robe, Lubec became Rising Wolf, Cadmus was changed to Gunsight, and Egan to Grizzly.

Vigorous solicitation and active upgrading of passenger offices, including the new one on New York's Fifth Avenue were added to the campaign, along with special tours, often in cooperation with others. Some were short, such as an excursion taking businessmen from the Twin Cities to towns in Minnesota and North Dakota. Louis Hill, who was particularly cordial with newspapermen, hosted writers in 1924 on the "Publisher's Edition of the *Oriental Limited*." En route, the journalists collected information, visited farms and factories, and met local residents.[21]

The "Upper Missouri Historical Expedition," which Ralph Budd led in July 1925, was the most publicized tour. Arranged under the auspices of governors and historical associations of four states in cooperation with the GN, the trip attracted a large number of writers and others interested in the history and lore of the Northwest. During the expedition the company dedicated monuments to commemorate explorers: a large sphere at Verendrye, N.D., honoring David Thompson; a rose-colored shaft at Meriwether, Montana, farthest north reached by the Lewis and Clark expedition; and a bronze statue of John F. Stevens at Summit, Montana, celebrating his locating Marias Pass through the Rockies. At Willis-

ton, N.D., Indians of many tribes took part in colorful ceremonies depicting for tour members a slice of western history; and at Lake McDonald in Glacier National Park, Charles M. Russell, famed painter, joined the travelers.

In all, the 1929 advertising budget topped $1 million. Expressed as a percentage of passenger revenues, these costs rose sharply— meaning that passenger revenues throughout the decade, except for the isolated years 1923 and 1925, declined in spite of new equipment, excellent service, and advanced advertising. Indeed, statistical measures of the GN's passenger business for the eleven years from 1920 to 1931 revealed a long-term trend. From a high in 1920, the decline was almost constant. Passenger-train revenue dropped from $30.4 million in 1920 to $11 million in 1931; passenger fares fell from $20.6 million to $6 million. Not many more than a million passengers traveled on GN trains in 1931, compared with 8.5 million in 1920. It was a bitter disappointment for Budd and for those who directed passenger activities. Could they hope for much of a future with that record?

22

Expansion and Development

The Great Northern in the 1920s found it had to reevaluate two traditional ways of generating freight traffic: building lines and selecting programs for economic development. Historically, a prominent corporate railroad strategy was to construct lines as feeders for main arteries, broaden the service area, and protect against competitive encroachment. As a corollary, railroad companies, especially those building through essentially unsettled areas, promoted a variety of undertakings designed to encourage settlement and economic growth. After World War I, however, GN managers faced the need to adapt to changed circumstances and, as a consequence, to formulate new policies.[1]

More Branch Lines

Although the decade of the 1920s was not marked by extensive branch-line expansion, the GN did experience scattered growth. For instance, it acquired the electrically operated Spokane & Inland Empire Railroad in 1927 for $1.25 million. The GN had investment in this company since 1910, and its bankruptcy nine years later rather forced the GN's hand. Restyled the Spokane, Coeur

D'Alene & Palouse Railway under Great
Northern ownership, the 179-mile company offered interurban passenger service, but its real
utility came in service to various lumber mills
in Idaho and grain elevators in the rich Palouse country.

To reach grain-producing areas elsewhere,
the GN extended one feeder in Montana and
constructed another. Between 1910 and 1913,
the company had built a branch from Bainville
on the main line northwest to Plentywood and
then west to Scobey. There the track ended
until the mid-1920s, when farmers' requests
and threatened expansion by the Soo Line got
construction under way again. Indeed, the Soo
had stated publicly that it intended to lengthen
its route from Sanish, N.D., across the Missouri River to Fairview, Montana, and surveyors were reportedly working between there and
Great Falls, a major GN traffic center. Here
the Great Northern prevailed, not the Soo. The
forty-nine-mile line from Scobey to Opheim
was completed during the summer of 1926. A
more ambitious branch extended from Saco,
on the GN's main line, north and west to
Hogeland. As early as 1917, the GN had considered building in the "Big Flat" country,
but World War I interrupted. Late in the
1920s, company planners again took up the
project, inspired by local demand, improved
economic conditions, and discovery that the
Canadian Pacific was hauling a large volume
of the grain produced in that area. Begun in
April 1928, the new line of seventy-eight
miles was formally opened eight months later.

Another project dated from 1910, when GN
directors authorized a route from New Rockford, N.D., to Lewistown, Montana. This
route was meant to protect territory and to in-

crease plant capacity by providing a second
and shorter main line west. By 1916, though,
only a few short pieces in North Dakota and
Montana had been built. One 34-mile segment
ran from the Great Falls–Billings line to Lewistown, and other portions, totaling 108 miles,
included track from Snowden, Montana, south
to Sidney; from Fairview, Montana, east to
Watford City, N.D.; and from Newlon Junction, Montana, west to Richey. Running rights
over the Northern Pacific extended operations
from Sidney to Newlon Junction. No further

construction on the projected line was undertaken for some years.

Late in the 1920s, however, construction
became an issue between the GN and the NP,
arousing a vigorous, if small "railroad war."
The NP opened hostilities by announcing plans
to construct a branch from Glendive west
through Circle to Brockway. This struck the
GN as an invasion of the territory for its long-
planned second main line and, Ralph Budd
said, the GN determined to oppose the NP
"not because we want to interfere with their

183

Expansion and Development

plans, but because they have come forward with plans which interfere with ours of long standing.'' Regulatory agencies finally undertook to settle the dispute. The Montana Board of Railroad Commissioners recommended that the NP's application be approved and the GN's be denied. When the ICC accepted this recommendation, the matter seemed settled. Instead, Montana's ''railroad war'' escalated. In 1929, the NP made application to build from Woodrow, on its new Brockway line, to Bloomfield, a town only 14 miles from the GN's Richey line. Stung, the GN first asked for permission to extend its rail 32 miles from Richey west to Hamblin, then petitioned to

By 1927, the Spokane & Inland Empire Railroad became the Spokane, Coeur D'Alene & Palouse Railway.

add 73 miles to Jordan. Offended in kind, the NP sought to build west from Brockway to Edwards, adding insult to injury by proposing an extension through Jordan. The GN then revived the entire New Rockford–Lewistown project, and asked for authority to build 195 miles from Richey through Jordan to an intersection with the Milwaukee at Winnett, whence trackage rights could open a route to Lewistown. Not to be outdone, the NP sought to build from Edwards to Lewistown, along a route that would parallel the projected GN line.[2]

The Great Depression terminated the war in eastern Montana, where local traffic could hardly be expected to support one new railroad, let alone two. By 1930, the contestants considered joint trackage to reduce construction costs, but then as hard times deepened they abandoned the entire project. Indeed, this flurry of jousting ended significant railroad construction in both Montana and North Dakota.

Lure of California

More important by far was the opening of a route to California, a project which James J. Hill had long dreamed of. In this the Great Northern and the Northern Pacific acted more or less cooperatively. They had, of course, operated coastal steamers from Oregon to San Francisco, and they had jointly sponsored the Spokane, Portland & Seattle Railroad, completed from Spokane to Portland in 1908. Then they had looked south of the Columbia River, where they acquired—through the SP&S—the Oregon Electric in the Willamette Valley, and where they tilted with Harriman in the Deschutes River campaign. In the process they had utilized the Oregon Trunk

Railway, which ran south from Wishram, Washington, on the Columbia River, to Bend, in central Oregon, where its rails pointed tantalizingly toward California.

The Southern Pacific, on the other hand, considered western Oregon its domain and California its province. In 1923, economic conditions improved and the SP, left intact following government attempts to divide its properties, sought to strengthen its hold in Oregon by new construction and impressive betterments. Its original route from the Bay Area to Oregon, the Siskiyou line via Medford and Ashland, had sharp curves and heavy grades, but the Siskiyou was supplanted when the SP completed the Natron Cutoff from Springfield, Oregon, to Klamath Falls, south of Bend. The SP then added the Alturas Cutoff from Klamath Falls to Alturas, California, and upgraded a branch line from Alturas to Fernley, Nevada. All this trackage opened massive sources of lumber, provided a shorter and easier route from Portland and Eugene to the Overland Route at Ogden, and vastly improved the SP's competitive position.

This collective activity on the part of the SP, and a growing demand by Oregonians for even more rail miles and better service, awakened the latent interest of the GN, and to a lesser extent the NP, in building onward from Bend. The most feasible route was south to a junction with the SP's Natron Cutoff and trackage rights thereon to Klamath Falls. The SP, however, looked unfavorably on this possibility, and sought to further solidify its position in the region by negotiating for control of the Oregon, California & Eastern (OC&E), a short line extending east from Klamath Falls. For Ralph Budd, though, California was simply too alluring. He would, if necessary, challenge SP's supremacy by initially seeking

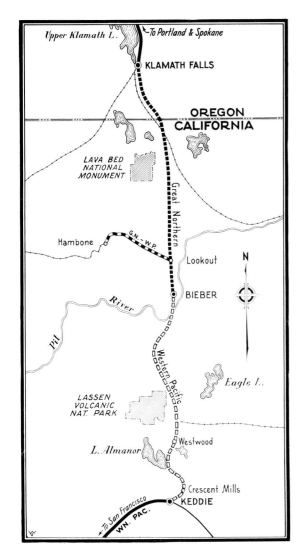

In June 1930, the ICC approved Great Northern's plans for an "inside gateway."

entry to Klamath Falls, under the flag of the Oregon Trunk.

In May 1926, the ICC authorized the Oregon Trunk to construct a line from Bend to a junction with either the SP's Natron Cutoff, or to an extension of the OC&E—provided that equitable arrangements could be worked out among the railroads involved. If the SP declined to grant trackage rights, the Trunk could gain authority to locate and build its own line. The SP, understandably, refused terms, and so the Trunk, late in 1926, asked the ICC for permission to construct a line from Bend via Paunina and Sprague River into Klamath Falls. In 1927, the regulatory body granted the request.

All was not well, though, between the GN and the NP. Indeed, the NP eventually concluded that extending the jointly owned Oregon Trunk would attract too little new traffic to benefit its main routes and, more important, did not wish to offend the SP, with which it had preferential traffic arrangements at Portland. The NP also felt that the Trunk's extension would benefit the GN at its expense, and that Oregon lumber, competing with shipments from the NP's established sources in Washington and Idaho, would hurt those shippers. Moreover, on the new line, some lumber loaded on the NP might move south, depriving that company of the long-haul business to eastern markets. The NP therefore backed out, halting construction work.

But the GN was not to be denied. In the spring of 1927, Budd gained permission for the GN to replace the Oregon Trunk in proceedings before the ICC. The SP felt pressured, for it could no longer play the NP against the GN and, finally, after prolonged and often heated negotiations, the SP agreed to grant both joint use of its line from Chemult to

E. C. Leedy recruited Mennonites to farm the area around Deer Park, Washington, during the late 1920s.

Klamath Falls and the GN's right to purchase a half interest in the OC&E.[3]

The Great Northern completed the necessary link from Bend to Chemult and opened it for service in May 1928. As finished, the extension consisted of 23.4 miles of newly improved logging railroad south from Bend, then 46.3 miles of construction to Chemult; from there, running rights on nearly 75 miles of the SP's Natron Cutoff completed the new route to Klamath Falls. The GN also now owned a half interest in the 38.5-mile OC&E, which soon completed a 26.5-mile extension to the town of Bly, deep in lumber country.

Unsatisfied with this major coup, Budd had already turned to California. Indeed, while negotiations for entrance into Klamath Falls were under way, he became convinced that, by itself, extension into southern Oregon would be of questionable value. W. P. Kenney commented that the Klamath Falls region had little but its timber to offer; when that was sawed, the GN would have more than 400 miles of railroad south of the Columbia River in

"about as poor a country as could possibly be picked out," unless the Bend–Klamath Falls line became an integral step toward the central Pacific coast.[4]

Budd studied options. Northern California, he knew, was rich in resources with some of the finest timber in the United States and the promise of irrigated farming for the future. Also, a line south from Klamath Falls could meet the Western Pacific (WP), thus opening the possibility of freight crossing the Sierra Nevadas by WP's relatively easy Feather River route, an inviting gateway to Sacramento and San Francisco. In this, the GN could anticipate growth in traffic with new markets, for the WP had an important connection at Stockton with the Santa Fe. And a route south of Klamath Falls could be expected to increase traffic by reducing the rail distance between San Francisco and inland points, such as Spokane, as well as by connecting dissimilar producing areas such as the northern Great Plains and California. Louis Hill agreed in theory, but proposed that the GN build its own tracks to San Francisco. Ralph Budd, however, believed cooperating with other railroads was the best policy and, as he told Hill, executives of the WP were receptive. Budd prevailed. Eventually, the GN and the WP agreed that the GN should build 91.6 miles from Klamath Falls south to Bieber, California, to which the WP would construct 112 miles of line north from its main stem at Keddie. Also, the two parties agreed to acquire in California a logging branch from Hambone east to Lookout on the GN's portion of the projected road, giving the WP running rights thereon to collect lumber moving south.

When the joint proposal was submitted to the ICC, the SP vigorously campaigned in opposition. The contest was glorified by the Se-

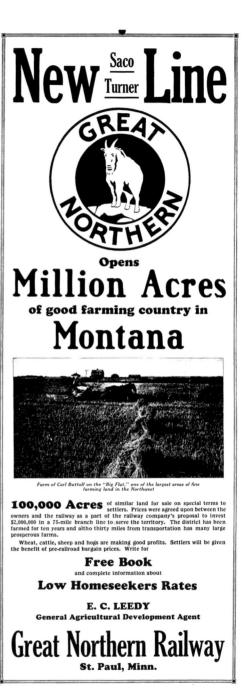

Street signs in the middle of wheat shocks suggest optimistic growth for Hogeland, Montana, in 1928.

attle Daily Times as ''one of the epic battles of modern railroading.'' Nevertheless, the ICC was not impressed by the SP's contention that no new lines were needed, believing that ''benefits of competition'' justified an affirmative answer. Approval followed in June 1930. In August the GN began work on the northern part, grading with machinery powered by internal combustion engines. The first section from Klamath Falls had easy grades and curves, but farther south was a difficult lava bed. Still, the GN reached the Pit River Valley at Bieber in September 1931, and the WP completed its more demanding road two months later.[5]

James J. Hill's dream finally had been achieved, as had Arthur Curtiss James's wish to effect a junction between the WP and the GN. As chairman of the WP's board, and as a large stockholder and active director of the GN, James properly wielded the maul at the golden-spike ceremony held at Bieber on November 10, 1931.

Frustrations in Colonizing

Constructing new lines was one way of generating traffic; developmental programs were another. After World War I, management lost no time in reactivating promotional programs that had proved.so successful. As in the past, the home office handled inquiries, designed expansive advertising, and produced promotional literature for distribution to prospective homeseekers. Agents toured the country, such as the older Midwest, where Edwin C. Leedy, head of the agricultural department, thought prospects for finding

suitable settlers were best. Between 1927 and 1931, the company also maintained an immigration agent in Europe.[6]

When experience showed that the Northwest had no large blocks of cultivable land still to be settled, Leedy focused on specific, smaller areas. Constructing the Saco–Hogeland line in Montana during 1928 opened to wheat production a region hitherto used primarily for grazing; for a time Leedy directed his department's promotional routine there. Just before the line opened, he reported that his men had been instrumental in selling 13,000 acres to new set-

tlers. Leedy likewise believed that cutover lands in northern Minnesota, northern Idaho, and Washington held significant opportunities for successful colonizing. The GN operated special trains to show how such lands could be readied for the plow, and late in the 1920s and into the next decade, Leedy attempted to combine colonization on cutover land with older techniques for settling church groups. Establishing contact with discontented Mennonites in Indiana and Kansas, and with refugees from the Soviet Union, Leedy directed them to northeastern Washington. Few individuals had capital enough to develop a farm, though, and some who did take land quickly failed. The campaign collapsed in 1930, with little to show except "bitter disappointments."[7]

Leedy also continued trying to settle irrigated lands, but with mixed success. Throughout the decade his department encouraged homeseekers to go to the Milk River in north-central Montana. A refinery built at Chinook in 1925 by the Utah-Idaho Sugar Company was progress, but keeping beet growers on the land proved to be a long struggle. During the 1920s, representatives also directed settlers to the Lower Yellowstone, Sun River, and other projects.[8]

Inducing homeseekers to occupy lands abandoned earlier was a more significant goal. Although Leedy knew that moving settlers among regions provided no simple answer to complex problems in northwestern agriculture, he thought that many skilled and well-equipped farmers in the Midwest would leave high-priced property in their native states for cheaper lands. Beginning in 1923, the railroad's agricultural-development department listed farms for sale or rent, cooperating closely with both local improvement groups and state promotional agencies. The scope was not spectacular, but it was steady, and in 1931 Leedy could report that all improved farms in western Minnesota and eastern North Dakota were occupied.[9]

Attempts at colonizing in the 1920s were disappointing. Leedy reported that between 1917 and 1927 he moved roughly one-third as many as in the ten years before 1917. Bowing to reality, Kenney in 1934 doubted that "we will have any more settlement in our country." He was essentially correct if he meant large movements of settlers as in earlier de-

cades. Nonetheless, Leedy continued his devoted labors until he retired in 1939.[10]

Agricultural Diversification and Irrigation

While Leedy did all he could to swell rural population in the Northwest, he was also trying to help farmers expand, or at least improve and stabilize their production of field crops and livestock. One of his approaches— agricultural diversification—although not new, was given much of the department's time. In many areas of the Northwest, diversification meant introducing livestock and dairying, a change hampered by rural inertia and the farmers' lack of experience and capital. Nevertheless, Leedy pushed ahead, distributing educational literature, sending subordinates to preach the doctrine at country meetings, and cooperating with the agricultural extension service and other organizations working toward the same end.

Leedy especially emphasized development of livestock. In 1924, the railroad gave twenty-four purebred bulls to farmers in Minnesota, North Dakota, and Montana; arrangements with recipients were similar to those outlined by James J. Hill years earlier. Leedy estimated that within four seasons the bulls would produce 2,000 animals of an improved type. In subsequent years, however, the GN changed its program as company officials came to believe that a farmer who paid for an animal would be motivated to take proper care of it and to make maximum use of it. Thereafter, the GN limited its work with livestock to cooperative ventures, and farmers themselves took greater responsibility.

Such a program was run by the Agricultural

Credit Corporation, an agency proposed by President Calvin Coolidge and financed by business interests to rehabilitate the banking structure in the northern Great Plains. Among the leading subscribers were northwestern railroads; the GN put up $60,000. By the end of 1924, after about ten months of operation, the credit corporation, having lent over $5 million to 236 banks, had just about completed its program for stabilization. The Agricultural Credit Corporation then shifted to diversification. It agreed to lend up to $1,000, at 6 percent, to individual farmers for purchasing high-grade livestock, which served as security for the loans. Under these arrangements the corporation functioned through 1930, lending $6,718,114 to 13,929 farmers, who purchased about 26,000 cattle and 256,000 sheep. Almost half the animals went to farms in GN territory.

Diversification included raising livestock and also introducing new field crops. Some areas needed new cash crops, as in the Wenatchee and Okanogan valleys of Washington, where apples had been the major crop for twenty years. To improve agricultural stability, additional kinds of fruit and garden produce were introduced. Sugar beets and potatoes were especially promising in both the Red River Valley and the irrigated areas of Montana. Highly resistant to disease and adverse weather, sugar beets gave farmers a cash crop fitted to a desirable system of crop rotation; the tops and pulp of beets were valuable too as feed for livestock. This crop, Leedy pointedly observed, also generated heavy tonnage for railroads serving producing districts. Meanwhile, if more potatoes were produced, markets had to be developed and varieties standardized. Company agents worked with

Leedy gave special importance to the production of sugar beets in the irrigated areas of Montana.

growers to improve selection of seed and packing of potatoes, and they also established relations with agricultural colleges and growers in the South to open that promising market to northwestern producers of seed potatoes.

Washington's apple industry received help, too, in the form of expert advice and financial assistance. When local resources from 1926 through 1928 proved inadequate for constructing needed warehouses, the GN agreed to make low-interest loans to cold-storage firms. During the depression repayment was slow, necessitating many waivers and postponements of interest, and yet the GN achieved its major objective — encouraging the apple industry and expanding the railroad's traffic.

Irrigation remained on the list of activities to be promoted. Few were more alert than Leedy to irrigated farming's potential for generating traffic. After 1916, however, as the federal government assumed most responsibility for planning and constructing irrigation projects, the GN ended direct participation, financial and otherwise, in such programs. Although the railroad continued to encourage the federal government to increase and improve irrigation facilities, it thereafter limited itself chiefly to colonization and educational work with farmers who utilized irrigation.

Perhaps the GN's supportive role was best demonstrated during the early stages of the Columbia Basin project in north-central Washington. James J. Hill and others had launched pioneer projects in the Big Bend country, and when World War I increased demand for food production, coupled with drought years, others decided to promote irrigation. Subsequently,

two groups urged governmental action. One, in Wenatchee and Ephrata, formulated plans for constructing a low dam and installing a pumping unit at Grand Coulee. In Spokane, others believed that the Basin could best be irrigated by diverting water from Pend d'Oreille Lake and rivers in Idaho. The GN gave financial support to the Spokane-based Columbia Basin Irrigation League between 1926 and 1932, and although time would show that the railroad did not back the accepted approach, the league helped popularize the idea of irrigation in the Columbia Basin.

Although promoting irrigation and agricul-

tural diversification was a major objective of the GN's agricultural development department, it took part in many other activities. Much of the work was routine, but all was calculated to enhance the agricultural economy and thus generate traffic for the railroad. Setting an example, Leedy's men regularly helped organize and manage local fairs, often serving as judges. They also conducted farm tours and participated in meetings and events sponsored by the agricultural extension service or agricultural colleges or both. Furthermore, the GN contributed to groups working to improve agriculture or to solve specific agricultural problems. Between 1922 and 1931, the railroad gave generously to the Conference for the Prevention of Grain Rust, on occasion to local groups such as the Northern Montana Potato Growers' Association, and regularly to rural youth organizations.

Northern Montana: Special Problems

No section of the company's territory challenged the agricultural development department more than northern Montana. During the decade ending in 1917, as hordes of homeseekers hurried to take up land, the vast expanse of rolling prairie and bench land was the scene of the last great land rush in American history. In promoting that movement, few agencies had been more influential than the Great Northern. James J. Hill himself, in his last years, had been a leader in promoting settlement there, believing sincerely that difficulties in converting former range land into traditional farms were no greater than had been encountered on other frontiers.

The bonanza years ended, however, and by 1920 much of northern Montana was near economic collapse. One drought after another, combined with plagues of insects, sharply cut farm production. Despair displaced hope. One observer wrote to Ralph Budd in 1924: "It is a pitiful picture that parts of Montana offer today." Studies showed that 63 percent of farmers had lost their lands or were in danger of doing so. Nor was the shock limited to farmers. Country towns fell ghostlike as merchants, bankers, and others joined in the exodus.[11]

The debacle disturbed and embarrassed GN management. The company had done much to attract settlers, but after the economic collapse in the early 1920s, GN managers privately admitted their mistake in encouraging that northern Montana be converted to a land of small, general farms. "It seems . . . that before any more colonizing is done in the western states," Louis W. Hill observed in 1922, "those who have at heart the interest of all concerned . . . must be sure that the land it is proposed to convert from the range to the small farm is more suitable to the latter than former uses." Ralph Budd added that "the best agriculturists . . . agree that the prevailing conditions must be considered in order to farm successfully in that country. . . . What the country needs is farmers who know how to farm. . . ."[12]

The question in the 1920s was how to find or develop "farmers who know how to farm." Milburn L. Wilson of Montana State College applied himself to that problem. In studies conducted early in the decade, Wilson showed that methods proved successful in the Midwest could not be relied on in Montana, where years of big crops were followed by failures. It appeared that where precipitation was low, farmers needed to avoid one-crop farming, to be as self-sufficient as possible, and to have financial and feed reserves to carry them through bad years. More corn for silage, alfalfa, and other forage crops should be grown to support a livestock industry. Wheat, however, should remain the basic cash crop, produced by dry-land farming methods with tractor-powered implements designed especially for that type of work. In 1923, Wilson launched his "Fairway Farms" project. Managing five farms in different sections of the state, he soon concluded that the key to successful dry-land farming was extensive and efficient operation. Holdings should be large, and farmers must use the most modern and specialized machinery available.[13]

Wilson's work pointed the way for Mon-

The Great Northern followed its historic course in 1928 and 1929 with the operation of low-cost wheat demonstration trains.

tana's farmers, but they had to know about his findings, and the best way of reaching them was the educational train. In February and April 1923, the GN's Big Hitch and Dry Farming Special stopped at forty-four towns in northeastern Montana. The 11,000 who visited the train saw exhibits of dry-farming equipment, and demonstrations showed how several teams of horses could be hitched together to move heavy equipment if tractors were not available. In 1928, Wilson again asked for assistance in taking the lessons of his "Fairway Farms" project to farmers, and again the railroad responded. The resulting Low Cost Wheat and Mechanical Farming Special spent two months in 1929 touring northern Montana. Almost 12,000 people attended fifty meetings, saw large modern tractors and other equipment, and heard experts explain the value of using such implements.

"Montana's agriculture," wrote Edwin C. Leedy in 1926, "has been revolutionized in the past five years." His evaluation may have been premature, but it was essentially correct. Gone was the dream of copying on Montana's bench lands the small-unit, highly diversified agriculture of the Midwest. Instead, extensive dry-land farms were devoted to producing wheat by a sparse population using heavy, expensive equipment. The GN, like others, had made earlier mistakes of this kind, but in the 1920s it did its part to promote a viable agriculture in that vast state.[14]

Generating traffic, whether by constructing new lines or by development programs, was a long-term proposition. Although results in tons of freight and in operating income might not be discernible for years, top management did not doubt that outlays for new trackage and for agricultural and industrial promotion were justified. Data are elusive, however. "It would be impossible," wrote Leedy in 1931, "to estimate the value of the development work. . . . It is to a considerable extent educational and cumulative. . . ." It was the same with new mileage. For instance, that between Bend and Bieber clearly stimulated additional traffic, but it would not be until World War II that the full importance was realized. Ralph Budd counseled patience. It was, he often observed, a matter of building for the future.[15]

23

An Attempted Merger

"The trouble with the Northwestern carriers," Ralph Budd wrote in 1925, "is that there are too many." This unpleasant circumstance had come about when the third and last northern trunk line in the United States—the Chicago, Milwaukee & St. Paul Railway (later reorganized as the Chicago, Milwaukee, St. Paul & Pacific Railroad)—was built after the turn of the century in an "abiding faith that the Northwest would continue to develop for many years." When growth slowed, however, it meant receivership for the Milwaukee and disappointing revenues for the Great Northern and the Northern Pacific. As Great Northern executives came to view the situation, a merger of the Great Northern and the Northern Pacific offered a sensible solution.[1]

Indeed, the question of railroad mergers was an important topic of discussion and focus of legislation throughout the 1920s. Congress had recognized the nation's need for strong railroads in the Transportation Act of 1920, by which the Interstate Commerce Commission was ordered to "prepare and adopt a plan for the consolidation of the railroad properties of the continental United States into a limited number of systems." In formulating such a plan, the commission was directed to preserve

competition and existing channels of trade, where possible, and to establish systems that, under uniform rates, might be expected to generate approximately equal revenues. Acceptance of the ICC's proposals by the nation's carriers was not to be mandatory. Nevertheless, the congressional directive marked a significant reversal in the government's policy on railway consolidations—rejecting, in fact, the doctrine underlying the Supreme Court's 1904 decision that broke up an earlier GN and NP combination.[2]

Congress, foreseeing that a comprehensive plan for mergers might take years, further authorized the commission to approve voluntary combinations found to be in the public interest. But the implication was clear: any voluntary plan would have to harmonize with ICC proposals. Specifically, the regulatory agency might permit one railroad to acquire control of another "either under a lease or by the purchase of stock or in any manner not involving the consolidation of such carriers into a single system for ownership and operation. . . ." The commission might also grant certificates of convenience and necessity to cover acquisition and control.[3]

The Act of 1920 gave Budd and his associates equal doses of hope and worry. Quite clearly, the provision for voluntary combination implied a new era; presumably such moves would no longer be blocked on antitrust grounds, which had caused dissolution of the Northern Securities Company. On the other hand, the ICC's comprehensive plan might well violate relationships and communities of interest, such as those which had developed over the past quarter of a century between GN and NP, on the one hand, and their major jointly owned affiliates, the Chicago, Burlington & Quincy and the Spokane, Portland & Seattle, on the other.

Such disruption of relationships seemed easily possible early in the decade. Within six months after the Transportation Act was passed in 1920, the ICC took up the task of drawing tentative comprehensive plans, asking William Z. Ripley, a transportation authority at Harvard University, to gather information and devise general recommendations. Ripley proposed grouping all railroads into twenty-one great systems, and placed the Burlington with the NP, and the GN with the Milwaukee. The ICC's own tentative plan, dated August 3, 1921, reduced the number of suggested systems to nineteen, but left intact Ripley's arrangement for the Northwest. To System No. 15, the Great Northern–Milwaukee alliance, the commission added two iron-ore roads, three minor lines, and suggested that the Spokane, Portland & Seattle could be placed in either the Northern Pacific–Burlington or the Great Northern–Milwaukee system.

The ICC's plan aroused no more enthusiasm among GN and NP officials than among railroaders generally. During the two years of hearings on the subject, practically every major carrier objected to some feature and offered its own recommendations. Representatives of the GN, NP, and Burlington predictably urged that their three companies be placed in the same system. Brought together by some of the ablest pioneers in American railroading, they noted, these companies had long-established and highly successful relationships that were of major importance to the Northwest.

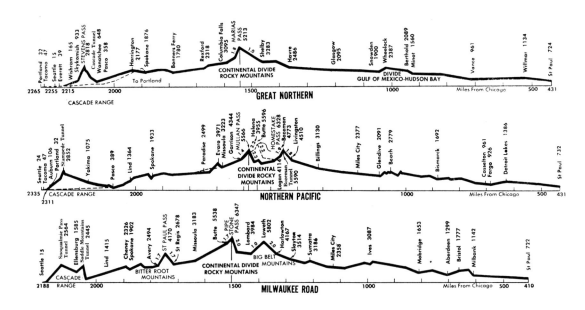

Furthermore, top management of the three companies contended that the problems of the weak Milwaukee could be solved without creating "unnatural alliances." If the GN and the NP were to be placed in different systems, officers of each hoped to be allied with the Burlington, not saddled with the Milwaukee. For his part, Ralph Budd maintained that "the Great Northern and the St. Paul [the Milwaukee] should not be combined, and, in the event the Hill lines cannot be kept together and one of them must be placed with the St. Paul, and the other with the Burlington, I think the Great Northern and the Burlington should be kept together." According to William J. Cunningham, professor of transportation at Harvard University, the "efforts of each of the northern lines to wish the poor St. Paul on the other was one of the entertaining features" of the hearings.[4]

As for the Milwaukee, its executives were ready to accept any arrangement which would

The relative advantages of the Great Northern's profile compared to those of the Northern Pacific and the Milwaukee Road are immediately apparent. (Courtesy of Trains Magazine)

place that company with any road stronger than itself and which would separate the Hill roads. Milwaukee's president, Harry E. Byram, observed that "having heard both the Northern Pacific and the Great Northern set forth the advantages that accrue each to the other by an alliance with the St. Paul, I am prepared to agree with both of them." In fact, he preferred a Milwaukee–Union Pacific combination.[5]

Hearings on the ICC's tentative plan for consolidation illustrated the tremendous complexity in producing a final grouping. The agency accumulated a vast body of often contradictory information, and in 1925, ICC members expressed doubt that an acceptable comprehensive plan for consolidations could be designed. They regularly recommended, rather, that Congress relieve the agency of that task.

Meanwhile, voluntary combinations were going ahead. Almost 30 percent of the aggregate railroad mileage changed hands during the 1920s. The ICC regarded most of these shifts not as consolidations but as "acquisitions of control" by means of lease or stock purchase or both.

Especially interesting to the northern lines was the relationship between the Southern Pacific and the Central Pacific (CP). In 1922, the Supreme Court ordered the former to terminate control of the latter, citing the Sherman Antitrust Act. Yet, less than a year later, acting under the Transportation Act of 1920, the ICC permitted the SP to reacquire control of the CP by lease and stock ownership—and federal courts subsequently upheld the ICC. Apparently, concluded Budd, the commission and the courts were prepared to abandon previous convictions where acquiring control did not amount to complete consolidation.

Executives of the GN and the NP thus began to explore the possibility of merger. In the background was James J. Hill's grand design, destroyed two decades earlier but still remembered favorably by senior officers of both northern railroads. Most influential, though, was Ralph Budd's conviction, as leading spirit in the project, that potential operating efficiencies made unification highly desirable, if not imperative. Preliminary discussions involved Arthur Curtiss James, the GN's major stockholder; Howard Elliott, NP president; Hale Holden, president of the Burlington; and Budd. In 1925, they decided to proceed. The object was to create a new operating company, the Great Northern Pacific Railway Company, to be incorporated in Delaware with capital

Ralph Budd was the leading spirit in the project to merge the Great Northern and the Northern Pacific.

stock of five million shares that would be exchanged for stock of the two merging companies. The Burlington would be left to operate as an entity effectively controlled through stock ownership, and the Spokane, Portland, & Seattle would be acquired and operated under lease. In all, the Great Northern Pacific would directly control 15,000 miles of road, and, through the Burlington, 11,000 miles more.

Events moved rapidly. Stockholders of the GN and the NP were asked to place their stock with designated New York banking houses,

where more than 70 percent of the two roads was soon deposited. Meanwhile, the northern lines began an extensive campaign to build favorable public opinion. On July 8, 1927, applications for merger were filed with the ICC.[6]

Hearings before ICC examiners began October 24, 1927, and continued intermittently until March 31, 1928. Oral arguments were given before the full commission October 3–5, 1928. During these proceedings, 147 local associations, eleven state agencies, three counties, six individuals, eleven smaller railroads, and four Class 1 carriers intervened to support or oppose the applications. Four thousand pages of testimony and 285 exhibits were presented at the October hearing alone.

In making the case for merger, GN and NP spokesmen restated arguments offered in opposition to the ICC's tentative consolidation plan: the community of interest among the roads had proved its value to the Northwest for thirty years and was itself a major justification; unification would result in operating and other savings estimated at $10.1 million annually; operating savings in due course would reduce the cost of transportation; proposed changes would bring the Northwest a stronger and more aggressive rail system, which would provide better service and enhance the area's competitive position; and the Great Northern Pacific would be stronger than the total of its components, hence better able to raise funds for improvements and developmental programs. In short, public interest demanded merger.

Competition, or its diminution, was the primary issue, but GN and NP managers insisted that shippers, passengers, and workers had nothing to fear from combination. Vigorous transcontinental competition would continue with the Milwaukee, the Union Pacific, and water transport via the Panama Canal. Roads such as the Soo Line, the Chicago, St. Paul, Minneapolis & Omaha, and the Chicago & North Western would remain vigorous regional carriers, and throughout the territory highway competition was a clear reality. Spokesmen contended that, contrary to uninformed opinion, little competition would be eliminated by unification. Although the GN and the NP paralleled each other, they were more complementary than competitive. Indeed, more than 98 percent of the two roads' tonnage was either noncompetitive or would continue competitive after merger. As for labor, merger proponents anticipated no sudden layoffs. Any reduction in work force could be handled in the normal turnover of workers; employees would be reassigned so as to minimize problems.

Finally, attorneys for the northern lines cited drastic changes in economic and legal conditions since the Northern Securities decision. New rail and severe modal competition had arisen. The Sherman Antitrust Act of 1890 had been the basis for the Supreme Court decision in the Northern Securities case; now the Transportation Act of 1920 provided that railroads, under specified conditions, were freed from older statutes and were encouraged to form combinations.

Nevertheless, the proposal aroused strong opposition from state regulatory agencies, municipalities, businessmen and farmers, and railroads. Six state railway commissions registered their opposition, primarily on grounds that unification would destroy competition and do violence to the Milwaukee in particular. Chambers of commerce in several cities were opposed for a host of reasons, simple self-interest being by far the commonest.

The receiver of the Minneapolis & St. Louis Railway, a bankrupt Class I reaching southeast from the Twin Cities into Iowa and to Peoria, Illinois, complained that the merger was counter to law and to public interest in that it would create an imbalance among northwestern carriers. Probably more to the point, spokesmen for the M&StL feared loss of business at Minneapolis. Interestingly, of the short lines that intervened, nine wanted to be included in the merger.

The bankrupt Milwaukee's management of course spoke loudest in opposition. As soon as the plan was announced, Harry E. Byram, as receiver, proclaimed his road's determination to fight the project to the bitter end. When Milwaukee officials appeared before the ICC, they flatly contradicted arguments presented earlier by proponents and claimed that the community of interest among the GN, NP, and CB&Q was not a valid reason for approval of the merger. According to Milwaukee officers, the proposed unification would be, in effect, a consolidation, counter to the Act of 1920. Further, it would violate the purpose of that act by establishing unbalanced railroad systems in the Northwest, and by blocking hopes for the ICC's success in creating a general plan for consolidation. Competition and channels of trade would be destroyed or badly disarrayed, and savings arising from the merger would in no way compensate for its evils. To be sure, if the Great Northern Pacific was combined with the Burlington, it would have almost two and a half times as many miles of track as the Milwaukee, and in 1929 a net income twelve times larger. Moreover, Milwaukee spokesmen carefully pointed out that the northern lines said nothing specific about reduced rates, in spite of their emphasis on savings in cost of

operation. Byram and others also objected that the merger would have the practical effect of making the Burlington an integral part of the Great Northern Pacific. Finally, the Milwaukee contended that public opinion, as reflected in the testimony, was firmly opposed to the merger.

Officers of the GN and the NP, attempting to refute the opposition's arguments, understandably sought to put the proposed combination in the best possible light. They even expressed willingness to absorb five connecting short lines and the weak M&StL to meet aims of the Act of 1920.

While the Great Northern Pacific case was still before the ICC, on December 9, 1929, the commission released its long-delayed national consolidation plan. Proposing twenty-one railroad systems, it placed the GN and NP together, thrust the Burlington into another system, and left the Milwaukee to be merged with two prosperous iron-ore roads. The ICC's announcement attracted little attention. The *New York Times* said wearily: The "groupings . . . provide a basis for discussion. They show what combinations could obtain approval. They accomplish little more." The plan, however, did foreshadow the ICC's views in the pending merger case.[7]

On February 11, 1930, the ICC made public its decision. A majority of commissioners found that the proposal of the Great Northern and the Northern Pacific was in the public interest and was compatible with the Transportation Act of 1920. Approval, however, was subject to four conditions. Although three of these were minor, the fourth presented the northern lines with a dilemma, requiring the GN and the NP to divest themselves of the Burlington and sever all ties with it.[8]

The ICC's objectives were obvious. Members of the commission wanted to protect the Milwaukee and to placate those who maintained that the Great Northern Pacific, with effective control of the Burlington, would dominate rail transportation from Chicago and St. Louis to the Pacific Northwest. Moreover, the Great Northern Pacific, with ties to the Burlington intact, would not square with the regulatory agency's general plan for consolidation. A majority of commissioners noted flatly that, although "the applicants' plan does not contemplate actual consolidation [with the Burlington] it is of such permanent character that our approval of it, with control of the Burlington passing into the same hands that would control the northern lines, would be clearly incompatible with our consolidation program."[9]

Meeting the ICC's onerous condition would be not only distasteful but difficult for the northern lines; both needed a strong link with Chicago. Moreover, the GN and the NP together owned 97 percent of Burlington stock, serving as security for bonds totaling approximately $200 million, and locating a buyer for the Burlington promised to be difficult in a sagging money market.

Meanwhile, opposition to the merger increased as economic conditions deteriorated. Organized labor, which had been passive, now became militant. By early spring 1930, Budd observed, the brotherhoods and others launched "an elaborate attack . . . against railroad consolidation with particular reference" to the merger of the northern lines. Soon were added voices of politicians, with Montana's Senator Burton K. Wheeler leading the pack. The Senate adopted an antimerger resolution, and, reacting to pressure from many sources,

the ICC on October 17, 1930, determined to reopen hearings. Railroad consolidation, observed the embittered *Traffic World*, might as well be settled in political primaries.[10]

Vigorous political opposition, presumably reflecting hostile public opinion, was the final blow to the proposed Great Northern Pacific. Even assuming that consolidation advocates had been able to dispose of the Burlington, the matter would have to be reargued before the ICC, a chance for opponents to whip up still more public opposition. "Tales of distress and the complaints of the State Commissions might well arouse a feeling of resentment against the Northern lines," Budd concluded in October 1930. Louis Hill agreed that neither the GN nor the NP wished to oppose public opinion in the Northwest. Consequently, in January 1931, the northern lines withdrew their application. The dreams of James J. Hill and Ralph Budd were thus deferred.[11]

24

Corporate Health

No railroader knew better than Ralph Budd that profits depended on efficient operation, an adequate traffic base, and sound financial management. Under Budd's effective leadership, the Great Northern steadily upgraded equipment, roadbed, and structures, completed line extensions, and prosecuted development campaigns. Concurrently, Budd found ways of financing these programs and also of refunding the GN's half of the twenty-year bonds issued with the Northern Pacific in 1901 to take control of the Chicago, Burlington & Quincy.[1]

Growth in Funded Debt

When Budd became president, the GN's financial structure appeared exemplary. As of December 31, 1919, it had issued $249.5 million of stock, and funded debt totaled $270.5 million. Composed of four parts, the bonds, given here in order of their due dates, were: Collateral Trust Gold ($20 million); one-half of the GN–NP Joint 4s (GN's share, $107.6 million); bonds of affiliated or merged companies ($107.2 million); and the First and Refunding Gold, issued in 1911 under GN's First and Refunding indenture ($35.7

million). Great Northern officers anticipated postwar prosperity, so that neither paying the Collateral Trust Gold notes, due September 1, 1920, nor refunding the Joint 4s on July 1, 1921, appeared to be really problematic.

In 1920, as in 1919, the GN reduced debt by paying off its $20 million Collateral Trust 5 percent Gold Notes. When the postwar recession struck in 1920–1921, however, the larger 1921 refunding operation demanded judgment, courage, and financial skill. The railroad's costs rose more rapidly than revenues, and net operating income declined sharply. Only payments made under federal guarantee enabled the GN to achieve satisfactory net earnings, and the company's credit sank. In the tight money market of 1921, refunding $107.6 million in Joint 4 percent bonds suddenly looked a formidable burden. Furthermore, interest rates had risen; the prevailing Federal Reserve discount rate early in 1921 was 7 percent, higher than the company was permitted to pay under its 1911 mortgage indenture.

Refunding was complicated by the necessary involvement of the Burlington, the Northern Pacific, the Interstate Commerce Commission, and bankers. Budd realized, too, that he should gain approval of investors and shippers as well as governors and state regulatory commissions. The northern lines formally submitted a new two-step program. The first element was issuance of $230 million GN–NP joint fifteen-year, 6½ percent convertible gold bonds, dated July 1, 1921, callable at 103½ and backed by a new joint trust indenture and additional collateral security. As a second step, for exchange of the 6½s the GN and the NP were to issue $115 million in bonds each, those of the GN to be backed by a new general mortgage. At the insistence of New York bankers, the NP bonds were to bear 6 percent

Table 6. General Mortgage Bonds Issued by Great Northern Railway Company to the Public, 1921–1931

Year	Series	Amount par value	Date of maturity	Interest rate, %	Selling price by GN	Net interest rate
1921	A[a]	$115,000,000	1936	7	91½	7.65
1922	B	30,000,000	1952	5½	93⅛	5.91
1924	C	15,000,000	1973	5	90	5.55
1926	D	15,000,000	1976	4½	91½	4.91
1927	E	20,000,000	1977	4½	97	4.66
1930	E	20,000,000	1977	4½	95	4.74

a. Issued to enable refunding of GN's share of the maturing GN–NP Joint 4 percent bonds.

Sources: GNAR, 1921–1931.

and mature in 125 years, those of the GN were to pay 7 percent and be due in 15 years. On April 25, 1921, the ICC approved this program. On the same day, an underwriting syndicate headed by J. P. Morgan & Company and the First National Bank of the City of New York (the First National Bank) announced a refunding program. Inasmuch as these joint bonds were the largest issue of railroad securities ever, the number of participating financial houses was enlarged from the original eight in New York and Boston by adding fifty-seven, ranging from Philadelphia to the Twin Cities.[2]

Such careful preparation paid off handsomely. On May 16, 1921, the subscription was completed. The sale of $230 million Joint 6½s at 91½, after deducting the banker's discount and expenses, netted $210.1 million. To retire the remaining Joint 4s ($5.1 million),

the GN and the NP had to make up the difference.[3]

The bankers' insistence on allowing issuance of NP bonds at 6 percent while obliging the GN to 7 percent galled Ralph Budd, and he asked for an adjustment. Insisting that the two companies should bear equally the costs of refunding, he demanded that the NP pay $2.6 million compensation to the GN. The NP offered $1 million, but a blue-ribbon board of arbitration awarded the GN $1.5 million. Partial equalization did little to lessen the negative reaction by GN executives, who could not accept with equanimity actions that resulted in a net increase of $7.4 million in funded debt and $3.7 million in extra annual interest charges. In their irritation, though, they underemphasized possible desirable effects: if fifteen years later interest rates were lower than in 1921, the GN, compared with the NP, stood to gain.

Table 7. Great Northern Railway Operating Data, 1919–1931

Year	Railway operating revenues (in millions of dollars)			Railway operating expenditures		Net revenue from railway operations		Net railway operating income[a]	
	Freight	All other	Total	Millions of dollars	Percentage of total railway operating revenues	Millions of dollars	Percentage of total railway operating revenues	Millions of dollars	Percentage of total railway operating revenues
1919	$ 77.4	$29.2	$106.6	$ 87.1	81.7%	$19.5	18.3%	b	b
1920	89.8	32.8	122.6	114.0	93.0	8.6	7.0	b	b
1921	74.7	26.6	101.3	80.5	79.5	20.8	20.5	$12.9	12.7%
1922	78.1	25.4	103.5	79.6	76.9	23.9	23.1	17.3	16.7
1923	93.7	26.4	120.1	86.8	72.3	33.3	27.7	24.7	20.6
1924	86.1	24.1	110.2	75.2	68.2	35.0	31.8	24.2	22.0
1925	90.1	24.8	114.9	75.8	66.0	39.1	34.0	28.3	24.6
1926	93.3	24.1	117.4	75.3	64.1	42.1	35.9	31.3	26.7
1927	94.4	23.5	117.9	78.4	66.5	39.5	33.5	29.2	24.8
1928	104.0	22.7	126.7	83.2	65.7	43.5	34.3	31.3	24.7
1929	101.2	24.7	125.9	82.9	65.8	43.0	34.2	32.5	25.8
1930	85.8	19.2	105.0	72.6	69.1	32.4	30.9	21.9	20.9
1931	63.3	13.8	77.1	55.3	71.7	21.8	28.3	12.7	16.5

a. Net income from railway operations (NROI) is the remainder after deducting from net revenue from railway operations not only railway tax accruals, but also uncollectable revenues and net equipment rents.

b. Not published in GNAR for 1919 and 1920, when the railroads were still under United States government control.

Sources: GNAR, 1919–1931.

Reminiscing in the late 1930s, a First National Bank officer thought that if he could change his recommendations, given in 1921, it would be to advise the companies to make their mortgage bonds convertible into stock at par. Both issues would have been converted into stock in 1929 and "the burden of fixed charges of the two roads much reduced before the subsequent depression."[4]

However heavy the burden of debt arising from ownership of the CB&Q shares may have seemed at times, the GN and the NP used their power as stockholders to authorize actions bolstering their own strategic positions. In 1921, the Burlington declared a dividend of

600,000 shares, raising the number outstanding to 1,708,391. Its directors then voted a 10 percent dividend from current earnings and an additional 15 percent from surplus accumulated over a number of years before 1921. As a result, the GN received from the Burlington $17.5 million more in cash dividends in 1921 than in 1920. *Barron's* correctly observed that the extra dividend "was clearly intended to carry dividends of the controlling roads over a period of depression and readjustment."[5]

Meanwhile, to finance Budd's extensive improvement program, the GN resorted to bonds (see Table 6). The ICC would not permit sales of new stock at less than par, and the market value of GN shares did not rise that high until the late 1920s. During Budd's regime, in addition to the $115 million 7 percent bonds of 1921, the company issued $100 million under the new General Mortgage. All purchases of GN's bonds were made in routine fashion by Morgan & Company and the First National Bank, either for an underwriting syndicate or for their own accounts.

From 1920 to 1925, the GN contracted almost $25 million in new equipment obligations, and it continued to use the Great Northern Equipment Company (GNEC), modifying only the method for providing funds for purchasing equipment. From 1911 to 1920, to avoid putting rolling stock under the First and Refunding Mortgage, the GN had provided funds by buying stock of GNEC, which in turn bought locomotives and cars and leased them to the parent firm. Beginning in 1923, however, the GN advanced necessary sums directly to the equipment company. In these contracts, GNEC was the vendor, the First National Bank the lessor and trustee, and the GN the lessee. At the end of 1931, the railroad's outstanding advances to GNEC totaled $23.8 million.

While expanding the GN's funded debt, officers sought to safeguard and improve the company's credit. Being sure to meet every financial obligation on time or earlier, Budd took other steps to reduce pressure. In 1927, through a subsidiary, Somers Lumber Company, the GN paid about $10 million to redeem bonds due in 1933 and 1936, reducing both the amount of outstanding debt and the interest thereon.

Despite all efforts to reduce the financial burden, however, the GN during Budd's administration issued more obligations than it retired, and interest charges grew accordingly. The funded debt rose $83.8 million, from $270.5 million at the end of 1919, to $354.3 million on December 31, 1931, the net growth being 31 percent. Annual carrying charges on funded debt jumped 62 percent over the same period, from $11.7 million to $19 million.

Performance

Partly because passenger and freight rates declined after 1920, the GN's railway operating revenues did not keep pace with the rising volume of traffic. Only in 1928 and 1929 did gross operating revenues exceed the $122.6 million of 1920. The GN's average revenue per ton mile fell from 1.3 cents in 1921 to 0.98 cent in 1930, and revenue per passenger mile from 3.44 cents in 1921 to 3.07 cents in 1929. Passenger revenues, reflecting the decline in numbers carried, dropped from $20.5 million in 1920 to $11.3 million in 1929.

The GN's net railway operating income (NROI) nevertheless rose markedly during the 1920s, from $5.3 million in 1920 to $32.5 million nine years later. Among GN's railroad competitors only the Union Pacific made a better record during the decade, and for the last four years of that period the GN's net railway operating income actually exceeded that of the UP.

The GN's net income (after nonoperating credits and charges) was disappointing at the beginning of the period, but exceeded $25 million in 1928 and 1929. The GN's net income never approached that of the UP, but it exceeded that of the NP with pleasing consistency and far outstripped that of the Milwaukee, which reported deficits in six of the ten years in the 1920s.

With the depression, though, Budd's financial brew turned sour; from 1929 to 1931, Great Northern's NROI dropped 58 percent. This decrease was greater than that recorded by the Northern Pacific or Union Pacific, but smaller than corresponding figures for the Milwaukee. This drop occurred despite Budd's strenuous efforts to compensate for declining revenues by reducing costs. In 1931, the company's outlays for additions and betterments to road and equipment were 74 percent below those of 1928. Between 1929 and 1931, the GN also cut train miles by 20 percent, the work force by 29 percent, and annual compensation to employees by 33 percent. Nevertheless, the company ended 1931 with an operating ratio of 71.7, highest since 1923. And more bad news came: net income dropped from $25.7 million to $5.3 million between 1929 and 1931, or more than 79 percent. The Milwaukee showed even more spectacular declines, but both NP and UP registered less drastic drops. The GN's heavy interest charges had begun to take their toll.[6] (See Table 7 for GN's operating data, 1919–1931.)

Faced with all this difficulty and uncertain about the future, GN officials decided to reduce dividend payments. In 1931, they reluctantly informed the 37,931 stockholders of a cut in the annual payment from $5.00 to $4.00. That decision, they nervously admitted, might have come earlier had not the Burlington voted an extra 5 percent dividend in 1930.

These difficulties aside, Ralph Budd welcomed a new challenge late in 1931. When Frederick E. Williamson resigned as president of the Burlington to take the same post with the New York Central, Burlington directors decided that Budd was the best candidate to step into that vacancy, and he accepted their invitation. The Burlington had more mileage than the GN and a distinguished record, and it promised impressive new possibilities for the erstwhile Iowa farm boy, now an experienced and respected railroad executive.

When Budd left the GN at the end of 1931, he bequeathed to his successor a strong railroad, though burdened by the Great Depression. The company's policy of upgrading plant and service not only had enhanced operating efficiency but had reduced unit costs and increased the company's net earnings. Budd had also succeeded in restoring GN's credit, and in keeping it high until recently. The outstanding problem at the beginning of 1932 was that Budd's refunding and physical-improvement activities had added substantial interest to the GN's annual fixed charges. This cost could be harmful if the Burlington failed to pay dividends and if the GN's net railway operating income long remained at the disappointing 1931 level.

25

The Tangled Ways of Finance

When Great Northern directors met to elect a successor to Ralph Budd the depression was nearing its depths. The man chosen for the president's office would have to be a talented manager, capable of holding expenses to an absolute minimum while attracting traffic under the most adverse conditions. Simultaneously, he would have to be adept in financial management, for the company faced heavy fixed charges and huge bond issues were maturing. Failure of the new president to perform satisfactorily in any way might risk bankruptcy for the Great Northern.[1]

Setting the Course

Directors chose William P. Kenney as the new president, although he had yet to demonstrate all the talents desired. Throughout his career he had been a highly competent traffic man, and, during his brief federal managership during World War I and even shorter service as the company's president, he had performed adequately. Perhaps the directors believed that Kenney—with his background in sales—could procure enough business and that, with good advice, he could master finan-

cial management. At least, as the political elections of 1932 would show, Kenney belonged to the "right" political party: he was a Democrat.

On the board of directors, Arthur Curtiss James and Louis W. Hill remained as dominant personalities, but deaths and resignations brought new members. Shreve M. Archer of Archer-Daniels-Midland, Minneapolis grain dealers, filled the vacancy left by Budd's departure. After Edward T. Nichols's death in 1934, Frank F. Henry from General Mills in Buffalo was elected; other new faces were Alexander C. Nagle of the First National Bank of the City of New York and F. Peavey Heffelinger, spokesman for a Minneapolis grain and milling company. Hill, James, and Kenney were, of course, the key members of the executive committee from 1932 through 1938.

The new president's tasks were easier because several veteran officers remained and outstanding newcomers had climbed. C. O. Jenks continued to head the operations department and F. G. Dorety remained as general counsel. L. C. Gilman retired as vice president at Seattle in 1937, but his successor, Thomas Balmer, had outstanding ability. The loss of Nichols was filled by Vernon P. Turnburke. An appointment with promise for the future was that of Frank J. Gavin, an operating man, as assistant to the president in 1936.

Kenney wrote in his first annual report that the Northwest had been "favored with much moisture during the winter" and that "bounteous rains" during the spring gave "every indication" of "a good crop year" for the territory. Other hopeful news was scarce. In fact, the 1931 report was filled with frustration and pessimism. Several cutbacks in steel production already had drastically curtailed iron-ore tonnage and promised still lower demand for the immediate future. With construction in the doldrums, lumbermen slashed shipments, and low prices and drought together threatened most of the rural economy, already having driven many farmers off the land.[2]

Kenney was constantly agonized by disappointing net railway operating revenues, and the end was not in sight. The Burlington failed to declare a dividend, and the Spokane, Portland & Seattle was paying only token interest on its bonds. Looking ahead, GN officers forecast a deficit greater than $8 million for 1932, a sad comparison to net income of $5.3 million in 1931 and a sharp contrast to the $19.4 million average net earnings from 1927 through 1931.

Financial Management

Amid these grim prospects, financial troubles over the next few years would be management's greatest challenge. The company's financial obligations were, in fact, enormous: almost $19 million annual interest on loans, $6.5 million owed to the federal government, and equipment notes of $1.2 million annually. Even those obligations paled beside refunding problems. Bonds outstanding were as listed in Table 8.

Previous policies accounted for part of the dilemma. James J. Hill's penchant in the 1880s for fifty-year bonds was bearing bitter fruit, and because of Ralph Budd's issuance of General Mortgage 7 percents due in 1936, the Burlington affiliation for the first time was a burden. During a conference in Washington, D.C., one ICC official ''lightly tossed off'' the suggestion that perhaps the GN could best solve its financial problems by taking advan-

Table 8

Company	Amounts (in thousands)	Percentage of interest	Due date
The St. Paul, Minneapolis and Manitoba Ry. Co. Consolidated Mortgage	$ 41,963	4, 4½ and 6	July 1, 1933
Great Northern General Mortgage Gold Bonds Series A	105,859	7	July 1, 1936
The St. Paul, Minneapolis and Manitoba Ry. Co. Montana Extension	10,185	4	July 1, 1937
The Montana Central Ry. Co. First Mortgage	10,000	5 and 6	July 1, 1937
The Willmar and Sioux Falls Ry. Co. First Mortgage	3,625	5	June 1, 1938

tage of the Bankruptcy Act, but Kenney refused to consider such action.[3]

The roof appeared to fall on Kenney, however, as it did on millions of others. Passenger revenues dropped almost 35 percent, freight tonnage an appalling 42 percent, and freight revenues more than 27 percent. As usual, operating expenses went down more slowly than revenues, and so the operating ratio jumped 10.5 points to 82.2. Net railway operating income declined 89 percent from that for 1931, itself hardly a satisfactory year. Only fixed charges remained firm. The GN closed its books in 1932 with an alarming $13.4-million deficit.

With that onerous burden of red ink facing him, Kenney asked his legal and financial advisers how to handle the $42.0 million due when the Manitoba's Consolidated Mortgage

bonds matured July 1, 1933. He was given several options. A bank loan of the required size was out of the question, and even if sale of new General Mortgage bonds could be negotiated, which was doubtful, it would be on terms that would make those of 1921 look good. Any attempt to force an exchange of maturing Manitoba bonds for General Mortgage bonds would have to be made at less than par for the new issue, an action destructive of the GN's credit rating and accompanied by risk of failure and resultant receivership. A loan from the Reconstruction Finance Corporation (RFC) was a possibility, but by turning to that bank of last resort the railroad might well violate its reputation.[4]

One adviser, Henry S. Sturgis of New York's First National Bank, recommended another option: extending maturities of Manitoba

bonds. A waiver was required, though, because these had a prior lien to the GN's First and Refunding Mortgage bonds of 1911, the indenture of that date safeguarding new investors by a stipulation banning extension of maturity for bonds of an earlier date. Kenney embraced Sturgis's suggestion and directed his advisers to proceed with details. Sturgis induced several large holders of GN First and Refunding bonds to form a committee urging others to waive for ten years the part of their contract forbidding extension of time on earlier bonds, and he devised a formula for refunding. Finally, to obviate a dissatisfied minority's throwing the GN into receivership, the First National headed a syndicate that tentatively agreed to buy and approve extension of up to $15 million in Consolidated bonds.

Under a contract dated May 6, 1933, the GN and holders of the outstanding Manitoba Consolidated Mortgage bonds agreed to extend the maturity for ten years. Those who deposited their securities with J. P. Morgan & Company were to receive certificates of deposit in return, and if the railroad had a net income of $4 million or more in 1938, or in any subsequent year, it agreed to pay $2 million annually to the mortgage trustees for redemption of bonds at not more than the price set for that period. The transaction proceeded smoothly, and nearly all bonds were presented by midsummer 1933. Although underwriters had to buy and find purchasers for $7.1 million of the maturities, all bondholders received full dollar value, and the First National Bank's expenses

Passenger revenues plummeted during the Great Depression. Seattle's King Street Station was as stately as ever, but fewer and fewer patrons boarded the cars under its lordly tower. Hard times also affected express volume.

and charges were moderate. Kenney, the traffic specialist, was learning the ways of finance.[5]

One result of this new financial direction was that a reduction in long-term debt was traded for an increase in short-term obligations. The company borrowed $12 million in 1933 from the Railroad Credit Corporation, the Reconstruction Finance Corporation, and the First National Bank of New York, but much of it was paid back quickly. Short-term loans at the end of the year aggregated $5.8 million.

The financial accomplishments of 1933 were great, but seemed small compared with the task ahead. For fifteen years the high interest rate on $105.9 million in General Mortgage 7 percent gold bonds due in 1936 had hung over the road like Damocles' sword. Now the crisis

was approaching. Regardless of the method utilized for refunding these bonds, it was imperative that the GN display the best possible physical condition and operating ratio for 1935. Kenney decided to expand maintenance sharply in 1934. Not only would he get the property into good shape, but he would supply jobs during the depression and get work done while wages remained low and ''cheap money'' was available. The Public Works Administration loaned the GN $5.8 million ($5.1 million in 1934 and $.7 million early in 1935) at 4 percent.[6]

Traffic forecasts in 1934 went unmet and the GN suffered a net deficit of $1.1 million, but Kenney did achieve the operating results he wanted in 1935. A rise of $10.4 million in railway operating revenue over 1934 was effected, following slight improvement in the

Hard times were not restricted to the United States; Canada suffered too. This GN train from Vancouver is a host for hobos (see top of second car).

nation's economy, minor increases in agricultural production in the Northwest, and several government construction projects, especially Fort Peck Dam on the Missouri River near the GN main line in Montana. Moreover, operating expenses, with economies in maintenance after Kenney's 1934 drive, went up only $1.5 million. Even after heavy interest charges were paid, net income shifted from the embarrassing $1.1 million red in 1934 to $7.1 million black in 1935. The company paid its taxes promptly, reimbursed the Railroad Credit Corporation by $319,340, and retired the $3-million loan from the First National Bank.

Over the Hurdle

During the spring of 1935, financial observers became more optimistic about the GN's refunding problem. Bankers made inquiries, and in June 1935 *The Wall Street Journal* saw new strength in the company's securities. Arthur Curtiss James also reported that New York financiers thought the refunding operation should be initiated promptly. Kenney was confident that he could go into the money market through investment bankers in New York, or through the Reconstruction Finance Corporation, or both. At the least, Kenney thought he could play the RFC off against investment bankers. President Franklin Roosevelt himself had said that railroads should reduce their bonded indebtedness, and he had indicated his desire to help them toward that goal.[7]

At mid-year 1935, GN directors moved to give the company a psychological boost by reducing the amount to be refunded in 1936 from $105.9 million to no more than $100 million—and that amount by acquiring bonds in the open market. The company paid cash, ultimately acquiring General Mortgage 7s worth $6.4 million and reducing the maturing obligation to $99.5 million. At the same time, Kenney got assurances from the First National Bank, and reminded his advisers that the RFC remained an alternative. Even earlier, the GN's chief executive had sought to persuade Jesse Jones "to appreciate the necessity for, at least, mentally counting us in on some of the RFC money for our 1936 maturity." Jones responded with a tentative commitment to finance half the refunding operation by a loan of $50 million at 4 percent. The GN might then redeem with cash half of the 7s and exchange new bonds for the remainder.[8]

Prior to any firm decision by Jones, the RFC studied in detail the GN's property and management. Its examiners found that track, structures, and rolling stock had been "adequately and thriftily maintained," that the fixed plant was "stout and solid," and that the equipment was "well fitted to the needs" of

This station scene at Crooks, South Dakota, during the 1930s was all too common along the GN. Only two cars were in the yard.

the road. These investigators stated further that operations were "efficiently handled," company expenses "well controlled," and management "well coordinated, effective and forward looking.'' These findings helped Jones to adjust his commitment from tentative to firm, making it public October 1, 1935. The RFC would lend GN all or part of $50 million. The plan was to have the railroad issue $100 million in 4½ percent bonds maturing in twenty or twenty-five years.[9]

Kenney and the directors considered all possibilities. New York bankers, whose task it would be to handle $50 million in the new bonds, disliked the RFC proposal. Henry Sturgis held out for 5 percent, ten-year bonds, convertible into stock. Kenney was finally persuaded. ''While Henry [Sturgis] dresses it up nicely and he has convinced me, it does seem damn funny that you can be better off paying 5 percent for your money than 4½,'' wrote Kenney, whose education in the details of finance was proceeding rapidly.[10]

The board of directors, on November 1, 1935, recommended general proposals to implement refunding. At Sturgis's insistence, a group of investment bankers organized a syndicate to float the entire $100-million issue. Half was to be convertible into stock at $40 a share, the other half at $75, providing one type of security attractive to conservative institutions and another appealing to those more speculatively inclined. The syndicate oversubscribed the issue by 50 percent.

Suddenly, Jesse Jones forced a change in plans. On December 15, the RFC offered to take the whole issue, or any part of it, at 4 percent. ''The bankers probably think I am a goddam fool, and a renegade,'' wrote Jones, ''but I . . . want to help the railroad.'' Subject to approval by the ICC, the RFC would take that part of a $100-million 4 percent issue not sold on July 1, 1936, charging no underwriting fee. Jones's motives were clear. He believed that the GN should not have to pay more than 4 percent interest. The railroad, Jones maintained, was ''one of our best systems,'' it had ''never been in receivership, and . . . had never missed paying dividends'' until the depression struck in full fury. Moreover, if the GN paid more than 4 percent, it would be ''hurting all railroad financing, and unnecessarily penalizing'' its own security holders. Perhaps more important, Jones's decision represented Roosevelt's economic policy. By using the RFC rather than the Federal Reserve Board, the president was intentionally keeping interest rates low in an effort to stimulate the economy. The offer to the Great Northern was a happy by-product of that policy.[11]

After arranging minor modifications and changes, GN directors accepted Jones's offer on January 21, 1936. They really had no alternative; it promised to save the GN $1 million in interest annually for the next ten years, or until the bonds were converted, and underwriters' charges would be avoided. The formal contract between the GN and the RFC was signed March 13.

To implement refunding of General Mortgage 7s, the railroad offered the new bonds to stockholders on March 21 and to bondholders four days later. The sum of the par value of the two equal series amounted to $99.4 million. Dated June 1, 1936, and maturing July 1, 1946, bonds of Series G could be exchanged for shares of $40 each, those of Series H at $75 a share. Payment could be made in cash or in General Mortgage Series A 7s. The GN could call and redeem them, and, until July 1, 1941, the railroad would pay 105 percent, after which the price could be reduced during the remaining five years before the bonds' maturity. Shareholders subscribed for $94.1 million of the two series, leaving only $5.3 million of them for the bondholders. The RFC did not have to assume any obligation.

In one major stroke Kenney restored GN's credit. The refunding cost was light, the GN's indebtedness was reduced, the annual interest charge on almost $100 million of bonds was cut from 7 percent to 4, and a satisfactory basis had been established for future financing. ''You can now roll over and go to sleep,'' Sturgis wired Kenney June 1, 1936. The refunding was the ''finest piece of work I have ever seen of a similar nature,'' wrote Arthur Curtiss James, who expected the reduction in interest charges to be a ''permanent stimulant over the ten ensuing years.'' *The Wall Street Journal* said that ''probably none of the country's leading steam carriers experienced a more dramatic change in fortunes over the past year than the Great Northern Railway.''[12]

Having succeeded so well in this, Kenney and his associates turned at once to the next problem. On July 1, 1937, maturity would be reached for $20.2 million in the Manitoba's Montana Extension and Montana Central Railway Company bonds. The prevailing interest rate was low and railway operating revenues were rising, so the time also seemed favorable for acquiring $40.8 million in outstanding Manitoba Consolidated Mortgage bonds that had been extended at 5 percent to 1943, but could be redeemed for a premium of $612,585 after July 1, 1937. Part of the redemption could be met out of current income and short-term loans, but some refunding was also necessary. Henry Sturgis agreed that interest on a bond issue could be as low as 4 percent, or even lower if Kenney was willing to sell at a slight discount. Morgan, Stanley & Company, representing ten major underwriters, took this issue of General Mortgage bonds, and generated net proceeds of $47.8 million for the railroad.

The large redemption of bonds, some before their maturity, gave Kenney and his subordinates the satisfaction of knowing that they had engineered a most economical operation further enhancing the company's credit. Bonded debt was reduced $11.8 million in one year, but issuing new equipment trust certificates, the first in Kenney's administration, increased equipment obligations. Nonetheless, funded debt was reduced $9 million, and for the first time since 1921, the GN's annual interest obligation was less than that of the neighboring Northern Pacific. Moreover, its average interest rate was lower than the NP had paid since its reorganization in 1897.

Changes in accounting methods also helped improve the balance sheet during Kenney's years. In 1936, investment in equipment was shifted to the GN account from the Great Northern Equipment Company, eliminating $24 million in advances to that affiliate. At the same time, accountants removed from both Deferred Assets and Deferred Liabilities $22.8 million, representing accrued and unpaid interest on Spokane, Portland & Seattle bonds owned by the GN. Directors also authorized writing off losses of more than $1.6 million in conjunction with abandoning two affiliates in Canada: the Brandon, Saskatchewan & Hudson's Bay Railway Company and the Crow's Nest Southern Railway Company.

Controlling Expenses

While managing finances with skill worthy of John S. Kennedy or James J. Hill, Kenney also held railway expenditures to

Even the proud *Oriental Limited* was a victim of Kenney's efficiency programs as he labored to give the Great Northern a steady helm during the grim days of the 1930s.

the minimum needed to maintain efficient operations while offering adequate service. This feat was made easier by the excellent condition in which Ralph Budd had left the property, but it still required a delicate balancing act. Kenney believed that aggressively soliciting freight was more essential than ever, so he approved maintaining personnel at on-line and off-line offices at close to full strength. He was, however, willing to downgrade advertising, for which the 1937 expenditure was only 40 percent as great as in 1929. The agricultural development budget was similarly reduced. A major reduction was achieved by stopping capital construction. For that matter, plant size was actually reduced. Between 1932 and 1938, the GN took up 276 miles of track. The longest stretches were from St. John, N.D., to Brandon, Manitoba; from Rexford,

Montana, to Elko, British Columbia; in British Columbia from Hedley to Brookmere; and, in Washington, from Curlew to Molson.

Sharp reductions in capital expenditures for improving structures, way, and new equipment were possible because of the extensive work undertaken in the previous decade. Few additions were made to the GN's fleet of locomotives and cars; in fact, their number was reduced. Nevertheless, C. O. Jenks pondered adopting diesel-electric motive power. The GN had purchased one unit, a switcher, in 1926, and then waited for improvement in this new motive power. Price was a strong consideration, for diesels cost 150 to 200 percent more than comparable locomotives, but operating officers pointed to the diesel's "availability" —in other words, its reliability, and its lower maintenance requirements. Diesels also pro-

The Tangled Ways of Finance

One way to cut expenses was to institute more mixed train service on branch lines. This homely scene on a North Dakota line speaks to the validity of combining passenger and freight service on low-density lines. The short train has only a "peddler car" for less-than-carload freight, two tanks, a "packing house products car," and an elderly combine bringing up the rear.

duced less wear and tear on track structure.[13]

In the late 1930s, as financial pressures eased, the GN laid the foundation for its diesel fleet. An authorization in 1937 covered two 900-horsepower units; by the next January, one was in yard service at Willmar and the other handled local trains between Fargo and Devil's Lake. In 1938, the GN ordered two 600-horsepower units and ten 1,000-horse-power switchers for use at eastern terminals. Operating officers urged additional investment in them, but Kenney refused, citing other needs.

New rolling stock was purchased on about the same schedule as diesel power. Early in his tenure Kenney remarked on the obvious—the company had "an immense surplus of cars all over," but as shipments improved later on, the GN was forced to place large orders, including 1,000 fifty-ton box cars and 500 fifty-ton steel gondolas. In all, however, only 2,500 freight cars were purchased from 1932 through 1938. On another front, the president made every effort to discourage requests for new passenger cars, saying: "We have too much

equipment for the business they [passenger trains] are turning in." Jenks was able to meet needs only by leasing coaches and diners from other railroads. Kenney did keep up with streamlined passenger trains being developed in the 1930s, but he remained opposed to them on the GN.[14]

Rarely a diplomat with his subordinates, Kenney was blunt in his demand that all costs be held to the minimum. When he received an AFE for $123,000 to repair ore docks at Allouez, Kenney commented caustically that the chief engineer had "the idea that we are earning a lot of money and he wants to spend it." Furthermore, he groused, "it seems too bad that we are obligated to earn any net money because just as quickly as we do, everybody looks for a place to spend it."[15]

One approach to reducing costs was to curtail or terminate services, either temporarily or permanently. The entire system was carefully studied to determine where freight and passenger operations might be rearranged, reduced, or eliminated. Train miles were minimized while retaining enough service to handle the

traffic offered and to discourage competitors. the GN cut branch-line operations by about 10 percent.

Savings in passenger service were effected in several ways. The company decided not to institute regular passenger service on the new California line, and changes in schedules elsewhere made it possible to cut trains. The once-proud *Oriental Limited* became "a combination of locals with a lengthened schedule," and sleeping, dining, and parlor cars were discontinued where businesses did not justify their use. Also, pooled trains between Seattle and Portland were cut from five to three daily in each direction. Ironically, however, GN officers rejected a proposal by the president of the Milwaukee that the Great Northern, Northern Pacific, and Milwaukee pool their transcontinental runs. Each company could have saved expensive passenger train miles by running a train every third day, but Kenney and Jenks argued that instituting local trains for communities whose only service was provided by the company's transcontinentals was an offsetting liability.[16]

Passenger service would have been cut even more extensively if public authorities had not refused to grant permission in some instances. For example, in July 1935, the GN asked the Montana Railroad Commission for authorization to take off three passenger trains between Great Falls and Butte, Great Falls and Lewistown, and Shelby and Sweet Grass. The commission bluntly rejected the petition, and one commissioner stated publicly that he was going "to keep the railroad running those trains, even though they are empty." The GN took that case into federal court, but received less than full satisfaction. In the hearings, counsel for the Montana Commission admitted that because "few people use the service of the trains," the "plaintiff sustained some loss," but he contended that the GN should be required to operate the trains unless it could show that the company's system-wide earnings did not represent a fair return. In the fall of 1936, the court allowed the GN to take off only one of the three trains, the one from Great Falls to Butte. Kenney was disappointed, but, given the political climate in Montana, he concluded that the decision represented a victory.[17]

Changes comparable to those in passenger service were made in freight operations. Schedules of some through trains were arranged to provide service to small communities along the line, eliminating the need for locals, and inaugurating mixed service on some branches enabled one train to do the work of two. In a few places, the GN even utilized trucks where trains were unprofitable.

The reduction in wage rates during the 1930s was short-lived and, before the depression was over, wages and salaries rose again. Average annual earnings per worker, which had been $1,796 in 1929, rose to $2,031 by 1938. In that year the GN employed 42 percent fewer employees than in 1928, but the payroll was only 33 percent less. Furthermore, social-security legislation was beginning to affect the cost of labor.

In the long struggle to carry the company through the depression, Kenney achieved notable success in two phases of his strategic plan.

He reduced the debt and refunded a large volume of bonds at a low rate of interest. At the same time, expense for railway operations had been slashed. Both programs depended, of course, on the volume of traffic generated and revenues gained therefrom. Fortunately for the Great Northern, Kenney focused similar energies in this field.

Traffic and Profits in Adversity

Cost reduction and strong financial programs were two essential elements in Great Northern management during the Great Depression; an almost desperate try to attract and hold business was another.[1]

During these difficult days, Harry H. Brown, Kenney's successor as vice president of traffic, was charged with generating traffic. A veteran of thirty-six years with the GN, Brown was a nationally recognized authority on rates. In practice, Kenney reduced the position of vice president to little more than that of a clerk, and in effect managed the department himself. Yet the president held the unfortunate Brown strictly accountable for any failure, real or alleged, to hold or obtain traffic.

Kenney's sharp tongue and short temper no doubt made Brown's life miserable. Angered by the poor showing during his first month as president, Kenney concluded that "conditions in the traffic department . . . are indeed alarming." In July 1932, he shrilly told Brown that every "man that can get an available car of freight should be out getting it, from you down. . . ." Nor was Kenney hesitant in giving pointed advice: "Your desk is piled with stuff that should be handled by your subordinates. . . . By this time you should have

Glacier Park always presented special opportunities for the Great Northern's passenger department.

known thousands of people who are in a position to give us business. . . .'' Answering Kenney's demands and attempting to follow his detailed instructions, however, left Brown little time to act on his own initiative. Then, when the vice president fell to a serious illness in 1937, Kenney declared that the department needed ''new blood.'' Going outside the organization for a replacement, Kenney selected Frank R. Newman, vice president-traffic of the Soo Line since 1925. After Newman took office on January 1, 1938, Kenney's attitude toward the traffic department changed little, although he found that he could not dominate the new vice president as he had Brown.[2]

The Passenger Department

During the 1930s, economic conditions cut express traffic and travel for business as well as pleasure; meanwhile, competition from other modes was gaining. Long-distance as well as local passenger travel by rail fell sharply. Decreases in revenue from passengers

for each year, from 1930 to 1933, compared with the previous year, were respectively 20.3, 32.9, 34.8, and 4.6 percent; thus, receipts for 1933 of less than $4 million were not even a fifth of the high point, 1920. Even passenger-service revenue (including returns from passengers, express, mail, and baggage) for 1933 was only $7.3 million.

Throughout the early 1930s, GN management urged reduction in fares to stimulate travel. Eastern carriers, however, with business falling less than on western roads, generally opposed change. Impatient, Kenney decided to be a price leader in the Northwest. On August 1, 1933, the GN reduced fares in its coaches and newly renovated tourist sleepers. The ''New Deal,'' Kenney boasted, was ''2 cents a mile every day on the Great Northern'' with ''comfort, security, and economy.''[3]

This action triggered others. For some time the Pullman Company had objected to differentials between its fares and special excursion offerings by the railroads. Kenney, long an advocate of cheaper first-class tickets, agreed that changes were necessary. Western carriers, accepting a new basic rate of 2 cents per mile for coach and tourist travel, on December 1, 1933, joined in reducing fares on Pullman cars from 3.6 to 3 cents per mile. The GN also reduced the price of its round-trip tickets and quoted especially low weekend rates and summer fares. The charge from the Twin Cities to the Pacific Coast was $32.50—plus 50 cents for the return trip. The GN likewise sold mileage scrip books at a discount of 25 percent and advertised ''mystery excursions'' at about a cent per mile. At the same time, it offered inexpensive meals; fifty-cent dinners were pleasing to passengers but aroused criticism from competitors and increased deficits in the dining-car service.[4]

Glacier National Park always presented special opportunities. Opened in 1933, the spectacular Going-to-the-Sun Highway over Logan Pass was advertised as a beautiful ''detour'' by bus or automobile from Glacier Park station to Belton. For those who wanted their own car in the park, the GN treated an automobile as baggage; the railroad charged five fares for two passengers and moved the automobile by train to either Glacier Park station or Belton.

Sometimes the GN did not initiate improvements but was forced into them. When the Union Pacific decided to air-condition one of its Chicago–Portland trains, Kenney huffed that "the lid seems to have blown off on the air-conditioning of passenger equipment." He reluctantly authorized this significant feature for GN trains in 1934, at first only on the *Empire Builder*, and restricted to observation-lounge cars and diners. By 1935, however, the GN advertised the *Empire Builder* as the "first completely air-conditioned transcontinental train throughout the Northwest." Pleased with the favorable comments, Kenney eventually approved an accelerated program, including the *Winnipeg Limited* and the Seattle–Spokane run.[5]

To justify air-conditioning and other improvements, Kenney needled subordinates to "get more business." Convinced that "optimistic and hustling solicitation" would increase volume, he exhorted salesmen to rid their minds of the idea that "the passenger business was hardly worth saving." He bluntly told them to "resurrect themselves from their proximity to the undertaker and meet people with a smile."[6]

Meanwhile, the GN continued to dabble in the bus business. As highways were improved in Montana, the company faced a challenge like that which it had experienced in Minnesota during the 1920s. Consequently, on May

Air-conditioning may not always have been required along the route of the *Empire Builder* in western Montana, but in other portions of the GN's service area, it proved a great blessing.

7, 1934, Great Northern Stages began service between Butte and Great Falls. Soon GN buses were on other runs, including Great Falls–Cutbank, Great Falls via Shelby to Sweet Grass, Great Falls–Lewistown, and Havre–Browning. Thereafter, however, GN contracted for service with Northland Greyhound Lines.[7]

During the early 1930s, along with stock in Northland Greyhound, the GN held indirect interest in the Pacific Greyhound Company. Kenney, often angered at competition by buses, questioned whether the GN should be involved with these rivals, and even objected to his officers serving as directors of Northland

Greyhound. "I would like very much to get out of these companies," he wrote in 1934, "if we can without too much loss." Changes followed: The GN exchanged its stock in Pacific Greyhound for that of Northland Greyhound, but in that way increased its interest in Northland to almost 50 percent. But this close relationship was short-lived. In the late 1930s, ICC decisions showed that, if a railroad was a major stockholder in a bus company, the latter's privileges to purchase other bus lines might be limited. Thus, in 1938 and 1939, the GN canceled its contracts for bus operations in Montana, and reduced its holdings in Northland Greyhound.[8]

Kenney did not lavish the company's finest on the *International*. Locomotive 453 is shown here getting the train together at Vancouver in 1938.

These collective alterations on the passenger front bore mixed results. Years of declining revenues in the early 1930s were followed by periods of improvement. In 1937, receipts from passengers topped $5 million for the first time since 1931. Kenney attributed this upswing to two-cent fares, but other variables were at work. For several years moving personnel for the Civilian Conservation Corps contributed significant revenues, and air-conditioned equipment was another factor. But passenger revenues fell off sharply in 1938. Kenney blasted his salesmen for lacking "original thought" and for following along "like sheep," but the decline was caused by forces over which Kenney's long-suffering subordinates had little control: the general economy and government movements had both slumped. At the same time, several competing railroads boasted new streamlined trains; an unusually open winter encouraged travel on improved highways; automobiles became speedier and more comfortable; relatively low fares attracted passengers to buses for longer distances; and airplanes were carrying increasing, though still small, numbers.[9]

Truck Competition

Modal alternatives preempted a growing percentage of passenger business during the 1930s, and trucks simultaneously took large segments of freight traffic. Trucks registered in the Northwest rose swiftly from 114,469 in 1920 to 371,751 in 1931, and to 482,004 in 1938. Moreover, as better roads were built, trucks were gaining greater capacity, reliability, and speed. The highway transport industry also became better organized. Hard times accelerated the evolution of trucking. After all, the price of transportation was paramount to hard-pressed shippers and merchants. In addition, during this period of high unemployment, many men tried to support themselves with "gypsy" trucking operations or by working for other trucking concerns at wages that made cost competition difficult for the railroads. Some truckers even hauled intercity freight simply for "gas money."

Truck competition did not affect all commodities, but damage was pervasive. Iron-ore shipments, of course, were not disturbed, and forest products too were mostly immune. Trucks, however, began to carry apples from Washington's Wenatchee Valley, and more and more farmers in Minnesota and North Dakota moved grain and livestock in vehicles that hauled building materials and other supplies on return trips.

Competition was especially sharp for LCL freight. Traditionally, high-rated commodities such as merchandise and miscellaneous manufactured goods had moved in carload lots to distribution centers and then by LCL to local wholesalers, retailers, and other consignees. Now, because many orders were small and trucks could expedite handling of such shipments, the GN's LCL shipments decreased 43

percent for the five years ending December 31, 1934, compared to the preceding five-year period. Some of this loss was attributable to general economic conditions, but truck competition too had to be significant.

In partial if ineffective response, the GN continued to advocate stricter regulation for truck operations. "The Great Northern is opposed to the use of trucks on the public highway," fumed Kenney in 1935. "We will support any legislation against the trucks, and we will work as hard against the trucks as we possibly can, to the extent of forcing them to cut out trailers, to reduce the size of loads, to pay more taxes, and to observe the same hours of service as the railroads are forced to observe." Controlling highway transportation was an objective shared by various groups. Ship-by-Rail clubs, which GN workers launched in St. Paul, soon had members in five states; and the Citizens' Transportation League, with a much larger membership, especially in Minnesota, favored regulation not only for highway but also for water transport. These organizations and others called for rigid enforcement of laws governing trucks, more restrictions on weight limits, and prohibition of trailers. The GN had no official connection with such groups, but welcomed their activities.[10]

These and similar campaigns had mixed results. Early in the 1930s, control over common carriers was fixed in some states by laws covering licensing and standards protecting the public and employees, but control over contract and private truckers was limited, and the distinctions among types of carriers were indistinctly drawn. Legislation was tightened in several states, and in 1935 the federal government passed the Motor Carrier Act, making the ICC responsible for certifying common carriers engaged in interstate commerce, for controlling mergers in the industry, and for setting maximum rates.

Kenney later hoped that unionizing bus and truck drivers would hurt highway carriers and thus improve the railroads' position. He thought it would be a great help if "a strong union such as the Teamsters" did the organizing, and he hoped that the "unionization of all these trucks and bus people" would continue. It did, but to no advantage for the railroad industry.[11]

Despite his frequent obtuseness, Kenney understood that competitive conditions had changed. "What I am trying to beat into the heads of our people," he wrote in 1935, "is that we no longer have a monopoly. . . ." Thus, the GN revived its program for employees' soliciting traffic as in the previous decade and sought to build goodwill at strategic locations. Traffic agents were urged to ever greater efforts and were even threatened with reductions in salary or layoffs if they did not produce. Supervisory personnel also coached local agents to help them become better solicitors.[12]

Kenney further recognized that the GN had to improve quality, speed its service, and reduce its charges. Accordingly, the company installed night locals on critical runs, moved an increased volume of LCL by passenger train and through freights, and tried to provide at least minimal daily freight service at each significant point. Procedures were improved, freight-station hours were made more flexible, and greater attention was devoted to transfer-

E. C. Leedy expended great effort to develop the production of fruits and vegetables along the GN's route in the state of Washington. His goal was to add tonnage to trains like this one near P. A. tower, west of Grand Forks, North Dakota.

As the depression ended, the GN handled a growing tonnage in forest products.

212

The Great Northern Railway: A History/Part II 1916 to 1970

ring LCL at junctions. The GN also reduced carload minimums, liberalized stop-in-transit privileges, and switched specified cars free of charge. Kenney made additions to Ralph Budd's experimental use of motor carriers working under contract to handle short-haul freight between stations. The aim was pickup-and-delivery service to counteract trucks' greater flexibility. Early experiments indicated that the expense of store-door delivery was too high compared with the line haul between stations, but when Pacific Coast rail competitors began such service at selected points in 1931, the GN introduced experimental operations at Portland and Klamath Falls. Within a year the railroad extended pickup and delivery to other locations in Oregon as well as in the Spokane – Palouse area and from Wenatchee to Pacific Coast ports. Rather than providing its own motor-transport facilities, the railroad made contracts with local drayage firms, offering rates competitive with those of licensed truckers. Profit levels were acceptable because of generally higher Pacific Northwest freight rates that provided a greater margin out of which drayers could be paid.

Elsewhere in the GN's service area conditions were less favorable, and the company was reluctant to expand such offerings. Before the close of 1934, however, the GN's hesitancy evaporated. When the Northern Pacific announced that it had permission from the Montana Railroad Commission to put trucks and buses on several routes in Montana and to abandon rail service on four branches, the GN immediately applied to the same body for authority to replace rail service with motor carriage, including pickup and delivery, along stretches of its main line. Approval was granted effective March 1, 1935, on condition that if motor operation was disrupted by ad-

verse weather or for other reasons, the railroad would provide rail service. The results were heartening. Between Havre and Shelby a bus-truck combination made it possible to eliminate fourteen stops for through passenger trains. Elsewhere, the GN in 1935 also placed its own trucks in service between Breckenridge and Fargo. The railroad already had contracts with truckers for a few other routes in Minnesota and North Dakota.

For years the value of these trucking operations was debated internally. Kenney, never enthusiastic about highway transport, was soon lamenting the mere "hatful of traffic," small gross revenue, and insignificant net income from trucking. A thorough study made in 1938 concluded, though, that "the trucking service results in sufficient savings in operations to warrant continuing it, particularly in view of the improved service" that the GN was rendering. The report pointed out that if the trucks were taken off, the company would either lose traffic or would have to put on more rail service — supplemented by provisions for pickup and delivery that would substantially increase expenditures. Persuaded, Kenney conceded: "I don't think we need worry any more about what we should do."[13]

In expanding general pickup-and-delivery service, the GN chose to rely on local draymen, as it had earlier. During 1935 and 1936, the company made contracts with almost 850 such firms where the railroad did not operate its own trucks. Most rates — including pickup, rail haul, and delivery — were competitive with those of authorized truckers, and shippers who used their own vehicles received discounts of five cents per hundredweight. By the spring of 1936, the GN reported that throughout its system it was providing the same service for the same charge as did truckers.

Kenney was never convinced, however, that pickup-and-delivery service generated profits, and he was disappointed that its inauguration did not deter the general growth of trucking. In 1936, he expressed the unwarranted hope that in time the highways would be restored "to the use of the people, rather than having them usurped for commercial purposes," but most railroaders, and undoubtedly Kenney himself, were aware that growing truck competition was a reality with which all rail carriers would be required to live.[14]

Developmental Programs and Federal Stimulants

Continuing exertions to promote growth in the Northwest were unevenly effective. E. C. Leedy, energetic head of the agricultural development department, kept some of his earlier programs going, and vigorously supported private and public relief programs that yielded solid business during the depression. But Leedy labored under the misapprehension that hard times would drive men to cutover lands and irrigated farms, and was disappointed when the anticipated back-to-the-farm movement proved an illusion. Leedy therefore shifted to helping families stay on the land, or relocate along other GN lines. Many had already left the farms, and others who lived on "dust and charity" were disposed to decamp as well. Leedy understood that anything possible had to be done to prevent that. The "interests of the Great Northern can best be served by having settlers remain where they are," he correctly observed.[15]

In 1931, Leedy had begun to promote truck gardening in Washington, a policy that helped diversify farm production and generate heavy tonnage per acre harvested. Lettuce was the first followed by peas, asparagus, and other favored vegetables. Late in the decade, with appreciable acreage of these crops in production, GN agents helped to bring canning factories to the Northwest.

At the same time, Leedy continued to encourage farmers to plant potatoes and sugar beets, and he convinced Kenney that growing sugar beets was "the best industry in any agricultural section that could possibly be secured from the railroad and the farmers' standpoint." Leedy's men encouraged farmers to adopt, along with established forms of assistance, feeding beet pulp to livestock; they helped recruit and transport migratory workers at reduced rates, and urged bankers to liberalize credit terms for hard-pressed farmers.[16]

Leedy's department also continued to distribute educational literature. Most popular of the publications they issued in the 1930s was a pamphlet on strip farming. Part of a broader federally sponsored program, it included contour plowing, designed to control wind erosion and other harmful effects of drought. Strip farming soon became a standard technique, widely used on wheat lands throughout the Northwest.

Educational trains, which had been so effective, were again used in 1938 when a Farm Day Exhibition Train toured Minnesota, eastern South Dakota, and the Red River Valley. Sponsored by several interests, including the GN, it was meant to promote commercial fertilizers and show how they could best be utilized. A similar Farm Progress Train followed a year later.

Throughout the 1930s, the GN cooperated with agencies in meeting emergencies caused by adverse weather and the depression. This activity began in response to President Hoover's request that western carriers help drought-stricken farmers. With other railroads,

the GN cut rates on feed shipped into and livestock moved out of such areas. The company further helped livestock producers find farmers in Iowa and elsewhere who were willing to take animals for fattening and supported the federal government's emergency programs. Company agents in 1931 held meetings to inform farmers about federal loans for seed, and in 1933, the GN hauled at reduced rates goods provided by the Federal Emergency Relief Administration. In the next year it carried, also at reduced rates, cattle purchased by the government. Although many railroad men were skeptical of the New Deal's measures for controlling production, agents were directed to explain the program's provisions to farmers.

During the hard times of the 1930s grasshoppers added insult to injury. The GN lobbied for federal funds to fight this menace, and reduced rates for hauling arsenic and bran used as poison. The engineering department set an example by destroying the insects and their breeding places along rights-of-way, and held innumerable meetings to educate farmers in using poison. By 1935, even Secretary of Agriculture Henry A. Wallace, no friend of railroads, acknowledged the GN's assistance in combating grasshoppers.

In this time of need, the GN found still other ways to assist. After local banks failed in 1931, the GN helped Washington state apple growers establish local credit associations, which then got them loans from the Reconstruction Finance Corporation. By 1937, the GN had invested $103,000 in these organizations, some of the company's outlays turning out to be outright gifts.

The depression's vicissitudes aside, Kenney grew dissatisfied with the GN's efforts to stimulate growth, especially outside agricultural endeavors. In 1934, he decided that the agent

in charge of industrial promotion was "too old for the kind of work that should be done"; some young, dynamic man was needed. The traffic department failed to act, and in 1937 Kenney authorized the vigorous Charles E. Finley, then land and tax agent in Seattle, to survey established plants, industrial sites, and business possibilities along the GN's lines. One year in the making, Finley's report showed clearly, Kenney said, that industrial development had been "neglected in two ways, first, securing inadequate property for locating industries; second, not going after industries." Finley was soon given the task of establishing a modern industrial development department.[17]

Though Finley was not responsible for securing them, he rejoiced in revenues derived from two federal projects. The Fort Peck dam near Glasgow, Montana, built for navigation and flood control on the Missouri River, was included in President Roosevelt's 1933 public-works program. Largest of its kind in the world, this giant dam would create a reservoir 180 miles long and up to 16 miles wide. Although the site was only 14 miles from the GN's station at Wiota, Kenney feared that the NP might get some of the traffic, and instructed subordinates to give the competitor no "chance to edge in any way in taking any of this construction material." The GN succeeded: Construction commenced in fall 1933, and by December 1939, when the dam was nearing completion, the railroad had hauled to the site 207,000 carloads of freight. Aggregate revenues were $14.7 million, or more than 3 percent of GN's freight revenues from 1934 to 1939. Kenney wondered what the GN was "going to do for traffic when this . . . business is terminated."[18]

A second large federal project brought a

Table 9

Years	Net railway operating income	Net income
1932	1,290,551	$13,405,439[a]
1933	11,810,227	3,187,760[a]
1934	14,101,650	1,074,480[a]
1935	23,483,854	7,139,860
1936	23,559,571	9,903,986
1937	23,769,408	10,089,920
1938	14,479,276	2,712,560

a. Indicated deficit.

Sources: Great Northern Railway Company, Annual Reports, 1932–1938.

partial answer: the Grand Coulee dam, planned early in the depression and funded initially under the National Industrial Recovery Act. Ultimately this huge central-Washington structure extended 550 feet above bedrock, with 11 million cubic yards of concrete. The NP won the direct connection, but most of the cement originated on the GN. Shipments began in October 1935, continued to June 1942, and contributed $2.5 million in revenue.

Survival

Kenney was reasonably successful in generating freight traffic during the wretched economic conditions of the 1930s. In fact, in almost every year after 1932, the GN was able to increase its volume. Despite setbacks in wheat shipments during the dry years of 1934 and 1936, total tonnage of agricultural products rose from 3.4 million in 1932 to 5.6 million in the recession year of 1938. Iron-ore shipments soared from 0.8 million short tons in 1932, lowest since the 1890s, to 23.1 million in 1937, before a precipitous if temporary drop in 1938. Forest-products tonnage tripled between the low of 1932 and the high of 1937, and in 1938 reached 235 percent of the 1932 figure. Manufactured and miscellaneous commodities, even in 1938, were almost 50 percent higher than in the first devasting year of Kenney's administration. Tonnage handled rose from 11.7 million in 1932 to 41.5 million in 1937, before declining temporarily to 23.3 million in 1938. Still, average volumes for the Kenney years were a mere fraction of those for the prosperous 1925–1929 period.

Although the ICC authorized small general increases in freight tariffs during the 1930s, competition from other railroads and from other modes led the GN to make innumerable voluntary reductions. These cuts stimulated increases in tonnage, but they also depressed dollar volume. The average revenue per ton-mile therefore fell after 1932; in 1937 it was 0.859 cent, compared with 1.063 cents in 1932 and 0.997 cent in 1929. The average revenue per passenger mile in 1937 was 1.63 cents, about half that for 1924 and 1.45 cents below 1930.

Other statistics were more favorable. The GN's railway revenue for the years 1932 through 1938 was 63 percent of the 1925 through 1929 figure, but its operating ratio dropped from 82.2 in 1932 to 61.7 in 1935 and 68.8 in the recession year of 1938. C. O. Jenks proudly pointed out that GN figures were lower than those of the NP and the Milwaukee, and in several years even lower than those of the UP.

These positive figures, however, did not provide pleasant net income for the Great Depression years. The figures in Table 9 tell the story.

Two elements in the company's accounts contributed substantially to depressed net income. Earnings from the Burlington and the Spokane, Portland & Seattle fell to extremely low levels: the Burlington declared annual dividends of 4 percent or less instead of the previous 10 percent, and the SP&S record was much worse. Meanwhile, the much-anticipated reduction in interest payments amounted to relatively little until 1938, when this saving became a very positive factor in allowing the company to show a profit. Understandably, from 1932 through 1938, GN directors voted only one dividend—$2.00 in 1937. Earnings looked good compared to those of the NP, which recorded a net deficit for the period, and the Milwaukee, which registered titanic losses in every year. Kenney, of course, would have preferred to emulate the UP performance—black ink in every annual report.

At the end of 1938, Kenney could reflect on his stewardship with at least modest pleasure. Ralph Budd had left the property in such fine condition that Kenney had been able to cut maintenance and operating expenses without ruining service. At the same time, Kenney had spurred his salesmen to scramble for every scrap of traffic, had adjusted to highway competition, had upgraded passenger equipment, and had begun a study of diesel power. For the long run, though, Kenney's refunding of the GN's debt and reduction in interest charges were his finest achievements.

27

The Pressures of War —Again

During the years 1939 through 1945, the Great Northern functioned under conditions markedly different from those in the preceding decade. Instead of serving a public restrained by a long depression, the GN now struggled to keep pace with demands set by a booming economy driven by a massive world conflict.[1]

Gavin's Preparations

Following William P. Kenney's death on January 24, 1939, GN directors delayed choosing his successor. At first, a majority favored Duncan J. Kerr, a former company officer who was currently president of the Lehigh Valley Railroad Company. Kerr was suddenly incapacitated, and so the board in February turned to Frank J. Gavin, assistant to the president, as the interim chief executive officer. When it became clear that Kerr's illness was incurable, the board on September 26, 1939, chose Gavin as president.

Born in 1880, on Prince Edward Island, Canada, Gavin started work for the GN as a clerk in 1897, gained experience in operations, and won several promotions. In 1919, he was sent to the Lake Superior Division, where he

did much to expedite and make more efficient the movement of iron ore. Ten years later he was appointed general manager–lines east, and in 1936 he was named assistant to the president in St. Paul.

Gavin's performance as interim chief executive demonstrated that his temperament and abilities were generally adequate for the presidency. Unassuming, imperturbable, and quietly confident, he won respect inside and outside the company for firm and sound decisions. Above all, Gavin knew how to get most transportation from least equipment with fewest men. Fully aware that he had no monopoly on talent and experience, he believed in and practiced delegation of authority. Fortunately for Gavin and the company he headed, his subordinates were of proven ability and well-deserved reputation. Among them were C. O. Jenks (operations), F. R. Newman (traffic), G. H. Hess (accounting), F. L. Paetzold (secretary-treasurer), and F. G. Dorety (law). Thomas Balmer, an attorney who had recently replaced L. C. Gilman as vice president–executive department in Seattle, gained steadily in influence, as did financial expert Vernon P. Turnburke.

The strict-economy policy, indispensable in the 1930s, had left the GN in uncertain condition for handling rapidly growing traffic. The company's locomotive fleet was especially problematic because the road still largely depended on steam power, to which it had made no major addition since 1930. Indeed, more than three-fourths of its road engines were more than fifteen years old, and its switch engines averaged forty years of age. In addition, the total number and aggregate capacity of its freight cars had declined; only 2,500 had been placed in service during the seven years before 1939. Though it had 108 steel passenger cars,

Frank J. Gavin became president of the Great Northern in 1939.

the other 181 were lamentably of wooden construction, including some that were thirty years old. Upgrading of track too had lagged; during the 1930s, purchase of rail had averaged 8,000 tons a year, far short of the 25,000 tons that the engineering department deemed desirable.

C. O. Jenks greeted the new president with a long list of suggested improvements. The GN needed, he said, 7,800 new freight cars, 37 new locomotives, and much work equipment of all kinds; renovation of power and water-treating plants, coaling stations, and roundhouses; and expanded yards at Allouez, Minot, and Hillyard (Spokane). Furthermore, track work was necessary in every category: stabilized roadbed, upgraded bridges, large amounts of heavy rail and treated ties, and additional automatic block signals on heavily used lines. Finally, said Jenks, electrification from Skykomish to Gold Bar in the Cascade Mountains would bring substantial savings.

Gavin's most immediate decision was to commit the Great Northern to diesel power. The new president did permit Jenks to buy four used steam locomotives, two in 1939 and two six years later, but in 1939, Gavin ordered fourteen 1,000-horsepower switchers. By the end of the year, the GN had twenty-nine units. Before 1942, a massive 4,050-horsepower diesel was in helper service over the Continental Divide in the Montana Rockies, and three 2,700-horsepower machines were used on freight and passenger runs elsewhere. As a result, when the United States entered World War II, the GN had forty-nine diesels, all financed under conditional sales contracts, with payments spread over a number of years.

During Gavin's first three years as president, the company also upgraded and expanded its fleet of freight cars, purchasing 6,505 new ones, including double-sheathed box cars, all-steel ore cars, and seventy-ton covered hoppers for carrying cement in bulk, and repairing and modernizing much of the rolling stock. In December 1941, the GN owned 47,772 freight cars, 3,000 fewer than in 1938, but the average capacity per car had grown from 44.6 tons to 47.0.

Better rolling stock was matched by increased expenditures for roadway. The company's policy dictated acquiring an average of 22,000 gross tons of rail (mostly 112 pounds per yard) each year, increasing tie renewals, and spending more for daylighting cuts, ballasting, widening banks, upgrading bridges, and expanding freight yards. Nineteen changes of line resulted in better alignment and reduced grades. At Allouez the company improved its system for steaming iron ore to facilitate unloading and began to rebuild Ore Dock No. 3.

Events proved that the company had initiated this rapid improvement in plant and equipment at an extremely opportune time. The German invasion of Poland in 1939 was followed by brisk demand for iron and then a war-stimulated upturn in general economic activity, quickly reflected by rail traffic. The GN carried 53 percent more freight tonnage in 1941 than in 1939.

Despite improved net income, GN directors decided to continue reducing bonded debt rather than effecting early resumption of divi-

C. O. Jenks worried that the GN's fleet of steam locomotives would prove inadequate for the flood of business during World War II. Shop crews performed heroically, however, and the *Fast Mail* and the road's other trains—heavily laden though they were—went through as scheduled.

dends, which, discontinued in depressed 1932, had been paid only in 1937. Consequently the railroad did not disburse payments until the last quarter of 1940, and then only at 50 cents a share (per quarter) through 1944.

Mobilization

American railroad leaders knew that the industry's wartime performance would be closely watched not only by government authorities, but also by advocates of public ownership. If the carriers failed to meet challenges, precipitating government control of the railroads for a second time, private railway operation might well disappear forever. At the same time, however, responsible government officials knew better than to repeat the mistakes made twenty-five years earlier. The na-

tion's railroads and the government eagerly sought to develop, under private ownership and operation, procedures that would meet the unprecented demands of a two-front war.

The railroad industry was better prepared to meet emergencies in 1941 than it had been in 1917. The collective improvement programs of the 1920s had poured huge amounts of capital into roadbed and rolling stock, enhancing speed, dependability, and efficiency. Moreover, the Car Service Division of the Association of American Railroads (AAR) had expanded its staff and by 1941 was ready to administer the association's rules on supplying and distributing cars in a period of increased demand. Months in advance, the Regional Shippers' Advisory Boards provided forecasts of the number of cars needed, and in other ways promoted efficient use of rolling stock.

On May 28, 1940, President Roosevelt revived the World War I Council of National Defense, and appointed an Advisory Commission to assist the council in its tasks. As a member of the commission, titled Commissioner of Transportation, Ralph Budd, then president of the Chicago, Burlington & Quincy, assumed responsibility for establishing a system that could handle any transportation problems that might arise. Limited to persuasion and suggestion, Budd chose to work through the Interstate Commerce Commission, the AAR, and the shippers' advisory groups to correct or avoid causes behind the 1917 congestion and breakdown of the rail transportation system. He made significant progress. Some 7,000 new freight cars went into service

The heavy flow of war materiel put a strain on the Great Northern's physical plant.

The Great Northern Railway: A History/Part II 1916 to 1970

during the twelve months ending October 1, 1941, and freight cars unfit for service were reduced from 12 percent to 4.4 percent, one of the lowest levels in the history of American railroads.[2]

After Pearl Harbor, however, Roosevelt and his advisers concluded that the emergency required a new agency empowered to act as well as to advise. On December 18, 1941, the president created, within the Office of Emergency Management, the Office of Defense Transportation (ODT) and appointed Joseph B. Eastman, ICC chairman, as its head.

The ODT, according to Eastman, was to lend the "authority of the government to the maintenance and development of transportation services" in a way that would "effectively and efficiently meet the needs of the country in its war effort." Forming the new agency

placed real governmental power behind policies that for a year and a half Ralph Budd had been promoting by suggestion and voluntary action. Specifically, the agency determined adequacy of surface transportation, formulated policies intended to achieve maximal use of equipment, and to advise the government's allocation boards on the transportation industry's material needs. Working through the Interstate Commerce Commission, the ODT established priorities for transportation, joined with shipping authorities to eliminate congestion at seaports, and assumed direction of warehousing at crucial points. The ODT also spoke for the government in rate matters and advised authorities on the need for emergency legislation.[3]

Among the ODT's programs the ones that counted were those designed to get the most out of freight and passenger equipment. Analysis of traffic data, collected in detail from carriers, enabled the railroads and public authorities to identify potential congestion and to mitigate problems before they became acute. Directives required that freight cars be loaded to capacity, froze passenger schedules and, with some exceptions, prohibited special passenger trains or extra sections. During the last

Military passenger traffic peaked during the last months of the war. This is a westbound troop train near Chumstick, Washington, in 1945. *(Photo by Wm. J. Pontin, collection of Norman F. Priebe)*

months of the war, when military passenger traffic reached its peak, directives were more restrictive, eliminating seasonal travel to resorts, lightly used trains, and sleeper service on runs shorter than 450 miles. In effect, these orders placed all sleepers and head-end cars at the disposal of the military.

Other directives pertained to export-import traffic and to specialized freight cars. This utilization required close cooperation with shipping authorities, establishing storage-in-transit facilities, and instituting a permit system for commercial traffic. In this way the nation's fleets of refrigerator, open-top, and grain cars were pooled. Also, when submarines became a grave threat to oceangoing vessels, the ODT and other agencies ordered tank cars moved in special trains and restricted such cars chiefly to oil and oil products.

TRAIN SALES SERVICE

Food and beverages are served on principal Great Northern trains by the Train Salesmen, as follows:

Meat Sandwich	15c
American Cheese Sandwich	15c
Ginger Snaps, Package	10c
Lemon Snaps, Package	10c
Cheese Crackers, Package	10c
Soda Crackers, Package	10c
Oatmeal Cookies, Package	10c
Pie, Individual	10c
Pork and Beans, Individual	15c
Potato Chips, Package	10c
Tomato Juice, Individual	10c
Coffee, Per Cup	10c
Milk, Bottle	10c
Assorted Pop	10c
Orange Drink	10c
Whole Orange	10c
Wenatchee Apple	5c

CONTINUOUS MEAL SERVICE

The ICC shared control over wartime traffic with the ODT. In a number of cases, the ICC increased demurrage charges and decreased free time permitted under current tariffs, encouraging prompt handling of cars. Other orders restricted diversion and reconsignment provisions, embargoed routes to reduce circuitous travel and backhauling, and freed carriers from counterproductive state laws covering lengths of freight trains.

Other government agencies too influenced railroad operations, though less directly than the ODT and the ICC. The War Production Board (WPB) allocated materials, and the Office of Price Administration (OPA) at times intervened in rate cases. The War Manpower Commission was influential in recruiting and training workers and in meeting other labor issues. Because of their purchases, if not otherwise, the railroads had to deal with the Petroleum Administration for War and the Solid Fuel Administration for War. At all times, the Navy and War departments were deeply involved in moving men and materials, and even the Department of Agriculture exercised some control over movement of traffic. The Office of War Mobilization, created in May 1943 to unify the activities of other emergency agencies, had to resolve several interagency disputes among railroads and other modes of transportation.

Cooperation under Regulation

Efficient operation in accordance with steady outpourings of often confusing and conflicting orders and directives was more and more difficult. Emphasizing cooperation instead of competition, railway officers had to shift from underutilizing plant and equipment to full utilization, and, simultaneously, to con-

form with wartime rules demanding that they fulfill requirements beyond normal expectations. Meanwhile, adjustments were needed to meet shortages in materiel and personnel and changes in traffic patterns.

Before the Japanese attack on Pearl Harbor, GN officials believed their railroad could handle any business offered. In September 1939, C. O. Jenks observed testily that the GN could do as well as any other line, but admitted that the railroad's capacity had not been tested since the new Cascade Tunnel was completed in 1928. Nevertheless, Frank Gavin assured the AAR six months before Pearl Harbor that the GN was prepared "to take care of any possible increase in traffic." Neither Gavin nor Jenks could foresee, however, the incredible flood of business that came as the war gained momentum.[4]

Early in 1942, Gavin set the tone for the GN's war effort. "We are in a very serious war," he told subordinates, "and one that is going to take every resource at our command to win." Railroads would have to "cut out the frills," and concentrate on providing a maximum of transportation. Cooperation would take many forms. As early as 1940, recruiting posters had appeared in stations and publications, and after December 1941, the company participated in war-bond drives, with award-winning programs of sales to employees. Security guards were posted at crucial points, as at the Allouez ore docks, and employees were impressed with the need to maintain secrecy about movement of men and materiels.[5]

The GN anticipated some of the government's desires and conformed to others. The company had already cut its passenger service substantially, and could do little more to elimi-

Security guards were posted at the busy ore docks at Allouez.

The GN moved entire trains of oil from Laurel, Montana, to Seattle.

nate unnecessary trains. When the ODT later sought to discourage nonessential travel, however, the railroad closed its facilities for summer visitors at Glacier National Park, reduced advertising, and took club cars off the *Empire Builder*, replacing them with ten-section observation and sleeping cars obtained from the Pullman Company.

The GN's improvement program was fully in accord with government efforts to keep cars and locomotives available. Employees were instructed to handle rolling stock promptly and to unload materials quickly. When transcontinental lines farther south were overburdened, the company accepted traffic diverted to it by the ODT. The GN also moved special oil trains from Laurel, Montana, to Seattle; the Western Fruit Express Company, a GN subsidiary, placed its refrigerator cars in the industry-wide pool; special trains expedited empty freight cars to areas where they were needed; and, following ODT directives, the GN increased the average LCL load from 2.5 tons per car during the first six months of 1941 to

11 tons by June 1945, releasing hundreds of cars for other uses.

Despite careful attention to detail, the GN suffered scarcity in supplies and equipment. In 1941, the purchasing department had attempted to increase inventory, but difficulties were evident even before the attack on Pearl Harbor. Motive power was especially critical. In 1942, the WPB took control of allocating not only completed locomotives in manufacturers' hands, but also all future output. The GN had twenty diesels on order, including thirteen four-unit, 5,400-horsepower Titans for service in the Rockies. The diversion of these locomotives to other roads caused Gavin to complain: "There is not much chance to get anything, the Pennsylvania, Southern, and a few other lines run the show." In November 1942, a WPB decision gave the GN no diesels suitable for regular road work, but allowed the Northern Pacific to obtain twenty-two; Jenks, in desperation, recommended that steam locomotives be purchased.[6]

Gavin angrily rejected that idea and earned

for the GN the reputation at ODT and AAR of being "rather particular." He was not amused. At issue was not just the present but also the future. "One thing we will have to do if we are going to stay in business . . . is to operate the railroad efficiently," Gavin correctly pointed out. The advantages of diesels were so great, he maintained, that "the whole future of the railroad depends on what we do now. . . ."[7]

The government relented somewhat; allocation of motive power to the GN improved as the war progressed. During 1942, the company acquired six diesels (all small units for switching and light road service) and three in the next year—one of which, however, was the first of the thirteen 5,400-horsepower heavy freight locomotives ordered in 1941. Then, in 1944 and 1945, respectively, the GN substantially increased its inventory.

Deliveries of freight cars too were delayed by government restraints. Of the 1941 order, 2,000 fifty-ton double-sheathed cars were to be built by car manufacturers, and 1,000 were to

FREIGHT TRAIN PERFORMANCE

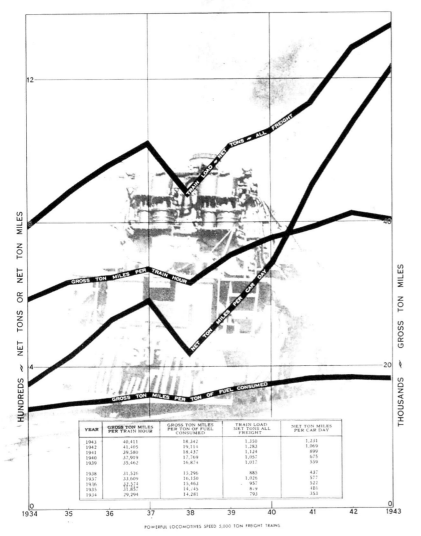

YEAR	GROSS TON MILES PER TRAIN HOUR	GROSS TON MILES PER TON OF FUEL CONSUMED	TRAIN LOAD NET TONS ALL FREIGHT	NET TON MILES PER CAR DAY
1943	40,411	18,342	1,350	1,231
1942	41,405	19,114	1,283	1,069
1941	39,580	18,437	1,124	899
1940	37,919	17,769	1,057	675
1939	35,462	16,874	1,017	559
1938	31,526	15,296	885	437
1937	33,609	16,150	1,026	577
1936	32,574	15,463	957	522
1935	31,857	14,745	849	486
1934	29,294	14,281	793	353

POWERFUL LOCOMOTIVES SPEED 5,000 TON FREIGHT TRAINS

REVENUE PASSENGER TRAFFIC

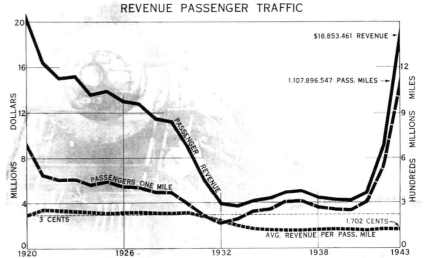

$18,853,461 REVENUE

1,107,896,547 PASS. MILES

PASSENGER REVENUE

PASSENGERS ONE MILE

3 CENTS

1.702 CENTS

AVG. REVENUE PER PASS. MILE

Minnesota's Mesabi Range remained a bastion of steam throughout the war years with massive N-3s handling most tonnage to the docks at Superior.

be constructed in the railroad's own shops. Nevertheless, only 1,126 of the "boxes" went into service in 1942, the remainder trickling in. Later on, the GN did succeed in acquiring,

after a short delay, 250 flat cars, 500 all-steel gondolas, and 1,000 seventy-five-ton ore cars.

After the WPB began allocating critical materials in 1942, company officers gradually

learned to manage within wartime procedures. Requests for rail and fastenings went through the AAR and the ODT to the WPB, which drew up a priority list based on supply and de-

223

The Pressures of War — Again

Diesel-electrics for passenger service finally arrived in 1945. *(Collection of Norman Priebe)*

mand. Shortages were severe. During the war years railroads were allocated only 70 percent of the 9.2 million tons of rail requests, and the companies actually acquired still less. In 1941, the GN contracted for 23,000 gross tons for delivery in the next year, but received only 16,100 tons. When the company asked for 23,000 gross tons for 1943, the WPB allotment was 22,000 net tons, half the amount granted the Northern Pacific. Gavin was furious: "We tried to play fair . . . and asked for only what we thought was absolutely necessary . . . we played the game wrong because if we asked for twice as much as we needed we would have gotten what we wanted." He, too, would play the game. In 1944, the GN reported its need as 50,000 net tons and obtained 37,326 tons.[8]

Despite shortages, the GN succeeded in making improvements. New shops were built at Havre and at Great Falls, and in 1945 the company commenced construction of a 1.25 million-bushel grain elevator at Superior, replacing one destroyed in a spectacular explosion and fire. Roadway improvements included new or lengthened passing tracks, expanded yards, automatic interlockers and spring switches, and upgraded bridges and culverts. Line changes on the west slope of the Rockies as well as others in Washington and in North Dakota improved alignment, lowered grades, and reduced curvature.

The shortage of new rolling stock was less harmful than the scarcity of manpower, especially of skilled workers, for whom competition was sharp. The tremendous increase in war-produced traffic coincided with a drain on the company's labor pool by enlistments, the draft, and expanded war industries. Altogether, 8,775 GN employees went into the armed forces, of whom 898, including future

President John M. Budd, served in either the 704th Railway Grand Division or the 732nd Railway Operating Battalion in campaigns from North Africa to Germany. After losses to the military grew heavy, the GN took workers where it could find them, with unpredictable results. Recruiting drives drew some response, occasionally with embarrassing consequences. In 1945, a hastily hired switch tender in Minneapolis proved to have "spent most of his time during working hours cracking safes around the city"; although highly recommended by a local trucking firm, he had actually spent the preceding years in "three or four penitentiaries."[9]

Innovation was required. By January 1944, more than 200 Mexican nationals were on the payroll. They worked hard, but a brief experiment with a few Nazi prisoners of war was less successful. Women were a huge and heretofore untapped pool, but by September 1943, more than 1,500 of them were in the GN work force—not only in typical secretarial or clerical jobs but also working as coach cleaners and roundhouse laborers.[10]

Problems remained. Early in 1944, the company sought to fill 2,000 openings, mostly skilled positions. So bad was the shortage by spring 1945 that President Truman, speaking from Potsdam, Germany, urged Americans as a patriotic duty to take railroad jobs. The War Manpower Commission accorded top priority for interregional recruiting to roads in the West, where the need was most acute. When the military was finally induced to furlough 4,000 men to join the railroads' work force, the GN welcomed its allotment. By 1945, the company boosted employment rolls from 18,461 in 1939 to 27,995, an increase of 52 percent.

Shifts in traffic patterns presented other dif-

The handful of diesel switchers turned in stellar performances during the hectic years of World War II.

ficulties. In 1942, for the first time since the 1890s, westbound volume surpassed eastbound. The new balance was mainly caused by two developments: rapidly evolving industry on the Pacific Coast that required shipment of supplies west, and the two-front war, with Seattle and Portland's gaining status as entrepôts. Because much of the westbound freight moved in open cars useless for hauling eastbound grain and lumber, the GN unfortunately had to move empty cars in both directions. Similarly, passenger traffic was heavily westbound until after Japan surrendered, when it became even more predominantly eastbound.[11]

Despite the AAR Car Service Division's good work, equipment was returned slowly. In 1943, an extreme maladjustment upset car supply. Inadequacies in refrigerator and livestock cars were dwarfed by a critical box-car short-

When adequate diesel locomotives were not forthcoming, C. O. Jenks recommended the purchase of steam locomotives.

practice of falling down,'' wrote one shipper in Montana. In reality, little could be done, given the wartime demand for transportation.[13]

Despite the company's best efforts, GN passenger service was similarly criticized. Struggling under government orders to move loaded and empty troop trains on schedules comparable to those of regular passenger service, C. O. Jenks properly attributed the difficulty to scarce manpower and equipment and to the heavy crush of business. "Facilities were never thought of that would take care of such passenger business as we have at the present time,'' he wrote in December 1945. The problem would disappear only after the flow of men from battlefields to their homes had eased.[14]

Performance and Financial Policy

The GN after all met emergency traffic demands with remarkable success, handling an unprecedented volume of freight. The total rose from 32.8 million tons in 1939, peaking at 59.7 million in 1942. Although declines came in the next three years, the tonnage in 1945 was still 32 percent above the highest prewar figure. New tonnage records were set in nearly all categories: in 1942 mine products; two years later wheat, animal products, and other agricultural commodities; and in 1945 manufactured and miscellaneous goods. Only coal, merchandise, and LCL shipments fell below 1920 levels. Longer average hauls made an obvious difference in some statistics. In fact, the GN moved 47 percent more tonnage in 1944 than in 1929 and produced 93 percent more ton miles. The company piled up still

age. Numerous on-line grain elevators were blocked (full), and wheat was stored on the ground because almost 20,000 of GN's box cars were off-line on other assignments.[12]

Problems peaked in 1944 and 1945. The GN started the 1944 grain-moving season with only 74 percent of its cars on line, and dropped to an all-time low of 39 percent in March 1945. A month earlier, managers of 250 blocked elevators pleaded for relief that

the GN could not immediately grant. Even working day and night, car repair shops with many inexperienced workers were not able to turn out equipment fast enough. For its part, the AAR ordered companies holding cars from western roads to return them to St. Louis or Chicago, in special trains if necessary. Nevertheless, many cars were diverted before reaching home roads. Public criticism was loud and bitter. "The Great Northern seems to make a

Passenger traffic tended to be heavily west-bound until after the surrender of Japan, when it became predominantly eastbound. Here a veteran P-2 wheels expectant GIs toward Minneapolis.

more striking measures in railway operating efficiency—gross ton miles per train hour, train load in net tons, ton miles per car day, and gross miles per ton of fuel consumed.

Wartime gains in the volume of passenger traffic were even more spectacular than those in freight. Passengers carried in 1944, 3.1 million, although fewer than half as many as in the peak year 1920, topped the 1939 figure by more than 180 percent. Moreover, with the average journey sharply longer under wartime conditions, the gain in passenger miles was much greater than the increase in passengers over those of recent years. The 8.5 million people transported by the GN in 1920 averaged 80 miles; the 3.1 million in 1945 averaged 438 miles.

Heavy traffic did not automatically produce new highs in earnings; World War II brought no bonanza to the GN. Costs rose, despite the government's efforts to stabilize them. Labor settlements drove up the average hourly wage by 32 percent between 1939 and 1945; that jump, combined with the larger work force, elevated the aggregate annual employee compensation by 120 percent. The relatively small increases in freight rates that the ICC granted were not at all compensatory, yet Gavin was able to maintain a favorable operating ratio until the last year of the war. Standing at 65.9 in 1939, this vital indicator fell to 56.5 in 1942, lowest since 1916, but rose into the low 60s in 1943 and 1944, then shot to 79.9 in 1945.

The GN did reduce one major expense during the war—interest on funded debt. Vernon P. Turnburke was instrumental in restructuring

finances to reduce fixed costs. With great facility for numbers and everything pertaining to them, he had already made his mark when in 1942 he was moved from his position as general auditor to the executive office as assistant to President Gavin. After experience on the Chicago, Milwaukee & St. Paul, Turnburke had joined the GN to head the statistical office when it was made part of the accounting department in 1917. During World War I, he was assistant manager, then manager, of the

operating statistical section of the United States Railroad Administration. Returning to the GN, he directed special studies, including "spade work" for President Kenney's refinancing in the 1930s. Turnburke analyzed the company's needs, recorded each move in the nation's capital markets, periodically estimated financial options open to the company, and took advantage of changes in investment markets and competition in money markets to design the GN's financial strategy.

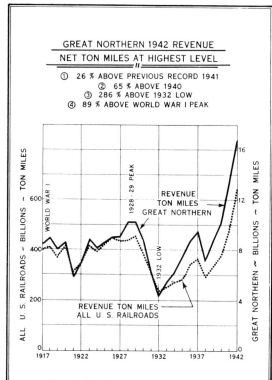

GREAT NORTHERN 1942 REVENUE
NET TON MILES AT HIGHEST LEVEL

① 26 % ABOVE PREVIOUS RECORD 1941
② 65 % ABOVE 1940
③ 286 % ABOVE 1932 LOW
④ 89 % ABOVE WORLD WAR I PEAK

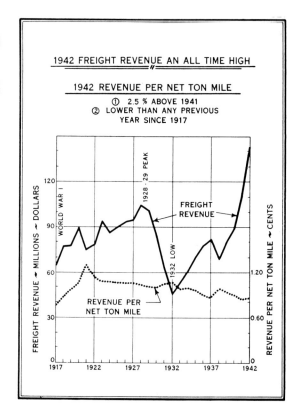

1942 FREIGHT REVENUE AN ALL TIME HIGH
1942 REVENUE PER NET TON MILE

① 2.5 % ABOVE 1941
② LOWER THAN ANY PREVIOUS
YEAR SINCE 1917

Heavier power was assigned west of Minot, lighter power on the prairie lines to the east. Top, an eastbound manifest hurries tonnage over Gassman Coulee; bottom, a maid-of-all-work lugs dead freight and empties westbound near Wayzata, Minnesota.

When Gavin became president in 1939, funded debt was composed of two main parts. One made up the company's equipment obligations, essentially equipment trusts, due in relatively few years and payable serially. Most of the GN's funded debt, however, was in the form of bonds in three general categories: (1) bonds of antecedent and affiliated companies, whose properties, built with proceeds of these securities, provided bondholders with a first claim on the railroad; (2) First and Refunding Mortgage bonds of 1911, with a second lien on the properties; (3) bonds of 1921 and later, issued under indenture of 1921 and subject to the two prior liens.

During the first three years of Gavin's administration, the GN made only modest reductions in funded debt. When the last of the St. Paul, Minneapolis & Manitoba Railway Company's bonds (4 percent Pacific Extension) became due in 1940, the GN met the remaining $28.1 million of these, in part by refunding. To meet this obligation, the railroad issued 4 percent Collateral Trust bonds, aggregating $20 million. It also made small reductions in other outstanding issues annually from 1939 to 1941, so that during these three years, bonded debt was cut by $12.8 million, bringing it to the lowest point since 1925. Annual interest was less than for any year since 1920.

The GN's policy of retiring bonds before their due dates gained momentum in 1942. Turnburke gave special attention to issues with near maturities, especially the Convertible and Collateral Trust bonds, which had grown out of earlier refunding, and carried relatively high interest rates. To achieve its aim, the GN varied its approaches, calling some bonds with that provision, buying others in the open market, and issuing an invitation for tenders.

The company's moves to lower the number of its bonds held by the public is shown by the handling of convertible bonds, Series G and H, which, issued in the 1936 refunding, bore interest at 4 percent and amounted to $98.9 million at the beginning of 1939. They were due in 1946. The company encouraged owners to exchange them for stock, an action reflected in the increase in GN's shares during the mid-1940s.

No large maturity faced the GN in 1944, but conditions were favorable for major refunding. Interest rates were low, the company's credit was good, and the price of its stock was up. Thus the GN issued $100 million in General Mortgage bonds in three series, maturing severally in 1960, 1970, and 1980, and bearing interest of up to 3½ percent. The GN sold these bonds above par and realized $100,645,500. By adding treasury funds to proceeds from this and future sales of bonds, the company was able to redeem several earlier issues under very favorable conditions.

Meanwhile, Turnburke carefully attended to the other part of funded debt—equipment obligations. Kenney's orders for locomotives and Gavin's emphasis on converting to diesel had increased this debt to $4.8 million in 1938,

In addition to heavy military movement westbound, the GN handled the usual flow of fruit eastbound from Wenatchee, Washington.

The Pressures of War—Again

then to $23.5 million in 1942, before declining to $19.4 million in 1945. The cost of carrying this liability was held down by carefully studying the market for short-term obligations. Trust certificates had been utilized in the 1930s, but in 1939 the GN began to use notes based on conditional sales contracts to purchase motive power and equipment, and by the end of 1942, such contracts made up 91 percent of the GN's equipment obligations. In that year, the company's typical notes carried 2 percent interest.

From 1939 on, the GN effected a remarkable change in its capitalization and fixed costs. Funded debt was reduced from $330.8 million at the start of 1939 to $247.9 million at the end of 1945; interest on bonds was lowered from a range of 4 to 6 percent to less than 4 percent on three-quarters of the bonded debt; and maturities were spread in relatively manageable amounts from 1952 to 2000. The proportion of stocks and bonds, making up the total capitalization, changed from 42.96 and 57.04 percent, respectively, in 1938, to 52.39 and 47.61 percent in 1945. By reducing both funded debt and interest rates, the annual charge for interest was cut from $14.1 million in 1938 to $9.8 million in 1945.

These favorable results did not fully extend to final net income, primarily because of wartime taxes. Net revenues from railway operations before fixed costs reached a high of $77.8 million in 1943 and averaged $62.4 million from 1941 to 1945. Although the "fixed cost" for use of capital was reduced, taxes rose to $48.5 million in 1943, a tremendous jump of 379 percent since 1939. After taking into account all these items, net income rose from $8.7 million in 1939 to a high of $29.1 million in 1942 and averaged $18.9 million

per annum during Gavin's first seven years at the helm.

As World War II ended in August 1945, railroaders, including those of the Great Northern, could look back with pride on their hard work and ingenuity. With relatively little expansion in their facilities, the country's railroads in 1944 had registered 97 percent more intercity ton miles and 295 percent more passenger miles than in 1940. Indeed, during the war years rail carriers moved 90 percent of the military freight and 98 percent of organized group travel of servicemen in the continental United States. The GN, as a major carrier, had a great part in this outstanding performance. That fine record was matched by remodeling in the railroad's debt structure. Great Northern executives worried, though, that adjustments after this conflict might prove as difficult as those which had followed World War I.

28

Labor-Management Relations in Depression and War

Presidents William P. Kenney and Frank J. Gavin had very different experiences in relations with employees. Depression and then prosperity were the major variables, and issues were settled according to those conditions, often with little thought to future effects.[1]

Cooperation in Hard Times

During the depression, the Great Northern's labor relations were typical of those experienced by the industry. Despite conscientious efforts to maintain employment, the carriers had to cut payrolls by 10 percent in 1930 and by 15 percent in 1931. The average number of employees dropped 48 percent between 1929 and 1933, from 28,258 to 14,695.

For the most part, C. O. Jenks encouraged labor organizations to work out share-the-work and layoff plans. Shopmen in 1932 chose to work two weeks a month rather than three-day weeks. In the same year firemen and trainmen voluntarily consented to reductions in their maximum mileage allowances. Conductors and engineers, who under seniority rules could take jobs as trainmen and firemen, were less cooperative. In another matter, the general feeling that married women with working husbands should not hold jobs resulted in a sharp cut in the number of female employees, especially among clerks, whose union's agreement temporarily forbade employment of married women. Telegraphers had special problems because at many isolated stations husband-and-wife teams shared the work. Maintenance-of-way personnel resisted the proposal that they accept half-time work, and their union president declared that "such low paid" men could not stand "any reduction in earning power." That refusal, coupled with growing mechanization, resulted in cutting alternate sections on branches and secondary lines as early as 1933.[2]

Pension plans were yet another special problem. Turnover of employees had been low throughout the 1920s, increasing workers' average age as more employees stayed until retirement. Pensions were based on wages in the last ten years of service, increasing payments to retirees at a time when the companies were less able to meet them. Nevertheless, GN managers agreed that workers' rights had to be safeguarded. Some consideration was given to partly financing the system by employees' contributions, but company officers did not wish to relinquish full control. Then, in 1937, anticipating federal legislation, the GN modified its own plan. The company continued to pay out to those already retired, but for the time being added no new names to its list.[3]

A national approach to pension problems was only one part of a general shift in union objectives. From 1931 on, labor spokesmen demanded laws that would provide both jobs and security. The Railway Labor Executives' Association (RLEA) was primarily responsible for formulating these goals — provisions for dismissal, wages, retirement and unemployment programs, stipulated length of trains and number of train crews, the six-hour day, and a long list of "safety" measures. In 1935, the RLEA also asked for laws providing for uniform inspection of dispatchers' offices, signal systems, tracks and bridges, and empowering the Interstate Commerce Commission to order repair work. Several labor leaders even urged government ownership of railroads, and a few resurrected the old Plumb plan.

Franklin Roosevelt's New Deal often reflected labor's goals. In 1937, Congress passed the Railroad Retirement Act, which provided a Railroad Retirement Board that would manage a program of life annuities for all railroad workers either at age sixty-five, or, if the retiree so chose, after thirty years of work. Disabled workers with fewer years of service could receive lower payments. To finance these pensions, both the employee and the employer were to pay a tax, scheduled to rise from 2¾ to 3¾ percent by 1949. On July 1, 1937, the new program, retroactive to August 29, 1935, superseded the individual railroads' plans.

The GN's management decided to go further. If a pensioner received less from the government than under the company's earlier plan, the railroad would make up the difference. "In any event, you will not receive less than you are now receiving under the company plan," Jenks assured a former employee. For nonunion (exempt) help, such as supervisory personnel, whose positions justified annuities larger than those under the government's plan, the GN retained its own program.[4]

During the New Deal years, railroad workers also gained unemployment protection. At first, this coverage was under the Social Security Act of 1935 and state legislation, but the federal Railroad Unemployment Insurance Act of 1938 provided for compensation by a tax on employers for the first $300 per month of each worker's earnings.

These innovations in social legislation together placed sizable burdens on the railroads just when they were least able to carry them. For the GN, 1940 payroll taxes totaled $2,330,983, in contrast to $292,511 paid for pensions in 1929 and $494,166 in 1933.

Labor relations were greatly shaped during the 1930s and after by the Railway Labor Act of 1926, as amended in 1934. Earlier legislation had created a national Board of Mediation, its five members appointed by the president. When mediation was unsuccessful, the board notified the president, who appointed a fact-finding board to examine the issues and submit a report to him. Although an emergency board's findings were not binding, they were expected to carry great weight. The law also provided that no strike could occur in a sixty-day cooling-off period, during which the parties might come to agreement. The Railway Labor Act of 1926 further provided for boards of adjustment, but the scope of their activities — whether they should be national, regional, or limited to one carrier, and whether they should cover all employees or specific groups of workers — was left to the carriers and their employees.

The 1934 amendments clearly reflected the New Deal philosophy. Changes strengthened workers' right to bargain collectively through unions of their choice, prohibited railroads from contributing to company unions, and outlawed any form of the so-called yellow-dog contract. The Board of Mediation was replaced by a National Mediation Board, with somewhat broader powers, but the format of arbitration and emergency boards remained substantially unchanged. The new legislation also created a permanent National Railroad Adjustment Board, with jurisdiction over all disputes about wages, work rules, and working conditions when such disputes were referred to it by either management or labor. With headquarters in Chicago, the thirty-six members of this board, chosen equally by the carriers and labor, were grouped in four divisions, each responsible for specific crafts or classes of workers. Where a decision could not be reached, either the National Railroad Adjustment Board or the National Mediation Board was empowered to appoint a neutral referee. Although findings by the board or referee were binding and judicially enforceable, the original petitioner might appeal decisions to the courts.

The nation's railroads soon found that the unions had won a powerful weapon in the National Railroad Adjustment Board, if only because they functioned nationally. By the end of the 1930s, railroad managers were increasingly critical of decisions handed down by the board, especially those by referees, whose neutrality was at times questioned. Management believed that board decisions, as a group, built up a body of rigid work rules, reduced savings inherent in technological innovation, and in other ways limited the carriers' ability to achieve operating efficiency. Some officers, moreover, believed that the National Railroad Adjustment Board discouraged true collective bargaining, for union leaders saw no need to negotiate with employers if better terms could be obtained from the board or from presumably neutral referees. Finally, the Burlington's Ralph Budd stated in 1940, "No

appeal or court review has been found to be available to railroads under the present law."[5]

The new structure for handling labor disputes started out less onerous for the GN than for many other roads because GN employees made relatively little use of the National Railroad Adjustment Board, contributing only thirteen of the two thousand cases brought before it by the end of 1936. Both the company and its employees preferred to settle issues at home. Jenks knew most of the general chairmen and many of the workers with whom he dealt, and they believed that they were as likely to get just treatment from him as from an impersonal national board. Jenks said that the company's employees "generally are agreed that they are properly paid for services performed, and that if a mistake is found in their payment or handling, it is properly and equitably adjusted."[6]

Meanwhile, national labor leaders pushed for wage increases — calling for complete and immediate restoration to wage levels prevailing before 1932 plus a 10 percent increase. Labor won. Then, in 1937, encouraged by gradual improvement in the economy, fourteen nonoperating brotherhoods sought an increase of 20 cents an hour, and five operating brotherhoods, a flat 20 percent raise. Compromise gave the nonoperating personnel an increase of 5 cents an hour, and the operating brotherhoods got 44 cents a day.

Unfortunately for the carriers, soon after these agreements had been formalized, the recession of 1938 struck the country. In February, railway net earnings were lower than at any time in the dark days of 1932 and 1933. Two months later, when management proposed a 15 percent reduction, labor leaders threatened to strike. In September, under the Railway Labor Act, President Roosevelt ap-

pointed an emergency board. It concluded that no reduction in wages was justified: railroad wages were not high compared with those in other industries, the carriers' immediate difficulties were temporary, and the more basic problems could not be solved by reduction in wages. Although not convinced that the board's reasoning was valid, the carriers withdrew their proposal.[7]

Rail managers understandably felt boxed in by the unions and the federal government. When the ICC in 1938 pared the carriers' request for a 15 percent raise in freight rates to only 5.3 percent, management concluded that government policy had destroyed the balance between rates and prevailing prices, that the principal cause of the railroads' low earnings was the rise in labor costs, and that the amended Railway Labor Act promoted injustice and discord. In the future, management's ability to operate efficiently and to increase productivity would be severely limited, despite technological advances. The depression's devastation and the New Deal had given railway labor power it had never had. It had also helped create an environment conducive to great conflict in later decades.[8]

War and Prosperity

With wartime boom and postwar prosperity, workers' desires and managers' reaction changed dramatically. Negotiators for labor shifted their emphasis from jobs and security to increased wages and real income. Aided by a favorable political climate and gradual inflation, unions were in a position to be militant. Railway officers were painfully aware that circumstances favored labor, but

Railroading very often was a family tradition: the Mahers, from left, Frank, Joe, and Harry.

Labor-Management Relations in Depression and War

234

The Great Northern Railway: A History/Part II 1916 to 1970

they also understood, if labor did not, that higher wages meant higher costs and increased competitive pressures. On the other hand, railroads during most of the 1940s were faced with the need to produce the maximum of transportation with an inadequate supply of labor. Unpleasant concessions would be required.

Long experienced as an operating man, Frank Gavin, as successor to W. P. Kenney, had pleasant relations with members of the work force and was generally respected by union officials. Throughout his administration he emphasized that management and labor were members of a team working together for the common good. One official of the Railway Labor Executives' Association knew of "nobody whose sincere acquaintance I enjoy more" than Gavin's, and he praised the railroad president for his "always just and fair attitude." In 1939, Gavin initiated publication of the *Annual Report to Employees* to enable workers to understand the company's operations and progress. He said, most "of us . . . feel that we have a very real interest in the industry and in the Company which makes our jobs possible."[9]

Such sentiments at the Great Northern, however, did little to soften the railway labor unions' new power or to temper their demands at the national level. One major issue was the size and type of crews on diesel locomotives. Discussions on this topic sharply focused the whole question of antiquated work rules. Diesel locomotives gave management greater speed and power, more flexibility and availability, and extensive operating economies. For

Enginemen insisted that the weight-on-drivers classification used to establish rates of pay for work on steam locomotives be extended to include diesels.

firemen, however, the new motive power threatened jobs and their union's existence. The issue was difficult to compromise.

Soon after diesel locomotives appeared in large numbers, union leaders sought a national policy on crews; hitherto they had negotiated with individual roads. In the fall of 1936, the Brotherhood of Locomotive Firemen and Enginemen had demanded two-man crews, an engineer and a fireman, for such power; the Carriers' Joint Conference Committee offered only light opposition. After all, only a few roads at that time had diesels, unemployment was still a big problem, and according to the Santa Fe's Fred G. Gurley, "many railroad officials had considerable doubts . . . as to whether or not the diesel locomotive would ever become an important factor on the American railroads."[10]

The Firemen's National Diesel Agreement, signed by the Carriers' Committee and the BLF&E in February 1937, thus stipulated that a fireman-helper should be employed on electric as well as diesel and other internal-combustion locomotives pulling main-line or streamline passenger trains, and on all such locomotives having 90,000 pounds of weight or more on the drivers. This settlement recognized 230 jobs for firemen on diesels and increased the carriers' payrolls at the time by only $445,000. And so was set a crucial industry-wide standard. Ralph Budd later correctly observed that there were "no manual duties for a fireman to perform on this diesel-electric equipment, and the request of the Brotherhood was presented solely under the guise that it is necessary for the safety of the employees and the traveling public."[11]

Nevertheless, as more multiple-unit diesel locomotives went into service, the Brotherhood of Locomotive Engineers insisted that an

"assistant engineer" was needed on such locomotives, and the BLF&E demanded a second fireman. Soon both groups asked that the weight-on-drivers classification, used to set graduated pay scales for crews on steam locomotives, be extended to include diesels. A presidential emergency board considered these issues in 1943. The so-called Swacker Board approved the weight-on-driver request but rejected others. The board recommended that at all times two men should be in the cab on multiple-unit diesels in high-speed passenger service, and that, if a third man was needed in engine rooms, he should be a fireman. Both brotherhoods professed to be displeased with the proposals, but they subsequently signed contracts embodying them.

The question came up again in 1948. Claiming that firemen were performing duties that rightfully belonged to engineers, the BLE reiterated its demand for a second engineer. Not to be outdone, the BLF&E reasserted its request for a second fireman. An emergency board found no justification for either, a decision that both unions quickly rejected. After consideration, however, the BLE decided not to strike, ending the struggle for a second engineer after almost fifteen years of negotiation. The firemen were more militant, and in May 1950 struck for six days against four railroads. Although negotiators worked out compromises on minor points, the principle was firmly established that only one fireman was needed on multiple-unit diesels· in ordinary road service.

Labor's greatest overall interest, however, was in gaining further wage increases. During World War II the government's economic stabilization program was a restraint, yet two major conflicts arose. In 1941, the brotherhoods demanded increases and paid vacations, rejected an emergency board's recommendations, and scheduled a nation-wide strike for December 5. The attack on Pearl Harbor came two days later, and to prevent chaos, President Roosevelt reconvened the emergency board, which effected a settlement by proposing terms more liberal than its original recommendations and retroactive to September 1, 1941. For the GN, the payroll swelled by $1.9 million in 1941 and $7.2 million in 1942. Labor's success on the "second try" would be regarded by management as the cause behind the unions' rejection of several emergency-board decisions in later years.

A more telling controversy erupted in 1943 when unions put forth still more demands. Nonoperating employees wanted an increase of 20 cents an hour, with a minimum hourly rate of 70 cents. Under White House pressure, an emergency board ultimately settled the matter by awarding raises of from 9 to 11 cents an hour, effective December 26, 1943, with an additional 4 to 10 cents retroactive to the preceding February 1. The operating crafts demanded a 30 percent raise in pay, with a minimal increase of $3.00 a day. An emergency board recommended, and the carriers placed in effect, an increase of 4 cents an hour, retroactive to April 1, 1943, but workers resolved to strike. President Roosevelt then made himself mediator and induced the engineers and trainmen to accept an award of an additional 5 cents, effective December 27. The firemen, conductors, and switchmen rejected that offer, however, and the government took control of the roads to avoid a strike. With no hope of success, dissatisfied workers soon accepted the same terms that had been given to engineers and trainmen. Government control of the roads ended on January 18, 1944. Together, increases in wages for 1943 added

$4.9 million to the GN's outlay for labor in the next season.

Although negotiations during the war were difficult, they were mild compared with disputes that came later. Even before the end of international hostilities, fifteen nonoperating unions and five operating organizations submitted demands for pay increases ranging from 30 cents per hour for nonoperating men to $2.80 per basic eight-hour day for operating personnel. Furthermore, changes in work rules were sought by each group. Early in 1946, after lengthy negotiations, the nonoperating unions and the BLF&E, the Order of Railway Conductors, and the Switchmen's Union of North America agreed to withdraw or defer demands for rule changes and to submit wage disputes to arbitration. Four months later, a board awarded train-service personnel an increase of $1.28 per day, retroactive to January 1, 1946. Labor accepted with great reluctance.

The unions soon demonstrated their dissatisfaction. The BLE and the Brotherhood of Railroad Trainmen, after refusing to drop requests for rule changes or to submit the matter to arbitration, rejected an emergency board's recommendation for an increase of $1.28 a day, and scheduled a strike. Moreover, now dissatisfied with their gains of a few weeks earlier, the nonoperating unions and the BLF&E, ORC, and SUNA asked for an additional 14 cents an hour and prepared to support their demands by striking.

To prevent interruption of rail service, the government again took over the roads on May 17, 1946. Undeterred, the BLE and BRT walked out on May 23, but accepted a settlement two days later after President Truman promised harsh measures. The rebellious engineers and trainmen got an increase of $1.28

per day, retroactive to January 1, and all railway employees received an additional 2½ cents an hour in lieu of desired rule changes or other wage increases, a compromise Truman had suggested. With labor peace restored, at least temporarily, the government returned the properties to owners May 26, 1946.

Yet another round of very unpleasant controversy surfaced in 1947, when all unions asked for sizable increases in pay. On September 2, an arbitration board awarded nonoperating unions a raise of 15½ cents an hour; a few weeks later the BRT and ORC accepted the same increase, but the BLE, BLF&E, and SUNA rejected a similar offer. In January 1948, President Truman appointed an emergency board but the unions rejected its offer and resolved to strike on May 11. A day before that deadline, however, Truman took control of the railroads, returning them to private management July 9, 1948. During government operation, though, union leaders were persuaded to accept the 15½-cents raise offered earlier, retroactive to November 1, 1947.

Even before this chapter in the conflict had ended, another began. In April 1948, several nonoperating unions, representing 80 percent of railroad employees, demanded that the work week be reduced from forty-eight to forty hours, with simultaneous increase in pay of 25 cents an hour. Again an emergency board was formed, and its decision, as accepted September 1, 1948, provided nonoperating employees a forty-hour week with an arrangement for a staggered work schedule, allowing the companies to avoid penalty rates on Saturdays and Sundays. The board also gave workers an increase of 7 cents an hour, effective October 1, 1948. Concurrently, the operating unions' request for increases before the carriers gained a

10-cents-an-hour boost, effective October 16, 1948.

Although relative calm prevailed in 1949, controversies arising from demands in that year extended well into the next decade and significantly changed contracts. In September, SUNA requested a five-day, forty-hour week, a 44 percent raise in basic daily wage rate, double time for overtime, and miscellaneous other increases. The usual negotiations and customary rejection of findings by an emergency board were followed by a short-lived strike on five western roads, including the GN. Agreement was reached September 1, 1950, when the switchmen received an increase of 23 cents an hour, and the carriers accepted in principle the five-day, forty-hour week. A new clause for a major railroad labor contract provided for a quarterly adjustment in basic wage rates according to changes in the consumers' cost-of-living index. The carriers accepted this arrangement to gain the union's agreement for a three-year moratorium on change in wages and work rules.

The clash with the switchmen had been sharp enough, but disputes with other unions, also begun in 1949, were even more intense and lasted longer. In March the conductors and trainmen submitted demands for changed rules and wages, specifying a work week of 40 hours with no reduction in take-home pay. The firemen and engineers made similar requests in November. When the conductors and trainmen announced a strike in August, Truman seized the carriers, directing that they be operated by the Secretary of the Army. Negotiations continued amid charges and countercharges. On December 21, 1950, the companies and the unions signed a memorandum, repudiated a month later by negotiating

Table 10. Employee Compensation, 1939–1951

Year	Average wages per hour worked[a]	Average fringe benefits[b] per hour worked	Total labor cost per hour worked	Productivity in traffic units[c] per dollar of labor costs
1939	$0.80	$0.04	$0.84	234
1940	.79	.05	.84	247
1941	.81	.05	.86	265
1942	.89	.07	.96	280
1943	.91	.08	.99	269
1944	1.02	.08	1.10	244
1945	1.03	.09	1.12	224
1946	1.22	.11	1.33	172
1947	1.27	.15	1.42	170
1948	1.44	.13	1.57	154
1949	1.55	.15	1.70	144
1950	1.71	.17	1.88	147
1951	1.90	.22	2.12	143

a. Excluded: pay for vacations, sick leave, and holidays.
b. Fringe benefits include retirement and pension payments; unemployment insurance and health, welfare, and group insurance premiums; pay for vacations, sick leave, and holidays; and meals and lodging.
c. Traffic units are the sum of net ton miles and passengers carried one mile.

Source: Comptroller's Department, Great Northern Railway Company.

committees and chairmen of the four brotherhoods. Spokesmen close to Truman accused the unions of bad faith, and workers went out on wildcat strikes that the Army declared were handicapping the war effort in Korea. Court orders directing the trainmen to desist were obeyed only after the striking unions had been fined $100,000 for contempt of court.

In 1951, the BRT, breaking away from the other unions, signed an agreement with the carriers. The men it represented won a forty-hour week and a 12½-cent increase in hourly wages, in three stages. The settlement also provided for substantial adjustments in wages according to advances in the cost-of-living index, in return for a moratorium on other changes in wages and work rules, this time to October 1953.

The confrontation with the engineers, conductors, and firemen continued until May 1952, when new contracts gave them increases of up to 23 cents an hour, retroactive to October 1950. The now-standard moratorium promised labor peace for three years, but the carriers were saddled with a back-pay bill of about $100 million with future cost-of-living adjustments and, much more significant, no offsetting gains in productivity.

During these protracted negotiations, the nonoperating unions also sought raises. Late in 1950 their leaders asked for an increase of 25 cents an hour, and after bargaining, railroad and union representatives agreed to a 12½-cent-an-hour increase effective February 1, 1951, with later changes to be based on the cost-of-living index. Again, the carriers granted much with no benefits in productivity.

Legislation too added to labor costs, above all the Crosser Act, approved on July 1, 1946. This comprehensive amendment to the Railroad Retirement Act and the Railroad Unemployment Insurance Act created a new system of annuities for survivors, increased payment to unemployed workers, and applied the same schedule of benefits for disability from any cause, including maternity. It also raised the payroll tax paid by employees to 5¾ percent and by employers to 8¾ percent and provided for subsequent increases in rates to 6¼ and 9¼ percent respectively by January 1951.

These constant demands spectacularly increased the GN's outlay for labor. From 1939 to 1951 annual compensation jumped from

$1,982 to $4,048, or 106 percent, and employee compensation was $122.2 million in 1951, a startling 234 percent above the 1939 level. Table 10 suggests the great surge.

Changes in management–labor relations during the 1930s and 1940s created a legacy certain to leave major problems for future management. With unprecedented demand for railroad services during the 1940s, company officers found it extremely difficult to deny workers' requests for security as well as higher wages and more liberal working conditions. At the same time, the government, wanting labor peace during and after the war, was motivated by a philosophy born in the depression — pragmatic solutions for immediate problems. Accordingly, the remarkable increase in workers' direct compensation in the 1940s, combined with legislative aftereffects from the 1930s, set patterns that could be changed only with great difficulty. It was a frightening development. Indeed, the average number of traffic units produced per dollar of labor cost dropped almost 50 percent from 1943 through 1951. The problem was clear: neither the volume of business nor advances in technology had kept pace with the extreme growth in compensation. Labor leaders would strive to hold all they had gained and ask for more, but the railroads could not permit their unit costs for employee compensation to continue rising at the same rate as in the 1940s. In the highly competitive world of transportation, railroad managers would have to find some way of squaring labor output with labor costs if their companies were to survive.

29

Prosperity Under Stress

With World War II over, the Great Northern's management looked ahead, balancing confidence and apprehension. The company was much stronger than it had been a half dozen years earlier, but President Frank Gavin and his associates knew that postwar adjustments would require major changes in company policies. Indeed, Gavin perceived that GN was entering a "most critical period." If satisfactory earnings were to be registered, he knew, the company had to maximize operating efficiency while preparing for the future.[1]

Expectations and Realities

Postwar prospects were especially confused by an uncertain general economy. Some economists anticipated an immediate and sharp recession, possibly even a severe depression, which would constrict traffic and profits. Conversely, removing wartime controls might trigger inflation, with costs spiraling upward. Such mixed circumstances would catch carriers in a price squeeze if, as the past suggested, they failed to gain adequate rate increases. On the other hand, higher rates could open the door to even more competition from all modes of transportation.

Nevertheless, the GN's potential for freight traffic looked at least moderately encouraging. Despite rapid depletion of high-grade iron ore during World War II, the steel industry would certainly continue to draw much of its raw material from Minnesota. As a carrier of lumber between the Pacific Northwest and the Midwest, the GN was in a position to prosper from newly resumed housing construction and related expansion. Diversification in agriculture, application of agricultural science, especially improved rust- and drought-resistant wheat, and expanded irrigation also implied that the disastrous drops in farm production during the 1920s and 1930s would not be repeated. Furthermore, in the Pacific Northwest, a growing population and increased industrialization, much of it based on inexpensive hydroelectric power, promised expanding traffic of all kinds both immediately and in the future.

The other side of the planning equation was less hopeful. Officers assumed that wage schedules could not be reduced and that if they gained higher passenger and freight rates, always difficult to win, these might adversely affect the volume of business. They also anticipated that shipments would drop temporarily and change somewhat in character, with more low-rated freight, shorter average hauls, and lighter loads. Management similarly estimated that the ratio of passenger revenue to freight income would decline sharply as most travelers returned to the highways and others took to the air.

Against this background, Gavin reviewed the company's strengths in personnel. Although several senior officers were near retirement, their successors were well trained and already experienced. Vernon P. Turnburke's remarkable talents were rewarded in 1946 when he was made vice president – executive department. Charles E. Finley took over as head of the traffic department, and when C.

O. Jenks terminated his fine career as the company's chief operating officer, he relinquished that post to Thomas F. Dixon. After the latter's death, the board chose John M. Budd to fill the position of vice president – operations. John Budd, son of the railroad's former president, Ralph Budd, had been trained on the GN until elected president of the Chicago & Eastern Illinois, from which position he resigned to return to the home road.

The board of directors underwent similar changes. In 1945, Frederick K. Weyerhaeuser joined the board after the death of his uncle, Frederick E., and Grant Keehn replaced Alexander C. Nagle, a fellow officer at the First National Bank of New York. Two years later

Escalation of sleeping car rates notwithstanding, passengers flocked to Glacier Park during the early postwar years. The attractions of Glacier were obvious.

Thomas L. Daniels, of Archer-Daniels-Midland Company, took the seat of Shreve M. Archer, who had long been director. In 1948, Louis W. Hill died, ending his forty-six years of service on the board.

Contrary to predictions by many, the period from 1945 through 1951 brought general prosperity and economic growth. Demobilization proceeded rapidly and unemployment benefits and educational allowances for veterans helped sustain purchasing power. Price controls were soon removed, stimulating the economy; pent-up demand for consumer goods encouraged speedy conversion to peacetime production; government spending for domestic programs remained high; and a decision to aid both allies and former enemies resulted in large expenditures. The Cold War and the Korean conflict in 1950 occasioned additional outlays. Under such forced draft, the American economy slowed slightly in 1946 and 1949, but no depression marred the general prosperity in the six years following World War II. On the negative side, the wholesale price index (1910–1914 = 100) rose from 151.7 in 1945 to 253.4 in 1951. Inflation had become a fact of American life.

An immediate effect for the GN, as for other railroads, was a steep rise in costs of operation. The new forty-hour week, combined with continued high levels of business, expanded the work force by almost 7 percent between 1945 and 1951. This growth, coupled with higher pay scales, elevated the GN's annual outlay for wages 52 percent in only six years. Costs for materials also inflated. Treated crossties jumped from $1.93 in 1945 to $3.05 six years later, a gain of 58 percent. Fuel for locomotives, the largest expense of railway operation after labor, rose in price even more; coal by 76 percent, fuel oil by 64

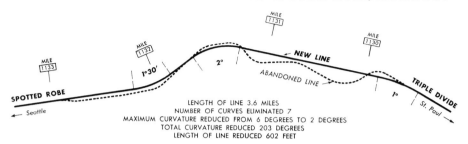

3.6 MILE LINE CHANGE – TRIPLE DIVIDE – SPOTTED ROBE, MONTANA

LENGTH OF LINE 3.6 MILES
NUMBER OF CURVES ELIMINATED 7
MAXIMUM CURVATURE REDUCED FROM 6 DEGREES TO 2 DEGREES
TOTAL CURVATURE REDUCED 203 DEGREES
LENGTH OF LINE REDUCED 602 FEET

percent, and diesel oil by 90 percent. A box car that cost $3,200 in 1937 was priced at $5,700 in 1951. Costs for other equipment were comparable. As early as 1948, Gavin reported that expenditures for materials and supplies as a whole had tripled in ten years.

Faced with rising expenses, the carriers reluctantly sought relief in higher rates. Although many officials contended that escalation would drive more business into the arms of modal competitors, between 1946 and 1951 the nation's railways on four occasions asked the ICC for general increases in freight rates. In no instance did the commission grant the carriers the full hikes sought, but recognizing the price squeeze, it did allow sizable jumps.

Rates for traffic other than freight were similarly adjusted. After lengthy negotiations with the Post Office Department, the ICC permitted three increments in rates for carrying mail between 1947 and the end of 1951, and it also allowed successive increases in express tariffs. The temporary 10 percent escalation in passenger fares that the commission had authorized during the war was made permanent in 1946. Additional boosts in 1948 and 1949 enabled roads in the western district to raise basic one-way coach fares to 2.5 cents per mile and parlor and sleeping-car fares to 3.5 cents a mile.

As usual, the company's voluntary cuts in rates and fares to meet competition and to expand traffic offset some of these gains. Consequently, the company's average revenue per ton mile rose only 30 percent—from 0.92 cent in 1945 to 1.192 cents in 1951. Average revenue per passenger mile showed a larger but still unsatisfactory increase—from 1.6 cents to 2.29 cents, or 43 percent, substantially less than the rise in prices in general as measured by the wholesale price index.

Maximizing Efficiency

The disparity between authorized rates and ascending costs soon became a major factor in shaping company policies. Greater operating efficiency was imperative. Such planning demanded new motive power. Acting on Gavin's conviction that the steam locomotive was technologically obsolete, the GN continued to move systematically toward diesels. At the end of 1945, the company owned 104 of them, which produced only 17 percent of its train miles; six years later, however, 301 diesels were responsible for 63 percent of train miles. Steam locomotives on the roster fell from 805 to 511, of which all, except 60 used chiefly during periods of peak business, had been converted to oil burners for economy. At first, diesels won greatest acceptance in passenger service, pulling the company's transcontinentals by 1947, and all the main-line passenger trains by 1950. Because oil delivered in the West cost less than coal, the western portion of the system was completely dieselized first. By the end of 1950, except on the line south of Bend, Oregon, no steam ran west and south of Havre, Montana.

To reduce costs and to provide better service in the Cascades, the GN also added to its electric locomotive fleet. As early as 1942, operating officers had been convinced that the fifteen electrics acquired earlier were inadequate for the job. The exigencies of war and then slow delivery, however, delayed acquisition of new units until 1947, when the GN received two 5,000-horsepower streamlined giants, costing $500,000 each.

To provide stable track for faster passenger and heavier freight trains, and to otherwise improve its physical plant, the GN expanded its traditional program of roadway improvements. Under Chief Engineer H. J. Seyton's direction, the company began to replace gravel ballast with crushed rock. Grouting, done by pumping cement, fine sand, and water into the roadbed to increase stability, proved especially effective for gumbo soils, as in the Red River Valley, and in eastern North Dakota. Simultaneously, bridges were strengthened and cuts widened.

Ties and rail got special attention. Beginning in 1946, all new ties for the main line were creosote-treated, and with few exceptions were 8½ feet long. At the same time, Seyton oversaw installation of additional 112- and 115-pound rail on the main line; the 90- and 110-pound steel that it replaced was cascaded to improve branches. Following earlier experiments in Montana, the GN also laid continu-

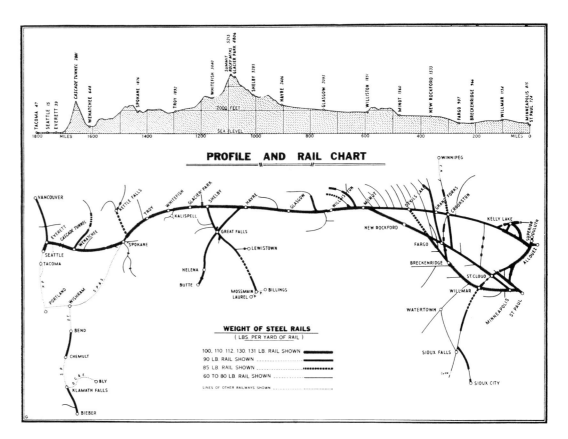

ous welded rail in the Cascade Tunnel, both to provide a smoother ride and to cut upkeep.

In the historic pattern James J. Hill had begun years before, Gavin relocated lines to facilitate faster, safer, and more efficient operations. The most noteworthy, near Merritt, Washington, was completed in 1949. Although this change straightened only a mile of track immediately east of the Cascade Tunnel, it required constructing a new 740-foot tunnel, and a 650-foot bridge. Elsewhere, a change of location on the east slope of the Rocky Mountains in Montana, from Triple Divide to Spotted Robe, was almost as helpful, taking out 203 degrees of curvature and shortening

the route by 620 feet. Then, in the spring and summer of 1948, floods in Montana, Idaho, and Washington occasioned heavy repair work, bringing about further improvements to line.

Other efficiencies derived from reducing services and personnel not required for safe or efficient operation. Passenger service was curtailed on branches, eliminated on Sundays, or relegated to mixed trains. Stations were closed on weekends and at other times when demand was little. Indeed, the GN's efficiency program followed a very broad path. For example, equipping the *Internationals* with coffee-shop cars meant fewer dining-car employees; a

new grain unloader at Superior dumped up to ten cars an hour; modern dictating and transcribing machines and calculators mechanized some work at headquarters; power ballasters, cribbing machines, tie saws, and tie removers did much to revolutionize track maintenance; and a machine designed and built by GN workers flame-cleaned rails exposed to salt-water corrosion.[2]

Holding down expenses was only one part of the struggle for efficiency; satisfactory performance also depended on strong traffic. Finding the volume was more and more difficult, however, as highway and air competition grew menacingly. Private automobile registrations in the Northwest climbed 62 percent between 1945 and 1951, and the number of trucks increased 59 percent and their aggregate carrying capacity even more.

The GN resorted to time-honored techniques to fight highway competition. It advocated stricter regulation of commercial truckers, opposed petitions for new or expanded bus and truck service, and constantly watched truck rates and schedules. Staying abreast of this threat was so vital that in 1951 Charles E. Finley wrote: "The establishment of rates to meet motor carriers competition, or the defensive work to prevent unduly low motor carrier rates has become a greater part of the work of the Traffic Department. . . . We consider this to be the number one issue in transportation competition today."[3]

Although GN managers' defensive tactics were often ineffective, they also embraced positive competitive weapons. Providing enough of all types of high-quality freight cars remained a primary objective. From 1946

In 1943, Frank Gavin and his subordinates agreed that an entirely new *Empire Builder* should be built as soon as possible after World War II, but it was not until February 23, 1947 that the handsome streamlined train was placed in service. The first run began at Seattle and was christened by Gavin, right, and the mayor of Seattle.

through 1951, the company purchased or built almost 4,000 box cars, 750 gondolas, and 275 covered hoppers. The trend toward fewer but larger cars also continued. The GN owned 6,028 fewer cars at the end of 1951 than the 49,523 on its roster in 1945, but the average capacity per car increased from 50.9 to 53.5 tons.

Innovating design and construction of cars was crucial. New covered hoppers were espe-

242

cially effective in handling bulk cement and similar commodities, and larger gondolas pleased shippers of pulpwood, construction steel, and other goods. Earlier, when the industry began to move toward steel box cars, the GN had rejected them, partly to avoid antagonizing producers of lumber, and partly because little steel was available during the middle 1940s. Thus it built 1,950 box cars with plywood sides, but, C. O. Jenks observed: "There is no question but what the all-steel box car is the best." Consequently, almost 80 percent of the box cars added from 1946 through 1951 were constructed of steel. In addition, the Western Fruit Express Company experimented with mechanically cooled reefers for traditional as well as frozen lading and had 165 of them in service by the end of 1951.[4]

Numerous technological innovations further improved freight service. Modern facilities for servicing the company's growing diesel fleet ensured adequate maintenance. Automatic block signals were installed on 336 miles of heavily used track in Minnesota and North Dakota, and radio equipment for trains and at stations, first used in 1943, was increased. At Allouez the company enlarged its ore-steaming facilities and installed equipment capable of unloading a car in only five minutes.

The GN also speeded its freight service between major terminals while building an admirable on-time record. In 1945, for trains 401 and 402, operating between Minneapolis and Seattle, the company reestablished the prewar schedule of 109 hours and 25 minutes, reducing it another three hours in 1951. Elsewhere, cooperating with the Santa Fe and the Western Pacific, the GN cut twenty-four hours from freight schedules between Los Angeles and Seattle or Spokane via the "Inside Gateway."

Meanwhile, private automobiles, buses, and airplanes offered service in intercity passenger carriage that railroads found almost impossible to meet. After World War II, more than 90 percent of intercity travel in the United States was by private automobile, but bus companies, because of low fuel costs, low taxes, and a publicly provided right-of-way, were able to expand their business with low fares. At the same time, speed-loving, time-conscious travelers flocked to airlines, accelerating long-haul passenger traffic into deeper decline. Inroads became worse after air coach service was inaugurated in 1948. Fares for this type of travel usually exceeded railway-coach tariffs, but they were below first-class charges, strongly motivating railroaders to hold down their rates.

Where attracting and holding passengers was possible, the GN moved vigorously. Concentrating on long- and intermediate-distance travel, the company determined to upgrade

Truckers skimmed shorter hauls in the livestock-carrying business, but during the mid-1950s the GN handled full trainloads from western ranges.

equipment and service. Frank Gavin and his associates had decided in 1943 that an entirely new *Empire Builder* should be built as soon as possible after World War II. Almost twenty years had elapsed since the company had purchased a new train, the first *Empire Builder*, leaving it without the fine new equipment many other carriers could advertise. So fast was such modern rolling stock being added that by the mid-1940s twenty-four companies operated streamliners, some in direct competition with the GN. Improved earnings and Internal Revenue Service rules permitting rapid amortization also encouraged the company to invest the large sums necessary for acquiring modern passenger trains.[5]

The GN arranged with Pullman Standard to purchase equipment for the streamlined *Empire Builder*. The order called for five complete train sets, each diesel powered and consisting of twelve cars. (A dozen of the cars were bought by the Chicago, Burlington & Quincy, for it would handle the trains between Chicago and St. Paul.) The projected forty-five-hour schedule between Chicago and Seattle, via New Rockford, would make the new train thirteen hours faster than the old *Builder*, though six hours slower than the Union Pacific's *City of Portland* service to the Northwest. The GN did not want an uncomfortably fast train, said Gavin, but rather one that would provide a luxuriously smooth ride.

When the new *Empire Builder* began service on February 23, 1947, it was modern railroad passenger service at its best. All train sets consisted of three sleeping cars, three forty-eight-seat coaches, and one each baggage-mail, sixty-seat coach, diner, coffee shop-kitchen-dormitory, all-bedroom sleeper, and bedroom-lounge sleeper. Painted in the GN's bright orange and green, the fully air-conditioned cars were finished inside with light-colored fabrics. Other innovations included a public address system and an onboard passenger representative.

The reequipped *Empire Builder* promptly established itself as a popular and profitable train. During the first year of operation, it averaged 75 percent occupancy, contributed more than $5 million in revenue, and generated almost twice as much average revenue per train mile as the GN's second transcontinental, the *Oriental Limited*, to which cars from the first *Empire Builder* were now assigned.

New equipment for the *Empire Builder* resulted in renovated cars for the *Winnipeg Limited*, shown here arriving in St. Paul.

Within the year, both the NP's *North Coast Limited* and the Milwaukee's *Olympian Hiawatha* were operating with new equipment on schedules comparable to that of the *Builder*, but the GN's new train more than held its own against them.

Pleased with favorable acceptance of the streamlined *Empire Builder*, Gavin approved yet another large purchase of passenger equipment. In 1949, the company ordered sixty-six new cars at a cost of $8.4 million to equip the "mid-century" *Empire Builder*, which went into service on June 31, 1951. At the same time, Gavin embraced the suggestion by Charles W. Moore, director of public relations, to rename the *Oriental Limited* as *Western Star*. In that way the *Star* became the GN's second transcontinental passenger train, inheriting the *Builder*'s 1947 equipment.

The GN could now offer daily service with two modern trains between Chicago and the Pacific Northwest. The "mid-century" *Empire Builder* continued a forty-five-hour schedule from Chicago to Seattle, the *Western Star* operated on a fifty-eight-hour run via Grand Forks. Both were fine, but the *Builder* was distinctly a luxury train with the widest possible accommodations, including berths, roomettes, bedrooms, and compartments. The *Builder* had a fine diner, and also a handsome if utilitarian coffee shop-lounge car, decorated in a western motif, and named the G-Bar-N Ranch Car.

Having acquired streamlined cars for major runs, the company could renovate its entire passenger-car fleet. The high-quality equipment that once had graced its transcontinental runs was now allocated to the *Gopher*, *Badger*, *Cascadian*, *Winnipeg Limited*, *Dakotan*, and the *Fast Mail*.

A peripheral change was made in the railroad's relationship with the Pullman Company. A federal court ordered Pullman, Incorporated, a holding company, to divest itself of either its car-manufacturing enterprise or its sleeping-car business. It chose to do the latter and sold the Pullman Company to those carriers, including the GN, which offered sleeping-car service. As a practical matter ownership made little difference: Pullman continued to operate the equipment in much the same manner as before.

The Operating and Financial Record

The Great Northern's record of performance reflected the general prosperity following World War II. Revenue tons in 1946 dropped 12 million below the 1942 peak, but a favorable increase in tonnage came in the following years. From 1946 through 1950, the company averaged 53.9 million tons per year, a satisfying 6.3 percent above the average for 1939 through 1945. The length of haul held up almost as well: the comparable ton-mile figure was 5.4 percent higher than in the earlier period. Passenger business, too, was better than forecasters had predicted in 1945. Numbers fell from the wartime peak, but the annual average of 1.8 million passengers from 1946 through 1950 was 50 percent above the comparable number for 1935 through 1940, and average passenger miles were 120 percent higher than in that earlier period (see Table 11).

The rising volume of traffic and higher rates authorized by regulatory agencies resulted in increased operating revenues. Although passenger returns registered declines in some years, the average from 1946 through 1950 exceeded that for 1939 through 1945 by 8.5 percent, and the rise in average annual freight revenues was 31 percent. Railway operating

Table 11. Selected Traffic Statistics, 1946–1950

(In Millions)

Date	Revenue freight tons[a]	Freight ton miles	Passengers carried	Passenger miles
1946	47.7	14,765	2.3	870
1947	55.6	16,271	1.9	630
1948	59.3	16,392	1.7	543
1949	52.7	15,373	1.7	502
1950	54.1	16,040	1.5	494

a. Excludes motor-vehicle operations.

Source: Great Northern Railway Company, Statistical Supplement, Annual Report 1950.

Table 12. Selected Financial Data, 1939–1950

(In Millions)

	Railway operating revenues	Less railway operating expenses	Less railway tax accruals	Less equipment and joint facility rentals paid	Net railway operating income	Plus other income	Less miscellaneous deductions	Less fixed charges	Net income
1939	$ 91.8	$ 60.5	$10.1	$1.6	$19.6	$4.1	$ .8	$14.2	$ 8.7
1940	101.7	65.9	12.3	1.7	21.8	3.2	.6	14.2	10.2
1941	125.0	78.3	16.9	1.8	28.0	3.6	.9	13.9	16.8
1942	165.2	93.3	30.7	1.7	39.5	4.6	1.3	13.7	29.1
1943	200.6	122.8	48.5	.8	28.5	5.1	1.5	12.5	19.6
1944	207.7	132.6	40.0	2.1	33.0	5.0	1.7	12.9	23.4
1945	200.1	159.5	11.3	.9	28.4	6.7	1.0	9.9	24.2
1946	167.4	129.8	11.0	1.6	25.0	7.7	.6	8.7	23.4
1947	193.8	143.5	24.5	2.0	23.8	6.8	.4	7.7	22.5
1948	216.3	162.2	24.0	2.9	27.2	8.3	.4	7.5	27.6
1949	212.3	162.0	26.0	3.7	20.6	6.3	.5	7.7	18.7
1950	227.5	162.1	34.5	3.5	27.4	9.2	.5	7.9	28.2

Source: Great Northern Railway Company, Statistical Supplement, Annual Report, 1951.

revenues from 1946 through 1950 averaged 30.4 percent more than in 1939 through 1945. In only two years (1946 and 1947) of the later period did these fall below the previous all-time high of $207.7 million, recorded in 1944. In 1950, the figure of $227.5 million was 8.7 percent above that wartime peak.

Despite the company's sustained efforts to maximize efficiency, its operating expenditures rose faster than operating revenues. Attempts to control expenses simply failed to withstand the pressure from compensation for employees and higher cost of materials. After setting a postwar low of $129.8 million in 1946, railway operating expenses swelled to $162.1 million in 1950, and for the period 1946–1950 their annual average was 49.3 percent above that for 1939–1945. (See Table 12.) A small portion of the increase—less than $700,000 per year on average—arose from Internal Revenue Service rules permitting rapid amortization of defense expenditures, a procedure that allowed the GN to sacrifice immediate income for long-term upgrading of road and equipment.

With a lag in operating revenues compared with operating expenses, the operating ratio stayed relatively high during the five-year period 1946–1950. The five-year average was 74.9, close to that of the UP but substantially better than those of the Milwaukee and NP.

The imbalance between operating revenues and operating expenses was increased by growing tax bills. In 1946, carry-back credit for wartime excess-profits taxes helped to hold total tax accruals to $11.0 million; of that amount, state and local levies accounted for $8.9 million. By 1950, reflecting larger income and higher wage payments, taxes on income and payroll climbed. Consequently, the company's aggregate liability jumped to $34.5 million. Of this total, state and local taxes accounted for $11.7 million, and payroll taxes for about $6.0 million.

Combined, the heavy tax payments and the rise in railway operating expenses kept net railway operating income relatively low in the years just after the war. It averaged $24.8 million for the 1946–1950 period, or almost 13 percent less than for the years 1939–1945. Even more striking, the average operating income for 1946–1950 was only about $1 million above that for William P. Kenney's best years, 1935–1937, when the company and the nation were still in the deep depression.

Fortunately, the GN's other income rose significantly after the war. Most of this increase resulted from resumption of annual dividends by the Burlington, continued dividends from Northland Greyhound Lines, and interest on investment in the Spokane, Portland & Seattle Railroad. These additions made the GN's average annual income during the years 1946–1950, before fixed charges, almost equal to that of the war years—approximately $32 million.

In the late 1940s, a favorable feature affecting total net income, after deducting fixed charges, was the continuing reduction in the price of capital. Between 1938 and 1945, the GN had cut its funded debt by about 25 per-

Unhandsome but functional, RS-1s from Alco frequently found themselves in branch line service.

cent and the interest by 30 percent. With careful preparation, Vernon Turnburke continued this policy. With interest rates low and the company's credit high, during 1946 the railroad issued new bonds in three series totaling $100 million and bearing very low interest. As with earlier refinancing, these bonds aggregated a smaller dollar total than those redeemed, were at lower interest, and had more satisfactory due dates. On January 1, 1952, the GN's bonds outstanding were $203.7 million, in contrast to $252 million at the end of 1938. No interest charge exceeded 5 percent,

and the majority were at less than 3 percent.

Starting in 1948, however, the cost of new locomotives and cars was reflected in additional equipment obligations. By the last full year of Gavin's presidency, 1950, these obligations rose to $48.7 million, and by the end of 1951 to $70.3 million. This debt was mainly in equipment trust certificates, carrying from 2 to 3 percent, and due serially from 1963 to 1966.

Although increases in short-term obligations caused total funded debt to rise at the end of the 1940s, this increase detracted little from

the general trend of reduction. Standing at $330.9 million in 1938, the total funded debt had been lowered to $235.6 million in 1947, before rising at the end of 1951 to $275 million. In the twenty years from 1931 to 1951, however, while the bonded debt was cut 41 percent, the total funded debt was reduced 22 percent. Meanwhile, the saving in interest charges had been considerable—$19 million in 1931 to about $8 million in 1951, a drop of more than 57 percent.[6]

With handsome revenues from all sources and relatively low interest costs, the GN during the years 1945 to 1950 made quite a satisfactory net income—averaging $24.1 million annually. Favorable circumstances enabled the GN to resume dividends and to raise them gradually. The long series of regular payments, broken during the 1930s, was resumed at the moderate rate of 50 cents per share in the last quarter of 1940, and the board voted the same rate, $2 per share annually, through 1944. Directors followed with a $3 rate for the next three years, $3.50 in 1948 and 1950, and $4 in 1949.

When Frank J. Gavin retired as president in May 1951, to become chairman of the board, he could look back with pride on his twelve-year stewardship. Admittedly, he had the good fortune to serve during a period of general prosperity, but that luck did not diminish his accomplishments. He had effectively led a team of officers with markedly diverse personalities and skills, and delegated to them great autonomy in managing their respective provinces. These men, with effective support by employees down the chain of command to brakemen and section hands, had substantially improved the property, upgraded standards of service, and handled an unprecedented volume of traffic. The GN had raised workers' remu-

neration, increased the company's profits, and greatly enhanced its credit by wise financial management. Perhaps unique among large American railroads, the GN's bonded debt was under one mortgage, and the new president, John M. Budd, would not be confronted, as his three predecessors had been, by the impending early maturity of a large issue of bonds. The company was in good shape to meet changing conditions.

30

John Budd and a Changing Environment

In 1951, Frank J. Gavin, having headed the Great Northern Railway through twelve years of war and prosperity, retired from the presidency. As his successor, the directors chose John M. Budd, whose administration would span almost two decades of meteoric change in American railroading.[1]

The New Team

John Budd spent most of his life with the Great Northern. Born in Des Moines, Iowa, in 1907, he did not at first aspire to a career in railroading although, a subordinate later recalled, he "grew up at the knee of his father"—Ralph Budd. During vacations from his civil-engineering curriculum at Yale University, John Budd held summer jobs at the GN, working as a chainman on the Cascade Tunnel and Chumstick line projects. After graduating and spending a summer in his father's group inspecting railroads in the Soviet Union, the younger Budd was employed during the fall of 1930 as assistant to the GN's chief electrical engineer. He would not, it turned out, escape the railroad industry. Following a Yale postgraduate course in transportation in 1932–1933, he became assistant trainmaster on the Willmar Division, and by the early 1940s he was a division superintendent. His knowledge of railroading was deepened and broadened by a period with the Military Railroad Service, including an assignment as commanding officer of the 704th Railway Grand Division. Budd returned from World War II in November 1945, to the post of assistant general manager, lines east of Williston, but two years later, at thirty-nine, he was elected president of the Chicago & Eastern Illinois, youngest president of a Class I railroad in the United States. In 1949, Budd came back to the GN as vice president-operations, from which position he was elevated to the presidency in May 1951.

John Budd gave the railroad a balanced, unpretentious style of leadership. A transportation man rather than merely a railroader, he looked first at the overall task: moving goods and people. Then he would consider how rails could handle the job. Throughout his career, Budd was remarkably alert to new ideas, though he never sought innovation simply to be first or to advocate a new way of doing things. Budd preferred to test new machines or ideas, timing their adoption for greatest potential gains. Those who knew him considered John Budd extremely ethical, thoughtful, sound of judgment, loyal, reserved in manner, fair-minded, perhaps even a little on the soft side. He was a good man to work for, asking associates their viewpoints and not afraid to learn from anybody. Not a publicity seeker, Budd avoided drama simply for effect, but his positions reflected careful analysis. He was well respected both within and outside of the railroad industry.

During Budd's tenure several changes were made on the board of directors and among senior officers. Other than Budd himself, only

John M. Budd spent most of his life with the Great Northern.

four who were directors in 1951 remained in 1970: Thomas L. Daniels of the Archer-Daniels-Midland Company, F. Peavey Heffelfinger of the Peavey Company, Frederick K. Weyerhaeuser of Weyerhaeuser Company, and Grant Keehn, of the Equitable Life Assurance Society. Major changes also replaced top officers. John A. Tauer, only senior executive to serve from 1951 through 1970, became vice president in 1953, continuing as comptroller. Ira G. Pool, John Budd's successor in the operations department, retired as vice president in 1957, and was followed by quietly competent Thomas A. Jerrow until 1965. Then the position was held by John L. Robson who, like Ira Pool, was unusual in GN history in having reached the post through the mechanical de-

partment. When Charles E. Finley retired as vice president-traffic in 1966, his place was taken by M. M. Scanlan, with thirty-eight years of experience. Two other retirements in 1957 were followed by promotions within the company: Edwin C. Matthias, after serving forty-five years, was succeeded as vice president and general counsel by Anthony Kane, who had background in both Seattle and St. Paul. After thirty-seven years as secretary and treasurer, F. L. Paetzold was succeeded by Richard M. O'Kelly, who had served in the New York fiscal office. In 1958, retiring vice presidents in the executive department, Thomas Balmer in Seattle and Vernon P. Turnburke in St. Paul, were replaced, respectively, by Clark A. Eckart, from lines west, and Robert W. Downing, formerly assistant to the president.

Two other high-ranking positions were added, carrying on John Budd's desire to improve employee relations and to benefit from technological innovations. Thomas C. DeButts was chosen vice president-labor relations, a new title separating union-management relations from other phases of personnel administration. And in 1967, Thomas J. Lamphier was elected vice president-administration, a post with varied responsibilities, among them expanding application of computers to communications and decision making.

In the tradition of James J. Hill and his own father, Budd enthusiastically held that top management needed a continuous program for maintaining or improving the company's position. Dieselization had to be completed; rolling stock had to be adjusted to customers' changing needs; track structure, yards, and other facilities required customary attention; new technology, such as computers, required evaluation and adoption when feasible; and, in pro-

moting regional economic development, the GN had to modify its methods to fit new conditions. Finally, the possibility of merger also merited consideration.

Budd's burden was to lead the Great Northern in a troublesome and confusing time for the entire industry. A major worry was broadly categorized as the "passenger problem." The airplane's speed and the flexibility in highway travel continued to reduce train patronage, and labor-intensive passenger service resisted economies. The outlook for freight was little more encouraging. Railroads moved 56 percent of intercity freight in 1950, but only 41 percent nineteen years later. Yet a price squeeze on railroads had prevailed since 1945, and the return on investment for many carriers was clearly unsatisfactory.

Railroads and Public Policy

John Budd's views were those of the industry. Transportation policy, he argued, should be considered as a whole. The government, of course, could not induce Americans to reject airplanes and private automobiles, nor could rail carriers regain near monopoly in moving intercity freight. Budd was confident, however, that railroads provided services for which the need was real, and they could do so more economically than their competitors. He argued, then, that government should give equitable treatment to the various modes of transportation, and that railroads should be allowed to compete as vigorously as possible.

Budd and other railroaders had ample reason to complain. After all, the carriers bore relatively heavy taxation, paid high wages, and

Railroads yearned for equity even as they laid out massive capital for dieselization. (Rail Photo Service by H. W. Pontin)

faced labor leaders insistent on retaining antiquated work rules. At the same time, they were forced to compete with heavily subsidized, inadequately regulated rivals, even though the rail carriers themselves fell under strict if archaic regulations that were designed, it appeared, to protect modal competitors. Although a few western railroads had earned land grants to foster early construction, most of the nation's rail mileage had been privately financed, built, and maintained. On the other hand, highways used by buses and trucks—their competitors—derived from and were maintained by public funds. Federal financial aid to highway construction, begun in 1916, aggregated $11.2 billion by the end of 1951; state and local outlays were $76 billion, and both were to soar in the next two decades. By 1969, public expenditure for highways reached $285.4 billion, of which the federal government provided $61.3 billion.

Inland waterway operators also benefited from government largess. For more than a century, the federal government had been responsible for most improvement and maintenance in navigation channels. Railroad managers estimated that $13.8 billion had been spent through 1960 by all governments in the United States on waterways, exclusive of the St. Lawrence Seaway and the Tennessee Valley Authority.

Air transport got help in many forms: installation, maintenance, and operation of navigational and terminal facilities, mail subsidies, and benefits from government research and development projects. By 1969, estimated federal assistance to airlines was $13.4 billion, and state and local expenditures for that purpose, mostly for airport construction and operation, were $7.5 billion.

Highway, waterway, and air transport also profited by facilities that governments provided to users at much less than the cost of building and maintenance. Operators of trucks and buses correctly considered excise taxes on fuel as de facto user charges, but operators of heavy trucks did not pay their fair share of the costs for constructing and maintaining highways. This inequity remained even after Congress passed the Highway Act of 1956, which John Budd characterized as "a long step forward in recognizing the validity of the user charge concept." This legislation provided for new interstate highways with pay-as-you-go financing, and assigned to a Highway Trust Fund proceeds of various taxes. Authorities agreed almost unanimously that airline payments to governments did not compensate for the facilities they utilized, although these paid some special charges, such as excise tax on fuel plus landing fees and hangar rentals varying from airport to airport. Not until later was an excise tax on airline passenger tickets

Regulatory agencies often demanded retention of passenger trains, even on branches, long after they had become unprofitable.

added. Water carriers were special beneficiaries. They were completely free of user charges and federal tolls, except for the St. Lawrence Seaway and the Panama Canal.[2]

Budd and other railroad leaders complained of further discrimination at the state level. Regulatory agencies often demanded that passenger trains continue long after absence of patronage had made them unprofitable, and as late as 1953 sixteen states, including five in GN territory, held over "full-crew" laws from days when a fireman and a third brakeman had real duties.

Taxes imposed other inequities. Federal income taxes were universal, of course, but on rail transport the wartime taxes of 15 percent on passengers and 3 percent on freight continued for years after V-J Day. John Budd called their effect "devastating," for it encouraged diversion of business to other modes and weighed heavily on small shippers and those far from markets. Even after the passenger tax had been reduced by 5 percent in 1954, and the freight tax four years later, a 10 percent tax on passenger tickets remained. Railroads also paid for employees far more in retirement and unemployment taxes than did competing forms of transportation. Testifying before a Senate subcommittee in 1958, Budd said that "according to the latest figures, the railroad industry pays out almost 3 percent of its gross operating revenues in payroll taxes, compared with 1 percent paid by highway, air, and water carriers." There was more. The impact of state and local property levies was heavier on railroads than on others. One instance of many was that, GN officers heatedly pointed out, their company in 1956 contributed $2,241 toward support of the airport at Cut Bank, Montana, but Western Airlines, which used the field, paid only $22.92 in *ad valorem* taxes.

Such inequities were brought on by the roads' large amount of property but also by unfair assessments. Rail carriers were the only mode of transportation that owned and paid taxes on roadway, and tax officials seemed to approach them with a Robin Hood complex, using entirely different formulas to assess their property. In 1961, twenty-four states assessed railroad holdings at from 28 to 100 percent of their value, while assessing other property at from 7.4 to 46 percent.[3]

Indeed, Budd could logically assert that inequality was pervasive in public transportation policy. Railroads, he observed, were bound by at least eighty years of regulation and precedent—based generally on outmoded premises. Rail carriers had long since lost their dominance over intercity traffic, but regulatory legislation and policy obstinately resisted recognizing that reality. Here was the rub, as Budd so thoroughly understood.

Several provisions of the Motor Carrier Act of 1935 especially angered railroad managers. That statute, designed to exert some control over common carriers and contract carriers, mostly ignored private haulers. Because these remained essentially unregulated, common and contract carriers had an incentive to pass themselves off as private carriers. Even more objectionable were the so-called agricultural exemptions, excusing from rate regulation all trucks owned and used by farmers to transport their commodities, trucks owned or used by agricultural cooperatives, and trucks of common and contract carriers hauling livestock, other agricultural commodities, and fish. This already substantial list was further expanded by ICC and court decisions, using a "substantial identity test." Including other trucks and extending the types of freight had the obvious effect of depressing rates and diverting traffic,

which, of course, deeply hurt most railroads, and especially the Great Northern. In 1958 Budd declared that the GN "depended for one-third of its total freight revenues on the transportation of commodities which now moved by truck without regulation." He favored eliminating exemptions from regulation of agricultural commodities transported by motor vehicles.[4]

Exemptions for barge operators were equally distasteful. The Transportation Act of 1940 excluded from control transportation of liquids in bulk and hauling of other commodities in bulk when barges carried no more than three types of goods in the same tow. Other exemptions covered private carriers, contract carriers under specified circumstances, and those in purely local service. The ICC itself estimated that only 10 percent of the tonnage shipped on inland waterways was effectively regulated.

Gradual Changes

"If all forms of transport were operated under the same rules," asserted John Budd in 1958, "our industry would have little or no difficulty maintaining its rightful position." Many agreed. The U.S. Senate undertook to investigate conditions in the transportation industry as early as 1950. At those hearings, railroad spokesmen blamed government policies for the carriers' inability to gain a rate of return high enough to sustain financial health. Further, they complained, government subsidies to other modes of transport prevented railroads from fully utilizing their inherent advantages. In turn, shippers had to bear both heavier taxes and higher costs for transporting freight. The Senate agreed, re-

Rail carriers were the only mode of transportation that owned and paid taxes on roadway.

John Budd and a Changing Environment

marking that competing modes thrived under protective legislation while regulatory authorities perceived the nation's railroad industry as "in the nature of a monopoly."[5]

The Senate report was followed in 1954 by creation of a Cabinet Committee on Transport Policy and Organization, with Secretary of Commerce Sinclair Weeks as its chairman. Released in April 1955, the Weeks Report made a comprehensive statement on the evolution of transportation in the United States, noting in particular the rapid changes that had confronted railroads in the competitive arena since 1920. The Weeks Report also carried an analysis of the way in which the federal government had spent "vast sums of the general taxpayer's funds" to aid in developing highways, waterways, and airways. Although government agencies had stimulated vigorous modal competition, public regulation continued to be based "on the historic assumption" that rail transportation was monopolistic. There was reason for hope, Budd predicted.[6]

He was right. Strongly influenced by the Weeks study, Congress in 1958 passed a comprehensive rail transportation act. It extended the ICC's authority to passenger train discontinuance cases, previously governed by state regulatory agencies, and attended to both agricultural exemptions and questions arising from private trucking. Other clauses were meant to protect from adverse court decisions the ICC's power to raise intrastate rates and fares that discriminated against interstate commerce. Changes for ratemaking were more helpful. Designed to help railroads meet competition from truckers and barge lines, the new legislation stated clearly that railroads' rates should not be held high simply to protect the traffic of another type of transport. Railroads were limited only by a general statement prohibiting

unfair or destructive competitive practices. Finally, the ICC was ordered to recognize and preserve the advantages inherent in each mode of transportation.

Shortly after passage of the Transportation Act of 1958, an ICC report admitted that one of the industry's most vexing problems was its deficit-ridden passenger business. Following rather convoluted logic, the ICC agreed that this loss was large, growing, and dangerous to the industry, concluding, nevertheless, that public interest demanded that ample passenger service be retained. To help, said the ICC, the federal government should repeal its excise tax on rail tickets and, if the public demanded passenger trains that the railroads could not profitably provide, the government should arrange a cost plus reasonable return for the service.[7]

In April 1962, President John F. Kennedy, aware of growing problems, submitted to Congress a momentous message on transportation. Treating transportation as an entity, Kennedy recognized that its various modes needed to mesh if public needs were to be met. The nation, he said, required "a more coordinated Federal policy and a less segmented approach to transportation." The regulatory structure was "a chaotic patchwork of inconsistent and often obsolete legislation," subjecting management to "excessive, cumbersome, and time-consuming . . . supervision that shackles and distorts managerial initiative. Some parts of the transportation system are restrained unnecessarily; others are promoted or taxed unevenly and inconsistently." Kennedy further believed in "greater reliance on the forces of competition and less reliance on the restraints of regulation."[8]

Kennedy's specific proposals dealt with strengthening competition and creating a better

balance in government relationships with the different modes of transportation. He asked for repeal (or extension to all modes) of both the exemption for bulk commodities moving by water and the agricultural exemption for trucks. The range of tax changes Kennedy proposed was broad. To encourage train travel and "clear the way for an equitable system of user charges for aviation," he asked that the 10 percent excise on rail passenger tickets be repealed, that a 5 percent tax be imposed on airline tickets, and that a 2 percent tax be levied on airline fuel. He also suggested the same tax on fuel for water carriers, to have them "pay a small share" as users of government facilities. Another of Kennedy's recommendations was that the depreciation allowance be revised to make income taxes more equitable among the several modes of transportation, and he looked toward eliminating mail subsidies for air carriers.[9]

Railroad spokesmen received the presidential message enthusiastically. Daniel P. Loomis of the Association of American Railroads thought it went "a long way in helping to develop a sound overall transportation system." John Budd was more restrained, commenting to GN stockholders that "for the first time in history" a United States president had "sent to Congress recommendations for legislative changes dealing with transportation" in all its forms.[10]

Substantive change, nevertheless, was slow in coming. On more than one occasion, President Lyndon B. Johnson urged that the regulatory structure be revised, that legislation be enacted to encourage competition, and that user charges be imposed on operators of airlines and barges. The congressional response however, was mixed and piecemeal. A 1961 Treasury Department study confirmed that depreciation policies were too restrictive to encourage railroads to replace obsolete facilities, and eventually more favorable guidelines were established, including an investment credit to foster modernization. For the GN, as for other railroads, this clause reduced current income taxes and encouraged technological progress. In addition, the 10 percent tax on passenger tickets was finally removed in 1962, as the levy on freight had been in 1958. Also, in 1962, a 5 percent tax was imposed on air travel, applying the principle of user taxation as in the 1956 highway legislation.

Other improvements were made at the state level. Although railroads continued to be, Association of American Railroads' Gregory S. Prince wrote, "plagued by tax discrimination at the state and local level," the Transportation Act of 1958, having broken state regulatory agencies' hold over passenger-train operations, had brought the public service commissions to a more cooperative policy. And, in some states, including Minnesota, permission was granted to reduce or do away with agencies at many small stations, allowing railroads to adjust their resources to actual need. By 1966, only nine states retained full-crew laws; sixteen states had them thirteen years earlier; among those which had abandoned such archaic restrictions were North Dakota, Oregon, and Washington.[11]

Despite these legislative and regulatory improvements, the country's railroads—including the Great Northern—were left with a growing dilemma: the "passenger-train problem." Between 1939 and 1965, intercity passenger miles for all modes increased by 671 billion, but the railroad's portion fell 5 billion. In 1939, rail carriers had handled about two-thirds of for-hire travel; in 1965, they handled less than one-fifth. The passenger deficit still

hung over the railroads. Collective losses averaged $417 million annually from 1960 through 1966.

Railroaders differed on the approach they should take in seeking relief. All recognized that branch-line business was gone, but some industry representatives felt that the carriers should continue to run their premier, long-haul trains. Nevertheless, a Stanford University study sponsored by the Southern Pacific concluded in 1966 that passenger service in that railroad's territory had little future. The implication, though, was much broader. As if to prove the point, in the next year the New York Central discontinued its famous *Twentieth Century Limited*, and the Pennsylvania downgraded its equally renowned *Broadway Limited*. In 1968, the chairman of the newly created Penn Central stated simply that the long-haul passenger business was "dead."[12]

Government reports were just as negative. The Doyle Report concluded that railroad "intercity passenger service meets no important needs that cannot be supplied by other carriers," and an ICC examiner wrote that "in a decade or so [the railroad passenger coach] may take its place in the transportation museums." Federal Railroad Administrator A. Scheffer Lang stated the railroad's problem with an example: The public, he said, should not expect railroads to run trains for "a few people who want to go from Chicago to Keokuk, Iowa, even though there is no adequate bus or airline service." As early as 1959, the ICC had even ventured the idea that public subsidies might be required if the railroads were to continue passenger service. Five years later, ordering the Pennsylvania to operate its *Spirit of St. Louis* for another year, the commission suggested that, if communities between New York and St. Louis really wanted

this train, they should contribute to its cost.[13]

Public attitudes did nothing to ease the problem. An average citizen who might not have used a passenger train for years was disturbed, even so, as the service was gradually curtailed. Many felt that railroads were unalterably responsible for maintaining enough standby service to meet emergencies. When highways were impassable and airliners grounded, "snowbirds" and "jet-age Johnnies" (railroaders' names for them) appeared at stations to complain bitterly if sudden crowds were not handled satisfactorily. In any event, a public hostility to further contraction of passenger service was widespread, along with a tendency to attribute all actual or imagined declines in service to managerial inadequacy.[14]

John Budd personally framed the Great Northern's passenger-train policy—one that seemingly followed a middle course between industry activists who promoted passenger service and others who energetically discouraged it. Budd emphasized that losses had to be reduced by eliminating the worst performers, but he demanded that GN's remaining trains be run in a way that the company could be proud of.

The privately operated passenger train was one of many railroad questions left unanswered at the end of the 1960s. One industry spokesman summed it up: "Practically every facet of the railroad problem has been investigated, studied, reviewed, scrutinized, analyzed, probed into and reported upon. Vitally needed solutions have been recommended. Implementation of those recommendations has rarely occurred." Although a few changes had been made, uniform treatment for the modes of transportation remained elusive.[15]

31

Labor Tensions and Personnel Policies

In addition to political constraints and regulatory shackles, John Budd and other railroad officers of his time had to contend with inflexibilities in the labor force. Budd understood that if the Great Northern was to continue to provide adequate service levels and to earn a satisfactory return on investment, the upward trend in costs had to be blunted and the productivity of workers significantly improved. The company's profits, if any, rested on the strenuous race between labor costs and productivity.[1]

As with other railroads, GN personnel policies often reflected union contracts and the web of work rules inherited from more than a century of railroading. Adjustment boards' interpretations of ambiguous rules often broadened the original intent, and in bargaining, the carriers had usually reacted to union demands rather than responding aggressively and innovatively. By the early 1950s many policies were anachronistic and very costly.

John Budd decided that the GN's increasingly complex personnel problem demanded systematic attention. Company-wide recruiting and training policies had never been carefully enunciated, most employees were engaged by the supervisor who required their services at

the moment, and training was done chiefly on the job with much variation in effectiveness. Relations with unions, traditionally handled by the vice president of operations, now demanded more time and more specialized techniques. Therefore Clyde A. Pearson was appointed assistant to the president in 1953, and given the task of gathering information, developing personnel policies and practices, and keeping the executive department fully informed on all employee issues. For a time, union–management relations were left with the operating department, but in 1955 they were added to Pearson's responsibilities. Three years later, his title was made vice president-personnel, recognizing the office's growing importance and giving the incumbent more authority in negotiating with union representatives and in handling all personnel matters.

When Pearson retired in 1965, Budd decided that responsibilities for relations with employees should be divided. Thomas C. DeButts, succeeding Pearson, was elected vice president-labor relations, with responsibility for collective bargaining and issues arising out of contracts with employees. Within the executive department, a new and distinct personnel department, headed by Harold H. Holmquist, took charge of the other tasks Pearson had handled. Holmquist's assignment included supervision of hiring and training practices, maintenance of personnel records, and administration of safety and pension programs, as well as communication between management and employees.

Maneuvers and Crisis

There could be no doubt as to problems faced by the industry regarding unions. In 1951, the country's railroads experienced

twenty-one work stoppages, most in any season since the Railway Labor Act of 1926. Moreover, labor organizations were now militant. Since 1941, impasse in bargaining meant heavier use of emergency boards.

Union leaders knew that expanded mechanization, technological improvements, and productivity in revenue ton miles per employee had risen at least marginally. Citing this advance, and pointing to the rising cost of living, labor organizations in 1952 demanded ''annual improvement wage increases.'' President Harry Truman asked Paul N. Guthrie, a professor at the University of North Carolina, to determine whether a raise was permissible under the government's wage-stabilization policies and, if so, what amount was justified. When Guthrie decided that railway employees were entitled to a boost of 4 cents an hour, retroactive to December 1, 1952, the productivity factor found a formal place in railway labor negotiations and remained there for more than ten years.

Labor relations in the 1950s took on other new configurations when union leaders asked for more concessions, with greater emphasis on fringe benefits. The latter had already risen from 4 cents out of a total compensation of 84 cents per hour worked in 1939, to 22 cents out of $2.12 in 1951. At the same time, company representatives made proposals for modernizing work rules. A major confrontation was inevitable. Maneuvering throughout the decade was frenetic; issues were almost continually in negotiation. After union representatives made uniform demands on all railroads, the GN and the other companies, through organizations such as the Association of Western Railroads (AWR) and later the National Railway Labor Conference (NRLC), engaged in collective bargaining. If negotiations failed to resolve issues, demands could become subject to mediation, then either arbitration or a presidential emergency board.

Only a few examples of demands and counterproposals can be cited here. In 1953, nonoperating unions asked for longer paid vacations, extra pay for work on holidays and Sundays, expanded pass privileges, and group life, medical, and surgical insurance. The resulting controversy finally reached a presidential emergency board in 1954. The board recommended that for these workers, employers assume half the premiums for health, medical, and surgical insurance, grant pay for seven recognized holidays a year, and increase the annual paid vacation to three weeks for employees with fifteen years of continuous service. Agreements approximated the board's recommendations. Other gains followed. In 1955, another emergency board's recommendations led to nation-wide agreements between these unions and carriers that increased pay by 14½ cents an hour. At the same time, the carriers agreed to assume the entire cost of health and welfare benefits, which, as of December 1, 1955, also covered employees' dependents.

Contracts with operating unions paralleled those for nonoperating groups. After threatening to strike in 1955, the former gained several concessions, including a 5-cent-an-hour increase in pay (later supplemented by additional changes in wage schedules), increases for cost of living, pay for seven holidays, and after fifteen years of service, three rather than two weeks of vacation with pay. In November 1956, union demands reached a new peak. The engineers asked for a 15 percent increase in wages, the switchmen and conductors for

Chiefly through technological advances, the GN was able to pare employment from 28,490 in 1950 to 20,539 in 1959.

25 percent, and the firemen and trainmen for a raise of $3 a day. The BLF&E also requested a company-financed hospital, surgical, and medical plan, and the BRT asked for an extra $2.50 a day for members in short-turn service. The ORC&B demanded a six-hour day for road freight and passenger service, an eight-hour day for short-turn runs, a 10 percent night-pay differential, and four weeks of paid vacation for men with more than fifteen years of service.

The carriers responded with counterproposals. They now suggested to locomotive engineers that instead of the traditional basic day of 100 miles in freight service, it should be 160 miles, and for passenger runs, 180 miles. To trainmen, the comparable suggestion was for 160 miles or 8 hours on freight trains, in lieu of the prevailing 100 or 8, and 240 miles or 8 hours on passenger trains, instead of 150 or 7½. Management plainly was arguing for greater flexibility. Most important for the future were the carriers' proposals for the BLF&E. On locomotives other than steam,

managements wanted to eliminate firemen in freight and yard service.

Budd, like other railroad leaders, chafed under prevailing patterns in labor relations and labor costs. Chiefly by adopting technological innovations, the GN had been able to reduce the average number of employees from 28,490 in 1950 to 20,539 in 1959, but the aggregate annual compensation, exclusive of fringe benefits, had risen from $105.8 million in 1950 to $136.4 million in 1957. More significantly, in dollars, labor productivity had declined sharply; traffic units (net ton miles plus passenger miles) per dollar of labor costs had fallen 19 percent—from 147 in 1950 to 119 in 1960. Depressed by the downtrend in labor productivity as well as current economic conditions, the GN's net income plummeted. After peaking at $32.2 million in 1956, it dropped a full 18 percent in 1957. During those years, Budd remarked, compensation to employees accounted for a whopping 64 percent of expenditures for railway operations. Implications were ominous. Simply stated, the continuous increase in wages and fringe benefits, combined with outdated work rules and practices, constituted a very real threat to the health of the company.

Work Rules and Compensation

By the late 1950s, railroad managers were convinced that they must have more freedom to eliminate jobs, reduce total employment, and obtain from each worker a full day's work for a full day's pay. Managers were especially frustrated by work rules that materially reduced benefits from new technology. Moreover, the wage structure was far out of balance, not only between railroad employees and workers in other industries, but also among groups within a company. To correct these and other inequities, managers believed that in many places craft barriers should be eliminated. They also proposed reducing the so-called arbitraries and devoting strong attention to productivity.

Labor leaders, however, were determined to protect union members' jobs, even if technological advances had left some of them superfluous. In May 1957, maintenance-of-way workers asked for compulsory negotiation on changes in length of sections, and in rates of pay when new roadway machines were introduced. They also wanted to participate in planning annual budgets, and to have job-protection benefits extended to employees affected by changed methods of work or by reduction in number of employees. The *New York Times* reported that management's "demand for efficient and profitable operation" had "collided head-on with labor's demand for job security."[2]

In their decision to fight over work rules and declining productivity, managers were encouraged by an apparent change in public sympathies. In neighboring Canada, after a battle that lasted from 1954 to 1958, the Canadian Pacific won the right to take firemen off diesels in yard and freight service, provided that jobs were gradually eliminated and displaced workers' rights were protected. Writing to President N. R. Crump of the Canadian Pacific, John Budd said, "you have certainly opened up a fine roadway and smoothed the path for us to follow."[3]

Daniel P. Loomis, president of the Association of American Railroads, became the industry's point man. In 1959, he urged "a thorough-going revision and modernization of the internal wage structure" of the railroads, and he invited labor leaders to join carriers in "seeking the appointment of a Presidential Commission to study the impact of our present rules on the public welfare." Unproductive labor policies were, he said, a form of "featherbedding"—"an economic albatross around the neck of American progress" and the "handmaiden of the ruinous inflationary spiral."[4]

That the railroad industry was strapped with numerous work rules that not only restricted management's ability to function but also gave the carriers no competitive benefits against other modes of transportation was clear enough. Yet the expression "featherbedding" was ill chosen. It implied that all contract employees were lazy and that all sought to gouge their employers. John Budd frankly disapproved of the term, considering its use inflammatory and unproductive. He quietly passed the word that GN officers should not use it, although he unhesitatingly supported the campaign to reform work rules.

Other industry leaders, though, lacked Budd's insight and continued to talk of featherbedding. Labor leaders were galvanized into a stiff campaign of resistance. President H. E. Gilbert of the BLF&E concluded that his organization should "institute . . . an intensive campaign of education in connection with our diesel program and related issues." His union also sought to drum up backing for full-crew laws in states lacking such legislation, and also for passage of municipal ordinances requiring firemen on diesels in the interest of public health and safety. Subsequently, the Railway Labor Executives' Association, representing twenty-three organizations, joined the battle, contending that if any featherbedding was to be found on the railroads, it was in management, "which requires more and more executives to supervise fewer and fewer employees."[5]

To concentrate on work rules, the carriers quickly agreed to new wage schedules, then returned to the rules issue. Managers believed that pay for work on the road should be set according to one category—hours or miles, whichever resulted in the larger sum. Moreover, they asked that arbitraries and special allowances higher than standard rates be abolished. The carriers also requested modification of rules limiting employees' mileage and restricting types of work done by crews in freight and yard services.

Before bargaining began, rail management put on an extensive public-relations campaign setting forth the industry's position. Loomis and members of the AAR staff prepared speeches, press releases, and letters that went to 20,000 "thought leaders" across the nation. The GN enthusiastically supported this drive, synchronizing its own program with those of other roads. Budd spoke to business leaders, legislators, city officials, and educators, and other officers stayed in touch with editors along the line.

A management–labor conference convened on July 6, 1960, achieving only the first clash in a long struggle over work rules. Management offered to submit the entire controversy to arbitration, and labor indicated again that it favored a commission to investigate and study many issues. Negotiations foundered, and President Eisenhower empaneled a special commission. Among the fifteen members was the GN's vice president-operations, Thomas A. Jerrow.

On February 28, 1962, after extensive hearings, the commission rendered its lengthy report, upholding with remarkable fidelity the carriers' contentions. The railroads should be permitted to gradually eliminate firemen from diesels in freight and yard service, to use any technological advances in operating trains, and to modify the pay basis for operating personnel. Work schedules should be revised to equalize working hours of employees performing similar tasks, and requirements for changing crews at division points should be altered to conform to modern high-speed operations. Effects on workers touched by these changes were to be minimized by lowering the retirement age and by providing severance pay, job retraining, and preferential rehiring of workers displaced by technological change. The commission's findings strengthened management but outraged union leaders. One labor spokesman found the report "the most vicious document that has ever come to my attention in the field of railroad labor." Another contended that it reflected "the combination of bias, ignorance, and insensitivity to the truth, exhibited by the Eisenhower appointees."[6]

Bargaining began again April 2, 1962. Spokesmen for the industry insisted that negotiations should begin at the commission's findings, a position that labor representatives rejected out of hand. Neither side budged, and the dispute went to the National Mediation Board, where again nothing was accomplished. The carriers agreed to arbitration, but labor refused. The companies then were legally free to put the commission's recommendations into effect, but doing so probably would cause a crippling, nation-wide strike.

When President John F. Kennedy's public appeal made no noticeable difference, he turned to Congress, which created an arbitration board empowered to make a binding decision on the union's demand for firemen on diesels and the general issue of crew consists. The board's decision of November 26, 1963, permitted railroads to separate firemen who had less than two years of service; those with from two to nine years might be transferred to other jobs with no immediate reduction in pay, or offered compensation upon separation. Firemen with ten or more years of seniority were to be retained. Union leaders, harshly criticizing the board's findings, carried the issue to the Supreme Court, but lost.

Meanwhile, the railroads pressed other issues. On April 21, 1964, mediators announced settlement on many issues. The unions got seven paid annual holidays for most employees, a 3.5 percent increase in pay for yard workers, and suitable lodging and a meal allowance for road crews who had to lay over four or more hours away from home. The carriers could make some reductions in crews of self-propelled machines and have more freedom in managing yard work. The brotherhoods were to abandon their demand for overtime and premium pay for night shifts, and the railroads were to yield on mileage-pay schedules.

Wages and fringe benefits continued their upward spiral. An agreement with the clerks provided a 5 percent increase in compensation on January 1, 1967, another 6 percent for 1968, and yet another 5 percent to be added in 1969. Together, these gains pushed the average wage of clerks by July 1, 1969, to $3.56 an hour and, including fringe benefits, represented a rise of 50½ cents an hour in two years. Increases for others were comparable. Firemen and trainmen got 5 percent raises in

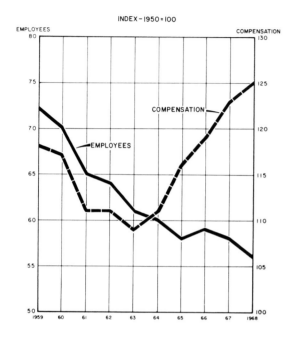

INDEX–1950=100

1966, and almost all other unions took home between 5 and 6 percent. At the same time, under laws covering railroaders' retirement, both benefits and taxes in support were increased. In 1967, fringe benefits accounted for more than 21 percent of the GN's average labor cost per hour.

Job security received greater attention in the 1960s than ever before. Improved technology, new ways of organizing work, and a new wave of mergers all frightened employees. In 1965, the GN became party to a special national contract for "stabilization of employment," the accepted euphemism for protecting jobs in a period of rapid technological change and mergers. By 1968, the GN had signed contracts with all major unions including such protection.

Those who did not belong to unions also benefited from their gains, for the GN's policy was to provide comparable compensation for so-called exempt employees. These received the same or similar holidays, paid vacations, sick leave, and moving allowances. They were also accorded group insurance plans, including, beyond the regular Railroad Retirement payments, the GN's supplements, for which, by 1968, the company paid all premiums.

All GN employees made substantial gains in the 1960s. Between 1958 and 1969 their average annual earnings rose from $5,884 to $8,953 — a 52 percent jump, far exceeding the rise in cost of living.

Personnel Policies

Wounds from the "anti-featherbed" campaign healed slowly. The Great Northern, and the industry at large, certainly needed fewer employees to gain operating efficiency required in an increasingly competitive environment. But to maintain its position or expand its market share, the company also needed the goodwill of all hands, a difficult balance. John Budd was realistic enough to know that ideal conditions probably were beyond grasp, but he insisted on cultivating awareness of the company's needs as a meaningful goal. Budd and his subordinates labored to create a loyal, interested, and productive group of employees. Budd demanded that new hires receive a constructive introduction to the company and be assured of help in preparing them for advancement. He affirmed that communication especially needed channeling in both directions between managers and employees. Clearly, said Budd, all workers had to

feel that their welfare was tied securely to the company.

Few personnel policies mattered more, GN officers believed, than promotion from within, complemented by judicious recruitment. Periodic tests of workers for such aptitudes in computer programming, gave clerical and other employees incentives and opportunities for such positions. Training was no less vital. Intracompany education and training ultimately covered almost every position. Beginning in 1957, written lessons supplied by the Railway Education Bureau supplemented traditional on-the-job learning in the mechanical department, and maintenance-of-way employees attended special classes on operating new roadway machines such as the Electromatic Autojack Tamper, which leveled track with an electronic beam and gyroscope. Nor was training limited to the rank and file. Student officer training, begun in the 1920s in the operating department, was expanded, and middle managers and upper-echelon personnel attended special

In 1962, President John F. Kennedy urged Congress to finally repeal the tax on rail passenger tickets.

schools for advanced training at Harvard and other universities.

In common with many other large business firms, the GN instituted an employee stock-purchase plan, stimulating response to it after 1964 by pledging to pay brokerage fees. Earlier, in 1951, to attract strong candidates and give senior officers and others in key positions greater incentives, the GN established a stock option plan, purchasing shares and making them available to participants at the market price of an announced date. Within ten years key officers held almost 300,000 shares.

The company also worked for better internal communications. *The Goat*, first issued in 1924, was aimed at a wide and diverse readership, but the *Annual Report to Employees*, first issued in 1939, grew rather stereotyped in quality and message; studies suggested that changes were advisable. *The Goat*, retaining much the same form, continued to tell outsiders about the company, and was joined in 1958 by *Talking It Over*, an informal, newsy monthly periodical directed specifically to employees. Later, an annual supplement took over from the *Annual Report to Employees*, which was terminated in 1964.

Articles in *Talking It Over* were diverse. Numerous items dealt with the functions of railroad offices and departments or with company history. Changes in federal legislation were given good coverage, and frequent columns brought messages from officers, information on revenues and expenditures, and discussions of company activities. The magazine told of personnel shifts, retirements, and additions to the list of "veterans" (employees with twenty-five years of service on the GN). Honors and awards as well as employees' acts beyond the call of duty were often featured.

Although safety on the job was not a new idea, John Budd's interest in it grew almost to a fetish. All internal communication focused on it with good cause, for railroading can be a dangerous occupation. Under Budd's direction, managers tried to keep the topic always before the employees with posters and exhortations by supervisors and senior officers. Departments and divisions with outstanding records received certificates of commendation, and to honor highly unusual achievements, the company gave dinners for employees and their spouses. All workers felt proud when the company received favorable recognition from the Minnesota Safety Council and when one or more units of the GN received honors from the National Safety Council. Most noteworthy was the GN's receipt in a number of years of the coveted Harriman Award from the American Museum of Safety.

At the end of the 1960s GN leaders could feel reasonably satisfied that they had helped employees reach their highest potential. Statistical measures of performance, however, were less glowing. Although the average number of employees declined almost 45 percent (from 28,490 to 15,776) between 1950 and 1969, the GN's outlay for their compensation rose 26 percent, from $105.8 million to $133.4 million. Furthermore, the average number of traffic units produced by GN workers for each dollar of labor costs dropped from 143 in 1951 to 117 in 1958, but rose from 119 in 1960 to 136 in 1966. The variations reflected fluctuations in volume of traffic, but where productivity declined, it put heavy pressure on the railroad's net income during a period of rising costs in an industry then consistently making modest returns. Such improved performance as did occur was principally related to two factors —an improved quality of employee and massive investment in advanced technology.

32

Economic Development Programs

The Great Northern's senior management was not occupied solely with problems of labor, regulation, and finance. Company officers constantly looked with energy and optimism for ways to increase business. It required a team effort. To this end, John Budd assigned numerous subordinates the task of encouraging long-term development of agriculture, mining, and industry; others were responsible for adequate car supply as well as reliable and efficient operation; and still others were charged with developing modern techniques to sell the service.[1]

Following its long tradition, the GN continued to cultivate development programs for the Northwest. Changing conditions in the region dictated, however, that some approaches be modified or abandoned and new ones activated. Internally, Edwin C. Leedy's retirement in 1939 as head of the agricultural development department ended an era. Since 1909, Leedy had devoted himself to attracting settlers to the Northwest and helping them to improve their methods of farming.

Shortly after Leedy's departure, the GN found itself preoccupied with the heavy business of World War II, deferring alterations in promotional plans and coordination of them.

The Great Northern Railway: A History/Part II 1916 to 1970

Even after the war, however, little was done. It remained for Budd to return the company to its traditional aggressiveness.

In 1951, Budd directed that two groups undertake this work. A mineral research and development department was set up with several experts. Also in 1951, Everett N. Duncan, whose varied experience included agricultural extension programs, the United States Farm Security Administration, and promotion for an oil company, was appointed to head the new industrial and agricultural development group.

When the traffic department was reorganized as the marketing wing in 1967, more changes were made in personnel. M. M. Scanlan became vice president-marketing, but Budd believed that with the growing need to locate new industries, one officer in the executive department should be responsible. Thus James C. Kenady, formerly land and tax commissioner, took over the promotion of industrial and mineral development, reporting to Robert W. Downing, the executive vice president. Everett Duncan remained in marketing, in charge of agricultural development with emphasis on farm products, especially grain.

Promoting Agribusiness

The Great Northern emphasized programs on raising animals, poultry, and all sorts of grains, fruits, and vegetables. Agents encouraged youth programs, and spread information by distributing literature and by promoting several feeding tours. In 1947, GN agents prepared a pamphlet on the care and feeding of turkeys to help expand production by working

Efforts on the part of E. C. Leedy and others resulted in the development of Wenatchee as a great producer of fruit and heavy traffic for the Great Northern.

with farmers, feed manufacturers, and poultry-processing firms. They also helped develop the green corn industry at Bellingham, Washington, and in Montana and North Dakota they urged planting of sunflowers and safflowers, both to provide useful oil and to free farmers from dependence on wheat. Throughout the territory, agents helped to organize and plan projects for soil conservation districts, and promoted use of commercial fertilizers and chemicals for controlling weeds and pests. As a part of these projects, in 1952, the GN operated its last demonstration train. During a North Dakota tour, this four-car exhibit attracted 50,000 people.

For the Great Northern, all of this represented a historic campaign, with roots as deep as the era of James J. Hill. The company continued its policy of cooperating with diverse organizations interested in the success of farming, especially upon special threat to some aspect of production. During a severe 1952 outbreak of hoof-and-mouth disease in Canada, GN agents served on a study committee and organized a patrol at the international border to prevent the disease's spread into the

The GN's ultimate goal in promoting agribusiness was to make more efficient producers in its service area and thus provide a steady and renumerative flow of traffic. The company had a special interest in funneling grain to the elevators at Superior, Wisconsin.

United States. A few months later representatives cooperated in a program to eradicate brucellosis. The GN similarly returned to its practice of giving financial aid to an anti−wheat-rust campaign, and for a time John Budd served on the governing board of the Rust Prevention Association.

In another endeavor, the GN pursued its traditional interest in water resources. "Throughout our territory," said one official, "our agricultural development agents work with constituted authorities . . . in the creation of initiatives . . . designed to bring about desirable water legislation." Even before construction began on the Columbia River's Chief Joseph Dam, the company joined other groups in urging that facilities for irrigation be included. Similar patterns were followed where both hydroelectric power and irrigation were possible.[2]

The company, however, shifted the emphasis to fit changing economic conditions. Agricultural evolution across the Columbia Basin testified to the wisdom of the GN's long-term support for irrigation, but more and more, management stressed opportunities for industrialization in the Northwest. As the federal government built dams there, GN managers, alert to the advantages of low-cost electric power, sought to expand the company's position. In North Dakota, they considered the industrial as well as the agricultural implications of the Garrison Diversion Project. Similarly, the giant Libby Dam to be built on the Kootenai River in northwestern Montana during the late 1960s was certain, they understood, to enhance the industrial potential of a broad area.

During the 1950s and 1960s, industrial and agricultural development agents, as they were now named, gradually shifted their attention from production of farm commodities to agricultural processing and marketing. In the Red River Valley the company helped to attract businesses that would store, flake, dehydrate, or freeze potatoes. Also, at Moorhead and Crookston, Minnesota, the railroad took a significant part in encouraging establishment of sugar-beet refineries.

All these were admittedly matters of self-interest, benign self-interest. As John Budd said in 1962, "Because agriculture is a basic industry on which Great Northern depends for a substantial portion of its revenue, our development forces devote a large part of their total effort to attracting to the railway industries utilizing farm and ranch products."[3]

Stimulating Industrial Growth

Promoting industrial development was more complex. Positive relations had to be sought with businessmen who might locate plants on or near the Great Northern, and the program meant acquiring suitable land for manufacturing or storage, leasing or selling sites and other property, and constructing spur tracks. Moreover, success depended on close cooperation among several of the railroad's departments. Local agents often made the first contact while traffic representatives were assessing the potential volume of freight. When railroad property was to be used, the land and tax department sold it or arranged leases, and the engineering department calculated the cost of construction. For a large transaction, approval by top management was required.

The company's promotional material emphasized attractions for industry, as in the GN's *Great Resources* and brochures boosting selected on-line cities. They included data on population, markets, labor, power and water supplies, tax structure, schools, and miscellaneous facts useful to businessmen seeking new plant locations.

The GN significantly changed its procedures as competitive pressures grew. By the 1950s, truck competition forced the company to assume costs for more spur tracks, because truck transportation imposed no such outlay on shippers, and top management made a concerted effort to handle swiftly applications for site locations and spur tracks. Frank Gavin had once complained that GN procedures lacked snap; by the time the company acted, the applicant often had either gone to another road or changed plans. Improvement was especially rapid after 1953, when clarified functions gave the land and tax department primary responsibility for negotiating with prospective lessees.

Financial and other assistance granted to encourage location of plants occasionally created perplexing problems. Help given one firm might lead to requests from others as well as to competitive bidding among carriers, and the ICC limited such aid. Companies seeking support were often financially weak, often leaving the carriers with unwanted facilities. Furthermore, a new firm's location might be detrimental to established customers, possibly causing net decreases in traffic. Nevertheless, reports that other carriers were assisting shippers were a challenge that the GN could not ignore. Neither Gavin nor Budd was eager to embark on such a program, but neither was willing to abandon the field. The policy settled upon was aiding "carefully screened prospects."[4]

A prerequisite for successfully recruiting industry was an abundance of attractive sites. The GN, of course, had acquired suitable properties as opportunity offered, but land in the developing Northwest was being taken up rapidly and competition for such properties increased accordingly. Purchasing additional parcels thus became a major challenge for the land and tax commissioner, expanding greatly after 1950.

Seattle offered special advantages. Following advice from Thomas Balmer, the company's vice president there, the GN purchased the Pacific Coast Railroad Company, a local pike used by the rival Milwaukee Road to reach Seattle. It had well-located terminal trackage in that city and extensive holdings suitable for industrial use at nearby Renton, Washington. The GN also expanded opportunities by filling in an area adjacent to its historic Smith Cove ocean terminal in the Seattle harbor area.

Rewards from this campaign came surely if gradually. Most installations were for agribusiness: storage facilities, factories for fertilizer and farm machinery, packinghouses, canneries and freezing facilities for vegetables and fruits, dehydrating plants for apples and potatoes, and refineries for sugar. Nonagribusiness enterprises varied from little sawmills to enormous paper mills, and from local bulk plants to oil refineries.

Other efforts were made on behalf of firms ranging from small metal-working shops with local markets to huge aluminum reduction plants. The $65 million facility of Anaconda Aluminum Company at Columbia Falls, Montana, began production in 1955. Eleven years later a joint enterprise began in Ferndale, Washington, on Puget Sound at the large Intalco plant. Other aluminum producers served by the GN in Washington were Alcoa at Malaga (near Wenatchee), Kaiser at Tacoma and Spokane, and Reynolds at Longview. Altogether, the GN served establishments that produced one-fourth of that primary product in

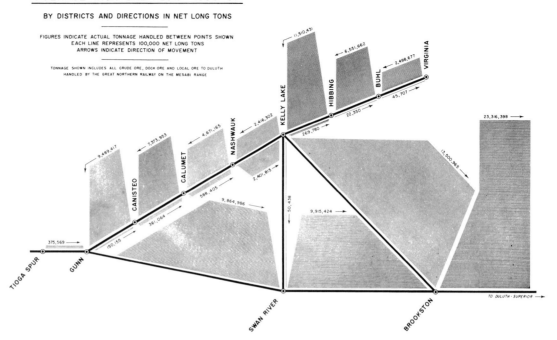

AVERAGE IRON ORE FLOW · 1956-57

BY DISTRICTS AND DIRECTIONS IN NET LONG TONS

FIGURES INDICATE ACTUAL TONNAGE HANDLED BETWEEN POINTS SHOWN
EACH LINE REPRESENTS 100,000 NET LONG TONS
ARROWS INDICATE DIRECTION OF MOVEMENT

TONNAGE SHOWN INCLUDES ALL CRUDE ORE, DOCK ORE AND LOCAL ORE TO DULUTH
HANDLED BY THE GREAT NORTHERN RAILWAY ON THE MESABI RANGE

The GN moved its first taconite in 1967.

the United States. The resulting traffic, practically nonexistent for the GN prior to World War II, amounted to more than 25,000 carloads by 1967, and yielded over $13 million in revenues.

Encouraging the Mining Industry

Because it relied on iron ore for significant tonnage and revenue, the GN followed developments in taconite processing with especially keen interest. Even before World War II ended, both public and private authorities warned that Minnesota's Iron Range depended on methods for utilizing the region's vast deposits of magnetic and nonmagnetic taconite. Several steel companies committed themselves to large-scale operations on the eastern end of the Range, and by 1954 they had three plants active or under construction. These crushed magnetic taconite, separated iron from waste, and concentrated the metal into pellets containing 64–68 percent iron.[5]

The GN's lines, however, served the western Mesabi Range, where most of the taconite was believed to be the nonmagnetic type. Hence in 1956, management authorized financial support for research at the University of Minnesota on the types of ore found in the GN's service area, as well as on practical methods for processing them. The GN also supported the University of North Dakota in a related study begun in 1959 to determine whether a roasting-beneficiating process, using carbon gases from lignite, was workable for converting nonmagnetic ore into the magnetic type.

These projects yielded mixed results. The Minnesota study demonstrated that nonmagnetic taconite responded to the roasting-magnetic method and that the concentrate could

subsequently be upgraded. Experiments by the North Dakota school showed lignite to be a satisfactory fuel for the roasting. Because the scientific findings did not determine that the method was economically practicable, though, no steel companies undertook to use it.

Magnetic ore was, however, discovered in the western Mesabi Range, and after Minnesota voters approved a 1964 constitutional amendment guaranteeing taconite processors a nondiscriminatory tax for twenty-five years, location of beneficiating plants along GN lines was ensured. National Steel built one at Keewatin and Butler Taconite another at Nashwauk, both almost immediately put into production. In 1967, the GN moved its first shipment of pellets.

Meanwhile, the company sought other mineral or mineral-based traffic in other areas, revealing to the Ashland Chemical Company, for example, a large bentonite deposit (clay used as binder for taconite pellets) southwest of Glasgow, Montana. And in 1965 the GN set aside monies for the University of North Dakota to see if lignite would yield a liquid that could be used as fuel or a chemical. The stakes were enormous: authorities estimated North Dakota's lignite reserves at 350 billion tons.

Although some of the GN's long-term developmental efforts were slow in showing results, as a whole they improved traffic. The outlay, exclusive of that for industrial land, from 1939 to 1970 was more than $7 million, but GN managers considered it well spent.

Nothing compared to the primeval excitement produced by an R-2 with a tonnage train or an S-2 at track speed.

33

SD45s and Univac III

When John M. Budd became president of the Great Northern in 1951, the United States was well into an era of technological innovation that some called the second industrial revolution. During and after World War II many scientific and technological breakthroughs altered life and work for most Americans. Changed and changing circumstances predictably presented GN managers with a blend of opportunities and problems. On the one hand, the new environment included several traffic-inducing elements, but on the other, costs of doing business—especially labor costs—were rising continuously. The Great Northern's officers, like those of other railroads, were hard put to improve efficiency. They understood, however, that they had no choice. Consequently, the carriers spent billions to better their plants and meet competitive pressures. Under John Budd's able leadership, the Great Northern became one of the pacesetters.[1]

Motive Power and Rolling Stock

A major technological change long since under way was the shift to diesel power. In 1951, the company owned 466 diesel units, 511 steam locomotives, and 20 electrics, but three years later management decided to retire all steam power—and as quickly as possible. To that end, between 1952 and 1958, the GN purchased 192 diesel units, and all without ceremony during August 1957, the fire was dropped for the last time on a GN steam locomotive in revenue service. (Six were retained, not in locomotive accounts, for steaming ore at Allouez.) It was a proper and dry-eyed business decision, earnestly advocated in the executive suite since early in Frank Gavin's presidency. Nevertheless, not even the most dedicated industrial engineer could feel for internal combustion the primeval excitement set off by an R-2 starting a tonnage train or an S-2 running at track speed.

At about the same time, after extensive study, GN officers also decided to abandon electric power in the Cascades. The two modern electric locomotives acquired in the 1940s had not obviated exchanging power at Wenatchee and Skykomish, and although experimental diesel-locomotive runs through the Cascade Tunnel during World War II had resulted in overheated engines and a potentially

Roundhouse foremen received few calls for steam, but in 1956 the wheat rush required one final burst. There were occasions, such as this, when the diesels stubbed their toes and had to be rescued by external combustion. Southwest of St. Cloud, Minnesota, in September 1956. *(Photo by Don L. Hofsommer)*

The end came for the Great Northern's electrics on August 1, 1956.

dangerous residue of nitrogen oxides in the bore, engineers decided that most of these problems could be solved by improved ventilation. The powerful fans and automatic door installed at the east portal spelled doom for the electrics. They were only a memory after August 1, 1956.

Having completed dieselization just as a general recession began, the GN brought no new locomotives from 1959 to 1962. But in 1963, the company purchased seventeen "second-generation" diesel locomotives, rated at 2,250 horsepower; each of these replaced one of 1,350 horsepower. During the next two years, the railroad further upgraded its roster by acquiring forty-eight units of 2,500 horsepower. Then, in 1966, the first eight giant 3,600-horsepower SD45s, part of a planned twenty-six, went into service. Other additions in the late 1960s included twelve smaller road units and ten for switching. By the end of 1969, the GN had reduced its locomotive fleet, but made it more efficient than ever.

All of this was reflected at maintenance points. The shop for steam locomotives at Hillyard in Spokane was extensively modified to service and repair diesels; former steam facilities at Superior were transformed to serve the large inventory of maintenance-of-way equipment; and additions were made at Havre and at Dale Street in St. Paul. Car shops were similarly improved. St. Cloud continued to maintain rolling stock and to build new equipment on demand, and St. Paul's Jackson Street Shop was outfitted with machine tools. These would more efficiently handle car and locomotive wheel and axle work.

The entire roster of rolling stock got special attention, including common box cars, which changed markedly. Many were made more versatile and dependable by new steel wheels, roller bearings, ride-control trucks, nailable steel floors, cushion underframes, and devices to facilitate loading and reduce damage to lading. The GN likewise acquired doubledoor cars, and equipped others with "plug doors" to improve versatility in hauling grain. In the late 1960s the company's sixty-foot, ninety-ton box cars with wide openings were welcomed at lumber- and paper-shipping points in the Pacific Northwest.

New cars designed for specific commodities began arriving in 1954. The GN acquired the first in a fleet of air-slide covered hopper cars designed to carry bulk flour, bulk sugar, and other granular materials. The company also added more and bigger covered hoppers, purchasing in 1962 the first of its giant 100-ton

"Second generation" diesels were ordered in 1962 and the process of renewing the fleet continued throughout the 1960s.

Domes finally came to the *Empire Builder*.

The Great Northern Railway: A History/Part II 1916 to 1970

cylindrical aluminum and steel cars. By the end of the 1960s, the GN proudly claimed 2,000 "jumbo" covered hoppers for grain service, a foundation for unit trains later on. Gondolas of various types were added, too. Some, 65 feet long, were to haul structural steel, and others with compartments carried ferro-silicon and ferro-alloys. Huge tank cars, each capable of moving 25,000 gallons, were acquired in the late 1950s, and in the next decade new 60-foot, doubledecker livestock cars were received for carrying hogs. For freight such as canned goods, insulated cars were equipped with special loading devices. At the same time, Western Fruit Express, an affiliate, bought more mechanical refrigerator cars.

During the Budd years, the GN purchased more than 14,000 freight cars, rebuilt many, leased still others, and disposed of smaller and less efficient equipment. The trend to larger cars continued, so that although cars went from 43,897 in 1950 to 43,364 at the end of 1969, the aggregate capacity was increased by about a fourth. The GN could now handle large volumes of traffic, as in the 1966 season, when poor crops in Asia found the GN carrying an astonishing 137,862 carloads of grain.

Passenger equipment too was improved. Despite unfavorable trends in passenger carriage, the railroad resolved to provide competitive equipment. During the 1950s, several coaches and sleepers were rebuilt into mail and baggage cars, and in the next decade the GN bought from other roads thirty-one cars, of which twenty-five were streamlined coaches. Among other modernization programs, dome cars were added to the *Empire Builder*. Some directors re-

By the end of the 1960s, the GN proudly claimed 2,000 covered hoppers in grain service.

jected the idea at first as too costly and unnecessary. Although Burlington's management was pleased with public response to Vista Dome cars on its *Zephyrs*, GN traffic officers believed the company could compete without such cars, which would be expensive to air-condition and heat because of extreme weather on the northern route. The *Builder*'s operating schedule too made dome cars less attractive.

In 1952, however, these same officers were forced to change their opinions. They knew that the Milwaukee had ordered such equipment, and they had heard rumors that the Northern Pacific would do so. "In 1951, we were cited as the outstanding railroad in the United States for progress in passenger equipment," Vice President Finley wrote, "and if we do not furnish dome cars we are falling behind in the race." He added that "good passenger service attracts new and repeat freight business" and that it was a "creator of good will"—without which all aspects of the company's operations would suffer. Budd, who at first had not favored the large expenditure, was finally convinced.[2]

In October 1953, the board of directors approved purchase of twenty-two domes for the *Empire Builder*. Plans called for one full-length "Great Dome" and three dome coaches in each of the five train sets. The "Great Domes," designed for Pullman passengers, featured a lounge on the lower level decorated with art and colors of the Haida (North Pacific Coast) Indians. Although the manufacturer promised delivery in June 1955, in time for the vacation season, it was October before the last of the order reached St. Paul. These new cars cost $5.6 million, and became the last big step in the GN's struggle to achieve a profitable long-distance passenger business in the age of the jet airliner and the superhighway.

Road and Yard Facilities

Creating an even more efficient plant was an unending challenge. During the twenty years after 1950 more than sixty line relocations were completed, and to facilitate movement of loads that were both high and wide, the GN changed bridges, daylighted tunnels, and widened cuts. By early 1965, the GN boasted that on its main line from St. Paul to Seattle, the governing clearance had been increased to nineteen feet above the rail—best among the northern transcontinentals.

Several of the improved stretches of line were in the state of Washington. Constructing 1.5 miles of new line between Seattle and Everett protected the railroad against mud slides along Puget Sound. Elsewhere, on the west slope of the Cascades, relocating 8 miles of line, including new bridges, cost more than $8 million, but reduced distance by 7,420 feet and eliminated 864 degrees of curvature, reducing rail wear and allowing higher train speeds. In addition, the railroad undertook, at federal expense, to replace 24 miles of the Wenatchee-Oroville branch that was flooded by the Rocky Reach Dam on the Columbia River.

One short piece of construction demanded special engineering to accommodate important freight. In the 1960s, to assemble its giant 747s, Boeing added to its plants at Seattle and Renton, and decided to build a larger one south of Everett. Reaching the latter required a 1.7-mile spur spiraling up Japan Gulch to the plant, about 500 feet above the main line.

Other new branches were longer but none as difficult to operate. Among these were two, aggregating 34.5 miles, which the GN built in the late 1950s to air bases: one near Minot, North Dakota, the other at Glasgow, Montana.

Also, large bentonite deposits discovered southwest of Glasgow moved the GN to put down 18 miles of track to connect that site with the main line.

More extensive work was undertaken in northwestern Montana, where a change of line was required by construction of the Libby Dam on the Kootenai River. When this work was completed, the impounded water flooded about fifty miles of track between Whitefish and Libby, and the federal government was called upon to finance construction of sixty miles of line, including the seven-mile Flathead Tunnel—the second longest rail tunnel in the western hemisphere. Begun in April 1966, and guided by laser beams, work on the bore progressed rapidly; on June 21, 1968, President Lyndon B. Johnson, from his office in the White House, fired the shot that completed "holing out."

One enterprise that never reached fruition—but consumed large volumes of managerial energy—had historic roots as well as contemporary potential. Early in the century, the GN had thrust its Fernie Branch into British Columbia to serve Crow's Nest Coal Company mines, but the route was abandoned in the 1930s and a Canadian Pacific line was used thereafter to handle colliery shipments. In the late 1960s, however, Crow's Nest had an opportunity to sell a large tonnage of coking coal to Japanese steelmakers if economical rail rates to tidewater could be arranged. The CPR proved obdurate and William Prentice, president of the coal company, asked John Budd if the GN would reestablish rail service for unit train operation. Thus was born the romantic-sounding Kootenay & Elk Railway, chartered by the coal firm in British Columbia.

The project attracted both strong supporters and determined detractors. Crow's Nest Coal soon passed to a new Canadian company, Kaiser Resources, Ltd., which received hearty support from the British Columbia Provincial Government. With that the GN pledged to build to the boundary from nearby Eureka, Montana, and the Kootenay & Elk agreed to construct and operate to a connection. The entire project, however, appeared to the Canadian Pacific as the dark and historic shadow of James J. Hill. Its opposition was intense. In the end CPR prevailed, agreeing to upgrade its line to the coal fields. By the early 1970s its unit trains were running to Roberts Bank, just above the international border along the Straits of Georgia. Ironically, though, to reach that location the Canadian Pacific was obliged to gain rights over a short piece of track owned by the Great Northern.

Meanwhile, in keeping with long tradition, Chief Engineer H. J. Seyton stressed careful and regular attention to track structure. All ties were now treated, crushed rock replaced gravel as ballast, and the GN's new standard, 115-pound rail, by 1966 was installed on more than a quarter of the main line. During the same period, the GN fully embraced ribbon or continuously welded rail. By the mid-1950s improved welding techniques and new track-laying machines had cut the cost of installing 1,400-foot segments enough that, with maintenance lowered by more than a fourth, welded rail was favored over standard 39-foot lengths. By the end of the 1960s, much of the company's track was of that type.

Throughout these years the GN mechanized maintenance-of-way work ever more rapidly. Purchases included spike pullers and drivers, tie removers and inserters, ballast tampers, power jacks and surfacers, self-propelled track liners and brooms, and sled-tie ejector units. By 1966, more than $11 million in roadway equipment demonstrated the GN's commitment to mechanization and enabled the company to better maintain track and at lower cost. Between 1950 and 1969, the number of sections was cut in half and employees were substantially reduced. By the mid-1960s, most maintenance was performed by machines operated by district gangs.

The GN adopted still other technological innovations. A rail-welding plant was established at Havre, and improved service and reduced costs were achieved by rail lubricators on sharp curves, snowblowers to keep switches operating in severe winter weather, and protective fences to control snow and rock slides. Mechanical cleaners quickly removed rubbish from cars and helped get the equipment promptly back in service. At the St. Cloud shops, an assembly line with a traveling paint-spray booth speeded construction and repair of freight cars.

On a more dramatic note, the company pledged in 1954 to build an imposing, modern, retarder-controlled classification yard near Minot. Teams of officers studied similar yards and meticulously planned the facility, which would be built where the GN's two principal lines—from the Twin Cities and from the Head of the Lakes—joined east of town. Grading began in spring 1955 and on October 12, 1956, the 417-acre hump yard entered service.

By centralizing much main-line freight classification at Gavin Yard (named in honor of the former president) the GN improved operations throughout the system. Switching expense was reduced, through traffic was expedited, and per diem charges were lowered. Officials calculated that the new yard saved 60,000 car-days per year. Budd was especially pleased with the $707,000 saved in the first year. James J. Hill's 1907 prediction that Minot would be the site of a major yard had finally proved true, but railroading had reached a sophistication beyond any that even he could have visualized a half century earlier.[3]

A capital investment as great as that in Gavin Yard was required for new taconite-handling and storage facilities on the Iron Range. In 1967, when Hanna Mining Company was to begin year-round operation of taconite plants at Keewatin and Nashwauk, Minnesota, the GN laid seven miles of track and began operating 200-car unit trains that made the round trip of 230 miles with 15,000 tons of pellets in thirteen to fourteen hours. Modern equipment at the Allouez terminal near Superior added to efficient operation. At 3,000 tons an hour, taconite pellets from the nearby storage area could be automatically fed and weighed on a conveyor that carried the continuous load two miles to the waiting pockets of refurbished Dock No. 1. When water transport ceased for winter, pellets were unloaded and deposited on both sides of the conveyor belt—itself straddled by a 160-foot boom equipped with an 85-foot-high stacker to lift taconite for stockpiling. In the spring when water transportation resumed, a huge bucket wheel reclaimed and passed pellets to the conveyor belt.

Although Gavin Yard and the taconite facilities at Allouez were the GN's most spectacular new terminals, the railroad also provided improved plant and service elsewhere. At a cost of $2.5 million it enlarged and changed Interbay Yard at Seattle into a modern, electronically controlled facility renamed Balmer Yard in honor of the former vice president who had done so much for the railroad and for Seattle.

Gavin Yard at Minot opened in 1956.

274

The Great Northern Railway: A History/Part II 1916 to 1970

The old and the new. A dispatcher wearing a green eyeshade, with telegraph instruments at his right, attends to a CTC board.

Centralized Traffic Control, Communications, and Computers

Electronics, a magic word in the years after World War II, was indispensable at Gavin Yard and in handling ore; it was also associated with Centralized Traffic Control (CTC). The company waited until the 1950s to install its first CTC, although as early as the 1920s a few railroads had tried remote control in limited application. Seeing how effective CTC was on the Burlington, the Southern Pacific, and other roads, operating officers near the end of World War II had recommended installing it on stretches west of Minneapolis and near Minot. Frank Gavin, however, had doubts. "Something tells me that we do not need Centralized Traffic Control on the Great Northern," he wrote. John Budd had other thoughts. Although the original cost was large, he was convinced that savings, better service, and greater safety justified the expenditure on high-density lines. Thus, in 1954, the GN installed CTC on short stretches in Montana and on the Iron Range. A larger application went from Delano 64.8 miles west to Willmar, at that time the track with the heaviest year-round traffic density. Results were heartening, and 100 miles or so of centralized traffic control was installed each year after 1954. By the end of 1969, the GN was operating more than 1,300 miles of its busiest trackage by remote control—replacing the time-honored system of written orders issued by dispatchers to trains through telegraph operators at wayside stations.[4]

Radio was applied in the drive to improve communications mostly after 1950. The GN and other railroads had experimented with radio since the 1920s, but it was not a reliable tool until the late 1940s. The GN began to utilize it regularly in 1952, especially for iron-ore traffic, placing sets on engines and cabooses and at stations from Kelly Lake to Allouez. Soon radios were installed on all transcontinental trains, both passenger and freight, and then elsewhere on secondary routes. After initial reluctance, railroaders, especially in the operating, mechanical, and maintenance departments, wondered how they had functioned without it.

In another phase of communications, the company modernized its telephone system. During World War I it had established a private double-wire connection between St. Paul and Seattle, but with that exception, the railroad paid telephone companies to provide long-distance service. During the 1950s, four carrier circuits were installed along the main line, and in the 1960s many private telephone circuits were added, incorporating transmission into Bell Telephone's microwave relay system. Meanwhile, the GN had installed a direct-dialing arrangement with automatic exchanges. These innovations connected the St. Paul offices with all major on-line stations. Company personnel could now reach other employees promptly via the company's own lines, saving both time and money and improving service to shippers.

In the 1950s, the GN also sought a substitute for telegraphy. Purchasing a microwave was considered but rejected, and a teletype system was embraced to speed transmission of various kinds of routine information. West-Coast traffic offices were connected to St. Paul, and also linked the Kelly Lake dispatchers and mining-company offices on the Range with the docks at Allouez. Soon the system was extended by leased lines to all important on- and off-line freight agencies and to selected passenger ticket offices. Telegraphy, once the railroad's communication backbone, thereafter was used primarily for local or intradivisional transmission and for supplemental communication.

Significant though each of these changes was, even more dramatic was the utilization of an entirely new tool, the electronic computer. It could speed routine tasks of accounting and help find answers for innumerable questions. In the 1930s, punched cards processed by electromechanical machines handled bookkeeping and statistical chores, and the GN was receptive to the electronic computer, made possible by scientific breakthroughs during and after World War II. Quickly adopting the most modern machines as they became available, and applying them innovatively, the GN was among the industry's pioneers in this field.

The railroad acquired two UNIVAC 120s (punched-card computers) in 1953. Installed in the St. Paul General Office Building, these were immediately valuable in interline accounting and in routinely handling bond purchases, tax withholdings, and railroad-retirement deductions. A special computer, placed in service at Allouez Yard in the early 1950s, was built into the track scale over which all loads moved—weighing while in motion up to 2,500 cars of ore per day. With information on weights furnished by teletype, instructions could be issued promptly by the mining company's ore graders to guide the railroad in dockside mixing and loading of lake vessels. Expedited switching and improved utility in the car fleet, of course, benefited shippers and carriers alike.

Fully convinced that computers would be desirable in more activities, management quickly sought additional equipment. By 1955, Remington Rand announced its UNIVAC I, capable of performing complex data-processing chores in an amazingly short time and of making available information hitherto inaccessible because of high cost. When studies showed that using a UNIVAC I just for labor and payroll accounting would save enough to pay the rental ($22,500 per month, applicable to purchase), the directors responded promptly. Installed in the General Office Building, the machine was in use by 1957. Three years later the railroad changed from renter to owner.

Expansion followed. The accounting department soon asked for a UNIVAC Solid State Computer, a transistorized machine with extensive technological advances. This second-generation computer rented for $12,600 a month, but company officers estimated it would effect a large annual saving. By mid-summer 1961, the new machine was installed and, supplementing UNIVAC I, made it possible to retire most unit records equipment remaining in the accounting department. Less than two years after the solid-state machine was installed, current and potential tasks for computers at the General Office Building exceeded capacity. Accounting officers recommended, and the directors approved, acquisition of a UNIVAC III, an electronic marvel, up to ten times faster than UNIVAC I and capable of far more sophisticated work. The new machine was installed in November 1963. As expected, it rendered obsolete the solid-state computer and gradually took over some of the work previously performed by UNIVAC I. Then, in 1968, the GN acquired an IBM 360/40, smaller and cheaper to operate than the UNIVAC I, with ten times greater memory capacity. The company retired the UNIVAC I accordingly.

The company's UNIVAC I was used for payroll accounting and ICC records. It was in place by 1957.

Within comparatively few years, the GN was putting computers to broader and more complex use. The first major task for UNIVAC I had been payroll accounting, but many other jobs were turned over to computers after Thomas J. Lamphier was given company-wide responsibility for data processing, and as employees became more experienced and creative in designing systems. Computers became more than accounting tools: by 1960, the Central Car Bureau relied on them in its daily work. Eight years later, with solid-state computers (UNIVAC 418s) the company could have information almost instantaneously on any of the more than 40,000 cars on its lines.

The new car-reporting arrangement and heavy dependence upon computers were backed up by innovative systems for measuring performance in various areas of operation. Terminal Performance Control, inaugurated at the Spokane complex in 1968, established time standards for moves that a car might make within a yard. Managers could now spot potential bottlenecks, move freight faster, and ease car shortages. Officials estimated that at Hillyard alone, the new technique in effect added 200 cars to the company's car fleet and would save $168,000 annually. The new method was soon extended to the Twin Cities, Seattle, and other terminals.

A system related to Terminal Performance Control that applied its methods and concepts to the entire railroad was Freight Service Management. By comparing actual performance with predetermined standards, division superintendents and other officials could pinpoint locations where performance was substandard, and then take the necessary remedial measures. These quality-control procedures, combined with the new car-information system, were labeled Transportation Service Control (TSC). Although TSC would cost $1.5 million a year, GN managers believed the expense would be justified by better service to customers, more efficient distribution of cars, and improved control of costs. The whole complex was compatible with the Automatic Car Identification System and the TeleRail Automated Information Network, industry-wide programs for improving service.

Quite apart from simplifying record keeping and aiding in operations, computers answered complex questions helpful in making decisions. Answering management's inquiries, the equipment provided new and comprehensive information that led directly to savings or to better service, or promised both in the future. Not surprisingly, the division of economic research, established in 1958, used computers extensively to analyze marketing costs as well as railroad operations.

The technological revolution that was so much a part of postwar America deeply affected the Great Northern. Budd and his associates were fully aware, however, that stimulating long-term economic development in the company's service area and investment in technology had to be supplemented by innovative and energetic marketing of the railroad's services.

A reservation service for meals typified procedures on the *Empire Builder* and the *Western Star*. Excellent cuisine was available on both trains.

Where patronage continued, the GN maintained fine food service. Aboard the *Empire Builder*, January 1970. *(Photo by Don L. Hofsommer)*

34

"No Sacred Cows — or Goats"

During John Budd's administration the Great Northern Railway faced change, yet many circumstances stubbornly stayed the same. Customers had to be satisfied, competition had to be met, and, as always, innovative approaches had to be found and unprofitable operations had to be modified or dropped.[1]

The Passenger Dilemma

Company officers had reason to be hopeful about the Great Northern's passenger business during the 1950s. The *Empire Builder* and the *Western Star* were among the very best trains in the country, and location brought the railroad much long-distance passenger traffic. At the same time, head-end business—principally mail—was growing in volume. Moreover, the GN's top managers believed that high-quality passenger trains created a favorable public impression that helped attract shippers. Many were convinced too that excellent passenger service improved workers' morale.[2]

Statistically, however, passenger operations presented a mixed picture. In 1952, the GN had higher passenger-service revenues, $27.2 million, than for any of the previous five years, and of that, $14.1 million was from tickets. In that year it carried 1.7 million persons an average of 352 miles, and offered passenger service on 5,338 miles of line. On the other hand, under ICC accounting rules, adding a set percentage of railroad fixed costs to direct costs of operating passenger trains, the service showed a deficit that increased over the next two decades.[3]

Senior managers agonized over the passenger problem incessantly. In 1959 and again in 1969, their comprehensive studies showed, in part, that much of the terminal-to-terminal business—Chicago–Seattle/Portland and Twin Cities–Seattle/Portland ticketing—had been lost to air competition. These studies also showed, however, that long-haul volume to and from terminals and intermediate points such as Minot, Williston, and Havre remained high. Using this information, the company changed operations and tested the market in a sincere and dedicated effort to attract passengers in profitable numbers.

Improving equipment and plant was one approach to the problem. Acquiring dome cars for the *Empire Builder* was a major step, and continuously improving the track structure to assure travelers of reliable, smooth, and fast service was another. In 1957, the *Builder* operated between St. Paul and Seattle on a 36-hour and 25 minute schedule, and the *Star* covered its route in 41 hours and 15 minutes. Meanwhile, several station buildings were improved, and a few were replaced by new ones. King's Street Station in Seattle was renovated, and the company opened a new restaurant in the recently refurbished Minneapolis station.

In these varied ways, the GN sought to make train travel more attractive. A reservation service for meals, popular on the *Empire Builder*, was introduced on the *Western Star*, a

The Great Northern sold its hotel and bus assets at Glacier Park in 1960.

passenger representative was added to its crew, and on all trains GN dining cars sustained their reputation for culinary excellence. The railroad joined Western Airlines in offering single reservations and tickets for the two modes of travel, and in tune with the times, the GN honored credit cards and for a time advertised a "Go Now, Pay Later" plan.

As in the past, tours were popular. Special "Rocky" excursions attracted patronage, especially to Glacier Park, although the railroad's relationship with facilities there underwent major change. In 1955, the affiliated Glacier Park Company, which owned and operated hotels at the park, was merged with the Glacier Park Transport Company, which operated buses.

Two years later, management was turned over to the Knutson Hotel Corporation of Minneapolis and, in 1960, the railroad's park facilities were sold to an Arizona-based group. For the first time in eighty years, the GN was out of the hotel business. In 1962, tours to the Seattle World's Fair helped to give GN passenger returns for that year a million-dollar boost.

Fares and their relation to volume were abundantly debated. According to studies, raising them invariably lost patronage, and so management frequently opposed increases in basic fares. Like other railroads, however, the GN experimented with special rates. Seat fares were cut on some trains, and occasionally coach tickets were honored in parlor and

Omaha orange and GN green, used since 1939, gradually gave way to "Big Sky Blue."

sleeping cars. A variety of round-trip fares was available, and excursion tickets at reduced rates encouraged travel to numerous special events. Servicemen on furlough enjoyed lower rates, as did family members traveling together.

In a period of generally rising prices, the GN's average revenue per passenger mile

The *Gopher* provided convenient early evening service between the Twin Cities and the Lakehead. Near Cedar, Minnesota, in September 1967. *(Photo by Don L. Hofsommer)*

changed relatively little, falling from 2.29 cents in 1951 to 2.15 cents four years later. With minor increases in rates, and despite a decline in local coach travel, the average rose to only 2.59 cents by 1969.

Throughout this period, the GN continued to advertise itself. In an industry that spent relatively little on promotion, the GN, with an annual outlay averaging $1.2 million, ranked among the first ten railroads; in several years, only the Santa Fe and the Union Pacific spent more. Several media were tried. During the 1950s, the GN allocated a relatively large amount to television, leading the industry in spot commercials, often with animated cartoons. But as television rates rose, the GN shifted more of its advertising budget to newspapers, magazines, and radio. In 1966, the 23 percent allocated to television was spent to sponsor local programs in the Twin Cities, Spokane, and Seattle. Spot commercials were disseminated by radio throughout the service area, but most newspaper advertising was done in cities served by the GN, as well as off-line in large metropolitan dailies. Consumer and trade periodicals too were used to reach the traveling public and those who influenced freight routing.

Related to the company's advertising broadcast were changes in its corporate colors and trademark. The GN's popular symbol, "Rocky" the goat, had not changed in appearance since 1936. Budd therefore hired an industrial design and marketing firm to make suggestions, adding that they had "absolutely no sacred cows—or goats—to consider." After thorough study, the consultants urged small changes to "bring out the best in Rocky." Thus, in the late 1960s, he grew trim, better proportioned, and more agile—a truly attractive, "vibrant, virile, and dynamic character."

At the same time, the GN adopted new corporate colors. Omaha orange and GN green, used since 1939, gradually gave way to "Big Sky Blue" to publicize the "Big Sky Country" of the great Northwest, GN's broad service area.[4]

Just as they labored diligently to promote train travel, Budd and his associates sought to cut related expenses. Sleeping-, dining-, and parlor-car service was reduced as demand slipped. Some trains were replaced by buses or bus-and-truck combinations, and in Montana by one new self-propelled diesel motor car. Although the company faced stiff and often unreasonable opposition from state regulatory agencies, passenger train miles inexorably shrank. From 1951 to 1957, the GN dropped at least thirty-four trains, mostly locals, and in the next two years twenty-six more joined the list; the pattern continued in the next decade.

On the main line changes frequently were achieved by rerouting or combining to minimize train miles. The *Western Star* was rerouted several times, and finally was consolidated with the *Fast Mail*, whose proud name disappeared. *The Cascadian* between Spokane and Seattle made its last runs in 1959, and one of the three daily *Internationals* between Seattle and Vancouver was removed in 1960. *The Red River* went in 1968. Even the elite *Empire Builder* was combined westbound between Chicago and St. Paul with the Burlington's *Afternoon Zephyr* and eastbound with the Northern Pacific's *North Coast Limited*.

By 1969, the GN's passenger business was skeletal. The transcontinental *Empire Builder* and *Western Star* were alone except for a few trains on intermediate runs. The *Winnipeg Limited* connected the Canadian city with St. Paul; the *Badger* and the *Gopher* ran between

St. Paul and the Head of the Lakes. The *Da-kotan* served Fargo and St. Paul via Alexandria, and another train ran between Havre and Great Falls. On the west end, the *Internationals* operated between Seattle and Vancouver, and the GN ran one train in the three-carrier pool between Portland and Seattle. Elsewhere, buses, including some owned by the GN, provided service where trains had once operated. In the eighteen years after 1951, the GN reduced the miles of line over which it operated passenger trains by 46 percent — to 3,033.

The reduction in passenger service was clearly related to changes in handling mail and express. For the GN, the major mail-carrying road between St. Paul and the Pacific Northwest, postal revenue was critical. It had grown from $8.6 million in 1951 to $9.4 million in 1967, when it made up 44 percent of passenger-train revenue. The Post Office Department, however, canceled contracts on some trains in the 1950s, and in the late 1960s began a massive shift to airlines, truckers, and to trailer-on-flat-car (TOFC) service. All railroads had suffered from the ''passenger problem,'' but the loss of en route sorting revenue was the last straw for most. On the GN, the department's decision to remove Railway Post Office cars from the *Red River* was the major factor in that train's discontinuance. Problems with express service were similar. Railway Express Agency's inability to compete with parcel post and trucking service led to its reorganization as REA Express in 1962, but the new firm failed to prosper. Between 1951 and 1969, the GN lost about half its revenues from express business.

Despite all efforts, the passenger business had become a heavy burden, piling up large deficits annually. Where patronage continued, the GN maintained good service, but manage-

ment knew that it must eventually face heavy equipment renewals. John Budd said as much in March 1968.[5]

New Departures in Freight Traffic

Freight business presented its own problems as well as its own opportunities. Improvements in track structure, motive power, and rolling stock made possible speedier service. In 1951, the GN's premier freight train was scheduled to run between Minneapolis and Seattle in 106 hours and 25 minutes. By 1964, however, the GN established eastbound and westbound schedules of 47 hours — only 11 hours and 35 minutes more than that of the *Empire Builder* — allowing the company to make fourth-morning delivery at either Chicago or Pacific Coast points. This improved schedule, of course, especially mattered to the

Reductions in passenger offerings became the order of the day as revenues plunged. The *Fast Mail*, shown here leaving St. Paul Union Depot for the west, was later combined with the *Western Star*.

freight forwarders who had picked up most of the long-haul LCL business and were competing with truckers for time-sensitive traffic.[6]

Bulk shippers received similar attention as the GN joined in the industry-wide operation of unit trains. These gave customers economy of scale as well as speedier transit and offered the carriers higher utilization of cars, attracting traffic that might have been lost to other modes. In 1964, for instance, the GN billed twenty-seven trainloads of iron ore to a steel mill in Granite City, Illinois, and later in the decade the company used unit trains to haul Pacific Northwest lumber, Montana wheat to

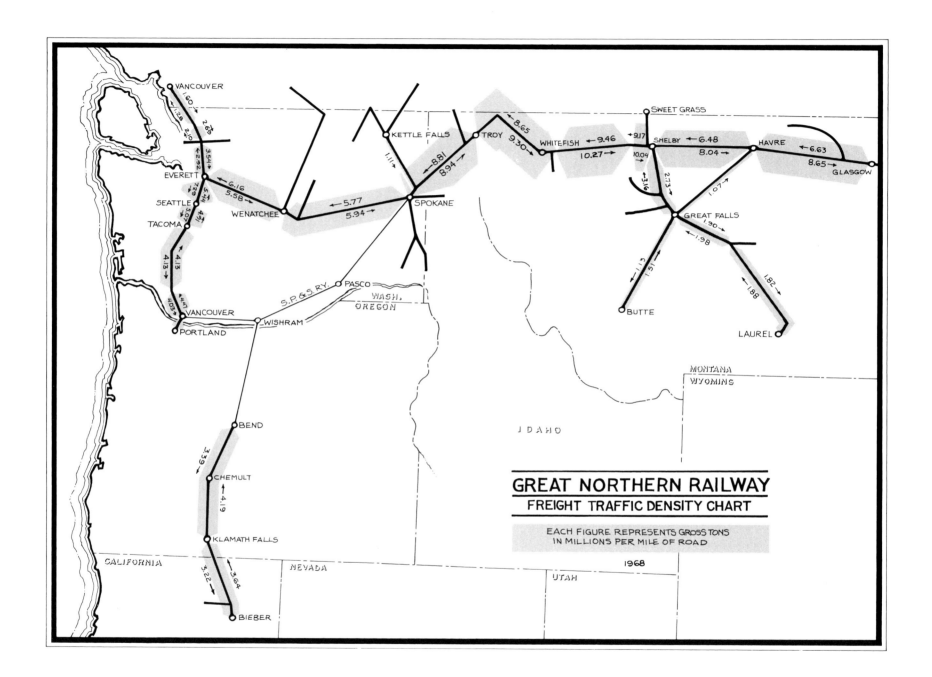

GREAT NORTHERN RAILWAY
FREIGHT TRAFFIC DENSITY CHART

EACH FIGURE REPRESENTS GROSS TONS
IN MILLIONS PER MILE OF ROAD

1968

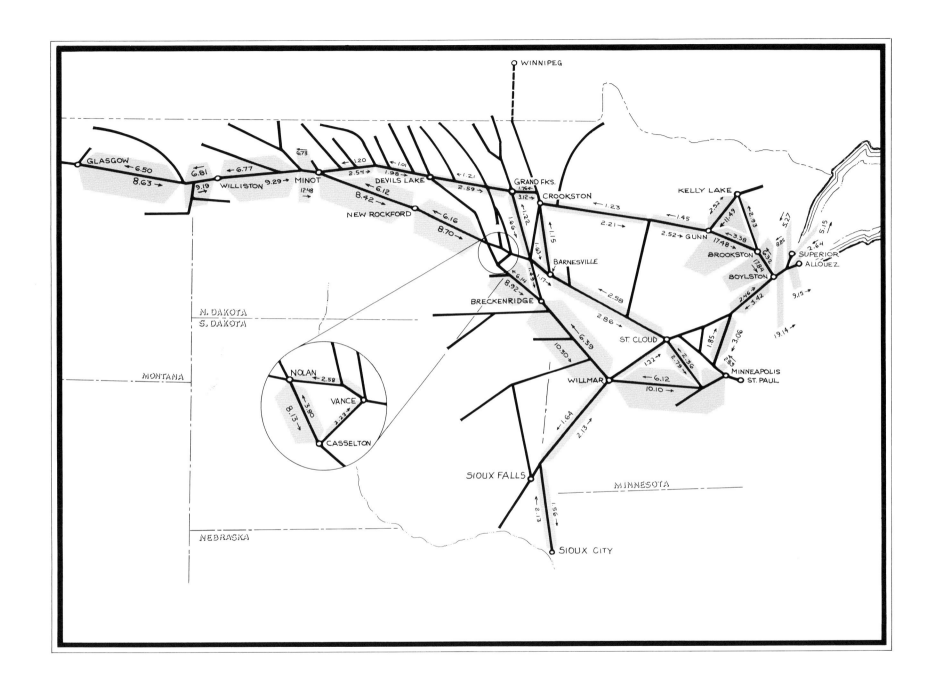

"No Sacred Cows—or Goats"

Loss of en route sorting contracts administered the coup de grace to much of the nation's rail passenger service. *(Photo by Don L. Hofsommer)*

Portland for export, and Saskatchewan potash, via Northgate, N.D., to the Midwest. In 1967, unit trains on the Iron Range began regularly carrying taconite pellets.

A decade earlier the GN had initiated TOFC or piggybacking, giving shippers the flexibility of truck service while retaining rail transport's inherent advantages, including economy. Piggybacking had been tried much earlier, but not

until the mid-1950s, encouraged by ICC decisions, did it begin to boom. Nation-wide carloadings grew from 168,000 in 1955 to 1,344,000 in 1969.

The industry eventually established several types of TOFC operation. By Plan I, a motor carrier gave "substitute service," moving its trailers by flat car, paying the railroad a fee per trailer based on weight and distance. Under Plan II, a railroad provided its own trailers and flat cars, giving complete door-to-door service, employing either railroad-owned tractors or local draymen to handle trailers over

Taconite was billed on unit-train rates.

the road. Plan III was a ramp-to-ramp arrangement, the customers providing trailers and doing the loading, unloading, and terminal hauling. Under Plan IV, railroads handled trailers and flat cars owned or leased by the shipper, providing only terminal-to-terminal line-haul movement. In Plan V, truck and rail facilities were coordinated to give a joint-rate, through-route service. This arrangement differed from Plan I only in that the motor carrier moved the trailer beyond communities reached

284

among TOFC Plans II, II½, III, and IV. The GN ultimately installed ramps at all major points and set up an adequate supply of flat cars. In 1963, TOFC operations generated almost $4 million in revenues; its future was assured.[7]

Piggybacking also suggested a new method of transporting automobiles. For several years manufacturers had used trucks to haul their product to dealers, but in the 1950s railroads bid for that business by transporting automobile trailers on flat cars. Bi- and tri-level auto racks later increased the capacity to twelve or more autos, instead of the four that the railroads had once hauled in modified box cars. By 1964, railroads using the new equipment handled 28 percent of automobiles moving from assembly plants to dealers.

The GN moved into this new business in 1959 by participating in a pooling arrangement for the movement of automobiles from California assembly points to the Pacific Northwest. A year later, when hauling automobiles from the Midwest opened new opportunities, the company purchased its first automobile racks, and in 1963, the five-year revenue from moving automobiles and trucks was up almost 400 percent.

The GN experimented also with containerized domestic mail and LCL shipments, but this method of handling freight seemed more promising for the export-import business. From origin to destination, sealed boxes could be handled by forklift trucks or other devices, cutting costs, damage, and pilferage. Commodities packed in standard-size containers could be easily transferred to and handled by air, rail, truck, and ship. In 1967, the GN billed its first shipment from the Far East, a consignment of soft goods bound for Chicago, and on the return trip, the 7 × 8 × 7-foot

by the railroad. Several variations followed. In Plan II½, railroads provided trailers and moved them from ramp to ramp; customers loaded, unloaded, and moved trailers to and from rail ramps with their own tractors.

The GN offered its first TOFC service in 1954, between the Twin Cities and Duluth–Superior and the Twin Cities and Red River points. The company at first piggybacked only LCL goods, but within the year it was hauling truckloads on flat cars. Quoting door-to-door through rates for customers, the railroad used its regularly scheduled trains to destinations

Hauling trailers on flat cars, or piggybacking, gave shippers the flexibility of truck service while retaining the inherent advantages of rail transport. *(Photo by Ted Bronstein for Great Northern)*

where contract truckers moved the trailers to shipper docks. As volume warranted, service was expanded along the main line from St. Paul to Seattle. The company's "Coordinated Shipping Service," announced in 1961, effectively wedded rail and highway transportation, giving the customer rail, truck, and piggyback equipment for a complete range of choices

285

boxes carried radios and television sets. So promising was this business that the GN appointed a market manager for containerized and export-import traffic, opened an office in Japan, and arranged for an adequate supply of equipment.

Under competitive pressure, the GN ventured into allied modes of transportation. The Canadian National's Seatrain was a special challenge; the GN responded by joining with three other railroads and a shipping firm to operate their own "trainship" between New Westminster, British Columbia, and Whittier, Alaska. This 520-foot vessel carried up to 56 freight cars on its covered decks; a stern-loading arrangement that adjusted tracks to dock level allowed cars to be rolled on and off at each terminal. At Whittier the vessel connected with the Alaska Railroad, giving GN shippers direct access to Anchorage, Fairbanks, and other points.

The opening of oil production in the GN's service area provided another opportunity for the Great Northern to diversify its transportation offerings. While new discoveries of oil in Montana were of general interest to the Great Northern, it was the rapid development of the petroleum business in the Williston Basin of North Dakota that in 1960 led to organization of the Great Northern Pipe Line Company, a wholly owned subsidiary, which soon had fifty miles of gathering lines to carry crude oil from Newburg, Wiley, and Glenburn Fields to Minot where it was loaded into tank cars. Producers enjoyed the low rates of pipeline gathering service, and the GN, instead of hauling tank cars to several points, gained the economies of centralized loading.

The enterprise was soon altered, though, when the GN formed, with two partners, Hunt Oil Company of Dallas and Northwestern Re-

Bulkhead flat cars offered lumber shippers convenient loading.

fining Company of St. Paul, the Portal Pipeline Company, which took over the Great Northern Pipe Line. The GN retained a 45 percent interest in Portal, and later increased it to 50 percent after Northwestern dropped out. In 1963, Portal had 366 miles of ten-inch and sixteen-inch pipeline from Lignite, North Dakota, to Clearbrook, Minnesota, where it connected with other systems, one east to Buffalo, New York, and another south to the Twin Cities. Portal later added an extension to tap oil-producing areas in eastern Montana.

Such departures mirrored the GN's philosophy of tailoring transportation to needs of individual shippers. The handling of lumber provides one of several possible examples.

That commodity had always been hand-loaded in box cars, but when rising labor costs forced lumbermen into mechanical loading, the GN supplied cars with wide doors. Later, the lumber industry came up with a technique for wrapping lumber in protective paper, in which form it was best handled on bulkhead flat cars, and the GN acquired these in large number. Elsewhere, the GN substituted trucks for rails in moving livestock from Minneapolis switching yards to South St. Paul stockyards, and in 1967 a new car-barge slip at Vancouver enabled Canadian pulp and paper manufacturers to load cars at mills on the British Columbia

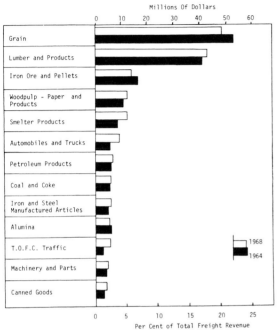

PRINCIPAL REVENUE PRODUCING PRODUCTS
1964 - 1968

Millions Of Dollars

Grain
Lumber and Products
Iron Ore and Pellets
Woodpulp - Paper and Products
Smelter Products
Automobiles and Trucks
Petroleum Products
Coal and Coke
Iron and Steel Manufactured Articles
Alumina
T.O.F.C. Traffic
Machinery and Parts
Canned Goods

1968
1964

Per Cent of Total Freight Revenue

Note: In 1968 these commodities accounted for 72.4% of Great Northern freight revenue.

coast and in Alaska that were not served by rail, moving them by barge to the railroad.[8]

Solicitation remained an important element in the generation of traffic, but salesmen increasingly were urged to study the needs of shippers and to be prepared to deliver a full package of transportation to them. Pricing was crucial. The GN and all other rail carriers depended, however, on the ICC for the general level of tariffs. Reacting to the rise in labor and other costs, the ICC granted five increases between 1952 and 1958, and a small boost in 1960. For the next seven years, though, the commission held the line on rates, assuming that further raises would diminish volume. At long last, the ICC—admitting that railroad

wages had gone up 27 percent since 1960—granted a general increase in 1967; the amount was 3 percent. Additional increases of 3, 2, and 6 percent came in 1968 and 1969, as the carriers and the ICC sought to adjust to spiraling inflation.[9]

Nevertheless, rates set by the ICC were points of departure for a multitude of specific reductions. One of the most knowledgeable ratemakers in the industry, Vincent Brown, performed this delicate task for the GN, assuming that federal regulation left the railroads substantial flexibility. Brown argued that it was necessary to lower tariffs to meet modal competition, to ensure continued market competition, and to help develop new or expanding industries. In 1958 rates for alumina from Gulf Coast ports to the Pacific Northwest were reduced to encourage the aluminum industry in Montana and Washington. The company also substantially reduced rates on Wenatchee apples so that growers could dispose of a large crop in eastern markets. Similarly, cuts during the 1960s enabled tinplate producers in the East to sell their product in the Pacific Northwest.

Modal competition naturally inspired most reductions. As an example, competition by barge, pipeline, and truck forced cuts in moving light petroleum products from refineries in Wyoming and Montana to points in central Washington. Later, when salesmen found that ships were carrying more newsprint, the GN reduced rates on that commodity from British Columbia to California. Truck competition for various products remained the most difficult to counter. Only a few examples, representative of a larger number, can be cited here. In 1954, lowered rates on Wenatchee apples bound for the Midwest protected the company's long haul of that commodity, and in the

next year other rates were lowered. These reductions included refined sugar from Minnesota, potatoes from the Red River Valley, and farm tractors from assembly plants in Illinois and Wisconsin.

Some downward adjustments had indirect or dual purposes, especially those affecting two-way traffic. In 1954, rates on fresh fruit moving from California to Washington were cut to reduce the number of trucks available for hauling Wenatchee apples on the return trip. Similarly, in 1961, rates were lowered on bagged cement from Duluth–Superior and the Twin Cities to destinations within a 300-mile radius to ensure movement of cement by rail and to discourage truckers who might cut into the GN's wheat traffic. Rates were lowered too on fresh meats and other refrigerated products moving from the Midwest to the North Pacific Coast, where the company needed refrigerated cars to handle Wenatchee apples moving east.

Although management felt that these and other reductions were necessary to preserve traffic, clearly the company could not continue to cut charges indefinitely. "Rate adjustments without cost reduction," said one spokesman, "can only lead to disaster." Although the GN did not flatly reject rate revisions in the 1960s, it did attempt to couple them with changes in operating procedures that would reduce the cost of providing service.[10]

The company tried several ways of cutting costs. Some rates were lowered contingent on an annual minimum volume—an arrangement that better utilized rolling stock. Shippers who could move commodities in multiple-car lots also received reduced rates, for terminal costs were lower. Heavier loading of cars further lowered rates, as did use of unit trains. Iron ore moved to Granite City, Illinois, went at a rate 32 percent below the standard.

Average revenue per ton mile usually paralleled trends in rates, despite fluctuating proportions of high- and low-rated goods. As ICC-authorized tariff increases went into effect during the 1950s, average revenue per ton mile moved irregularly upward from 1.195 cents in 1951 to an all-time high of 1.465 cents in 1958, a 23 percent increase in seven years. This rise was followed by a decline. Slight general increases in rates granted in 1958 and 1960 did not offset special reductions, and the average revenue per ton mile fell further in the 1960s. In 1969, the revenue was 1.368 cents, only 14 percent above the 1951 figure.

A New Marketing Structure

By 1966, top management was convinced that the Great Northern's future did not appear "very bright because inevitable forces of higher costs and keener competition" restricted its earning capacity. The GN engaged an independent consulting firm for an outside assessment. These experts essentially confirmed the internal study. The company's basic business and traffic patterns, they calculated, could not be expected to change. "No matter how you look at it," said the consultants, "those who believed that Great Northern need only wait for more business . . . will have a very long wait indeed." To improve its position, the company would "have to do a better job at what it's been doing all along." They recommended that the GN expand its commitment to new equipment, particularly in easier-to-load and higher-capacity rolling stock, and try still harder to meet individual customers' specific needs, paying special attention to the place of transportation expenses in their distribution costs.[11]

Table 13. Traffic on Great Northern Railway, 1951–1969

(000 omitted)

	Freight				Passengers	
	Total tons	*Tons iron ore*	*Tons exclusive of iron ore*	*Net ton miles*	*Number carried*	*Carried one mile*
1951	62,979	33,538	29,441	18,041,425	1,707	589,519
1952	59,442	30,069	29,373	17,518,226	1,741	612,030
1953	66,335	36,876	29,459	18,586,111	1,580	558,784
1954	53,797	23,869	29,928	17,255,531	1,463	497,173
1955	66,769	36,449	30,320	19,056,847	1,486	508,634
1956	63,524	31,624	31,900	19,443,847	1,383	476,432
1957	60,456	29,701	30,755	17,677,654	1,288	450,061
1958	44,038	16,251	27,787	15,284,452	1,252	433,508
1959	41,077	12,570	28,507	15,666,564	1,249	435,185
1960	48,060	19,923	28,137	15,839,450	1,122	409,356
1961	44,097	16,865	27,232	15,099,590	1,078	432,010
1962	43,981	16,068	27,893	16,137,419	1,122	502,782
1963	44,593	16,438	28,155	16,761,747	1,026	411,971
1964	47,044[a]	16,855	30,189	17,192,710	1,072	422,553
1965	49,167	17,499	31,668	18,424,713	1,102	424,383
1966	49,744	16,278	33,466	19,342,186	1,150	435,996
1967	44,124	13,627	30,497	17,948,264	1,084	397,978
1968	44,823	14,695	30,128	18,087,083	953	350,531
1969	49,259	16,732	32,527	19,143,418	822	329,828

a. In 1969 GNAR, SS, figure revised to 47,047; component data not given.

Sources: GNAR SS, 1951–1969; ARGN-ICC, 1951–1969.

These recommendations reinforced John Budd's consistent view that a precisely defined, customer-oriented approach was required. The traffic department thus was replaced with a marketing department in 1967. Budd's desire was to come up with an "aggressive, customer-oriented program" in which research, "market study, service innovation, operational changes, equipment acquisition and planning and pricing policies" were coordinated and "focused imaginatively on a common target."[12]

In this new structure each market manager was responsible for ten to fifteen large shippers in the same commodity group. These positions reflected Budd's recognition that, even though the GN dealt with 37,000 freight customers in a year, the top one hundred shippers provided 76 percent of freight revenues. Market managers, given authority to deal with and coordinate the railroad's relationship with these major shippers, were expected to be decision makers and to know as much about the customers' businesses as the customers themselves.

Pricing was assigned to new offices — pricing analysis and pricing services. The former was responsible for system analysis of rates on all commodities except grain, the latter for the more technical work of producing tariffs and handling division of rates. Collectively, these offices considered and reached decisions on all rate proposals. Because of its importance, grain was handled by special sections in both analysis and pricing. The new arrangement was expected to provide expert support for the overall marketing program, emphasize sound, thorough analysis of rate questions, and produce decisions promptly.

Other innovations included a market-research office and extensive changes in the

Table 14. Employment Data, Great Northern Railway Company, 1951–1969

Year	Employees average number (midmonth count)	Average earnings per employee year	Average total compensation[a] per hour worked	Total compensation,[b] % of railway operating expense	Productivity (traffic units[c] per dollar labor cost)
1951	29,907	$4,085	$1.97	63.8%	143
1952	29,157	4,366	2.07	63.5	*
1953	28,606	4,428	2.13	62.8	*
1954	26,970	4,566	2.22	63.6	*
1955	26,782	4,712	2.29	63.9	*
1956	26,399	5,138	2.48	62.9	*
1957	24,968	5,462	2.66	63.0	*
1958	20,931	5,884	2.91	62.7	*
1959	20,539	6,095	3.03	61.1	*
1960	19,863	6,240	3.11	61.3	119
1961	18,619	6,299	3.20	61.0	118
1962	18,128	6,508	3.30	61.2	126
1963	17,439	6,614	3.34	59.9	133
1964	17,003	6,932	3.42	58.8	132
1965	16,655	7,366	3.67	59.8	135
1966	16,797	7,495	3.76	58.6	136
1967	16,517	7,880	4.01	59.4	122
1968	15,913	8,320	4.22	59.3	119
1969	15,776	8,953	4.50	56.1	119

*Data not readily available.
a. Including fringe benefits.
b. Chargeable to railway operating expense.
c. Traffic units are net ton miles plus passenger miles.

Sources: GNAR and GNAR-SS, 1951–1969.

company's development organizations. The director of market research was charged with supplying other marketing-department units with detailed statistical data that their personnel needed to perform assigned tasks. In addition, industrial development, mineral promotion activities, and a new office of industrial research were combined under one head for better coordination among all departments for locating industries.

Performance: A Mixed Record

Despite cyclical fluctuations and growing competition from trucks, the Great Northern performed well in attracting tonnage from 1951 through 1969. (See Table 13.) Only assiduous and continuous work achieved this success. The company lost iron-ore tonnage, because deposits of red ore were depleted but the loss was partly offset by developing merchantable taconite. Programs to develop long-term growth clearly increased tonnage of grain, chemicals, fertilizers, sugar beets and sugar, and alumina and aluminum. Favorable rates and new equipment helped generate larger shipments of automobiles and trucks, and declining tonnage of canned foods was offset by increases in frozen foods, reflecting changes in food packaging and the GN's providing advanced refrigerator cars. Gains were also scored in forest products. Long association with that increasingly integrated Pacific Northwest industry, advantageous location, and effective marketing all contributed to the GN's rapidly growing movement of pulpwood, wood pulp, fiberboard, newsprint, and other paper products. Meanwhile, the company maintained its competitive position in lumber and plywood.

Laboring to maintain or even expand its

market portion, Budd's team simultaneously sought to control or reduce the cost of providing transportation. But labor expenses were critical. Although employees were reduced from 29,907 in 1951 to 15,776 in 1969, payment for labor, not counting payroll taxes, rose 16.2 percent. Over these nineteen years, average compensation per hour and earnings per employee per year more than doubled. (See Table 14.)

Between 1951 and 1969, the year-to-year changes in railway operating revenues roughly paralleled those of net ton miles, reflecting both annual variations and cyclical fluctuations in the economy. Each of the three peaks in revenue — 1956 ($280.5 million), 1966 ($281.8 million), and 1969 ($289.1 million) — was a new high for the company. Perhaps more significant, the low for the period, $233 million in 1961, was higher than in any comparable year prior to 1951. Moreover, revenues for the 1951–1969 period in almost every year substantially surpassed those of the Northern Pacific and the Milwaukee. Nevertheless, between 1951 and 1969, revenues rose less than 17 percent but expenditures increased 29 percent.

Although GN managers failed to hold down railway expenditures as much as they desired during these years, they did achieve an operating ratio that compared favorably with those of the company's competitors, if not with its own past. For most years railway operating expenditures averaged less than 76 percent of operating revenues; those of the Northern Pacific and the Milwaukee were around 82 percent. In the last years of the 1960s, however, the GN's operating ratio also went over 80.

From 1951 to 1969, net railway operating income, affected by so many variables, fluctuated widely. A rise of 31 percent from the

$23.2 million of 1951 to 1956 was followed by a 44.7 percent drop to 1961. Then a 96.4 percent climb to 1965 brought the figure to the peak for the period, $33 million. (See Table 15.) From that date forward, the GN's net railway operating income was below the average for the decade.

The company's nonoperating income did grow significantly, with only minor fluctuations, during John Budd's presidency, a welcome contribution to total income. Although amounts for other components also increased, this expansion was primarily attributable to increased dividends and interest income. The only sizable new investments during Budd's presidency were in shares of the Pacific Coast Railroad Company ($1,700,000), Portal Pipe Line Company ($900,000), Trailer Train Company ($123,395), and Western Pacific Railroad Company ($4,390,837). Dividends from long-owned Burlington stock and interest income from short-term investment of surplus funds were notable.

During these two decades the interest on funded debt was relatively stable, falling and rising in a narrow range from $7.9 million in 1952 to a high of $9.8 million in 1969. Interest charges were affected by two changes, the size of the debt and an increase in interest rates. The bonded debt was reduced by $36.7 million by retirement of outstanding bonds, but equipment trusts rose with acquisition of new equipment, and on such debt, the average interest increased from $2\frac{4}{5}$ percent in the early 1950s to $4\frac{1}{2}$ percent in later years, with a range from $3\frac{3}{8}$ percent to $7\frac{1}{2}$ percent.

The Great Northern's debt, however, was manageable. Even after the new equipment trusts of 1969, the total funded debt of $255.4 million was $20.1 million less than that of 1951. Only six series of bonds, totaling

Table 15. Income Account of Great Northern Railway Company, 1951–1969 *(In Millions)*

	Railway operating revenues	Railway operating expenditures	Net revenue from railway operations	Railway tax accruals[a]	Net railway operating income[b]	Other income[a]	Total income	Fixed charges and misc. deductions	Net income
1951	$248.0	$184.2	$ 63.8	$ 36.9	$ 23.2	$ 9.4	$ 32.6	$ 8.6	$ 24.0
1952	260.2	191.4	68.8	38.1	25.9	10.1	36.0	8.3	27.7
1953	268.0	194.9	73.1	39.6	27.5	10.9	36.4	8.5	29.9
1954	250.2	188.6	61.6	30.4	24.2	9.8	34.0	8.6	25.4
1955	267.1	194.4	72.7	37.8	30.2	10.3	40.5	8.4	32.1
1956	280.5	209.4	71.1	35.9	30.4	10.3	40.7	8.5	32.2
1957	275.4	212.2	63.2	33.4	24.9	10.5	35.4	8.7	26.7
1958	251.7	190.9	60.8	32.4	25.8	11.0	36.8	9.2	27.6
1959	254.6	197.1	57.5	29.9	24.2	11.3	35.5	8.9	26.6
1960	246.0	194.0	52.0	28.7	18.4	11.5	29.9	9.2	20.7
1961	233.0	185.1	47.9	27.7	16.8	10.9	27.7	9.1	18.6
1962	238.9	187.8	51.1	25.7	23.2	11.0	34.2	9.2	25.0
1963	242.8	186.4	56.4	26.4	27.0	11.5	38.5	9.2	29.3
1964	250.4	195.0	55.4	25.8	25.5	12.3	37.8	8.9	28.9
1965	265.6	200.7	64.9	28.7	33.0	13.3	46.3	9.4	36.9
1966	281.8	207.9	73.9	37.3	32.3	14.3	46.6	10.1	36.5
1967	260.2	212.8	47.4	27.5	15.6	13.9	29.5	10.2	19.3
1968	266.3	217.3	49.0	26.6	20.6	13.4	34.0	12.2	21.8
1969	289.1	237.7	51.4	30.1	19.3	15.3	34.6	11.2	23.4[c]

a. For greater detail on Tax accruals, Other income, and Fixed charges, see Table 17.
b. Net railway operating income is the remainder after deducting from Net revenue from railway operations, not only railway tax accruals, but also rentals for equipment and joint facilities, which are not listed in this table.
c. This figure of $23.4 million was prior to deduction of $12.9 million for costs incurred during arrangements for merger of GN into Burlington Northern, Inc., in 1970.

Sources: GNAR-SS, 1951–1969.

"No Sacred Cows—or Goats"

Table 16. Details on Tax Accruals, Other Income, and Fixed Charges, Great Northern Railway Company, 1951–1969 *(In Millions)*

| | Railway tax accruals | | | | | Other income | | | | Fixed charges | | |
	Federal income	Payroll	All other	Total	Dividends	Interest earned	All other[a]	Total	Interest on funded debt	All other[b]	Total
1951	$17.9	$ 6.7	$12.3	$36.9	$5.8	$2.9	$0.7	$ 9.4	$8.1	$0.1	$8.2
1952	18.7	6.9	12.5	38.1	6.5	2.6	1.0	10.1	7.9	0.1	8.0
1953	20.4	6.9	12.3	39.6	6.3	3.5	1.1	10.9	7.9	0.2	8.1
1954	11.1	6.9	12.4	30.4	6.4	2.2	1.2	9.8	8.0	0.1	8.1
1955	17.5	7.3	13.0	37.8	6.8	2.1	1.4	10.3	8.0	0.1	8.1
1956	14.1	8.6	13.2	35.9	6.4	2.3	1.6	10.3	7.9	0.1	8.0
1957	10.7	8.9	13.8	33.4	6.3	2.4	1.8	10.5	8.0	0.1	8.1
1958	11.4	8.0	13.0	32.4	6.4	2.2	2.4	11.0	8.2	0.1	8.3
1959	7.8	9.7	12.4	29.9	6.3	2.6	2.4	11.3	8.3	0.1	8.4
1960	5.9	10.1	12.7	28.7	6.3	2.9	2.3	11.5	8.3	0.2	8.5
1961	5.8	9.5	12.4	27.7	6.8	2.2	1.9	10.9	8.0	0.2	8.2
1962	3.8	9.9	12.0	25.7	6.9	2.1	2.0	11.0	7.8	0.2	8.0
1963	5.0	9.6	11.8	26.4	6.9	2.5	2.1	11.5	7.8	0.2	8.0
1964	4.2	10.1	11.5	25.8	7.1	3.1	2.1	12.3	8.0	0.1	8.1
1965	5.8	10.6	12.3	28.7	6.9	4.4	2.0	13.3	8.3	0.2	8.5
1966	12.7	12.0	12.6	37.3	7.4	4.9	2.0	14.3	8.7	0.2	8.9
1967	1.9	13.3	12.3	27.5	6.9	4.6	2.4	13.9	9.0	0.2	9.2
1968	1.2	14.1	11.3	26.6	7.1	4.0	2.3	13.4	9.6	0.2	9.8
1969	3.2	14.9	12.0	30.1	7.4	4.6	3.3	15.3	9.8	0.2	10.0

a. All other income includes rents received, income from nonoperating properties, profits from separately operated properties, income from sinking and other reserve funds, and receipts from miscellaneous unspecified sources.

b. Included in other fixed charges were several components. In 1958, 1967, 1968, and 1969, interest on unfunded debt ranged from $2,000 to $3,000. Rent on leased road equipment during the entire nineteen-year period amounted annually to between $1,000 and $4,000. Amortization of discount on funded debt throughout the period ranged between $100,000 and $200,000.

Sources: GNAR-SS, 1951–1969.

$178.7 million, remained outstanding. Maturity dates were spaced and spread over the years 1973 to 2010, with no more than a maximum of $40 million due at any one time. Savings in interest over many years had been substantial, and continued so.

Total net income, after deducting fixed charges, was characterized by marked fluctuations. It rose 34.2 percent from 1951 to 1956, then fell 42.2 percent between 1956 and 1961. The average annual net income for 1962–1969 was more than $3.5 million above that for the depressed period 1957–1961. Net income per share ranged from a low of $3.07 in 1961 to a high of $6.01 four years later.

In 1954, a year of good income, directors determined to make several changes in the company's stock. The charter empowered issuance of both common and preferred stock, but only preferred had been issued, although it was treated as common. Now the preferred was converted to common, and each share split into two, increasing the number from 3 to 6 million. The market price per share dropped less than 50 percent. Before the split the low and high for the first half of 1954 had been 45⅝ and 59⅝, and for the second half of the year the comparable figures were 27 and 38½. The company's credit was sound and stockholder's interest was stimulated.

In allocating retained income, the GN also changed the dividend rate. From 1951 to 1953 it was $2, then raised gradually to $3 in 1957, the amount paid annually for thirteen years. Meanwhile, the number of stockholders climbed from 32,387 in 1951 to a high of 45,014 in 1965, followed by a slight decline.

Despite a generally positive record, Budd and his fellows were not satisfied with the company's performance as measured by several widely accepted indexes. The ratio of total

Table 17. Great Northern Railway—Various Statistical Data, 1951–1969

	Number of times fixed charges earned[a]	Return on property investment	Net income per share	Dividend per share[b]
1951	3.92	3.6	$3.91	$2.00
1952	4.48	4.0	4.55	2.00
1953	4.71	4.1	4.92	2.00
1954	4.14	3.6	4.21	2.10
1955	4.95	4.4	5.27	2.35
1956	5.00	4.3	5.32	2.63
1957	4.27	3.5	4.38	3.00
1958	4.31	3.7	4.52	3.00
1959	4.16	3.5	4.35	3.00
1960	3.44	2.6	3.41	3.00
1961	3.29	2.4	3.07	3.00
1962	4.13	3.4	4.12	3.00
1963	4.68	4.0	4.80	3.00
1964	4.55	3.7	4.71	3.00
1965	5.36	4.7	6.01	3.00
1966	5.12	4.5	5.94	3.00
1967	3.11	2.1	3.14	3.00
1968	3.22	2.7	3.54	3.00
1969	3.35	2.6	1.71[c]	3.00

a. The figures for calculating this column were taken after deducting federal income taxes.
b. The entries for 1951–1954 are adjusted to make them comparable to those after the stock split in 1954.
c. This figure would have been $3.80 without the extraordinary charge against net income in 1969.

Sources: GNAR and GNAR-SS, 1951–1969.

"No Sacred Cows—or Goats"

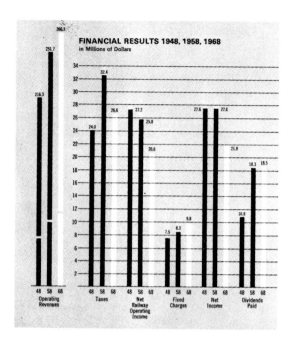

FINANCIAL RESULTS 1948, 1958, 1968
in Millions of Dollars

income to fixed charges reached 5 or more only three years out of the nineteen from 1951 to 1969, and in no year was the return on property investment as much as 5 percent. In fact, the rate exceeded 4 percent in only five years. These results, however, were neither the highest nor the lowest in the railroad industry, one of the lowest earners in the American economy at that time. (See Table 17.)

John Budd could take pride in the Great Northern's general performance from 1951 through 1969, and he could afford to be at least cautiously optimistic about the property's potential for the future. The company was physically stronger than when he had taken office in 1951, he had diligently pursued the GN's historic pattern, upgrading plant to gain operating efficiencies, he had pared passenger offerings as loadings decreased and mail and

express business faltered, he had improved freight service and forged a modern marketing approach, and he had moved the company into the computer era. Moreover, the GN had a stable of powerful diesel locomotives, a fleet of modern freight cars, and an enviable physical plant. All this achievement was required, Budd commented, to keep the GN from "running to stand still." The fly in the ointment was that the GN required a strong increase in traffic. Yet, on its own, prospects for that improvement appeared elusive in the extreme. Merger with strong rail partners, on the other hand, might be just the right prescription.[13]

35

The Last Spike is Never Driven

The Great Northern Railway's performance during the 1950s was modestly satisfactory, but as they looked to the future, senior officers came to believe that the Great Northern, the Northern Pacific, and the properties they owned cooperatively must be unified if all were to prosper. The idea, of course, was not new. James J. Hill had worked to that end early in the century, only to be defeated by popular opinion and the courts. Hill's successors had tried again two decades later, but conditions attached by the Interstate Commerce Commission were intolerable and combination failed again. John Budd understood, however, that much had changed since the last attempt. Indeed, the railroad industry after the war was faced with monumental difficulties, a fact gradually perceived by the public and by elected representatives. Budd thus determined to try again, but the path would prove serpentine.[1]

Budd was not alone among industry leaders in advocating mergers. The continued growth of modal competition, the resultant erosion of rail traffic, and the low return on investment all pointed to serious financial problems for the country's railroads. Technological im-

294

provements such as conversion to diesel were useful, but wage rates and other costs were rising, and much of the industry was piled high with deferred maintenance. An intense squeeze on earnings was inevitable. In view of that, many industry leaders considered consolidation essential in order to improve operations, reduce costs, and make reasonable profits.

Fortunately, the political climate in the 1950s was more favorable for achieving combinations than it had been for many years. The Transportation Act of 1940 had authorized the ICC to examine individual proposals for consolidation and to approve those consistent with the public interest. In evaluating any proposed merger, the commission was to assess the weight of fixed charges for the new company, the effects of such combination on the public's transportation needs, and the impact of inclusions or exclusions on other railroads. The ICC was also to attempt to ensure that jobs would not be adversely touched. Unifications were to be judged against antitrust laws, but the railroads had only to show that a merger was not harmful; that is, they might balance anticipated advantages against disruptions caused by curtailed competition.

Railroad leaders tarried, however. Initially they were occupied by the tremendous volume of traffic accompanying World War II, and then by the need to restore physical plant and to convert from steam to diesel. Except for the Gulf, Mobile & Ohio Railroad created in 1947, industry leaders gave little attention to the possibilities of combination until the squeeze between rising costs and lagging rates grew extreme.

The new consolidation movement got under way in 1955 when the Louisville & Nashville Railroad asked the ICC for consent to merge with its affiliate, the Nashville, Chattanooga & St. Louis Railroad. After two years of preliminaries, the commission approved this request. Also, after hearings, Congress urged railroads to use their own initiative in recommending mergers. A surge of applications ensued, gradually picking up momentum.

In the West, interest was focused on the tiny but potentially important Western Pacific Railroad. The much larger Southern Pacific perceived that improved transportation service would derive from economies and efficiencies should it be allowed to acquire the WP. After all, the two served a common territory from northern California into Utah. Consequently, the SP purchased a 10 percent interest in the WP and asked the Interstate Commerce Commission for permission to issue additional common stock to exchange share for share with owners of WP. Exceptions were instant and vigorous. The Great Northern was joined by the Santa Fe in leading the charge.[2]

John Budd was caught in a dilemma familiar to railroad leaders: he wanted the merger movement to prosper, but he was obliged to protect his company's parochial interests. At issue, of course, was the "Inside Gateway" — serving the respective interests of the Great Northern, Western Pacific, and Santa Fe. As Budd reminded his board of directors, the GN was locked in bitter rivalry with the SP for traffic moving to and from the Pacific Northwest and Southern California. Should the SP win, the larger road was certain to favor its own single-line route, damaging the tripartite arrangement via Bieber. The board saw it likewise, and authorized Director Grant Keehn and Vice President Robert W. Downing to acquire in the GN's name a 10 percent block of WP. The mood was much the same at Santa

Fe, which quickly purchased 20 percent of WP's common and at Union Pacific, which also acquired 10 percent. An acrimonious struggle followed and, in the end, the ICC directed that the Western Pacific remain independent. Budd breathed easier — the Inside Gateway had been protected. More important, the general merger movement appeared unimpaired by the WP case.[3]

The Northern Lines — Again

Against this mixed but generally favorable climate, Great Northern officers reviewed their company's long-range strategic situation. John Budd firmly believed that the Great Northern and Northern Pacific with their shared affiliates (Chicago, Burlington & Quincy Railroad and the Spokane, Portland & Seattle Railway), were prime candidates for successful combination. Budd contended, further, that the ICC's insistence upon excluding the CB&Q from the proposed merger in the 1920s would no longer be a factor. Moreover, in many ways, the GN and the NP were complementary instead of competitive. Their main lines across North Dakota, Montana, and Washington were widely separated; the GN was particularly potent on its eastern lines, which originated heavy grain and iron-ore shipments, and the NP was especially strong in the West, with growing lumber traffic. From the start, merger between the northern lines was planned as a combining of equals.

After preliminary talks in 1955, John Budd and NP president Robert S. MacFarlane took up the question of merger with their boards of directors. Formal action was taken by the GN's board January 20, 1956, when it adopted a resolution providing for an exploratory study. It also established a special consolidation committee of five members, chaired by the president, to act with a similar body from the NP; these formed the Joint Committee on Consolidation.

At the first meeting of the Joint Committee on April 9, 1956, its members decided to separate economic from legal and corporate matters. Analysis of the latter, particularly the roads' mortgages, required extensive work, which was delegated to the outside New York counsel of each railroad, in conjunction with the respective general counsels in St. Paul, Anthony Kane of the GN and M. L. Countryman of the NP.

The engineering and economic facets of consolidation were to be explored by an independent consulting firm, which would work with both railroads. On August 20, 1956, William Wyer & Company (later Wyer, Dick & Company) was engaged. Members of this firm, experts on railroad matters, would help to resolve conflicting GN and NP opinions. Furthermore, if these consultants favored merger, their objectivity would assure fiduciaries and security analysts that the move was sound. In September, a steering committee was set up, including William Wyer, his deputy Corwin E. Dick, Robert W. Downing of the GN, and Douglas H. Shoemaker of the NP. This group was responsible for directing work utilizing, as much as possible, experienced personnel from the GN and NP and, to a lesser extent, the CB&Q and the SP&S.

Help was required in other matters. Each of the two companies selected an investment banker to prepare and support plans for financial negotiation. The GN engaged the First Boston Corporation and the NP employed Morgan, Stanley & Company of New York.

To help in evaluating the NP's natural resources, the GN employed experts in timber, oil, and gas, and the NP's regular consultants prepared their own estimates.

On December 1, 1957, Wyer, Dick & Company issued a report favoring combination. In their judgment, unification would result in an annual net gain, before taxes, of $40.7 million within five years. The full GN board met January 17, 1958, to approve the special committee's recommendation to undertake negotiations with the NP. Pending completion of the NP's own study of its resources, however, the GN did not immediately propose terms.

Establishing the value of each property was an especially challenging task. The GN had the better of it in railroad properties, with 1,500 more miles of line and a shorter and more efficient transcontinental route with lower grades and better alignment. The GN also had a more favorable history of earnings, dividends, and market price on stock; its revenues were higher, and its funded debt and fixed charges were substantially lower than those of the NP. On the other hand, some of the NP's lines were particularly attractive, and its nonrail assets — 2.5 million acres of timber lands and massive mineral rights — were extremely impressive. Indeed, the NP's income from natural resources had surged when oil was discovered in the Williston Basin of North Dakota and returns from timber resources grew.

One difficulty was uppermost: How should the northern companies' stock be exchanged for that of the new company? At a Joint Committee meeting on May 27, 1959, several proposals were considered, but no solution was in sight; impasse resulted.

Because the major problem was estimating the future earning power of the NP's natural resources, legal counsel was asked to explore the possibility of spinning off those assets to NP stockholders prior to merger. Counsel advised, however, that because of restrictions in the NP's mortgage, such handling of land-grant properties was not possible without an order from the courts. The suggestion perished.

During the latter part of 1959 and early in 1960 agreement seemed doubtful. Several options for exchanging stock were considered but all were rejected, and on January 12, 1960, NP officers suggested waiting two or three years and then reconsidering prospects. Directors of both companies disagreed, contending that delay would be a bad mistake.

An accommodation was finally struck on June 2, 1960, when Budd and MacFarlane agreed to general principles. Since the number of shares in the two companies was about equal, holders would exchange old for new on a share-for-share basis. In addition, GN stockholders were to receive, for each GN share, a half share of nonvoting and nonconvertible preferred stock, bearing a 5½ percent dividend and with a par value of $10. By this means GN stockholders would have a premium of about $31 million. Other essential terms were soon worked out and presented to the Joint Committee, which approved the plan effective July 13, 1960. The boards of the two roads followed suit shortly thereafter.

Presidents of the GN and the NP and chief counsels of each company agreed the case would have to be presented by an experienced law firm with an able staff and large resources. They selected Sidney, Austin, Burgess & Smith, one of whose senior partners, Kenneth F. Burgess, was an authority on railroad law and had been general solicitor and later a director of the CB&Q. Burgess died in 1965 and was succeeded in direct charge of the case by D. Robert Thomas, another senior partner.

The next step was to submit to the Interstate Commerce Commission an application for permission to merge the Great Northern, the Northern Pacific, and their affiliates into a system of about 27,000 miles of line in nineteen states and two Canadian provinces. Filed with the ICC on February 17, 1961, the formal document carried a cumbersome name for the new company: the Great Northern Pacific & Burlington Lines, Inc.

Meanwhile, stockholders of both northern companies approved the proposed combination. Despite criticism of terms by the Northern Pacific Stockholders Protective Association at a Northern Pacific stockholders' meeting on April 26, 1961, only 6.6 percent of the stock represented was voted against consolidation, and 73.8 percent of the stock was voted in favor. At the GN stockholders' annual meeting on May 11, 1961, the vote was 81 percent for the consolidation and less than 1 percent against.

Beginning in St. Paul during October 1961, ICC hearings extended over many months throughout the railroads' wide service area. Robert H. Murphy, the examiner, heard views expressed by 623 witnesses during eighty-two days of testimony, all of it assembled in 15,000 pages of transcript and 243 exhibits.

Justification for the merger, proponents argued, clearly overshadowed any possible objection. Building and improving on the community of interest shared by the applicant lines for more than sixty years, the new company would provide faster and better service for shippers. The GN's Robert W. Downing said that the merged companies would "utilize

those routes which are productive of the most efficient and economical operations." After combination, the main transcontinental freight line — the best parts of the GN and NP system — would be shorter, with lower grades and less curvature than either predecessor company could offer alone. Furthermore, one-carrier service would result in economies — fewer interchanges, shorter routes, better-balanced traffic flow, and unified handling of LCL shipments — that would improve the supply of cars, provide better transit times, and facilitate diversion privileges. The new company would also retain passenger service so long as "public patronage in sufficient volume" made that possible. Finally, the merged company's size and financial strength, combined with savings

John M. Budd, seated at left, was joined by subordinates (Robert W. Downing, Anthony Kane, Clark A. Eckart, John L. Robson, Thomas A. DeButts, Malachy M. Scanlan, Richard M. O'Kelly, and John A. Tauer) in planning for the gigantic merger.

in operations, would enable it to raise capital more easily.[4]

Supporters maintained that the proposed merger would cause no significant decline in competition, nor would it harm individuals or communities. Some 92 percent of the shared communities on the applicants' lines also were served by other railroads as well as modal competitors, and a stronger consolidated company could offer more vigorous rivalry for opponents while strengthening the position, in distant markets, of northwestern producers. Estimates indicated that the merged company would require about 8 percent fewer workers, but this number would be accounted for by normal turnover. Furthermore, provisions were being made to protect those workers who had to be relocated. Proponents pointed out that the merger met legal requirements of the Transportation Act of 1940, and, because a strong majority of Northwest shippers favored it, consolidation obviously suited the public interest.

A majority of witnesses supported the merger, but a vociferous minority opposed it. Maintaining that the proposed merger would greatly damage their roads, representatives of the Milwaukee and of the Chicago & North Western requested conditions that the northern lines considered unreasonable. Spokesmen for the Milwaukee contended that their company would lose $6.5 million in revenues, unless numerous conditions were imposed. The C&NW fixed its potential losses at more than $4 million annually and listed several demands that its management deemed essential.

Objections by these railroads were mild compared with those of labor. Spokesmen for unions strongly opposed the plan from the start, arguing that merger would lead to great loss of jobs. Union leaders questioned potential savings and held that even if such economies were possible, the threatened monopoly and widespread employee distress were prices too high to pay. According to Leon Keyserling, an economist who testified on behalf of labor, the merger would not forward the national interest, requirements of a growing economy, the workers' fair interest or preservation of competition. Instead it promised only the savings of ''some millions of dollars for . . . stockholders by rendering more efficient service narrowly conceived.''[5]

Spokesmen for opposing state regulatory agencies and local communities presented many arguments, but with common themes. They maintained that merger inevitably would mean jobs lost and that as facilities and services were downgraded or shifted, the railroad's role at some places would be lessened. They further predicted loss in tax revenues and a blow to local and state economies. Most important, those who testified for states and local communities contended that rail competition was beneficial and should not be reduced.

In opposing the merger, spokesmen for two federal departments feared its monopolistic aspects. Representatives of the Department of Agriculture stated that, although not opposed to consolidation in general, they viewed with disfavor the possible decline in railroad competition in the Northwest. Inspired in part by the Minnesota Public Service Commission, the Attorney General of the United States, Robert F. Kennedy, asserted that merging the northern lines was inconsistent with relevant sections of the Interstate Commerce Act. Combination would create a rail monopoly in the Northwest that would adversely affect other railroads, shippers, communities, some federal establishments, and perhaps even national defense. It was not, said Kennedy, in the public interest.

Those fears and complaints notwithstanding, on August 24, 1964, two years after the hearings were concluded, Examiner Murphy recommended that the GN, NP, and their affiliates consolidate. Unification, he found, fully accorded with requirements stipulated in the Transportation Act of 1940, and with guidelines laid down by the ICC in approving other recent mergers. After estimating annual savings in operations of $39.9 million following merger, Murphy wrote: ''The proposed unification will promote public interest by en-

abling the new company to provide more economical and efficient service. . . . The . . . proposal is entirely sound in principle, and is entitled to serious consideration as a step toward ultimately reducing the cost of transportation.'' At the same time, he considered that the merger would not materially lessen competition, nor would it work a hardship on labor. Moreover, consolidation was justified by the northern lines' clearly deteriorating competitive position since 1945. That trend, Murphy believed, would continue with adverse effect on all parties unless the carriers were permitted to help themselves by unification. ''Efficiency and economy are essential to the survival of railroad common carriers as private enterprises in these years of increased competition from other modes of . . . transportation,'' he stated.[6]

To his approval, the examiner attached conditions designed to strengthen rail competition in the Northwest. The Milwaukee was to be allowed to operate over the merged company's lines into Portland, north from the Seattle area to the Canadian border; also, between the Twin Cities and Tacoma, eleven new gateways were to be opened to help the Milwaukee compete for longer hauls on interline traffic. For the C&NW, new gateways should be opened at Crawford, Nebraska, and Oakes, North Dakota. Moreover, to improve the Milwaukee's position, the consolidated company was to introduce equitable switching arrangements in the Twin Cities, and to help the C&NW, better interchange terms were recommended.

Murphy's report was greeted with varied reactions. Officials of the northern lines were pleased and the president of the Milwaukee expressed conditional acceptance. Labor leaders, however, denounced the report, labeling it ''another victory for monopoly interests.''

298

Some political leaders, notably Senator Mike Mansfield of Montana, strenuously objected. Urging the ICC to reject the merger, he asked the Senate antitrust committee to start hearings on a dangerous tendency toward monopoly through railway consolidation. The Department of Justice reiterated its contention that the marriage would violate both antitrust law and purposes of the Tranportation Act of 1940, and continued to declare that railroad mergers should be judged by standards set up for other industries, refusing to recognize any difference between these antitrust rules and those prescribed by railroad legislation. Formal exceptions to the examiner's report and replies to them were filed with the ICC early in 1965.[7]

After reviewing these arguments the Interstate Commerce Commission on April 27, 1966, announced its decision in a 6–5 vote. The majority of commissioners rejected Murphy's findings, and denied approval. As defined by the majority, the problem was to decide whether "the disadvantages of a substantial lessening of competition, coupled with the adverse effects on the carrier employees, outweigh the advantage that would be derived by applicants and the shipping public." The majority of commissioners saw nothing in the applicants' financial health requiring merger, and asserted that both the railroads and the examiner had overestimated economies that might accrue with unification. The proposed merger, the majority concluded, would harm labor and substantially reduce competition in the Northwest. Accordingly, they said, the merger was not "consistent with the public interest."[8]

Even as GN managers planned for merger, they prepared for the possible need to go it alone. Welded rail promised greater efficiency as well as a smoother ride for passengers and freight.

All five of the ICC's dissenting commissioners registered opinions critical of the majority decision. They accused the six of misapplying the law, of ignoring the 1940 legal changes that were designed to facilitate such proposed mergers, and of failing to stand for an enlightened transportation policy. Wedded to a theory of competition based on nineteenth-century conditions, opponents of the merger failed to recognize how intense modal competition had grown. A suitably conditioned merger, the minority contended, would have shown that the ICC was willing to permit the companies to exercise managerial initiative and to support moves that would help establish a national transportation system.

With the possible exception of the recent Western Pacific case, disapproval of this application was the first setback in the general merger movement of the 1960s. The commission's rationale was difficult to understand because on the day it rejected the northern lines' application it approved the Pennsylvania and the New York Central railroads' unification. Perhaps the majority among the commissioners were influenced by the relatively sound financial health of GN, NP, and the CB&Q, which were generally regarded as large, strong, and prosperous railroads. And, aware of the growing complexity in the consolidation movement among western railroads, the majority may have chosen to delay further until the picture was clearer.

As always, GN managers looked for ways to reduce grades and curvature in order to make the company's profile more efficient. One example was the $8-million line change near Index, Washington. Here new U33C locomotives lift an eastbound freight over a new bridge on a 1.1% grade.

Continuing the Campaign

Whatever the reason or reasons for the ICC's decision, Great Northern and Northern Pacific managers now had to choose among three options. They could give up, turn to the courts, or ask the ICC to reconsider. On July 27, 1966, they chose the latter. Competition did not let up, and other roads were proposing mergers, leading the GN and the NP to consider their own marriage imperative. Even if they fully satisfied demands by the Milwaukee Road and the C&NW, savings from combination would still be larger than the ICC's estimates. Furthermore, the GN and the NP had signed contracts with several unions to protect jobs after combination, and they were arranging other agreements that would bring job security to current workers.

Nonetheless, when the company announced that it would appeal the ICC's decision, adverse reaction set in. Minnesota Governor Karl F. Rolvaag denounced the companies, contending that "every merger has resulted in grave unemployment problems for railway workers. . . ." St. Paul Mayor Thomas Byrne branded the possibility "a threat to the economic life of the city." For a time some unions remained unreconciled; Chairman Robert M. Curran of the Brotherhood of Railway Clerks maintained that any guarantees management might give to labor were "meaningless and deceptive" and that widespread hardship would follow merger.[9]

Criticism of the merger continued, and opposition spread. Protective agreements signed with several unions undermined the credibility of critics such as Rolvaag, Byrne, and Curran, and placated by voluntary settlements worked out with the GN and the NP, the Milwaukee and the C&NW became at least lukewarm advocates. A number of state regulatory agencies

withdrew their opposition, and some agreed to support the proposed unification. The United States Department of Agriculture then announced that it no longer opposed consolidation.

Against this opposition, the ICC could do no other than reconsider. In January 1967, when hearings were reopened, advocates and their opponents restated their positions, and again the ICC balanced savings arising from combination against possible damage to other carriers, to employees, and to the public. Now, however, the ICC estimated that annual operating savings could be $39.7 million, an amount nearly matching the $43.2 million forecast in the application. Concessions made to the Milwaukee and the C&NW would strengthen both of those rivals, and at the same time, by giving better service to shippers, the consolidated company could offer stronger competition to highway, water, and air carriers. Finally, job security for employees covered in contracts, signed or promised, was deemed satisfactory, and standards for merger laid down in the Transportation Act of 1940 were met. Thus the Interstate Commerce Commission was obliged to reverse itself. On November 30, 1967, in an 8–2 decision, its members approved merger.

Despite the overwhelmingly favorable ICC vote, controversy continued. On the day that the new decision was announced, Senator Mansfield and seven fellows introduced a bill to strip the commission of authority to approve such consolidations and giving Congress three years to pass new legislation on railway unification. Senator Warren G. Magnuson of Washington, chairman of the Senate Commerce Committee, promised hearings on the question and expressed deep uneasiness for railroad labor. Spokesmen for the Denver &

Rio Grande Western Railway (D&RGW), which had appeared as plaintiff for the first time in the 1967 hearings, were unreconciled in their failure to influence the commission either to deny the merger or to exclude the CB&Q from it. The D&RGW now asked that the effective date of unification be delayed, that evidence be reheard, and that the commission reconsider. Jumping on the bandwagon, representatives of the Milwaukee, the Soo Line, and the Union Pacific asked for minor modifications in merger provisions. And the Northern Pacific Stockholders Protective Association reiterated its objections.[10]

Again bowing to pressure, the ICC in January 1968 postponed the effective date for merger and scheduled additional hearings. The GN and NP officers acceded to requests by the Milwaukee and the Soo, but asked that delay sought by the D&RGW and modifications asked for by the UP and others be dismissed. On the other side, lawyers for the antitrust division of the U.S. Department of Justice again trotted out their objections to merger. Nevertheless, after three months, by a 7–2 vote, the commission dismissed these and other objections, reaffirmed its earlier decision, and authorized consummation on May 10, 1968.

With the regulatory agency's blessing in hand, GN and NP officers—as well as those of the Burlington and the Spokane, Portland & Seattle—went about the business of preparing for implementation. New stationery, business forms, and even timetables were printed, all bearing the inscription Burlington Northern Incorporated, the name chosen for the new company, implying bold plans for diversification. All was in order. *Railway Age* said that "May 10 will be merger day," adding ominously, however, "unless something unforseen intervenes."[11]

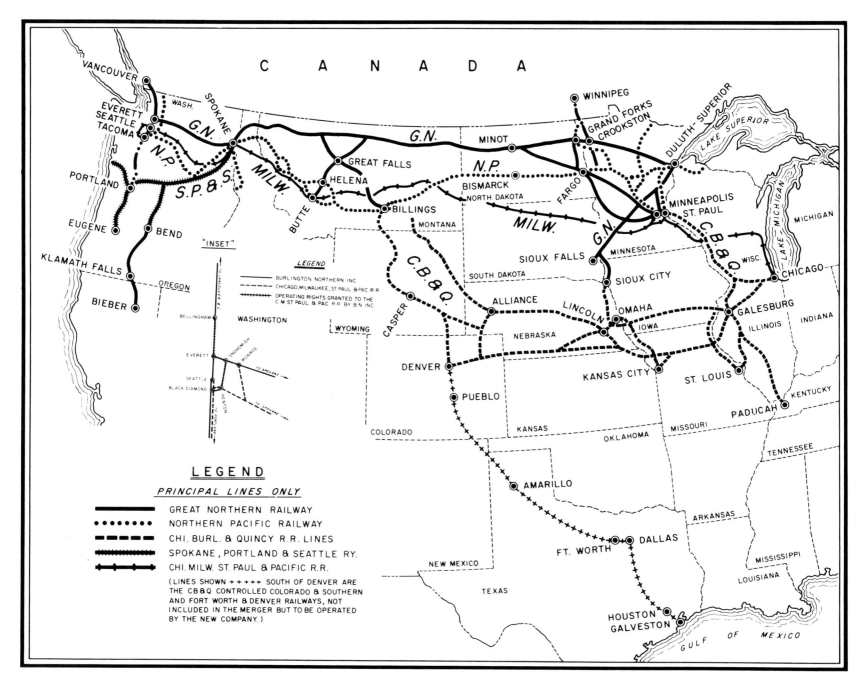

CANADA

VANCOUVER
EVERETT
SEATTLE
TACOMA
PORTLAND
EUGENE
BEND
KLAMATH FALLS
BIEBER

WASH.
SPOKANE
G.N.
N.P.
S.P.&S.
MILW.
GREAT FALLS
HELENA
BUTTE
BILLINGS

MINOT
N.P.
BISMARCK
NORTH DAKOTA
FARGO

WINNIPEG
GRAND FORKS
CROOKSTON
DULUTH-SUPERIOR
LAKE SUPERIOR

MINNEAPOLIS
ST. PAUL
MILW.
G.N.
C.B.&Q.
LAKE MICHIGAN
MICHIGAN

"INSET"

LEGEND
—— BURLINGTON NORTHERN INC.
---- CHICAGO, MILWAUKEE, ST. PAUL & PAC. R.R.
++++ OPERATING RIGHTS GRANTED TO THE
     C.M.ST PAUL & PAC. R.R. BY B.N. INC.

WASHINGTON
TO VANCOUVER B.C.
BELLINGHAM
EVERETT
SNOHOMISH
MONROE
TO SPOKANE
SEATTLE
BLACK DIAMOND
RENTON
TO PORTLAND
TO SPOKANE

MONTANA

WYOMING
CASPER

C.B.&Q.
ALLIANCE
DENVER

PUEBLO

AMARILLO

FT. WORTH
DALLAS

HOUSTON
GALVESTON

SOUTH DAKOTA

SIOUX FALLS
MINNESOTA
SIOUX CITY
IOWA
OMAHA
LINCOLN
NEBRASKA

KANSAS CITY

COLORADO
KANSAS

NEW MEXICO

TEXAS

WISC.
CHICAGO
GALESBURG
ILLINOIS
INDIANA

ST. LOUIS

MISSOURI
OKLAHOMA

ARKANSAS

PADUCAH
KENTUCKY

TENNESSEE

MISSISSIPPI
LOUISIANA

GULF OF MEXICO

LEGEND
PRINCIPAL LINES ONLY
———— GREAT NORTHERN RAILWAY
•••••• NORTHERN PACIFIC RAILWAY
– – – CHI. BURL. & QUINCY R.R. LINES
++++ SPOKANE, PORTLAND & SEATTLE RY.
◆◆◆◆ CHI. MILW. ST. PAUL & PACIFIC R.R.

(LINES SHOWN ++++ SOUTH OF DENVER ARE
THE CB&Q CONTROLLED COLORADO & SOUTHERN
AND FORT WORTH & DENVER RAILWAYS, NOT
INCLUDED IN THE MERGER BUT TO BE OPERATED
BY THE NEW COMPANY.)

The Great Northern Railway: A History/Part II 1916 to 1970

Perhaps the writer for *Railway Age* had a premonition, because on May 9, the U.S. Department of Justice asked a district judge in Washington, D.C. to issue a temporary restraining order postponing the effective date. In language verging on the extreme, the department's lawyers characterized the ICC's recent decision as "arbitrary, capricious, an abuse of discretion, unsupported by substantial evidence, the product of improper procedure, lacking a rational basis, and . . . otherwise not in accordance with law." Other appeals were made to federal district courts. Unimpressed, the district-court judges rejected these, but minutes before the complex merger procedures were scheduled to begin, an appeal by the Department of Justice to Chief Justice Earl Warren of the U.S. Supreme Court resulted in a ten-day staying order.[12]

The long-sought merger now hung on a bizarre legal battle between two wings of the federal government. A statutory three-judge court was empaneled to hear the case. On May 15, 1968, the Department of Justice asked for an indefinite stay, and for judicial review of the ICC's decision. Next day the three judges granted the request and authorized other opponents to intervene in the case. Plaintiffs' and defendants' briefs were to be filed by July 1, and oral arguments were to be presented later in the same month.

Before this three-judge court, Department of Justice lawyers asserted again that the Interstate Commerce Commission's approval of the merger failed to protect the public interest as directed by the Transportation Act of 1940, and, concentrating on savings expected from the merger, the commission had not determined whether these were sufficient to balance diminished competition—especially that between the GN and the NP. They also pointed

out that the commission earlier had used essentially the same facts and estimates to reach conclusions diametrically opposed in its later favorable decision. As to possible precedents, Justice Department attorneys contended that the ICC's recent approval of the Pennsylvania–New York Central unification was for a merger not comparable to the proposed union among the northern lines because economic conditions differed so markedly between East and West.

As interveners in the case, the GN and the NP were in a stronger position to demonstrate the advantages of merger than they had been earlier. Except for the Antitrust Division of the U.S. Department of Justice, active opposition had been practically eliminated. Above all, the two northern lines had made peace with labor. Attorneys for the northern lines could argue convincingly that the proposed consolidation, approved by the ICC, complied with the law and furthered the public interest. Managers of the GN and NP were relieved on November 20, 1968, to hear the three-judge unanimous opinion that the ICC decision indeed had been correct on every account, but even though the court dismissed all complaints, it stayed the effective date of merger fifteen days to give plaintiffs the opportunity to appeal to the Supreme Court should they so choose.

As expected, the Department of Justice, with three other plaintiffs, did appeal. On December 16, 1968, the Supreme Court issued an order blocking consummation of the merger until further notice. To the interested railroads it seemed that delays would never cease. Not until the fall of 1969 did the justices hear oral arguments. The basic question before the court, the Department of Justice maintained, was whether the ICC's approval of the merger was "supported by the requisite showing that

The general offices of the Great Northern and the Northern Pacific were housed in a common building at St. Paul, but stout walls separated the two companies. The barriers were breached after M-Day with numerous doors. The Burlington Northern, the culmination of historic dreams, had come to life.

benefits to the public interest outweigh the elimination of substantial competition in the northern tier of the United States." According to the department, the regulatory agency, in its 1967 affirmative decision, had assessed inaccurately not only the Milwaukee's potential strength and that of other railroad competitors in the Northwest, but also the benefits arising from the merger. The result, lawyers for the plaintiff insisted, had been approval of a unification having "no beneficial consequences to the public except the conventional results of such combination of competitors—predicted savings to the parties. . . .''[13]

VICTORY

At long last, on February 2, 1970, the U.S. Supreme Court announced its decision. By a 7–0 vote, the judges upheld findings of the lower court, and also those of the Interstate Commerce Commission. Chief Justice Warren F. Burger, author of the decision, stated that the Transportation Act of 1940 clearly expressed ''the desire of the Congress that the railroad industry proceed toward an integrated national transportation system through substantial corporate simplification'' so long as it was in the public interest. ''The benefits to the public from this merger are important,'' Burger concluded.[14]

The first freight train under Burlington Northern colors roars out of Chicago. Twenty-four hours later it would be in Montana, rolling over former Great Northern trackage toward Puget Sound. *(Photo by Harold A. Edmonson for Trains Magazine)*

On the day of the court's decision, John Budd of the GN and the NP's Louis W. Menk issued a joint statement in St. Paul applauding the Supreme Court opinion. ''We have finally gained a long-sought opportunity to prove our merger will result in a dynamic new transportation system that shall benefit not only the American West, but the nation as a whole.'' Facing the gigantic task of consolidating properties, the presidents declared ''we are beginning the job immediately.''[15]

March 3, 1970 was M-Day. On that date Burlington Northern, possessor of the world's longest privately owned railroad system, commenced operation as a combined business. The Great Northern, the Northern Pacific, and the Chicago, Burlington & Quincy ceased to exist as separate companies as their properties were integrated in the Burlington Northern; the Spokane, Portland & Seattle would follow later. James J. Hill would have smiled broadly and applauded with gusto.

After 114 years, the Great Northern Railway had come to the end of its corporate existence. Founded in 1856, under a Minnesota territorial charter, the railroad had originally taken the modest name Minneapolis & St. Cloud Railroad Company, but in 1889 its title was changed to the Great Northern Railway—better to identify the regional system that was about to become a grand transcontinental contender.

Until James J. Hill died in 1916, the GN had enjoyed his energetic and talented personal leadership. Yet even thereafter the Hill spirit was present in the values passed from one generation of managers to the next. Indeed, a Great Northern hallmark in all seasons was ardent dedication to lowering operating costs by reducing grade and curvature, by adopting advanced motive power, or by taking on any

program or device that would help make the company the Northwest's low-cost producer of rail transportation. Hill's insistence that the company pay strict attention to the welfare and the building up of its service area had been just as vital. This intense work was neither merely selfless nor simply selfish, but rather a tasteful balance of the two. Hill, after all, understood the symbiotic relationship between the company and those it served; he knew that the railroad would prosper only if its customers prospered. This ideal became an integral part of the Great Northern's corporate culture and was firmly embraced by those who followed Hill in the executive suite.

John Budd, of course, accomplished much that neither his father nor Hill had been able to achieve. But like both of these well-known predecessors, he had a full sense of history and profound personal attachment to the GN. John Budd was fond of saying that which he firmly believed: The proud heritage of the Great Northern Railway would not die, but would live on in new colors—those of the Burlington Northern.

BURLINGTON NORTHERN

Notes

Chapter 1

1. Material on the Minnesota & Pacific Railroad Company, 1857–1862, is scarce and scattered. Items of interest were located at the Hill Reference Library, the Great Northern Museum, and the Minnesota Historical Society. Valuable internal materials included S. P. Folsom, *Statement of the Inception of the Minnesota & Pacific Railroad Company and Its Successors* (np, 1894); James Crosby Morrison, "Brief History of the Minnesota & Pacific, St. Paul & Pacific, St. Paul, Minneapolis & Manitoba and the Great Northern Railway Company" (typed manuscript, dated March 18, 1898).

   Most information on the Minnesota & Pacific financial history was gleaned from several law cases: 2 Minn., p. 13, Minnesota & Pacific Railroad Company v. H. H. Sibley (1858); 4 Minn., p. 313; James J. Winslow v. The Minnesota & Pacific R.R. Co. et al. (1860); 14 Minn., p. 297, First Division of the St. Paul & Pacific Railroad Co. v. Frank M. Parcher et al. (1869); 92 Otto 49, Farnsworth et al., trustees v. Minnesota & Pacific Railroad Company et al., U.S. Supreme Court, October Term, 1875; Edwin A. C. Hatch v. Thomas B. Coddington and the First National Bank of St. Paul, State of Minnesota, Supreme Court, October Term, 1883, Appeal from District Court Second Judicial District, Exhibit A, Transcript of Record, Supreme Court of the United States No. 13, Edwin A. C. Hatch, plaintiff in error v. Thomas B. Coddington, September 29, 1874, especially pp. 45, 65, and testimony of Edmund Rice, pp. 70–71 and 94; Report of Railroad Commission of Minnesota, 1872, pp. 2–9; Third annual report of the directors of the Minnesota and Pacific Railroad

   Company, quoted by Folsom, *Minnesota & Pacific*, p. 5.

   Throughout this and subsequent chapters dealing with the early history of the Great Northern, its antecedents, and the regional economy, these proved valuable:
   William Watts Folwell, *A History of Minnesota*, vols. I & II (St. Paul: Minnesota Historical Society, 1924).
   Theodore C. Blegen, "James Wickes Taylor: A Biographical Sketch," *Minnesota History Bulletin*, vol. 1 (May 1915), pp. 153–219.
   Arthur J. Larson, "Roads and the Settlement of Minnesota," *Minnesota History*, vol. 21 (Sept. 1940), pp. 225–244.
   Captain Russel Blakely, "Opening of the Red River of the North to Commerce and Civilization," *Collections of the Minnesota Historical Society*, vol. 8 (1896).
   David Stanchfield, "History of Pioneer Lumbering on the Upper Mississippi and Its Tributaries, with Biographical Sketches," *Collections of the Minnesota Historical Society*, vol. 9 (1901).
   S. Saby Rasmus, "Railroad Legislation in Minnesota, 1849–1875." *Collections of the Minnesota Historical Society*, vol. 15 (1915).
   Reports of the Railroad Commissioner of Minnesota, 1871, 1872. For greater detail on important statutes, see: Act of Territorial Legislature of Minnesota 1849–1857; Acts of State Legislature of Minnesota; Minnesota Supreme Court Records.

2. 11 U.S. Statutes at Large 195, "An Act Making a Grant of Land to the Territory of Minnesota, in alternate sections, to and in the construction of certain railroads in said Territory; Territorial Laws of Minnesota, Extra Session, ch. 1, Act approved May 22, 1857.

3. GN Museum, First Report, Chief Engineer, Minnesota & Pacific, Jan. 9, 1858.

4. A statement by Hon. John M. Berry.

5. *Weekly Pioneer and Democrat* (St. Paul), Dec. 9, 1858.

6. *Minnesota State News*, Jan. 14, 21, Sept. 17, 1859; *Mankato Weekly Record*, Oct. 25, 1859.

7. SP. Laws Minnesota, 1861, ch. 5, "An Act to Facilitate the Construction of the Minnesota and Pacific Railroad," approved March 8, 1861; 14 Minn., p. 297, First Division, St. Paul & Pacific Railroad Company v. Parcher; *St. Paul Daily Press*, May 3, 1861.

8. *St. Paul Pioneer and Democrat*, Sept. 10, 1861; Walter F. Becker, "Railway Equipment up the River to Minnesota: 1861–1869," The Railway & Locomotive Historical Society, *Bulletin No. 95* (Oct. 1956), pp. 47–56.

9. *Minnesota State News*, Feb. 1, 1862.

10. *St. Paul Daily Press*, June 29, 1862.

Chapter 2

1. Area newspapers were invaluable in preparing this chapter. Particularly useful were the *Minneapolis Tribune*, *St. Paul Pioneer*, *Minneapolis Chronicle*, *St. Paul Daily Press*, and *St. Anthony Falls Democrat*. We have utilized numerous secondary sources, correspondence files of the Great Northern's executive department, and materials at the Minnesota Historical Society and the Hill Reference Library. Laws of the territory and the state were also of great service.

2. Rice v. First Division, Affidavits to Oppose Motion for Receiver, Main Line, Affidavit, F. R. Delano, June 5, 1874.

3. Circuit Court of the United States for the District of Minnesota in Equity, The St. Paul, Minneapolis and Manitoba v. Charles W. Greenhalgh et al., map; *St. Paul Daily Press*, April 27, 1864.

4. *Minneapolis Chronicle*, July 21, 1866.

5. Information from Martha Bray, Minneapolis Public Library; *Minneapolis Tribune*, Jan. 7, 1868.

6. *St. Paul Daily Press*, Nov. 17, 1869.

7. Steenerson v. Great Northern, Testimony, vol. II, pp. 5–6, 11–12 (quotation—Testimony of William Crooks, June 17, 1895.

8. Sahlgaard v. John S. Kennedy et al., Deposition on Part of Plaintiff, p. 12. Testimony of George L. Becker, Dec. 6, 1880.

Chapter 3

1. Among the most useful sources for this chapter were reports of the railroad itself and those of the Railroad Commissioner of Minnesota, the local newspapers in St. Paul and Minneapolis, which were greatly interested in the railroad's progress and service, many pamphlets at the Great Northern and in the collection of pamphlets on immigration at the MHS, and testimony in several law cases.

On James J. Hill, see Stewart H. Holbrook, *James J. Hill: A Great Life in Brief* (New York: Alfred A. Knopf, 1955); Albro Martin, *James J. Hill and the Opening of the Northwest* (New York: Oxford University Press, 1976); and Joseph Gilpin Pyle, *The Life of James J. Hill*, 2 vols. (New York: Appleton Century, 1917). GN, Report of F. R. Delano, Supt., First Division of the St. Paul & Pacific Railroad, to G. L. Becker, Pres., March 4, 1871.

2. *St. Paul Daily Press*, July 23, 1863.
3. *St. Paul Pioneer Press*, Jan. 19, 1864.
4. *St. Paul Pioneer*, May 27 and Sept. 2, 1866.
5. *Pioneer and Democrat*, July 6, 26, 1862.
6. St. Paul Pioneer, Aug. 25, Sept. 1, 1867; Rufus Blanchard, *Handbook of Minnesota* (Chicago: Blanchard & Cram, 1867), p. 25; *Minneapolis Chronicle*, Oct. 17, 1866; *Minneapolis Tribune*, May 25, 1967.
7. *Minneapolis Chronicle*, April 25, 1867; *St. Paul Pioneer*, Nov. 7, 1866; *Minneapolis Tribune*, July 5, 1869.
8. Report of the Railroad Commissioner, Minnesota, 1871, Appendix, Report of First Division of the St. Paul and Pacific Railroad Co.
9. Delano Report, March 4, 1871.
10. Sahlgaard v. Kennedy et al., Depositions on part of Plaintiff, Depositions of Becker, Dec. 6, 1880, and Trott, Dec. 8, 1880, pp. 28–29, 48.
11. GN, Becker, *Timber, Meadow and Prairie Lands,* passim; *St. Paul Pioneer*, April 20, 1864.
12. E. Rice et al. v. First Division, Affidavit, John H. Kloos, April 14, 1874; GN, John H. Kloos, *Report relative to the Resources, Population & Products of the country along the Brainerd and St. Vincent Extensions of the St. Paul & Pacific Railroad and to the Land Grant, Traffic and Prospects of these Railroad Lines* (St. Paul, 1871).
13. Becker, *Timber, Meadow and Prairie Land;* Contract Form, First Division of the St. Paul & Pacific Railroad Company, Contract for 1869.
14. GN, *Minnesota and Its Advantages to Settlers* (1867), pp. 4–5.
15. Ibid.
16. Delano Report, March 4, 1871.
17. James J. Hill to ''Grandmother,'' Aug. 4, 1856, letter made available by courtesy of Louis W. Hill, Jr.; Martin, pp. 1–26.
18. Material on the early business career of James J. Hill is found in the Hill Records and the U.S. Circuit Court, District of Minnesota, in Equity, Jesse P. Farley v. Norman W. Kittson, J. J. Hill and the St. Paul, Minneapolis & Manitoba Railway Co., Defendant's Testimony, James J. Hill, March 26, 1888.
19. Thomas B. Walker, ''Memories of the Early Life and Development of Minnesota,'' *Coll. MHS*, vol. 15 (1915), pp. 459–461; Baker Library, Harvard University, Dun & Bradstreet Records; Martin, pp. 27–58.
20. Henrietta M. Larson, *The Wheat Market and the Farmers in Minnesota, 1858–1900* (New York: Columbia University, 1926), pp. 57–90, passim.
21. GN, Agreement of First Division and W. B. Litchfield, Dec. 30, 1865; two contracts, First Division and W. F. Davidson, April 20, 1868.
22. [Annual] Report of First Division of St. Paul & Pacific, 1871.
23. Report of Railroad Commission of Minnesota, 1871, Appendix, Report of First Division, p. 6.

Chapter 4

1. This chapter was constructed from a blend of regional news accounts, internal materials, and usual secondary accounts. Especially useful were the laws of Minnesota and the United States and GN records from the offices of the secretary and the treasurer, land and tax department, and engineering office. Vital background material came from Eugene V. Smalley, *History of the Northern Pacific Railroad* (New York: G. P. Putnam's Sons, 1883) and Henrietta Larson, *Jay Cooke, Private Banker* (Cambridge: Harvard University Press, 1936).
2. Taylor papers, Taylor to N. W. Kittson, May 15, 1869.
3. Taylor papers, Taylor to Becker, Oct. 2, 1869.
4. *Minneapolis Tribune*, Dec. 29, 1870.
5. Lewis v. De Graff, Deposition of Frederick Billings, April 24, 1875.
6. *St. Anthony Falls Democrat*, Oct. 26, 1871.
7. Hodges, *Forest Tree Planting*, passim; *Duluth Daily Tribune*, Oct. 28, 1872; *St. Paul Daily Press*, May 24, 1873.
8. 16. U.S. Statutes at Large 588, ''An Act . . . St. Paul and Pacific. . . .'' March 3, 1871.
9. Wetmore v. St. Paul & Pacific et al., Defendant's Testimony, Exhibit No. 1, Willmar to Becker, Feb. 11, 1871.
10. Wetmore v. St. Paul & Pacific et al., Defendant's Testimony, Exhibit No. 4, Moorhead to Becker, June 25, 1872 and July 10, 1872.
11. Steenerson v. Great Northern, Paper Book, vol. II, Testimony, pp. 9–10.

Chapter 5

1. General and Special Laws of Minnesota, reports of the Railroad Commission of Minnesota, and the report of the Special Joint Railroad Investigating Committee (1871) were indispensable in preparing this chapter. Also of great use were the *Minneapolis Tribune, St. Paul Daily Press, St. Anthony Falls Democrat, St. Paul Pioneer Press, St. Paul Dispatch,* and *Little Falls Transcript.* St. Paul & Pacific records, letters, and memoranda, and scrapbooks at the GN Museum were helpful, as were First Division letterbooks and the Farley file at the Hill Reference Library. See also James P. Shannon, *Catholic Colonization of the Western Frontier* (New Haven: Yale University Press, 1957).
    The quotation from Carp derives from GN, St. Paul & Pacific Records, 1 (7), Johan Carp to Kennedy & Co., Dec. 23, 1873.
2. *Minneapolis Tribune*, Jan. 8, 1874.
3. GN Museum, St. Paul & Pacific Records 1 (14), Farley to Kennedy, Feb. 5, 18, 20, 1874; GN Museum, Farley v. Kittson et al., Plaintiff's Testimony, pp. 22 ff. (Jesse P. Farley).
4. Wetmore v. St. Paul & Pacific et al., Evidence, Feb. 1878, pp. 52 ff. (W. H. Fisher); U.S. Circuit Court, District of Minnesota, Northern Pacific Railroad Co. v. the St. Paul & Pacific Railroad Co. et al., Testimony on part of Plaintiff, p. 13, Thomas L. Rossa (quotation).
5. HRLH, Farley File, Farley to Kennedy & Co., Dec. 2, 1873; *St. Paul Daily Press*, Dec. 23, 1873.
6. GN Museum, St. Paul & Pacific Records, 1 (14), Farley to Kennedy, Feb. 5, 18, 20, 1874.
7. GN Museum, R44, Carp to J. S. Barnes, Nov. 6, 1873.
8. GN Museum, StP&PR 1 (7), Carp to Kennedy & Co., Dec. 23, 1873.
9. *St. Anthony Falls Democrat*, Feb. 11, 1870.
10. GN Museum; St P&PR 1 (14), Farley to Kennedy & Co., Feb. 5, 18, 20, 1874.

Chapter 6

1. The major sources for this chapter were legal cases, the James J. Hill Records, and materials in Great Northern files. Among the latter were the St. Paul and Pacific Records, the Nichols file, and several court cases.

    Along with the relevant General Laws of Minnesota and the Reports of the state railroad commission, these items provided much useful information: Donald Creighton, *John A. MacDonald, The Old Chieftain* (Boston: Houghton Mifflin, 1956); Heather Gilbert, *Awakening Continent: The Life of Lord Mount Stephen* (Aberdeen, Scotland: Aberdeen University Press, 1965); Henrietta M. Larson, *Jay Cooke, Private Banker* (Cambridge: Harvard University Press, 1936); E. D. Neill, *History of Ramsey County and City of St. Paul* (St. Paul, 1881); Joseph G. Pyle, *The Life of James J. Hill*, 2 vols. (New York: Appleton Century, 1917); C. W. Rife, "Norman W. Kittson, a Fur-Trader at Pembina," *Minnesota History*, vol. 6 (Sept. 1925), pp. 225–252; and Beckles Willson, *The Life of Lord Strathcona and Mount Royal*, 2 vols. (Boston and New York, 1915).
2. Donald Creighton, *John A. MacDonald, The Old Chieftain* (Boston: Houghton Mifflin, 1956), pp. 284–285, 334–344.
3. Joseph G. Pyle, *The Life of James J. Hill*, 2 vols. (New York: Appleton Century, 1917), vol. 1, p. 224.
4. Ibid.; Appendix 6, pp. 432–444; Albro Martin, *James J. Hill and the Opening of the Northwest* (New York: Oxford University Press, 1976), pp. 114–145.
5. HR, Hill to Stephen, Jan. 14, 1879.
6. *St. Paul Pioneer Press*, no. 5, 1878.
7. *St. Paul Globe*, Nov. 19, Dec. 15, 1878; *Minneapolis Tribune*, Nov. 23, 1878.
8. StP&P Records, Hill to Kennedy and Co., April 15, 1878; Ibid., Stephen to E. C. Litchfield, Oct. 8, 1878; Martin, pp. 146–173.
9. GN, Nichols File, Angus to J. Kennedy Tod, July 28, 1880; StPM&M Minutes Book, May 12, 1880.
10. GN, Barnes to Hill, June 24, 1879; Martin, pp. 174–198.
11. 19 HR, Barnes to Kennedy, June 9, 1879 (excerpt).
12. HR, Kennedy to G. B. Young, defense lawyer, Oct. 25, 1880.

Chapter 7

1. We have made extensive use of court records, the James J. Hill Records, and Great Northern files in preparing this chapter; *St. Paul Globe*, Feb. 15, June 22, 1879.
2. Farley v. Kittson, Defendant's Exhibit 131, Hill to Stephen, Dec. 26, 1878; GN, Hill to Stephen, March 12, 1879, citing report of E. B. Wakeman; Stephen to Hill, Sept. 6, 1879.
3. GN, Hill to Kennedy & Co., Sept. 13, 1879.
4. GN, Stephen to Hill, Sept. 6, Oct. 18, 1879.
5. HR, Angus to L. J. Sergeant, Dec. 4, 1879, Jan. 6, 1880; Angus to Stephen, Jan. 5, 6, 1880.
6. HR, Hill to Angus, Oct. 14, 1881; Hill to A. B. Rogers, Sept. 15, 1881; Albro Martin, *James J. Hill and the Opening of the Northwest* (New York: Oxford University Press, 1976), pp. 237–272.
7. HR, Hill to Stephen, Dec. 15, 1881; HR, Stephen to Hill, March 4, 1882.
8. This discussion is based on GN Records of Agents and Station Men (General Manager's office), 1882; Personal Records of Train Men, 1882; many letters from supervisors and other workers to Hill and Manvel; and circulars; HR, StPM&M letterbooks 1879–1883.
9. GN, Ackerly to Hill, Aug. 21, 1880; HR, Hill to Stephen, Dec. 17, 1881.
10. GN, Stephen to Kennedy & Co. March 26, 1879; Stephen to F. Billings, Aug. 17, 1880; Railroad Commission of Minnesota Annual Report, 1881, p. 4; 1882, p. 4.
11. HR, Angus to Stephen, Sept. 24, 1880; Angus to Sir Richard Cartwright, Nov. 9, 1880; Hill to Kennedy, Oct. 16, 1880.
12. HR, Memorandum of the Proposed Basis for an Agreement between the Northern Pacific Company and the St. Paul, Minneapolis & Manitoba Railway Company . . ., July 23, 1881, cited hereafter as Memo., July 23, 1881; HR, Angus to Kennedy & Co., May 18, 1880.
13. Railroad Commission of Minnesota Annual Report, 1882, p. 82.
14. GN, Sullivan to Hill, Feb. 12, Dec. 29, 1880, April 13, 1881.
15. GN, D. K. Smith to Manvel, July 1, Aug. 5, 1882.
16. HR, Stephen to Hill, Dec. 19, 1881; Villard Papers, Harvard University, H. Villard to F. Oakes, July 23, 1881. (Notes by kindness of John Cochran.)
17. HR, Hill to Oakes, Oct. 22, 1881; Memo., July 23, 1881.
18. GN, Agreements between StPM&M and NP, March 20, 1882 and Oct. 1, 1882; StPM&M, 1182–1883, p. 16.
19. Frank P. Donovan, Jr., *Mileposts on the Prairie: The Story of the Minneapolis & St. Louis Railway* (New York: Simmons-Boardman, 1950), pp. 69–75.
20. Minnesota Laws, An act relating to the St. Paul Union Depot Company, March 4, 1879.
21. GN v. Railway Commission, pp. 108, 209, 211 (Clough testimony).
22. StPM&M AR, 1881–1882, p. 13; 1882–1883, p. 11; Kennedy v. GN, vol. 11, p. 1248 (Hill testimony).
23. GN, StPM&M Asst. Gen. Supt. Office, Circular no. 2, July 11, 1882.
24. *Railroad Gazette*, vol. 13 (Dec. 30, 1881), p. 748
25. StPM&M AR, 1884–1885, pp. 13–14.
26. HR, Stephen to Hill, Dec. 19, 1881.
27. HR, Stephen to Hill, Dec. 19, 1881.
28. The companies that sold to StPM&M the properties for the amount that had been advanced for their building were: St. Cloud & Lake Traverse Railway (47 miles, Morris to Brown's Valley), and Barnesville & Moorhead Railway (22 miles, Barnesville to Moorhead).
29. The companies the properties of which were consolidated with StPM&M in 1883 were: Minneapolis and Northwestern Railway Co. (Minneapolis to St. Cloud, 63.5 miles); Minneapolis & St. Cloud Railway Co. (East St. Cloud to Hinckley, 66.5 miles); Sauk Centre Northern Railway Co. (Sauk Centre to Clarissa, 31.5 miles); Red River and Lake of the Woods Railway Co. (Shirley to St. Hilaire, 21.5 miles); Minnesota and Dakota Railroad Co. (Moorhead north to Norman County, 34 miles); Northern Pacific, Fergus Falls and Black Hills Railroad Co. (Fergus Falls to Pelican Rapids, 21.6 miles); Casselton Branch Railroad (Everest and Mayville to border, 160 miles). The last two lines named were built by NP and their properties were purchased as a whole or in part. The other companies had been given advances by StPM&M to do their building; separate franchises were necessary because StPM&M's charter did not include these rights; GN, StPM&M Directors' Minutes, March 19, April 12, 1883; Mortgage Indenture, May 1, 1883.

30. StPM&M AR, 1882–1883, p. 17; HR, Hill to Thomas W. Pearsall, July 26, 1883; Hill to Lord Mount Stephen, June 15, 1904.

Chapter 8

1. Indispensable background for this chapter was *Railway Age*; W. Kaye Lamb, *History of the Canadian Pacific Railway* (New York: Macmillan, 1977); and Richard C. Overton, *The Burlington Route: A History of the Burlington Lines* (New York: Alfred A. Knopf, 1965). The chief source was the full and frank correspondence among members of StPM&M's board of directors, some of which we examined in the GN files and others in the James J. Hill papers.
2. HR, George Stephen to Hill, Nov. 14, 1883; HR, Stephen to Hill, Sept. 10, 1882, June 7, Nov. 14, 1883; Albro Martin, *James J. Hill and the Opening of the Northwest* (New York: Oxford University Press, 1976), pp. 237–270.
3. HR, Hill to J. S. Kennedy, May 17, 1884.
4. GN, Kennedy to Hill, July 3, 1885.
5. HR, Hill to Stephen, Sept. 5, 1883; GN, D. Willis James to Hill, Feb. 10, 1885.
6. HR, Hill to E. T. Nichols, Feb. 5, 6, 10, 1885.
7. HR, Stephen to Hill, July 9, 1883; HR, John W. Sterling, agent CPR, NY, to Hill, Aug. 15, 1883; HR, Kennedy to Hill, Oct. 11, 1884.
8. *Railway Age*, vol. 9 (May 29, 1884), p. 399.
9. StPM&M AR, 1883–1884, p. 12; StPM&M Directors' Minutes, Dec. 15, 1884; GN, Hill to Oyens & Zonen, Oct. 13, 1884.
10. HR, Kennedy to Hill, Jan. 12, 13, 1885.
11. HR, Hill to Kennedy, July 20, 1885.
12. C. E. Perkins to J. J. Forbes, Oct. 20, 1883, by the kindness of Richard C. Overton.
13. GN, Kennedy to Hill, July 18, 1885.
14. HR, Hill to Tutein, Nolthenius & De Haan, Oct. 31, 1885.
15. HR, A. E. Touzalin to Greenleaf Clark, Feb. 3, 1885.

Chapter 9

1. These sources were significant in preparing this chapter. From the Hill Records, the most useful were letters of Paris Gibson, C. A. Broadwater, and John H. Hammond; the letterbooks in the alphabet series; Minute Books of the StPM&M Executive and Finance committees; the Minot letterbooks, 1886–1889; the Record Book of W. G. Tubby, Construction Storekeeper, and in the Louis W. Hill, Sr., Collection, the letters of Samuel Thorne.

The Great Northern Records included letters from Hill to Mark Hanna, John Gordon, and Henry Minot, as well as minutes of directors' and stockholders' meetings of the Climax Coal Company, Eastern Railway Company of Minnesota, Montana Railway Company, Lake Superior and Southwestern Railway Company, and the St. Paul, Minneapolis and Manitoba Railway Company.

Excerpts from the Samuel T. Hauser Records, with notes from the Hauser Papers and clippings from Montana newspapers, especially the *Helena Weekly Independent* and the *Helena Weekly Herald*, provided through the kindness of John W. Hakola, were informative, as his unpublished doctoral dissertation was: "Samuel T. Hauser and the Economic Development of Montana" (Indiana University, 1961), and the books and articles in the Bibliography on Montana and railroad competitors at the eastern end of the StPM&M system.
2. HR, Minot to Kennedy, Feb. 17, Oct. 11, 1886, March 10, 1887.
3. HR, Hill to Frank Thomson, April 3, 1886. HR, Minot to Kennedy, Sept. 25, 1886. GN, Minot to A. F. Priest, Jan. 4, 1889. GN, Minot to James, Feb. 18, 1889.
4. HR, Hill to James, Jan. 10, 1887; Hill to Kennedy, April 12, 1888.
5. HR, Kennedy to Hill, April 11, 1887.
6. GN, Thomas Dowse to Hill, June 20, 1879; GN, Paris Gibson to Hill, March 15, 1880; Albro Martin, *James J. Hill and the Opening of the Northwest* (New York: Oxford University Press, 1976), pp. 301–305.
7. HR, Hill to Gibson, Dec. 30, 1879; Hill to Hon. M. Maginnis, April 26, 1881.
8. HR, Kennedy to Hill, March 20, 1886.
9. HR in L. W. Hill, Sr., Collection, Thorne to Hill, Dec. 24, 1886; HR, Hill to Kennedy, Jan. 23, April 10, 1886; Kennedy to Minot, Feb. 10, 1886.
10. GN, A. H. Hogeland to George Hess, Oct. 31, 1924.
11. HR, Hill to Kennedy, Oct. 22, 1886; Minot to James, Aug. 26, 1886; Hill to James, Oct. 15, 1886; *Railroad Gazette*, vol. 18 (March 19, 1886), p. 207.
12. HR in L. W. Hill, Sr., Collection, Thorne to Hill, Nov. 4, 1886.
13. HR, Minot to Kennedy, Nov. 26, 1886.
14. GN, "Montana Extension Records."
15. Charles Dudley Warner, "Studies of the Great West," *Harper's Magazine* vol. 76 (March 1888), p. 564; StPM&M AR, 1887–1888, p. 17.
16. HR, Hill to Kennedy, May 7, 1887.
17. Shepard, *Memoirs*, Feb. 20, 1898.
18. HR, Kennedy to Hill, June 6, 1884.
19. HR, Hill to Marvin Hughitt, Sept. 22, 1885; Hill to Kennedy, Jan. 23, 1886; Minot to Kennedy, Jan. 22, 1886.
20. HR, Hill to Kennedy, Feb. 17, 1886.
21. HR, Minot to Hill, Aug. 6, 1887.
22. GN, Lake Superior & Southwestern Railway Co. Directors' Minutes, 1886–1887; HR, letters between Hill and John H. Hammond, 1885.
23. HR, Hill to C. R. Cummings, Nov. 29, 1886; Minot to Kennedy, Nov. 8, 1886, quoting Chicago grain dealer.
24. GN, Howard James to W. A. Foot, Aug. 31, 1888.
25. StPM&M AR, 1888–1889, p. 18; HR, Hill to Exec. Comm., May 18, 1887.
26. GN, John Gordon to Minot, June 24, 1889; Martin, pp. 468–469.
27. *Railroad Gazette*, vol. 18 (May 14, 1886), p. 343.

Chapter 10

1. For this chapter GN accounting department records were useful, including corporate histories and primary records on finance.
2. HR, J. S. Kennedy to Hill, Oct. 20, 1886.
3. HR, Hill to Kennedy, Oct. 22, 1886.
4. HR, Kennedy to Hill, Feb. 11, 1887; Hill to Kennedy, July 22, 1887.
5. GN, Nichols to Hill, 1886–1889, especially Oct. 15, 1887.
6. HR, LWH Coll., Samuel Thorne to Hill, Feb. 10, 1887.
7. GN, StPM&M Finance Committee Minutes, Nov. 16, 1887; HR, Kennedy to Hill, Nov. 19, 1887.
8. GN, T. J. Coolidge to Kennedy, Dec. 24, 1887.
9. GN, W. P. Clough to Hill, Dec. 14, 1887, Jan. 1888, passim; HR, LWH Collection, Thorne to Hill, Jan. 4, 1888; Hill to T. B. Walker, Jan. 12, 1888.
10. HR, Hill to Lord Mount Stephen, June 15, 1904. HR, Hill to J. W. Cannon, April 15, 1888.

11. HR, Kuhn, Loeb & Co. to Nichols, March 19, 1888, enclosed in Nichols to Hill, March 20, 1888; Nichols to Hill, May 31, 1888.
12. GN, Nichols to Hill, Sept. 4, 1889.
13. HR, Kennedy to Hill, Nov. 19, 1887.
14. GN, StPM&M AR, 1887–1888, p. 18.

Chapter 11

1. This chapter rests upon research in the Hill Records and Great Northern files of the executive, operating, secretary, and comptroller departments. In the Hill Records the correspondence between James J. Hill and George Stephen, E. H. Beckler, and Baring Brothers and Co. was most useful. The files of the operating department of GN have letters from Beckler to his engineers, which give a complete picture of construction problems and progress. A wealth of material is printed in sources on the building of the Pacific Extension, which caught the fancy of a great many writers. *Railway Gazette* was informative as always, and *Engineering News* and *Northwest Magazine* carried many useful articles. The newspapers in St. Paul and Seattle devoted much space to the extension of Hill's railroad to Puget Sound. Of those newspapers the *Seattle Post-Intelligencer* was most informative.
2. StPM&M AR 1889–1890, p. 7; Albro Martin, *James J. Hill and the Opening of the Northwest* (New York: Oxford University Press, 1976), pp. 366–398.
3. GN, J. J. Hill to Sir George Stephen, Feb. 23, 1890.
4. GN, Directors' Minutes, June 1, 1890.
5. E. H. Beckler, ''Location of the Pacific Extension of the Great Northern,'' *Railway Gazette*, vol. 25 (Oct. 11, 1893), pp. 744–745.
6. Ibid.
7. GN, E. H. Beckler to J. J. Hill, Dec. 7, 1889; GN, E. H. Beckler to J. J. Hill, July 3, 1890.
8. GN, J. J. Hill to Beckler, June 18, 1890.
9. *Seattle Post-Intelligencer*, Oct. 5, 1890; ibid., Oct. 1, 1890.
10. *Seattle Telegraph*, Nov. 15, 1890.
11. Ibid., Nov. 15, 1890.
12. HR, J. J. Hill to Baring Brothers and Co., May 3, 1890.
13. GN, J. J. Hill to George F. Thayer, Aug. 6, 1891.
14. GN, J. J. Hill to E. H. Beckler, June 18, 1890.
15. GN, E. H. Beckler to J. J. Hill, June 11, 1890.
16. *Railway Gazette*, vol. 25 (Jan. 6, 1893), p. 2.

17. GN, E. H. Beckler to Shephard, Siems and Co., Dec. 3, 1890.
18. GN, J. J. Hill to J. S. Kennedy, Dec. 25, 1891.
19. GN, E. H. Beckler to J. J. Hill, Nov. 20, 1892.
20. *Engineering News*, vol. 30 (Oct. 5, 1893), p. 272; *New York Times*, Nov. 23, 1892.
21. S. F. Van Oss, *American Railroads as Investments: A Handbook for Investors in American Railroad Securities* (New York, 1893), pp. 653–673, especially pp. 656, 657, 660.

Chapter 12

1. This chapter rests on research in the Hill Records and the files of GN's executive department. They hold many pivotal letters between Hill and such influential figures as Lord Mount Stephen, William Van Horne, and Hill's bankers, especially J. P. Morgan and representatives of his firm. Discussion of the Northern Securities case follows accounts in B. H. Meyer, *A History of the Northern Securities Case* (Madison: University of Wisconsin, 1906) and Richard C. Overton, *Burlington Route: A History of the Burlington Lines* (New York: Alfred A. Knopf, 1965).
2. *St. Paul Pioneer Press*, Oct. 1, 1885.
3. HR, J. J. Hill to E. T. Nichols, Sept. 26, 1892.
4. GN, J. J. Hill to A. R. Ledoux, Aug. 8, 1895.
5. Papers on the Duluth and Winnipeg Railway, Memorandum, Feb. 2, 1897; Walter Vaughan, *The Life and Work of Sir William Van Horne* (New York: Century, 1920), p. 254.
6. ''Committee on Investigation of the United States Steel Corporation,'' U.S. House, *Hearings*, 62nd Cong., 2nd Sess. (1912), p. 3171. Cited hereafter as ''Investigation of the United States Steel Corporation''; Edmund J. Longyear, *Reminiscences of Edmund J. Longyear, Mesabi Pioneer* (St. Paul, 1951), pp. 61–62.
7. Unidentified clipping from Hill Records, Feb. 16, 1898.
8. ''Investigation of the United States Steel Corporation,'' pp. 3219–3220.
9. HR, Mount Stephen to J. J. Hill, Oct. 18, 1894; Albro Martin, *James J. Hill and the Opening of the Northwest* (New York: Oxford University Press, 1976), pp. 439–459.
10. HR, ibid., Nov. 6, 1894; HR, Report from GN comptroller's department, ''Year Ending June 30, 1894.''

11. HR, Mount Stephen to J. J. Hill, Sept. 8, 27, 1895; HR, J. J. Hill to Mount Stephen, Feb. 15, 1896.
12. HR, ibid., Dec. 17, 1895.
13. HR, Memorandum of a Conference held in London, April 2, 1896.
14. HR, J. J. Hill to Mount Stephen, May 23, July 3, Aug. 21, 1896.
15. HR, J. J. Hill to Gaspard Farrer, Nov. 22, 1897; HR, J. J. Hill to Arthur Gwinner, March 28, 1898.
16. HR, J. J. Hill to D. S. Lamont, July 17, 1898.
17. HR, J. J. Hill to J. P. Morgan, Oct. 1, 1898.
18. HR, Morgan and Company to J. J. Hill, Oct. 8, 1898. HR, J. J. Hill to Morgan and Company, Nov. 8, 1898.
19. HR, J. S. Kennedy to J. J. Hill, July 12, 1899; *Railway Gazette*, vol. 31 (June 23, 1899), p. 457; *Railway Age*, vol. 28 (July 7, 1899), p. 495.
20. HR, J. J. Hill to D. S. Lamont, March 31, 1900.
21. Martin, pp. 477–523.
22. Overton, pp. 244–263.
23. George Kennan, *E. H. Harriman: A Biography*, 2 vols. (Boston: Houghton Mifflin, 1922), vol. I, pp. 286–339.
24. Brief of Counsel for the United States, U.S. v. Northern Securities Company, p. 30; Kennan, vol. I, pp. 387–404.
25. *The Wall Street Journal*, Jan. 28, 1910.
26. *Railway Age*, vol. 28 (Sept. 8, 1899), p. 657.
27. Don L. Hofsommer, *The Southern Pacific, 1901–1985* (College Station: Texas A&M University Press, 1986), pp. 37–42.
28. Ibid., p. 40.
29. Ibid., p. 56.
30. HR, J. J. Hill to T. J. Shaughnessy, June 16, 1899.
31. *Railway Gazette*, vol. 40 (May 18, 1906), p. 491; *St. Paul Dispatch*, April 10, 1907.
32. *New York Herald*, Aug. 24, 1906.

Chapter 13

1. The chapter is based on materials from Great Northern executive, traffic, and land department files. Hill's correspondence with Thomas Shaw is especially enlightening. Chester C. Morrison, ''A History of the Immigration and Agricultural Development Departments of the Great Northern Railway,'' an account prepared by a former officer of those departments, is very useful. Hill's views on agricul-

ture and conservation are set forth conveniently in his *Highways of Progress* (New York: Doubleday 1910), and in a number of articles in *World's Work*. Howard L. Dickman's doctoral dissertation, "James Jerome Hill and the Agricultural Development of the Northwest" (University of Michigan, 1977), proved helpful and generally substantiated our earlier research. For an account of railroads in early twentieth-century agricultural education, see Roy V. Scott, *The Reluctant Farmer: The Rise of Agricultural Education to 1914* (Urbana: University of Illinois Press, 1970), ch. 6, and on the general theme of promotional activities see Roy V. Scott, *Railroad Development Programs in the Twentieth Century* (Ames: Iowa State University Press, 1985). The citation from *Northwest Magazine* is in vol. 11 (March 1893), pp. 31–32.

2. GN, J. J. Hill to C. H. Coster, Oct. 1, 1898; Hill to J. A. Wheelock, June 21, 1891; GN, J. J. Hill to Knute Nelson, Oct. 19, 1891.

3. *Commercial West*, vol. 20 (Nov. 30, 1911), p. 7.

4. GN, Co-operative Work in Dry Farming in Montana, undated memo; Thomas Shaw to L. W. Hill, Oct. 1, 1909.

5. GN, J. J. Hill to A. B. Stevenson, March 12, 1914.

6. Fred A. Shannon, *The Farmer's Last Frontier: Agriculture, 1860–1897* (New York: Holt, Rinehart & Winston, 1945), p. 220.

7. Albro Martin, *James J. Hill and the Opening of the Northwest* (New York: Oxford University Press, 1976), pp. 309–314, 450–451.

8. *Railway and Engineering Review*, vol. 45 (Sept. 9, 1905), pp. 654–655; *Commercial West*, vol. 5 (Sept. 26, 1903), p. 14.

9. James J. Hill, *Highways of Progress* (New York: Doubleday, 1910), p. 45.

10. Randall H. Howard, "Following the Colonists: An Account of the Great Semi-Annual Movement of Homeseekers," *Pacific Monthly*, vol. 23 (May 1910), p. 529.

Chapter 14

1. In preparing this chapter, the authors relied upon materials in the Hill Records and in the files of Great Northern executive, comptroller, and engineering departments. An interview with C. C. Morrison, a retired GN officer, was helpful. Along with the standard trade journals, *Iron Age, Commercial and Financial Chronicle*, and *Railway and Engineering Review* provided much information. The Interstate Commerce Commission's valuation of the Great Northern has plentiful information on various topics; it is found in Great Northern Railway Company et al., 133 ICC 1. For our discussion of GN motive power we found a vital source in Paul T. Warner, "The Great Northern Railway and Its Locomotives," *Baldwin Locomotives*, vol. 3 (Jan. 1925), pp. 3–33. Most of our account of how the ore lands were acquired and how ore traffic was handled comes from "Committee on Investigation of the U.S. Steel Corporation," U.S. House, *Hearings*, 62nd Cong., 2nd Sess. (1912), and Joseph W. Thompson, "The Genesis of Great Northern's Mesabi Ore Traffic," *Journal of Economic History*, vol. 16 (Dec. 1956), pp. 551–557. Useful, too, were Duluth and Iron Range Railroad Company, *Transportation of Iron Ore and the History of the Duluth and Iron Range* (np, 1927), and Duluth, Missabe and Northern Railway Company, *The Missabe Road* (Duluth, 1927).

2. GN, A. L. Mohler to J. J. Hill, May 10, 1893.

3. GN, E. T. Nichols to Samuel Hill, Jan. 10, 1894; HR, J. J. Hill to Nichols, Nov. 5, 1893.

4. HR, J. J. Hill to Jacob H. Schiff, June 7, 1896; HR, J. J. Hill to Mount Stephen, Dec. 17, 1895.

5. GN AR, 1892–1893, p. 17.

6. HR, J. J. Hill to C. S. Mellen, Feb. 19, 1900.

7. HR in L. W. Hill, Sr., Collection, L. W. Hill to J. J. Hill, Sept. 26, 1904.

8. "Committee on Investigation of the United States Steel Corporation," U.S. House, *Hearings*, 62nd Cong., 2nd Sess. (1912), pp. 3162, 3171. Cited hereafter as "Committee on Investigation of the United States Steel Corporation"; HR, J. J. Hill to Kennedy, July 30, 1898.

9. GN AR, 1899–1900, pp. 10–11; "Committee on Investigation of the United States Steel Corporation," p. 3204.

10. Ibid., p. 3164.

11. James J. Hill, as reported in *St. Paul Pioneer Press*, Dec. 20, 1906.

12. See Albro Martin, *Enterprise Denied: Origins of the Decline of American Railroads, 1897–1917* (New York: Columbia University Press, 1971).

13. GN AR, 1895–1896, p. 9.

Chapter 15

1. Material for this chapter comes from the Hill Records and from Great Northern executive, legal, and passenger department files. The timetables, brochures, and other items issued by the company to advertise and promote travel on his trains were most useful. We also consulted the railway trade journals and major metropolitan newspapers along the GN line, especially those of Chicago, St. Paul, and Seattle.

2. GN Book of Advertisements, No. 2, 1895. GN *Time Table*, Oct. and Dec., 1906; *The Oriental Limited: The Comfortable Way* (np, nd); *Washington Herald*, Sept. 3, 1905; *St. Louis Globe Democrat*, Sept. 1, 1905. GN *Time Table*, 1906.

3. GN Book of Advertisements, No. 19, 1895, quoting McKinley to John Gordon.

4. GN, F. C. Cruger to Howard Jones, Oct. 27, 1911.

5. GN *Time Table*, Aug., 1905; W. Kaye Lamb, "Trans-Pacific Venture of James J. Hill," *The American Neptune* (July 1943), pp. 185–204.

6. GN *Time Table*, Aug., 1906.

7. HR, J. J. Hill to E. F. Warner, Feb. 18, 1880.

8. GN AR, 1898–1899, pp. 9, 19.

9. HR, J. J. Hill to J. C. Stubbs, April 11, 1892; HR, J. J. Hill to Sir Donald Smith, June 14, 1893.

10. *Railway Age*, vol. 29 (May 25, 1900), p. 517.

11. GN, W. P. Clough to F. C. Power, Feb. 22, 1894; HR, J. J. Hill to Sydney Dillon, Jan. 2, 1891; GN, L. W. Hill to Will H. Thompson, Jan. 24, 1899.

12. GN, J. J. Hill to Nichols, July 31, 1900.

Chapter 16

1. For this chapter, in addition to oft-cited annual reports and minute books of GN and StPM&M, AR GN-ICC, and GN Executive Department files, the corporate histories of GN and StPM&M, GN's account books, the Financial History of the Great Northern by R. I. Farrington, June 30, 1912 (manuscript), ICC Valuation Report No. 327, ICC Valuation Report Papers, and J. A. Tauer, statement of highs and lows of Great Northern Capital stock from 1890 onward, were particularly helpful.

2. GN AR, 1894, p. 18.

3. GN, E. T. Nichols to Samuel Hill, Jan. 10, 1894; HR, Hill to Nichols, April 1, 1898.

Notes

4. HR, Hill to Nichols, June 7, 1898; 169 U.S. 466, 546–547; HR, J. S. Kennedy to Hill, March 10, 1898; Hill to Kennedy, March 12, 1898; Hill to Jacob Schiff, March 28, 1898.

5. HR, Hill to Schiff, March 28, 1898.

6. GN, clipping, *N.Y. Commercial Advertiser*, Aug. 7, 1898; HR, Hill to Stephen, May 23, 1897.

7. GN, Directors' and Stockholders' Minutes, Oct. 19, 1898.

8. GN, Directors' Minutes, April 20, 1900.

9. Dow, Jones & Co. News Bulletin, July 24, 1907.

10. HR, M. D. Grover to Hill, April 3, 1899.

11. HR, Hill to Tuck, July 22, 1904.

Chapter 17

1. Most information for this chapter came from GN files in the executive (especially Personnel Note Books, containing schedules and agreements with unions), operating, accounting, law, and secretary departments, and the Nichols file. Supplementary sources were the HR, GN AR, and AR GN-ICC, plus histories of the unions involved and of the Pullman Strike and biographies of Debs and Hill. HR, clipping, no designation, Book 11, p. 117.

2. GN, F. E. Ward to D. A. Robinson, May 28, 1897.

3. HR, J. J. Hill to A. Hutton, Aug. 7, 1895; GN, Hill to Henry Minot, Aug. 25, 1888.

4. HR, clipping, *Buffalo Commercial*, Jan. 21, 1910; HR, F. B. Walker to W. Hauser, May 17, 1914; GN, P. C. Schwartz to E. N. Duncan, June 17, 1958.

5. HR, clipping, *Buffalo Commercial*, Jan. 21, 1910.

6. GN, Hill to D. R. Maginnis, Jan. 8, 1891; GN, Gen. Mgr. Circular No. 35, March 10, 1893; GN, Gen. Mgr. C. H. Warren Circular No. 8, Oct. 3, 1894; HR, clipping, *New York World*, Dec. 15, 1909.

7. HR, clipping, no designation, Book II, p. 117. See also GN, Hill to H. B. Wilkins, April 7, 1891.

8. GN, Samuel Hill to Lewis Stockett, Dec. 26, 1896.

9. GN, A. L. Mohler to C. W. Case, Dec. 14, 1892.

10. GN, "1890 Schedule proposed by B. L. E. Committee and as finally adopted, 11-1-1890."

11. GN, Hill to Mohler, Aug. 7, 8, 1893; Hill to N. C. Hay, Oct. 11, 1893.

12. GN, Hill to C. A. Pillsbury and others, April 30, 1894.

13. GN, Hill to F. P. Sargent and P. M. Arthur, April 14, 1894.

14. GN, Hill to John C. Curtin, April 15, 1894; Hill to W. H. Brahen, Secy. ARU, April 15, 1894.

15. Gerald G. Eggert, *Railroad Labor Disputes: The Beginning of Federal Strike Policy* (Ann Arbor: University of Michigan Press, 1967), p. 149.

16. GN, Hill to President Grover Cleveland, April 28, 1894.

17. Ray Ginger, *The Bending Cross: A Biography of Eugene Victor Debs* (New Brunswick: Rutgers University Press, 1949), p. 106.

18. GN, Hill to D. J. Jones, May 4, 1894.

19. GN, Ward to P. T. Downs, June 1, 1901.

20. GN, C. R. Gray to Gruber, May 23, 1913.

Chapter 18

1. For this chapter, covering the years 1916–1920, the major sources of information were the GN AR, AR GN-ICC, GN Records Book, including the Subrecord, and the files of GN Executive Department, including several special memos and reports to the president. Supplementary data came from GN's passenger, personnel, purchasing, traffic, and industrial and agricultural development departments, as well as from railway trade journals, annual reports and dockets of the ICC, newspapers in Seattle and the Twin Cities, and the books, listed in the Bibliography, pertaining to railroads and World War I, especially Aaron Austin Godfrey, *Government Operation of the Railroad, 1918–1920*, (Austin, Texas: Jenkins, 1974).

2. *New York Times*, June 14, 1916.

3. Albert W. Atwood, "Why Has My Stock Declined?" *Minneapolis Journal*, Magazine Section, Nov. 20, 1916.

4. Walker D. Hines, "The Permanent Solution of the Railroad Problem," *Railway Age*, vol. 67 (July 4, 1919), pp. 18–20, from an address before the New England Bankers Association in Swampscott, Mass., June 21, 1919; GN AR, 1915, p. 13.

5. *Railway Age Gazette*, vol. 61 (Sept. 8, 1916), p. 394.

6. 42 ICC 661.

7. GN, W. P. Kenney to F. R. Newman, Feb. 17, 1938.

8. GN, *Railway Review*, April 21, 1917, clipping.

9. GN Minutes Book, Dec. 16, 1918, copy of agreement and approval of directors and stockholders.

10. GN Minutes Book, Dec. 16, 1918, copy of agreement and approval of directors and stockholders.

11. GN, C. E. Stone to G. H. Smitton, March 1, 1919.

12. GN Minutes Book, Sub-record, Aug. 3, 1919.

13. K. Austin Kerr, *American Railroad Politics, 1914–1920: Rates, Wages, and Efficiency* (Pittsburgh: University of Pittsburgh Press, 1968), p. 222.

14. U.S. Statutes at Large, XLI, p. 456.

Chapter 19

1. In preparing this chapter and later ones on the 1920s, we found useful the minutes of the GN's board of directors and of the executive committee. A vast correspondence in the files of the executive department, especially letters between Budd and his several vice presidents, filled out the account. Ralph Hidy and Muriel Hidy benefited from a series of interviews with Ralph Budd and C. O. Jenks, which extended over several years. In the 1920s the Annual Reports of the GN became much more informative, carrying more narrative material. The Annual Reports of the Great Northern Railway Company to the Interstate Commerce Commission, required by law, provided a great deal of statistical data not easily available elsewhere. The Annual Reports and dockets of the ICC provided information on rates and related matters. The newspapers of St. Paul and other cities and the industry trade journals, especially *Railway Age*, were consulted. *Skilling's Mining Review* had information on the iron-ore traffic. Of the many books and articles that we consulted, these were especially useful: George Soule, *Prosperity Decade: From War to Depression* (New York, 1947); F. H. Dixon, *Railroads and Government* (New York: Scribner, 1922); I. L. Sharfman, *The American Railroad Problem* (New York: The Century Co., 1921); Eliot Jones, *Principles of Railway Transportation* (New York: Macmillan, 1924); Richard C. Overton, "Ralph Budd: Railroad Entrepreneur," *The Palimpsest*, vol. 36 (Nov. 1955), pp. 421–484; and Ralph W. Hidy, Frank E. Hill, and Allan Nevins, *Timber and Men: The Weyerhaeuser Story* (New York, 1963).

2. Richard C. Overton, "Ralph Budd: Railroad Entrepreneur," *The Palimpsest*, vol. 36 (Nov. 1955), pp. 427–443.

3. Interview with Jackson E. Reynolds by Ralph Hidy and Muriel Hidy, June 6, 1955.

4. Interview with Charles W. ''Dinty'' Moore by Don L. Hofsommer, Nov. 20, 1985.
5. GN, R. Budd to E. C. Lindley, Feb. 9, 1920.
6. GN, W. P. Kenney to Budd, May 5, 1920.
7. GN, Budd to Kenney, Feb. 4, 1921.
8. GN, Budd to E. T. Nichols, Aug. 16, 1923.
9. GN, Budd to E. C. Wilkinson, vice president, Moody's Investor's Service, Jan. 24, 1922.
10. U.S. Railroad Labor Board, Decision No. 299, Docket No. 845, Oct. 29, 1921.
11. (St. Paul) Pioneer Press, Dec. 5, 1921.
12. GN, The Sunday Oregonian, Portland, Feb. 26, 1922, clipping.
13. GN, M. L. Countryman to C. O. Jenks, Sept. 28, 1922.

Chapter 20

1. GN, Ralph Budd, Addresses, April 10, 1922, April 13, 1928. In preparing this chapter the authors used the files of the executive, law, purchasing, and engineering departments. Especially useful was Ralph Budd's correspondence with his vice presidents, W. P. Kenney and C. O. Jenks. Texts of Budd's speeches often gave insight into managerial decisions as well as operating problems. Important, too, was a memo by W. B. Irwin of the operations department entitled ''Changes in Operating Practices and Procedures since March 1, 1920.'' *Railway Age* and the more important newspapers along the line were also consulted. Alfred W. Bruce, *The Steam Locomotive in America* (New York: W. W. Norton, 1952), gives an excellent account of the technological evolution of engines. For GN motive power in this period, the files of the *Great Northern Semaphore* and Great Northern Railway Company, *Steam Locomotives* (St. Paul, nd) were informative. See also Norman C. Keyes and Kenneth R. Middleton, ''The Great Northern Railway Company: All-Time Locomotive Roster, 1861–1920,'' *Railroad History, No. 143* (Autumn 1980), pp. 20–162. The changing pattern in freight rates may be followed through the appropriate reports of the ICC. Useful in understanding Cascade Tunnel construction were several articles by participants that appeared in the *Railway and Marine News* and reports by D. J. Kerr, Frederick Mears, and J. C. Baxter in American Society of Civil Engineers, *Transactions*, vol. 96 (1932), pp. 917–998. Over

several years, informal interviews by Ralph Hidy and Muriel Hidy with Ralph Budd and with C. O. Jenks were most helpful.
2. GN, Budd to Frank Devery, Dec. 5, 1923.
3. GN AR, 1929, p. 7.
4. GN, J. Arten to Jenks, July 7, 1923.
5. GN, Budd to L. W. Hill, Nov. 11, 1925.
6. W. E. Conroy, ''Construction Problems of the 8-Mile Tunnel,'' *Railway and Marine News*, vol. 26 (Jan. 1929), p. 40; ''Mr. Budd Dedicates the Tunnel,'' *Railway and Marine News*, vol. 26 (Jan. 1929), p. 41.
7. Great Northern Railway, *Dedication and Opening of the New Cascade Tunnel* (1929), pp. 2–5, 7; Westinghouse Electric & Manufacturing Company, *The Great Northern Railway Electrification* (1929), pp. 5–8, 14, 21–23. See also William D. Middleton, *When the Steam Railroads Electrified* (Milwaukee: Kalmbach Publishing, 1974), pp. 155–173, 399–400.
8. GN, W. P. Kenney to Budd, Sept. 25, 1923, Aug. 22, 1928.
9. GN, Kenney to Budd, Sept. 14, 1923.
10. Wood, Struthers and Company, *Great Northern Railway Company, Northern Pacific: A Review of Their Operations in the Period 1916–1923* (New York, 1924), p. 36.
11. GN, Kenney to Budd, Sept. 24, 1923.
12. GN, Kenney to Budd, Aug. 12, 1921; GN, Budd to W. A. Emerson, March 24, 1922.

Chapter 21

1. No facet of railroading in the 1920s presented us with a more complex and challenging situation than the passenger business, and the volume of materials on the subject in the Great Northern's files is large. It illustrates, among other things, the relationship between Ralph Budd and L. W. Hill, relations between railroad and state and local government, changing competition between modes of transportation, and the possibilities in their relationship. In the GN records the most useful sources were the passenger department annual reports, informative timetables, advertising materials, special statistical compilations, and voluminous correspondence, especially the letters of Ralph Budd, Alex Janes, W. P. Kenney, A. J. Dickinson, and C. Eric Wickman. Several interviews by

Muriel E. Hidy with GN's executives were helpful; these were with Ralph Budd, Alex Janes, A. J. Dickinson, and W. H. Wilde. The printed material studied included the many speeches of Ralph Budd and articles in national trade journals, such as *Railway Age*. Files of several newspapers were informative, especially those of St. Paul.
2. *St. Paul Press*, July 14, 1914.
3. *Railway Age*, vol. 68 (May 21, 1920), p. 1442.
4. GN, Budd to C. E. Wickman, Dec. 12, 1930.
5. GN, G. R. Martin to Budd, June 13, 1921; Budd to W. F. Turner, April 29, 1924; Ralph Budd, ''The Relation of Highway Transportation to the Railway,'' *American Society of Civil Engineers, Transactions*, vol. 92 (1928), p. 394; GN, Alex Janes to Budd, July 31, 1922.
6. GN, Budd to Chauncy McCormick, June 18, 1928; interviews of Muriel E. Hidy with Ralph Budd, Aug. 2, 1954, and A. L. Janes, Aug. 4, 1954; GN, Budd to Harry Curran, May 23, 1925.
7. GN, Budd to Freeman, Nov. 7, 1928; C. E. Wickman, ''Great Northern Using Buses to Regain Lost Short-Haul Business in Minnesota,'' *Bus Transportation*, vol. 8 (June 1926), p. 315.
8. GN, Memo., 1929, about Northland Transportation Company and sale of its stock to the Motor Transit Co.; Budd to Wickman, Jan. 6, 1930. See also Carlton Jackson, *Hounds of the Road: A History of the Greyhound Bus Company* (Bowling Green: Bowling Green University Press, 1984), especially pp. 8, 13.
9. GN, Budd to McCormick, June 18, 1928; Budd to Samuel O. Dunn, Feb. 5, 1931.
10. GN, Budd, Address to Passenger Ticket Agents, Chicago, Oct. 20, 1921 (quotation); Kenney to Budd, Oct. 14, 1929.
11. *Railway Age*, vol. 77 (Aug. 30, 1924), p. 370.
12. GN, Budd to Kenney, July 25, 1923.
13. GN, GN Timetable, Aug. 1923, p. 1; Oct. 1923, p. 1; Dec. 1923, p. 30; Dec. 1925, p. 1.
14. GN, Kenney to Budd, Dec. 27, 1923.
15. GN AR, 1923 pp. 8, 13; 1925, pp. 8, 13. On the *Oriental Limited*, see Arthur D. Dubin, *Some Classic Trains* (Milwaukee: Kalmbach Publishing, 1964), pp. 297–303, and Lucius Beebe and Charles Clegg, *The Trains We Rode*, 2 vols. (Berkeley: Howell-North Books, 1965), I, pp. 228–239.
16. GN, Budd to Kenney, April 7, 1924; Kenney to Budd, Oct. 15, 1924; Jenks to Budd, Oct. 10, 1924; GN Timetable, Jan.–Feb. 1923, p. 47.

17. *Railway and Marine News*, vol. 26 (Oct. 1929), p. 37. On the *Empire Builder*, see Dubin, pp. 304–307, and Beebe and Clegg, pp. 240–255.
18. Interview with Robert W. Downing by Don L. Hofsommer, July 24, 1985.
19. "63 Hour Service," *Railway and Marine News*, vol. 26 (Jan. 29, 1929), p. 13; GN, Dickinson to Kenney, Feb. 24, 1928, 1929 (quotation).
20. GN, Dickinson to Kenney, June 16, 1922.
21. GN, Dickinson to Kenney, Feb. 8, 1924.

Chapter 22

1. This chapter depends upon materials in the files of the executive, law and agricultural development departments of Great Northern and on *Railway Age* and other printed sources. Budd's correspondence with major stockholder Arthur Curtiss James was especially helpful. For understanding the complexities of branch-line construction and purchase, the decisions of the Interstate Commerce Commission are essential. E. C. Leedy, head of the company's agricultural department, supplied his superiors with remarkably detailed accounts of his office's activities, often including copies of reports that originated with subordinate agents in the field. A helpful source was Chester C. Morrison, "History of the Immigration and Agricultural Development Departments of the Great Northern Railway," a lengthy manuscript prepared by a retired employee of those departments. Interviews with Chester C. Morrison were appreciated, because he had worked for the GN for many years. A number of the company's promotional pamphlets, such as *New Branch Lines, Saco-Turner Branch, Montana* (St. Paul, 1928), were also useful. The unique problems in northern Montana are discussed critically by Joseph K. Howard in *Montana: High, Wide, and Handsome* (New Haven: Yale University Press, 1943) and by K. Ross Toole in *Montana: An Uncommon Land* (Norman: Oklahoma University Press, 1959). More specific are Milburn L. Wilson, "Dry Farming in the North Central Montana 'Triangle,'" Montana Agricultural Extension Service, *Bulletin* 66 (Bozeman, 1923); and Elmer A. Starch, "Economic Changes in Montana's Wheat Area," Montana Agricultural Experiment Station, *Bulletin* 295 (Bozeman, 1935). Important for background is Mary W. M. Hargreaves, *Dry Farming in the Northern Great Plains*

1900–1925 (Cambridge: Harvard University Press, 1957). For information on North Dakota, see Elwyn B. Robinson, *History of North Dakota* (Lincoln: University of Nebraska Press, 1966); and for Washington, see Dorothy O. Johansen and Charles M. Gates, *Empire on the Columbia: A History of the Pacific Northwest* (New York: Harper, 1957). For a study of agricultural programs that another carrier had, see C. Clyde Jones, "The Burlington Railroad and Agricultural Policy in the 1920s," *Agricultural History*, vol. 31 (Oct. 1957), pp. 67–74. Useful, too, is Howard L. Dickman, "James Jerome Hill and the Agriculture Development of the Northwest" (Ph.D. dissertation, University of Michigan, 1977). On the Southern Pacific, see Don L. Hofsommer, *The Southern Pacific, 1901–1985* (College Station: Texas A&M University Press, 1986).
2. GN, Ralph Budd to F. G. Dorety, Dec. 1, 1926; GN, W. P. Kenney to Budd, April 23, 1927.
3. Hofsommer, pp. 93–97.
4. GN, Kenney to Budd, Sept. 3, 1924.
5. *Seattle Daily Times*, Sept. 10, 1931; *Great Northern Railway Company Construction*, 166 ICC 3.
6. Quoted in *St. Paul Dispatch*, Nov. 22, 1920.
7. GN, F. H. Reeves to Fred Graham, June 17, 1936.
8. GN, William Blonder to E. C. Leedy, June 30, 1935.
9. GN, Leedy to Reeves, June 23, 1936.
10. GN, Kenney to H. H. Brown, Aug. 25, 1934.
11. GN, C. T. Fairfield to Budd, May 15, 1924.
12. GN, L. W. Hill to John H. Worst, Jan. 11, 1922; GN, Budd to Arthur W. Page, Aug. 7, 1924.
13. Roy V. Scott, *Railroad Development Programs in the Twentieth Century* (Ames: Iowa State University Press, 1985), p. 102.
14. GN, Leedy to Kenney, Nov. 27, 1926.
15. GN, Leedy to Kenney, Oct. 23, 1931.

Chapter 23

1. GN, Ralph Budd to W. D. Hines, Nov. 9, 1925; Budd to E. E. Loomis, Feb. 15, 1923; Budd, Address before the Transportation Club of St. Paul, Jan. 30, 1923. The executive department files have abundant correspondence between Ralph Budd and Arthur Curtiss James, Howard Elliott of the Northern Pacific, Hale Holden of the Burlington, and bankers Jackson E. Reynolds and George F. Baker, all active in the merger attempt. Those files also include the le-

gal briefs, statements, and documents prepared by all parties in the long struggle to unite the northern lines. *Railway Age* and *Commercial and Financial Chronicle* carried detailed accounts of the issues. The ICC's tentative plan is in *Consolidation of Railroads*, 63 ICC 455, and its final plan is *In the Matter of Consolidation of Railway Properties of the United States into a Limited Number of Systems*, 159 ICC 522. The ICC's decision in the northern merger case is in *Great Northern Pacific Railway Company Acquisition*, 162 ICC 37. Walker D. Hines analyzes issues at an early stage in "The Relationship of the Burlington-Great Northern-Northern Pacific Group to the Federal Railroad Consolidation Law," *Harvard Business Review*, vol. 1 (July 1923), pp. 398–413. Among secondary accounts, these are indispensable: Stuart Daggett, *Railroad Consolidation West of the Mississippi River* (Berkeley: University of California Press, 1933); William N. Leonard, *Railroad Consolidation under the Transportation Act of 1920* (New York: Columbia University Press, 1946); Richard C. Overton, *Burlington Route: A History of the Burlington Lines* (New York: Alfred A. Knopf, 1965).
2. U.S. Statutes at Large, XLI, p. 481.
3. Ibid.
4. GN, Stenographers' Minutes of Testimony on ICC Docket No. 12964, Nov. 18, 20, 1922; William J. Cunningham, "Railroad Unification in the Northwest," *The Annalist*, vol. 29 (March 25, 1927), p. 428.
5. GN, Stenographers' Minutes of Testimony of ICC Docket No. 12964, Nov. 20, 1922.
6. Ralph Budd, *Address before the Minneapolis Civic and Commerce Association*.
7. *New York Times*, Dec. 21, 1929, quoted in William N. Leonard, *Railroad Consolidation under the Transportation Act of 1920* (New York: Columbia University Press, 1946), p. 190.
8. *Great Northern Pacific Railroad Company Acquisition*, 162 ICC 69–71.
9. Ibid., p. 47.
10. GN, Hines to Budd, April 1, 1930.
11. GN, Budd to Hines, Oct. 18, Dec. 17, 1930.

Chapter 24

1. In preparing this chapter we drew from voluminous correspondence in the files of GN's executive depart-

313

Notes

ment, the minutes of the board of directors and of the executive committee, and the relevant ICC finance dockets and reports. Most significant were Budd's letters to and from Hale Holden, Howard Elliott, Jackson E. Reynolds, Henry S. Sturgis, and officers of Morgan & Company. Useful, too, was Budd's correspondence with GN officials, including L. W. Hill, G. H. Hess, I. C. Lindley, G. R. Martin, E. T. Nichols, and F. L. Paetzold. The Annual Reports of the Great Northern Railway to the ICC supplied financial and other data. The commission's valuation of the GN is in 133 ICC, Valuation Docket No. 327. Among useful interviews by Ralph W. Hidy and Muriel E. Hidy were several with Ralph Budd and one with Jackson E. Reynolds, July 6, 1955. Richard C. Overton, *Burlington Route: A History of the Burlington Lines* (New York: Alfred A. Knopf, 1965) is especially useful in this chapter.

2. GN, ICC Order, Finance Docket No. 1374.
3. *New York Evening Post*, Nov. 2, 1921.
4. GN, unsigned memo by Henry S. Sturgis, undated but written in July 1937, as indicated by context and accompanying correspondence.
5. *Barron's*, Dec. 19, 1921.
6. GN, Ralph Budd to W. D. Hines, Aug. 29, 1931.

Chapter 25

1. Most of the material for this chapter came from files in the executive and comptroller departments and from the directors' and executive committee's record books. Important for the financial part of the chapter was W. P. Kenney's correspondence with GN's director, Arthur Curtiss James, Henry S. Sturgis of the First National Bank of the City of New York, C. H. Hand, Jr., a partner in a New York law firm that handled many of Great Northern's legal affairs, and G. H. Hess, comptroller. For the second part of the chapter communications with C. O. Jenks were helpful. *Railway Age* continued to be a prime source, along with *The Wall Street Journal* on financial matters. Statistical data came from GN's Annual Report to Stockholders and the Annual Report of the Great Northern Railway Company to the Interstate Commerce Commission, and comparative data were available in that agency's *Statistics of Railways in the United States* for appropriate years. These were informative: Thor Hultgren, *American Transportation*

in Prosperity and Depression (New York: National Bureau of Economic Research, 1948); Harold G. Moulton and others, *The American Transportation Problem* (Washington, D.C.: Brookings Institution, 1933); and Charles F. Foell and M. E. Thompson, *Diesel-Electric Locomotives* (New York: Diesel, 1946).

2. GN AR, 1931, p. 9.
3. GN, W. P. Kenney to C. H. Hand, Jr., July 3, 1933.
4. GN, Henry S. Sturgis, "That Banker Domination of Railroads," unpublished memorandum, July 1937.
5. GN, Kenney to Hand, July 3, 1933.
6. GN, Kenney to Hand, Jan. 4, 1934.
7. GN, Hand to Kenney, May 22, 1935.
8. GN, Kenney to directors, June 27, 1935; GN, Kenney to Hand, Feb. 12, 1935.
9. GN, Reconstruction Finance Corporation Report, Great Northern Railway Company, March 1936; GN, Jesse Jones to Kenney, Sept. 27, 1935.
10. GN, H. S. Sturgis to Kenney, Oct. 2, 1935; GN, Kenney to Hand, Oct. 24, 1935.
11. GN, Kenney, Memorandum of telephone conversation with Jesse Jones, Dec. 15, 1935; GN, Jones to Kenney, Dec. 15, 1935.
12. GN, Sturgis to Kenney, June 3, 1936, GN, A. C. James to Kenney, June 3, 1936; *The Wall Street Journal*, May 30, 1936.
13. GN, C. O. Jenks to F. J. Gavin, Sept. 14, 1939.
14. GN, Kenney to Jenks, Oct. 19, 1933, and May 4, 1934; GN, Kenney to H. H. Brown, May 28, 1937.
15. GN, Kenney to Gavin, Dec. 1, 1936.
16. GN, A. J. Dickinson, Memorandum, Dec. 30, 1931; GN, Memorandum, Dickinson on Joseph B. Eastman's Comments, Dec. 30, 1931.
17. GN, Kenney to F. G. Dorety, Feb. 14, 1935; GN, A. L. Janes to Kenney, March 5, 1936.

Chapter 26

1. This chapter is based mainly on materials from files of the executive, vice president-traffic, and agricultural development departments. E. C. Leedy continued to be remarkably thorough in his reports, and H. H. Brown had the difficult task of explaining to W. P. Kenney why traffic volume was always smaller than the president expected. *Railway Age* was consulted, and the GN annual reports to the ICC and the ICC's annual statistical volumes continued to supply

basic data. Our discussion of rising highway competition comes in part from Charles A. Taff, *Commercial Motor Transportation* (Chicago: R. D. Irwin, 1950), and from U.S. Federal Works Agency, *Highway Statistics: Summary to 1945* (Washington, D.C., 1947). The establishment of irrigation in Washington's Big Bend Country is discussed in U.S. Bureau of Reclamation, *General Information—Columbia Basin Project, Washington* (Washington, D. C.: GPO, 1939), and the GN's interest in the matter is manifested in the company's *Columbia Basin Development* (St. Paul, nd) and in its *Three Great Dams* (St. Paul, nd).

2. GN, W. P. Kenney to H. H. Brown, Feb. 11, July 12, 1932; GN, Kenney to Brown, Sept. 26, 1933; GN, Kenney to F. J. Gavin, July 29, 1937.
3. GN, *Time Tables*, Dec. 1933, p. 9.
4. GN, Kenney to Budd, April 24, 1930.
5. GN, Kenney to Brown, Oct. 26, 1933; GN public relations department, News Release, March 20, 1935.
6. GN, Kenney to A. J. Dickinson, Sept. 23, 1933; GN, Kenney to Brown, Aug. 5, 1933; GN, Kenney to Budd, Jan. 23, 1936.
7. GN, Kenney to F. G. Dorety, Nov. 25, 1933.
8. GN, Kenney to G. H. Hess, May 24, 1934.
9. GN, Kenney to F. R. Newman, Nov. 2, 1938.
10. GN, Kenney to A. L. Janes, Oct. 10, 1935.
11. GN, Kenney to Thomas Balmer, Oct. 22, 1937.
12. GN, Kenney to Brown, Aug. 20, 1935.
13. GN, C. O. Jenks to Kenney, Jan. 16, Sept. 29, 1938; GN, Kenney to Jenks, Sept. 30, 1938.
14. GN, Kenney to Janes, Feb. 10, 1936; GN, E. B. Duncan to E. C. Leedy, Jan. 29, 1935.
15. GN, Kenney to Brown, Sept. 9, 1937; Leedy to Brown, Dec. 19, 1934.
16. GN, Kenney to J. B. Bingham, Feb. 4, 1932.
17. GN, Kenney to Brown, Dec. 10, 1934; GN, Kenney to C. E. Finley, Oct. 14, 1937.
18. GN, Kenney to Brown, May 19, July 5, 1933; GN, Kenney to Brown, March 12, 1935, Nov. 16, 1936.

Chapter 27

1. Executive and public relations department files were essential in preparing this chapter. The correspondence of Vice President C. O. Jenks with President F. J. Gavin was especially meaningful, for it was Jenks who handled the difficult problem of providing rolling stock needed to move the unprecedented vol-

ume of wartime traffic. *Railway Age, Traffic World*, and the St. Paul newspapers were useful. The standard account of wartime transportation problems by Joseph R. Rose, *American Wartime Transportation* (New York, 1953), may be supplemented by reading Claude M. Fuess, *Joseph B. Eastman: Servant of the People* (New York: Columbia University Press, 1952). Other sources include Richard C. Overton, "Ralph Budd: Railroad Entrepreneur," *The Palimpsest*, vol. 36 (Nov. 1955), in which the government's first effort to mobilize transportation is discussed, and Elliot Janeway, *Struggle for Survival* (New Haven: Yale University Press, 1951), in which those efforts are criticized. U.S. Office of Defense Transportation, *Civilian War Transport* (Washington, D.C.: GPO, 1948), and the Annual Reports of the ICC provide information on how government direction of the nation's transportation facilities evolved; Carl R. Gray, Jr., *Railroading in Eighteen Countries* (New York: Scribner, 1955), gives an account of the military rail units. Several interviews by Ralph W. Hidy and Muriel E. Hidy with Frank J. Gavin and Vernon P. Turnburke were most helpful.

2. Excerpts from *AAR Weekly Information Letter*, No. 378, Oct. 12, 1940. John F. Stover, *The Life and Decline of the American Railroad* (New York: Oxford University Press, 1970), pp. 176–191.
3. Quoted in *Railway Age*, vol. 112 (Jan. 17, 1942), p. 215.
4. GN, Gavin to J. J. Pelley, May 15, 1941.
5. GN, Gavin to C. O. Jenks, Jan. 22, 1942.
6. GN, Gavin to A. Price, May 26, 1942.
7. GN, Gavin to Jenks, Dec. 29, 1942.
8. GN, Gavin to Pelley, May 10, 1943.
9. GN, Gavin to Jenks, Sept. 21, 1945.
10. GN, Jenks to Gavin, Aug. 25, 1943.
11. GN, Gavin to Pelley, Aug. 19, 1940.
12. GN, A. E. Dypwich to Gavin, March 17, 1943.
13. GN, E. B. Smith to C. E. Finley, Aug. 6, 1945.
14. GN, Jenks to Gavin, Dec. 16, 1945.

Chapter 28

1. For this chapter the letters in the executive department were the primary source, especially the correspondence of the presidents, W. P. Kenney and F. J. Gavin, with the vice presidents of Operations, C. O. Jenks and his successors. The annual reports of the ICC and the annual *Review of Railway Operations* of the Association of American Railroads are convenient guides to national legislation and to industry-wide problems. Both D. Phillip Locklin, *Economics of Transportation* (Homewood: R. D. Irwin, 1966), and Julius H. Parmelee, *The Modern Railway* (New York: Longman, Green, 1940) are indispensable textbooks for many aspects of modern railroad history, including that of labor–management relations. Among other books utilized were: Jacob J. Kaufman, *Collective Bargaining in the Railroad Industry* (New York: King's Crown Press, 1954); P. Harvey Middleton, *Railways and Organized Labor* (Chicago, 1941); Leonard A. Lecht, *Experience under Railway Labor Legislation* (New York: AMS Press, 1955); *History of the Brotherhood of Maintenance of Way Employees: Its History and Growth* (Washington, D.C., 1955); R. C. Richardson, *The Locomotive Engineer, 1863–1963: A Century of Railway Labor Relations and Work Rules* (Ann Arbor: University of Michigan, Graduate School of Business, 1963); and Harold M. Levinson, Charles M. Rehonus, Joseph P. Goldberg, and Mark L. Kahn, *Collective Bargaining and Technological Change in American Transportation*, The Transportation Center of Northwestern University (Evanston, Ill., 1971).
2. GN, F. H. Fljozdal to Ralph Budd, Jan. 8, 1931.
3. GN, C. O. Jenks to Ralph Budd, April 27, 1931.
4. GN, Jenks to C. McDonough, Feb. 25, 1937.
5. Quoted in Richard C. Overton, *Burlington Route: A History of the Burlington Lines* (New York: Alfred A. Knopf, 1965), p. 442.
6. GN, Jenks to Kenney, Dec. 6, 1936; GN, Jenks to Kenney, Sept. 8, 1937.
7. *Railway Age*, vol. 104 (Jan. 8, 1938), p. 128.
8. *Railway Age*, vol. 105 (Oct. 8, 1938), pp. 503–504.
9. GN, J. G. Luhrsen to Gavin, April 10, 1945; GN, F. J. Gavin to All Employees, May 18, 1940.
10. Arbitration Board, Use of Firemen on Other Than Steam Power Consist of Road and Yard Crews, The 1937 Firemen's National Diesel Agreement, Excerpt from the Stenographic Transcript of the Proceedings, Statement of Mr. Fred G. Gurley, Presented by Counsel for the Carriers (np, Sept.–Nov. 1963), p. 13.
11. Quoted in Overton, *Burlington Route*, p. 435.

Chapter 29

1. GN, F. J. Gavin to C. O. Jenks, Oct. 16, 1945. This chapter is based primarily on material from executive department files, especially President Gavin's correspondence with V. P. Turnburke, C. E. Finley, and J. A. Tauer, GN AR and AR GN-ICC, and several interviews with F. J. Gavin and Vernon P. Turnburke by Ralph W. Hidy and Muriel E. Hidy. The trade journals, *Railway Age* and *Traffic World*, *Railway Mechanical and Electrical Engineer*, and *Diesel Power and Diesel Transportation* provided supplementary information on technological change.
2. GN, Gavin to John M. Budd and others, July 18, 1949.
3. GN, C. E. Finley to Gavin, March 28, 1951.
4. GN, Jenks to Gavin, March 4, 1947.
5. GN, F. R. Newman to Gavin, Oct. 26, 1939; Gavin to T. H. Henkle, May 21, 1941.
6. Interview with F. J. Gavin, by the Hidys, Aug. 12, 1953.

Chapter 30

1. This chapter draws upon John M. Budd's correspondence with his vice presidents and upon the standard trade journals, including *Railway Age* and *Traffic World*. The Great Northern's *Talking It Over*, a house periodical, was useful, and the Association of American Railroad's annual *Review of Railway Operations* and *Yearbook of Railroad Facts* provided basic data. Standard accounts of the modern railroad problem are found in John F. Stover, *The Life and Decline of the American Railroad* (New York: Oxford University Press, 1970) and James C. Nelson, *Railroad Transportation and Public Policy* (Washington, D.C., 1959). Some economic problems of the period are described in Harold G. Vatter, *The U.S. Economy in the 1950s* (New York, 1963). The Association of American Railroads, *The High Cost of Conflicting Public Transportation Policies* (Washington, D.C.: AAR, 1951), presents the industry's point of view.

Among the many studies of the railroad problem these are the most important: "Problems of the Railroads," U.S. Senate, *Hearings before the Subcommittee on Surface Transportation of the Committee on Interstate and Foreign Commerce*, 85th Cong., 2nd Sess. (1958); "Adequacy of Transportation Systems in Support of the National Defense Effort in the Event of Mobilization," U.S. House, *Hearings before a Subcommittee of the Committee on Armed Forces*, 86th Cong., 1st Sess. (1959); U.S. Department of Commerce, *Modern Transport Policy* (Washington, D.C., 1956); U.S. Department of Commerce, *Federal Transportation Policy and Program* (Washington, D.C., 1960); and "National Transportation Problems," U.S. Senate, *Report* No. 445, 87th Cong., 1st Sess. (1961).

For details on the passenger problem, see *Railway Passenger Train Deficit*, 306 ICC 417; Association of American Railroads, *Statistics of Railroad Passenger Service* (Washington, D.C., 1966), and Association of American Railroads, *The Case of the Disappearing Passenger Train* (Washington, D.C., nd). Peter Lyon's *To Hell in a Day Coach* (Philadelphia: Lippincott, 1968) is a journalistic account of the horrors, alleged and otherwise, of traveling by rail. See also Donald M. Itzkoff, *Off the Track: The Decline of the Intercity Passenger Train in the United States* (Westport, Conn.: Greenwood, 1985).

Some of the problems arising from modal competition and pricing policies may be seen in John R. Meyer and others, *The Economics of Competition in the Transportation Industries* (Cambridge: Oelgeschlager, 1960); *Ingot Molds from Pennsylvania to Steelton, Ky.*, 323 ICC 758; W. J. Baumol and others, "The Role of Cost in the Minimum Pricing of Railroad Services," *The Journal of Business*, vol. 35 (Oct., 1962), pp. 357–366; and Howard W. Davis, "A Review of Federal Rate Regulation and Its Impact upon the Railway Industry," *Land Economics*, vol. 44 (Feb., 1968), pp. 1–10.

For the standard account of the major piece of national legislation enacted during the period see George W. Hilton, *The Transportation Act of 1958* (Bloomington: Indiana University Press, 1969); and for an early analysis see Robert W. Harbeson, "The Transportation Act of 1958," *Land Economics*, vol. 35 (May 1959), pp. 156–171.

2. "Adequacy of Transportation Systems in Support of the National Defense Effort in the Event of Mobilization," U.S. House, *Hearings Before a Subcommittee of the Committee on Armed Forces*, 86th Cong., 1st Sess. (1959), p. 338.

3. "Problems of the Railroads," U.S. Senate, *Hearings before the Subcommittee on Surface Transportation of the Committee on Interstate and Foreign Commerce,*

85th Cong., 2nd Sess. (1958), p. 435.

4. "Adequacy of Transportation Systems," p. 336.

5. "Problems of the Railroads," p. 429, quoted in *Railway Age*, vol. 131 (Oct. 29, 1951), p. 11.

6. U.S. Department of Commerce, *Modern Transport Policy* (Washington, D.C., 1956), pp. 1–10.

7. *Railroad Passenger Train Deficit*, 306 ICC 417; ICC, Annual Report, 1959, pp. 2–3.

8. U.S. Department of Commerce, *Federal Transportation Policy and Program* (Washington, D.C., 1960), p. 11.

9. Kennedy's speech is given in full in *Railway Age*, vol. 152 (April 16, 1962), pp. 12–19.

10. Ibid., pp. 9–10; GN AR, 1962, p. 2.

11. GN, Gregory S. Prince to Willard Deason, May 11, 1967.

12. *Modern Railroads*, vol. 23 (March 1968), p. 11.

13. "National Transportation Policy," U.S. Senate, *Report* No. 445, 87th Cong., 1st Sess. (1961), pp. 322, 323. *Railway Age*, vol. 164 (April 22, 1968), p. 40.

14. ICC, *Annual Report*, 1961, pp. 189–190.

15. GN, David I. Mackie, Address, Pittsburgh, Feb. 14, 1961.

Chapter 31

1. Information for this chapter is from the files of Great Northern and a variety of publications. The files of the executive department and those of the vice presidents dealing with labor were examined. Among the significant papers were John M. Budd's correspondence with C. A. Pearson, and in the operating department, letters of successive vice presidents and of M. C. Anderson. Also in the files mentioned were circulars, information to superintendents, and a large correspondence of Pearson with many men. There was also a mass of reports, such as those of the National Mediation Board, and several special studies, including some dealing with the struggle over employment of firemen on diesels and other work rules in union contracts. Helpful publications included GN's *Talking It Over*, standard trade journals, and the Minneapolis and St. Paul newspapers, which devoted a great deal of attention to labor and personnel problems. The Association of American Railroads' annual *Review of Railway Operations* was a convenient guide to major industry-wide developments. Among the books with useful material were R. C.

Richardson, *The Locomotive Engineer, 1863–1963: A Century of Railway Labor Relations and Work Rules* (Ann Arbor: University of Michigan, Graduate School of Business, 1963); William F. Cottrell, *Technological Change and Labor in the Railroad Industry: A Comparative Study* (Lexington, 1970); Harold M. Levinson and others, *Collective Bargaining and Technological Change in American Transportation* (Evanston: Transportation Center at Northwestern University, 1971); and Summer H. Slichter, James J. Healy, and E. Robert Livernash, *The Impact of Collective Bargaining on Management* (Washington, D.C.: Brookings Institution, 1960).

2. *New York Times*, July 14, 1963.

3. GN, John Budd to N. R. Crump, May 19, 1958.

4. GN, D. P. Loomis to Labor Leaders, Feb. 10, 1959; GN, Loomis to Executives of Member Roads, Feb. 13, 1959.

5. GN, H. E. Gilbert to all members, June 15, 1958; *St. Paul Dispatch*, Feb. 20, 1959.

6. GN, BLE Press Release, Feb. 23, 1962.

Chapter 32

1. This chapter depends upon materials in the files of these departments—executive vice president-traffic, law, land and tax—and from others dealing with development work. Also serviceable were extensive interviews with men involved in the work. *Railway Age* devotes some attention to development work; *Industrial Development* is especially helpful on industrial promotion. Great Northern's *Great Resources* and *Report to Shippers* had extensive information. *In the Matter of Leases and Grants of Property by Carriers to Shippers*, 73 ICC 677, suggests something of early industrial development work, and Donald R. Gilmore, *Developing the "Little" Economies* (Committee for Economic Development, Supplementary Paper No. 10, np, nd) describes the work in a more recent period. On taconite, see *Engineering and Mining Journal, Skilling's Mining Review*, and E. W. Davis, *Pioneering with Taconite* (St. Paul, 1964).

2. GN, E. B. Duncan to F. R. Newman, June 12, 1944.

3. *Railway Age*, vol. 153 (Aug. 6, 1962), pp. 30–31.

4. Interview of R. V. Scott with B. J. Stasson, May 14, 1959.

5. GN, A. J. Haley to C. E. Finley, May 15, 1958.

Notes

Chapter 33

1. In preparing this chapter, we relied upon the files of the Great Northern. Especially important were those of the executive and public relations departments, supplemented by GN ''Reports to the Interstate Commerce Commission,'' some significant AFEs, and letters from operating men, chiefly I. G. Pool, T. A. Jerrow, J. L. Robson, and Comptroller J. A. Tauer. Circulars in the operating department were informative, as were interviews with officials of the operating, engineering, and other departments involved in the technical aspects of railway operations. *Railway Age* and *Modern Railroads* had many useful articles. Helpful also were the company's house organs: *Talking It Over* and the *Goat*. A new publication by GN, the annual *Progress Report to Shippers*, carried much valuable information. The construction of Gavin Yard is described in the GN's pamphlet *Gavin Yard, Minot, North Dakota* (St. Paul, 1956), and the early development of computers was outlined in *Electronic Data Processing at Great Northern* (St. Paul, 1957). Among informative interviews were: R. V. Scott with C. D. Archibald, Aug. 3, 5, 1964; R. V. Scott with C. H. Wesman, signals and communications, Aug. 3, 1964; and Muriel Hidy with Margaret Holden, who gave a great deal of help based on her years of dedication to computers. Useful books on the industry as a whole were William F. Cottrell, *Technological Change and Labor in the Railroad Industry: A Comparative Study* (Lexington, 1970), and Donald M. Street, *Railroad Equipment Financing* (New York: Columbia University Press, 1959).
2. GN, C. E. Finley to J. M. Budd, May 13, 1952; GN, Finley to Budd, Jan. 14, Oct. 6, 1953.
3. GN, Budd to Directors, April 11, 1958; T. A. Jerrow to Budd, April 11, 1958.
4. GN, F. J. Gavin to C. O. Jenks, July 19, 1945.

Chapter 34

1. This chapter rests on executive and vice president-traffic department files, as well as a mass of company brochures and other publications issued in the 1950s and 1960s. Especially useful was GN's *Progress Report to Shippers*, describing the innovations adopted to meet customers' needs. Developments within the industry are well covered in *Railway Age, Traffic World*, and *Modern Railroads*. New services offered by GN are often described in layman's language in *Talking It Over*, and industry-wide changes in services may be followed in the Association of American Railroads, *Yearbook of Railroad Facts*.
2. GN AR, 1957, p. 7.
3. GN, C. E. Finley to J. A. Tauer, Feb. 14, 1952.
4. *Talking It Over*, vol. 10 (May 1967), pp. 2–3; *Railway Age*, vol. 162 (May 8, 1967), pp. 20–21.
5. GN AR, 1967, p. 2.
6. GN, *Progress Report to Shippers*, 1967, p. 3.
7. GN AR, 1959, p. 14.
8. *Talking It Over*, vol. 9 (May 1966), p. 10; GN, *Progress Report to Shippers*, 1967, p. 3.
9. Numerous advertisements, provided by GN public relations department.
10. GN AR, 1961, p. 7.
11. *Talking It Over*, vol. 10 (July 1967), p. 3; *Railway Age*, vol. 163 (July 31, 1967), p. 34.
12. GN AR, 1967, p. 14.
13. GN, J. M. Budd, Statement before the West Coast General Management Conference, Jan. 27, 1959.

Chapter 35

1. This chapter is based upon material from executive, law, and public relations department files, which contain correspondence and copies of the legal briefs and other documents prepared by both advocates and opponents of the merger. Because of wide interest in the outcome of the case, *Railway Age, Traffic World, Business Week, The Wall Street Journal, New York Times*, and the Minneapolis and St. Paul newspapers provided continuous coverage as the proceedings progressed through the Interstate Commerce Commission and the federal courts. Great Northern Railway Company and others, *Consolidation, Key to Transportation Progress* (np, 1961) is perhaps the clearest statement of the companies' point of view. The ICC decisions are in *Great Northern Pacific and Burlington Lines, Inc. Merger*, 328 ICC 460 and 331 ICC 228, 869. The Supreme Court decision that brought the issue to a close is United States v. Interstate Commerce Commission, 396 U.S. 491. Among secondary accounts of the merger movement, of which creation of the Burlington Northern was a part, Michael Conant, *Railroad Mergers and Abandonments* (Berkeley and Los Angeles: University of California Press, 1964), and Richard Saunders, *The Railroad Mergers and the Coming of Conrail* (Westport, Conn.: Greenwood, 1978) were most useful. Interviews of Ralph W. Hidy with John M. Budd and a detailed statement by John Budd were significant. Additional interviews and correspondence of Don L. Hofsommer with Robert W. Downing, Thomas J. Lamphier, Anthony Kane, Charles W. Moore, John Robson, Frank Perrin, and Pat Stafford were especially pertinent.
2. *Railway Age* (Oct. 17, 1960), p. 9; ibid., Oct. 31, 1960, p. 9; Don L. Hofsommer, *The Southern Pacific, 1901–1985* (College Station: Texas A&M University Press, 1986), p. 262.
3. Interview of Don L. Hofsommer with Robert W. Downing, Jan. 26, 1987.
4. *Talking It Over*, vol. 4 (Nov. 1961), p. 5; Great Northern Railway Company, *Consolidation, Key to Transportation Progress* (np, 1961).
5. *Railway Age*, vol. 152 (June 4, 1962), p. 13.
6. Report of the Examiner, ICC Dockets 21478–21480, *Great Northern Pacific and Burlington Lines, Inc., Merger*.
7. *New York Times*, Aug. 25, 1964, p. 52.
8. *Great Northern Pacific and Burlington Lines, Inc., Merger*, 328 ICC 522, 528.
9. *St. Paul Pioneer Press*, July 28, 1966, p. 27; *St. Paul Dispatch*, Aug. 1, 1966, p. 15; Aug. 24, 1966, Part III, p. 1.
10. *Traffic World*, vol. 132 (Dec. 23, 1967), p. 55.
11. *Railway Age*, vol. 164 (April 29, 1968), p. 11.
12. U.S. Department of Justice, Applicants for Preliminary Injunction and for Temporary Restraining Order, U.S. District Court for the District of Columbia, May 9, 1968.
13. Brief for the United States in the Supreme Court of the United States, October Term, 1969, United States v. Interstate Commerce Commission.
14. United States v. Interstate Commerce Commission, 396 U.S. 510–511, 514, 516, 530.
15. *St. Paul Dispatch*, Feb. 2, 1970, p. 2; *Burlington Northern News*, March 2, 1970.

APPENDIX A

Original Track-laying Record

Year	Description	Miles	Total Miles
1862	St. Paul to Minneapolis, MN	9.90	9.90
1864	Minneapolis to Elk River, MN	28.60	28.60
1866	Elk River to East St. Cloud, MN	36.40	36.40
1867	East St. Cloud to Sauk Rapids, MN	2.14	
	Minneapolis Jct. to East Minneapolis, MN	0.70	
	East Minneapolis to 0.6 Ms. east of Lake Jct., MN	14.00	
			16.84
1868	0.6 Ms. east of Lake Jct. to Howard Lake, MN	29.00	29.00
1869	Howard Lake to Willmar, MN	49.00	49.00
1870	Willmar to 0.6 Ms. west of Benson, MN	31.00	31.00
1871	0.6 Ms. west of Benson to Breckenridge, MN	81.12	81.12
1872	East St. Cloud to Melrose, MN	35.00	
	4.9 Ms. N. of Barnesville to 2.3 Ms. S. of Warren, MN	104.00	
			139.00
1875	Crookston to 6.5 Ms. E. of Mallory, MN	10.50	10.50
1877	4.9 Ms. N. of Barnesville to 1.4 Ms. N. of Barnesville, MN	3.50	
	Breckenridge to Barnesville, MN	29.00	
			32.50
1878	Melrose to Alexandria, MN	31.50	
	2.3 Ms. S. of Warren to St. Vincent, MN	62.10	
	St. Vincent Jct. to boundary (rebuilt in 1902), MN	2.62	
			96.22
1879	Alexandria to Fergus Falls, MN	45.01	
	Fergus Falls to 1.4 Ms. N. of Barnesville, MN	32.26	
	6.5 Ms. E. of Mallory, MN to 1 Mi. W. of Grand Forks, ND	14.54	
			91.81
1880	Barnesville, MN to 0.4 Ms. W. of Reynolds, ND	81.63	
	Breckenridge, MN to Durbin, ND	48.00	
	1 Mi. W. of Grand Forks to 2 Ms. W. of Ojata, ND	12.00	
	Morris to Brown's Valley, MN	46.68	
	Casselton to Mayville (acquired from NP), ND	43.33	
			231.64
1881	0.4 Ms. W. of Reynolds to Grand Forks Jct., ND	16.00	
	Grand Forks to Grafton, ND	40.00	
	Durbin to Portland, ND	53.10	
	2 Ms. W. of Ojata to 1.6 Ms. W. of Larimore, ND	16.30	
	Osseo Jct. to 0.5 Ms. W. of Clearwater, MN	50.57	
	Fergus Falls to Pelican Rapids (acquired from NP), MN	21.65	
	Carlisle Jct. to Elizabeth, MN	3.52	
	Minnetonka North Shore Line, MN	5.93	
			207.07
1882	0.5 Ms. W. of Clearwater to St. Cloud, MN incl. N. Wye	12.50	
	East St. Cloud to Hinckley, MN	66.43	
	Sauk Centre to 0.54 Ms. E. of Browerville, MN	25.47	
	Grafton to boundary, ND	40.94	
	Everest to Casselton, ND	3.00	
	Ripon to Hope, ND	29.50	

	1.6 Ms. W. of Larimore to 1 Mi. W. of Bartlett, ND	39.80	
			217.64
1883	Hamline to University Switch (Short Line), MN	3.35	
	0.54 Ms. E. of Browerville to Eagle Bend, MN	10.97	
	Shirley to St. Hilaire, MN	21.55	
	Moorhead Jct. to Halstad, MN	34.09	
	1 Mi. W. of Bartlett to Devils Lake, ND	20.26	
	University Switch to Minneapolis (Mpls. Union Ry.), MN	2.62	
			92.84
1884	St. Vincent Jct. Switch to end of track via old depot, MN	2.12	
	Portland to Larimore, ND	30.90	
	Mayville to Portland Jct., ND	4.11	
	Park River Jct. to Park River, ND	34.78	
			71.91
1885	State Fair Grounds Spur, St. Paul, MN	0.64	
	St. Cloud to 4.79 Ms. E. of Rockville, MN	14.12	
			14.76
1886	Elk River to Milaca, MN	31.80	
	4.79 Ms. E. of Rockville to 0.65 Ms. E. of Willmar Jct., MN	41.08	
	Hutchinson Jct. to Hutchinson, MN	53.13	
	Aberdeen Line Jct., SD (Yarmouth) to Rutland, ND	55.10	
	Rutland Jct., ND to Aberdeen, SD	64.00	
	Devils Lake to 4.23 Ms. W. of Minot, ND	121.16	
			366.27
1887	Evansville to Tintah, MN	32.03	
	Rutland to Ellendale, ND	49.22	
	Benson, MN to Watertown, SD	91.62	
	Moorhead, MN to Wahpeton, ND	42.91	
	Park River to Langdon, ND	39.10	
	Rugby Jct. to Bottineau, ND	38.66	
	4.23 Ms. W. of Minot, ND to S. side of Sun River (Great Falls), MT	545.02	
	Johnstown Jct. to jct. with Sand Coulee Br., MT	3.10	
	Red Mountain Br. Helena, MT	1.47	
	Great Falls to Helena, MT	96.56	
			939.69
1888	Hinckley, MN to West Superior, WI	69.78	
	Crookston Jct. (Carman) to Fosston, MN	44.69	
	Church's Ferry to St. John, ND	55.21	
	Montana Silver & Lead Smelting Co. Branch (Great Falls), MT	5.33	
	Great Falls to Sand Coulee, MT	14.53	
	Fair Grounds Spur at Helena, MT	0.85	
	Helena to Butte, MT	72.78	
	Watertown to Huron (DW&P Ry.), MN	69.84	
	Willmar, MN to Sioux Falls (W&SF Ry.), SD	146.91	
	Duluth Terminal Ry., MN	1.78	
	Kettle River Branch (Sandstone), MN	2.61	
	St. Cloud Mill Spur to Dam (off Osseo Line), MN	2.53	
	Sioux Falls (SF Term. RR.), SD	3.00	
			489.84
1889	Garretson, SD to Sioux City, IA (SC&N Ry.)	96.00	
	South Bellingham (Fairhaven) to Sedro (F&S Rd.), WA	25.71	
	Spokane to Colville (SF&N Ry.), WA	88.15	
	Sioux City (SCT RR. & Whse. Co.), IA	1.28	
			211.14
1890	0.65 Ms. E. of Willmar Jct. to Willmar Jct., MN	0.65	
	Grafton to Cavalier, ND	31.71	
	Great Falls to B&M Smelter, MT	5.04	
	GF&C Connection at Great Falls, MT	1.26	
	Gerber (Allen) to Neihart, MT	56.34	
	Monarch to Barker, MT	10.69	
	Pacific Jct. to 98.92 Ms. W. of Pacific Jct., MT	98.92	
	South Bellingham (Fairhaven) to boundary (F&S Rd.), WA	24.25	

Year	Description	Miles	Total Miles
	Sedro to 1.10 Ms. E. of Sedro (E. Skagit Div., F&S Rd.), WA	1.10	
	New Westminster Southern Ry., BC	23.51	
	Anacortes to 28.07 Ms. E. of Anacortes, WA	28.07	
	Cloquet to Paupores (Acquired D&W), MN	24.38	
	Colville to Little Dalles (SF&N Ry.), WA	35.90	
			341.82
1891	Minneapolis Western Ry., MN	1.69	
	Eagle Bend to Park Rapids, MN	54.52	
	Halstad, MN to Alton, ND	10.38	
	98.92 Ms. W. of Pacific Jct. to 256.4 Ms. W. of Pacific Jct., MT	157.48	
	Seattle to F&S Jct. (S&M Ry.), WA	78.50	
	1.10 Ms. E. of Sedro to 3.11 Ms. E. of (E. Skagit Div., F&S Rd.), WA	2.01	
	3.11 Ms. E. of Sedro to coal mines (F&S Rd.), WA	3.79	
	New Westminster Southern Ry., BC	0.59	
	28.07 Ms. E. of Anacortes to Hamilton, WA	6.07	
	Paupores to La Prairie (Acquired D&W), MN	43.90	
			358.93
1892	St. Hilaire to Thief River Falls, MN	7.59	
	St. Hilaire to Red Lake Falls, MN	10.13	
	Mountain View Branch, Butte, MT	3.38	
	256.4 Ms. W. of Pacific Jct., MT to jct. with UP at Spokane, WA	254.90	
	Jct. with UP at Spokane to point ½ mile west of Embro, WA	244.32	
	1¾ Ms. W. of Scenic to jct. with EMC Ry. at Lowell, WA	59.13	
	Saunders to Allouez (Omaha Crossing), WI	5.33	
	La Prairie to Deer River (acquired D&W), MN	16.82	
	Part of line, Mississippi – Dewey Lake Line (DMR&N), MN	12.76	
	Little Dalles to Northport (SF&N), WA	6.40	
	Allouez (D&WT Co.), WI	0.92	
			621.68
1893	North "Y" at Minneapolis Jct., MN	0.25	
	"Y" with Minneapolis Union Ry., MN ("Y" removed in 1913 and replaced in 1925 — 14 mi. lg.)	0.08	
	Sioux Falls to Yankton, SD	58.34	
	Addison West Line, ND	11.78	
	½ Mi. west of Embro to 1¾ Ms. west of Scenic, WA	6.98	
	Part of Mississippi – Dewey Lake Line (DMR&N), MN	8.38	
	Northport to boundary (SF&N), WA	10.21	
	Boundary to Troup Jct. (N&FS), BC	55.42	
			151.44
1894	Part of Mississippi – Dewey Lake Line (DMR&N), MN	11.19	11.19
1895	Casselton to Fleming, ND	4.35	
	Part of Mississippi – Dewey Lake Line (DMR&N), MN	2.10	
			6.45
1896	Hope to Aneta, ND	28.07	
	Halstad to Crookston Jct. (Carman), MN	32.23	
	Part of Mississippi – Dewey Lake Line (DMR&N), MN	1.76	
	Northport to boundary (C&RM Ry.), WA	7.51	
	Boundary to Rossland (RM Ry.), BC	9.59	
			79.16
1897	Park Rapids to Akeley, MN	18.32	
	Cavalier to Walhalla, ND	16.13	
	Langdon to Hannah, ND	21.06	
	Lewis Jct. to Stockett — Cottonwood Branch, MT	5.21	
	Part of Mississippi – Dewey Lake Line (DMR&N), MN	13.45	
			74.17

Original Track-laying record

1898	Akeley to Cass Lake incl. W. Wye, MN	30.69	
	Fosston to Deer River, MN	98.59	
	Cloquet, MN to Boylston, WI incl. Cutoff	27.53	
			156.81
1899	Coon Creek to Hinckley, MN	64.71	
	Hibbing to Virginia incl. track to Commodore Mine, MN	18.78	
	Bonners Ferry to boundary (KV Ry.), ID	25.79	
	Boundary to Kuskonook (B&N Ry.), BC	14.98	
	Dean (Colbert) to connection with SF&N near Wayside, WA	3.57	
			127.83
1900	Spring Park to St. Bonifacius, MN	8.22	
	Hamilton to Sauk, WA	18.84	
	Kalispell to Somers — Tie Plant, MT	10.32	
	Cascade Tunnel Line, WA	3.52	
			40.90
1901	Bottineau to Souris, ND	12.72	
	Brookston to Ellis incl. "Y" at Ellis, MN	46.49	
	Jennings to 17.35 Ms. N. of Jennings, MT	17.35	
	Sauk to Rockport including "Y," WA	2.36	
			78.92
1902	0/00, Devils Lake, to 1268/39, Starkweather (FG&S Co. Ry.), ND	24.02	
	Kelly Lake to Kinney — Hawkins Mine, MN	10.42	
	Lakota to Edmore incl. "Y," ND	27.72	
	17.35 Ms. N. of Jennings, MI to Swinton, BC	77.90	
	Belleville to So. Bellingham (Fairhaven), WA	18.82	
	Marcus to Laurier, incl. "Y" (W&GN), WA	27.66	
	Laurier to Danville (VV&E), WA	14.40	
	Danville to Republic (W&GN), WA	31.90	
	Eureka Gulch Branch at Republic, WA	8.37	
	Mtn. Lion, Lone Pine & Quilp Spurs (Eureka Gulch), WA	1.45	
	Grand Forks Jct. to Grand Forks, BC incl. W. "Y"	2.10	

	Willard to Shelby, MT	97.93	
	Virden to Sweet Grass incl. Virden "Y," MT	36.54	
	Floweree to Great Falls, MT	21.77	
			401.00
1903	Cloverdale to Ladner (Port Guichon) incl. "Y" (VT Ry. & F. Co.), BC	17.49	
	Souris to Westhope, ND	16.41	
	Kelly Lake to Flanders, South Range Line, MN	9.69	
	Granville to Mohall, incl. W. "Y," ND	46.97	
	Columbia Falls to Whitefish incl. W. "Y," MT	8.75	
	Part of New Westminster – Vancouver Line (VW&Y), BC	4.93	
	Spokane, WA to Coeur d'Alene (SC&P Ry.), ID	30.74	
			134.98
1904	Colton to Sioux Falls (W&SF Ry.), SD	20.50	
	Whitefish to Rexford, MT	60.42	
	Swinton to Fernie, BC	9.82	
	Mohall to Sherwood, ND	14.85	
	Edmore to Munich, ND	24.87	
	Thief River Falls to Greenbush, MN	41.09	
	Granby Smelter Line incl. N. "Y" at Columbia Jct. (VV&E), BC	4.74	
	Part of Copper Jct. – Phoenix Line incl. "Y"'s & Sw. Bks. (VV&E), BC	22.86	
	Part of New Westminster – Vancouver Line (VW&Y), BC	9.86	
			209.01
1905	1246/62 = 1276/78.5, Starkweather, to 2845/40, Rock Lake (FG&S Co. Ry.), ND	29.71	
	2845/40, Rock Lake to 3534/40, Hansboro, ND (BDL&S Ry.)	13.05	
	Rutland to Colton (W&SF Ry.), SD	19.78	
	Part of Copper Jct. – Phoenix Line incl. "Y"'s & Sw. Bks. (VV&E), BC	1.76	
	Westhope to Antler (D&GN), ND	12.76	
	Towner to Maxbass (D&GN), ND	46.12	
	York to Thorne incl. "Y," ND	34.67	

Year	Description	Miles	Total Miles
	St. John to boundary (0.11 Ms. GN) (3.77 Ms. D&GN), ND	3.88	
	Boundary of St. John to 0.87 Ms. N. (BS&HB), Man.	0.87	
	Munich to Sarles, ND	20.54	
	Ellendale to Forbes (0.75 Ms. GN) (13.36 Ms. D&GN), ND	14.11	
	Curlew to boundary at Midway incl. "Y" (W&GN), WA	14.52	
	Red Lake Falls, connection to NP Ry., MN	1.70	
	Spokane to Moran (SC&P Ry.), WA	6.56	
			220.03
1906	Moran to Rosalia (SC&P Ry.), WA	38.82	
	Spring Valley to Geary (SC&P Ry.), WA	10.73	
	Ladow to Palouse (SC&P Ry.), WA	6.98	
	East leg of "Y" and tail track at Oroville (made main trk. in 1914), WA	0.67	
	Berthold to 1.93 Ms. N. of Aurelia incl. "Y," (D&GN), ND	15.17	
	Thorne to Dunseith (D&GN), ND	7.83	
	0.87 Ms. N. of boundary (St. John) to Brandon (BS&HB), Man.	68.59	
	Neche to boundary, ND	0.64	
	Boundary of Neche to Portage La Prairie (M. Ry. of M.), Man.	77.02	
	Boundary at Midway to boundary E. of Molson (VV&E), BC	28.89	
	Boundary E. of Molson to 0.86 Ms. E. of Oroville (W&GN), WA	26.33	
	Brown's Valley Extension, MN	1.64	
	Aneta to 2.03 Ms. W. of Tokio (D&GN), ND	45.53	
	Schurmeir Jct. to Schurmeir incl. W. "Y," ND	4.52	
			333.36
1907	Geary to Ladow (SC&P Ry.), WA	18.18	
	Rosalia to Colfax (SC&P Ry.), WA	30.37	
	West leg of Oroville "Y" (made main track in 1914), WA	0.33	

Year	Description	Miles	Total Miles
	0.86 Ms. E. of Oroville to boundary at Chopaka (W&GN), WA	22.13	
	2.03 Ms. W. of Tokio to Devils Lake, ND	12.14	
	Fermoy to Kelly Lake, MN	23.38	
	Boundary at Chopaka to 1.39 Ms. W. of Keremeos (VV&E), BC	18.19	
	1.93 Ms. N. of Aurelia to Crosby, ND	73.99	
	Walhalla to boundary, ND	5.34	
	Boundary to Morden (M. Ry. of M.), Man.	15.25	
	Fernie to 3.26 Ms. north (CNS), BC	3.26	
	Armington to 2.6 Ms. S. of Merino (B&N), MT	32.21	
	Cloverdale to 1.38 Ms. E. of Cloverdale (VV&E), BC	1.38	
	Watertown to Rutland (W&SF Ry.), SD	62.72	
			318.87
1908	Palouse, WA to Moscow (SC&P Ry.), ID	14.89	
	Coeur d'Alene on former Hayden Lake line (SC&P Ry.), ID	0.98	
	2.6 Ms. S. of Merino to Mossmain (GN Jct.) incl. "Y" (B&N), MT	162.32	
	3.26 Ms. N. of Fernie to Michel (CNS), BC	17.72	
	Greenbush to Warroad, MN	43.16	
	1.38 Ms. E. of Cloverdale to boundary at Sumas (VV&E), BC	27.88	
			266.95
1909	Spear to Flora (SC&P Ry.), WA	6.48	
	Oliver Jct. (Blaine) to boundary, WA	2.94	
	Boundary to Colebrook (VV&E), BC	11.32	
	Colebrook to Brownsville (VV&E), BC	9.73	
	Burrard Inlet line, Vancouver, (VV&E), BC	1.93	
	Keremeos to Princeton (VV&E), BC	40.92	
	Columbia River to Mansfield, WA	60.62	
	Nashwauk to Gunn incl. "Y," MN	22.04	
			155.98
1910	Monroe to Carnation (Tolt) (E&CV Ry.), WA	17.84	
	SP&S connection at Spokane, WA	2.16	
	Bainville to Plentywood, MT	53.20	

	Surrey to 3.5 Ms. E. of Simcoe (F-S line), ND	17.60	
			90.80
1911	Princeton to Coalmont (VV&E), BC	12.15	
	Vaughn to Sun River Crossing, MT	8.36	
	3.5 E. of Simcoe to 4.12 Ms. E. of Simcoe (F-S line), ND	0.62	
	0.26 Ms. E. of Nolan to 1.31 Ms. W. of Luverne (F-S line), ND	20.60	
	Stanley to Wildrose, ND	50.75	
	Winnipeg Frt. Terminal to St. James Jct. (M. Ry. of M.), Man.	6.05	
			98.53
1912	Fargo to 0.26 Ms. E. of Nolan (F-S line), ND	40.10	
	1.31 Ms. W. of Luverne to 4.12 Ms. E. of Simcoe (F-S line), ND	146.26	
	Sun River Crossing to Gilman, MT	31.92	
	Abbotsford to 7.82 Ms. east (VV&E), BC	7.82	
	Niobe to 2.54 Ms. north, ND	2.54	
	Moccasin to Lewistown, incl. "Y," MT	30.27	
	Station 619+00 S. of Snowden, MT to Sta. 213+00 S. of Dore (ME Ry.), ND	7.69	
	1.52 Ms. S. of Oroville to 3.32 Ms. S. of Oroville, WA	1.80	
	2.57 Ms. N. of Wenatchee to 3.80 Ms. N. of Wenatchee, WA	1.23	
	West of Coalmont (VV&E), BC	0.21	
			269.84
1913	2.54 Ms. N. of Niobe to Northgate incl. "Y," ND	19.14	
	Power to Bynum incl. "Y" (GF&TC Ry.), MT	42.97	
	Plentywood to Scobey, MT	44.66	
	7.82 Ms. E. of Abbotsford to 12.86 Ms. E. of Abbotsford, BC	5.04	
	Snowden to Sidney (less No. 234) incl. "Y" (ME Ry.), MT	17.03	
	Fairview to Arnegard, incl. Fairview "Y" (ME Ry.), ND	30.26	
	3.32 Ms. S. of Oroville to Pateros, WA	75.49	

	3.80 Ms. N. of Wenatchee depot to Chelan River, WA	34.18	
	H.B. on Pass. Trk. at Wenatchee sta.—44+00 to sta.—1+35, WA	0.81	
			269.58
1914	Sta. 1904+00 at Arnegard to 1507+35 at Watford City (ME Ry.), ND	7.51	
	Newlon Jct.—0+65 to Lambert—1160+10 (ME Ry.), MT	21.99	
	Chelan River 1872+00 to Pateros 2953+00, WA	20.46	
	West of Coalmont 2217+00 to Brookmere 868+67 (VV&E), BC	25.19	
	Lehigh Mine Br. M.L. 2377+59.8 to 249+41, MT	4.72	
			79.87
1915	No track-laying		
1916	Wildrose 2685+03 to Grenora 4602+00 (GN Ry.), ND	36.33	
	Lewistown East to 1861+29 (GN Ry.), MT	1.28	
	Lewistown East 1718+70 to 1861+29 (ME Ry.), MT	2.71	
	Lambert 1161+10 to Richey 2446+00 (ME Ry.), MT	23.80	
	Bynum 682+93 to Pendroy 1143+58 (GF&T Co. Ry.), MT	8.72	
	At Hope, BC (VV&E)	0.17	
	12.86 Ms. E. of Abbotsford 1297+70 to Cannor 1352+555 (VV&E), BC	1.04	
			74.05
1917	Connecting Track at Sioux Falls (W&SF Ry.), SD	0.19	
	Branch line to Lehigh Mine No. 2, MT	2.36	
			2.55
1918–1921	No track-laying		
1922	Gilman to Augusta Sta. 2125+70 to Sta. 2208+03, MT	1.57	1.57

1923	No track-laying		
1924	Augusta Sta. 2208+03 to Sta. 2226+54, MT	0.35	0.35
1925	Augusta Sta. 2226+54 to Sta. 2236+32, MT	0.18	
	Scobey to Peerless Sta. 5304+90 to Sta. 6359+43, MT	20.03	
			20.21
1926	Peerless to Opheim Sta. 6359+43 to Sta. 4787+69.4, MT	28.74	28.74
1927	Connection at Bend Sta. 48+38.3 to Sta. 19+11.9, OR	0.36	
	Stearns to Chemult Sta. 67+80.7 to Sta. 2108+99, OR	46.30	
	Conn. Trk. bet. GN Ry. & SC&P Ry. at Spokane, WA (made main trk. in 1943)	.19	
			46.85
1928	Depot at Klamath Falls south to Sta. 143+72.7, OR	3.29	
	Chumstick Revision from Peshastin to Winton, WA	19.37	
	Jct. at Saco to Hogeland, MT	77.44	
	Hambone to Sta. 1241+60 at White Horse, CA	23.30	
			123.40
	Monarch to Barker, MT (reconstr. as a private line for St. Joseph Lead Co.; GN owns .05 Mi. conn. at Monarch)	11.10	
1929	New Cascade Tunnel Line from Berne to Scenic, WA	10.29	10.29
1930	White Horse (Sta. 1241+60) to Jct. at Lookout, WA	10.19	
	Giffen Jct. near Stockett to Sta. 309+50.5 at Giffen, MT	5.84	
			16.03

1931	Jct. at Klamath Falls, OR to Sta. 4899+73.7 at Bieber, CA	91.58	91.58
1932	Bend to Lava Jct., Sta. 122+22.5 to 125+22.7, OR	13.84	13.84
1933	No track-laying		
1934	Marion to Bitter Root (acquired from SL Co. 1942), MT	4.66	4.66
1935–1939	No track-laying		
1940	Bitter Root to Hubbard (acquired from SL Co. 1942), MT	2.55	2.55
1941	Jct. at Kettle Falls to Sta. 1135+55.5 at Boyds, WA	13.02	
	Jct. at Galena to Sta. 430+80 at East Galena, WA	8.16	
			21.18
1942–1956	No track-laying		
1957	Minot to Tatman, Sta. 0+00 to Sta. 887+31.2, ND	16.81	16.81
1958	Glasgow to Glasgow Air Base, Sta. 0+00 to 960+58.6, MT	18.31	18.31
1959–1960	No track-laying		
1961	Volin to Mission Hill—acquired from C&NW Ry., SD	5.19	
	Townsend to Deas Island, BC	4.10	
			9.29
1962–1964	No track-laying		
1965	Custer to Lake Terrell, WA	8.87	
	Stanwood–Twin City Food Co. Spur, WA	2.37	
			11.24
1966–1967	Boeing Spur at Mukilteo, WA	2.09	
	Noshwauk Taconite Plant	2.50	
	Keewatin Taconite Plant	3.54	
			8.13

Original Track-laying record

1968–
1969   No track-laying

MINNEAPOLIS TO SEATTLE

Great Northern
    via Willmar and New Rockford   1,769 miles
Northern Pacific
    via Helena and St. Regis   1,923 miles

APPENDIX B

Track Removals

Year	Description	Miles	Total Miles
1890	Breckenridge to Barnesville, MN	29.00	29.00
1896	Everest to Fleming, ND	4.75	4.75
1898	Carlisle Jct. to Elizabeth, MN	3.52	3.52
1900	Hillyard to Wayside (SF&N), WA	14.51	
	Alton to Halstad (Part of), ND	1.33	
	F.S. Jct. to Sedro, Sedro to Cokedale Jct., WA	14.66	
	Red Mountain Branch, Helena, MT	1.47	
			31.97
1901	Hopkins to St. Bonifacius, MN	19.66	19.66
1902	Floweree to Willard, MT	21.93	21.93
1903	So. Bellingham to Yukon, WA	9.16	9.16
1904	Monarch to Barker, MT	10.69	10.69
1905	Cokedale Jct. to Cokedale, WA	3.79	
	Jennings to Melbourne, MT	29.03	
			32.82
1906	Shirley to Ives, MN	7.52	7.52
1907	Ives to Wylie, MN	5.80	
	Grand Forks to Schurmeir, ND	4.74	
			10.54

Year	Description	Miles	Total Miles
1908	Melbourne to Lakeview, MT	11.86	
	Alton to Halstad (Part of), ND	8.50	
			20.36
1909	Lakeview to Marion, MT	10.69	
	Dewey Lake Line, MN	6.93	
			17.62
1911	Chisholm North, MN	3.07	3.07
1913	Ripon to Mason Jct., WI	8.47	
	Sirdar Jct. to Kuskonook, BC	3.26	
			11.73
1916	Port Hill to Wilkes, BC	11.72	
	Brownsville to Port Kells, BC	8.55	
			20.27
1917	Chisholm to Flanders, MN	1.48	
	Eureka Gulch Line, WA	3.83	
	Monroe to Carnation, WA	17.84	
	Yukon to Belleville, WA	11.07	
			34.22
1918	Blaine to Hazelmere, BC	2.69	2.69
1919	Hazelmere to Port Kells, BC	7.81	7.81
1920	Kelly Lake to Hibbing, MN	1.41	
	Grand Forks to Phoenix Line to Granby Smelter, BC	31.36	
	Cannor to Bridge 176, BC	1.04	
	Chisholm to Flanders, MN	0.74	
			34.55
1922	Boundary to Rossland, BC	9.59	
	Mountain View Branch, MT	3.38	
			12.97
1923	Northport to Boundary, WA	7.51	7.51
1924	Kilgard to Cannor (Bridge 176), BC	5.04	5.04
1925	Fermoy to Ellis, MN	20.65	
	Windham to Lehigh, MT	2.36	
			23.01
1926	Windham to Lehigh, MT	4.72	
	Elko to Michel, BC	40.12	
	Portage La Prairie to Gretna, Man.	76.14	
			120.98
1927	Gretna to Neche, ND	1.52	1.52
1928	Peshastin to Winton, WA	17.22	
	Lewistown East, MT	3.99	
			21.21
1929	Abbotsford to Kilgard, BC	4.73	
	Cloverdale to Sumas, BC	29.15	
	Berne to Scenic, WA	17.59	
			51.47
1930	Fairgrounds Spur (Helena), MT	0.67	
	Grand Forks Jct. to Grand Forks, BC	1.57	
	Columbia Jct. to Weston, BC	1.00	
			3.24
1931	Oroville to Molson, WA	23.49	
	Colebrook to Cloverdale, BC	6.25	
			29.74
1932	Bend to Lava Jct., OR	15.41	15.41
	Lewis Jct. to Stockett, MT	1.42	
	Lewis Jct. to Sand Coulee, MT	1.45	
			2.87
1933	Brookmere to Princeton, BC	37.47	37.47
1935	Molson to Curlew, WA and BC	45.59	
	Colebrook to Ladner, BC	10.00	
			55.59
1936	Brandon to St. John, Man.	73.05	
	Morden to Walhalla, Man. and ND	20.54	
	Rexford to Elko, MT and BC	42.63	
			136.22

Track Removals

1937	Princeton to Hedley, BC	23.49	
	Mississippi Jct. to Swan River, MN	5.41	
			28.90
1940	Kettle River Branch (Sandstone), MN	2.61	2.61
1941	Marcus to Boyds, WA	6.21	
	Eureka Gulch Branch, WA	4.58	
			10.79
1943	Tintah to Elbow Lake, MN	15.81	
	Wylie to St. Hilaire, MN	6.81	
			22.62
1944	Superior to Duluth, MN	1.82	1.82
1945	Armington to Neihart, MT	38.22	38.22
1952	Kila to Hubbard, MT	20.18	
	Spokane to Mt. Hope, WA	27.65	
	St. Vincent Jct. to St. Vincent, MN	1.94	
			49.67
1954	Giffen to Browns Spur, MT	8.27	8.27
1955	Hedley to Keremeos, BC	17.57	17.57
1956	Aberdeen Line Jct. to Hankinson, MN and ND	28.37	28.37
1957	Kalispell to Kila, MT	9.42	
	Evansville to Elbow Lake, MN	16.19	
	Swan River to Kelly Lake, MN	23.08	
	Flora to Vera, WA	1.33	
			50.02
1960	Hankinson to Geneseo, ND	15.26	
	Clifford to Portland, ND	9.93	
			25.19
1960– 1961	Elliott Siding to Wacootah, MN	4.93	4.93
1962	Elliott Siding to Wacootah, MN	0.35	
	Vancouver, BC	0.70	
	Concrete to Rockport, WA	9.24	
			10.29

1963	Vera to Dishman, WA	5.15	5.15
1964	Neche Jct. – West Wye, ND	0.30	0.30
1967	Manning to Colfax, WA	5.62	5.62
1969	At Chisholm, MN	0.37	0.37

Appendix B

APPENDIX C

Great Northern Railway Ruling Grades on Main Freight Routes

Main Line	Westbound	Eastbound
Minneapolis – Minot (via Willmar)	.4%	.4%
Minot – Williston	.6%	.6%
Williston – Havre	.4%	.4%
*Havre – Whitefish	1.0%	*.8%
Whitefish – Spokane	.6%	.7%
Spokane – Wenatchee	1.0%	1.0%
**Wenatchee – Seattle	*1.0%	*1.0%

*Helper grade eastbound 1.8% for 14 miles Nimrod to Summit, MT.
**Helper grade westbound 1.6% to 2.2%, 33 miles Peshastin to Berne, WA.
**Helper grade eastbound 2.2% for 11 miles, Skykomish to Scenic, WA.

Mesabi Range Iron Ore Lines

Kelly Lake to Allouez via Fermoy	.3% loaded ore trains / .6% empty ore trains
Kelly Lake to Allouez via Gunn (loaded trains from Keewatin to Allouez)	.4% loaded ore trains / .4% empty ore trains

APPENDIX D

Northern Pacific Main Line Ruling Grades Minneapolis – Seattle

	Westbound	Eastbound
Minneapolis – Mandan, ND — Both WB and EB there are short stretches in excess of the ruling grade shown above.	1.0% (between Fargo and Mandan)	0.4%
Mandan – Glendive, MT	1.0%	1.0%
Glendive – Livingston, MT	0.5%	Down
Livingston – Helena, MT (Belt Range)	1.0% — Helper District Livingston to Bozeman both directions — 12 miles 1.8% Livingston – Bozeman Tunnel	1.0% — 7 miles 1.9% Bozeman – Livingston Tunnel
Helena – Missoula, MT (Continental Divide)	Down — Helper required — 15 miles 1.6% – 2.2% Helena – Blossburg	1.0% — Helper required on many trains — 8 miles 1.4% Elliston – Blossburg
Missoula – Spokane, WA	Down to 0.8% — Ruling grade is 0.8% for 2.6 miles east of Athol, ID — Remainder of the district is 0.4% maximum.	0.4%
Spokane – Pasco, WA	1.14%	1.0%
Pasco – Seattle, WA (Cascade Mountains)	0.8% — Helper District Easton to Lester — 6 miles 2.2%	1.1% — 10.25 miles 2.2%

Bibliography and Notes on Sources

As originally conceived, this study was to appear in two volumes and, indeed, it was written to that end. The size of it being, however, enough to repel even the most sanguine of publishers, compromise was required. In the end, Burlington Northern Incorporated agreed to stand the cost of placing copies of the original "long version" in selected libraries: Baker (Harvard Business School), Newberry (Chicago), James J. Hill Reference (St. Paul), University of Montana (Missoula), University of Washington (Seattle), and California State Railroad Museum (Sacramento). The full story and documentation is thus available to those who have particular interest in the Great Northern's experience. Meanwhile, attention focused on the need to pare the manuscript to an attractive size for publication. With this aim, the authors determined to embrace the styles of documentation used in Macmillan's Railroad Series (Keith L. Bryant, *History of the Atchison, Topeka & Santa Fe Railway*, 1974; Maury Klein, *History of the Louisville & Nashville Railroad*, 1972; W. K. Lamb, *History of the Canadian Pacific Railway*, 1976; G. R. Stevens, *Canadian National Railways*, 1973; and, John F. Stover, *History of the Illinois Central Railroad*, 1975.) This system allows for the maximum number of pages of text and at the same time provides adequate information on sources.

Materials consulted as a part of this undertaking were many and varied, but the authors relied greatly on the company's massive record base. During the time of principal research these records were housed in the General Office Building of the Great Northern at St. Paul. (Much of the material subsequently has been moved to the Minnesota Historical Society in St. Paul and to the Great Northern Railway Historical Society in Mankato, Minnesota). Along with the usual secondary sources — books, periodicals, newspapers, reports, court cases — the authors gained insight from interviews held with many of the company's officers. Outside papers, particularly those of James J. Hill and Louis W. Hill, were similarly meaningful. (These are now open and available at the James J. Hill Reference Library, St. Paul.)

Books, Pamphlets, and Reports

Abdill, George B. *Pacific Slope Railroads from 1854 to 1900* (Seattle: Superior Publishing, 1959).

Adams, Brooks, and Frederick O. Downs. *Railways as Public Agents: A Study in Sovereignty: With an Historical Financial Analysis of the Great Northern Railway System* (Boston, 1910).

Adler, Cyrus. *Jacob H. Schiff: His Life and Letters*, 2 vols. (New York: American Jewish Committee, 1928).

Adler, Dorothy R. (ed. by Muriel E. Hidy). *British Investment in American Railways, 1834–1898* (Charlottesville: University Press of Virginia, 1970).

Agricultural Credit Corporation. *Report for Fiscal Year Ended December 31, 1930* (Minneapolis, 1931).

American Crystal Sugar Company. *Facts about Beet Sugar in Minnesota* (np, nd).

Anderson, Eva. *Rails Across the Cascades* (Wenatchee, Wash., 1952).

Andrews, Frank. "Railroads and Farming," U.S. Bureau of Statistics, *Bulletin 100* (Washington, D.C., 1912).

Association of American Railroads. *The Case of the Disappearing Passenger Train* (Washington, D.C., nd).

———. *The Gathering Transportation Storm* (Washington, D.C., 1961).

———. *The High Cost of Conflicting Public Transportation Policies* (Washington, D.C., 1951).

———. *Railroad Review and Outlook* (Washington, D.C., 1969–1970).

———. *Review of Railway Operations, 1932–1968* (Washington, D.C., nd).

———. *Statistics of Railway Passenger Service* (Washington, D.C., 1966).

———. *Yearbook of Railroad Facts* (Washington, D.C., 1968).

Athearn, Robert G. *Rebel of the Rockies: A History of the Denver and Rio Grande Western Railway* (New Haven: Yale University Press, 1962).

———. *Union Pacific Country* (Chicago: Rand McNally, 1971).

Atkinson, Gail Shay, and Jim C. Atkinson. *Izaak Walton Inn: A History of the Izaak Walton Inn and Essex, Montana* (Kalispell, Mont., np, 1985).

Atwater, Isaac, ed. *History of the City of Minneapolis, Minnesota* (New York: Munsell, 1893).

Avery, Mary W. *Washington: A History of the Evergreen State* (Seattle: University of Washington Press, 1965).

Babcock, Kendric C. *The Scandinavian Element in the United States* (Urbana: University of Illinois, 1914).

Bagley, Clarence B. *History of Seattle from the Earliest Settlement to the Present Time*, 3 vols. (Chicago, 1916).

Baker, George F., and others. *Unification of Northern Pacific Railway Company, Plan and Deposit Agreement*, Feb. 7, 1927 (New York, nd).

Beaton, Welford. *The City That Made Itself: A Literary and Pictorial Record of the Building of Seattle* (Seattle: Terminal Publishing, 1914).

Beebe, Lucius, and Charles Clegg. *The Trains We Rode*, 2 vols. (Berkeley: Howell-North Books, 1965).

Bell, Edward J. *Homesteading in Montana, 1911–1923: Life in the Blue Mountain Country* (Bozeman, 1975).

Benson, Ramsey. *Hill Country* (New York: Stokes, 1928).

Blanchard, Rufus. *Hand Book of Minnesota* (Chicago: Blanchard & Cram, 1867).

Blegen, Theodore C. *Building Minnesota* (Boston, 1938).

Bonbright, James C. *Railroad Capitalization* (New York: Columbia University, 1920).

Borak, Arthur M. "The Financial History of the Chicago, Milwaukee and St. Paul Railway Company" (Ph.D. dissertation, University of Minnesota, 1929).

Bosch, Kornelis Douwe. *De Nederlandse Beleggingen in de Vereingde Staten* (Amsterdam: Elsevier, 1948).

Bridges, Leonard Hal. *Iron Millionaire: Life of Charlemagne Tower* (Philadelphia: University of Pennsylvania Press, 1952).

Brosnan, Cornelius James. *History of the State of Idaho* (New York, 1948).

Brown, Dee. *Hear That Lonesome Whistle Blow: Railroads in the West* (New York: Holt, Rinehart & Winston, 1977).

Bruce, Alfred W. *The Steam Locomotive in America* (New York: W. W. Norton, 1952).

Bryan, Enoch A. *Orient Meets Occident: Advent of Railways to the Pacific* (Pullman, Wash.: Student's Book Corp., 1936).

Bryant, Keith L., Jr. *History of the Atchison, Topeka and Santa Fe Railway* (New York: Macmillan, 1974).

Budd, Ralph. *In the Matter of Consolidation of the Railway Properties of the United States into a Limited Number of Systems . . . Statement* (Washington, D.C., 1923).

———. *Essentials for Low Railroad Rates.* Address before the Montana Bankers' Association, Bozeman, Mont., 1924.

———. *The Relations of Highway Transportation to the Railway.* Address before the American Society of Civil Engineers, Kansas City, Mo., April 14, 1926.

———. *Significance of the Rocky Mountains to Transcontinental Railways.* Address before the National Association of Railroad and Utilities Commissioners at Glacier Park, Mont., Aug. 28, 1929.

———. *The Changing Transportation Situation.* Address before Des Moines Chamber of Commerce at Its Annual Meeting, Des Moines, Iowa, Jan. 7, 1931.

———. *Railway Routes Across the Rocky Mountains.* Newcomen Society Address, April 20, 1938.

Burdick, Usher L. *History of the Farmer's Political Action in North Dakota* (Baltimore, 1944).

Burlingame, Merrill G. *The Montana Frontier* (Helena, 1942).

Campbell, Edward G. *The Reorganization of the American Railroad System, 1893–1900: A Study of the Effects of the Panic of 1893, the Ensuing Depression, and the First Years of Recovery on Railroad Organization and Finance* (New York: Columbia University Press, 1928).

Carson, Robert B. *Main Line to Oblivion: The Disintegration of New York Railroads in the Twentieth Century* (Port Washington, N.Y.: Associated Faculty Press, 1971).

Casey, Robert J., and W. A. S. Douglas. *Pioneer Railroad: The Story of the Chicago and North Western System* (New York: Whittlesey House, 1948).

Chandler, Alfred Dupont. *The Railroads, the Nation's First Big Business: Sources and Readings* (New York: Harcourt, Brace & World, 1965).

Chandler, Alfred D., Jr. *The Visible Hand: The Managerial Revolution in American Business* (Cambridge: Harvard University Press, 1977).

Christianson, Theodore. *Minnesota: The Land of Sky-Tinted Waters. A History of the State and Its People*, 5 vols. (Chicago: American Historical Society, 1935).

Cleveland, Frederick A., and Fred W. Powell. *Railroad Promotion and Capitalization in the United States* (New York: Longmans, Green, 1909).

———. *Railroad Finance* (New York: D. Appleton, 1912).

Clews, Henry. *Twenty-Eight Years in Wall Street* (New York: Irving, 1909).

Cochran, Thomas C. *Railroad Leaders, 1845–1890: The Business Mind in Action* (Cambridge: Harvard University Press, 1953).

Cole, Arthur H. *Business Enterprise in Its Social Setting* (Cambridge: Harvard University Press, 1959).

Conant, Michael. *Railroad Mergers and Abandonments* (Berkeley: University of California Press, 1964).

Cottrell, William F. *Technological Change and Labor in the Railroad Industry: A Comparative Study* (Lexington, 1970).

Crawford, Lewis Fernandia. *History of North Dakota*, 3 vols. (Chicago, 1931).

Creighton, Donald. *John A. Macdonald: The Young Politician* (Toronto: Macmillan of Canada, 1955).

———. *John A. Macdonald: The Old Chieftain* (Boston: Houghton Mifflin, 1956).

Cunningham, W. J. *American Railroads: Government Control and Reconstruction Policies* (Chicago, 1922).

Daggett, Stuart. *Principles of Inland Transportation* (New York: Harper, 1941).

———. *Railroad Consolidation West of the Mississippi River* (Berkeley: University of California Press, 1933).

———. *Railroad Reorganization* (Cambridge: Houghton Mifflin, 1908).

Davis, E. W. *Pioneering with Taconite* (St. Paul, 1964).

Bibliography and Notes on Sources

Davis, Patricia T. *End of the Line: Alexander J. Cassatt and the Pennsylvania Railroad* (New York: Watson, 1978).

Derleth, August. *The Milwaukee Road: Its First Hundred Years* (New York: Creative Age Press, 1948).

Dickman, Howard L. "James Jerome Hill and the Agricultural Development of the Northwest" (Ph.D. dissertation, University of Michigan, 1977).

Dixon, F. H. *Railroads and Government* (New York: Scribner, 1922).

Donovan, Frank P., Jr. *Mileposts on the Prairie: The Story of the Minneapolis and St. Louis Railway* (New York: Simmons-Boardman, 1950).

———. *Gateway to the Northwest: The Story of the Minnesota Transfer Railway* (Minneapolis: np, 1954).

Drache, Hiram M. *The Day of the Bonanza: A History of Bonanza Farming in the Red River Valley of the North* (Fargo, N.D.: Interstate, 1964).

Droege, John Albert. *Passenger Terminals and Trains* (New York: McGraw-Hill, 1916).

Dubin, Arthur D. *Some Classic Trains* (Milwaukee: Kalmbach Publishing, 1967).

Ducker, James H. *Men of the Steel Rails: Workers on the Atchison, Topeka & Santa Fe Railroad, 1869–1900* (Lincoln: University of Nebraska Press, 1983).

Duluth and Iron Range Railroad. *Transportation of Iron Ore and the History of the Duluth and Iron Range* (np, 1927).

Duluth, Missabe & Northern Railway. *The Missabe Road* (Duluth, 1927).

Dyar, Ralph E. *News for an Empire: The Story of the Spokesman-Review of Spokane, Washington, and of the Field It Serves* (Caldwell, Idaho: Caxton, 1952).

Eggert, Gerald G. *Railroad Labor Disputes: The Beginnings of Federal Strike Policy* (Ann Arbor: University of Michigan Press, 1967).

Elliott, Howard. *Minnesota: The Railways and Advertising* (St. Paul, 1911).

Epstein, Ralph C. *The Automobile Industry: Its Economic and Commercial Development* (Chicago: A. W. Shaw, 1928).

Fahey, John. *Inland Empire: D. C. Corbin and Spokane* (Seattle: University of Washington Press, 1965).

Farrington, S. Kip. *Railroading the Modern Way* (New York: Coward McCann, 1951).

———. *Railroads of Today* (New York: Coward McCann, 1949).

———. *Railroads at War* (New York: Coward McCann, 1944).

Faulkner, Harold U. *The Decline of Laissez Faire, 1897–1917* (New York: Holt, Rinehart & Winston, 1951).

Federal Writers Project. *North Dakota: A Guide to the Northern Prairie State* (New York, 1950).

Fishlow, Albert. *American Railroads and the Transformation of the Anti-Bellum Economy* (Cambridge: Harvard University Press, 1965).

Flynn, Edward F. *James J. Hill—Empire Builder*, Address before the Twin City Market Week audience in St. Paul, Minn., Aug. 2, 1939.

Foell, Charles F., and M. E. Thompson. *Diesel-Electric Locomotives* (New York: Diesel, 1946).

Fogarty, Kate Hammond. *The Story of Montana* (Chicago: A. S. Barnes, 1916).

Fogel, Robert W. *Railroads and American Economic Growth: Essays in Econometric History* (Baltimore: Johns Hopkins University Press, 1964).

———. *The Union Pacific Railroad: A Case in Premature Enterprise* (Baltimore: Johns Hopkins University Press, 1960).

Folwell, William Watts. *A History of Minnesota*, 4 vols. (St. Paul: Minnesota Historical Society, 1921–1930).

Fossum, Paul R. *The Agrarian Movement in North Dakota* (Baltimore: Johns Hopkins University Press, 1925).

Freedman, Bernard I. "How to Get Cheap Farms: The Land Colonization Policies of the Great Northern Railway and Its Progenitors in Minnesota" (M.A. thesis, Brooklyn College, 1947).

French, Hiram T. *History of Idaho: A Narrative Account of Its Historical Progress, Its People, and Its Principal Interest* (Chicago, 1914).

Friedheim, R. L. *The Seattle General Strike* (Seattle: University of Washington Press, 1965).

Fuess, Claude M. *Joseph B. Eastman, Servant of the People* (New York: Columbia University Press, 1952).

Gates, Paul W. *The Illinois Central Railroad and Its Colonization Work* (Cambridge: Harvard University Press, 1934).

Gibbon, J. M. *The Romantic History of the Canadian Pacific: The Northwest of Today* (New York, 1937).

Gilbert, Heather. *The End of the Road: The Life of Lord Mount Stephen* (Aberdeen: Aberdeen University Press, 1977).

Gilbreath, W. C. *North Dakota and Her Magnificent Resources: What Twenty-two Years Has Accomplished for This Thriving and Progressive State* (Bismarck, 1912).

Gilmore, Donald R. *Developing the "Little" Economies, Supplemental Paper* No. 10 (New York: Committee for Economic Development, 1960).

Ginger, Ray. *The Bending Cross: A Biography of Eugene Victor Debs* (New Brunswick: Rutgers University Press, 1949).

Gjevre, John A. *Saga of the Soo: West from Shoreham* (La Crosse, Wis.: np, 1973).

Gluck, Alvin C., Jr. *Minnesota and the Manifest Destiny of the Canadian Northwest* (Toronto, 1965).

Godfrey, Aaron A. *Government Operation of the Railroads, 1918–1920: Its Necessity, Success, and Consequences* (Austin: Jenkins, 1974).

Goetzmann, William H. *Army Exploration in the American West, 1803–1863* (New Haven: Yale University Press, 1959).

Goodrich, Carter. *Government Promotion of American Canals and Railroads, 1800–1890* (New York: Columbia University Press, 1960).

Grant, Frederick J., ed. *History of Seattle, Washington* (New York, 1891).

Gray, Carl R., Jr. *Railroading in Eighteen Countries: The Story of American Railroad Men Serving in the Military Railway Service, 1862 to 1953* (New York: Scribner, 1955).

Great Northern Railway Company and Its Antecedents "Across America via the Great Northern" (1894).

———. "Alaska, Land of Gold and Glacier" (1898).

———. Annual Reports (GN) to stockholders, 1890–1969.

———. Annual Reports (St. Paul, Minneapolis & Manitoba, 1880–1899).

———. "Brief History of the Minnesota & Pacific, St. Paul, Minneapolis & Manitoba, and the Great Northern Railway Company" (March 18, 1898). By James Crosby Morrison. Typescript.

———. "Business Openings along the Line of the Great Northern Railway" (1904).

———. "Columbia Basin Development" (nd).

———. "Condensed History of the Great Northern Railway" (1953).

———. "Dedication and Opening of the New Cascade Tunnel." Addresses delivered during the coast-to-coast broadcasting program and at the banquet, Scenic, Washington (Jan. 12, 1929).

———. "Electric Data Processing at Great Northern" (1957).

———. "Facts About Minnesota: Reliable Practical Information for Immigrants with a Valuable Map." By D. A. McKinley (1879).

———. "Gavin Yard, Minot, North Dakota" (1956).

———. "Geography and Geology of Glacier Park" (1912).

———. "Helps for Home Seekers: A Number of Recent Letters from Washington" (1889).

———. "Historic Adventure Land of the Northwest." By Grace Flandrau (1927).

———. "History of the Great Northern Railway, 1882–1940." By H. M. Sims (nd). Typescript.

———. "Local Trains and Highways" (nd).

———. "Long Tunnel Through Cascade Range" (1926).

———. "Manual of Instructions for Agents and Other Station Personnel" (1954).

———. "Manuscript Covering History of the Immigration, Agricultural and Mineral Development Departments of the Great Northern Railway." By C. C. Morrison (1919 or 1920?). Typescript.

———. "Minnesota and Its Advantages to Settlers" (1867).

———. "New Cascade Tunnel" (192?).

———. "New Line — Saco-Turner Branch, Montana" (1928).

———. "New Oil-Electric Locomotives" (nd).

———. "Oregon, Back to the Farm, 320 Acres Free" (1911).

———. "Program of Events, Columbia River Historical Expedition: Itinerary of Columbia River Special via Great Northern Railway, July 15–27, 1926."

———. "Progress Report to Shippers" (Annually, 1963–1969).

———. "Red River Trails." By Grace Flandrau (1925).

———. "Report Relative to the Resources, Population & Products of the Country Along the Brainerd and St. Vincent & Extensions of the St. Paul & Pacific Railroad and the Land Grant, Traffic and Prospects of these Railroad Lines." By John H. Kloos (1871).

———. "Seattle and the Great Northern Railway" (nd).

———. "Seven Sunsets." By Grace Flandrau (1925).

———. "Statement of the Inception of the Minnesota & Pacific Railroad and Its Successors." By S. P. Folsom (1894).

———. "Steam Locomotives" (nd).

———. "The Story of Marias Pass." By Grace Flandrau (nd).

———. "Strip Farming" (1935).

———. "Sugar Beets" (1943).

———. "Talking It Over" (1961–1969).

———. "Three Great Dams" (nd).

———. "Timber, Meadow and Prairie Lands." By George L. Becker (1867?).

———. Time Tables (1893–1970).

———. "Track Laying Record." (System diagram showing track built for each year plus abandonments. Issued and updated periodically by the Engineering Department).

———. "Turkey Production and Management" (1947).

———. "Valley, Plain and Peak" (1894).

———. "West Okanogan Valley Irrigation District" (1915).

Great Northern Railway Company and others, *Consolidation, Key to Transportation Progress* (np, 1961).

Grodinsky, Julius. *The Iowa Pool: A Study in Railroad Competition, 1870–1884.* (Chicago: University of Chicago Press, 1950).

———. *Jay Gould: His Business Career, 1867–1892* (Philadelphia: University of Pennsylvania Press, 1957).

———. *Railroad Consolidation: Its Economics and Controlling Principles.* (New York: Appleton, 1930).

———. *Transcontinental Railway Strategy, 1869–1893: A Study of Businessmen* (Philadelphia: University of Pennsylvania Press, 1962).

Hakola, John W. "Samuel T. Hauser and Economic Development of Montana" (Ph.D. dissertation, Indiana University, 1961).

Hammer, Kenneth M. "Dakota Railroads" (Ph.D. dissertation, South Dakota State University, 1966).

Haney, Lewis Henry. *A Congressional History of Railways in the United States* (New York: Kelley, 1968).

Harbaugh, W. H. *Power and Responsibility: The Life and Times of Theodore Roosevelt* (New York: Farrar, Straus & Cudahy, 1961).

Hargreaves, Mary W. M. *Dry Farming in the Northern Great Plains, 1900–1925* (Cambridge: Harvard University Press, 1957).

Harnsberger, John L. "Jay Cooke and Minnesota: The Formative Years of the Northern Pacific, 1868–1873" (Ph.D. dissertation, University of Minnesota, 1956).

Harris, Forbes & Co. *The Hill Roads: A Short History and Description of Railroads Comprising the Hill System* (New York, 1921).

Harrison, Milton W. *The A B C of Railroad Consolidations* (New York, 1930).

Hartsough, Mildred L. *The Development of the Twin Cities as a Metropolitan Market* (Minneapolis: University of Minnesota, 1925).

Haskell, Daniel C. *On Reconnaissance for the Great Northern: Letters of C. F. B. Haskell, 1889–1891* (New York: New York Public Library, 1948).

Hayes, William E. *Iron Road to Empire: The History of 100 Years of the Progress and Achievements of the Rock Island Lines* (New York: Simons-Boardman, 1953).

Hedges, James B. *Building the Canadian West: The Land and Colonization Policies of the Canadian Pacific Railway* (New York: Macmillan, 1939).

———. *Henry Villard and the Railways of the Northwest* (New Haven: Yale University Press, 1930).

Henry, Robert S. *This Fascinating Railroad Business* (Indianapolis: Bobbs-Merrill, 1942).

Hertel, D. W. *History of the Brotherhood of Maintenance of Way Employees: Its Birth and Growth, 1887–1955* (Randell, Wash., 1955).

Hess, George H., Jr. *Accuracy, Speed and Economy Feature Great Northern's Payroll Procedure.* Reprinted from *Savings Bank Journal* (November 1944).

Hewitt, Girart. *Minnesota: Its Advantages to Settlers* (St. Paul: np, 1867).

Hidy, Ralph W. *The House of Baring in American Trade and Finance: English Merchant Bankers at Work, 1763–1861* (Cambridge, 1949).

Hidy, Ralph W., and others. *Timber and Men: The Weyerhaeuser Story* (New York: Macmillan, 1963).

Hill, James J. *The Great Northern and the Northwest* (St. Paul, 1912).

———. *Highways of Progress* (New York: Doubleday, 1910).

———. *Addresses by James J. Hill.* (Collection of pamphlets, addresses, and papers read by James J. Hill, bound in three volumes in Executive Department of Great Northern Railway Company. Collections, as well as separate pamphlets, are available in some libraries.)

Hill, James J., and Charles R. Flint, James H. Bridge, S. C. T. Dodd, and Francis B. Thurber (James H. Bridge, ed.). *The Trust: Its Book, Being a Presentation of the Several Aspects of the Latest Form of Industrial Evolution* (New York, 1902).

Hillman, Jordan Jay. *Competition and Railroad Price Discrimination: Legal Precedent and Economic Policy* (Evanston, Ill., 1968).

Hilton, George W. *The Transportation Act of 1958: A Decade of Experience* (Bloomington: Indiana University Press, 1969).

Hines, Walker D. *War History of American Railroads* (New Haven: Yale University Press, 1928).

Hofsommer, Don L. *The Southern Pacific, 1901–1985* (College Station: Texas A&M University Press, 1986).

Holbrook, Stewart H. *The Age of the Moguls* (Garden City: Doubleday, 1953).

———. *James J. Hill: A Great Life in Brief* (New York: Alfred A. Knopf, 1955).

———. *The Story of American Railroads* (New York: Crown, 1947).

Howard, Joseph K. *Montana: High, Wide and Handsome* (New Haven: Yale University Press, 1943).

Hubbard, Freeman H. *Railroad Avenue: Great Stories and Legends of American Railroading* (New York: Whittlesey House, 1945).

Hudson, Horace B., ed. *A Half Century of Minneapolis* (Minneapolis, 1908).

Hultgren, Thor. *American Transportation in Prosperity and Depression* (New York: National Bureau of Economic Research, 1948).

Hunkins, Ralph V., and John C. Lindsay. *South Dakota: Its Past, Present and Future* (New York: Macmillan, 1932).

Hunter, Louis C. *Steamboats on Western Rivers* (Cambridge: Harvard University Press, 1949).

Innes, H. A. *A History of the Canadian Pacific Railway* (London: P. S. King & Sons, Ltd., 1923).

Irwin, Leonard B. *Pacific Railways and Nationalism in the Canadian-American Northwest, 1845–1873* (New York: Greenwood, 1968).

Jackson, Carlton. *Hounds of the Road: A History of the Greyhound Bus Company* (Bowling Green: Bowling Green University Press, 1984).

Jackson, W. Turrentine. *The Enterprising Scot: Investors in the American West After 1873* (Edinburgh, 1968).

Janeway, Eliot. *The Struggle for Survival* (New Haven: Yale University Press, 1951).

Jarchow, Merrill E. *The Earth Brought Forth: A History of Minnesota Agriculture to 1885* (St. Paul, 1949).

Johansen, Dorothy O., and Charles M. Gates. *Empire of the Columbia: A History of the Pacific Northwest* (New York: Harper, 1957).

Johnson, Arthur M., and Barry E. Supple. *Boston Capitalists and Western Railroads: A Study in the Nineteenth-Century Railroad Investment Process* (Cambridge: Harvard University Press, 1967).

Johnson, John A. *Minnesota and the Railroads* (Minneapolis, 1906).

Jones, C. Clyde. "The Agricultural Development Program of the Chicago, Burlington and Quincy Railroad" (Ph.D. dissertation, Northwestern University, 1954).

Jones, Eliot. *Principles of Railway Transportation* (New York: Macmillan, 1924).

Jones, Jesse H., with Edward Angly. *Fifty Billion Dollars: My Thirteen Years with the RFC, 1932–1945* (New York: Macmillan, 1951).

Josephson, Matthew. *The Robber Barons: The Great American Capitalists, 1861–1901* (New York: Harcourt, Brace, 1934).

Kaufman, Jacob J. *Collective Bargaining in the Railroad Industry* (New York: King's Crown Press, 1954).

Kelsey, Vera. *Red River Runs North* (New York: Harper, 1951).

Kennan, George. *E. H. Harriman: A Biography*, 2 vols. (Boston: Houghton Mifflin, 1922).

Kerr, Duncan John. *The Story of the Great Northern Railway Company and James J. Hill*. A Newcomen address (Princeton: Princeton University Press, 1939).

Kerr, K. Austin. *American Railroad Politics, 1914–1920: Rates, Wages, and Efficiency* (Pittsburgh: University of Pittsburgh Press, 1968).

King, Frank A. *The Missabe Road: The Duluth, Missabe and Iron Range Railway* (San Marino, Calif.: Golden West, 1972).

Kirkland, Edward C. *Dream and Thought in the Business Community, 1860–1900* (Ithaca: Cornell University Press, 1956).

———. *Industry Comes of Age: Business, Labor and Public Policy, 1860–1897* (New York: Holt, Rinehart & Winston, 1961).

———. *Men, Cities and Transportation: A Study in New England History, 1820–1900*, 2 vols. (Cambridge: Harvard University Press, 1948).

Kloos, J. H. *Minnesota (Vereenigde Staten von Noord-Amerika) in zijne Hulpbronnen, vruchtbaarheid en ontwikkeling geschetst voor landverhuizers en kapitalisten* (Amsterdam, 1867).

———. *Rapport omtrent den St. Paul en Pacific Spoorweg en de waarde der Landerijen nitmakende het onderpand der 7 pct. obligatien* (St. Paul, 1866).

Kolko, Gabriel. *Railroads and Regulation, 1877–1916* (Princeton: Princeton University Press, 1965).

Kuhlman, Charles B. *The Development of the Flour Milling Industry in the United States, with Special Reference to the Industry in Minneapolis* (Boston, 1929).

Lamar, Howard R. *Dakota Territory, 1861–1889: A Study of Frontier Politics* (New Haven: Yale University Press, 1956).

Lamb, W. Kaye. *History of the Canadian Pacific Railway* (New York: Macmillan, 1977).

Larrabee, William. *The Railroad Question: A Historical and Practical Treatise on Railroads, and Remedies for their Abuses* (Chicago: Schulte, 1893).

Larson, Agnes M. *History of the White Pine Industry in Minnesota* (Minneapolis, 1949).

Larson, Henrietta M. *Jay Cooke, Private Banker* (Cambridge: Harvard University Press, 1936).

———. *The Wheat Market and the Farmer in Minnesota, 1858–1900* (New York: Columbia University, 1926).

Laut, Agnes. *The Blazed Trail of the Old Frontier* (New York: McBride, 1926).

Lecht, Leonard A. *Experience Under Railway Labor Legislation* (New York: AMS Press, 1955).

Leith, Charles K. *The Mesabi Iron-Bearing District of Minnesota* (Washington, D.C.: Geological Survey, 1903).

Lemley, James H. *The Gulf, Mobile and Ohio: A Railroad That Had to Expand or Expire* (Homewood, Ill.: Irwin, 1953).

Leonard, William N. *Railroad Consolidation Under the Transportation Act of 1920* (New York: Columbia University Press, 1946).

Levinson, Harold M., and others. *Collective Bargaining and Technological Change in American Transportation* (Evanston, Ill.: Transportation Center at Northwestern University, 1971).

Lewis, Edwin H. *Minnesota's Interstate Trade* (Minneapolis, 1953).

Lewis, Elmer A., comp. *Laws Relating to Interstate and Foreign Commerce* (Washington, D.C.: GPO, 1946).

Licht, Walter. *Working for the Railroad: The Organization of Work in the Nineteenth Century* (Princeton: Princeton University Press, 1983).

Lindley, Clara Hill. *James J. and Mary T. Hill: An Unfinished Chronicle by Their Daughter* (New York, 1948).

Lindsey, Almont. *The Pullman Strike* (Chicago: University of Chicago Press, 1942).

Locklin, D. Philip. *Economics of Transportation* (Homewood, Ill.: Irwin, 1966).

Longyear, Edmund J. *Reminiscences of Edmund J. Longyear, Mesabi Pioneer* (St. Paul, 1951).

Lounsberry, Clement Augustus. *Early History of North Dakota: Essential Outlines of American History* (Washington, D.C.: Liberty Press, 1919).

Lyon, Peter. *To Hell in a Day Coach* (Philadelphia: Lippincott, 1968).

MacAvoy, Paul W. *The Economic Effects of Regulation: The Trunk-Line Railroad Cartels and the Interstate Commerce Commission Before 1900* (Cambridge: MIT Press, 1965).

MacBeth, R. G. *The Romance of the Canadian Pacific Railway* (Toronto: Ryerson, 1924).

McCague, James. *Moguls and Iron Men: The Story of the First Transcontinental Railroad* (New York: Harper & Row, 1964).

McClung, J. W. *Minnesota as It Is in 1870: Its General Resources and Attractions* (St. Paul: np, 1870).

McDougall, J. Lorne. *Canadian Pacific: A Brief History* (Montreal: McGill, 1968).

McMechen, Edgar C. *The Moffat Tunnel of Colorado*, 2 vols. (Denver: Wahlgreen, 1927).

McMurray, Donald L. *The Great Burlington Strike of 1888: A Case History in Labor Relations* (Cambridge: Harvard University Press, 1956).

Marquis, Albert N. *The Book of Minnesotans* (Chicago, 1907).

Martin, Albro. *Enterprise Denied: Origins of the Decline of American Railroads, 1897–1917* (New York: Columbia University Press, 1971).

———. *James J. Hill and the Opening of the Northwest* (New York: Oxford University Press, 1976).

Martin, Charles F. *Locomotives of the Empire Builder* (Chicago, Normandie House, nd).

Mattson, Hans. *Reminiscences: The Story of an Emigrant* (St. Paul: Merrill, 1891).

Meeks, Carroll Louis Vanderslive. *The Railroad Station: An Architectural History* (New Haven: Yale University Press, 1956).

Meinig, Donald W. *The Great Columbia Plain: A Historical Geography, 1805–1910* (Seattle: University of Washington Press, 1968).

Mercer, Lloyd J. *E. H. Harriman: Master Railroader* (Boston: G. K. Hall, 1985).

Meyer, B. H. "A History of the Northern Securities Case," University of Wisconsin, *Economics and Political Science Series*, vol. 1, no. 3, pp. 215–350. (Madison: University of Wisconsin, 1906).

Meyer, John R., and others. *The Economics of Competition in the Transportation Industries* (Cambridge: Oelgeschlager, 1960).

Middleton, Harvey P. *Railways and Organized Labor* (Chicago, 1941).

Middleton, William D. *When the Steam Railroads Electrified* (Milwaukee: Kalmbach Publishing, 1974).

Miller, George Hall. *Railroads and the Granger Laws* (Madison: University of Wisconsin Press, 1971).

Minnesota State Board of Immigration. *Minnesota, the Land of Opportunity for Agriculture, Horticulture, Livestock, Manufactures, Mining, Education and Everything That Attracts the Immigrant* (St. Paul, 1919?).

Mitchell, Broadus. *Depression Decade: From New Era through New Deal, 1929–1941* (New York: Holt, Rinehart & Winston, 1947).

Moody, John. *The Railroad Builders.* Johnson, Allen, ed., The Chronicle of America Series (New Haven: Yale University Press, 1919).

Morse, Frank P. *Cavalcade of the Rails* (New York: E. P. Dutton, 1940).

Moulton, Harold G., and others. *The American Transportation Problem, Prepared for the National Transportation Committee* (Washington, D.C.: Brookings Institution, 1933).

Moynihan, James H. *The Life of Archbishop John Ireland* (New York: Harper, 1953).

Murray, Stanley N. *The Valley Comes of Age: A History of Agriculture in the Valley of the Red River of the North, 1812–1920* (Fargo, N.D., 1967).

National Industrial Conference Board. *The Consolidation of Railroads in the United States* (New York, 1923).

Neill, E. D. *History of Ramsey County and the City of St. Paul, Including the Explorers and Pioneers of Minnesota* (St. Paul, 1881).

Nelson, James C. *Railroad Transportation and Public Policy* (Washington, D. C., 1959).

Nesbit, Robert C. *"He Built Seattle": A Biography of Judge Thomas Burke* (Seattle: University of Washington Press, 1961).

Olson, Sherry H. *The Depletion Myth: A History of Railroad Use of Timber* (Cambridge: Harvard University Press, 1971).

Overton, Richard C. *Burlington Route: A History of the Burlington Lines* (New York: Alfred A. Knopf, 1965).

———. *Burlington West: A Colonization History of the Burlington Railroad* (Cambridge: Harvard University Press, 1941).

———. *Gulf to Rockies: The Heritage of the Fort Worth and Denver—Colorado and Southern Railways* (Austin: University of Texas Press, 1953).

Parmelee, Julius H. *The Modern Railway* (New York: Longmans, Green, 1940).

Pickett, Victor G., and Roland S. Vaile. *The Decline of Northwestern Flour Milling* (Minneapolis, 1933).

Preston, W. T. R. *Life and Times of Lord Strathcona* (London, 1914).

Pringle, H. F. *Theodore Roosevelt: A Biography* (New York: Harcourt, Brace, 1931).

Prosser, Richard S. *Rails to the North Star: One Hundred Years of Railroad Evolution in Minnesota* (Minneapolis: Dillon Press, 1966).

Pyle, Joseph G. *The Life of James J. Hill*, 2 vols. (New York: Appleton Century, 1917).

Quiett, Glenn C. *They Built the West: An Epic of Rails and Cities* (New York: D. Appleton-Century, 1934).

Rae, John B. *The American Automobile: A Brief History* (Chicago: University of Chicago Press, 1965).

Regehr, T. D. *The Canadian Northern Railway: Pioneer Road of the Northern Prairies, 1895–1918* (Toronto: Macmillan, 1976).

Renz, Louis Tuck. *The History of the Northern Pacific Railroad* (Fairfield, Wash.: Ye Galleon Press, 1980).

Richardson, R. C. *The Locomotive Engineer, 1863–1963: A Century of Railway Labor Relations and Work Rules* (Ann Arbor: University of Michigan, Graduate School of Business, 1963).

Ridgley, Ronald H. "Railroads and the Development of the Dakotas: 1872–1914" (Ph.D. dissertation, Indiana University, 1967).

Riegel, Robert E. *The Story of Western Railroads* (New York: Macmillan, 1926).

Riegger, Hal. *The Kettle Valley and Its Railroads* (Edmonds, Wash., 1983).

Ripley, William Z. *Railroads, Finance and Organization* (New York: Longmans, Green, 1915).

———. *Railroads, Rates and Regulations* (New York: Longmans, Green, 1912).

———, ed. *Railway Problems* (Boston: Ginn, 1913).

———. *Trusts, Pools and Corporations* (Boston: Ginn, 1905).

Robbins, Edwin C. *Railway Conductors: A Study in Organized Labor* (New York: Columbia University, 1970).

Robinson, Edward V. *Early Economic Conditions and the Development of Agriculture in Minnesota* (Minneapolis: University of Minnesota, 1915).

Robinson, Elwyn B. *History of North Dakota* (Lincoln: University of Nebraska Press, 1966).

Roth, Lottie R., ed. *History of Whatcom County*, 2 vols. (Chicago, 1926).

Ruffner, W. H. *A Report on Washington Territory* (New York, Seattle, Lake Shore, and Eastern Railway, 1889).

Sanborn, John B. *Congressional Grants of Land in Aid of Railways.* (Madison: University of Wisconsin, 1899).

Sanford, Barrie. *McCulloch's Wonder: The Story of the Kettle Valley Railway* (West Vancouver, B.C., 1977).
———. *The Pictorial History of Railroads in British Columbia* (Vancouver, B.C., 1981).

Saunders, Richard. *The Railroad Mergers and the Coming of Conrail* (Westport, Conn.: Greenwood, 1978).

Schell, Herbert S. *History of South Dakota* (Lincoln: University of Nebraska Press, 1961).

Scott, Roy V. *Railroad Development Programs in the Twentieth Century* (Ames: Iowa State University Press, 1985).
———. *The Reluctant Farmer: The Rise of Agricultural Extension to 1914* (Urbana: University of Illinois Press, 1970).

Shannon, Fred A. *The Farmer's Last Frontier: Agriculture, 1860–1897* (New York: Holt, Rinehart & Winston, 1945).

Shannon, James P. *Catholic Colonization of the Western Frontier* (New Haven: Yale University Press, 1957).

Sharfman, I. L. *The American Railroad Problem: A Study in War and Reconstruction* (New York: The Century Co., 1921).
———. *The Interstate Commerce Commission: A Study in Administrative Law and Procedure*, 5 vols. (New York: Commonwealth Fund, 1931–1937).

Shideler, James H. *Farm Crisis, 1919–1923.* (Berkeley: University of California Press, 1957).

Shott, John G. *The Railroad Monopoly: An Instrument of Banker Control of the American Economy* (Washington, D.C., 1950).

Shutter, Marion D., and J. S. McLain, eds. *Progressive Men of Minnesota* (Minneapolis, 1897).

Slichter, Sumner H., James J. Healy, and E. Robert Livernash. *The Impact of Collective Bargaining on Management* (Washington, D.C.: Brookings Institution, 1960).

Smalley, E. V. *History of the Northern Pacific Railroad* (New York: G. P. Putnam's, 1883).

Snyder, Carl. *American Railways as Investments* (New York: Moody Corporation, 1907).

Soule, George. *Prosperity Decade: From War to Depression, 1917–1929* (New York, 1947).

Spero, Herbert. *Reconstruction Finance Corporation Loans to the Railroads, 1932–1937* (New York, 1939).

Splawn, Walter M. W. *Consolidation of Railroads* (New York: Macmillan, 1925).

Starr, John T., Jr. *The Evolution of the Unit Train, 1960–1969* (Chicago: Department of Geography, University of Chicago, 1976).

Stevens, Isaac I. *Narrative and Final Report of Exploration for a Route for a Pacific Railroad Near the 47th and 49th Parallels of North Latitude from St. Paul to Puget Sound* (Washington, D.C., 1860).

Stevens, John F. *An Engineer's Recollections* (New York: McGraw-Hill, 1936).

Stilgoe, John R. *Metropolitan Corridor: Railroads and the American Scene* (New Haven: Yale University Press, 1983).

Stover, John F. *History of the Illinois Central Railroad* (New York: Macmillan, 1975).
———. *The Life and Decline of the American Railroad* (New York: Oxford University Press, 1970).

Street, Donald M. *Railroad Equipment Financing* (New York: Columbia University Press, 1959).

Sullivan, Oscar M. *The Empire Builder* (New York: The Century Co., 1928).

Taff, Charles A. *Commercial Motor Transportation* (Chicago: R. D. Irwin, 1950).

Taylor, George R., and Irene Neu. *The American Railroad Network, 1861–1890* (Cambridge: Harvard University Press, 1956).

Thompson, Joseph W. "An Economic History of the Mesabi Division of the Great Northern Railway Company to 1915" (Ph.D. dissertation, University of Illinois, 1956).

Thompson, Slason, *The Railway Library, 1912* (Chicago: Stromberg, Allen & Co., 1913).
———. *A Short History of American Railways, Covering Ten Decades* (Freeport: Ayer, 1971).

Thomson, R. H. *That Man Thomson* (Seattle: University of Washington Press, 1950).

Timpe, Georg. *Durch die Nordwest Staaten von U.S.A.* (Hamburg, 1929).

Toole, K. Ross. *Montana: An Uncommon Land* (Norman: University of Oklahoma Press, 1959).
———. *Twentieth-Century Montana: A State of Extremes* (Norman: University of Oklahoma Press, 1972).

Trottman, Nelson. *History of the Union Pacific: A Financial and Economic Survey* (New York: Ronald Press, 1923).

True, Alfred C. *A History of the Agricultural Extension Work in the United States* (Washington: U.S. Department of Agriculture, 1928).

Tuhy, John E. *Sam Hill: The Prince of Castle Nowhere* (Portland: Timber Press, 1983).

Van Barneveld, Charles Edwin. *Iron Mining in Minnesota* (Minneapolis, 1912).

Van Oss, S. F. *American Railroads as Investments: A Handbook for Investors in American Railroad Securities* (New York, 1893).

Vatter, Harold G. *The U.S. Economy in the 1950s: An Economic History* (New York, 1963).

Vaughan, Walter. *The Life and Work of Sir William Van Horne* (New York: Century, 1920).
———. *Sir William Van Horne* (London, 1926).

Villard, Henry. *Memoirs of Henry Villard, Journalist and Financier, 1835–1900*, 2 vols. (New York: Houghton, 1904).

Vinnedge, W. W. *The Pacific Northwest Lumber Industry and Its Development* (New Haven, 1923).

Walker, David A. *Iron Frontier: The Discovery and Early Development of Minnesota's Three Ranges* (St. Paul: Minnesota Historical Society, 1979).

Ward, James A. *Railroads and the Character of America, 1820–1887* (Knoxville: University of Tennessee Press, 1986).

Westinghouse Electric and Manufacturing Company. *The Great Northern Railway Electrification* (np, 1929).

White, John H., Jr. *American Locomotives: An Engineering History, 1830–1880* (Baltimore: Johns Hopkins University Press, 1968).

———. *The Great Yellow Fleet: A History of American Refrigerator Cars* (San Marino, Calif.: Golden West Books, 1986).

Widtsoe, John A. *Success on Irrigation Projects* (New York, 1928).

Wiebe, Robert H. *Businessmen and Reform: A Study of the Progressive Movement* (Cambridge, 1962).

Wilkinson, William. *Memorials of the Minnesota Forest Fires in the Year 1894* (Minneapolis, 1895).

Williams, J. F. *The Minnesota Guide: A Hand Book of Information for Travellers, Pleasure Seekers & Immigrants* (St. Paul, 1869).

Willson, Beckles. *The Life of Lord Strathcona and Mount Royal*, 2 vols. (Boston, 1915).

Wilson, Neill C., and Frank J. Taylor. *Southern Pacific: The Roaring Story of a Fighting Railroad* (New York: McGraw-Hill, 1952).

Winchell, Newton H., and H. V. Winchell. *The Iron Ores of Minnesota, Their Geology, Discovery, Development, Qualities and Origin, and Comparison with those of Other Iron Districts* (Minneapolis, 1891).

Winther, Oscar O. *The Transportation Frontier: Trans-Mississippi West, 1865–1890* (New York: Holt, Rinehart & Winston, 1964).

Wirth, Fremont P. *The Discovery and Exploitation of the Minnesota Iron Lands* (Cedar Rapids, 1937).

Wood, Charles R. *Lines West: A Pictorial History of the Great Northern Railway Operations and Motive Power from 1887 to 1967* (Seattle: Superior Publishing, 1967).

Wood, Charles R., and Dorothy Wood. *The Great Northern Railway: A Pictorial Study* (Edmonds, Wash.: PFM Publishing, 1979).

———. *The Spokane, Portland & Seattle Railway* (Seattle: Superior Publishing, 1974).

Wood, Struthers and Company. *Great Northern Railway Company, Northern Pacific: A Review of Their Operations in the Period 1916–1923* (New York, 1924).

———. *Great Northern Railway Preferred: A Brief Analysis and Recommendation* (New York, 1952).

Articles

Adams, E. E. "Great Northern Railway Improvements at Seattle, Washington." *Engineering News*, vol. 72 (Aug. 20, 1914), pp. 377–379.

Anderson, Willard V. "It Takes Money to Make Money." *Trains and Travel*, vol. 12 (November 1951), pp. 36–41.

Andrews, F. B. "Arbitraging Formula Simple: Technique Applied to Great Northern Rail Issues." *Barron's, The National Financial Weekly*, vol. 16 (Aug. 10, 1936), p. 9.

Appel, Livia, and Theodore C. Blegen. "Official Encouragement of Immigration to Minnesota During the Territorial Period." *Minnesota History Bulletin*, vol. 5 (August 1923), pp. 167–203.

Arrington, Leonard J. "The Transcontinental Railroad and the Development of the West." *Utah Historical Quarterly*, vol. 37 (Winter 1969), pp. 3–15.

Atwood, Albert W. "Why Has My Stock Declined?" *Minneapolis Journal* (Nov. 20, 1916).

Bailey, W. F. "Story of the Great Northern." *Pacific Monthly*, vol. 21 (February 1909), pp. 177–179.

Baldwin, E. F. "Two Leaders in Rural Progress." *The Outlook*, vol. 96 (Dec. 10, 1910), pp. 828–831.

Bancroft, G. J. "Central Idaho—Rugged Mining Region." *Engineering and Mining Journal*, pp. 428–441.

Barron's, 1921–1970.

Bartholemy, P. P. "Freight Car Conditions in the Northwest." Car Department Officers Association, *Proceedings*, Sept. 23–24, 1941. Abstract of, in *Railway Age*, vol. III (Nov. 8, 1941), pp. 749–750.

Bartlett, Guy. "Great Northern Railway Obtains Largest Motor-Generator Electric Locomotives." *Locomotive Firemen and Enginemen's Magazine*, vol. 83 (November 1927), pp. 413–415.

Baston, C. E. "Great Northern, Motor-Generator Locomotives." *Railway Electrical Engineer*, vol. 18 (February 1927), pp. 53–55.

Baumol, William J., and others. "The Role of Cost in the Minimum Pricing of Railroad Services." *The Journal of Business*, vol. 35 (October 1962), pp. 357–366.

Baxter, J. C. "Construction Plans and Methods." American Society of Civil Engineers, *Transactions*, vol. 96 (1932), pp. 950–988.

———. "New Cascade Tunnel for Great Northern Railway." *Journal of Western Society of Engineers*, vol. 32 (February 1927), pp. 52–68.

Beahan, Willard. "Notes of Experience in Driving the Cascade Tunnel." *Engineering News and American Railway Journal*, vol. XLV (Feb. 28, 1901), pp. 154–155.

Becker, Walter F. "Railway Equipment up the River to Minnesota, 1861–1869." Railway & Locomotive Society *Bulletin No. 95* (October 1956), pp. 47–56.

Beckler, E. H. "Location of the Pacific Extension of the Great Northern." *Railway Gazette*, vol. 25 (Oct. 11, 1893), pp. 744–745.

Bell, R. N. "Mining in Idaho in 1913." *Engineering and Mining Journal*, vol. 97 (Jan. 10, 1914), pp. 118–120.

Berglund, Abraham. "Valuation of Railroads in the State of Washington." *Journal of Political Economy*, vol. 21 (April 1913), pp. 332–344.

Blakely, Captain Russell. "Opening of the Red River of the North to Commerce and Civilization." *Collections of the Minnesota Historical Society*, vol. 8 (1896).

Blanchard, Henry. "Single Expansion Articulated Locomotives in Mountain Service on the Great Northern Railway." *Baldwin Locomotives*, vol. 5 (July 1926), pp. 52–56.

Blegen, Theodore C. "James Wickes Taylor: A Biographical Sketch." *Minnesota History Bulletin*, vol. 1 (May 1915), pp. 153–219.

Blossom, Mary C. "James J. Hill: The Development and the Characteristics of the Man Who Worked Out the Transportation Problems of the Northwest—The Significance and Interest of Transcontinental Steamship and Railroad System." *World's Work*, vol. 2 (May 1901), pp. 721–728.

Boeing, Rose M. "History of Irrigation in the State of Washington." *Washington Historical Quarterly*, vol. 9 (October 1918), pp. 259–276.

———. "History of Irrigation in the State of Washington." *Washington Historical Quarterly*, vol. 10 (January 1919), pp. 21–45.

"The Bonanza Farms of the West." *Atlantic Monthly*, vol. 45 (January 1880), pp. 33–44.

Borah, L. A. "North Dakota Comes into Its Own." *National Geographic Magazine*, vol. 100 (September 1951), pp. 283–322.

Briggs, Harold E. "The Development of Agriculture in Territorial Dakota." *The Culver Stockton Quarterly*, vol. 7 (January 1931), p. 138.

"Budd Defends Northern's Plan." *Wall Street News*, Jan. 21, 1950, p. 4.

Budd, Ralph. "Conquering the Cascades." *Railway and Marine News*, vol. 26 (January 1929), pp. 41, 56.

———. "The Relation of Highway Transportation to the Railway." American Society of Civil Engineers, Paper No. 1663, *Transactions*, vol. 92 (1928), pp. 394–433.

Burlington Northern News, March 2, 1970.

Carlson, R. "Potentials for Western Rails as Pacific War Intensifies." *The Magazine of Wall Street*, vol. 75 (Nov. 25, 1944), p. 194.

Carr, F. "Great Railway Builder." *The Outlook*, vol. 87 (Oct. 26, 1907), pp. 390–398.

Carson, Robert B. "Railroads and Regulation Revisited: A Note on Problems of Historiography and Ideology." *The Historian*, vol. 34 (May 1972), pp. 437–446.

Clark, Earl. "John F. Stevens: Pathfinder for Western Railroads." *The American West*, vol. 8 (May 1971), pp. 28–33, 62–63.

Cochran, John S. "Economic Importance of Early Transcontinental Railroads: Pacific Northwest." *Oregon Historical Quarterly*, vol. 71 (March 1970), pp. 27–98.

Colley, Marion T. "Stevens Has Blasted and Bridged His Way Across America." *The American Magazine*, vol. 101 (February 1926), pp. 16–17.

Commercial West, 1903–1911.

Conroy, W. E. "Construction Problems of the 8-Mile Tunnel." *Railway and Marine News*, vol. 26 (January 1929), pp. 24–40.

Cook, W. W. "Industrial Democracy or Monopoly." *McClure's Magazine*, vol. 38 (January 1912), pp. 352–360.

Coolidge, G. H. "Hill Against Harriman." *The American Magazine*, vol. 68 (September 1909), pp. 419–429.

Cooper, W. O. "Railroads on the Air." *Railroad Stories*, vol. 7 (February 1932), pp. 388–391.

Cotroneo, Ross R. "Colonization of the Northern Pacific Land Grant, 1900–1920." *North Dakota History*, vol. 38 (Summer 1970), pp. 33–48.

———. "The History of the Northern Pacific Land Grant, 1900–1952." (Ph.D. dissertation, University of Idaho, 1967.)

———. "Western Land Marketing by the Northern Pacific Railway." *Pacific Historical Review*, vol. 37 (August 1968), pp. 299–320.

Coulter, Calvin B. "The Victory of National Irrigation in the Yakima Valley, 1902–1906." *Pacific Northwest Quarterly*, vol. 42 (April 1951), pp. 99–122.

Coulter, J. L. "Marketing of Agricultural Lands in Minnesota and North Dakota." *American Economic Review*, vol. 2 (June 1912), pp. 282–301.

Cox, F. B. "Electrical Operation on the Cascade Division of the Great Northern Railway." *General Electric Review*, vol. 35 (November 1932), pp. 583–590.

Crooks, Col. William. "The First Railroad in Minnesota." *Minnesota Historical Society Collections*, vol. X, pt. 1 (1900–1904).

Cunningham, William J. "Railroad Unification in the Northwest." *The Annalist: A Magazine of Finance, Commerce and Economics*, vol. 29 (March 25, 1927), pp. 427–430.

———. "James J. Hill's Philosophy of Railroad Management." *Railway Age*, vol. III (Dec. 27, 1941), pp. 1081–1082.

———. "James J. Hill's Philosophy of Railroad Management." *Bulletin of Business History Society*, vol. XV (November 1941), pp. 65–72.

———. "The Railroads Under Government Operation." *Quarterly Journal of Economics*, vol. 36 (November 1921), pp. 30–71.

Cushing, George H. "Hill Against Harriman: The Story of the Ten-Years' Struggle for the Railroad Supremacy of the West." *The American Magazine*, vol. LXVIII (September 1909), pp. 418–429.

Dalrymple, A. J. "The 'Internationals' are Launched." *Wheels*, vol. 6 (July-August 1950), pp. 13–17.

Danforth, G. H. "They Capitalized Opportunities: Life Sketches." *The Magazine of Wall Street*, vol. 53 (March 3, 1934), p. 494.

David, Q. J. "Campaign for Passenger Traffic." *Traffic World*, vol. 63 (June 3, 1939), p. 1238.

Davis, Howard W. "A Review of Federal Rate Regulation and Its Impact Upon the Railway Industry." *Land Economics*, vol. 44 (February 1968), pp. 1–10.

"[Ralph Budd] Dedicates the Tunnel." *Railway & Marine News*, vol. 26 (January 1929), pp. 41, 56.

"Describes Historic Bridges." *Railway Age* [over Mississippi River at Minneapolis], vol. 83 (Oct. 29, 1927), p. 832.

Devlin, Charles E. "Great Northern Moves First Plywood Built Freight Train." *Railway Purchases and Stores*, vol. 37 (August 1944), pp. 533–535.

Devlin, S. "High Yield Stocks." *The Magazine of Wall Street*, vol. 69 (Feb. 21, 1942), p. 561.

Dimon, George H. "Two Giants of the Northwest: Northern Pacific-Great Northern." *Financial World*, vol. 52 (Sept. 11, 1929), pp. 354–355.

Douglas, James. "American Transcontinental Railroads," Part II. *Cassier's Magazine*, vol. 19 (April 1901), pp. 469–485.

Drache, Hiram M. "The Economic Aspects of the Northern Pacific Railroad in North Dakota." *North Dakota History*, vol. 34 (Fall 1967), pp. 321–372.

Edwards, H. R. "Jim Hill's Great Adventure. If ever a mighty railroad was the lengthened shadow of one man, that railroad is the Great Northern." *Railroad Stories*, vol. 21 (February 1937), pp. 34–53.

Elmgreen, A. W. "Handling Ore Traffic at Great Northern Docks." *Railway Review*, vol. 76 (May 16, 1925), p. 910.

"Equipment Plans for Next Year Estimated." *Railway Review*, vol. 78 (Jan. 2, 1926), p. 15.

Escher, Franklin. "A Six-Hundred-Million-Dollar Mortgage." *Harper's Weekly*, vol. LV (June 17, 1911), p. 22.

Farmer, Hallie. "The Railroads and Frontier Populism." *The Mississippi Valley Historical Review*, vol. XIII (December 1926), pp. 387–397.

Fayant, Frank. "The Great Northern Railroad." *Moody's Magazine*, vol. 1 (March 1906), pp. 408–416.

Flinn, Alfred D. "A Feat of Railway Pioneering through the Rockies" (Stevens finds Marias Pass). *Stone and Webster Journal*, vol. 41 (July 1927), p. 61.

Flynn, E. F. "Stevens Monument Dedicated by Historical Expedition." *Engineering News Record*, vol. 95 (Sept. 10, 1925), pp. 428–430.

Frankel, H. D. "Railroad's Fight with Snow." *The World Today*, vol. 12 (March 1907), pp. 266–268.

Frewen, Moreton. "The Economics of James J. Hill." *The Living Age*, vol. 292 (Jan. 20, 1917), pp. 131–141.

————. "The Economics of James J. Hill." *The Nineteenth Century*, vol. LXXX (November 1916), pp. 1083–1096.

Fulton, H. P. "Great Northern Comes Back." *The Magazine of Wall Street*, vol. 57 (Dec. 21, 1935), pp. 274–275.

————. "Merging of the Northerns." *The Magazine of Wall Street*, vol. 45 (Feb. 22, 1930), pp. 690–692.

Gasner, James W. "The Northern Securities Case." *The Annals of the American Academy of Political and Social Science*, vol. XXIV, pp. 123–147.

Gates, Ward. "Higher Dividends for Great Northern?" *The Magazine of Wall Street*, vol. 42 (Oct. 20, 1928), pp. 1098 ff.

Gavin, F. J. "Statement . . . Written for Annual Review and Outlook Number of the Commercial and Financial Chronicle." *The Commercial and Financial Chronicle*, vol. 152 (Jan. 25, 1941), p. 486.

Gaynor, Joseph F. M. "Comparative Operating Results of Steam, Diesel Electric, and Electric Motive Power on the Great Northern Railway Electrification." A.I.E.E. Technical Paper, Presented at A.I.E.E. Winter Meeting, New York, January 1948. Summary in *Railway Age*, vol. 124 (Jan. 31, 1948), p. 251.

Gerst, H. A. "Great Northern Builds New Dock at Superior." *Railway Age*, vol. 74 (June 2, 1923), pp. 1311–1314.

Gilman, L. C. "The Spokane, Portland and Seattle Railroad Company." *The Washington Historical Quarterly*, vol. 14 (January 1923), pp. 14–20.

Ginger, Frank J. "In Pursuit of the Mail: Great Northern Wanted the Mail Contract, and Not Even a Landslide Could Hold It Back." *Trains*, vol. 10 (March 1950), pp. 40–42.

Glead, Charles S. "James Jerome Hill." *Cosmopolitan*, vol. 33 (June 1902), pp. 169–172.

Gras, N. S. B., and Henrietta M. Larson. "James J. Hill and the Great Northern, 1878–1916." *Casebook in American Business History*. New York: 1939, pp. 403–421.

"Great Northern Evaluation." *Railway Age*, vol. 75 (Dec. 15, 1923), p. 1125.

Greever, William S. "A Comparison of Railroad Land Grant Policies." *Agricultural History*, vol. 25 (April 1951), pp. 83–90.

Halpern, M. "Big Gains in Great Northern's Traffic Likely to Hold." *Barron's, The National Financial Weekly*, vol. 27 (July 21, 1947), p. 31.

Hamilton, John. "The Transportation Companies as Factors in Agricultural Extension." U.S. Office of Experiment Stations, *Circular* 112 (Washington, D.C., 1911).

Hamilton, Sam R. "Automatic Interlocking on Great Northern: Spring Switches Used to Convert Double Track to Single. . . ." *Signalman's Journal*, vol. 20 (September 1939), pp. 294–296.

Harbeson, Robert W. "The Transportation Act of 1958." *Land Economics*, vol. 35 (May 1959), pp. 156–171.

Harnsberger, John L. "Jay Cooke and the Financing of the Northern Pacific Railroad, 1869–1873." *North Dakota History*, vol. 37 (Autumn 1969), pp. 5–13.

Hayes, Howard. "The Great Northern Railway Remodels Its General Storehouse." *Railway Purchases and Stores*, vol. 35 (July 1942), pp. 343–345.

Hedges, James B. "The Colonization Work of the Northern Pacific Railroad." *Mississippi Valley Historical Review*, vol. 13 (December 1926), pp. 311–342.

————. "Promotion of Immigration to the Pacific Northwest by the Railroads." *Mississippi Valley Historical Review*, vol. 15 (September 1928), pp. 183–203.

Henry, Robert S. "The Railroad Land Grant Legend in American History Texts." *Mississippi Valley Historical Review*, vol. 32 (September 1945), pp. 171–194.

Herriott, Marion H. "An Emigrant Through Minnesota to the Canadian West in 1869." *Minnesota History*, vol. 24 (December 1943), pp. 328–335.

Hidy, Ralph W., and Muriel E. Hidy. "John F. Stevens, Great Northern Engineer." *Minnesota History*, vol. 41 (Winter 1969), pp. 345–361.

"James J. Hill: Master of Efficiency." *Independent*, vol. 86 (June 26, 1916), pp. 501–502.

Hill, William P. "Recent Utterances of Mr. Hill on Railway Problems." *The Journal of Political Economy*, vol. 14 (December 1906), pp. 627–632.

Hines, Walker D. "The Permanent Solutions of the Railroad Problems." *Railway Age*, vol. 67 (July 4, 1919), pp. 18–20.

———. "The Relationship of the Burlington-Great Northern Pacific Group to the Federal Railroad Consolidation Law." *Harvard Business Review*, vol. 1 (July 1923), pp. 398–416.

Holbrook, Stewart H. "Jim Hill Built an Empire." *The American Mercury*, vol. 65 (July 1947), pp. 103–110.

Hovey, D. "Prospects for Hill Roads: Great Northern, Northern Pacific, and Burlington." *Barron's, The National Financial Weekly*, vol. 13 (Aug. 7, 1933), pp. 8–9.

Howard, Randall H. "Following the Colonists: An Account of the Great Semi-Annual Movement of Homeseekers." *Pacific Monthly*, vol. 23 (May 1910), pp. 529–530.

Howard, R. R. "Railroad Fight for an Empire." *The World's Work*, vol. 21 (December 1910), pp. 13767–13782.

Howland, McClure M. "James J. Hill: The Man Who Built an Empire." *Railway Progress*, vol. 4 (August 1950), pp. 14–18.

Hutchinson, Cary T. "The Three-Phase Electric-Traction System of the Great Northern Railway Company at Cascade Tunnel." *Engineering News*, vol. 62 (Nov. 18, 1909), pp. 557–561.

Jansen, A. "Dividend Prospects." *Barron's, The National Financial Weekly*, vol. 20 (Aug. 19, 1940), p. 18.

———. "Great Northern Credit Re-established." *Barron's, The National Financial Weekly*, vol. 24 (Oct. 9, 1944), pp. 12 ff.

Jenks, Leland H. "Railroads as an Economic Force in American Development." *Journal of Economic History*, vol. 4 (May 1944), pp. 1–20.

Jones, C. Clyde. "The Burlington Railroad and Agricultural Policy in the 1920s." *Agricultural History*, vol. 31 (October 1957), pp. 67–74.

———. "A Survey of the Agricultural Development Program of the Chicago, Burlington and Quincy Railroad." *Nebraska History*, vol. 30 (September 1949), pp. 226–256.

Jones, David C. "The Strategy of Railway Abandonment: The Great Northern in Washington and British Columbia, 1917–1935." *The Western Historical Quarterly*, vol. 11 (April 1980), pp. 141–158.

Jones, Jesse H. "Billions Out and Billions Back: The Bankers Boss the Railroads." *Saturday Evening Post*, vol. 209 (June 26, 1937), pp. 23 ff.

———. "Great Northern Loan at 4%: Letter to Mr. Kenney." *The Commercial and Financial Chronicle*, vol. 142 (Jan. 18, 1936), pp. 460–461.

———. "Jones Discusses Great Northern Financing." *Railway Age*, vol. 108 (March 30, 1940), p. 606.

Kenney, W. P. "The Straight Road to Low-Cost Transportation." *Railway Age*, vol. 97 (Dec. 1, 1934), pp. 108–109.

———. "Great Northern Railway to Create New General Mortgage of Which $100,000,000 Will Be Issued." *The Commercial and Financial Chronicle*, vol. 141 (Nov. 23, 1935), pp. 3378–3379.

Kerr, D. J. "Preliminary Studies and Results of Improving Cascade Crossings." *Proceedings*, American Society of Civil Engineers, vol. 57 (February 1931), pp. 185–196.

Kerr, D. J., Frederick Mears, and J. C. Baxter. "The Eight-Mile Cascade Tunnel, Great Northern Railway: A Symposium." *Proceedings*, American Society of Civil Engineers, vol. 57 (February 1931), pp. 185–268.

Keyes, Norman C., and Kenneth R. Middleton. "The Great Northern Railway Company: All-Time Locomotive Roster, 1860–1920." *Railroad History No. 143* (Autumn 1980), pp. 20–162.

Keys, C. M. "A Country Ready for Capital." *World's Work*, vol. 18 (August 1909), pp. 11922–11930.

"Knute Steenerson's Recollections: The Story of a Pioneer." *Minnesota History Bulletin*, vol. 4 (August–November 1921), pp. 130–151.

Koyl, C. Herschel. "Treating Montana Water: Great Northern Installation on 1100 Miles of Main Line Yields Excellent Results." *Railway Maintenance Engineer*, vol. 15 (May 1919), pp. 154–157.

———. "Treating Water Reduces Boiler Troubles." *Railway Age*, vol. 66 (April 25, 1919), pp. 1053–1056.

Krantz, Shad O. "Railroad War in the Mountains." *Technical World*, vol. 18 (September 1912), pp. 27–34.

Lamb, W. Kaye. "The Trans-Pacific Venture of James J. Hill." *American Neptune*, vol. 3 (Salem, Ore., 1943), pp. 185–204.

"Large Land Holdings in North Dakota." *The American Monthly Review of Reviews*, vol. 72 (October 1925), pp. 431–432.

Larsen, Arthur J. "Roads and the Settlement of Minnesota." *Minnesota History*, vol. 21 (September 1940), pp. 225–244.

Larson, Agnes M. "On the Trail of the Woodsman in Minnesota." *Minnesota History*, vol. 13 (December 1932).

Latzke, P. "Builder of the Northwest Empire." *Everybody's Magazine*, vol. XVI (April 1907), pp. 435–450.

Ledoux, Albert R. "Stories from the Northwest." *The Outlook*, vol. 87 (Dec. 21, 1907), p. 879.

Lee, A. "Beckoning Northwest: A Shirt-sleeve Interview with James J. Hill on Railroading, Schools, and Farming." *Collier's, The National Weekly*, vol. 56 (Nov. 20, 1915), pp. 27–28.

"E. C. Leedy." *The Railroader*, vol. 8 (July 1933), p. 3.

Leupp, F. E. "As They See It in the Northwest." *The Outlook*, vol. 100 (March 9, 1912), pp. 537–539.

Lewis, John H. "Consolidation of Railroads and the Proposed Great Northern-Northern Pacific Unification." *Harvard Business Review*, vol. 6 (July 1928), pp. 458–471.

"The Livestock Special Train." Montana Extension Service, *Bulletin* 96 (Bozeman, 1928).

Loeffler, H. S. "Bridge Reinforcing under Difficulties." *Railway Review*, vol. 78 (May 1, 1926), pp. 779–782.

———. "Develops Ingenious Reinforcement for Old Bridge." *Railway Age,* vol. 80 (April 24, 1926), pp. 1133–1136.

Lord, Russell. "To Hold this Soil." U.S. Department of Agriculture, *Miscellaneous Publication* 321 (Washington, D.C., 1938).

Lux, Mabel. "Honyockers of Harlem, Scissorbills of Zurich." *Montana, The Magazine of Western History*, vol. 13 (Autumn 1963), pp. 2–14.

McGee, P. A. "The Great Northern Electrification." *Railroad Herald,* vol. 33 (January 1929), pp. 22–26.

McLaughlin, D. W. "How the Great Northern Conquered the Cascades." *Trains*, vol. XXII (November 1961), pp. 23–26; "The Reason for America's Longest Tunnel." *Trains*, vol. XXII (December 1961), pp. 23–26.

Marshall, Ernest. "Great Northern Electrification." *Railway Electrical Engineer*, vol. 16 (November 1925), pp. 359–361.

Martin, Albro. "The Troubled Subject of Railroad Regulation in the 'Gilded Age'—A Reappraisal." *Journal of American History*, vol. 41 (September 1974).

Martin, E. R. "Great Northern Electric Locomotives." *Railway Age*, vol. 82 (June 25, 1927), pp. 1997–1998.

———. "Great Northern Electric Locomotives: General Description of Rotating Apparatus and Operating Features." *Railway and Locomotive Engineering*, vol. 40 (July 1927), pp. 191–192.

"Marvelous Development of the Mesabi Range." *Iron Age*, vol. 92 (Sept. 4, 1913), pp. 510–511.

Mears, Frederick. "Conquering the Cascades." *Railway and Marine News*, vol. 26 (January 1929), pp. 14–22.

———. "Surveys, Construction Methods, and a Comparison of Routes." American Society of Civil Engineers, *Transactions*, vol. 96 (1932), pp. 926–949.

Mears, F., and others. "Great Northern Improvement Program." *General Electric Review*, vol. 30 (October 1927), pp. 472–484.

Mercer, Lloyd J. "Land Grants to American Railroads: Social Cost or Social Benefit?" *Business History Review*, vol. 43 (Summer 1969), pp. 134–151.

Merrill, H. S. "Ignatius Donnelly, James J. Hill, and Cleveland Administration Patronage." *Mississippi Valley Historical Review*, vol. 39 (December 1952), pp. 505–518.

"Methods and Progress in Driving the 8-Mile Great Northern Tunnel in the Cascades." *Engineering News-Record*, vol. 97 (Nov. 25, 1926), pp. 858–863.

Meyer, B. H. *A History of the Northern Securities Case*. Madison, Wisc., 1906. (*Bulletin* of the University of Wisconsin. Economic and Political Science Series, vol. 1, no. 3, July 1906, pp. 215–350.)

"Minnesota Rate Case." *Journal of Political Economy*, vol. 16 (May 1908), pp. 305–307.

Mitchell, T. W. "Southern Pacific and the Northern Securities Combination." *Quarterly Journal of Economics*, vol. 21 (August 1907), pp. 581–598.

Modern Railroads, 1968–1970.

Moody, J., and G. K. Turner. "Multimillionaires of the Great Northern System." *McClure's Magazine*, vol. 36 (December 1910), pp. 123–140.

Moreland, Edward L. "Electrification on the Great Northern." *The Military Engineer*, vol. 21 (November–December 1929), pp. 481–482.

Moreland, E. L., and R. D. Booth. "Great Northern Railway Electrification in the Cascades." *Journal of the American Institute of Electrical Engineers*, vol. 47 (November 1928), pp. 803–807.

Morrison, James C. "Early Days of Railroading in the Northwest." *The Constructor*, vol. 29 (August 1947), pp. 30–33.

Mumford, John K. "The Great One-Man Railroad of the West," Part I. *Harper's Weekly*, vol. LII (Oct. 31, 1908), pp. 24–25; Part II, vol. LII (Nov. 14, 1908), pp. 24–25.

Murray, Stanley N. "Railroads and the Agricultural Development of the Red River Valley of the North, 1870–1890." *Agricultural History*, vol. 31 (October 1957), pp. 57–66.

Myrick, D. C., and Roy M. Huffman. "Sugar Beet Production in Montana." Montana Agricultural Experiment Station, *Bulletin* 525 (Bozeman, 1956).

Northwest Magazine, 1893.

"The Operating Plan of the Proposed Merger." *Railway and Marine News*, vol. 25 (May 1928), p. 7.

Overton, Richard C. "Ralph Budd: Railroad Entrepreneur." *The Palimpsest*, vol. 36 (November 1955), pp. 421–484.

Parker, Raymond. "Everything's De Luxe These Days: *Oriental Limited* a Fine Example." *Transportation*, vol. 1 (May 1927), pp. 85–86.

Peterson, Harold F. "Some Colonization Projects of the Northern Pacific Railroad." *Minnesota History*, vol. 10 (June 1929), pp. 127–144.

Petty, G. R. "Two Granger Roads." *Commerce and Finance*, vol. 26 (May 29, 1937), pp. 373–374.

Price, M. "Outposts of Architecture: Monuments Marking Historic Spots on the Great Northern Railway." *Architectural Forum*, vol. 49 (July 1928), pp. 65–70.

Primmer, George H. "Railways at the Head of the Lake Superior." *Economic Geography*, vol. 13 (July 1937), pp. 269–280.

"Prosperous Idaho." *National Geographic Magazine*, vol. 17 (January 1906), pp. 16–20.

Pugsley, Edmund E. "Heads for St. Paul." *Railroad Magazine*, vol. 49 (September 1940), pp. 32–46.

Pyle, J. G. "Facts of the Northern Securities Case." *The World's Work*, vol. 33 (April 1917), pp. 678–684.

———. "James J. Hill." *Minnesota History Bulletin*, vol. 2 (February 1918), pp. 295–323.

Qualty, Carlton C. "Some National Groups in Minnesota." *Minnesota History*, vol. 31 (March 1950), pp. 18–32.

Rae, John B. "The Great Northern's Land Grant." *Journal of Economic History*, vol. 21 (Spring 1952), pp. 140–145.

Railroad Gazette, 1881–1906.

Railroad Review, 1917.

Railway Age, 1899–1970.

"Railway and Bus Transportation." *Engineering News Record*, vol. 104 (Feb. 27, 1930), pp. 352–354.

Railway & Engineering Review, 1905.

Ralph, J. "Dakotas." *Harper's Monthly*, vol. 84 (May 1892), pp. 895–908.

"The Reasons for Luxurious Passenger Equipment." *Railway Review*, vol. 74 (April 19, 1924), pp. 716–717.

Reed, A. "Empire of the Northern Prairies." *World Today*, vol. 14 (February 1908), pp. 184–188.

Reed, W. H. "Where Are We Headed for?" Harlem Development Association, *Bulletin* No. 1 (Harlem, Mont., 1920).

Remington, H. H., and R. B. Koeber. "Pacific Coast Transportation Favors Plant Location." *Chemical and Metallurgical Engineering*, vol. 42 (August 1935), pp. 452–453.

Rezneck, Samuel. "Patterns of Thought and Action in an American Depression, 1882–1886." *American Historical Review*, vol. 61 (January 1956), pp. 284–307.

Ridgley, Ronald. "The Railroads and Rural Development in the Dakotas." *North Dakota History*, vol. 36 (Spring 1969), pp. 163–187.

Rife, C. W. "Norman W. Kittson: A Fur-Trader at Pembina." *Minnesota History*, vol. 6 (September 1925), pp. 225–252.

Robins, W. B. "Description and Trials of Steamships *Great Northern* and *Northern Pacific*." *Journal of the American Society of Naval Engineers*, vol. 27 (February 1915), pp. 426–437.

Saby, Rasmus S. "Railroad Legislation in Minnesota, 1849–1875." *Collections of the Minnesota Historical Society* (St. Paul, 1915), pp. 1–188.

Schell, Herbert S. "Drought and Agriculture in South Dakota During the Eighteen-Nineties." *Agricultural History*, vol. 5 (October 1931), pp. 162–179.

Scott, Roy V. "American Railroads and Agricultural Extension, 1900–1914: A Study in Railway Developmental Techniques." *Business History Review*, vol. 39 (Spring 1965), pp. 74–98.

Seldon, G. C. "Analysis of Pacific Rails." *The Magazine of Wall Street*, vol. 21 (Nov. 3, 10, 1917), pp. 164–167.

Severance, Mary Harriman. "James J. Hill, a Builder of the Northwest: A Character Sketch of the Builder of the Great Northern Railroad." *The American Monthly Review of Reviews*, vol. XXI (June 1900), pp. 669–678.

Shafer, D. C. "Waterfall to Haul Mountain Trains." *The World's Work*, vol. 17 (December 1908), pp. 10982–10983.

Shannon, William O. "Eight-Mile Tunnel Through the Cascades and Great Northern Electrification." *Stone and Webster Journal*, vol. 40 (March 1927), pp. 283–294.

Sims, Harold M. "History of the Great Northern Railway Company." *Shipper and Carrier Magazine* (February 1926), pp. 4–10.

———. "Roads of Progress: The Story of the Great Northern Railway System." *Railroad Workers' Journal*, vol. 2 (November 1941), pp. 6 ff.

Slagsvold, P. L. "An Analysis of the Present Status of Agriculture on the Sun River Irrigation Project." Montana Agricultural Experiment Station, *Bulletin* 321 (Bozeman, 1936).

Slagsvold, P. L., and G. H. Bingham. "An Analysis of Agriculture on the Milk River Irrigation Project." Montana Agricultural Experiment Station, *Bulletin* 290 (Bozeman, 1934).

Smart, Douglas. "Spokane's Battle for Freight Rates." *Pacific Northwest Quarterly*, vol. 45 (January 1954), pp. 27–30.

Smith, Hoke. "A Railway Revolutionizes Farming." *Leslie's Weekly*, vol. 116 (April 3, 1913), p. 372.

Snyder, William L. "Railway Overcapitalization, I." *The Outlook*, vol. 85 (Feb. 9, 1907), pp. 312–316; "Railway Overcapitalization, II: The Case Against the Great Northern." op. cit., vol. 85 (March 9, 1907), pp. 559–562.

Stanchfield, David. "History of Pioneer Lumbering on the Upper Mississippi and Its Tributaries, with Biographical Sketches." *Collections of the Minnesota Historical Society*, vol. 9 (1901).

Starch, E. A. "Economic Changes in Montana's Wheat Area." Montana Agricultural Experiment Station, *Bulletin* 295 (Bozeman, 1935).

"Statement by President Budd." *Railway Age*, vol. 78 (May 23, 1925), p. 1302.

Stevens, John F. "The Cascade Tunnel: Great Northern Ry." *Engineering News and American Railway Journal*, vol. XLV (Jan. 10, 1901), pp. 23–26.

Stevens, J. F. "Engineer's Recollections: Discovery of Marias Pass." *Engineering News Record*, vol. 114 (May 9, 1935), pp. 672–675.

———. "Engineer's Recollections: Railway Reconnaissance over the Cascade Range." *Engineering News Record*, vol. 114 (May 23, 1935), pp. 749–751.

———. "Engineer's Recollections: Great Northern and Jas. J. Hill." *Engineering News Record*, vol. 114 (June 13, 1935), pp. 850–852.

———. "Engineer's Recollections: Railway Invasion of Central Oregon." *Engineering News Record*, vol. 114 (June 27, 1935), pp. 917–919.

Stickney, A. B. "Defense of the Great Northern." *The Outlook*, vol. 85 (March 9, 1907), pp. 557–559.

Tallmadge, G. E. "Great Northern Builds New Diesel Storehouse at Havre, Montana." *Railway Purchases and Stores*, vol. 39 (March 1946), pp. 106–108.

Tetu, V. A. "Conditioning the *Empire Builder*." *Railway Mechanical Engineer*, vol. 107 (August 1933), pp. 295–296.

Thompson, Joseph W. "The Genesis of Great Northern's Mesabi Ore Traffic." *Journal of Economic History*, vol. 16 (December 1956), pp. 551–557.

Traffic World, 1927–1970.

Virtue, G. O. "Minnesota Iron Ranges." U.S. Bureau of Labor, *Bulletin* 19 (September 1909), pp. 338–396.

———. "Minnesota Railway Valuation." *Quarterly Journal of Economics*, vol. 23 (May 1909), pp. 542–547.

Walker, F. B. "Mesabi Iron Range." *Journal of the Boston Society of Civil Engineers*, vol. 5 (March 1918), pp. 105–120.

Walker, Thomas B. "Memories of the Early Life and Development of Minnesota." *Collection of the Minnesota Historical Society*, vol. 15 (1915), pp. 459–461.

Walters, F. R. "Better Days: Earnings Sharply Higher." *The Magazine of Wall Street*, vol. 65 (Nov. 4, 1939), pp. 100–101.

Warner, Charles Dudley. "Studies of the West." *Harper's Magazine*, vol. 76 (March 1888), pp. 564–565.

Warner, Paul T. "The Great Northern Railway and Its Locomotives." *Baldwin Locomotives*, vol. 3 (January 1925), pp. 3–33.

Warren, D., Jr. "Minnesota and the Railway Trust." *Outlook*, vol. 69 (Dec. 14, 1901), pp. 975–978.

Webb, R. C. "Periodic Medical Examinations." *Railway Age*, vol. 82 (Feb. 19, 1927), p. 540.

Welch, Douglas. "Railroad Press Relations — A Communication by . . . *Seattle Post Intelli-*

gencer." *Railway Age*, vol. 120 (Jan. 26, 1946), pp. 242–243.

"What Congress Will Do Most Pressing Question." *Railway Age*, vol. 82 (Jan. 1, 1927), pp. 19–20.

White, Bruce M. "Working for the Railroad: Life in the General Offices of the Great Northern and Northern Pacific, 1915–1921." *Minnesota History*, vol. 46 (Spring 1978), pp. 24–30.

White, Victor H. "Through the Cascade Tunnel: Three Times the Great Northern Hurdled the Cascades to Get a Low Route to the Northwest." *Trains*, vol. 1 (June 1941), pp. 4–7.

White, W. Thomas. "Paris Gibson, James J. Hill and the 'New Minneapolis': The Great Falls Water Power and Townsite Company, 1882–1908." *Montana*, vol. 33 (Summer 1983).

———. "Race, Ethnicity, and Gender in the Railroad Work Force: The Case of the Far Northwest, 1883–1918." *Western Historical Quarterly*, vol. XVI (July 1985), pp. 265–283.

———. "Railroad Labor Protests, 1894–1917." *Pacific Northwest Quarterly*, vol. 75 (January 1984).

———. "Railroad Labor Relations in the Great War and After, 1917–1921." *Journal of the West*, vol. XXV (April 1986), pp. 27–35.

———. "The War of the Great Railroad Kings: Great Northern–Northern Pacific Rivalry in Montana, 1881–1896." *Montana and the West: Essays in Honor of K. Ross Toole*, Rex C. Myers and Harry W. Fritz, eds. (Boulder: Pruett Publishing, 1984), pp. 37–54.

Wickman, C. E. "Great Northern Railway Using Buses to Regain Lost Short-Haul Business in Minnesota." *Bus Transportation*, vol. 5 (June 1926), pp. 313–315.

Wiecking, H. R. "James J. Hill, Empire Builder, Father of Great Northern." *Pacific Coast Railroader*, vol. 3 (April 1945).

———. "Great Northern Route of the *Empire Builder*." *Brotherhood of Locomotive Firemen and Enginemen's Magazine*, vol. 120 (April 1946).

———. "Great Northern Railroad's Cascade Tunnel Is Longest on Continent." *Locomotive Engineer's Journal* (January 1948), p. 4.

Wiley, J. S. "Great Northern's New Outlook." *Barron's, The National Financial Weekly*, vol. 16 (March 2, 1936), pp. 10–11.

Williamson, R. A. "Great Northern Single-Cab 5,000 hp. . . . Built by General Electric. . . ." *Railway Mechanical Engineer*, vol. 121 (August 1947), pp. 432–433.

Wilson, M. L. "Dry Farming in the North Central Montana 'Triangle,'" Montana Agricultural Extension Service, *Bulletin* 66 (Bozeman, 1923).

Wright, A. M. "Inclined Catenary on the Great Northern: Installation Represents Application of a Much Discussed Overhead Construction." *Railway Electrical Engineer*, vol. 19 (April 1928), pp. 112–116.

———. "Overhead Construction on the Great Northern." *Railway Age*, vol. 84 (Feb. 25, 1928), pp. 445–448.

Newspapers

Buffalo Commercial, 1910.
Commercial & Financial Chronicle, 1900–1930.
Duluth Daily Tribune, 1872.
Great Falls Tribune, 1923–1959.
Mankato Weekly Record, 1859.
Minneapolis Chronicle, 1866–1869.
Minneapolis Journal, 1916.
Minneapolis Star, 1924–1970.
Minneapolis Tribune, 1868–1970.
Minnesota State News, 1859–1862.
Minot Daily News, 1946–1955.
New York Commercial Advertiser, 1898.
New York Evening Post, 1921.
New York Herald, 1906.
New York Times, 1892–1970.
New York World, 1909.
St. Anthony Falls Democratic, 1870–1871.
St. Louis Globe Democrat, 1905.
St. Paul Dispatch, 1920–1959.

St. Paul Globe, 1878–1879.
St. Paul Pioneer Press (title varies), 1858–1970.
Seattle Post-Intelligencer, 1890–1910.
Seattle Telegraph, 1890.
Seattle Times, 1931–1945.
Spokane Daily Chronicle, 1931.
Spokane Spokesman-Review, 1951.
Wall Street Journal, The, 1910–1970.
Washington Herald, 1905.

Government Materials

82 ICC 185 Natron Cutoff Construction.
99 ICC 432 Branch Line Extensions.
117 ICC 737 Construction . . . Eastern Oregon.
124 ICC 355 Acquisition of lines by the Spokane, Coeur d'Alene and Palouse Railway.
133 ICC 1 Valuation Docket 327 Great Northern Railway (1927).
162 ICC 37 Great Northern Pacific Railway Company Acquisition.
166 ICC 3 Great Northern Construction.
306 ICC 417 Railway Passenger Train Deficits.
323 ICC 758 Ingot Molds from Pennsylvania to Steelton, Ky.
328 ICC 460, and Ingot Molds from Pennsylvania to Steelton, Ky.
331 ICC 228, 869 Great Northern Pacific and Burlington Lines, Inc., Merger.
ICC. Annual Reports, 1920–1970.
ICC. Statistics of Railways in the United States, 1920–1945.
ICC. Transport Statistics in the United States, 1954–1966.
Reconstruction Finance Corporation, Railroad Division. Report, Great Northern Railway (March 1936).
Reports of the Railroad Commission of Minnesota (title varies), 1872–1970.
U.S., Bureau of Public Roads. Highway Statistics Summary to 1955 (1957).
U.S., Bureau of Reclamation. General Information —Columbia Basin Project, Washington (1939).

U.S., Committee on Interstate and Foreign Commerce. 71st Congress, 3rd Session, House Report No. 2789, Regulation of Stock Ownership in Railroads (1931).
U.S., Department of Commerce. Federal Transportation Policy and Program (1960).
U.S., Department of Commerce. Modern Transportation Policy (1956).
U.S., Federal Works Agency. Highway Statistics: Summary to 1945 (1947).
U.S. House. "Adequacy of Transportation in Support of the National Defense Effort in the Event of Mobilization." Hearings before a Subcommittee of the Committee on Armed Forces, 86th Congress, 1st Session (1959).
U.S. House. "Committee on Investigation of the U.S. Steel Corporation." Hearings, 62nd Congress, 2nd Session (1912).
U.S., Library of Congress, Division of Bibliography. Northern-Securities Company. Bibliography. A List of Books (with references to periodicals) relating to railroads in their relation to the Government and the public. With appendix: List of references on the Northern Securities Case. Compiled under the direction of Appleton Prentiss Clark Griffin, Chief Bibliographer. (1904).
U.S., National Mediation Board. Administration of the Railway Labor Act by the National Mediation Board, 1934–1970 (1970).
U.S., Office of Defense Transportation. Civilian War Transport (1948).
U.S., Office of Emergency Management. OEM Handbook: Functions and Administration (1942).
U.S., Railroad Commission. Final Settlement between the Director General of the Railroads and the Great Northern Railway Company and Other Corporations (1921).
U.S., Senate. "National Transportation Policy." Report No. 445, 87th Congress, 1st Session (1961).
U.S., Senate. "Problems of the Railroads." Hearings before the Subcommittee on Surface

Transportation of the Committee on Interstate and Foreign Commerce, 85th Congress, 2nd Session (1958).

Bridges and Dams Across Rivers

THE COLUMBIA RIVER

O'Neill, J. J. Interstate and Foreign Commerce. Bridging Columbia River by St. Paul, Minneapolis and Manitoba Railway recommended, July 12, 1892. (S.R. 3029. 27 S.L., 416.)
S. 4638, Act authorizing Great Northern Railway Company to maintain or reconstruct bridge across Columbia River at Marcus, Wash. Approved March 4, 1923. 1 p. (Public Law 510, 67th Congress.)

THE MISSOURI RIVER

Nelson, Knute. Report from Committee on Commerce, Favoring S. 6160, to authorize Great Northern Railway Company to construct bridge across Missouri River at or near mouth of Little Missouri River, N. Dak. April 16, 1912. 1 p. (Senate Report 627, 62nd Congress, 2nd Session. In Vol. 2; 6121.)
Stevens, F. C. Report from Committee on Interstate and Foreign Commerce, favoring S. 6160, to authorize Great Northern Railway Company to construct bridge across Missouri River at or near mouth of Little Missouri River, N. Dak. April 26, 1912. 1 p. (House Report 607, 62nd Congress, 2nd Session. In Vol. 3; 6131.)
Nelson, Knute. Report from Committee on Commerce, favoring S. 7195, to authorize Great Northern Railway Company to construct bridge across Missouri River either in county of McKenzie or Williams, N. Dak., or in county of Dawson or Valley, Mont. July 3, 1912. 1 p. (Senate Report 902, 62nd Congress, 2nd Session. In Vol. 3; 6122.)
Sims, T. W. Report from Committee on Interstate and Foreign Commerce, favoring S. 7195, to

authorize Great Northern Railway Company to construct bridge across Missouri River either in county of McKenzie or Williams, N. Dak., or in county of Dawson or Valley, Mont. July 13, 1912. 1 p. (House Report 996, 62nd Congress, 2nd Session. In Vol. 5; 6132.)

THE MISSISSIPPI RIVER

Stevens, F. C. Report from Committee on Interstate and Foreign Commerce, amending H. 25775, to authorize company to construct dam across Mississippi River at Coon Creek Rapids, Minn. December 13, 1910. 2 p. (House Report 1752, 61st Congress, 3rd Session. In Vol. 1; 5847.)

Commerce Committee. Bridge across Mississippi River, report to accompany S. 2497 to authorize construction of bridge across Mississippi River between Anoka and Hennepin counties, Minn., above Minneapolis, by Great Northern Railway Company; submitted by Mr. Sheppard. January 11, 1916. 1 p. (Senate Report, 64th Congress, 1st Session. In Vol. 1; 6897.)

Interstate and Foreign Commerce Committee. House. Bridge across Mississippi River in Minnesota, report to accompany H.R. 5767 to authorize construction of bridge across Mississippi River between Anoka and Hennepin counties, Minn., above Minneapolis, by Great Northern Railway Company; submitted by Mr. Dillon. February 8, 1916. 2 p. (House Report 154, 64th Congress, 1st Session. In Vol. 1; 6903.)

Congress. S. 2497, Act to authorize construction of bridge across Mississippi River between Anoka and Hennepin counties, Minn. above Minneapolis, by Great Northern Railway Company. Approved March 1, 1916. 1 p. (Public Law 27, 64th Congress.)

Bridge across Mississippi River, report to accompany S. 802 granting consent of Congress to maintenance and operation or reconstruction, maintenance, and operation of existing bridge owned and operated by Great Northern Rail-

way Company across Mississippi River, within Minneapolis, Minn., submitted by Mr. Ladd. January 23, 1924. 2 p. (Senate Report 92, 68th Congress, 1st Session. In Vol. 1; 8220.)

Congress. H.R. 4366, Act granting consent of Congress to Great Northern Railway Company to maintain and operate or reconstruct, maintain and operate bridge across Mississippi River within Minneapolis, Minn. Approved February 16, 1924. 1 p. (Public Law 27, 68th Congress.)

THE RED RIVER OF THE NORTH

O'Neill, J. J., Interstate and Foreign Commerce Committee. Bridging Red River of the North by St. Paul, Minneapolis and Manitoba Railroad, recommended June 28, 1892. 1 p. (House Report, 52-1, Vol. 7, No. 1687.)

Congress. N.R. 14428, Act granting consent of Congress to reconstruction of bridge across Red River between Moorhead, Minn., and Fargo, N. Dak. by Great Northern Railway Company. Approved March 4, 1923. 1 p. (Public Law 549, 67th Congress.)

Interstate and Foreign Commerce Committee. Report to accompany H.R. 14429; . . . reconstruction of bridge across Red River between East Grand Forks, Minn., and Grand Forks, N. Dak. by Great Northern Railway Company; submitted by Mr. Newton of Minnesota. March 2, 1923. 1 p. (House Report 1752, 67th Congress, 4th Session. In Vol. 2; 8158.)

Congress. H.R. 14429, Act granting consent of Congress to reconstruction of bridge across Red River between Grand Forks, N. Dak., and East Grand Forks, Minn. by Great Northern Railway Company. Approved March 4, 1923. 1 p. (Public Law 550, 67th Congress.)

THE YELLOWSTONE RIVER

Nelson, Knute. Report from Committee on Commerce, favoring S. 6161, to authorize Great Northern Railway Company to construct

bridge across Yellowstone River in county of Dawson, Mont., April 16, 1912. 1 p. (Senate Report 625, 62nd Congress, 2nd Session. In Vol. 2; 6121.) For Senate bill 6161 as it passed and became law, see Statutes at Large, Vol. 37, Pt. 1, p. 117.

Burlington, Northern Pacific and Great Northern Systems

Stockder, A. H. Burlington, Northern Pacific and Great Northern Systems, study of development in their corporate and intercorporate structures. (In House Report 2789, Pt. 3, pp. 1251–1409; 71st Congress, 3rd Session. In Vol. 5; 9330.)

Fort Spokane

Hawley, J. R. Report from Committee on Military Affairs, favoring S. 3561, to grant right-of-way through Fort Spokane, Wash., to St. Paul, Minneapolis and Manitoba Railway Company. February 4, 1897. 1 p. (Senate Report 1403, 54th Congress, 2nd Session. In Vol. 2.)

Hull, J. A. T. Report from Committee on Military Affairs, favoring H. 10062, to grant right-of-way through Fort Spokane, Wash., to St. Paul, Minneapolis and Manitoba Railway Company. February 23, 1897. 1 p. (House Report 3013, 54th Congress, 2nd Session. In Vol. 3.)

Glacier National Park, Montana

Public Lands Committee. Senate. Great Northern Railway right-of-way adjacent to Glacier National Park, Mont., report to accompany S. 3897 (to authorize Great Northern Railway Company to revise location of its right-of-way along south boundary of Glacier National Park, etc.); submitted by Mr. Pittman. April 20, 1914. 2 p. (Senate Report 433, 63rd Congress, 2nd Session. In Vol. 1; 6552.)

Congress. S. 3897, Act to Authorize Great Northern Railway Company to revise its rights-of-way [. . .] Approved February 27, 1915. 1 p. (Public Law 257, 63rd Congress.)

Indian Reservations

Robinson, J. T. Report from Committee on public lands, favoring H.J.R. 142, to declare and make certain authority of Attorney General to begin and maintain and of circuit court of eastern district of Washington, to entertain and decide suit or suits for purpose of having judicially declared forfeiture of rights granted by act granting to Washington Improvement Company right-of-way through Colville Reservation, Wash. which rights are now held by Great Northern Railway Company. August 5, 1911. 2 p. (House Report 122, 62nd Congress, 1st Session. In Vol. 1; 6078.) For House Joint Resolution 142 as it passed and became law, see Statutes at Large, Vol. 37, Pt. 1, p. 634.

McCumber, P. J. Report from Committee on Indian Affairs, amending by substitute H.J.R. 142, to grant hearing to Great Northern Railway Company and Spokane and British Columbia Railway Company in matter of their conflicting claims of right-of-way across Colville Reservation, Wash. in San Poil River Valley, and to readjust locations of said rights-of-way in such manner as to allow each company opportunity to construct railroad through said valley without interference with location and construction of the other. April 22, 1912. (Senate Report 649, 62nd Congress, 2nd Session. In Vol. 2; 6121.)

Public Lands Committee. House. Washington Improvement and Development Co., hearings on H.J.R. 142, to declare and make certain authority of Attorney General to begin and maintain and of circuit court of eastern district of Washington, to entertain and decide suit or suits for purpose of having judicially declared

forfeiture of rights granted by act granting to Washington Improvement and Development Co. right-of-way through Colville Reservation, Wash. which rights came to be held by Great Northern Railway Company, May 21, 1912. 10 p.

Indian Affairs Committee. Senate. Right-of-way through Colville Indian Reservation, hearing on H.J.R. 142, to declare and make certain authority of Attorney General to begin and maintain and of any court of competent jurisdiction to entertain and decide suit or suits for purpose of having judicially declared forfeiture of rights granted by act granting to Washington Improvement and Development Co. right-of-way through Colville Reservation, Wash. 1912. 2 pts. ii and 69 p.

Congress. S. 2711, Act for acquiring of station grounds by Great Northern Railway Company in Colville Indian Reservation, Wash. Approved, September 17, 1913. 1 p. (Public Law 12, 63rd Congress.)

Nelson, Knute. Indian Affairs Committee. Right-of-way to St. Paul, Minneapolis and Manitoba Railway through Indian reservations in Montana and Dakota recommended. December 16, 1886. H.B. 1056, 24 S.L. 402. House Report 49-2. Vol. 1, No. 3487, 3 p.

Nelson, Knute. Indian Affairs Committee. Right-of-way to St. Paul, Minneapolis and Manitoba Railway through White Earth Indian Reservation, Minn., recommended. February 5, 1889. H.B. 12443. 25 S.L. 696. H.R. 50-2, Vol. 2, No. 3941. 1 p.

Pettigrew, R. F. Report amending and favoring S. 1694, granting right-of-way to St. Paul, Minneapolis and Manitoba Railway through White Earth, Leech Lake, Chippewa and Fond du Lac Indian Reservations. April 13, 1894. 3 p.

Allen, J. M. Report favoring S. 1694, granting right-of-way to St. Paul, Minneapolis and Manitoba Railway through White Earth, Leech Lake, Chippewa, and Fond du Lac Indian Reservations, as substitute for H.R. 6340. June

21, 1894. 3 p. (House Report 1128, 2nd Session. In Vol. 3.)

Eddy, F. M. Report from Committee on Indian Affairs, favoring S. 3603, to extend time for completion of St. Paul, Minneapolis and Manitoba Railway through White Earth, Leech Lake, Chippewa and Fond du Lac Indian Reservations. February 4, 1897. 1 p. (House Report 2787, 54th Congress, 2nd Session. In Vol. 3.)

Dixon, J. M. Report from Committee on Indian Affairs, favoring S. 8439, to appraise lands in Fort Peck Reservation, Mont., and grant same to Great Northern Railway Company. January 14, 1909. 2 p. (Senate Report 763, 60th Congress, 2nd Session. In Vol. 1; 5380.)

Terminal and Stock Yards

Public Lands Committee. Report to accompany H.R. 6922 to sell and convey to Great Northern Railway Company lands in Montana for division terminal yards and other railway purposes; submitted by Mr. Stout. December 20, 1916. 5 p. (House Report 1233, 64th Congress, 2nd Session. In Vol. 1; 7110.)

Public Lands Committee. Senate. Report to accompany S. 7796 to sell and convey to Great Northern Railway Company lands in Montana for division terminal yards and other railway purposes; submitted by Mr. Myers. January 23, 1917. 3 p. (Senate Report 961, 64th Congress, 2nd Session. In Vol. 1; 7106.)

Congress. S. 7796, Act to sell and convey to Great Northern Railway Company lands in Montana for division terminal yards and other railway purposes. Approved February 26, 1917. 3 p. (Public Law 355, 64th Congress.)

Public Lands Committee. Senate. Report to accompany S. 3138 authorizing Secretary of Interior to sell and convey to Great Northern Railway Company lands for stockyards and for other purposes at Browning Station, Mont. submitted by Mr. Myers. January 10, 1920. 1 p.

(Senate Report 368, 66th Congress, 2nd Session. In Vol. A; 7650.)

Public Affairs Committee. House. Report to accompany S. 3138 to sell and convey to Great Northern Railway Company lands for stockyards and for other purposes at Browning Station, Mont. submitted by Mr. Hernandez. January 27, 1921. 1 p. (House Report 1248, 66th Congress, 3rd Session. In Vol. A; 7778.)

*Court Cases**

Edwin A. C. Hatch v. Thomas B. Coddington and the First National Bank of St. Paul. Minnesota Supreme Court, October Term (1883).

First Division of the St. Paul & Pacific Railroad Co. v. Frank M. Parcher et al. (1869). 14 Minnesota Reports, p. 297.

James J. Winslow v. The Minnesota & St. Paul R.R. Co. (1860). 4 Minnesota Reports, p. 313.

Minnesota & Pacific Railroad Co. v. H. H. Sibley (1858). 2 Minnesota Reports, p. 13.

United States Circuit Court, District of Minnesota, Case of Jesse P. Farley v. J. J. Hill, Norman Kittson, and the St. Paul, Minneapolis & Manitoba Railway Co., Vol. 39 (September 13, 1889).

United States Circuit Court, District of Minnesota, Minnesota Rate Case, John S. Kennedy et al., complainants, v. Great Northern Railway Co. et al., defendants.

161 U.S. 646 Pearsall v. Great Northern Railway Company.

193 U.S. 197 Northern Securities Company v. United States.

396 U.S. 491 United States v. Interstate Commerce Commission (Burlington Northern merger).

*Voluminous legal data, briefs, and so on were found in the Great Northern's law department.

Interviews

Muriel E. Hidy with Thomas Balmer, October 19–21, 1953
——— with Ralph Budd, August 2, 1954
——— with Margaret Holden, August 3, 1964
——— with William B. Irwin, August 20, 1953
——— with Alexander James, August 5, 1954
——— with Jacob H. Marthaler, August 21, 1953
——— with Jackson E. Reynolds, June 6, 1955
——— with Frederick E. Wiesner, October 22, 1953
Ralph W. Hidy with George Anderson, August 18, 1953
——— with P. H. Burnham, August 17, 1953
——— with E. I. Clarke, October 22, 1953
——— with Ira E. Clary, October 22, 1953
——— with A. J. Dickinson, August 25, 1953
——— with E. M. Duncan, July 19, 1967
——— with C. E. Finley, September 1, 1953
——— with Frank J. Gavin, August 12, 1953
——— with H. M. Goering, October 21, 1953
——— with Howard H. Hayes, August 20, 1954
——— with Chris McDonough, September 21, 1954
——— with James Maher, August 13, 1953
——— with Charles W. Moore, July 28, 1964
——— with F. L. Paetzold, August 27, 1953
——— with Harry J. Seyton, August 24, 1953
——— with Worthington Smith, July 24, 1968
——— with V. P. Turnburke, September 2, 1953
Muriel E. Hidy and Ralph Hidy with William J. Cunningham, November 19, 1953
——— with C. O. Jenks, August 31, 1953
——— with Harry W. Kask, August 14, 1953
——— with C. C. Morrison, July 12, 1954
——— with E. H. Wilde, August 10, 1953
Don L. Hofsommer with Robert W. Downing, July 22–24, 1985, May 1, 1986, January 26, 1987
——— with Tony Kane, August 28, 1985
——— with Thomas J. Lamphier, August 28, 1985 and April 14, 1986
——— with Frank F. Perrin, August 28, 1985
——— with John L. Robson, August 28, 1985
——— with Robert H. Shober, August 28, 1985
——— with Charles W. Moore, November 20, 1985
Roy V. Scott with C. D. Archibald, August 3–5, 1964
——— with Nick Blazovich, May 22, 1959 and August 10, 1964
——— with E. C. Bredeson, August 10, 1964
——— with E. N. Duncan, June 8, 1959
——— with C. E. Finley, August 28, 1958 and September 1, 1958
——— with J. C. Kenady, May 28, 1959
——— with M. M. Scanlan, August 28, 1958 and April 16, 1959
——— with B. J. Stasson, May 14, 1959
——— with C. H. Wesman, August 3, 1964

Index

359

Ralph W. Hidy and Muriel E. Hidy were professors of business history at the Harvard Business School. They also coauthored a history of the Standard Oil Company.

Don L. Hofsommer is professor of history at St. Cloud State University, where he specializes in transportation history. He is the author of several books, including *The Tootin' Louie: A History of the Minneapolis & St. Louis Railway, The Hook & Eye: A History of the Iowa Central Railway,* and *Minneapolis and the Age of Railways,* all published by the University of Minnesota Press.

Roy V. Scott is the William L. Giles Distinguished Professor of history at Mississippi State University. He has served as president of the Agricultural History Society and the Mississippi Historical Society. He is the author of several books, including *Wal-Mart: A History of Sam Walton's Retail Phenomenon* and *Railroad Development Programs in the Twentieth Century.*

Alfred D. Chandler, Jr. is the Isidor Straus Professor of Business History, Emeritus at the Harvard Business School.